THE ICSA DIRECTORS HANDBOOK

THE ICSA

DIRECTORS HANDBOOK

General editor: Rita Dattani

ICSA
PUBLISHING

Published by ICSA Information & Training Ltd
16 Park Crescent
London W1B 1AH

Typeset in 10 on 12½ pt Kuenstler by Hands Fotoset, Mapperley, Nottingham
Printed in Great Britain by Hobbs the Printers Ltd, Totton, Hampshire

British Library Cataloguing in Publication Data
A catalogue record for this book is available from the British Library

ISBN 978-1-86072-402-2

Contents

Preface

Directors are subject to increasing amounts of regulation and concomitant liabilities. This is well illustrated by the Companies Act 2006, which is the most significant recent law to affect directors. Having received royal assent on 8 November 2006, it is being brought into force piecemeal over some three years, with the final provisions expected to come into force this October. At 1300 clauses and 16 schedules it is also the longest Act ever to have been passed by a UK Parliament. Although intended as a de-regulatory measure, the sheer volume of the Act together with the numerous secondary legislation made under it as well as the fact that its implementation is being staggered over three years makes it difficult for directors to know and comply with the legal and regulatory obligations imposed on them in running a UK company. This Handbook seeks to cut through the morass of detail and to provide an accessible, practical guide to assist company directors with their duties and responsibilities, and with the laws and regulations that may affect the smooth running of their companies. It will also be useful to company secretaries, company advisers and persons dealing with companies.

The Handbook focuses on the changes introduced by the Companies Act 2006. It covers a broad range of topics affecting directors, from their appointment and qualifications, their removal, their powers and duties, restricted transactions, their responsibilities for the company's accounts, their roles as employees and shareholders, including the importance of compliance with share dealing rules, how they run the company through board and shareholder meetings, good corporate governance, their liabilities and how shareholders can hold them to account, the importance of directors' and officers' insurance, their duties if the company is facing insolvency, to their ultimate disqualification. Checklists, at a glance boxes and practical tips are included. The Handbook includes an index which gives readers quick access to specific subject areas. The Handbook also addresses future developments, such as the EU Shareholder Rights Directive, which is due to be implemented this August.

Almost all of the Companies Act 2006, including most of the provisions affecting directors, are already in force. The final tranche of provisions are expected to become effective this October. However, this Handbook is written as if the whole of the 2006 Act is in force. Where certain provisions, for instance, those relating to directors' residential addresses, are not yet in force, the Handbook addresses the position under both the 2006 Act and the Companies Act 1985. A full table of commencement dates is included to assist the reader.

The law is stated as at 31 January 2009.

Rita Dattani
General editor

Contributors

Oliver Barnes trained at Travers Smith and became a partner in the Corporate Department in 1980. Oliver advises on a broad spectrum of company law matters. He has extensive experience of major corporate transactions in the UK and overseas. He specialises in corporate finance, acting for both listed companies and financial intermediaries, particularly on public company takeovers, mergers, acquisitions, disposals and primary and secondary equity issues. He also advises on boardroom and shareholder issues and general matters of corporate governance.

Oliver is a member of the International Bar Association and the Institute of Advanced Legal Studies. He is also a member of the Company Law Committee of the Law Society.

Andrew Barton is a Counsel in Allen & Overy's London corporate department and is an insurance specialist with a background in corporate and commercial law. He regularly advises insurance and financial institution clients in relation to a wide range of insurance, regulatory and general corporate matters, including insurance company and general M&A, reinsurance, joint ventures and restructuring matters. He has extensive experience advising corporate clients on Directors & Officers' liability insurance and director indemnification. Andrew is Editor of the 10th edition of *Butterworths Insurance Law Handbook*, to be published in April 2009.

Marlies Braun is a Professional Support Lawyer at Wedlake Bell where she heads the knowledge management function of its corporate group. She is dual-qualified in England and the US and joined Wedlake Bell from Debevoise & Plimpton LLP (New York office 2001–3; London office 2003–6) where she gained extensive transactional experience in mergers and acquisitions, private equity and securities offerings. Prior to that Marlies worked at Freshfields Bruckhaus Deringer in Vienna.

Marlies has a wide range of experience covering mergers and acquisitions, capital markets, private equity and general corporate law. She has advised public and private companies and private equity investors on cross-border and domestic mergers and acquisitions, securities offerings and general corporate law matters.

Matthew Blows is a corporate partner at Macfarlanes LLP. He is involved in a wide range of both private and public company work but with an emphasis on transactions involving public companies. Over the last year he has advised on a number of cross-border mergers and acquisitions.

David Bridge is a Senior Associate and qualified solicitor-advocate in Allen & Overy LLP's commercial litigation and arbitration group. He has acted in numerous large-scale High Court cases and international arbitrations. His clients include major UK and international corporates in the engineering, energy and manufacturing sectors, as well as banks and private equity groups.

David has acted for both companies and insolvency practitioners in relation to court proceedings arising from a number of insolvency procedures, including schemes of arrangement and administrations. David advised on the court hearings and litigation aspects of the Marconi schemes of arrangement in 2003, then the largest scheme of arrangement ever created, and has since advised on the successful implementation of those schemes.

Jemima Coleman is a Professional Support Lawyer at Herbert Smith specialising in both contentious and non-contentious employment law. She writes regular client bulletins on developments, speaks at in-house client seminars and provides tailored client training on recent and forthcoming legislation.

Rita Dattani is a knowledge management lawyer in the corporate department at Freshfields Bruckhaus Deringer LLP. She concentrates on providing technical advice on company law, corporate finance and public mergers and acquisitions, analysing new law and regulation as part of a team working to ensure that Freshfields remains at the cutting edge of legal practice. She was previously at Norton Rose where she led its Companies Act 2006 team, including providing training and know-how to clients and the firm's lawyers. Before this, Rita was a senior associate at Allen & Overy LLP. Rita qualified in 1993 and has considerable transactional experience in mergers and acquisitions and equity capital markets.

Malcolm Davis-White QC. Malcolm is primarily a company lawyer with a particular specialisation in directors' duties. He has wide experience in conducting litigation (especially witness trials) and providing advice in the fields of company law (including shareholder disputes, directors' duties, corporate fraud and asset recovery, reductions of capital and schemes of arrangement), insolvency (corporate and personal), financial services, insurance transfer schemes, regulatory work (including Listing Rules, directors' disqualification, public interest winding up proceedings, insolvency practitioner tribunals, FSA tribunals, VAT carousel schemes) and commercial disputes. Malcolm is joint author of *Directors Disqualification and Bankruptcy Restrictions: Law and Practice* (Sweet & Maxwell, 2005, 2nd edition), and contributor on other publications such as *Atkins Court Forms*.

He was recommended as a leading silk in Chambers UK & Chambers Global and in the Legal 500 for company and restructuring/insolvency. Comments made about Malcolm include: 'His arguments are all so concise and to the point; there is no wasting time with him'; 'an opponent you do not wish to see on the other side'; 'a sterling reputation for an ability to pare down vastly complex issues with speed and accuracy'.

Michelle de Kluyver is a Senior Associate and Qualified Solicitor Advocate in Allen & Overy LLP's litigation department and has represented clients in major and complex litigation in the High Court, Court of Appeal and House of Lords, as well as in international arbitration disputes including ICSID, LCIA and SCCI arbitrations.

Michelle has also acted for clients in relation to restructurings and other insolvency procedures. Michelle has acted for financial institutions, listed companies, private equity partnerships, insolvency practitioners and shareholders.

Sara George is a specialist in investigations into criminal and regulatory contraventions. She joined Allen & Overy LLP from the Enforcement Division of the Financial Services Authority (FSA). She led the first prosecution of a director for making a misleading statement to the market for the FSA. She has extensive experience of regulatory investigations and advocacy before the Financial Services and Markets Tribunal and the Crown Court. Formerly a criminal barrister, Sara advises on all aspects of criminal law, including corruption, insider dealing, market abuse and fraud.

Stephanie Henshaw is a chartered accountant. She joined Francis Clark as the firm's Technical Partner in 2008 with responsibility for overseeing the firm's audit and corporate reporting function and providing high level technical support. As Stephanie Barber, she occupied a similar position as Technical Partner with MacIntyre Hudson LLP between 1995 and 2008. Stephanie has presented CPD training to the accountancy profession since 1991 and is a well-known trainer to the legal profession, specialising in helping lawyers understand how accounting concepts apply in the context of their work. She has been a member of various committees of the Institute of Chartered Accountants in England & Wales and is currently on the board of its new Financial Reporting Faculty.

Robin Hollington QC has been in practice since 1981. He took silk in 1999 and has sat as a Recorder (Civil) since 2004. Praised as *'absolutely the top man in his field'* by *Legal 500* (2008 edition), his practice encompasses virtually all aspects of contentious work in the Chancery Division, with emphasis on company law and insolvency (both corporate and individual). He has developed a particular specialisation in claims involving complaints of oppression of minority shareholders and is the author of a leading textbook in this field.

He has appeared in many recent heavy and complex court cases in the field of shareholders' disputes and has also represented parties in many foreign jurisdictions, including Gibraltar (most recently, a derivative claim in Gibraltar and breach of trust claim in the High Court in London concerning oil and gas fields held through complex off-shore trusts and companies).

Tony Hoskins is Chief Executive of The Virtuous Circle, a specialist management consultancy that works with national and international businesses in three areas: enhancing shareholder value through effective corporate reporting; building their reputation through developing and implementing their CSR strategies; and building an understanding of non-financial risks and their management. In addition to his consultancy work, he has undertaken CSR research reports in conjunction with The Work Foundation, the RSA, the DTI and CIPD, as well as research featured by the ASB in their review of corporate narrative reporting. He also speaks at conferences on CSR and the impact of narrative reporting, and on television and radio on reputation management. He is the author of five books, including the *ICSA Corporate Social Responsibility Handbook*, now in its second edition, and the *ICSA Company Reporting Handbook*.

Richard Isham is a partner at Wedlake Bell where he is head of the employment team. Richard advises on all aspects of employment law, both contentious and non-contentious. He is a member of the Employment Lawyers' Association and sits on their Legislative and Policy sub-committee which coordinates responses to the BERR and the Department of Work and Pensions' consultations on proposed new legislation.

Richard advises corporate clients on the full range of employment law issues, including collective cross-border issues, harmonisation of terms and conditions and policies, redundancies, TUPE, bonus schemes and corporate governance. He frequently speaks at seminars, presents training videos and has contributed to *Tolley's Employment Law*.

James Johnson is a partner in the Corporate Department of Trowers & Hamlins LLP, the City-based international law firm. James qualified as a solicitor in 1997 and his practice consists of advising companies on corporate and commercial matters and, in particular, mergers and acquisitions, commercial contracts, joint ventures and private equity-backed investments and acquisitions.

Alexander Keepin is a Partner in Charles Russell LLP. Alexander qualified in 1998 and joined Charles Russell in 2001, becoming partner in May 2005. He is a general corporate lawyer specialising in listings and fundraisings on the Official List and AIM and mergers and acquisitions. Whilst at Charles Russell he has been involved in a number of Class 1 acquisitions and disposals, as well as a number of admissions to and placings on AIM, including fast-track admissions and reverse takeovers. Alexander also has experience of pre-IPO fundraisings, venture capital investments, management buy-outs and buy-ins, and joint ventures. He also advises clients on regulatory issues relating to securities, including under the Financial Services and Markets Act 2000.

Alexander is the author of *A Practical Guide to AIM*, published by ICSA.

Martin Mankabady is a corporate partner at Mayer Brown International LLP. He specialises in mergers and acquisitions, both private and public, joint ventures and corporate finance, primarily in the insurance and financial services sectors. Martin also advises on company law issues. Martin is recommended by the leading legal directories as being 'a highly accomplished lawyer' and an 'up-and-coming individual'.

Beliz McKenzie trained at Freshfields Bruckhaus Deringer and qualified in 2002. She joined Travers Smith as an assistant in the Corporate Department in 2004. Since 2006 she has been working as a Professional Support Lawyer specialising in corporate finance as well as general mergers and acquisitions and Companies Act matters.

David Mensley, Director, Corporate Partners Ltd, has over 20 years' experience working with listed companies. His career has included relationship management roles with a number of key national organisations including the CBI and the London Stock Exchange. In 1998 David founded Catalyst Investor Relations Group plc, that now works with UK listed companies to help them to achieve best practice in areas such as listed company regulation, corporate governance and investor communication. His recent experience has included working with the boards of a large number of FTSE companies on their compliance with the Combined Code – particularly in the field of Board and individual director evaluation.

In addition to assisting UK listed and quoted companies to understand and implement the listing, disclosure and transparency rules – and to meet their subsequent continuing obligations, David currently facilitates several long-standing company secretary groups around the UK, some of which have been running since the early 1990's.

Rachel Mills is a senior lawyer within the Corporate Group of Lawrence Graham. Rachel specialises in mergers and acquisitions for small and medium-sized companies, shareholder agreements, limited liability partnerships and group reorganisations.

Nicky Morgan trained at Theodore Goddard and qualified in 1996. She subsequently moved to Allen & Overy, spending five years in their Company Department working on a number of high-profile deals before moving, in 2002, to Travers Smith as their second Professional Support Lawyer in the Corporate Department. She advises on general company law matters as well as issues relating to public mergers and acquisitions and corporate finance.

Claire Pardo After qualifying at the Bar, Claire Pardo joined Macfarlanes LLP in October 2007 and cross-qualified as a Solicitor. Claire works in the Corporate M&A department, assisting on private and public company work.

Megan Paul is an associate in the corporate team at Mayer Brown International LLP

Ian Redington is Development Director of The Virtuous Circle, a specialist management consultancy that works with national and international businesses in the areas enhancing shareholder value through effective corporate reporting; developing and implementing their CSR strategies; and building an understanding of non-financial risks and their management. Ian is a regular speaker at conferences on CSR and the impact of narrative reporting.

Carol Shutkever is a Corporate Partner at Herbert Smith. Carol has a broad range of experience in corporate finance, corporate and commercial transactions and technical expertise in corporate finance, including equity fund raising, takeovers and financial services regulation. She now concentrates on providing technical advice on company and corporate finance law issues, analysing new law and regulation and ensuring that Herbert Smith is at the forefront of corporate law and practice. Carol is a member of a number of the Law Society Company Law working parties on the Companies Act 2006 and has been involved in the discussions on the legislation with the government. She is leading the firm's Companies Act 2006 team, including providing education and know-how to clients and the firm's lawyers and analysing practical implications for companies.

Andrew Taggart is a Partner and Solicitor Advocate in Herbert Smith's Employment Pensions and Incentives Department and advises on all aspects of employment law. He has considerable experience of all types of corporate transactions (from both a UK and international perspective) and advises employers on disputes and strategic matters including claims in the Employment Tribunal and High Court, disputes with trade unions and other employee representatives and regulatory investigations. He is the co-author of the UK section of the European employment law textbook *Arbeitsrecht in Europa*.

Commencement table

Companies Act 2006 Table of Commencement Dates

The following table shows a summary of the commencement timetable for the Companies Act 2006 following the ministerial announcement on 13 December 2007.

Following the final commencement on 1 October 2009, four provisions will not have been commenced. These are:

- Section 327(2) (c)
- Section 330(6) (c)
- Section 1175 as it applies in Northern Ireland
- Part 2 of Schedule 9

Part	Title (section numbers)	Commencement
1	**General introductory provisions (1 – 6)** Section 2: 6 April 2007	1 October 2009
2	**Company formation (7 – 16)**	1 October 2009
3	**A company's constitution (17 – 38)** Sections 29 and 30: 1 October 2007	1 October 2009
4	**A company's capacity and related matters (39 – 52)** Section 44: 6 April 2008	1 October 2009
5	**A company's name (53 – 85)** Sections 69 to 74: 1 October 2008 Sections 82 to 85: 1 October 2008	1 October 2009
6	**A company's registered office (86 – 88)**	1 October 2009
7	**Re-registration as a means of altering a company's status (89 – 111)**	1 October 2009
8	**A company's members (112 – 144)** Sections 116 to 119: 1 October 2007 Sections 121 & 128: 6 April 2008	1 October 2009
9	**Exercise of members' rights (145 – 153)**	1 October 2007
10	**A company's directors (154 – 259)** Sections 155 to 159: 1 October 2008 Sections 162 to 167: 1 October 2009 Sections 175 to 177: 1 October 2008 Sections 180(1), (2)(in part), & (4)(b), and 181(2) & (3): 1 October 2008 Sections 182 to 187: 1 October 2008 Sections 240 to 247: 1 October 2009	1 October 2007

Part	Title (section numbers)	Commencement
11	**Derivative claims and proceedings by members (260 – 269)**	1 October 2007
12	**Company secretaries (270 – 280)** Sections 270(3)(b)(ii): 1 October 2009 Sections 275 to 279: 1 October 2009	6 April 2008
13	**Resolutions and meetings (281 – 361)** Sections 308 & 309: 20 January 2007 Section 333: 20 January 2007 Sections 327(2)(c) & 330(6)(c) are not being commenced.	1 October 2007
14	**Control of political donations and expenditure (362 – 379)** Provisions relating to independent election candidates: 1 October 2008 Part 14 comes into force in Northern Ireland on 1 November 2007, except for provisions relating to independent election candidates.	1 October 2007
15	**Accounts and reports (380 – 474)** Section 417: 1 October 2007 Section 463: 20 January 2007 for reports and statements first sent to members and others after that date	6 April 2008
16	**Audit (475 – 539)** Sections 485 to 488: 1 October 2007	1 October 2009
17	**A company's share capital (540 – 657)** Section 544: 6 April 2008 Sections 641(1)(a) & (2)–(6), 642–644, 652 (1) and (3), 654: 1 October 2008	1 October 2009
18	**Acquisition by limited company of its own shares (658 – 737)** Repeal of the restrictions under the Companies Act 1985 on financial assistance for acquisition of shares in private companies, including the "whitewash" procedure: 1 October 2008	1 October 2009
19	**Debentures (738 – 754)**	6 April 2008
20	**Private and public companies (755 – 767)**	6 April 2008
21	**Certification and transfer of securities (768 – 790)**	6 April 2008

Part	Title (section numbers)	Commencement
22	**Information about interests in a company's shares (791 – 828)** Sections 811(4), 812, 814: 6 April 2008	20 January 2007
23	**Distributions (829 – 853)**	6 April 2008
24	**A company's annual return (854 – 859)**	1 October 2009
25	**Company charges (860 – 894)**	1 October 2009
26	**Arrangements and reconstructions (895 – 901)**	6 April 2008
27	**Mergers and divisions of public companies (902 – 941)**	6 April 2008
28	**Takeovers etc (942 – 992)**	6 April 2007
29	**Fraudulent trading (993)**	1 October 2007
30	**Protection of members against unfair prejudice (994 – 999)**	1 October 2007
31	**Dissolution and restoration to the register (1000 – 1034)**	1 October 2009
32	**Company investigations: amendments (1035 – 1039)**	1 October 2007
33	**UK companies not formed under the Companies Acts (1040 – 1043)** **Section 1043: 6 April 2007**	1 October 2009
34	**Overseas companies (1044 – 1059)**	1 October 2009
35	The registrar of companies (1060 – 1120) Section 1063 (in respect of England, Wales and Scotland): 6 April 2007 Section 1068(5): 1 January 2007 Sections 1077 to 1080: 1 January 2007 Sections 1085 to 1092: 1 January 2007 Sections 1102 to 1107: 1 January 2007 Section 1111: 1 January 2007	1 October 2009
36	**Offences under the Companies Acts (1121 – 1133)** Section 1124: 1 October 2007 Section 1126: 6 April 2008	With relevant provisions
37	**Companies: supplementary provisions (1134 – 1157)** Section 1137(1), (4), (5)(b) and (6): 30 September 2007 Sections 1143 to 1148: 20 January 2007 Section 1157: 1 October 2008	With relevant provisions
38	**Companies: interpretation (1158 – 1174)** Sections 1161, 1162, 1164, 1165, 1167 and 1172: 6 April 2008 Section 1167: 30 September 2007 Section 1170: 6 April 2007	With relevant provisions

Part	Title (section numbers)	Commencement
39	**Companies: minor amendments (1175 – 1181)** Section 1175 (In relation to England & Wales and Scotland): 1 April 2008 Section 1180: 1 October 2009 Section 1181: 1 October 2009	6 April 2007
40	**Company directors: foreign disqualification etc (1182 – 1191)**	1 October 2009
41	**Business names (1192 – 1208)**	1 October 2009
42	**Statutory auditors (1209 – 1264)** **Sections 1242 to 1244: 29 June 2008**	6 April 2008
43	**Transparency obligations and related matters (1265 – 1273)**	Royal Assent
44	**Miscellaneous provisions (1274 – 1283)** Sections 1274 and 1276: Royal Assent Section 1275: 1 October 2009 Sections 1277 to 1280: 1 October 2008 Section 1281: 6 April 2007 Section 1282: 6 April 2008 Section 1283: 1 October 2009	
45	**Northern Ireland (1284 – 1287)**	With relevant provisions
46	**General supplementary provisions (1288 – 1297)** Section 1295: With relevant provisions	Royal Assent
47	**Final provisions (1298 – 1300)**	Royal Assent

Department for Business, Enterprise and Regulatory Reform www.berr.gov.uk

Table of cases

Main case reference is given together with paragraph number and/or footnote where it can be found in the text.

AG for Tuvalu v. Philatelic Distribution Co. [1990] 1 WLR 926, 14.45, n. 44
AP Besson Ltd v. Fulleon Ltd [1986] FSR 197, 14.41, n. 36
Aspden v. Webb Poulty [1996] IRLR 521, 8.89

Baker v. Potter [2005] BCC 855, 15.40, n. 48
Bamford v. Bamford [1970] Ch 212, 15.29, n. 38
Barings Futures (Singapore) Pte Ltd (in liquidation) v. Marra [2003] All ER (D) 294, 14.150, n. 75
Barings plc (in liquidation) v. Coopers & Lybrand (a firm) All ER (D) 294 14.150, n. 75
Barrett v. Duckett [1995] 1 BCLC 243, 15.9, n. 4, 15.15, n. 9
Barron. v. Potter [1914] 1 Ch 895, 4.16, n. 3
Beckett Investments Management Group Ltd v. Hall [2007] IRLR 793, 8.111
Bishopsgate Investment Management Ltd v. Maxwell (No. 2) [1994] 1 All ER 261, 19.23, n. 29
Blackmore v. Richardson [2006] BCC 276, 15.70, n. 78, 15.75, n. 83
Boardman v. Phipps [1942] 2 All ER 378, 5.14, n. 3, 5.16
Bondina Ltd v. Rollaway Shower Blinds Ltd [1986] 1 WLR 517, 4.33, n. 21
Boschoek Proprietary Company Limited v. Fuke [1906] 1 Ch 148, 4.30, n. 9
Boston Deep Sea Fishing and Ice Co. v. Ansell [1888] LR 39 ChD 339, 5.17, n. 7
Braymist Ltd and others v. Wise Finance Co. Ltd [2002] EWCA Civ 127, 14.31, n. 19
British Thomson-Houston Co. Ltd v. Sterling Accessories Ltd [1924] 41 RPC 311, 14.37, n. 27
Bushell v. Faith [1970] AC 1099, 3.14

Carmen v. The Cronos Group SA [2005] WL 3067026, 18.64, n. 26
CAS (Nominees) Ltd v. Nottingham Forest Football Club plc [2002] BCC 145, 14.8, n. 2
Charterhouse Investment Trust Ltd v. Tempest Diesels Ltd [1985] 1 BCC 99, 544, 4.16, n. 4
Cheyne Finance plc (in receivership) [2007] EWHC 2116, 18.3, n. 1
Claridge's Patent Asphalte Co. Ltd [1921] 1 Ch 543, 14.150, n. 76

Greenhalgh v. Aderne Cinemas [1951] Ch 286, 15.44, n. 55
Gross v. Rackind [2005] 1 WLR 3505, 15.42, n. 51
Haille v. Trax [2000] BCC 1020, 15.21, n. 18
Halls v. David and anor [1989] 5 BCC 399, 18.56, n. 19
Halton International Inc. (Holding) v. Kaddoura [2006] 1 BCLC 60, 15.30, n. 41
Hawkes v. Cuddy [2007] EWHC 2999, 15.40, n. 49, 15.42, n. 51, 15.72, n. 80, 15.82, n. 91
Hennelly v. Secretary of State for Trade and Industry [2004] EWCH 34, 19.81, n. 112
Heron International Ltd v .Grade [1983] BCLC 244, 15.29, n. 37
Highberry Ltd v. Colt Telecommunications [2003] BPR 324, 18.3, n. 2
Hill v. Spread Trustee Co. Ltd and Warr [2006] EWCA Civ 542, 18.87, n. 39
Howard Smith v. Ampol Petroleum [1974] AC 821, 5.12, n. 2
Howard v. Patent Ivory Mf Co. [1888] 38 ChD 156, 14.31, n. 18
Hunter v. Senate Support Services [2005] 1 BCLC 175, 15.29, n. 37

Industrial Development Consultants Limited v. Cooley [1972] All ER 162, 5.17, n. 6
Isaacs v. Benfield [2006] 2 BCLC 14, 15.51, n. 61

Jaybird Group v. Greenwood [1986] BCLC 319, 15.21, n. 16
Jenvey v. Australian Broadcasting Corporation [2002] IRLR 520, 8.89
Johnson v. Gore Wood (No. 1) [2002] CPR 19.9A(10), 15.29, nn. 36 and 37
Juer v. Lomes unrep. Ch D 28, 19.45, n. 60

Kappler v. Secretary of State for Trade and Industry [2008] 1 BCLC 120, 19.51, n. 65
Keen v. Commerzbank [2007] IRLR 132, 8.64, 8.65
Kelner v. Baxter [1867] LR 2 CP 174, 14.30, n. 14
Kinsella v. Russell Kinsella [1986] 4 NSWLR 722, 18.28, n. 6

Larvin v. Phoenix [2003] 1 BCLC 76, 15.69, n. 76
Liquidator of West Mercia Safetywear Ltd v. Dood [1988] BCLC 250, 18.28, n. 7
Lloyd v. Casey [2002] 1 BCLC 454, 15.39, n. 47

MacPherson v. European Strategic Bureau [2002] BCC 39, 14.8, n. 1
Mainstream Properties Ltd v. Young and ors [2007] 4 All ER 545, 8.118
Mancetter Developments Ltd v. Germanson Ltd [1986] 1 All ER 449, 14.41, n. 36
MCA Records Inc. v. Charity Records Ltd [2001] EWCA Civ 1441, 14.39, n. 31

Re Cannonquest Ltd [1997] 2 BCLC 473, 19.58, n. 69
Re Carecraft Construction Co. Ltd [1994] 1 WLR 172, 19.62, n. 75
Re Cedac Ltd [1991] Ch 402, 19.44, n. 56
Re Chime Corporation Ltd [2004] HKCF 85, 15.47, n. 59, 15.53, n. 63, 15.83, n. 93
Re City Equitable Fire Insurance Co. [1925] CH 407, 5.19, n. 8, 5.59, n. 25
Re Continental Assurance Co. of London (in liquidation) No. 1 [1997] 1 BCLC 48, 14.4, n. 4
Re Continental Assurance Co. of London plc [2001] All ER (D) 299, 18.52, n. 13
Re Copecrest Ltd [1996] 2 BCLC 477, 19.23, n. 16
Re Country Farms Inn Ltd [1997] 2 BCLC 334, 19.21, n. 14
Re Cumana [1986] 2 BCC 99, 15.54, n. 67
Re D [2008] UKHL 33, 19.54, n. 68
Re Dennis Hilton Ltd [2002] 1 BCLC 302, 19.39, n. 53
Re D'Jan of London Limited [1993] BCC 646, 5.20, n. 9, 14.50, n. 75
Re DKG Contractors Ltd [1990] BCC 569, 18.53, n. 14
Re DR Chemicals Ltd [1989] 5 BCC 39, 15.62, n. 72
Re Duomatic [1969] 2 Ch 365, 11.141, 14.153, n. 81
Re Estate Acquisition and Development Ltd [1991] BCLC 154, 15.76, n. 86
Re Finelist Ltd [2003] EWHC 1780, 19.44, n. 57, 19.81, n. 112
Re Fireproof Doors Ltd [1916] 2 Ch 132, 4.23, n. 7
Re Galeforce Pleating Co. [1999] 2 BCLC 704, 14.5, n. 5
Re Gibson Davies Ltd [1995] BCC 11, 19.80, n. 111
Re German Date Coffee [1882] 20 ChD 169, 15.74, n. 82, 15.75, n. 84
Re Gower Enterprises Ltd [1995] BCC 293, 19.19, n. 12
Re Gower Enterprises (No. 2) [1995] 2 BCLC 201, 19.58, n. 69
Re Grandactual [2006] BCC 73, 15.75, n. 84
Re Guidezone Ltd [2000] 2 BCLC 321, 15.47, n. 58, 15.86
Re Hawkes Hill Publishing Co. Ltd (in liquidation) [2007] All ER (D) 422, 18.25 n. 5, 18.92, n. 40
Re Hennelly's Utilities [2004] EWHC 34, 19.81, n. 112
Re Howglen Ltd [2002] EWCA Civ 947, 19.23, n. 24, 19.53, n. 67
Re Ins Realisations Ltd [2006] EWHC 135, 19.64, n. 80
Re J.A. Chapman & Co. Ltd [2003] EWHC 523, 19.28 n. 41
Re J. E. Cade & Son Ltd [1992] 2 BCLC 213, 15.43, n. 52
Re Jessel Trust Limited [1985] BCLC 119, 9.12
Re Kaytech International plc [1999] 2 BCLC 351, 19.18, n. 11
Re Lombard Shipping and Forwarding Ltd [1992] BCC 700, 19.53, n. 66
Re Leaf [2007] All ER (D) 52, 18.60, n. 21
Re Living Images Ltd [1996] BCC 112, 18.42, n. 10, 18.99, n. 43, 19.54, n. 68
Re Lo-Line Electric Motors Ltd [1988] Ch 477, 19.15 n. 7

Re Martin Coulter [1988] BCLC 12, 15.86, n. 96
Re MC Bacon Limited (No. 1) [1990] BCC 78, 18.87, n. 38, 18.93, n. 41
Re McNulty Interchange Ltd [1989] BCLC 709, 19.23, n .32
Re Metropolis Motorcycles Ltd [2007] 1 BCLC 520, 15.66, n. 74, 15.69, n.76, 15.70, n. 77
Re Moonlight Foods (UK) Ltd [1996] BCC 678, 19.44, n. 57
Re North Holdings v Southern Tropics [1999] 2 BCLC 625, 15.81, n. 90
Re Otto Electrical Manufacturing Company (1905) Limited, Jenkins's Claim [1906] 2 Ch 390, 14.35, n. 25
Re Pantmaenog Timber Co. Ltd [2003] UKHL 49, 19.44, n. 59
Re Park House Properties Ltd [1998] BCC 847, 19.44, n. 58
Re Produce Marketing Consortium Ltd [1989] 5 BCC 569, 18.53, n. 15, 18.56, n. 19
Re Prove Data Systems Ltd (No. 3) [1992] BCC 110, 19.50, n. 64
Re Purpoint Ltd [1991] BCC 121, 18.54, n. 16, 18.57, n. 20, 18.60, n. 22
Re Regional Airports Ltd [1999] 2 BCLC 30, 15.71, n. 79
Re Sam Weller & Sons Ltd [1990] Ch 682, 15.54, n. 65
Re Sanflex Limited [1979] Ch 592, 18.64, n. 24
*Re Saul D. Harrison & Sons pl*c [1995] 1 BCLC 14, 15.47, n. 58
Re Seagull Manufacturing Ltd (No. 3) [1995] BCC 1088, 19.58, n. 69
Re Sevenoaks Stationers (Retail) Ltd [1991] Ch 164, 19.23, n. 21
Re Sherborne Park Residents Co. Ltd [1987] BCLC 82, 15.29, n. 38
Re Skyward Builders plc [2002] EWHC 1788, 19.53, n. 67
Re Smith and Fawcett Limited [1942] Ch 402, 5.40, n. 17
Re Surrey Leisure [1999] 1 BCLC 731, 19.21, n. 13
Re Swift 736 Limited [1993] BCLC 896, 19.13, n. 6
Re Tech Textiles Ltd [1998] 259, 19.79, nn. 107 and 109, 19.81, n. 112
Re TLL Realisations Ltd [2000] 2 BCLC 223, 19.79, n. 107, 19.80, n. 110
Re Wendoflex Textiles Pty Ltd [1951] VLR 458, 15.61
Re Westminster Property Management Ltd (No. 2) [2001] BCC 305, 19.79, n. 107, 19.82, n. 114
Re Westmid Packing Services Ltd [1998] 2 All ER 124, 19.23, n. 29, 19.41, n. 54, 19.79, n. 108
Regal (Hastings) Ltd v. Gulliver [1942] 1 All ER 378, 5.14, n. 3, 5.15, 14.22, n. 9
Reid MDA Investment Management Ltd [2003] All ER (D) 128, 18.76, n. 36
Reid v. Ramlort Ltd [2002] All ER (D) 235, 18.76, nn. 34 and 35
Ridgway v. JP Morgan Chase Bank National Association [2007] EWHC 1325, 8.65
Rock Nominees v. RCO [2004] 1 BCLC 439, 15.46, n. 57
Rolled Steel Products Ltd v. BSC [1897] AC 22, 5.96, n. 37
Royal British Bank v. Turquand [1865] 25 LJQB 317, 4.44
Russell v. Northern Bank Development Co. Ltd [1992] 3 All ER 161, 3.15

Salomon v. Salomon & Co. Ltd [1897] AC 22, 5.96, n. 37
Samengo -Turner & ors v. J & H Marsh and McLennan (Services) Ltd and ors [2007] IRLR 237, 8.86
Sanderson v. Griffiths [2003] Ch 162, 4.72, n. 14
Sands v. Clitheroe [2006] BPIR 1000, 18.106, n. 47
Secretary of State for Trade and Industry v. Baker (No. 6) [1999] 1 BCLC 433, 4.25, n. 8
Secretary of State for Trade and Industry v. Baker [1999] 1 WLR 1985, 19.23, n. 18, 19.81, n. 112
Secretary of State for Trade and Industry v. Davies [1996] 4 All ER 289, 19.50, n. 64
Secretary of State for Trade and Industry v. Desai [1992] BCC 110, 19.50, n. 64
Secretary of State for Trade and Industry v. Glover unreported, 19.19, n. 12
Secretary of State for Trade and Industry v. Goldberg [2004] 1 BCLC 597, 19.23, nn. 19 and 22
Secretary of State for Trade and Industry v. Jabble [1998] 1 BCLC 598, 19.18, n. 11
Secretary of State for Trade and Industry v. Jonkler [2006] HC 135, 19.64, n. 80
Secretary of State for Trade and Industry v. Renwick unreported, 19.84, n. 117
Secretary of State for Trade and Industry v. Woolf [2005] WHC 3074, 19.18, n. 11
See of S for T & L v. Gash [1997] 1 BCLC 541, 18.44, n. 11
SG & R Valuation Services Co. v. Boudrais [2008] EWHC 1340, 8.100
Shepherds Investments Ltd v. Walters [2007] IRLR 110, 8.124
Sinclair Investments v. Versailles Trade Finance [2006] 1 BCLC 372, 15.30, n. 41
Smith v. Ampol [1974] AC 821, 15.54, n. 67
Smith v. Croft (No. 1) [1986] 1 WLR 580, 15.18, n. 12, 15.21, n. 24
Smith v. Croft (No. 2) [1988] Ch 114, 15.9, n. 3, 15.18, n. 14, 15.21, n. 24
Smith v. Fawcett Limited [1942] Ch 402, 5.40, n. 17
Smith v. Henniker Major and Co. [2003] Ch 182, 4.67, n. 14
Swan v. North British Australasian Co. [1952] 2 QB 147, 4.58, n.13
Symbian Ltd v. Christensen [2001] IRLR 7, 8.102
Symington's [1905] 8 F [Ct of Sess] 121, 15.69, n. 76

Takacs v. Barclays Services Jersey Ltd [2007] IRLR 877, 8.66
Taylor Fashions v. Liverpool Victoria Trustees [1981] 2 WLR 576, 15.56, n. 68, 15.62, n. 71
Thomas v. Farr plc and Hanover Park Commercial Ltd [2007] IRLR 419, 8.109
Thornton Springer v. NEM Insurance Co. Ltd and others [2000] 2 All E R 489, ch. 16, n. 3

UBA Ltd v. European American Banking Corporation [1984] QB 713, 14.34, n. 23
UBS Wealth Management (UK) Ltd v. Vestra Wealth LLP [2008] EWHC 1974, 8.119
University of Nottingham v. Fishel [2000] IRLR 471, 8.124

Virdi v Abbey Leisure [1990] BCLC 342, 15.74

Wallersteiner v. Moir (No. 2) [1975] QB 373, 15.20
Ward v. Perks and another [2007] All ER (D) 422, 18.25, n. 5, 18. 18.44, n. 12
Welham v. DPP [1961] AC 103, 18.65, n. 29
Wilkinson v. West Coast Capital [2005] WHC 3009, 15.45, n. 56
Williams v. Natural Health Foods Limited [1998] 1 WLR 830, 4.41, n. 10, 14.41, n. 36, 15.30, n. 40

Yuille v. B & B Fisheries (Leigh) Ltd [1958] 2 Lloyd's Rep 596, 14.43, n. 41

1 What is a director?

Introduction

1.1 'In the Companies Acts "director" includes any person occupying the position of director, by whatever name called.' (Companies Act 2006, s. 250)

1.2 The Companies Act 2006 (the 2006 Act) restates the description of 'director' previously included in the Companies Act 1985. The 2006 Act does not define what a director is. Instead it includes a broad description of the term 'director', which is designed to encompass anyone who has real power in the company, i.e. someone who effectively directs the affairs of the company even though he may not be called a director. In determining whether someone is a director, one must look not at the person's title but at what he does, especially in relation to a company's decision-making. Is he the directing mind of the company? This will clearly differ from company to company and will depend on the director's service contract (if there is one) and the company's constitutional document (commonly referred to as its articles of association).

1.3 Companies can either be incorporated with their own articles or can adopt government-drafted articles, known as 'Table A'. An interim form of Table A is applicable to companies incorporated between 1 October 2007 and 30 September 2009. This is based on the original Table A, but amended to reflect the 2006 Act. There are two versions of the interim Table A: one for private companies and one for public companies. Those companies incorporated on or after 1 October 2009 will be incorporated either using their own articles or government-drafted 'Model Articles'. This chapter refers to the regulations made under the 2006 Act in December 2008. These provide for three sets of Model Articles for the following types of company:

- private companies limited by shares ('Private Company Articles');
- private companies limited by guarantee; and
- public companies ('Public Company Articles').

1.4 Companies can describe their directors as council members, executive members, trustees, etc., and these persons will still be directors within the terms of the 2006 Act. The term 'director' does not apply to persons whose title includes the term but who do not exercise real power within a company (see **1.87** below for further details).

The statutory description of director refers to 'any person' rather than any individual, and thus includes corporate bodies with legal personality. One company can be a director of another company but the 2006 Act requires each company to have, in addition, at least one natural person, that is, an individual, on its board (see **1.10** below).

1.5 The Explanatory Notes to the 2006 Act, paragraph 278 refer to the term 'director' as including executive and non-executive directors who have been properly appointed by the company as well as de facto directors. A de facto director is a person who has assumed the status and functions of a director without being properly appointed as such. The term director does not, however, include shadow director, which is separately defined in the 2006 Act (see **1.74** below).

1.6 This chapter looks in detail at these and other types of director commonly found in UK companies. The company law duties owed by directors to their company, as well as their liabilities, depend on the type of director a person is, their service contract/letter of appointment (if any) with the company and the company's articles of association. Directors should also bear in mind that they are subject to a myriad of other duties as set out in statute, notably the Company Directors' Disqualification Act 1986 and the Insolvency Act 1986, regulations such as the City Code on Takeovers and Mergers which applies to public companies, the Listing Rules for companies whose shares are listed on the Official List of the London Stock Exchange and the AIM Rules for companies whose shares are traded on the Alternative Investment Market, and codes of best practice. More broadly, they must also comply with environmental and health and safety requirements, some of which are covered in other chapters of this book.

Eligibility

1.7 Unlike company secretaries, directors have never been expected to hold any formal qualification to qualify for the office. UK law has always been very liberal in allowing most persons to form a company and to act as directors. A director need not even be resident in the UK or a UK citizen to hold a directorship of a UK company.

1.8 The 2006 Act has now introduced some requirements to be satisfied by those acting as company directors. Key changes include:

- the introduction of a minimum age of 16; and
- the requirement to have at least one natural person on the board.

Minimum age of 16

1.9 To act as a director, a person must be at least 16 years old when he is appointed (s. 157). This is in contrast to the position under the Companies Act 1985, which did not specify a minimum age. The government has reserved the power to provide in the future the circumstances under which a person below the age of 16 could still validly be appointed as a director. (The 2006 Act also removed the requirement for the appointment of directors of public companies aged over 70 to be specifically approved by the shareholders.)

A natural person on the board

1.10 Every company must have at least one director who is a natural person, that is, an individual (s. 155). This is to ensure that where the company does a wrong, an individual director can be held personally accountable. Whilst corporate directors continue to be permitted, one company can no longer be the sole director of another company. This has important implications for corporate groups and company formation agents, both of which need to review their group structures, and newly formed companies respectively, to ensure that there is at least one individual on the board.

1.11 Except as discussed above, the 2006 Act does not stipulate any other requirements to be met by a person wishing to be a company director.

1.12 There are, however, some restrictions under the general law about who can be appointed a director, for example, persons who are disqualified may not act as directors. See **Chapter 2** for further information on who is eligible to act as a director and the appointment of directors.

Qualification

1.13 The director of a company need have no professional or other qualification, or have any previous experience. The Institute of Directors offers a 'Chartered Director' qualification to those directors wishing to take it. This, however, is optional.

1.14 A company's articles of association may, however, require a director to hold a specified qualification. This can be a requirement to hold a certain minimum number of shares in the company or, in a professional services company, for all the directors to be qualified to practise as architects, auditors, accountants, actuaries, etc.

Minimum number of directors

1.15 A private company must have at least one director who must be an individual (ss. 154–155). If a private company has more than a single director, then the others may be corporate directors. A public company must have a minimum of two directors, one of whom must be an individual.

1.16 A company's articles of association may stipulate a higher minimum number. For further information on the number of directors and what happens if that number falls below the specified minimum, see **Chapter 2**.

Directors in law: de jure and de facto directors

De jure directors

1.17 A director who has been appointed properly according to the rules, who has agreed to accept the appointment, who is not disqualified, whose details are entered in the company's register of directors and whose appointment has been notified to Companies House is a de jure director (a director as of right). He derives his authority from his office.

De facto directors

1.18 A person who acts as a director but who has not been properly appointed, or indeed appointed at all, is a de facto director (a director as a matter of fact). Notwithstanding any defects in such a director's appointment, a de facto director is one who openly takes part in board decisions on the same basis as the other directors.

1.19 There are a number of guidelines to help determine if someone is a de facto director:

- Is the person part of the corporate governing structure? (He will not be if he is at all times and in all decisions subordinate to the de jure directors.)
- Does he have the right to participate in strategic decisions?
- Is there a family or other relationship between the parties which would tend to establish a position of dominance?
- Has the company held him out as being a director, and did he have access to relevant company information?

1.20 Simply using the title director does not make someone a de facto director if they do not in fact direct the company.

1.21 Who might be deemed to be a de facto director?

- a parent company of a subsidiary;

- family members (e.g. parent, spouse or child) of a de jure director; and
- a substantial shareholder.

1.22 A person who acts as a de facto director is subject to the same duties and liabilities as a properly appointed director.

Note that de facto and shadow directorships are alternatives. A shadow director does not act openly as a de facto director does.

Executive and non-executive directors

Executive directors

1.23 The 2006 Act, like its predecessor, neither defines executive and non-executive directors nor distinguishes between them. All directors owe the same duties and have the same responsibilities and liabilities to the company, although executive directors will have additional responsibilities arising from their service contracts and, in practice, non-executives are expected to devote less time to company affairs. Notwithstanding the lack of definition, the terms 'executive' and 'non-executive' are well understood and commonly uscd, especially in large and listed companies.

1.24 Full-time working directors are often described as executive directors. So a sole director of a private company would usually be its executive director even though he may not describe himself as such. Executive directors have specific responsibilities additional to their responsibilities as members of the board of directors. They are responsible for managing the company's business or a specific part of it on a day-to-day basis. A company's finance director is an executive director responsible for managing the company's financial affairs. A managing director will be an executive director with overall responsibility for managing the company's business.

1.25 Executive directors are usually employees of the company working under an employment (or service) contract and as such have rights and duties separate from those arising from their office as director. For example, an employed executive director may be entitled to compensation under his service contract on dismissal by the company whereas he may not be so entitled simply by virtue of his directorship. Employed executive directors usually receive a salary and benefits under their contract. The company's articles usually grant the executive directors extensive powers. See **Chapter 8** for further information on directors as employees.

1.26 Article 3 in each of the Private and Public Company Articles provides that, 'Subject to the articles, the directors are responsible for the management of the company's business, for which purpose they may exercise all the powers of the company.'

Managing director or chief executive

1.27 A company's articles usually permit the directors to appoint one of their number as the company's managing director and to delegate to that individual such of the board's powers as deemed appropriate. 'Managing director' is the English term which tends to be used in private and smaller public companies in contrast to the American term 'chief executive' or 'chief executive officer', which is used in larger companies, especially those listed on the markets. All three terms are broadly equivalent.

1.28 A managing director is typically given overall responsibility for managing the company and is, therefore, normally the most senior full-time executive director. Where the company has an executive chairman, the chairman would be the most senior executive director of the company. The managing director is usually an employee of the company. Although regulation 72 of Table A provided specifically for the appointment of a managing director, this provision has not been carried forward into the Model Articles, which simply permit the directors to delegate their powers to 'such person or committee … as they think fit' without specifically mentioning a managing director (article 5 in each of the Private and Public Company Articles).

1.29 A managing director is normally given wide-ranging power by the articles to direct the affairs of the company. The managing director's powers will depend on the company's articles and the individual's service contract with the company. A managing director is often delegated the authority to manage the day-to-day business of the company. Such authority includes allowing the managing director to enter into contracts on behalf of the company either generally or limited to specific transactions. The managing director reports to the board or to the company's chairman (see **1.42** below).

1.30 Both the appointment of a managing director and the delegation of powers to such an individual can be made by a simple board resolution. The articles normally empower the board to revoke the appointment of a managing director at any time, subject to the terms of his service contract with the company. The managing director's appointment terminates when he ceases to be an employee of the company.

1.31 See **Appendix 2,** the ICSA Guidance Note on the role of the chief executive.

Non-executive directors

1.32 Non-executive directors owe the same duties to the company and have the same liabilities as their executive counterparts, although they do not devote their whole time to the company. They are part-time directors who are not usually employed by the company but operate under a contract for services or letter of appointment. They receive a fee for their work.

1.33 Non-executives are normally appointed to the boards of listed companies to provide an independent and impartial view of the board's deliberations and decisions. They are expected to exercise independence of judgement and to undertake a critical supervisory role, overseeing what the executive board does. They are also increasingly being recruited by large private companies. Non-executives often have quite extensive powers, especially to scrutinise the decisions of the executive directors. Recent years have seen a significant increase in the responsibilities and time commitment of non-executive directors. There is, however, little official guidance on the role and responsibilities of a non-executive director other than, in the context of listed companies, the provisions of the Combined Code on Corporate Governance (the 'Combined Code' or 'Code').[1] The Code is discussed in **Chapter 12**.

The Combined Code

1.34 Requirement for non-executive directors: Code principle A.3 recommends that listed companies should have a balance of executive and non-executive directors, with the aim of ensuring that no one individual or group of individuals can dominate the board. The Code also recommends that, except for smaller companies (those below the FTSE 350), the independent non-executives (excluding the chairman) should comprise at least half the board (Code provision A.3.2). The board should appoint one of the independent non-executives to be the senior independent director (see **1.40** below).

1.35 The role of the non-executive director: Supporting Principle A.1 of the Code provides specific guidance on the role and responsibilities of the non-executive director. They should:

- constructively challenge and help develop proposals on strategy;
- monitor the performance of the executive directors;
- satisfy themselves on the integrity of financial information and that financial controls and systems of risk management are robust and defensible;
- appoint and remove executive directors and become involved in succession planning; and
- participate in board committees, especially the audit, remuneration and nomination committees.

1.36 In relation to the audit committee, for example, the non-executive directors should ensure that the company's books are in order, hold the executives accountable for the expenditure of the company's funds and ensure that the interests of the company's shareholders are protected. In short, they are corporate watchdogs who, to discharge their duties effectively, need to maintain a certain distance from the executive directors.

1.37 Schedule B of the Combined Code (on the liability of non-executives) states that non-executives are likely to devote significantly less time to the company's affairs than the executive directors and are likely to have significantly less detailed knowledge and experience of the company's affairs than the executive directors. These matters may be relevant in assessing the knowledge, skill and experience to be expected of them. The Code goes on to provide that it is up to each individual non-executive director to determine what is necessary in the particular circumstances for him to comply with the duty of care, skill and diligence that he owes to the company (see **1.54** below).

1.38 The Institute of Directors suggests that non-executives should be expected to bring to a company the following qualities:

- independence;
- impartiality;
- wide experience;
- special knowledge; and
- personal qualities.

1.39 The European Commission in October 2004 recommended that EU member state governments should encourage non-executive participation in listed companies. The Commission's recommendation (which is not binding) contains minimum standards for the qualification, commitment and independence of non-executives. The recommendation follows a very similar approach to non-executive directors to that taken by the Combined Code. In particular, it suggests using the 'comply or explain' approach already in use in the UK as a result of the Combined Code and its predecessors. Because of its similarity to the Combined Code, no changes needed to be made to the Code as a result of the recommendation.

Senior independent director

1.40 In the listed company context, one of the independent non-executive directors should be identified as the senior independent director (SID) – someone with whom investors can raise concerns if contacting the chairman, the chief executive or the finance director has failed to resolve the issue or for which such contact is inappropriate (Code provision A.3.3). To discharge this role, SIDs should attend sufficient meetings with major shareholders to obtain a balanced understanding of the issues and concerns of such shareholders (Code provision D.1.1). Part of the SID's role is also to hold annual meetings with the non-executive directors, without the chairman present, to appraise the chairman's performance (Code provision A.1.3). They should also meet with the non-executive directors on such other occasions as are deemed appropriate.

Independence

1.41 Non-executive directors may or may not be independent. The Combined Code requires at least half the board to be independent non-executive directors. The board must consider the independence of each director and identify in its annual report each non-executive it considers to be independent (Code provision A.3.1). Independence includes independence of judgement and of character. Also relevant are whether there are relationships or circumstances which could affect, or appear to affect, a director's independence, including if the director:

- has been an employee of the company or group within the last five years;
- has had a material business relationship with the company in the last three years, including certain indirect relationships;
- receives or has received any additional remuneration from the company other than director's fees, participates in the company's share option or performance-related pay scheme or is a member of the company's pension scheme;
- has close family ties with any of the company's advisers, directors or senior employees;
- has cross-directorships or significant links with other directors;
- represents a major shareholder; or
- has been a director for more than nine years.

The board should state its reasons if it decides that a director is independent notwithstanding the existence of these relationships or circumstances.

Chairman

1.42 The chairman can be either an executive or a non-executive director. In private companies, the chairmanship tends to be combined with the role of managing director. However, in listed companies, the Combined Code recommends that the roles of chairman and chief executive should be separate and not filled by the same person (Code provision A.2.1). The Code also provides that a chief executive should not go on to be chairman of the same company (Code provision A.2.2). This is due to the difficulties that can arise from a former chief executive not having sufficient detachment to objectively assess executive management and strategy. According to Peter Montagnon, director of investment affairs at the Association of British Insurers, 'the chairman is supposed to oversee strategy and make sure the board tests it and decision-making is robust. If the chairman was the chief executive who developed the strategy, he is supervising himself. There are risks in that' (*The Financial Times*, 15–16 December 2007, p. 14). The chairman's role is to run the board. It is for the managing director or the chief executive to run the company. Institutional investors become concerned when one individual combines both roles, as Robert Maxwell of Mirror Group and Maxwell Communications Corporation and Conrad Black of Hollinger Group did, or when someone who has been the chief executive is then promoted to the chairmanship of the company, as happened to Stuart Rose (the chief executive of Marks & Spencer plc who was promoted to the chairmanship of the company in 2008). As Maxwell and Black demonstrated, the potential for wrongdoing, corporate abuse and even fraud is greatly increased when so much power is concentrated in the hands of a single person.

1.43 Like the chief executive, the chairman is appointed by the board. He can be either a full-time or part-time director.

1.44 The chairman's main role is to lead the board. He should support the managing director or chief executive (where there is one), and be the company's main spokesman in communicating with investors, the market and the media. He will take a leading role in determining the nature and composition of the board, including taking soundings from significant shareholders as to the suitability of candidates for the position of chief executive and the appropriateness of the non-executive directors. His most critical role, according to Lord Cuckney, former vice-chairman of Glaxo Wellcome plc, is to ensure that the right people are appointed to the board. He will also chair shareholder and board meetings.

1.45 The Model Articles permit the directors to appoint one of their number to act as chairman of the board (article 12 in each of the Private and Public Company Articles). The Private Company Articles provide:

> **'Chairing of directors' meetings**
> (1) The directors may appoint a director to chair their meetings.
> (2) The person so appointed for the time being is known as the chairman.
> (3) The directors may terminate the chairman's appointment at any time.
> (4) If the chairman is not participating in a directors' meeting within ten minutes of the time at which it was to start, the participating directors must appoint one of themselves to chair it.'

1.46 In addition, the Public Company Articles permit the appointment of a deputy or assistant chairman to act in the chairman's absence (article 12(3)):

> **'Chairing directors' meetings**
> (1) The directors may appoint a director to chair their meetings.
> (2) The person so appointed for the time being is known as the chairman.
> (3) The directors may appoint other directors as deputy or assistant chairmen to chair directors' meetings in the chairman's absence.
> (4) The directors may terminate the chairman's appointment at any time.
> (5) If neither the chairman nor any director appointed generally to chair directors' meetings in the chairman's absence is participating in a meeting within ten minutes of the time at which it was to start, the participating directors must appoint one of themselves to chair it.'

1.47 In the event that a majority vote cannot be reached on a board decision, the articles usually grant the chairman a second or casting vote. The Model Articles provide for this in identical terms in the Private and Public Company Articles (article 13, Private and article 14, Public Company Articles), as follows:

> **'Casting vote**
> (1) If the numbers of votes for and against a proposal are equal, the chairman or other director chairing the meeting has a casting vote.
> (2) But this does not apply if, in accordance with the articles, the chairman or other director is not to be counted as participating in the decision-making process for quorum or voting purposes.'

1.48 The chairman has complete discretion on how to exercise his casting vote, although it is customary for him to vote to maintain the staus quo on the grounds that there is no majority in favour of change.

1.49 A director who is appointed to chair board meetings is usually the same person who chairs meetings of the company's shareholders.

1.50 The Model Articles provide for the appointment of a chairman of a general meeting in identical terms in the Private and Public Company Articles (article 39, Private and article 31, Public Company) as follows:

> 'The chairman shall chair the general meetings if present and willing to do so.'

1.51 A director appointed to chair board meetings would, before the 2006 Act, have had a casting vote to exercise in addition to any vote he may have had as a shareholder of the company. For companies formed since 1 October 2007, the effect of ss. 281(3) and 282(3) is to abolish the concept of the chairman's casting vote in relation to general meetings of the company. Companies formed before 1 October 2007 whose articles permit the chairman to have a casting vote can continue with the provision (Fifth Commencement Order, Schedule 5, paragraph 2(5)). In publicly listed companies, however, it is the proxy votes held by a chairman rather than any casting vote which he has which determine the passing or otherwise of a resolution. (See **4.34**.)

1.52 For listed companies, Principle A.2 of the Combined Code provides that the chairman is responsible for:

- leading the board;
- ensuring that the directors receive accurate, timely and clear information;
- ensuring effective communication with shareholders;
- facilitating the effective contribution of non-executive directors; and
- ensuring constructive relations between the executive and non-executive directors.

1.53 A good chairman should also provide the company with a strategic vision and objectives. One former director of the Bank of England and chairman of many boards, the late Professor Sir Roland Smith, succinctly explained the chairman's role: 'I just help to develop strategies and advise on improving company performance.' (See **Appendix 2**, the ICSA Guidance Note on the role of the chairman.)

Duty of care, skill and diligence

1.54 Executive and non-executive directors have the same duties and liabilities. The duties of executive directors are typically set out in their service contract, whereas those of non-executives tend to be governed by their letter of appointment (if any) and the common law.

1.55 In recent years, there has been a trend to hold non-executives to a higher standard than previously. The 2006 Act follows this trend. In acting with due skill and care, directors must comply with the dual objective and subjective test set out in s. 174. The objective part of the test sets the minimum standard expected of all directors and requires that a director exercise the care, skill and diligence that would be exercised by a reasonably diligent person with the general knowledge, skill and experience that may be expected of a person carrying out the functions of that director. The subjective test requires a director to perform his functions with the general knowledge, skill and experience that the director in fact possesses. This dual test aims to ensure that directors with more experience and/or specialist knowledge, including non-executive directors, are subject to a higher test by virtue of their particular knowledge, skill and experience. For instance, a non-executive director who happens to be an accountant will be expected to bring his financial expertise to bear when discharging his duties as a non-executive director. Note that the application of this duty will vary depending on the nature of the company concerned, in particular its size and whether it is private, public or listed. In practice, a far higher standard of conduct is expected of directors of listed companies. Such directors have additional duties imposed on them by virtue of the Listing Rules or the AIM Rules, as appropriate, as well as the Disclosure and Transparency Rules and the Prospectus Rules. See **Chapter 5** for discussion of the duty of care, skill and diligence.

Conflicts of interest

1.56 The 2006 Act has codified the complicated common law position regulating directors' conflicts of interest. Section 175 provides that 'A director of a company must avoid a situation in which he has, or can have, a direct or indirect interest that conflicts, or possibly may conflict, with the interests of the company.'

1.57 The duty covers transactions between a director and a third party, including other companies, so it would, for example, catch any other directorships which the director held. This duty extends to directorships of other group companies as well as unrelated companies. The duty does not apply where the situation cannot reasonably be regarded as likely to give rise to a conflict of interest. This exception may be of limited use, however, as it is likely to be difficult to determine at the time a director accepts a directorship of another company whether the exception may be relied on.

1.58 Before the 2006 Act, directors managed the potential conflicts of interest that might arise between their directorships of multiple companies by absenting themselves from relevant board meetings. The 2006 Act does not permit conflicts to be managed in this way. Instead, directors who wish to accept an appointment as director of another company should consider taking the following steps:

- disclose the appointment to the board of the first company and obtain the board's specific approval to accept the appointment (this assumes that the board has the power to authorise such appointment);
- ensure that the board discusses what should happen if an actual conflict arises subsequently; and
- if a conflict does arise, the director should seek independent advice on how he should manage it. This is especially so where the conflict relates to confidential information.

1.59 Additional restrictions apply to directors of Official List and AIM companies. These are discussed in **Chapters 5** and **12**.

1.60 Many non-executives have more than one non-executive directorship. It is quite common for executives of one company to be non-executive directors of other companies. There is a very limited pool of non-executives from which companies can make their selection. There are concerns that the codification of directors' duties, particularly those relating to conflicts of interest, in the 2006 Act has significantly increased the burden on all directors, both executive and non-executive. This is especially so given the codification of the common law derivative action, which extends considerably the ability of shareholders to sue directors for wrongs done to the company. Non-executive directors may find themselves particularly exposed unless they keep themselves fully informed of the company's financial and other affairs. These concerns may have the effect of reducing further the already small pool of people willing to act as non-executive directors.

1.61 The Higgs Report (published in 2003 before the enactment of the 2006 Act) on the role and effectiveness of non-executive directors suggested that boards need to widen the pool of candidates from which they appoint non-executives. The Tyson Report (published later in 2003) on the recruitment and development of non-executives concluded that UK companies would benefit from more diversity among non-executives and that companies should recruit people of a different background from that from which non-executives are usually drawn. In particular, companies should aim to recruit non-executives from women and ethnic minorities. However, no progress has been made on widening the pool of non-executives: most non-executives are appointed from other large UK public companies; and there are still very few female or non-UK directors.

Alternate directors

1.62 It can be useful for a director to appoint someone to be his alternate or proxy at board meetings which the director is unable to attend because, for example, the director will be on vacation. However, as the office of director is personal, the 2006 Act does not authorise the directors to appoint an alternate to act on their behalf. A director can therefore only appoint an alternate if permitted to do so by the company's articles. It is normal for a company's articles to permit the appointment of alternates. With advances in technology, the appointment of alternates is becoming less common as directors can usually attend board meetings by conference call or video link.

1.63 The Public Company Articles permit the appointment of another director or a person approved by the board as an alternate, as follows:

> 'Appointment and removal of alternates
> (25.1) Any director (the 'appointor') may appoint as an alternate any other

director, or any other person approved by resolution of the directors, to –
(a) exercise that director's powers, and
(b) carry out that director's responsibilities,
in relation to the taking of decisions by the directors in the absence of the alternate's appointor.

(2) Any appointment or removal of an alternate must be effected by notice to the company signed by the appointor, or in any other manner approved by the directors.

(3) The notice must –
identify the proposed alternate, and
in the case of a notice of appointment, contain a statement signed by the proposed alternate that the proposed alternate is willing to act as the alternate of the director giving the notice.'

1.64 Note that there is no equivalent permission in the Private Company Articles as it was considered that few private companies would want to provide for the appointment of alternates. A private company may permit the appointment of alternates in its articles of association, and larger private companies may like the flexibility of allowing their directors to appoint alternates.

1.65 Where a company's articles permit the appointment of an alternate it is important to follow the article closely as it can differ considerably from company to company, not only in terms of who may be appointed to act as an alternate, but also the manner of appointment of the alternate and when his appointment will cease. For example, the Public Company Articles provide that an alternate must be either an existing director or a person approved by the board; his appointment must be effected by serving a notice on the company signed by his appointor, identifying the proposed alternate and containing a signed statement by the alternate that he is willing to act as an alternate for his appointor. It is also common for bespoke articles to permit directors to appoint other directors of the same company to act as their alternates without board approval.

1.66 Subject to a company's articles, there are no special formalities for appointing an alternate director. They are appointed in the same way as any other director and their appointment must be notified to Companies House. Their details must also be recorded in the company's register of directors. An alternate's appointment will automatically terminate when his appointor ceases to be a director. It will also terminate when his appointor notifies the company that he has revoked the alternate's appointment, on the death of the appointor or when the alternate would no longer be able to act as a director, for example, because he is disqualified. Thus article 27 of the Public Company Articles provides that:

> 'Termination of alternate directorship
> 27. An alternate director's appointment as an alternate terminates –
> (a) when the alternate's appointor revokes the appointment by notice to the company in writing specifying when it is to terminate;
> (b) on the occurrence in relation to the alternate of any event which, if it occurred in relation to the alternate's appointor, would result in the termination of the appointor's appointment as a director;
> (c) on the death of the alternate's appointor; or
> (d) when the alternate's appointor's appointment as a director terminates, except that an alternate's appointment as an alternate does not terminate when the appointor retires by rotation at a general meeting and is then re-appointed as a director at the same general meeting.'

1.67 Subject to contrary provision in the company's articles, an alternate is not regarded as the agent of the appointing director but is deemed for all purposes to be a director (s. 250 of the 2006 Act and article 26, Public Company Articles). Article 26(2) provides that:

> 'Except as the articles specify otherwise, alternate directors –
> (a) are deemed for all purposes to be directors;
> (b) are liable for their own acts and omissions;
> (c) are subject to the same restrictions as their appointors; and
> (d) are not deemed to be agents of or for their appointors.'

1.68 An alternate therefore enjoys the same status as other directors on the board and, in his appointor's absence, has the same rights and liabilities as those other directors. He is also responsible for his own acts and omissions. This means that an alternate is entitled to receive notice of board and (where the appointor is a committee member) committee meetings and, in his appointor's absence, to attend those meetings and to vote. However, an alternate is not entitled to remuneration from the company for his services. Note that by appointing an alternate, the appointor is not relieved of his duties and responsibilities as a director.

1.69 Who may act as an alternate? In principle, anyone. In practice, a company's articles may restrict who a director can appoint to act as his alternate. A common restriction is that directors may only appoint one of their fellow directors. Where a fellow director acts as an alternate for one of his colleagues, he has an additional vote to exercise at board meetings (and committee meetings, if appropriate), which is separate from his right to vote in his own capacity as a director.

Nominee directors

1.70 A director who is appointed to the board by a particular shareholder or group of shareholders, a major creditor or some other group of people is usually known as a nominee director, that is, he has been nominated to the board to represent and/or to protect the interests of the person who appointed him.

1.71 In what circumstances might a company have a nominee director on its board? Companies with outside investment, especially private equity investment, would usually, as a term of the investment, have a representative of the investor on the board. A lending bank may also wish to protect its interests by appointing a nominee to the board of the company to which it has loaned a significant amount. A joint venture company set up by two or more other companies would typically have an investment or subscription agreement stipulating for the appointment of a director from each of the founding companies. A parent company may require one of its directors to serve on the board of a subsidiary company.

1.72 Nominee directors are considered in law to be the same as other directors on the board and have the same rights and liabilities as those other directors. Equally, there are no special formalities for appointing a nominee director. They are appointed in the same way as any other director. They may be executive directors or non-executive.

1.73 One particular issue which nominee directors face, more so than other types of director, is that of conflicts of interest. On the one hand, a director owes duties to his company; on the other, he is probably an office holder or employee of the company which appointed him and thus feels he has obligations to that company also. As a company director, the nominee must exercise independent judgement (s. 173) in the interests of the company, ignoring the interests and wishes of his appointor, unless he is authorised to act in accordance with those interests and wishes by the company's articles. Although a nominee may follow instructions, he must comply with all his other duties as a company director and, in particular, with the new duty introduced by the 2006 Act to promote the success of the company. The nominee must act to promote the success of the company in the interests of the members as a whole (s. 172), rather than simply representing the interests of his appointor. The nominee cannot allow his interest in representing an investor or bank, for example, to conflict with the duty he owes the company. Although he can be a director of both his appointor and the nominee company this must not put him in a conflict of interest (s. 175). The position of nominees in a corporate group can be difficult as the nominee will owe a fiduciary duty to both the parent company and the subsidiary of which he has been appointed a nominee by the parent. **Chapter 5** discusses the issue of conflicts in more detail.

Shadow directors

1.74 '... "shadow director" ... means a person in accordance with whose directions or instructions the directors of the company are accustomed to act.' (s. 251(1))

1.75 Unlike the other types of director discussed above, the term shadow director is defined by the 2006 Act in identical terms to the definition included in the Companies Act 1985. It follows, therefore, that a shadow director does not fall within the description of 'director' set out in s. 250 of the 2006 Act, with all that that description entails.

1.76 As the term suggests, a person acting as a shadow director does not act openly as a director; instead, he remains in the background, directing the board while at the same time avoiding being appointed as a director. A shadow director can be distinguished from both de jure and de facto directors by three factors:

- he seeks to evade the duties and liabilities of de facto and de jure directors;
- he does not claim to be a director and prefers to exert his influence from behind the scenes; and
- the board is accustomed to act on the directions of a shadow director so he is the ultimate source of decision-making power in the company, unlike the other directors who will tend to be equal or similar in status and influence.

1.77 To be a shadow director, the person must have real influence over the affairs of the company and be able to direct and instruct a governing majority of the board (direction and instruction are to be determined on a case-by-case basis). Advice or guidance given to directors can amount to a direction or instruction. It is not necessary to show that the board surrendered its discretion to the shadow director. It is sufficient that the board were accustomed to act in accordance with a shadow director's 'guidance'.

1.78 There are two exceptions to the statutory definition of shadow director.

1.79 First, a person acting in a purely professional capacity will not be deemed to be a shadow director (s. 251(2)). This is understandable as professional advice tends to be limited to particular matters rather than the business as a whole. If a board follows advice given to it by its accountant in relation to, for instance, a proposed disposal of the business, then that accountant will not, simply by virtue of giving that advice in a professional capacity, be at risk of being found to be a shadow director. If, on the other hand, the accountant went beyond simply advising the board of its options by seeking to direct and instruct the board, and the board acted on the accountant's directions, then the accountant would be at risk of being held to be a shadow director.

1.80 Second, in certain limited circumstances, a parent company is not to be regarded as a shadow director of any of its subsidiaries (s. 251(3)). A parent company often exercises significant influence over a subsidiary and can be in danger of being categorised as a shadow director. The 2006 Act provides that in three specified situations a parent company is not to be regarded as a shadow director of its subsidiaries 'by reason only' that the subsidiary's directors are 'accustomed to act in accordance with' the parent company's directions or instructions. The three situations are:

- the general duties of directors found in Part 10, Chapter 2 of the 2006 Act;
- transactions between a company and its directors requiring shareholder approval found in Part 10, Chapter 4 of the 2006 Act; and
- contracts with a sole shareholder who is also a director found in s. 231 of the 2006 Act.

1.81 Where a parent company is held to be a shadow director of one of its subsidiaries, it does not necessarily follow that the directors of the parent company are also shadow directors of the subsidiary. Equally, in the three situations given above, even though a parent company is not to be regarded as a shadow director, the directors of the parent may, by what they do, be so regarded.

1.82 An individual or a company can be a shadow director for the purposes of the 2006 Act as well as the Insolvency Act 1986 and the Company Directors Disqualification Act 1986.

1.83 Persons who might be at risk of being deemed to be shadow directors include:

- a controlling or significant shareholder;
- a former director or chairman of the company;
- a disqualified director;
- a family member, such as a spouse or child of a director;
- a secured creditor;
- a company doctor;
- a board of a parent company in accordance with whose instructions a

subsidiary is accustomed to act, provided that the situation does not fall within one of the three exceptions in s. 251(3); and

- a bank, especially when a company is having financial difficulties (although banks are careful to ensure that their advice is given to avoid their becoming liable as shadow directors).

1.84 The 2006 Act does not codify the duties owed by shadow directors. Instead, the general duties of directors set out in Part 10, Chapter 2 of the 2006 Act apply to shadow directors where, and to the extent that, the common law rules or equitable principles which they replace so apply (s. 170(5)). This means that shadow directors must look at the 2006 Act as well as the previous common law and equitable principles to determine the duties they owe to a company. As a shadow director does not fall within the statutory description of a director, he will not owe the company the full range of fiduciary duties as are owed by a de facto director. Instead, depending on his position and on what he does, certain fiduciary obligations may arise. Some of the statutory provisions of the 2006 Act which apply to directors specifically extend to shadow directors also, as follows:

- the general duties of directors set out in ss. 171–177;
- the duty to declare an interest in existing transactions (s. 187);
- the provisions relating to transactions between a company and its directors requiring shareholder approval (s. 223);
- the provisions relating to directors' service contracts, although this is of limited relevance given that a shadow director is unlikely to have a service contract with the company (s. 230);
- the provisions regarding contracts with a sole shareholder who is also a director (s. 231); and
- the ratification of directors' acts by shareholders (s. 239).

1.85 A shadow director cannot avoid liability as a director simply by not having been formally appointed as a director.

1.86 Where the board acts in accordance with the instructions of a shadow director, the shadow directorship should be notified to Companies House on Form 288a. (Form 288a will continue to be used until s. 288 of the CA 1985 is repealed and replaced by s. 167 of the 2006 Act – this is expected to be on 1 October 2009.) Note that the shadow director may be unwilling to sign the 'consent to act declaration' on the form and in this case an existing officer of the company should sign it and send it to Companies House with an explanation of the circumstances of the appointment.

Other types of director

1.87 Many individuals with director in their title, such as sales director, marketing director, local, regional, associate or divisional director, are not 2006 Act directors. Such titles, especially in banks, are usually awarded to confer status on the individual concerned to facilitate their dealings with third parties, such as suppliers and customers. When used in this way, the 'director' titles have no standing in law as these individuals cannot be described as having the ability to direct the affairs of the company. They have no right to attend board meetings and are not subject to the responsibilities of a 2006 Act director. They may, however, by their actions, be judged to be de facto directors of the company (see **1.18**). If they are also judged to have been held out as directors of the company, they could commit the company to contracts which are beyond the company's powers to enter.

Sometimes, a company's articles will provide for the appointment of associate or divisional directors. These terms have no generally understood meaning, so one must examine the articles to check what authority and powers an individual with such a title has. The articles would typically provide that such persons have no right to attend board meetings.

Source

1 Although the Code is a voluntary one, listed companies are required by the Listing Rules to state whether they comply with it and, if not, to explain why not. Many AIM companies also comply with the Combined Code although they are not required to do so by the AIM Rules.

2

Appointment of directors

Introduction

2.1 The Companies Acts have historically said very little about the appointment of directors. The Companies Act 2006 (the Act) maintains this tradition but contains a few more requirements governing the appointment of directors. It stipulates:

- the number of directors a company must have: a private company must have at least one director and a public company at least two (s. 154);
- at least one director must be a natural person, i.e. an individual (s. 155);
- each director who is a natural person must be at least 16 years old (s. 157); and
- the directors may provide a service address for the company's register of directors rather than their residential address (s. 163).

2.2 Apart from the first requirement, these are all new; they were not a feature of the previous Companies Act 1985 (The 1985 Act). The Act has repealed (from April 2007) the maximum age limit of 70 years for directors of public companies.

2.3 There is no general requirement that directors should be chosen by the shareholders.

Eligibility to act as a director

2.4 Before a person may become a director, he must be eligible to be appointed as such. There are very few legal restrictions on who may be a director. The Act does not specify any qualification requirements and almost anyone can become a director. Two statutes, the Company Directors Disqualification Act 1986 and the Insolvency Act 1986, do, however, prohibit the following persons from being appointed as a director:

- a director convicted of a criminal offence in connection with the promotion, formation, management, liquidation or striking off of a company;
- a director who has persistently defaulted in filing or delivering returns, accounts or other documents specified by companies legislation;

- a director found guilty of fraudulent trading or any fraud or breach of duty in relation to a company which is being wound up;
- a director of an insolvent company who is adjudged by the court to be unfit to be concerned in the management of a company;
- an undischarged bankrupt who does not have leave of the court to act;
- a director in breach of competition laws;
- a director who has been ordered to contribute to the assets of a company which has been involved in fraudulent or wrongful trading; and
- a person who is prohibited for failing to pay amounts owing under a county court administration order.

2.5 Furthermore, a director of an insolvent company cannot, without court leave, be appointed as a director of a company with a 'prohibited' name (either the name of the company that went into insolvent liquidation or a name so similar that it suggests an association with that company).

Disqualification

2.6 The Secretary of State can disqualify a person from acting as a director if he considers that it would be in the public interest for the director to be disqualified. A person who is currently disqualified may not act as a director without court leave.

2.7 In a significant change to the law on director disqualification, from 1 October 2009 the Act empowers the government to make regulations to disqualify from being a director of a UK company persons who are disqualified in another country (Part 40, ss. 1182–1191). This means that persons disqualified in other countries will no longer be able to be involved in the conduct of UK companies, whether in the UK or in the country in which they were disqualified. See **Chapter 19** on disqualification.

Minimum and maximum ages

2.8 To comply with the age discrimination legislation, the Act has repealed the restriction on persons aged 70 or more from acting as directors of public companies or private company subsidiaries of public companies (with effect from April 2007). Now, persons over 70 can become or continue as directors of public companies (or their private company subsidiaries) without shareholder approval. This will be welcome news for directors as well as for companies and shareholders. It means that companies do not lose the wealth of experience, expertise and connections that such directors have built up over the years.

2.9 It has also introduced a new minimum age requirement (with effect from 1 October 2008). A person may only be appointed as a director once he has attained the age of 16, although a person under 16 may be appointed provided that his appointment does not take effect until he is 16 (s. 157). Where a person under 16 was already a director before the new law came into effect on 1 October 2008, he will have ceased to be a director on that day (s. 159). The company will then have to amend its register of directors accordingly, but need not notify the Registrar of Companies. If the company fails to amend its register, the Registrar can amend the public register by removing that director.

Natural person

2.10 Another new requirement is that (with effect from 1 October 2008) every company must have at least one natural person on its board as a director (s. 155). This is to ensure that there is a natural person who can, where the law provides, be held personally accountable for the company's failings. This requirement may particularly impact corporate groups with a number of subsidiaries which simply have corporate directors on their boards. Such groups will need to ensure that there is at least one natural person on the board of each company in the group, in addition to any corporate directors. There is a grace period until October 2010 which is the longstop date for compliance by those companies which did not have at least one natural person on the board on 8 November 2006, the date the Act received royal assent.

Articles of association

2.11 A company's articles of association may impose additional restrictions on eligibility. There is no set list of exclusions as each company will have its own requirements, but most will exclude minors (prior to the Act taking effect in October 2008), persons suffering from a mental disorder and persons who have made any arrangement or compromise with their creditors. The articles may also require a director to have a particular qualification, for example, a director of an architects' or auditors' practice may be required to be a qualified architect or capable of being appointed an auditor in his own right, respectively.

Shareholding qualification

2.12 There is no statutory requirement for a director to be a shareholder. A company's articles may, however, require each of its directors to hold a minimum number of shares in the company to ensure that they have an interest in its success. Such a share qualification is rarely found in articles nowadays. In private companies, especially small, closely held companies, it is quite common for the directors and the shareholders to be the same individuals. In such a case, it is important for the directors when fulfilling their role as directors to comply with their duties and responsibilities as directors, rather than as shareholders.

Other requirements

2.13 There is no restriction on the number of directorships an individual may hold, and many executive directors also hold non-executive directorships.

2.14 Finally, there is no nationality requirement for directors. Although most directors of UK companies are UK citizens, there are a number of high-profile directors of UK companies who are foreign nationals (at the time of writing, for example, Vittorio Colao of Vodafone and Clara Furse of the London Stock Exchange).

Chartered directors

2.15 Although there are no formal qualification requirements for a person wishing to become a director, the Institute of Directors has a Chartered Director qualification, which can be obtained after following a course of study and passing a rigorous examination. This is widely recognised as the professional qualification for directors, having been referred to as a 'gold standard in director training and development' by Co-operative Insurance and a 'must-have for all directors' by the Quoted Companies Alliance. The qualification aims to set a benchmark for directors and to raise their standards. Demand for the qualification, according to the Institute of Directors, is increasing strongly despite the stringent entry requirements.

2.16 Applicants must be a member of the Institute and must either have been a company director for three years (if they have a degree or recognised professional qualification) or if they do not have such a qualification, they need to have been a company director for seven years. Successful candidates must agree to adhere to the Institute's Chartered Director Code of Professional Conduct. This requires directors to serve the interests of the company's shareholders, act responsibly towards other stakeholders, refrain from anti-competitive behaviour and avoid conflicts of interest. They must also agree to at least 30 hours of further continuing professional development each year. Provided they satisfy those requirements, they can call themselves a Chartered Director and put C.Dir after their name.

Means of appointment

Appointment of first directors

2.17 The first directors of a company are those persons who have agreed to take office by signing Form 10 on the incorporation of a company. They automatically become directors once the company is formed. Subsequent appointments are governed by the company's articles of association.

2.18 There is no requirement that a director must be an individual, and it is common for corporate directors to be appointed as the first directors of a company, especially of shelf (or ready-made) companies. The Act constrains this by requiring each company to have at least one natural person as a director (s. 155). This has already had the effect of limiting the supply of shelf companies, with incorporation agents such as Jordans Limited encouraging clients to advise them of the names of the company's directors so that a tailor-made company can be established for the clients, rather than changing the names of the officers of a shelf company.

2.19 There is no similar requirement for a company secretary to be a natural person so it is possible for a public company to be incorporated with a corporate secretary, a corporate director (the same person can be both the corporate secretary and the corporate director) and a natural person as a director. Note that if the Act requires or authorises a thing to be done by or to *both* a director and the company secretary, it will not be satisfied if it is done by the same person acting in both capacities (s. 280). A private company can be incorporated with a single natural person as a director and no need for a secretary.

Which articles of association?

Until 1 October 2009, the articles of association set out in Table A will continue to be the default articles for companies incorporated before that date.

From 1 October 2009, the new Model Articles will apply to those companies incorporated on or after 1 October 2009 which either do not adopt their own articles or do not exclude the Model Articles.

Even once the Model Articles come into force in October 2009, companies incorporated after that date will be able to adopt Table A as their articles of association. So the provisions of Table A will continue to be relevant for some time to come. This chapter therefore discusses the position relating to directors' appointments under both Table A and the Model Articles. See also **1.3**

Appointment of subsequent directors

2.20 A company's articles of association usually provide for the appointment of subsequent directors by the company's directors or its shareholders. The articles may permit the appointment of subsequent directors by any of the following means:

- by the directors to fill a casual vacancy (this is a vacancy arising otherwise than on a director's term of office expiring, and so there will be a casual vacancy if a director resigns, or is removed, or dies, or becomes disqualified from holding office);

- by the directors to appoint additional directors;
- by the directors to appoint a managing director;
- by the directors to appoint alternate directors;
- by an ordinary resolution of the members;
- by notice in writing from a particular class of shareholder where, for instance, the company is a joint venture company or has outside investors who, as a condition of subscribing for shares, are given the right to appoint one or more directors to the board to protect their interests;
- by written notice from a parent company where the company is a wholly-owned subsidiary.

2.21 Both Table A (regulation 90) and the Model Articles (article 11) provide for an inquorate board to meet to appoint an additional director to make up its numbers or to convene a general meeting.

2.22 Whether the subsequent directors are to be appointed by the directors or the shareholders, the procedure for making the appointment will be as set out in the company's articles.

Appointment by the board

2.23 If a company's articles incorporate Table A, then regulation 79 empowers the board to appoint subsequent directors, provided that the appointment does not cause the number of directors to exceed any permitted maximum number of directors fixed by the articles. If the articles do not permit the board to make such appointments, then only the shareholders can appoint new directors (see **2.26** below).

2.24 If a company is incorporated with or adopts the Model Articles, then these too permit the directors to appoint new directors (article 17, Private Company Articles, article 20 Public Company Articles).

2.25 A director appointed by the board under regulation 79 of Table A only holds office until the next annual general meeting (AGM), unless his appointment is confirmed at that meeting. This does not apply to alternate directors, who hold office for as long their appointor does. The provision that a board appointee only holds office until the next AGM has not been carried forward into the Private Company Articles, which permit such a director to hold office indefinitely.

Appointment by the shareholders

2.26 If a company's articles incorporate Table A, then regulation 78 empowers the shareholders to appoint subsequent directors by passing an ordinary resolution. The Model Articles also permit shareholder appointments of directors (article 17 Private Company Articles, article 20 Public Company Articles).

2.27 If the person to be appointed to the board is not recommended by the board or standing for reappointment following retirement by rotation (see **2.29** below), then prior notice of at least 14 days and not more than 35 clear days must be given to the company by the shareholder proposing that person's appointment as director (regulation 76). The company is then required to give its shareholders not less than seven or more than 28 clear days' notice of a proposed appointment under regulation 78, whether the proposed candidate has been recommended by the board or proposed by a shareholder.

2.28 The Model Articles say very little about the procedure for appointing a director, except for the following. Any person who is willing to act as a director, and is permitted by law to do so, may be appointed a director either by ordinary resolution or by the directors (article 17 Private Company Articles, article 20 Public Company Articles). When a sole director of a private company, who is also its sole shareholder, dies his personal representatives can appoint someone to be a director (article 17(2) of the Private Company Articles).

Retirement of directors by rotation

2.29 Companies incorporated before 6 April 2008 which have Table A articles require one-third of the total number of directors to retire by rotation at each AGM (regulation 73). Private companies usually exclude this provision and, indeed, since 1 October 2007, regulation 73 has been repealed in relation to private companies limited by shares. The requirement for directors of public companies to retire by rotation has been retained in the Public Company Articles (article 21), but amended to comply with the Combined Code (Code provision A.7.1). This provides that directors must be subject to re-election by the shareholders at intervals of no more than three years.

2.30 The procedure to be followed for the retirement of directors by rotation depends on the wording of the company's articles. Table A sets out a full procedure for retirement by rotation in contrast to the Public Company Articles, which simply state that all the directors must retire from office at the first AGM and at every subsequent AGM directors who have been appointed since the last AGM or who were not appointed at one of the previous two AGMS must retire and may offer themselves for reappointment by the shareholders (article 21). For further information on retirement by rotation see **Chapter 3**.

What if the articles are silent on the appointment of directors?

2.31 If the articles are silent on the appointment of directors, then the power to appoint directors is exercisable by the members of the company in general meeting by ordinary resolution.

Additional requirements for public companies

2.32 When directors of a public company are appointed or re-appointed by the members in general meeting, their appointments must be voted on individually by separate resolutions unless there is unanimous agreement to a block resolution. The appointment of a director in breach of this requirement is void (s. 160). This provision enables members to express their disapproval of a particular director without having to reject the entire board. The provision restates s. 292 of the Companies Act 1985.

Additional requirements for listed companies

2.33 In addition to the Act, companies listed on the Official List need to bear in mind the following when appointing directors to the board:

- the Listing Rules (LR);
- the Combined Code; and
- best practice requirements set out by investor protection bodies such as the National Association of Pension Funds and Pensions & Investment Research Consultants.

Listing Rules

2.34 The Listing Rules require a director's appointment to be notified to a Regulatory Information Service by the end of the business day following the decision to appoint (LR 9.6.11R). (See paragraphs 5 and 6 of the Procedure for appointing a director for further information on the Listing Rule requirements.)

Combined Code

2.35 The Combined Code (see **Appendix 1**) gives guidance on board appointments. It requires listed companies to have 'a formal, rigorous and transparent procedure for the appointment of new directors to the board' (Main Principle A.4). This is underpinned by two Supporting Principles:

> 'Appointments to the board should be made on merit and against objective criteria. Care should be taken to ensure that appointees have enough time available to devote to the job. This is particularly important in the case of chairmanships.

The board should satisfy itself that plans are in place for orderly succession for appointments to the board and to senior management, so as to maintain an appropriate balance of skills and experience within the company and on the board.'

The Code Provisions state that:

- all listed companies should have a nomination committee to lead the process of board appointments and to make recommendations to the board (Code Provision A.4.1) (see **2.39** below);
- the nomination committee should evaluate the balance of skills, knowledge and experience of the board and prepare a description of the role and capabilities required for a particular appointment (Code provision A.4.2);
- the nomination committee should prepare a job specification for the appointment of a chairman. A chairman's other significant commitments should be disclosed to the board before his appointment. For accounting periods beginning on or after 29 June 2008, an individual may chair more than one FTSE 100 company (Code provision A.4.3);
- the terms and conditions of appointment of non-executive directors should be made available for inspection and a letter of appointment should set out the time commitment expected. Like a chairman, their other significant commitments should be disclosed to the board before appointment, with a broad indication of the time involved (Code provision A.4.4);
- a full-time executive director should not take on more than one non-executive directorship, or become chairman, of a FTSE 100 company (Code provision A.4.5);
- a separate section of the annual report should describe the work of the nomination committee and the process used in relation to board appointments (Code provision A.4.6).

2.36 The Combined Code also gives guidance on the composition of the board. It requires listed companies to have 'a balance of executive and non-executive directors (and in particular independent non executive directors) such that no individual or small group of individuals can dominate the board's decision-taking' (Main Principle A.3). This is underpinned by Supporting Principles which provide that:

- the board should not be so large as to be unwieldy. It should be of sufficient size that the balance of skills and experience is appropriate for the requirements of the business and that changes to the board's composition can be managed without undue disruption; and
- to ensure that power and information are not concentrated in one or two individuals, there should be a strong representation on the board of both executive and non-executive directors.

The Code Provisions state that:

- except for companies below the FTSE 350, independent non-executives should comprise at least half the board, excluding the chairman (Code provision A.3.2);
- it is for the board to determine whether a director is independent, having regard to the existence of relevant relationships or circumstances, including those specified in the Combined Code (Code provision A.3.1);
- all directors should be subject to election by shareholders at the first AGM after their appointment, and to re-election thereafter at intervals of not more than three years (Code provision A.7.1);
- non-executive directors should be appointed for specified terms, subject to re-election and to the provisions of the Act relating to the removal of directors; their re-appointment should not be automatic (Code provision A.7.2);
- the appointment of a non-executive director for a term beyond six years should be subject to particularly rigorous review (Code provision A.7.2);
- serving for more than nine years may affect the independence of a non-executive director (Code provision A.3.1); and
- non-executives who do in fact serve longer than nine years should be subject to annual re-election by the shareholders (Code provision A.3.1).

2.37 Although the Combined Code only applies to listed companies, its recommendations can serve as a useful starting point for companies not required to comply with it. Clearly, not every provision will be relevant to a small private company. (See **Chapter 12**.)

Investor protection bodies

2.38 The National Association of Pension Funds' Corporate Governance Policy and Voting Guidelines contain much information on the organisation's views on board appointments and composition. The Shareholder Voting Guidelines of the Pensions & Investment Research Consultants also contain best practice recommendations for board appointments and composition. It is beyond the scope of this chapter to discuss them.

Nomination committee

2.39 The role of the nomination committee is to recommend directors for appointment to the board. A majority of its members should be independent non-executive directors. The chairman of the nomination committee should be either the chairman of the board or an independent non-executive director. The committee should make available its terms of reference, explaining its role and the authority delegated to it by the board. The committee will consult with executive directors when considering appointments and may use external consultants to find suitable candidates. Its recommendations will be made to the full board, which will make the final choice of candidate, subject to the re-election of directors by the shareholders as required by the company's articles. Further details on the nomination committee can be found in **Chapter 12**.

What happens if a director has not been appointed properly?

2.40 In a restatement of the Companies Act 1985, s. 285, a defect in appointing a director does not invalidate the actions of the relevant director (s. 161). The director's acts remain valid even though it is later discovered that there was a defect in his appointment or that he was disqualified from acting as a director. Where the defect is discovered a long time after the particular act, it is prudent for the shareholders to ratify the act retrospectively by passing an ordinary resolution (s. 239). Although the director's acts are valid, the section does not validate his appointment as a director. A director who has not been properly appointed may nevertheless be a de facto director (see **1.18**).

Procedure for appointing a director

1. Company secretary should check the articles:
   (a) to determine whether new directors can be appointed by the board or whether they must be appointed by the shareholders in general meeting;
   (b) to see if they limit the maximum number of directors and if the proposed candidate is eligible and agrees to act as a director; and
   (c) for any necessary share qualification or other eligibility requirements.
2. The company and the director should both sign the director's service agreement or letter of appointment if the director is a non-executive.
3. Hold a board or shareholders' meeting to formally approve the appointment of the new director.
4. Company secretary writes to the director confirming his appointment and requesting the following:
   (a) his full name and address, including a service address, the country in which he is usually resident, his nationality, date of birth and business occupation;
   (b) details of any interests that the director has which may conflict with those of the company, including other directorships;
   (c) details of any interests in contracts with the company;
   (d) that the director purchase any shares required by the company's articles in order to be eligible to serve as a director;

(e) a specimen signature if the director is to be a signatory on company cheques; and
(f) the director's bank details so that his remuneration can be paid direct into the account.

Company secretary will also inform the director of the following:

(a) the director's duties under the Act and any relevant regulations to which the company is subject, including the AIM Rules or the Listing Rules;
(b) the dates of future board meetings;
(c) the nature of the company's business if the director is not already involved in the company. Copies of the memorandum and articles of association, annual reports and accounts, and, if the director requests, copies of interim reports, management reports and shareholder circulars;
(d) the company's share dealings rules, including any Model Code of dealings, with which the director must comply;
(e) any directors' and officers' insurance cover that will apply to the director;
(f) in the case of a director of an Official List or AIM or PLUS Markets company, that the director must comply with rules requiring the disclosure of stakes of 3% or more which are set out in DTR 5; directors of other companies need no longer notify the company of their interests in its shares (see Chapter 6); and
(g) in the case of a director of an Official List company, that the director must report transactions in the company's shares or financial instruments (including derivatives) as required by DTR 3 (see **Chapter 6**).

5. In the case of a listed company, the company secretary will require the following information from the director:
   (a) 'details of all directorships held by the director in any other publicly quoted company at any time in the previous five years, indicating whether or not he is still a director;
   (b) any unspent convictions in relation to indictable offences;
   (c) details of receiverships, compulsory liquidations, creditors voluntary liquidations, administrations, company voluntary arrangements or any compositions or arrangement with its creditors generally or any class of its creditors of any company where the director was an executive director at the time of, or within the 12 months preceding, such events;
   (d) details of any compulsory liquidations, administrations or partnership voluntary arrangements of any partnerships where the director was a partner at the time of, or within the 12 months preceding, such events;

(e) details of receiverships of any asset of such person or of a partnership of which the director was a partner at the time of, or within the 12 months preceding, such event; and
(f) details of any public criticisms of the director by statutory or regulatory authorities (including designated professional bodies) and whether the director has ever been disqualified by a court from acting as a director of a company or from acting in the management or conduct of the affairs of any company.'

(LR 9.6.13R)

6. If the company is listed, the company secretary needs to notify a Regulatory Information Service by the end of the business day following the decision to appoint the director of the following:
   (a) the director's name;
   (b) whether the position is executive, non-executive or chairman; and
   (c) the nature of any specific function or responsibility of the position.

   (LR 9.6.11R).

   The director's other business activities, convictions, public criticisms of the director and various other information as specified in 3 above must also be notified to a Regulatory Information Service as soon as possible following the decision to appoint the director and in any event within five business days of the decision (LR 9.6.13R). If there is no information relating to the director as set out in paragraph 5 above, that must be stated in the notification to the Regulatory Information Service (LR 9.6.15G).
7. Company secretary should enter the details of director in the company's register of directors (see 2.44 below).
8. Company secretary should notify Companies House of the appointment within 14 days.
9. Notify insurers of director's appointment to ensure that the directors' and officers' insurance policy also covers the new director.
10. If the company's notepaper includes directors' names, add the new director's name.
11. Consider publicising the director's appointment by a press notice.

Number of directors

2.41 In a restatement of the position under the Companies Act 1985, s. 282, the 2006 Act requires every private company to have at least one director and every public company to have at least two directors (s. 154). If a company fails to have the statutory requisite minimum, then a new provision in the Act enables the Secretary of State to direct the company to make an appointment (s. 156).

2.42 A company's articles of association may specify a higher minimum number of directors and/or limit the maximum number of directors to be appointed. Both of these may be changed by ordinary resolution. Table A, regulation 64 provides for a minimum of two directors, but does not specify a maximum. The Model Articles are silent on the number of directors a company should have as this is now provided for in the Act. The Association of British Insurers suggests that it is good practice for the articles of a listed company to specify the maximum number of directors that the company may have.

Notification of appointment

2.43 The provisions relating to the notification of director appointments to Companies House come into force on 1 October 2009. Until then, the provisions of the Companies Act 1985 continue to apply. These are largely unchanged except in relation to the 'required particulars' (see **2.50** below) to be filed in relation to a director who is an individual. The required particulars contain a new requirement to notify a director's service address (see **2.50** below) in addition to his usual residential address (s. 12).

Notification of the appointment of first directors

2.44 Notification of the appointment of the first directors of a company, containing the 'required particulars' of the directors (see **2.50** below) must be filed with the Registrar of Companies at the time of the application for registration of the company (s. 12). Until October 2009, this notification will continue to be made on Form 10 under the Companies Act 1985, s. 10.

Notification of subsequent appointments

2.45 Notification of the appointment of subsequent directors must be made to the Registrar of Companies within 14 days (s. 167). There is no change from the requirement to notify under Companies Act 1985, s. 288 other than the obligation to notify details of a director's service address and the removal of the requirement to use a 'prescribed form' to make the notification.

2.46 A company must give notice to the Registrar of Companies of the appointment and the date on which it occurred, as well as the particulars of the new director that are required to be included in the company's register of directors and its register of directors' residential addresses (see **2.48** below).

The notice of a new director's appointment must, as currently, be accompanied by the director's consent to act. Currently, directors' appointments are notified on prescribed Form 288a, but with effect from 1 October 2009 there may no longer be a prescribed form as s. 167 simply requires 'notice' to be given rather than 'notification in the prescribed form' which is required under Companies Act 1985, s. 288.

Other notifications

2.47 The company secretary should also consider notifying the new director's appointment to the company's bankers for bank mandate purposes and to its insurers for directors and officers' insurance.

Directors' registers

2.48 Details of a director's appointment must be recorded in the company's register of directors (ss. 162–166). These provisions of the Act come into effect from 1 October 2009. From that date, companies will be required to maintain two registers:

- a register of directors, containing a service address that is open to public inspection; and
- a register of directors' usual residential addresses that is *not* open to inspection.

2.49 The registers must be completed on the appointment of each director and when there is any change in the particulars required to be entered. Until October 2009, the Companies Act 1985 continues to apply. This requires a company to maintain a single register of directors containing the director's usual residential address (Companies Act 1985, s. 288).

Register of individual directors

2.50 The register of directors must contain the 'required particulars' (see **2.51** below) of each director (s. 162). It must be kept available for inspection at the company's registered office or such other place as the government may specify by regulations. The company must notify the Registrar of Companies of the place where the register is available for inspection and any change in that place, unless the register is always kept at the company's registered office. The register must be open for inspection, free of charge, by any shareholder and, on payment of a prescribed fee, by any other person

Which 'required particulars' must be filed?

2.51 Section 163 sets out the information that companies must file for a newly appointed individual director, as follows:

- name and any former name – name means forename and surname, except in the case of a peer or an individual usually known by a title, when that person's title may be stated instead; forename means a name by which an individual was formerly known for business purposes;
- service address – note that the Companies Act 1985 requires a director's usual residential address;
- the country or state (or part of the UK) in which the director is usually resident – this is a new requirement which is not in the Companies Act 1985;
- nationality;
- business occupation (if any); and
- date of birth.

2.52 The Act does not require particulars of a director's other directorships – this is a requirement of the Companies Act 1985, s. 289 and will need to be complied with until 1 October 2009. As far as directors' names are concerned, the Act changes the law by requiring the inclusion of any name by which the individual was formerly known for business purposes. There is no longer an exception for a married woman's former name so this must included in the register of directors.

Service addresses can be used

2.53 In a change to the law (with effect from 1 October 2009), the register of individual (as opposed to corporate) directors must include a service address for a director instead of his usual residential address (s. 163). A director's service address could be the same as or different from his usual residential address (e.g. a director may give the company's registered office address as his service address). It will not be apparent from the public record that the director's service address is the same as his usual residential address unless the person is already a director whose residential address is on the public record. The provision to permit the filing of a service address provides no protection for historic records already on the microfiches at Companies House. This means that members of the public will continue to have access to the residential addresses of current directors (unless a confidentiality order protecting the address is in place). The confidentiality order regime in the Companies Act 1985 will be repealed in October 2009 and replaced by ss. 240–246 of the 2006 Act. Transitional provisions provide for the protection afforded by confidentiality orders in place before October 2009 to continue in effect (Companies Act 2006 Eighth Commencement Order 2008, Schedule 2, paras 36–38). If an existing director (who does not have the benefit of a confidentiality order) wishes to protect his residential address from disclosure, the only practical way in which he can do so is to move house and then provide the company's registered office address as his service address for the required particulars.

Protecting directors' residential addresses from disclosure

2.54 Currently, under the Companies Act 1985 directors facing a serious risk of intimidation or violence can apply for a confidentiality order which enables them to keep details of their residential addresses confidential. From 1 October 2009, the Act will allow all directors to keep their residential addresses confidential (see **2.48** above), with only the service address being generally available to the public. As explained above, the service address can be the company's registered office address.

2.55 A company may not use or disclose a director's home address without his consent except for communicating with him, or to comply with an obligation to send information to the Registrar of Companies or when required by a court (s. 241). The Registrar can use a director's residential address to communicate with the director (s. 243). The Registrar can also disclose it to public authorities that have been specified by the Secretary of State. An extensive list of public authorities has been published in the Draft Companies (Disclosure of Address) Regulations 2008 (the Draft Regulations). It includes the Director of Public Prosecutions, the Serious Fraud Office, the Financial Services Authority, the Competition Commission, the Pensions Regulator, the Takeover Panel, the Office of Fair Trading, a local authority, an official receiver and the police. The Registrar can also disclose the director's residential address to credit reference agencies. Before the Registrar can disclose either to a public authority or to a credit reference agency, the conditions set out in the Draft Regulations must be satisfied.

2.56 A director (or proposed director) can apply to the Registrar to prevent the Registrar from disclosing the director's residential address on the grounds of serious risk of violence or intimidation (Draft Regulations, para. 5). Application may also be made on behalf of a director by his company. The application must contain the information set out in the Draft Regulations, including documentary evidence regarding the violence or intimidation.

2.57 A shareholder, liquidator or creditor can apply to the court for an order requiring the disclosure of a director's residential address (s. 244). The court may make the order if it is satisfied that documents are not being effectively served on the director at his service address or it is necessary or expedient for the information to be provided in connection with the enforcement of a court order. Section 245 sets out a procedure under which the Registrar may put a director's usual residential address on the public register if there is evidence that the service of documents at the service address is not effective to bring them to the notice of the director.

Register of directors' usual residential addresses

2.58 The Act also introduces a new obligation on companies to create and maintain a separate register of individual directors' usual residential addresses (s. 165). If the director's usual residential address is the same as his service address, an entry to that effect is sufficient unless he has chosen the company's registered office as his service address. Unlike the register of directors maintained under s. 162, this register will not be open to public inspection.

Register of corporate directors

2.59 The Act restates the previous position (Companies Act 1985, s. 289) that the corporate or firm name and the registered or principal office be recorded where the director is a body corporate or a firm that is a legal person. In a new requirement, directors that are EEA companies must provide particulars of the register where the company is registered and its registration number (s. 164). Corporate directors that are non-EEA companies will also need to disclose particulars of their legal form and the law by which the company is governed.

Induction

2.60 Once a director has been appointed, it is helpful for him to be given a formal induction covering such matters as an understanding of the company's business, the markets in which it operates, its employees and the company's main supplier and customer relationships. This will help to ensure that the newly appointed director makes an effective contribution to the board as soon as possible. The company secretary usually organises this. A formal induction is a requirement of the Combined Code for listed companies and it is also desirable for other companies. **Chapter 20** contains more detail on induction.

3

Removal of directors

Introduction

3.1 Directors, particularly executive directors, often have two roles:

- they are office holders, having been appointed to the office of director in accordance with the criteria set out in the preceding chapter. As office holders, their relationship with the company is usually governed by the Companies Acts, the Company's articles of association and, for public companies, the Model Code and the Combined Code and Listing Rules;
- they can also be, and usually are, employees of the companies that they serve, this relationship being governed by a formal contract of employment, usually called a 'service agreement'.

3.2 Whether he is just an officer or an officer and employee, the director's position can give rise to a potential conflict of interest in relation to the director negotiating his fee to act as a director (which must be paid subject to deduction of income tax and national insurance contributions) and/or the terms of the service agreement.

3.3 **Chapter 6** discusses the issues that arise when a director has direct or indirect personal transactions with the company of which he is a director and **Chapter 8** considers in detail the issues that arise when a director is also an employee of the company.

3.4 This chapter looks at a director in his capacity as an office holder only.

The Companies Act 2006

3.5 The relevant provisions of the 2006 Act covering removal of directors and compensation for loss of office were not designed to be a radical change or departure from the provisions of CA 1985; rather, Part 10 of 2006 Act was drafted more as a restatement of CA 1985, Part X.

3.6 The provisions of 2006 Act, Part 10, governing removal of directors, notification of such removal and compensation for loss of office, came into force with effect from 1 October 2007.

Means of removal

3.7 Under ss. 168 and 169 of the Act, removal of a director is by ordinary resolution, on special notice. The articles also often contain provisions for the removal of a director.

Model Articles

3.8 Section 19 of the 2006 Act confers on the Secretary of State powers to prescribe model articles of association for companies. The Department of Business, Enterprise and Regulatory Reform (BERR) published in December 2008 what is expected to be the final draft of The Companies (Model Articles) Regulations 2008, Schedule 1 of which sets out the Draft Model Articles for Private Companies Limited by Shares (the Model Articles).

3.9 Article 18 of the Private Company Model Articles deals with the termination of a director's appointment, as follows:

> '18 A person ceases to be a director as soon as:
> (a) that person ceases to be a director by virtue of any provision of the Companies Act 2006 or is prohibited from being a director by law;
> (b) a bankruptcy order is made against that person;
> (c) a composition is made with that person's creditors generally in satisfaction of that person's debts;
> (d) a registered medical practitioner who is treating that person gives a written opinion to the company stating that that person has become physically or mentally incapable of acting as a director and may remain so for more than three months;
> (e) by reason of that person's mental health, the Court makes an order which wholly or partly prevents that person from personally exercising any powers or rights which that person would otherwise have;
> (f) notifications received by the company from the director that the director is resigning or retiring from office and such resignation or retirement has taken effect in accordance with its terms.'

3.10 That said, s. 168 makes it clear that a company may remove a director before the expiration of his period of office 'notwithstanding anything in any agreement between it and [the director]'. As the Model Articles are not expected to take effect until 1 October 2009, Table A and ss. 303 and 304 of CA 1985 remain relevant. The provisions of CA 1985 make it clear that shareholders may remove a director at any time by ordinary resolution regardless of anything to the contrary in the company's articles of association. Under CA 1985 and Table A (which will remain relevant to existing companies even after 1 October 2009), special notice must be given to the company of the intention to propose a resolution to remove a director. Additionally, a copy of the notice must be sent to the director concerned so that he can make representations in writing to the company and request that these be circulated to the members.

Procedural requirements for removal

3.11 The requirements for removing a director by ordinary resolution are set out in s. 168:

> '(1) a company may by ordinary resolution at a meeting remove a director before the end of his term of office notwithstanding anything in any agreement between the director and the company. [That said, the company could, by removing the director, expose itself to significant liabilities under the terms of the director's service agreement and/or under the terms of any shareholders' agreement, if the director were also a shareholder – commonly the case in owner managed businesses – see (5) below and **Chapters 8** and **9**.]
>
> (2) Special notice is required of a resolution to remove or appoint a replacement for the director so removed. (Special notice requires at least 28 days' notice of the resolution being served on the company.)
>
> (3) A vacancy created by the removal of the director, if not filled at the meeting at which he is removed, may be filled as a casual vacancy.
>
> (4) A person appointed director in place of a person removed under s. 168 is treated, for the purposes of determining the time at which he or any other director is to retire, as if he had become director on the day on which the person in whose place he is appointed was last appointed as a director;
>
> (5) This section is not to be taken:
>
> (a) as depriving a person removed under it of compensation or damages payable to him in respect of the termination of his appointment as director or of any appointment terminating with that as director, or
>
> (b) as derogating from any power to remove a director that may exist apart from this section.'

3.12 Section 168(1) provides for the protection of the director in that the resolution to remove him has to be heard at a meeting and not just by vote on written resolutions. This gives the director the right to be heard on the resolution for his removal. This protection is further reinforced by the provisions of s. 169 (see **3.19** below).

Removal

3.13 The following steps and administrative matters should be dealt with when a director ceases to hold office:

- The board should formally minute the vacation of office.
- The date that the director ceases to be a director must be recorded in the register of directors and secretaries and the register of directors' share and debenture interests.
- Currently (until 1 October 2009) formal notice on Form 288b or the electronic equivalent should be sent to the Registrar of Companies within 14 days of the date of vacation of office. (Under 2006 Act, with effect from 1 October 2009, the time periods for notification will remain the same, but companies will not be required to use Form 288b. Notification will be in writing and the information that is required will be the same as that currently sent out in Form 288b, but notification will be by way of letter rather than standard form.)
- If the name of the director is shown on company stationery, it should be removed.
- In the case of a listed company, a Regulatory Information Service must be notified.
- If the director was authorised to sign cheques, the bank should be informed and any bank mandates changed as required.
- Any fees for the period to the date of cessation of office should be paid to the director or, if the director has died, to his personal representative. HM Revenue & Customs should be informed of the cessation. (It is customary in relation to executive directors that they do not receive fees. Rather, they are employees and receive salary and benefits. Accordingly, it is important that the company observe the requirements of the various employment laws – for example, Employment Rights Act 1996 as amended – in relation to any termination. See **Chapter 8**.)
- A press announcement should be sent via the company's PR agents for directing newspapers as appropriate.
- The director should be requested to return all documents and other company property. If the director had authority to work at home, consideration should be given to how to recover any company property from the director. Consider whether the information needs to be returned or irretrievably deleted from the director's computer(s). Furthermore, if the director had use of a company mobile, blackberry and/or company car, arrangements should be made for the return of these items. If the director has private email correspondence on the company's blackberry or computer

systems, arrangements should be made for these private emails to be deleted from the system or transferred to the director's own computer. Such transfer should, as a matter of policy, be supervised.

Weighted voting rights on resolutions for removal

3.14 A company's articles may provide for enhanced/weighted voting rights for a director who is also a shareholder when it comes to passing a resolution to remove the director from office. This is known as *Bushell v. Faith* protection (after *Bushell v. Faith* [1970] AC 1099). In that case, shares were held equally by three siblings, each of whom was a director of the company. The company's articles provided that on any vote to pass a resolution to remove a director, any share held by the director who was the subject of the resolution to remove would carry three votes. Although *Bushell v. Faith* protection is not suitable for public companies, it can be used in the private arena.

3.15 One noticeable difference between s. 168 of the 2006 Act and s. 303 of CA 1985 is that the latter was meant to apply notwithstanding anything in the company's articles to the contrary. This wording has not been repeated in s. 168. However, as some commentators have observed, this does not amount to a substantial change in the law, since a provision in the articles that purported to fetter a company's statutory powers would be unlawful and therefore unenforceable. See *Russell v. Northern Bank Development Company Limited* [1992] 3 All ER 161.

Director's right to protest against removal

3.16 On receipt of a notice of an intended resolution to remove a director the company must send a copy of the notice to the director concerned. Under s. 169, the director, whether or not a member of the company, can make his objections to the resolution known by having the company circulate his representations to members to whom notice of the meeting is sent. He can also exercise his right be heard on a resolution at the meeting.

3.17 Circulation by the company of the director's written representation is possible only if it is received within a reasonable time of notification of the resolution. In the event of his representation not being circulated as required, the director may (without prejudice to his right to be heard in person) require that the representation be read out at the meeting.

3.18 Copies of the representation need not be sent out and the representation need not be read at the meeting if, on the application of either the company or any other person who claims to be aggrieved, the court is satisfied that the rights conferred by this section are being abused.

3.19 The court may order the company's costs (in Scotland, expenses) on an application to be paid in whole or in part by the director, notwithstanding he is not a party to the application (s. 169(5)).

Notification of removal

3.20 As with the appointment of directors (see **Chapter 2**), s. 167 requires the company to notify the Registrar of Companies within 14 days if a person ceases to be a director.

3.21 As s. 167 is not expected to come into force until 1 October 2009 (the delayed implementation is partly due to the changes relating to service addresses for directors – see **Chapter 2**) the provisions of s. 288, CA 1985 remain in force, with the notification periods remaining the same as those under s. 167. As with the new s. 168, s. 288, CA 1985 requires that the appointment, departure or any change in the particulars of an existing director must be notified to the Registrar of Companies. Under s. 288, the notification is done on standard forms as follows:

Form 288a Appointment
Form 288b Resignation/removal
Form 288c Change in particulars

3.22 Section 167 dispenses with the requirement for the necessary information to be provided to the Registrar in the prescribed form. Accordingly, after 1 October 2009, Forms 288 a–c will no longer be required, but the information will still have to be supplied for filing by the Registrar.

Compensation for loss of office

3.23 A director may be an office holder and employee, and in private, owner-managed businesses, he may also be a shareholder, often through the award of share options. In such a situation, the director will have a number of potential claims if he is removed from office:

- as an office holder (see **3.24**);
- as an employee in relation to his notice period and statutory rights (such as unfair dismissal, redundancy, non-payment of wages, accrued holiday pay, breach of statutory dismissal procedures, etc. – see **Chapter 8**); and
- as a shareholder under the articles and any shareholders' agreement (the termination of the directorship may be a breach of the shareholders' agreement and may trigger transfer notices from other shareholders regarding the sale of their shares, or give the director the opportunity to sell his shares or, in a private company, bring claims to wind up the company on just and equitable grounds on the basis that his removal as a director amounts to a prejudice in

relation to his position as a minority shareholder in a company that operates as a quasi-partnership – see **Chapter 9**).

Substantial property transactions

3.24 Sections 190–196 govern substantial property transactions between directors, shadow directors and former directors and the company. They have the following effect:

- they enable directors, shadow directors and former directors to enter into substantial property transactions (so-called arrangements) which are conditional upon shareholder approval; and
- although the minimum value of relevant assets is £5,000, in calculating whether the £5,000 threshold has been reached, the aggregate value of all non-cash assets which are subject to the transfer have to be taken into account. (see **Chapter 6**).

Payments for loss of office

3.25 Payment for loss of office is defined by s. 215 as:

- in connection with the management of the affairs of the company; or
- any office (as director or otherwise) or employment in connection with the management of the affairs of any office as director of the company; or
- as consideration for or in connection with his retirement, while director of a subsidiary undertaking of the company;
- as consideration for or in connection with his retirement from the company or in connection with his ceasing to be a director of it; or
- from any other office or employment in connection with the management of the affairs of the company, or compensation for loss of office as director of the company; or
- compensation for loss, while director of the company or in connection with his ceasing to be a director of it; or
- any other office or employment; or
- any office (as director or otherwise) or employment in connection with the management of the affairs of any subsidiary undertaking of the company.

3.26 References to compensation and consideration include benefits otherwise than in cash. For the purposes of ss. 217–221 payments requiring members' approval are:

- payments to a person connected with a director; or
- payments to any person at the direction of, or for the benefit of, a director or a person connected with him.

These are treated as payments to the director.

3.27 Reference in those sections to payment by a person include 'payment by another person at the direction of, or on behalf of, the person referred to'.

3.28 Accordingly, a company may not make an ex gratia payment to a director or former director (or shadow director) for loss of office without it being approved, in advance, by a resolution of the shareholders. Such payments include:

- payments in respect of loss of any other office or employment with the company or any subsidiary of the company and payments in connection with retirement; and
- in relation to a former director, what matters is the *reason* for the payment. Accordingly, a director cannot resign and then receive an ex gratia payment on the basis that, as at the time the payment is made, he was not a director.

3.29 It is important to note that s. 215(2) makes it clear that it is immaterial whether payment is made in cash or the provision of other benefits. If other benefits or property are involved, then the rules governing substantial property transactions/arrangements may come into play (see **Chapter 6**).

Payments in connection with transfers of undertakings, property or shares

3.30 Section 216 brings certain other payments, made in connection with the transfer of the company's undertaking, property or shares, into the definition of a 'payment for loss of office' if the director of the company:

(a) is to cease to hold office, or
(b) is to cease to be the holder of –
  (i) any other office or employment in connection with the management of the affairs of the company, or
  (ii) any office (as director or otherwise) or employment in connection with the management of the affairs of any subsidiary undertaking of the company.

If, in connection with any such transfer:

(a) the price to be paid to the director for any shares in the company held by him is in excess of the price which could at the time have been obtained by other holders of like shares; or
(b) any valuable consideration is given to the director by a person other than the company, the excess or, as the case may be, the money value of the consideration is taken for the purposes of those sections to have been a payment for loss of office.

3.31 Section 216(2) makes it clear that, if there is a payment of money or other valuable consideration, which results in the director getting more than other shareholders in the same class, then that excess is treated as a payment for loss of office.

Prohibition on payments for loss of office

3.32 Section 217 provides that a company 'may not make a payment for loss of office to a director unless the payment has been approved by an ordinary resolution of the members'. This prohibition also applies to a director of the company's holding company. It should, however, be noted that the company's articles may impose more stringent requirements, for example a special resolution.

3.33 A director who is also a shareholder and/or member with voting rights is ordinarily not debarred from voting on the proposed resolution, even though he is the intended beneficiary of the proposed payment. However, in the public arena, regard should be had to the Listing Rules and the City Code on Takeovers and Mergers (see **Chapter 9**).

3.34 Payment for loss of office to a director of the company's holding company must be approved by a resolution of the members of both the company and the holding company (s. 217(2)). This is the case unless the subsidiary is wholly owned by the holding company, in which case the resolution only needs to be approved by members of the holding company (s. 217(4)(b)).

3.35 Private companies are permitted to grant approval by written resolution rather than at a formal meeting (s. 217(3)).

3.36 Section 217(4)(a) also makes it clear that approval is never required on the part of the members of an overseas company.

Prohibition on payments on a transfer of undertaking or property

3.37 Section 218 provides that shareholder approval is required in relation to any payment for loss of office in connection with the transfer of the whole or any part of the undertaking or property of the company or any subsidiary company. If the payment is in relation to the transfer of the undertaking or property of a subsidiary company, then the payment has to be approved by a resolution of the members of both the company and the subsidiary company, unless the subsidiary is wholly owned, in which case the payment must have the approval of the shareholders of the holding company only (s. 218(4)(b)).

3.38 As with s. 217, approval is never required on the part of the members of an overseas company (s. 218(4)(a)).

3.39 Section 218(5) makes it clear that a payment made in two specified instances is treated as a payment within the definition of the Act unless it can be shown otherwise. The two instances are where payment is made in pursuance of an arrangement:

- entered into as part of the agreement for the transfer in question, or within one year before or two years after that agreement; and
- to which the company whose undertaking or property is transferred, or any person to whom the transfer is made, is privy.

Prohibition on payments on transfer of shares

3.40 Section 219 deals with payments in connection with share transfers and is directed specifically at takeovers. Its aim is to avoid the risk that directors may obtain payments from parties initiating a takeover bid in circumstances in which such payments should, in reality, go to the shareholders. The section provides that shareholder approval is required if any person wishes to make a payment for loss of office to a director of the company in connection with the transfer of the shares of that company or in a subsidiary of the company resulting from the takeover bid. The approval that is required is that of the holders of the shares to which the bid relates and any other holders of shares in the same class, i.e. the shareholders of the target company.

3.41 Section 219 does not place a positive obligation on the director who is to receive the payment to take all reasonable steps to secure that the particulars of the proposed payment are brought to the attention of the shareholders at the time that the offer is made for their shares. Furthermore, s. 219(4) prevents 'the person making the offer [or] any associate of his (as defined in s. 988)' from voting on the proposed payment to the director. However, where the resolution is proposed as a written resolution, such persons are entitled to be sent a copy of the resolution and at any meeting to consider it. They are entitled to be given notice of the meeting and to attend and speak and, if present (in person or by proxy), to count towards the quorum for the meeting. As with ss. 217 and 218, no approval is required on the part of shareholders of a wholly owned subsidiary (it is the approval of the shareholders of the holding company that is required in these circumstances) or on the part of shareholders of any overseas company.

Additional prohibitions

3.42 Sections 215–222 make changes and extend the prohibitions on payments that can be made to directors on loss of office, in summary as follows:

- Section 215(3) extends the prohibitions to payments made to persons connected to the director.
- Section 215 extends the prohibition to include payments made to directors

in respect of loss of any office, or employment in connection with the management of the affairs of the company, not just any loss of office as a director.

- Section 217(2) extends the ambit of the prohibition to include payments by a company to a director of its holding company.
- Section 218(2) extends the prohibition to include payments made in connection with the transfer of the undertaking or property of the company, including such transfers in relation to a subsidiary.
- Section 219(1) extends the prohibition in relation to share transfers so as to include all transfers of shares in the company or in a subsidiary resulting from a takeover bid.
- Section 219(4) widens the ambit of the prohibition in relation to persons making the offer for shares in the company and any associate of such persons, preventing them from voting on any resolution to approve a payment for loss of office in connection with a share transfer.

Exceptions

3.43 Under s. 220(1), member approval is not required for payments made in good faith to directors in the following instances:

- In discharge of an existing legal obligation. Here, obligation can mean the following:
  - An obligation of the company, or any body corporate associated with it that was not entered into in connection with, or in consequence of, the event giving rise to the payment for loss of office (s. 220(2)).
  - In relation to a payment in connection with the transfer of undertaking, property or shares, an' existing legal obligation' means an obligation of the person making the payment that was not entered into for the purposes of, in connection with or in consequence of, the transfer in question (s. 220). However, in the case of a payment within both ss. 217 and 218, or within both ss. 217 and 219, the former meaning applies.
- Damages for breach of such an obligation.
- Settlement or compromise of any claim arising in connection with termination of a person's office or employment.
- A pension in respect of past services.

3.44 It is worth noting that s. 220(1)(d) does not define pension and therefore does not appear to be restricted to one to which the director has a contractual entitlement.

3.45 Section 220(5) allows a single payment to be divided into its constituent parts – the part that is a lawful payment and the part that amounts to an unlawful payment.

Small payments exception

3.46 Section 221 creates a further exception in relation to small payments. Member approval is not required for small payments of £200 or the equivalent value in kind or less. This applies only to payments made by the company or subsidiary companies and not to a payment made by a person making a take-over bid. Furthermore, there are anti-avoidance provisions within s. 221 to prevent a series of connected payments, the individual values of which fall below £200, from coming within the exception. Section 221(1)(b) provides that 'the amount or value of the payment, together with the amount or value of any other relevant payments, does not exceed £200'.

Contravention – civil consequences

3.47 The consequences of contravening ss. 217, 218 and 219 are dealt with by s. 222. Section 222(1) codifies the common law rule that unapproved payment for loss of office by the company (s. 217) is a misapplication of company funds and is therefore held by the recipient on trust for the company making the payment, and any director who authorised the payment is jointly and severally liable to indemnify the company who made the payment for any loss resulting from it.

3.48 A payment that contravenes s. 218 (payment in connection with a transfer of undertaking or property) is held by the recipient on trust for the company whose undertaking or property is or is proposed to be transferred and not the company making the payment (s. 222(2)).

3.49 Under s. 222(3) a contravention of s. 219, which deals with payment in connection with a share transfer, provides that the payment is held by the recipient on trust for the shareholders who have sold their shares as a result of the offer; and that the expenses incurred by the recipient in distributing that sum among those shareholders shall be borne by him and not retained out of the sum he received.

3.50 Where there is a contravention of both s. 217 (a payment by the company) and s. 218 (a payment in connection with the transfer of the company's undertaking or property) it is dealt with under s. 222(4), which makes it clear that s. 222(2) applies and not s. 222(1). Accordingly, the payment is held by the recipient on trust for the company whose undertaking or property is or is proposed to be transferred, and not the company making the payment.

3.51 By contrast, s 222(5) deals with the situation in which the payment is the contravention of both s. 217 and s. 219 (payment in connection with a share transfer). In this situation, the payment is held on trust for the persons who have sold their shares as a result of the offer (with the expense of doing so borne by the director or former director or other recipient of the payment and not retained out of the sum received) and not on trust for the company making the payment.

Transactions requiring member's approval – shadow directors

3.52 Section 223 provides that for the purposes of ss. 188 and 189 (directors' service contracts); ss. 190–196 (property transactions); ss. 197–214 (loans, etc. to directors) and ss. 215–222 (payments for loss of office), a shadow director is treated as a director (s. 223(1)(a)–(d)). However, s. 223(2) provides that:

> 'Any reference in those provisions to loss of office as a director does not apply in relation to loss of a person's status as a shadow director.'

3.53 A shadow director is not, at law, an officer of the company, but because such a person has such a high degree of influence over the board, s. 251 defines a shadow director as 'a person in accordance with whose directions or instructions the directors of the company are accustomed to act' – he is to be treated in the same way as a director for the purposes of ss. 188–222. However, because such a person is not an office holder, by definition, such a person cannot lose office and so any reference to 'loss of office as a director' in ss. 188–222 cannot apply to a person who falls within the definition of shadow director.

4

Powers of directors

Introduction

4.1 It is important for directors to understand fully their roles and capabilities as officers of the company for which they act; such understanding is necessary not only to enable directors to carry out their tasks and functions effectively, but also to prevent them from acting beyond their powers. This chapter examines the extent of the powers of directors to act on behalf of their company and the consequences that can arise if they do act beyond those powers.

4.2 The law relating to the powers of directors has not changed significantly as a result of the enactment of the Companies Act 2006 (the 2006 Act), and many provisions of the Companies Act 1985 (the 1985 Act) have been retained in identical form. One important change affecting the powers of directors is that, under the 1985 Act, a company's constitution comprised both the memorandum and articles of association. The objects clause governing the powers of the company (and therefore the powers that could be delegated to the directors) was included in the memorandum; it remained the only part of the memorandum to affect the constitution of a company following its initial incorporation. Following the relaxation of the requirement for companies to have detailed objects clauses under the Companies Act 1989, objects clauses became far more general in nature and tended to include far fewer restrictions on the powers of the company.

4.3 Under the 2006 Act, if a company wishes to include an objects clause in its constitution, this clause will now form part of the articles of the company and not the memorandum; the memorandum of a company will have no effect on the company after its initial incorporation and will no longer form part of the company's constitutional documents. In fact, under the 2006 Act, there is no longer a requirement for a company to have any form of objects clause in its constitution: section 31(1) of the 2006 Act provides that 'unless a company's articles specifically restrict the objects of the company, its objects are unrestricted'. It is anticipated that very few companies will choose to restrict themselves with objects clauses, although it may be necessary for certain types of company (for example, charities) to retain objects clauses in order to maintain tight control over the actions that the company is permitted to undertake.

4.4 Companies incorporated prior to the enactment of the 2006 Act will not have to amend their memorandum and articles to reflect the changes to the legislation unless they wish to remove the restrictions imposed by their objects clauses, as objects clauses will automatically be treated as provisions of the articles by virtue of s. 28 of the 2006 Act. A company subsequently wishing to amend or remove its objects clause can do so by amending its articles by special resolution. It should be noted that under s. 31(2) of the 2006 Act, where a company amends its articles in order to add, remove or alter a statement of the company's objects, the amendment will not be effective until notice of the amendment has been given to the Registrar and the Registrar has registered the notice.

Division of powers within a company

4.5 The division of powers within a company between the directors and the shareholders is primarily determined by the provisions of the company's articles of association and, subject to the provisions of the relevant statutes, a company is able to allocate and divide its powers as it wishes. The manner in which the powers of a company are divided will generally depend on the type and size of the company: smaller companies tend to have less detailed articles and fewer directors, who will hold the majority of the delegated powers, whereas larger companies, particularly publicly traded companies, tend to have full, detailed articles, which confer on the board of directors extensive powers to manage the business of the company and the ability to exercise all corporate powers not specifically reserved to the shareholders.

Powers to be exercised by shareholders

4.6 The ability of a company to divide powers between its shareholders and directors will always be subject to certain matters which, according to the 2006 Act and other relevant legislation, must be carried out by the company's shareholders. For example:

- Under ss. 617–620 and 641 of the 2006 Act, a limited company which has an authorised share capital may only increase or reduce its share capital or consolidate, subdivide or convert any of its shares if its shareholders have passed a resolution authorising it to do so.
- Under s. 21(1) of the 2006 Act, an alteration to the articles of association of a company can only be carried out by special resolution of its shareholders authorising it to do so.

- Under s. 84 of the Insolvency Act 1986, the voluntary liquidation of a company can be started either by an ordinary resolution of its shareholders when the period fixed for the duration of the company by the articles expires, or otherwise by special resolution of its shareholders.
- Under ss. 549–551 of the 2006 Act, the directors of a company cannot allot shares in the company unless they are authorised to do so under the company's articles or by resolution of the shareholders. However, under the 2006 Act, where a private company has only one class of share, the directors are automatically authorised to allot shares in the company except to the extent they are prohibited from doing so by the terms of the articles.
- Under s. 303 of the 2006 Act, shareholders of a company retain the power to compel the directors to call a general meeting of the company. The directors must convene a general meeting once they have received requests from:
  - shareholders holding at least 10% of the paid-up share capital of the company (provided, of course, those shares carry voting rights); or
  - shareholders holding at least 5% of the paid-up share capital of the company in the case of a private company where a period of twelve months has elapsed since the last general meeting which was (a) called in pursuance of a requirement under s. 303, or (b) in relation to which any shareholders had rights with respect to the circulation of a resolution no less extensive than they would have had if the meeting had been so called at their request.
- Under s. 188 of the 2006 Act, a company may not agree to a director's service contract with a guaranteed term in excess of two years unless approved by ordinary resolution of the shareholders.

Powers delegated to directors

4.7 The delegation of powers to directors of a company is primarily governed by the provisions of the company's articles of association. The articles of a significant number of private companies adopt, or are substantially based on, the provisions of Table A. The current version of Table A remains in force under the 2006 Act subject only to relatively few minor amendments.

4.8 Section 19 of the 2006 Act gives the Secretary of State the power to make regulations for three sets of model articles: one for private companies limited by shares, one for private companies limited by guarantee and one for public companies. The final draft of The Companies (Model Articles) Regulations 2008 was published in December 2008 with an implementation date of 1 October 2009 (the Model Articles). The implementation of the Model Articles will not affect any provision of Table A, although it is anticipated that new companies being incorporated after the introduction of the regulations will base their articles on the Model Articles rather than on Table A.

4.9 The division of powers within a company is dealt with in Regulation 70 of Table A, which states:

> 'Subject to the provisions of the Act, the memorandum and the articles and to any directions given by special resolution, the business of the company shall be managed by the directors who may exercise all the powers of the company. No alteration of the memorandum or articles and no such direction shall invalidate any prior act of the directors which would have been valid if that alteration had not been made or that direction had not been given. The powers given by this regulation shall not be limited to any special power given to the directors by the articles and a meeting of directors at which a quorum is present may exercise all powers exercisable by the directors.'

4.10 A key question that arises from the terms of Regulation 70, and that arose in relation to the previous enactments of this provision under Table A introduced by the Companies Act 1948, is whether the shareholders of a company have the power to override the decisions of the directors to whom they have delegated the company's powers.

4.11 Until the beginning of the twentieth century, the directors of a company were regarded only as agents of that company, and the generally accepted view was that shareholders in general meeting were entitled to direct the manner in which the directors exercised their powers to manage the company.[1] The approach to the powers of directors has, of course, changed since the initial case law in this area, although vestiges of the old approach remain:

- If a board of directors is unable to act because they lack the requisite quorum, for example, because they have reached a deadlock on a particular issue or because there is no board due to directors' retirement by rotation, the delegated powers revert to the shareholders. It should be noted, however, that the shareholders' residual powers will not arise where, in their discretion, the directors of a company have determined not to exercise a power delegated to them.
- If directors act in excess of their delegated powers or exercise their powers for an improper purpose (thereby making the decision voidable), their decision may be ratified by the shareholders. Ratification is discussed in **4.71–75** below.

4.12 If the articles of a company adopt Table A, or contain similar provisions to Regulation 70, it is now generally acknowledged that the directors (providing they act within their delegated powers) are entitled to act without interference from shareholders acting by ordinary resolution. Shareholders are still able to control directors to a limited extent by special resolutions (a principle which is also expressly stated in the Model Articles); a special resolution will not invalidate a prior decision of the directors but will merely prevent the directors acting in a manner they had previously decided on but which has now become contrary to the shareholders' special resolution.[2] The special resolution passed by the shareholders can require that the directors not only refrain from undertaking acts contrary to the special resolution but also require them to take any positive steps prescribed by the special resolution. Shareholders also retain the ultimate sanction against directors who act in a manner contrary to their wishes: removal from office under s. 168 of the 2006 Act by ordinary resolution.

4.13 Shareholders must, however, be careful not to exercise too much control over their appointed directors; if they do, they may be viewed as shadow directors and become subject to the corresponding obligations and liabilities under the 2006 Act.

4.14 Therefore, in general, the management of a company is delegated to its board of directors, subject only to the limited directions of the shareholders given by special resolution.

Delegation of powers

Delegation to the board of directors

4.15 In general, a person to whom powers have been delegated cannot delegate those powers. As a result the board will only be able to delegate their powers if such delegation has been authorised by the shareholders or provided for in the articles. The powers of management of a company are delegated by shareholders to the board of directors as a whole and not to each director individually; in the absence of any permissible further delegation by the board, the decisions regarding the management of the company must be made by the board as a whole and not by a lesser number of directors acting either without a meeting or at a meeting in respect of which not all directors have received notification.

4.16 Although board meetings are a convenient way for directors to make collective decisions, there is no restriction in the 2006 Act preventing directors from making management decisions other than at board meetings. For example, the articles of private limited companies often enable the directors to transact business through written resolutions. Where articles are silent as to the requirement for a board meeting, case law suggests that directors may hold informal meetings without proper notice (provided that no director objects)[3] and dispense with the requirement for a meeting altogether where the directors unanimously approve a proposed course of conduct.[4]

4.17 Many of these concepts which had previously only been addressed in common law and not in statute, have now been codified in the Model Articles, which include provisions in relation to the collective decision-making of directors, unanimous decisions and the calling of board meetings.

4.18 It is not necessary for every director of a company to be involved in every task in respect of which the directors have been authorised to act. A director is entitled, in the absence of any matters which should put him on notice to the contrary, to trust his fellow directors and other duly authorised officers of the company to perform tasks which have been properly assigned to them.[5] Directors are not prevented from entering into an agreement that would limit the exercise of their powers in the future, where such agreement would be in the best interests of the company, but directors must be careful not to fetter their discretion when they delegate their powers.[6] It is therefore advisable for any agreement which seeks to delegate directors' powers to be revocable.

Delegation to committees and to specific executives

4.19 In May 1991, the Cadbury Committee was established following a number of high-profile business scandals (notably, the BCCI and Maxwell affairs) to consider the financial aspects of corporate governance and tasked with the role of recommending a code of best practice for companies. In December 1992, the Cadbury Report was published and included the committee's recommended code which dealt with issues such as the composition and effective operation of the board, the division of responsibilities on the board, the roles of non-executive directors, the availability and access of advice to directors, and delegation, reporting and controls within the company. Following the Cadbury Report, further committees and reports, including the Greenbury and Hampel Reports, considered other financial aspects of corporate governance, and eventually led to the production and publication of the Combined Code.

4.20 Today, the Combined Code is the key source of corporate governance recommendations for listed companies in the UK and deals with directors, their remunerations, their relations with shareholders and their accountability (in Part 1), and with institutional investors (in Part 2). The Listing Rules require annual financial statements to state how the company has applied the principles of the Code, where it has and has not complied with the Code and, if applicable, an explanation of why it has not complied (see **Appendix 1**).

4.21 In addition to the consolidation in the Combined Code of the guidance outlined in the Cadbury, Greenbury, Hampel and other reports, the principles identified in those reports for effective corporate governance have been incorporated in the provisions of Table A. Table A contains provisions for the delegation to committees (Regulation 72), the delegation to a managing director (Regulation 84) and the delegation to a chairman (Regulation 91). The Model Articles contain very widely drafted delegation provisions stating that, subject to the articles, directors may delegate any powers conferred on them to any person or committee, by such means, to such extent, in relation to such matters or territories and on such terms and conditions as they think fit.

Delegation to committees

4.22 According to Regulation 72 of Table A:

> 'The directors may delegate any of their powers to any committee consisting of one or more directors. They may also delegate to any managing director or any director holding any other executive office such of their powers as they consider desirable to be exercised by him. Any such delegation may be made subject to any conditions the directors may impose, and either collaterally with or to the exclusion of their own powers and may be revoked or altered. Subject to any such conditions, the proceedings of a committee with two or more members shall be governed by the articles regulating the proceedings of directors so far as they are capable of applying.'

4.23 The delegation of the powers of directors to committees promotes the efficient running of a company, especially in companies with large boards, and enables key decisions to be made in a more straightforward, more time-efficient and less restricted manner. As outlined in Regulation 72, committees must consist of at least one director; in fact, there is no legal objection to a committee consisting of only one person.[7] However, a committee generally tends to consist of a number of directors and sometimes also a number of other key employees.

4.24 The power of the board to delegate authority to committees is generally found in the articles of association of the company. Any delegating authority should be clearly and carefully worded and should explain whether the powers granted to each committee are in addition to, or to the exclusion of, the corresponding powers of the directors. The delegation of powers to a committee must not be engineered to prevent directors who are properly entitled to participate in the management of the company from doing so.

4.25 While the directors are entitled to delegate particular functions or powers to a committee and trust that committee's competence and integrity to a reasonable extent, the delegation by the directors does not in itself absolve them from their duties in relation to those powers. Directors who have delegated their powers have a duty to supervise the discharge of that delegated function.[8] The extent of a director's duty to supervise the committee or person to whom he has delegated his powers and to assess and determine whether that delegated power has been correctly exercised will depend on the facts in each case.

4.26 The powers delegated to a committee can be revoked at any time simply by passing a board resolution to such effect. Even if certain powers have been delegated to a committee, the board is still entitled to exercise the delegated power, but it should be noted that the mere exercise of the power by the board will not automatically end the authority delegated to the committee; a board resolution must be passed bringing the authority to an end.

4.27 The Cadbury, Greenbury and Hampel Reports recommended that, where relevant (for example, in listed companies and large private companies), each company should, as a minimum, have an audit committee, a remuneration committee and a nominations committee:

- Audit committee – the purpose of the audit committee is to review the financial statements and reports of the company, compile and, as necessary, review the accounting and financial policies and procedures of the company and make the necessary recommendations to the company's auditors. The audit committee should be composed of at least three independent non-executive directors.
- Remuneration committee – the purpose of the remuneration committee is to make recommendations to the board in relation to the company's remuneration policies and to issue guidelines in relation to bonuses, incentive schemes, benefits and service contracts. The remuneration committee should be composed wholly or mainly of independent non-executive directors.
- Nominations committee – the purpose of the nominations committee is to recommend potential appointees for non-executive director positions in the company. The nominations committee should be composed mainly of non-executive directors and should be chaired by either the company's chairman or an independent non-executive director.

Delegation to specific executives

4.28 In addition to the delegation of powers to committees, the board of directors can delegate certain powers to individuals. Certain executive roles within a company, such as the roles of managing director and chairman, carry with them specific powers and duties.

4.29 Regulation 84 of Table A states:

> 'Subject to the provisions of the Act, the directors may appoint one or more of their number to the office of managing director or to any other

executive office under the company and may enter into an agreement or arrangement with any director for his employment by the company or for the provision by him of any services outside the scope of the ordinary duties of a director. Any such appointment, agreement or arrangement may be made upon such terms as the directors determine and they may remunerate any such director for his services as they think fit. Any appointment of a director to an executive office shall terminate if he ceases to be a director but without prejudice to any claim to damages for breach of the contract of service between the director and the company. A managing director and a director holding any other executive office shall not be subject to retirement by rotation.'

4.30 The managing director is generally the most important director from an operational perspective and is usually an employee of the company. If a chairman has not been appointed, often the company's managing director will perform both roles, although the Cadbury Report noted that such role-sharing is undesirable. A company will only be able to delegate specific powers to a managing director where its articles provide for such delegation.[9]

4.31 As stated in Regulation 84, a managing director will not generally retire by rotation in a private company as such retirement is expressly excluded under many private companies' articles; it is, however, usual practice for managing directors of public companies to retire as a director by rotation. Shareholders do not have the power to remove a managing director from his employment as managing director, but can of course remove him as a director by ordinary resolution under s. 168 of the 2006 Act (special notice of such a resolution is required).

4.32 Regulation 91 of Table A states:

> 'The directors may appoint one of their number to be the chairman of the board of directors and may at any time remove him from that office. Unless he is unwilling to do so, the director so appointed shall preside at every meeting of directors at which he is present.'

4.33 The main role of a chairman is to ensure that the board of directors operates effectively in its management of the company. The chairman is responsible for the size and composition of the board, the agenda for board meetings and ensuring that the non-executive directors are kept sufficiently informed on all necessary matters to enable them to make a full contribution to the management of the company.

4.34 It has been common practice for articles of association to include a provision granting a chairman a casting vote where there is an equality of votes.

However, ss. 281 and 282 of the 2006 Act require an ordinary resolution to be passed by a simple majority. A resolution is passed by a simple majority where it is passed by a simple majority of the votes cast by duly entitled members and/or their duly appointed proxies (s. 282(3)). Therefore, the 2006 Act appears to override any article giving the chairman a casting vote. Paragraph 2(5), Schedule 5 to the Fifth Commencement Order of the 2006 Act inserts a new paragraph 23A into Schedule 3 to the Third Commencement Order. Paragraph 23A provides that where, immediately before 1 October 2007, a company's articles provided for the chairman to have a casting vote in the case of an equality of votes, that article remains effective, notwithstanding ss. 281(3) and 282 of the 2006 Act. Paragraph 23A further provides that where, since 1 October 2007, a company has removed an existing article providing for a chairman's casting vote, it may validly reinstate that article. Therefore, existing companies which have historically given the chairman a casting vote can retain that provision, but companies formed on or after 1 October 2007 cannot put in place such an article.

4.35 The Model Articles do not contain any specific provisions in relation to managing directors and chairmen as Table A does, but merely contain a widely drafted clause under which the directors are authorised to delegate any powers conferred on them to any person or committee and by such means (including by power of attorney) as they think fit.

Specific powers

4.36 Table A and the 2006 Act contain numerous specific powers available to directors to enable them to manage a company. Three key specific powers are outlined below, and a more extensive list is contained in the table at the end of this chapter.

Powers of attorney

4.37 According to Regulation 71 of Table A, the directors may appoint any person to be an agent of the company by a power of attorney on such conditions as the directors determine. The directors may not, however, assign or grant a power of attorney over their own office. The power of attorney may include the power to delegate further the powers contained therein. The delegation of powers under a power of attorney is governed by the Powers of Attorney Act 1971, which states that any ambiguity in the drafting of the power will be construed against the donor. In addition, ss. 5 and 6 of the Powers of Attorney Act provide protection for the attorney and for third parties when the power has been revoked by the donor but the attorney and/or third party have not been notified and are therefore unaware of the revocation.

Company contracts and executing documents

4.38 Under s. 43 of the 2006 Act, a company may enter into a contract either by writing under its common seal or through a person acting under its authority (whether express or implied) executing the contract. Under s. 44 of the 2006 Act, the methods by which a company may execute a document as a deed through a person acting under its authority has been expanded: in addition to the signature of a document by two directors or one director and the secretary duly authorised by the company (as was permissible under the 1985 Act), it is now possible for a company to execute a document as a deed with the signature of one director in the presence of a witness who attests the signature.

Appointment of alternate directors

4.39 Under Regulations 65–69 of Table A, alternate directors may be appointed and removed by written notice signed by the director on whose behalf the person is acting as an alternate. Alternate directors are deemed to be directors themselves and not merely agents of the director for whom they act as an alternate, and therefore the appointment of an alternate director will not result in the assignment of a director's office. An alternate director has the same rights, responsibilities and liabilities as the director for whom he is an alternate and will therefore be entitled to receive notices of all board meetings and all committees meetings to which his director is entitled. An alternate director is not, however, entitled to any form of remuneration from the company by virtue of his role as alternate director.

4.40 The Model Articles produced for public limited companies include provisions similar to those in Table A, although the Model Articles produced for private limited companies contain no such provisions relating to alternate directors.

Directors exceeding their delegated powers and the protection of third parties

4.41 When a company wishes to enter into a commercial transaction, it is usually one of the directors acting on behalf, and in the name, of the company who undertakes the commercial negotiations, concludes the deal and executes the relevant documents. In these circumstances, the director will be acting as an agent of the principal company; the director will contract on behalf of the company and will not incur any personal liability in relation to the transaction unless he acts beyond his powers or extends a personal duty of care.[10]

4.42 However, when a director is carrying out his general duties and undertaking his role in the management of the company, he will not be acting as an agent of a company or its shareholders, but will be executing his role as an officer of the company as authorised by the articles of association. The consequence of this distinction is usually in relation to the level of control exercised by the company in respect of the director (although such distinctions are rarely clear cut): when acting as an officer of the company (as discussed earlier in this chapter) the director may use his discretion in exercising the powers delegated to him, whereas when a director is acting as an agent for the company, he is acting as specifically instructed by, and under a more significant level of control from, the company.

4.43 Although it would be prudent for someone dealing with a company to ensure that the director with whom he has been dealing is duly authorised and has the requisite authority to bind the company in relation to the proposed transaction, there are a number of principles, both common law and statutory, that will assist a third party if it later transpires that the director was not duly authorised.

Turquand's rule

4.44 Turquand's rule (the 'indoor management rule') arises out of the case of *Royal British Bank v. Turquand* (1865) 25 LJQB 317. In *Turquand*, the Royal British Bank sued Turquand as the official manager of the company in relation to a bond signed by two directors. The board of directors' power to borrow was subject to a limit of such sum or sums of money as from time to time, by resolution passed at a general meeting of the company, they were authorised to borrow. The directors were authorised by such a resolution but the resolution had not set a limit. The company later refused to acknowledge the indebtedness.

4.45 Turquand's rule applies in circumstances where, in relation to a transaction between a third party and a company, it later transpires that some matter of internal procedure was not correctly observed, or where there has been some other form of internal impropriety, which might mean that the transaction has not technically been concluded by the company. Turquand's rule states that third parties who deal with a company in good faith may assume that the internal procedures of the company have been properly and duly observed and further that those third parties are not bound to inquire into the internal management of the company.

4.46 Turquand's rule will not apply, however, where:

- the third party dealing with the company knows, or is taken to know, that the internal management procedures of the company have not been properly and duly observed;
- the document relied on is a forgery; or

- the third party dealing with the company has been put on inquiry that the requisite internal procedures of the company have not been followed.

4.47 Turquand's rule is therefore useful where questions arise as to whether the internal procedures that are required by a company before it can enter into a transaction have been carried out and completed correctly. However, where questions arise as to whether the director who agreed and executed a transaction on behalf of a company had the requisite authority to bind the company, it is necessary to consider the principles of agency; in particular, it is necessary to consider whether the director had any actual or apparent authority to act on behalf of the company.

Actual authority

4.48 Actual authority arises where a director has been given authority to act on behalf of a company and to bind that company in relation to transactions with third parties by way of an express or an implied consent. There are no formalities that must be satisfied in order to confer actual authority on a director and, in particular, there is no need for a formal contract between the director and the company. Any questions regarding the extent of the authority given to a director is determined by recourse to general contractual principles.

4.49 The actual authority granted to a director could be granted expressly by way of a shareholder's resolution in general meeting, as a result of a board resolution in a board meeting or under the terms of a director's contract of employment. Alternatively, the actual authority could be implied from the conduct of the parties. For example, the appointment of a person to the role of company sales director would imply that the company was delegating to that person the duties necessary to carry out his role as sales director; such delegated powers would be necessarily different from those delegated to someone appointed as company operations director or company financial officer.

4.50 If a director has been given actual authority to act on behalf of the company, he will implicitly have the authority to carry out the tasks and transactions that are usual in his particular trade or business sector, the tasks that are necessary to carry out the terms of any express authority and any matters incidental to those tasks and transactions.

Apparent authority

4.51 The question of apparent authority arises where a director has acted on behalf of a company in circumstances where he did not have actual authority or where he acted beyond the terms of the authority granted to him. The doctrine of apparent authority operates as a form of estoppel and arises where a third party wishes to claim that a company is bound by the actions of its director where that director had not been granted actual authority, but where the company has represented or allowed another person to represent that director did in fact have authority to act on its behalf.

4.52 The doctrine of apparent authority states that if a representation is made to a third party that a person has authority to act on behalf of the company and the third party acts in reliance on that representation, the company will be estopped from claiming that the director did not have the requisite authority and that as a result it is not bound.[11]

4.53 A third party is entitled to rely on the doctrine if it wants to enforce a contract entered into by a director on behalf of a company in circumstances where he had no authority or was acting in excess of the authority he had been granted. The doctrine cannot be relied on by the company itself to enforce a contract made by a director purportedly acting on its behalf; the company could, however, ratify the acts of the director and thereby bind itself to the transaction.

4.54 In order to establish a claim for apparent authority, a third party must establish that:[12]

1 a person having actual authority to manage the business of the company made a representation that the director had authority to enter into the transaction on behalf of the company;
2 the representation made was relied on by the third party to whom the representation was made; and
3 the third party altered its position as a result of its reliance upon the representation.

4.55 Each of these conditions is examined in further detail below.

4.56 In addition, the transaction entered into by the director on behalf of the company must have been *intra vires*: it must have been possible for the company to have entered into the contract under the terms of its constitution and it must have been possible for the company to have delegated its authority to the directors in relation to that type of contract and transaction.

Representation

4.57 The first condition that must be established in order to rely on the doctrine of apparent authority is that a representation was made as to the director's authority to act on behalf of the company. The representation may be made in any form or via any medium, but it must be a representation of fact and not of law, and the representation must have been made by a committee, body or person who had actual authority to make such a representation. The representation can arise from a number of different circumstances:

- by express notification, stating that a director is a duly authorised agent of the company;
- by general trade or business sector practice, such that a representation is made where a company holds an individual out in a role that would usually mean that they had the authority to enter into the particular transaction or contract on behalf of the company;
- by previous course of conduct, such that a representation is made where a director has acted on behalf of and bound a company in relation to a number of other obligations or transactions in the past, but where the company has subsequently revoked or reduced the director's authority without notifying the relevant third party;
- by the company allowing a director to continue to make representations to third parties about his authority, such that the company will be taken to have represented to the third party that the director had the usual authority of someone in his position.

4.58 The representation must have been made deliberately or negligently[13] and must have been made directly to the third party or have been sufficiently public for the third party to be able to claim that he knew about the representation and that he acted in relation to it.

4.59 The representation must be that the director was acting in his capacity as an agent of the company. The doctrine of apparent authority will not operate if the director purports to act as principal to the transaction himself and the third party accepts the director as principal.

Reliance

4.60 The second condition that must be established in order for the doctrine to operate is that the third party placed reliance on the representation that was made when entering into the transaction with the director. A third party will not be able to rely on the doctrine in circumstances where it knew, or ought to have known, that the representation was not accurate and as a result did not place reliance on it.

4.61 A third party will not be able to claim that it relied on the representation where it was put on inquiry and ought reasonably to have discovered that the director purporting to act as agent did not have the requisite authority to bind the company. However, a third party may still be able to rely on the doctrine if the results of the enquiries that it ought reasonably to have made would have led a reasonable person to conclude that there was nothing to be concerned about in relation to the director's authority.

4.62 Although there is no general duty on a third party entering into a transaction with a company to inquire as to a director's authority, there are circumstances that may give rise to a duty to inquire. In addition to events which may place a third party on inquiry, a duty to inquire may arise if the director with whom the third party is dealing acts beyond the usual scope of authority that someone undertaking his role would possess; for example, if the sales director of a company was entering into a bank facilities agreement. In these circumstances, it would be prudent for a third party to ask for clarification of the extent of the director's authority or confirmation that the director had been granted the requisite authority by the board of the company.

Change of position

4.63 The third condition that must be satisfied in order to rely on the doctrine of apparent authority is that the third party altered its position as a result of its reliance on the representation made. It has been unclear from previous case law what was required to demonstrate a sufficient change of position to satisfy this condition. In particular, it was not clear whether entering into the contract with the company was a sufficient change of position or whether, in addition, the third party had to demonstrate some additional change of position or whether it had to demonstrate that it had suffered some form of loss or detriment.

4.64 It is now accepted that in order to satisfy the third limb of the test for the doctrine of apparent authority, the only change of position that the third party must demonstrate is that it entered into the contract with the company in reliance on the representation made to it.

Statutory protection for third parties under s. 40 of the 2006 Act

4.65 In addition to the common law rules of Turquand's rule and the doctrines of actual and apparent authority, statutory protection is available for third parties who deal in good faith with a director of a company who is acting in the absence of, or in excess of, his authority. Sections 35A and 35B of the 1985 Act have now been replaced by and consolidated in s. 40 of the 2006 Act.

4.66 Section 40(1) of the 2006 Act states:

> 'In favour of a person dealing with a company in good faith, the power of the directors to bind the company, or authorise others to do so, is deemed to be free of any limitation under the company's constitution.'

4.67 As outlined in section 40(2)(a) of the 2006 Act, a person 'deals with' a company if he is a party to any transaction or other act to which the company is a party. The person dealing with the company need not be a third party; this provision may also include a director dealing with the company provided that the director is not himself responsible for the failure to observe the requirements of the company's constitution.[14]

4.68 The main limitations on a director's powers under the company's constitution are contained in the articles of the company, but limitations may also be found in resolutions of shareholders (or any class of shareholders) of the company or in any agreement between the company and its shareholders (or class of shareholders). A third party is not bound to inquire as to any limitation that might be contained in any of a company's constitutional documents in relation to the powers of the directors to act on behalf of the company, to bind the company or to authorise others to act on behalf of the company. This means that third parties will not be deemed to have constructive notice of the documents filed by a company at Companies House.

4.69 Under s. 40(2)(b)(ii) of the 2006 Act, a third party will be presumed to be acting in good faith unless the contrary is proved. A third party will not be deemed to be acting in bad faith, and therefore prevented from availing itself of this statutory protection, by reason only of it knowing that the director is acting beyond the powers granted to him by the company under the company's constitution.[15] It appears that in order for a third party to be found to be acting in bad faith, the third party must have had some form of fraudulent intent; for example, the third party must have tried deliberately to induce the director to enter into the transaction which it knew was beyond the director's authority or the third party must have otherwise knowingly participated in the breach of the director's duties to his company.

4.70 Section 40(4) of the 2006 Act makes it clear that the provisions of s. 40 do not affect any right of shareholders to bring proceedings to restrain a director from doing an action that is beyond the powers of the directors. In addition, s. 40(5) states that s. 40 will not operate to provide any reduction in a liability incurred by directors, or any other person, by reason of the directors exceeding their powers.

Ratification

4.71 Where a director has acted in the absence of any authority or beyond the scope of any authority granted to him by the company, that company may choose to ratify its director's actions. Ratification by the company operates retrospectively and validates any act which was invalid as result of a director's lack of authority and may make it fully effective as though the director had been granted the necessary authorisations from the outset. A company cannot ratify either illegal transactions or acts which are in breach of companies' legislation; for example, a company may not ratify an unlawful dividend.

4.72 A company will only be able to ratify in certain circumstances:

- The director in respect of whose actions the ratification is sought must have been acting as agent on behalf of a company and cannot have been purporting to act either as principal in a transaction or on behalf of an unnamed principal. The third party must have known the name of the company on whose behalf the director was purporting to act at the time of entering into the transaction.[16]
- The company on whose behalf the director purported to act must have been in existence at the time of the transaction. A company cannot ratify a transaction entered into by an agent prior to its incorporation because the company would not have been able to enter into the contract itself or have authorised agents to act on its behalf in such respect.
- At common law, the act must have been *intra vires* (that is, within the capacity of the company) although beyond the director's authority in order for the company to be able to ratify it – in these circumstances, the act can be ratified by way of ordinary resolution.[17] An ordinary resolution will not, however, be sufficient to circumvent a right that has been included in the articles.[18] In addition, under s. 35(3) of the 1985 Act, a company was able to ratify an act which was *ultra vires* (outside the scope of the company's powers) by means of a special resolution. There is, however, no corresponding section under the 2006 Act (see **4.77–4.81** below).

4.73 If a director acts beyond the powers granted to the board but still within the powers of the company, the act can be ratified by ordinary resolution of the shareholders of the company. If a director acts beyond the powers delegated to him individually but still within the powers of the board, the act can be ratified by a board resolution. If the act is ratified by means of a board resolution, the director who acted beyond his powers and whose act is being ratified should not form part of the quorum voting on the resolution.

4.74 Section 239 of the 2006 Act applies to the ratification by a company of conduct by a director amounting to negligence, default, breach of duty or breach of trust in relation to the company. Sections 239(3) and (4) of the 2006 Act, in a reversal of the House of Lords' decision in *North-West Transportation Co Ltd and Beatty v. Beatty* (1887) 12 App Cas 589, provide that an interested director who is a member of the company (and any member connected with him) is not eligible to vote on a resolution ratifying his acts.

4.75 The effects of the ratification of a director's act is that the act is treated as if it had been done with the requisite antecedent authority and the act is adopted as an act of the company itself and is no longer considered to be an act of the director acting as principal. The director or agent who entered into the transaction will cease to be a party to the contract. As a result, the third party will only have recourse against the company under the contract. The third party could still seek redress against the director or agent, however, by means of a claim for breach of warranty of authority, although establishing loss would be difficult in a situation where the contract had been ratified.

Ultra vires the company

4.76 The restrictions on a company and on the transactions it can enter into come from a number of sources: statutory provisions in the 2006 Act and other relevant legislation; the objects clause (if any); a company's articles of association; the duties of directors under the 2006 Act; and common law and the normal rules of agency.

4.77 The restrictions contained in an objects clause are restrictions as to the capacity of the company; if the company acts contrary to these restrictions, it will be acting *ultra vires*. The restrictions contained in the articles of association, in the directors' duties and in the normal rules of agency are restrictions as to the authority of the company to act in certain situations and transactions but are not restrictions on the capacity of the company; if the company acts in a manner that is contrary to these restrictions, its acts will not be *ultra vires* or void and will therefore be ratifiable.

4.78 Strictly, if a company acts *ultra vires*, its acts are void and are not ratifiable by the shareholders. However, without the ability to ratify an act or contract, the company could find itself in a position where it cannot enforce the contract.

4.79 Section 35(3) of the 1985 Act allowed a company to ratify a transaction in excess of the powers of the company by special resolution. A corresponding section has not been included in the 2006 Act, probably for two main reasons:

- Most companies will no longer retain an objects clause which means that there will be no *intra vires* and *ultra vires* division in the company's constitution. Therefore, the only way that a company will be able to act beyond its capacity will be if it acts in a manner that is illegal or against companies' legislation. As neither of these types of act is ratifiable a corresponding provision to s. 35(3) would be of no use.
- Objects clauses will now be contained in the articles of association, and as a result a breach of any objects clause will be dealt with in the same way as any other breach of the articles by the company, that is by shareholders' ratification through a special resolution.

4.80 Regardless of whether acts are inside or outside a company's powers, third parties are now provided with statutory protection and are able to enforce the contract. Under s. 39 of the 2006 Act, the validity of an act done by the company cannot be called into question on grounds of lack of capacity by reason of anything in the company's constitution. Therefore, if a company acts in a manner that is contrary to any restrictions imposed by the company's shareholders, this will have no effect on the enforceability of the transaction to a third party.

4.81 Practical tips for directors

- Check the extent of your delegated powers by checking:
  - articles of association and any relevant resolutions;
  - any other documents conferring special authority, e.g. terms of reference of any relevant committees.
- Act within your actual authority.
- If you are not sure of the extent of your actual authority, check with the board.
- Do not hold yourself out personally when entering into transactions.

Specific powers of directors

Table A or 2006 Act Provision	Specific power conferred
Regulation 2, Table A	Subject to the provisions of the 2006 Act and without prejudice to any rights attaching to existing shares, Regulation 2 authorises directors to issue shares with such rights or restrictions as the company determines by ordinary resolution.
Regulations 8–11, Table A	Authorise the directors to take a lien over partly paid shares with respect to liabilities on calls. The lien makes the company a secured creditor in the event of the bankruptcy of the shareholder and enables the directors to withhold dividends owing to that shareholder.
Regulations 12–22, Table A	Authorise the directors to make calls on members to pay up any money remaining unpaid on their shares and forfeit any shares which remain unpaid to the extent that the directors have called for payment.

Table A or 2006 Act Provision	Specific power conferred
Regulations 23–28, Table A	Authorise the directors to refuse to register a transfer of shares in certain circumstances.
Regulation 33, Table A	Where as a result of a consolidation of shares any shareholder would become entitled to a fraction of a share, Regulation 33 authorises the directors to sell the shares representing the fractions of the shares for the best price reasonably obtainable and distribute the net proceeds of sale in due proportion.
Regulation 37, Table A	Authorises the directors to call general meetings.
Regulation 44, Table A	Authorises the directors to attend and speak at any general meeting of the company and at any separate meeting of the holders of any class of shares of the company.
Regulations 65–69, Table A	Authorise the directors to appoint and remove alternate directors by signed written notice.
Regulations 70–71, Table A	Authorise the directors to manage the business of the company and to appoint any person as agent of the company by way of a power of attorney.
Regulation 72, Table A	Authorises the directors to further delegate their powers to committees of the company, to their appointed managing director or to any other director holding an executive office.
Regulation 84, Table A	Authorises the directors to appoint a managing director.
Regulations 88–98, Table A	Authorise the directors to regulate their proceedings as they see fit, including the appointment of a chairman of the board and the ability to make decisions by way of written resolution.
Regulation 99, Table A	Authorises the directors to appoint a secretary for such term, at such remuneration and on such conditions as they think fit.
Regulation 101, Table A	Authorises the directors to use the company seal and determine who may sign any instrument to which the company seal is affixed.

Table A or 2006 Act Provision	Specific power conferred
Regulations 102–108, Table A	Authorise the directors to limit the amount of the dividend that can be declared by the shareholders of the company and the date on which the dividend will be declared.
Regulation 109, Table A	Authorises the directors to enable shareholders to inspect the accounting records or documents of the company other than those available by right.
Regulation 110, Table A	Subject to the authorisation of an ordinary resolution of the company, Regulation 110 authorises the directors to resolve to capitalise any undivided profits of the company not required for paying any preferential dividend or any sum standing to the credit of the company's share premium account or capital redemption reserve. The directors may then appropriate the sum capitalised to the shareholders who would have been entitled to it by way of dividend by issuing fully paid-up bonus shares.
Section 44 of the 2006 Act	Authorises the directors to execute documents on behalf of the company either by signature of the document by two authorised signatories or by one director in the presence of a witness who attests the signature.
Section 247 of the 2006 Act	Authorises the directors to make provision for the benefit of persons employed or formerly employed by the company or any of its subsidiaries in connection with the cessation or transfer of the business.
Section 302 of the 2006 Act	Authorises the director of a company to call a general meeting.
Sections 394 and 415 of the 2006 Act	Authorise the directors to prepare accounts and a directors' report for the company for each of its financial years.
Sections 485, 489 and 492 of the 2006 Act	Authorise the directors to appoint an auditor or auditors of the company and to fix the remuneration of the auditor where the directors have so appointed him.
Section 550 of the 2006 Act	Subject to any limitations contained in the articles of association, section 550 authorises the directors of a private company which has only one class of shares to allot shares in the company and grant rights to subscribe for or to convert any security into such shares.

Sources

1 *Foss v. Harbottle* (1843) 2 Hare 461, Wigram VC at 492.
2 Regulation 70, Table A.
3 *Barron v. Potter* [1914] 1 Ch 895.
4 *Charterhouse Investment Trust Ltd v. Tempest Diesels Ltd* (1985) 1 BCLC 99, 544.
5 *Re Brazilian Rubber Plantations and Estates Ltd* [1911] 1 Ch 425.
6 *Fulham Football Club Limited v. Cabra Estates Plc* [1992] BCC 863; s. 173(2)(a), Companies Act 2006.
7 *Re Fireproof Doors Limited* [1916] 2 Ch 142.
8 *Secretary of State for Trade and Industry v. Baker (No. 5)/Re Barings Plc (No. 5)* [1999] 1 BCLC 433.
9 *Boschoek Proprietary Company Limited v. Fuke* [1906] 1 Ch 148.
10 *Williams v. Natural Life Health Foods Limited* [1998] 1 WLR 830.
11 *Freeman and Lockyer v. Buckhurst Park Properties (Mangal Limited)* [1964] 2 QB 480, at 498 per Pearson LJ.
12 *Rama Corporation Ltd v. Proved Tin and General Investments Ltd* [1952] 2 QB 147, at 149–150 per Slade J.
13 *Swan v. North British Australasian Co* (1863) 2 Hurl. &C 175.
14 *Smith v. Henniker-Major & Co* [2003] Ch 182.
15 S. 40(2)(b)(iii) of the 2006 Act.
16 *Sanderson v. Griffiths* (1826) 5 B&C 909.
17 *Grant v. United Kingdom Switchback Railway Co* (1888) 40 ChD 135.
18 *Quin & Axtens Ltd v. Salmon* [1909] AC 442.

5 Directors' duties

Introduction

Background

5.1 Historically, directors' duties have been a creation of common law and have therefore evolved through case law. The duties a director of a company incorporated within the United Kingdom had to abide by were not written down in a cohesive form in any one place. When considering what those duties comprised and how they were to be interpreted, an appraisal of a large number of often complex cases was required. As a result, there was no clarity regarding what the duties of a director were, and determining the duties at any one time involved an analysis of case law, which it is not easy for most directors to perform.

5.2 Broadly, the duties a director owed to a company under common law comprised:

- the duty to exercise skill and care;
- the duty to act in good faith in the best interests of the company;
- the duty to act within the powers conferred by the company's memorandum and articles of association and to exercise powers for proper purposes;
- the duty not to fetter discretion;
- the duty to avoid conflicting interests and conflicting duties; and
- the duty not to make a secret profit.

5.3 As we shall see later in this chapter, these common law duties are still relevant when it comes to interpreting the new codified duties set out in the Companies Act 2006 (the Act).

Recent developments

5.4 Given the failure to have one cohesive set of statutory duties, and the fact that the vast majority of companies incorporated within the UK are small, private limited companies, it was considered, by a number of different sources, including the Law Commission, that the rules by which a director had to abide were not clear and accessible to the directors of those entities. Consequently, it was thought that it would be helpful if the duties to which directors must abide were set out in statute with the aim being 'to make what is expected of directors clearer and to make the law more accessible to them and to others'.[1]

Companies Act 2006

5.5 One of the most controversial proposals of the Act as it was passing through Parliament, and which received the most press coverage, was Part 10 of the Act, which introduces the codified statutory statements of the directors' duties. Despite Lord Goldsmith stating that 'once the [Act] is passed, one will go to the statutory statement of duties to identify the duty the director' owes to a company, Part 10 of the Act does not set out all the duties a director owes. There are other duties (e.g. the duty to prepare and deliver accounts to the Registrar of Companies), which are set out in other Parts of the Act.

5.6 This chapter explores the duties owed by a director prior to the enactment of the Act, and explores the differences and similarities between common law duties and the new codified statutory duties.

The position before the Companies Act 2006

5.7 Whilst this section of the chapter refers to the common law and fiduciary duties in the past tense, they are still relevant when it comes to interpreting the new codified statutory duties. Accordingly, the impact and scope of these duties cannot be overlooked.

Fiduciary duties (including the director's position as trustee)

5.8 A director is often thought to be in a fiduciary relationship with the company he represents, owing duties to that company. This was especially true in the old cases where the post of director was thought to be analogous to that of a trustee. However, unlike a trustee, a director rarely has the property of the company vested in him as owner.

Exercise independent judgement and not fetter his discretion

5.9 Generally, a director could not agree to exercise his power in a certain way, even if that would not have prevented his other duties to the company, unless he was permitted to do so under the company's constitutional documents.

Duty to act in good faith in the best interests of the company

5.10 A director, historically, had to act at all times in what he considered to be the best interests of the company. The duty was subjective and, provided that the director had exercised his powers in good faith, it was immaterial what the outcome of his deliberations was. This did not mean that a director would be cleared by a court merely on a subjective test of his motives. Courts did become increasingly involved in considering the substantial or principal purpose for which the director had exercised his power, and provided that the exercise was for a proper purpose and the director had acted in good faith, the courts would not concern themselves with the merits of the decision from a commercial perspective. It was generally accepted that while the company was solvent, the best interests of the company meant the interests of the shareholders of the company.

5.11 Once a company was insolvent, the directors had to consider the interests of the creditors in advance of the interests of the shareholders of the company and take those interests into account when carrying out their duties. However, it was held that the duty was still owed to the company and not to the creditors directly.

Duty to act within the powers conferred by the company's constitution

5.12 A director could not cause the company to undertake activities outside that permitted by the company's constitutional documents or exercise its powers for any improper purpose. This applied even if the director thought that he was acting in good faith and conducting his activities in the best interests of the company.[2]

Duty to avoid conflicts

5.13 A director was under a duty not to place himself in a position where there was a conflict, or possible conflict, between the duties he owed to the company and his personal interests. If such a conflict arose, he was under a duty to disclose this conflict to the company and could be prohibited from taking part in various decisions at board level.

Duty not to profit out of his position

5.14 *Regal (Hastings) Ltd v. Gulliver*[3] and *Boardman v. Phipps*[4] are cases which held that a director must not profit from his position as a director.

5.15 In *Regal (Hastings)*, Regal brought an action against five former directors to recover sums of money which it was alleged were profits made by them on the acquisition and sale of shares in a subsidiary company, Hastings Amalgamated Cinemas Limited. The allegations were that the directors had used their positions to acquire the shares with a view to selling them immediately at a high profit, and that this profit had been obtained due to their position as directors of Regal. In this case, despite the fact that Regal would not have taken advantage of the situation, it was held that the directors had made a profit for themselves and that this profit had been made as a result of their position as directors of Regal. The directors sought no authority from Regal to make such profit and, therefore, were in breach of their fiduciary duties to Regal and were liable to account for that profit to the company.

5.16 *Boardman v. Phipps* involved a similar issue. In that case, shares in a private company were left to be divided among a wife and children as an asset under a will. The solicitor to the trustees of the will and a beneficiary under the will decided that the company was in an unsatisfactory position and that something had to be done to improve the situation. They attended a general meeting of the company as proxies for two of the trustees and, following that meeting, they decided, with the knowledge of the trustees, to endeavour to obtain control of the company by themselves purchasing the shares in the company. The negotiations for the shares were protracted and eventually a contract was entered into under which the solicitor and beneficiary acquired the shares. A considerable profit was then made on these shares through capital distributions. Both parties had acted honestly throughout the matter, but an order was made by the court that they had received information that the purchase of the shares would be a good investment and the opportunity to acquire the shares came to the solicitor and beneficiary as a result of their acting, or purporting to act, as trustees for certain purposes. Therefore, they were found liable to account for the profits they received.

5.17 Regulation 85 of Table A[5] specifically allows a director to be interested in a particular transaction and to keep any profit he derives from that transaction, provided that he has disclosed the nature and extent of his interest to his fellow directors. However, where a director profits from a particular transaction without proper authorisation, the courts will often provide a remedy to the company, requiring the director to repay the profits he wrongly received, on the basis that the director has breached his fiduciary relationship with the company. It is the fact that a director has profited from his position without disclosing it to his fellow directors which is the important factor to consider here, not how the profit was made and indeed whether the company would ever have taken up the opportunity,[6] or if it was in fact able legally or financially to take up the contract.[7] Additionally, a director can be found liable to repay profits that he has made where they are undisclosed even if the transaction also benefits the company, and where the director has incurred costs and expenses in connection with the profit made.

5.18 Whilst a director cannot, even after he has ceased to be a director, pursue and take on an opportunity which the company is actively pursuing, he cannot be prevented from using the knowledge he acquired as a director to his advantage once he has ceased to be a director, unless such knowledge was confidential, or the opportunity had developed to such a stage while he was a director that it should remain with the company and the director should not be capable of taking advantage of it.

Duty of skill and care

5.19 The classic statement of a director's obligation to act with skill and care was set out in *Re City Equitable Fire Insurance Co*[8] where Romer J stated:

> 'a director need not exhibit in the performance of his duties a greater degree of skill than may reasonably be expected from a person of his knowledge and experience. A director of a life assurance company does not guarantee that he has the skill of an actuary or of a physician.'

5.20 This means that a greater level of skill is expected of experienced businessmen than of an amateur. However, where a company has got into financial difficulties and is insolvent, it has been held that a more objective standard is required and the courts will require a general level of skill, knowledge and experience as may reasonably be expected of a person carrying out the same function as those carried out by the director. More recently, the courts have begun to employ a more objective assessment alongside the traditional subjective test by providing that a director had to take such actions as would be taken by

> 'a reasonably diligent person having both (a) the general knowledge, skill and experience that may reasonably be expected of a person carrying out the same functions as are carried out by the director in relation to that company and (b) the general knowledge, skill and experience that he has.'[9]

5.21 The level of care required from a director depends on the facts of each case. He must exhibit in the performance of his duties such care as an ordinary man might be expected to take on his own behalf. One director, among a board of ten directors, may not be expected to be as diligent as a sole director. However, it should not be forgotten that all directors are responsible for the proper management of the company and its affairs.

Background to the codification of duties

5.22 In 1998, the then Department of Trade and Industry (DTI) began a wide-ranging review of company law. The DTI published a consultation paper, the Company Law Review (CLR), one objective of which was feedback on the preparation and promotion of laws that provide straightforward and cost-effective regulation, balance the interests of shareholders, creditors and others, and promote consistency and transparency. One of the points examined in the consultation document was the question of whether the duties of directors should be codified in the Act so that they would be more widely accessible and understood. The CLR Steering Group, following its review, recommended that there should be a statutory statement of directors' duties contained in the Act and that this statement should codify the existing law. This codification was 'intended to provide greater clarity on what is expected of directors and make the law more accessible'.

5.23 These recommendations were accepted by the government in the preparation of the Act, and led to the introduction and enactment of the Companies Bill.

Companies Act 2006

5.24 Part 10, chapter 2, of the Act sets out the duties owed by a director of a company to that company.[10] (See **5.90–5.91** below for further details of who should abide by these duties.) The general duties are based on the old common law rules and equitable principles as they applied in relation to directors of companies and are stated to 'have effect in place of those rules and principles'[11] as regards the duties which a director owes to a company. However, the new codified statutory duties are to be interpreted and applied in the same way that the old common law rules were, and regard is to be had to the old common law rules and principles when interpreting these duties (see **5.106–5.109** below).

5.25 However, the new codified duties depart from the common law rules and equitable principles in two areas:

1 Section 175 provides that transactions or arrangements with the company do not have to be authorised by the board; instead interests in transactions or arrangements with the company must be declared under s. 177 or s. 182.
2 Board authorisation of conflicts of interest arising from third party dealings by the director are permitted, but the authorisation is effective only if the conflicted director(s) has (have) not participated in the taking of the decision or if the decision would have been valid even without the participation of the conflicted director(s).

5.26 The explanatory notes to the Act state that the general duties 'set out how directors are expected to behave; it does not tell them in terms what to do'.[12]

Codified duties

5.27 Seven codified duties are set out in the Act and this chapter considers each one in turn. However, in relation to the duty to promote the success of the company,[13] the Act sets out a non-exhaustive list of matters a director must take into account. It is clear, however, that the duty to promote the success of the company is the overriding duty and the non-exhaustive list of matters are simply ancillary factors which a director should consider when making his ultimate decision. Lord Goldsmith in the Lords Grand Committee[14] stated:

> 'The statement of general duties ... is not intended to be an exhaustive list of all the duties owed by a director to his company. The directors may owe a wide range of duties to their companies in addition to the general duties listed. Those are general, basic, duties which it is seen as right and important to set out in this way. The statement that these are the general duties does not allow a director to escape any other obligation he has, including obligations under the Insolvency Act 1986.'

5.28 A concern with regard to the introduction of these statutory duties, and the non-exhaustive list of matters to which the directors of a company must have regard when making their decision as to whether their action will promote the success of the company for the benefit of the members as a whole, is that directors may have to consider setting up new processes to ensure that they have adequately considered these matters, including more detail in board minutes thereby adding to what can already be quite lengthy documents, and effectively leading to more box-ticking and administration rather than less, which was one of the CLR's initial objectives when implementing the Act.

5.29 The GC 100, which brings together senior legal officers of more than 70 FTSE100 companies, published a paper relating to directors' duties under the Act on 7 February 2007.[15] The paper looked in particular at the level of support and the paper trail which should be put in place when directors are making decisions as to whether a particular act is likely to promote the success of the company. While the GC 100 is made up of representatives from public companies, the guidance from the GC 100 can be equally applied to private companies as the new legal regime for both types of company is broadly similar. The paper notes that, when a proposal is put to a board meeting, the subsequent decisions are nearly always supported by a background paper which will have been prepared and reviewed by management teams, possibly with advisers as well. It is likely that all the relevant considerations will have been made by the persons who compiled the paper, but it is still the responsibility of the directors to apply their own business judgement and review the papers and the recommendations contained in them.

5.30 If a factor is not relevant, the GC 100 does not believe that a negative statement to that effect should be included in the board documents. Board minutes are, as they always have been, simply a summary of the actions and discussions of the meeting. The GC 100, therefore, recommends that board minutes should not be used as a medium for recording the extent to which each of the relevant factors in the Act is discussed. This should mean that board minutes do not increase substantially in length or content and remain in a similar format to those recorded prior to the introduction of the Act. The GC 100 view is that, because the list of matters to be taken into consideration is non-exhaustive, directors should record in the board minutes that they have considered 'all relevant factors' when reaching their decision rather than recording the specific factors which they actually did consider when making a key decision. (See also **Appendix 4**.)

5.31 Directors can authorise conflicts in the case of:

- a private company incorporated on or after 1 October 2008, if there is nothing in its constitution to the contrary;
- a private company incorporated before 1 October 2008, if there is nothing in its constitution to the contrary and the members of the company have resolved by ordinary resolution that authorisation may be given in accordance with the Act. Such a resolution may be passed before, on or after 1 October 2008 and must be forwarded to the Registrar of Companies within 15 days after it is passed; and
- a public company, if its constitution provides for the directors to authorise the matter and they do so in accordance with that provision.

5.32 Even though there is no requirement for a private company's articles to contain provisions enabling the directors to authorise conflicts, there may be benefits in doing so. For instance, the articles can contain 'provisions for dealing with conflicts of interest'. The Act states that anything done (or omitted) by the directors in accordance with those provisions does not constitute a breach of their general duties. To utilise this safe harbour, the articles can, for instance, contain provisions that regulate the disclosure and use of confidential information that the director has as a result of the conflicted situation from a third party, the attendance at board and committee meetings (and voting at them) and the receiving of information. Private companies incorporated before 1 October 2008 that are amending their articles will also need to pass an ordinary resolution that authorisation may be given in accordance with the Act.

5.33 Authorisation must be given by independent directors, so an interested director's vote must be disregarded and he or she may not count in the quorum.

The seven codified duties

Act within powers – s. 171

5.34 Section 171 provides that 'a director of a company must act in accordance with the company's constitution and only exercise powers for the purposes for which they are conferred'. This section codifies the previous common law provision that a director should act within his powers, in accordance with the terms on which they were given, and should always do so for a proper purpose only. There are effectively two limbs to this duty: (a) the duty to act within the powers conferred by the constitution; and (b) the proper purpose duty.

5.35 The company's constitution comprises its articles of association and memorandum (the latter is now of much more limited significance) and any resolutions or agreements which affect the articles of association. It is usual for a company's constitution to limit a director's authority to act (e.g. in respect of borrowing powers) and so directors must ensure that they are aware of the content of the constitution of the company of which they are a director to be certain that they are acting within those powers so conferred.

5.36 A director who acts in breach of this duty is liable to compensate the company for any loss incurred. However, it is always worth remembering that an act undertaken by a director outside the scope of the constitution may be considered to be valid if the director has actual, apparent or ostensible authority to undertake such an act, thereby falling back on the common law fiduciary duties and the rules of agency (see **5.8**).[16]

5.37 What constitutes a proper purpose should be ascertained in the context of each situation and will vary depending on the given facts or circumstances. This decision will not always be an easy one. It could be that only part of a decision was made for an improper purpose. This means that the exercise will be tainted and will be deemed to be improper.

5.38 Nominee directors may find this duty hard to comply with as they may feel obliged to act in a way that advances the interests of their appointer even though this may not necessarily be in the interests of the company itself. If they do so, they may be in breach of this duty.

5.39 Formal procedures should be in place and followed when holding and attending a meeting of the board of directors as opposed to other meetings involving directors, for example, assisting one director in the performance of certain functions delegated to him by the board. Directors should be conscious of the contents of the constitutional documents of their company and ensure that they act within them at all times. If there is any doubt about the content of these documents, they should seek the advice of the company secretary or external legal advice.

Promote the success of the company – s. 172

5.40 This duty codifies, although it has altered the wording slightly, the duty to act in the best interests of the company. A director must now 'act in a way which he considers, in good faith, would be most likely to promote the success of the company for the benefit of its members as a whole'. It is hoped that this will put an end to the protracted debate as to the exact meaning of the words 'act in the best interests of the company'. Lord Greene MR, in Re *Smith & Fawcett Limited*[17] stated that directors are required to 'act bona fide in what they consider – not what a court may consider – is in the interests of the company, and not for any collateral purpose'.

5.41 This is the matter for consideration that prompted the most debate both in the press and also in Parliament. This is largely because, in addition to the main duty to promote the success of the company for the benefit of its members, there are six non-exhaustive factors to which a director must have regard (among other matters). These are:

1 the likely consequences of any decision in the long term;
2 the interests of the company's employees;
3 the need to foster the company's business relationships with customers, suppliers and others;
4 the impact of the company's operations on the community and the environment;
5 the desirability of the company maintaining a reputation for high standards of business conduct; and
6 the need to act fairly as between members of the company.

5.42 See **5.101** below for a consideration of the issues which may arise when one decision involves a number of these statutory considerations which may not necessarily sit comfortably with each other, and could, indeed, be in conflict.

The Rt. Hon Margaret Hodge MP stated:

> 'the words "have regard to" mean "think about"; they are absolutely not about just ticking boxes. If 'thinking about' leads to the conclusion, as we believe it will in many cases, that the proper course is to act positively to achieve the objectives in the clause, that will be what the director's duty is. In other words "have regard to" means "give proper consideration to" ... Consideration of the factors will be an integral part of the

duty to promote the success of the company for the benefit of its members as a whole. The clause makes it clear that a director is to have regard to the factors in fulfilling that duty. The decisions taken by a director and the weight given to the factors will continue to be a matter for his good faith judgment.'[18]

5.43 The Act makes it clear that the duty is to act for the benefit of the company's members as a whole, but the duties are generally owed to the company and enforceable by the company rather than its members (see below).

5.44 In having regard to the various factors listed in the Act, the duty to exercise reasonable care, skill and diligence (s. 174) will be relevant and should be taken into account.

5.45 Concern has been raised about taking these factors into account when there are already large bodies of statutes governing such matters which a company is already required to comply with. For example, there are rafts of environmental legislation already on the statute books. By including a duty on a director to have regard to the impact of the company's operation on the environment, the obligation to consider these matters increases in significance whereas previously it was simply an additional consideration. Additionally, it will extend the consideration to the overseas operations of a company incorporated in England and Wales whereas currently the scope of the environmental legislation is restricted to the United Kingdom. This itself introduces an argument raised by the Friends of the Earth. They reported that the UK's requirement for palm oil is destroying rainforests in South East Asia and threatening the survival of the orang-utan. Friends of the Earth palm oil campaigner, Ed Matthew, stated: 'the Company Law Reform Bill represents a great opportunity for MPs to make sure that UK companies clean up their act',[19] and he urged MPs to take advantage of the Company Law Reform Bill (as it was then known) to make UK companies responsible for the environmental impact of their operations. The counter-argument is that this may put UK companies at a disadvantage *vis-à-vis* overseas companies which are not required to have regard to the impact of their operations on the environment when making their decisions. Is this what was intended when this sub-section of the Act was introduced? Having said that, it is clear that the director owes his duties to the company only and not to any of the persons listed in the non-exhaustive list (e.g. employees or suppliers). Provided that a director fulfils the duty to promote the success of the company, and provided that he has made business decisions in good faith and has exercised reasonable skill, care and diligence, he is not likely to be found to be in breach of his duty to the company.

5.46 The Explanatory Notes to the Act make it clear that 'it will not be sufficient to pay lip service to the factors, and that in many cases, directors will need to take action to comply with' this aspect of the duty.[20] However, the Explanatory Notes also make it clear that it is not intended that a director will have to do more than act in good faith and exercise reasonable care, skill and diligence and it is not intended that a director who acts in good faith can be held liable for a process failure which would not have affected his decision as to which course of action to follow if he considered that it promoted the success of the company. Nevertheless, the enactment of this duty, together with the introduction of the statutory derivative action rules, has led many directors to believe that they are at risk of possible litigation if, with the benefit of hindsight, a shareholder alleges that a company was not successful or as successful as it could have been because a director did not take a relevant factor into account.

5.47 Additionally, debate was had about the meaning of the word 'success'. Is that financial success only, or could it be some other sort of success? For example, during the 2005–6 season Chelsea Football Club was one of the most successful teams in the UK on the football pitch, but, from a financial perspective, it was not one of the most successful of clubs (despite the fact that Chelsea had a very wealthy owner). What is success in Chelsea FC's case? This should be viewed alongside the fact that the majority of shares in public listed companies are held on a short-term basis, whether in hedge funds or other investment houses. Many shareholders do not invest long-term and may want to make a quick gain and then exit.

5.48 The Attorney-General, Lord Goldsmith, gave guidance that 'success' is to be determined on a case-by-case basis with the starting point being that it is essentially for the members of the company to define the objectives they wish to achieve, and he added that, for a commercial company, success will normally mean long-term increase in value, but the company's constitution and decisions made under it may also specify the appropriate success model.

5.49 In light of this, it may be advisable for directors to include a definition of success in the company's constitution so that it is clear to all parties what the aims and objectives of the company are.

5.50 The CLR thought it important to add a statement that required directors to consider success for the benefit of the members as a whole.

5.51 One of the essential principles of this duty is that it is for the directors of a company to make a decision, in good faith, as to whether a particular matter is likely to promote the success of the company or not. The courts will not enquire, objectively, whether a particular decision was the best decision for the company, or whether the directors' beliefs were honest and reasonable. In addition, directors should be aware that this duty is a personal one and cannot be delegated to others.

5.52 If a director acts without giving any thought at all to any of these factors, does this mean that he has acted in breach of his duties? It is thought that the court will look at the decision and decide whether there was any basis at all on which a director could reasonably have concluded that the specific action was likely to promote the success of the company. If there are no such grounds, then it is likely that he will be found to have breached this duty. This was stated by the Attorney-General, Lord Goldsmith, on 9 May 2006 during the House of Lords debate:

> 'we want the director to give such consideration to the factors identified as is necessary for the decision that he has to take, and no more than that. We do not intend a director to be required to do more than good faith and the duty of skill and care would require, nor do we want it to be possible for a director acting in good faith to be held liable for a process failure where it could not have affected the outcome.'[21]

5.53 However, a strict legal interpretation of this section is that a director could find his decision subjected to review if he fails to take into account all the identified factors.

5.54 Section 172(3) recognises that when a company is insolvent, the duty of the directors shifts from being focused on the members of the company to acting in the best interests of the creditors of the company. Directors should always have an eye on this if they consider the company is at risk of insolvency as the Insolvency Act 1986 contains provisions which allow a liquidator to require a director to contribute towards the assets of the company in the event that the company was trading when it had no reasonable prospect of being able to avoid insolvent liquidation.[22]

Exercise independent judgement – s. 173 of the Act

5.55 This duty codifies the previous common law rule to exercise the powers independently, without subordinating the powers to the will of others.[23] Additionally, the fact that directors can rely on others for advice, but then must consider all the advice received and make their own decision, was noted in the House of Commons debate on 11 July 2006, where it was said that 'the duty is about directors having to make their own judgements' and not following blindly the views of others. It was stated that:

> 'the duty does not prevent a director from relying on the advice or work of others, but the final judgement must be his responsibility. He clearly cannot be expected to do everything himself. Indeed, in certain circumstances directors may be in breach of duty if they fail to take appropriate advice, for example legal advice. As with all advice, slavish reliance is not acceptable and the obtaining of outside advice does not absolve directors from exercising their judgement on the basis of such advice.'[24]

5.56 Directors are allowed to limit their discretion provided they are acting in accordance with an agreement duly entered into by the company or in a way authorised by the company's articles of association. This reinforces the need for a director to be aware of the content of the constitutional documents of the company of which he is a director.

5.57 Interestingly, this duty does not permit a director to delegate some or all of his functions to others or to committees, unless this is agreed by the company (e.g. recorded in the board minutes) or stated in its articles. Accordingly, constitutional documents will need to be checked to ensure that delegation is permitted.

5.58 As a practical matter, a director should ensure that any personal concerns do not affect any judgement he makes with regard to the company. Where there is a conflict, he should absent himself from the discussion. He should, where appropriate, seek third party advice on particular matters but ensure that he does not simply follow it without thought since the ultimate decision is his responsibility and his judgement has to be independent.

Exercise reasonable care, skill and diligence – s. 174

5.59 This duty codifies the common law rule to exercise reasonable care, skill and diligence. The courts historically have interpreted this duty as being a subjective test,[25] looking at the skill and knowledge of the particular director and not requiring him to exhibit any greater skill or care than may be reasonably expected from a person with his skill and knowledge. This is confirmed by s. 174(2), which introduces an objective element to the test – it provides that the duty will be interpreted by reference to '(a) the general knowledge, skill and experience that may be reasonably expected of a person carrying out the functions carried out by the director in relation to the company, and (b) the general knowledge, skill and experience that director has'.

5.60 In effect, this means that a director with specialist knowledge or expertise such as a financial qualification would be expected to employ such knowledge or expertise in the discharge of his duties. The objective test sets the minimum standard with which a director must comply. The subjective test raises the standard based on the particular director's knowledge, skill and experience.

5.61 As a practical matter, a director must ensure that he acts as he deems fit and proper using his skill and experience, but he must also bear in mind how a 'reasonable person' would act in the same situation.

Avoid conflicts of interest – s. 175

5.62 The Act provides that a director must avoid a situation in which he has, or can have, a direct or indirect interest that conflicts, or may conflict, with the interests of the company. The duty applies in particular to the exploitation of any property, information or opportunity for personal purposes, whether or not the company itself could take advantage of the property, information or opportunity. There is no definition of 'interest' or 'conflict of interest' in the Act. A director is no longer under a duty merely to mitigate a conflict of interest; he is under a duty to avoid a potential conflict of interest and carries an ongoing duty to be vigilant of changing interests and circumstances that could lead to a conflict situation. It is thought that this duty may apply in a number of common situations, for example, where a director is a director of more than one company, especially if that second company is a competitor of or supplier to the first company, or he is a major shareholder of a competitor or supplier, as the duties that he owes to the two companies could compete with each other and put him in a position of conflict.

5.63 This duty applies to conflicts other than those arising in relation to transactions or arrangements with the company, which are dealt which separately under s. 177.

5.64 Section 175(4)–(6) provides means by which a potential conflict does not amount to a breach of the duty contained in s. 175(1). This can be where (a) the situation cannot reasonably be regarded as likely to give rise to a conflict of interest[26] or (b) if the matter is authorised by the directors.

5.65 A conflict must be authorised in advance in order to avoid a director being in breach of this duty. As noted in **5.31**, in order for the directors of a public company to authorise a conflict, the public company's constitution must permit the board to sanction such breaches. Accordingly, it is advisable, in the case of a public company, for the articles of association to be reviewed to ensure that they contain a provision enabling the directors to authorise conflicts and take advantage of the safe harbour provisions in s. 180(4) which allow the articles of association to permit certain actions. If this is not included in the articles, an amendment should be proposed. Some public companies have been including such an amendment in their 2008 AGM round.

Companies that have proposed amendments to their articles to allow the directors to approve certain conflicts also tend to include safeguards in the articles of association. For example, they have provided that the director who is interested cannot be counted in a quorum when considering whether or not to authorise the conflict and cannot vote on any resolution, and that the directors must act in good faith when considering what action they should take in relation to this conflict and whether allowing the conflict will promote the success of the company. In addition, the articles should specify what the consequences of a conflict which is not approved should be: should the director be excluded from debates, or even suspended?

5.66 The Act also retains the ability for the company to authorise a conflict, either through shareholder approval or in accordance with the provisions in the company's articles. The shareholder route may be useful where there are insufficient independent directors available to authorise a conflict or, in the case of a wholly-owned subsidiary, where it is decided that the holding company should authorise conflicts rather than the subsidiary's directors. Where the shareholders are concerned about giving the directors full authority to approve conflicts, the company's articles could provide for the members to have the sole power to authorise a conflict. It is unlikely to be a practicable approach in most cases, however, to have to convene a shareholder meeting (or pass a members' written resolution) every time a conflict or potential conflict arises.

5.67 The GC 100 has published guidance on conflicts of interests and the exercise of the power of directors to approve such conflicts.[27] The guidance advises that directors consider the matter for approval, and, if approved, that they record the nature of the matter they have approved, the duration of the approval (it is suggested that there be an annual review), any circumstances when the director must revert to the board for any part of the authority to be reviewed, and, where appropriate, include provisions relating to confidential company information such as provisions stating that, where a director obtains confidential information, he will not be obliged to disclose this to the company or use it in relation to the company's affairs if he would then be in breach of that confidence.

5.68 Section 232(4) is also relevant as it allows a company's articles to protect directors from liability by continuing to include provisions dealing with conflicts of interest where they were lawful prior to the Act coming into force. Therefore, companies will be able to continue to rely on the conflict provisions in their articles, including Table A 1985, Regulation 85, if applicable.

5.69 The CLR took the view that a requirement for shareholders to approve potential conflicts could stifle entrepreneurial activity. One of the aims of the CLR was to have a 'Think Small First' approach to regulation which was intended to make it easier for the majority of companies in the UK which are small, owner-managed businesses to operate and run. However, Lord Goldsmith, in Grand Committee, made it clear that 'any requirements under the common law for what is necessary for a valid authorisation remain in force'.[28] He added that the section states that the authorisation is 'effective only if' the stated matters are complied with, but does not state that those are the only matters which must be complied with to authorise the matter. He stated that 'there might be other conditions in relation to an authorisation that would be required – for example, the company's constitution may have some specific provision which it would need to comply with as well'.

5.70 The Act provides that this statutory duty covers conflicts of interest and also conflicts of duties.[29] Concern has been expressed that what previously amounted under case law to a disability, so that a conflict of interest would result in a director not being able to participate in the board's decision-making in relation to a matter unless shareholder approval were obtained, now amounts to a positive duty under the Act to avoid a conflict of interest. This has led to concerns about the position for directors with multiple directorships when conflicts of interest arise between their different directorships, in particular whether it is still possible for a director to deal with such a conflict by absenting himself from the meeting at which the relevant matter is discussed.

5.71 The new duty also creates problems in terms of any new directorships that a director may be considering taking up. Directors must avoid situations in which they have interests that conflict or 'possibly may conflict' with the company's interests. A director may find it difficult to reach the conclusion, before taking on a new directorship, that there is no possibility of such a conflict arising in the future. Similarly, a director may not be able to satisfy himself, at that stage, that the situation could not reasonably be regarded as likely to give rise to a conflict of interest so as to fall within the safe harbour available under the Act. For example, a director of an IT company looking for a non-executive directorship in the IT field where no actual conflict exists but where future conflict could be said to be at least 'possible', through the companies deciding to compete, at some point in the future, for the same business.

5.72 Companies should consider giving their directors the power to authorise conflicts, including authorising directors to take up board positions with other companies. Whether this will be sufficient to cover any conflicts that later arise will depend on the specific circumstances, including the scope of the authorisation given by the non-conflicted directors. If it is not sufficient, and a director needs to seek a further board authorisation when a specific conflict associated with his new directorship arises, this may cause practical difficulties given that the director – because of his duty of confidentiality to the other company – may not be in a position to disclose the conflict situation.

5.73 Internal company policies and procedures for the notification of conflicts or potential conflicts by individual directors should be reviewed. Notification to the company secretary or another officer is likely to be the most practical solution; the company secretary or other officer can then arrange for the conflict to be considered and, if appropriate, authorised by the other non-conflicted members of the board. Policies should also make clear what directors should do if they are unsure whether they can, for reasons of confidentiality, notify a specific conflict arising out of another directorship; for instance, that they should take independent legal advice. Even with policies of this kind in place and provision for independent advice, it remains possible that a director who is unable to notify a conflict of interest, due to his obligations of confidentiality, will have to resign the original directorship.

5.74 Companies with a diverse shareholder profile will need to consider whether shareholders are likely to support a change to the articles which grants the directors the power to authorise conflicts. Listed and AIM-traded companies should establish the likely attitude of the investor bodies and be ready to explain to the relevant general meeting the rationale behind the change. Shareholders may derive comfort, when considering whether to authorise such a change to the articles, from the fact that the directors would, in considering whether to exercise their powers to authorise a conflict, still be subject to their overall duties to the company and in particular to their duty to promote the success of the company.

5.75 As a practical matter, public companies should consider amending their articles of association as soon as possible to allow directors to approve certain conflicts of interest. A director should not have to act differently from how he historically has behaved. He should ensure that his personal or other interests do not conflict with those of the company. Where they could do, he should ensure that the directors on the board approve this conflict or potential conflict in advance. If there is a conflict, a director should ideally absent himself from meetings at which that interest is being discussed. When approving conflicts, directors should still act in the manner they consider is going to promote the success of the company.

Duty not to accept benefit from third parties – s. 176

5.76 The Act provides that a director must not accept a benefit from a third party conferred by reason of being a director or doing (or not doing) anything as director. This is intended to cover bribes and secret commissions, and again represents the codification of an equitable principle. It will catch non-financial benefits, such as the provision of corporate hospitality to directors.

5.77 The prohibition applies only to benefits the acceptance of which can reasonably be regarded as likely to give rise to a conflict of interest. So payments of small, non-material amounts are unlikely to be caught. If the benefit is more substantial, it will need to be considered in the light of all the relevant circumstances pertaining to the director, the company and the third party to ascertain if it could reasonably be likely to give rise to a conflict of interest.

5.78 By contrast with the duty to avoid conflicts of interests, the board authorisation route is not provided for. Whereas a strict no conflicts rule was thought to act as a fetter on entrepreneurial and business start-up activity by existing company directors, it was not thought that any similar rationale applied to justify board authorisation of the acceptance of benefits from third parties. Accordingly, in keeping with case law, these benefits may be authorised by the members or in accordance with provisions in the company's articles.

Declare interests in proposed transactions – s. 177

5.79 This duty replaces the equitable principle that a director cannot have any interest in a proposed transaction unless that interest is declared and authorised by the members of the company (whether contained in the constitution or separately). This historically was covered by Regulation 96 of Table A 1985. It also replaces s. 317 of the Companies Act 1985, which imposed a requirement on a director to disclose interests in any contracts or proposed contracts with the company.

5.80 The duty requires a director to declare to the other directors, before the company enters into a transaction or arrangement, if he is 'in any way, directly or indirectly, interested in a proposed transaction or arrangement with the company'.[30] He must declare the nature and the extent of the interest. Any declaration can be made at a meeting of the directors or by notice in writing to the directors.[31] If a declaration that has been previously made becomes inaccurate or incomplete, a further amending declaration must be made.[32] The fact that the interest can be direct or indirect means that it is not necessary for the director himself to be interested in the transaction. It could be that someone with whom he is associated is directly interested, making his interest an indirect interest, but this would still need to be declared.

5.81 The word 'proposed' was included in this section as the requirement to disclose an interest in an existing transaction or arrangement is within the ambit of s. 182 (being the duty of a director to declare an interest in existing transactions or arrangements). (See **5.87** for further details.)

5.82 The requirement for shareholder approval of an interest was removed as the CLR found that this provision was altered in the articles of association of most private companies before the introduction of the Act, with those articles providing simply that the matter had to be disclosed to the other directors, who could then vote on it. Consequently, there is no longer a requirement for shareholder or other approval of any particular interest. Nevertheless, it is always open for a company to impose a requirement for the shareholders to approve a certain matter in its articles of association.

5.83 An interesting issue for consideration is what disclosure, if any, is required where the company has a sole director. As the duty is only to disclose the arrangement to the other directors, the Explanatory Notes to the Act state that where there is only one director of the company, no disclosure is required.

5.84 Section 177(5) provides that a director is not required to make a declaration of an interest of which he is not aware, or where he is not aware of the transaction or arrangement in question. However, this is not a subjective test and the statute provides that a director is treated as being aware of matters of which he ought reasonably to be aware.

5.85 There are a few get-outs from this duty, specifically where the matter cannot reasonably be regarded as likely to give rise to a conflict of interest, or where the other directors are already aware of the matter (and, for this purpose, they are deemed to be aware of things that they ought reasonably to be aware) and if, or to the extent that, the matter concerns terms of his service contract that have been, or are to be, considered by a meeting of the directors, or by a committee of the directors appointed for the purpose under the company's constitution.

5.86 A director must ensure that he declares any interest before the transaction or arrangement is entered into by the company. He must also address any inaccurate or misleading declaration of interest before the transaction is concluded. This applies not only to those transactions or arrangements to which the director is a direct party, but also to any in which persons connected with him, such as his spouse and children, are a direct party.

Declaration of interest in existing transaction or arrangement

5.87 This duty expands on the duty to declare an interest in proposed transactions or arrangements and provides that interests in existing transactions or arrangements must also be disclosed. The disclosure must be made if the director is directly or indirectly interested in the transaction, and the nature and scope of the duty must be declared. However, where the director declared an interest in a proposed transaction or arrangement under s. 177, he does not need to make another declaration when that transaction or arrangement becomes actual. The declaration must be made in the same way as one in a proposed transaction or arrangement (i.e. by notice in writing to the directors or at a meeting of the directors), and must be updated if the declaration becomes inaccurate or incomplete. The disclosure must be made as soon as reasonably practicable.

5.88 A director who fails to make a disclosure under this section is guilty of an offence and is liable to a fine and/or conviction.

Relationship of the statutory duties and the articles of association

5.89 A company can set out more restrictive duties in its articles of association, but it cannot dilute the statutory duties unless the Act specifically provides that the company can do so. For example, the duty to exercise independent judgement is not infringed by a director 'acting in a way authorised by the company's constitution'.[33] This means that where a specific company's constitution, for example, requires a director not to deal with persons or companies located in certain jurisdictions, he cannot be deemed to have breached his duty to exercise independent judgement simply by complying with that constitutional provision. Equally, if a specific act would otherwise have been a conflict of interest, that act can be taken as approved by the directors of the company (acting without the director who would otherwise have the conflict of interest or, to the extent that he does vote on the matter, provided only that it would have been agreed to without his vote or if his vote had not been counted) provided that there is nothing in the company's constitution to invalidate such an authorisation.[34]

To whom do the general duties apply?

5.90 Section 170(1) makes it clear that the statutory duties are owed by a director of a company to that company. 'Director' for these purposes has the meaning set out in s. 250 ('includes any person occupying the position of a director, by whatever name called'). This covers both executive and non-executive directors.

5.91 In addition, 'the general duties apply to shadow directors where, and to the extent that, the corresponding common law rules or equitable principles so apply'.[35] This means that where a common law rule or equitable principle applied to a shadow director, the statutory duty which replaces the common law or equitable principle will apply to the shadow director in place of that common law rule or equitable principle. However, if case law has developed such that a common law rule or equitable principle does not apply to a shadow director, the statutory duty replacing that rule or principle will not apply to a shadow director. Rather than making this clearer for shadow directors, it has, arguably, made it more complex and confusing as shadow directors will now not only need to have an eye to the new statutory provisions, but will also need to bear in mind the common law rules and equitable provisions to ascertain whether a specific statutory duty applies to them. (See **1.74** for what constitutes a shadow director.)

To whom are the duties owed?

5.92 Historically, the duties owed by a director were owed to the company itself. This has now been codified in s. 170(1), which makes it clear that the general duties set out in ss. 171–177 are owed by a director of a company to the company itself. It therefore follows that the company itself is the only person who can bring an action against a director for breach of duty. Such actions can be initiated by the board of directors on behalf of the company (although it must be recognised that a board is unlikely to bring an action against itself and such an action is more likely to be brought following a takeover or change of management), a liquidator if the company has been put into liquidation, or by a member undertaking a derivative action. Part 11 of the Act (derivative claims and proceedings by members) sets out on a statutory footing for the first time the mechanism by which members of a company can enforce the new statutory duties against a director on behalf of the company. (See **Chapter 15** in relation to derivative claims.)

5.93 It was feared that the introduction of these statutory duties would lead to an increase in litigation against directors. However, given the limited number of people who are entitled to initiate an action on behalf of the company, and the requirement to prove a loss (which can only mean that the company was not as successful as it otherwise would have been) it is thought unlikely that there will be an opening of the floodgates with regard to claims.

Approval of a breach of duty by the shareholders of the company

5.94 Section 180 provides that where what would otherwise be a breach of the duty in s. 175 (duty to avoid conflicts of interest) has been approved by the directors of the company or, in the case of s. 177 (duty to declare interest in proposed transaction or arrangement), the director has declared his interest to the other directors, the transaction or arrangement is not liable to be set aside by virtue of any common law rule or equitable principle requiring consent or approval of the members of the company. However, if the articles of association of the company impose a requirement for there to be shareholder approval, this will override this statutory provision.

5.95 Additionally, s. 180(4) of the Act provides that the general duties (the seven statutory duties set out in ss. 171–177) will not be infringed by anything done (or omitted to be done) by the directors which is contained or set out within the articles of association of the company.

5.96 Shareholder ratification historically was available as a breach of a duty and simply made the transaction in question voidable. The Act now places this on a statutory footing. Prior to the Act, the principle was set out in *Rolled Steel Products Ltd v. BSC*[36] where it was stated that

> 'if an act is beyond the corporate capacity of a company, it is clear that it cannot be ratified. As against the company itself, an *ultra vires* agreement cannot become *intra vires* by means of estoppel, lapse of time, ratification, acquiescence or delay. However, the clear general principle is that any act which falls within the corporate capacity of a company will bind it if it is done with the unanimous consent of all the shareholders, or which is subsequently ratified by such consent (see *Salomon v. A Salomon & Co Ltd*).[37] This principle is not an unqualified one. In particular, it will not enable the shareholders of a company to bind the company itself to a transaction which constitutes a fraud on its creditors.'

5.97 Section 35(3) of the Companies Act 1985 provided an alternative route of ratification. It stated that directors must observe any limitation on their powers which flow from the company's constitution, but that the shareholders may, by special resolution, approve an act which would otherwise be beyond the company's constitution. The rationale for this would be that the shareholders could, by special resolution, amend the constitution of the company and so they should be able to ratify decisions which would otherwise involve an alteration of the company's constitution by such a majority. Some acts of directors are ratifiable by an ordinary resolution of the shareholders (e.g. making a secret profit, and the failure to exercise skill and care) but the few that are not permitted to be ratified in such a way are breaches involving the abridgement of rights of individual shareholders, acts that are fraudulent or dishonest, or acts for which the articles provide a procedure as these would require an amendment to the articles of association of the company.

Duration of the duties

5.98 The vast majority of the new statutory duties apply to directors only while they are directors of a company. However, there are a couple of instances in which a specific duty can continue to apply to a director even after he has ceased to be a director of a company.

5.99 A person who ceases to be a director continues to be subject to the duty to avoid conflicts of interests (s. 175) as regards the exploitation of any property, information or opportunity of which he became aware when he was a director, and to the duty not to accept benefits from third parties (s. 176) as regards things done or not done by him before he ceased to be a director.[38] The statute does make it clear that these extended duties are to be applied after making 'any necessary adaptations'. This means, it is thought, that the court can be a little more lenient or flexible when interpreting these duties and can take into account the fact that the person is no longer a director of the company but also may wish to consider the reason for his removal or resignation.

5.100 That these provisions continue after a person ceases to be a director of a company is intended to prevent, for example, a director becoming aware of an opportunity whilst managing the company's business and simply resigning his directorship in order to absolve himself from the requirement to seek shareholder approval.

Relationship between the various statutory duties

5.101 It is clear that a given set of facts may lead to a breach of more than one of the statutory duties (s. 179). For example, in the case of a decision as to whether or not to outsource a particular function of the company, the decision will obviously benefit the company as it will, or should, reduce costs, but is not likely to be in the best interests of the company's employees if a number of them are made redundant as a result. In this situation, the duty to take into account the interests of the employees is ancillary to the duty to promote the success of the company, and therefore, provided that the directors act in a way which they consider likely to promote the success of the company (by outsourcing) and they have considered the interests of the employees, they will have fulfilled their statutory duty. However, in a situation where two of the seven statutory duties conflict, it is important that the director complies with all the relevant statutory duties. The Explanatory Notes to the Act make it clear that the duties to which a director is subject in any one situation must be read in context. The fact that one duty permits a director to do a particular act does not mean that he can perform that act if it would also breach another duty. For example, if the director considers that by borrowing a large sum of money from a third party he would be promoting the success of the company for the benefit of its members as a whole, he would not be permitted to do this if the company's constitution does not permit the director to approve borrowings on behalf of the company.

5.102 As referred to above, the duty to avoid a conflict of interest is specifically stated not to apply to a conflict which arises in relation to a transaction or arrangement between the director and the company.[39] In such a situation, provided that the director has complied with his duties under s. 177 (to declare his interest in the proposed transaction or arrangement), he need not comply with s. 175.

Consequences of breach of duty

5.103 Section 178 preserves the common law rules and equitable principles when considering the consequence of a breach of duty. It makes clear, therefore, that the duties (with the exception of s. 174 – duty to exercise reasonable skill, care and diligence) are enforceable as fiduciary duties owed to a company by its director.

5.104 The Act does not set out in statutory form what these consequences are and reference must be made to existing case laws for guidance on consequences of breach.

5.105 Consequences of a breach of a fiduciary duty may include:

- damages or compensation where the company has suffered a loss;
- restoration of the company's property;
- an account of profits made by the director;
- rescission of a contract where the director failed to disclose an interest; and
- injunctions or declarations (although these are primarily used where a breach has not yet occurred).

Relationship between case law and the new duties

5.106 Section 170(3) provides that 'the general duties are based on certain common law rules and equitable principles as they apply in relation to directors and have effect in place of those rules and principles as regards the duties owed to a company by the directors'. It follows that any court deciding a case against a director for breach of duty will have to interpret these new statutory provisions, and not a breach of an older common law rule or equitable principle. How the rules are to be interpreted is unclear as no cases have yet been brought before the courts.

5.107 The recommendation that codification of the duties should not hinder the development of the law by the courts, and recognition that court judgments are based on a particular fact pattern and often state general principles rather than being exhaustive, is recognised by the Act as it provides that 'the general duties shall be interpreted and applied in the same way as common law rules or equitable principles, and regard shall be had to the corresponding common law rules and equitable principles in interpreting and applying the general duties'.[40] This was explained by David Howarth in the House of Commons, who said:

> 'the statutory statement of directors' duties was intended to reflect a refined version of where the case law has got to. Because part of [Parliament's] intention in passing the statute is to put into statutory form what already exists in some other form in case law, it would be legitimate to refer back to existing case law, because that would tend to clarify, rather than make more confusing, what we are doing.'[41]

The practical effect is that reference must be had to the statutory duties but that, in order to understand these duties, the case law must also be read.

5.108 In effect, it would appear that there has only been a partial codification. Since regard is to be had to the common law cases, this means that the codification of duties in the Act does not represent a cohesive set of rules. Directors, when interpreting the statutory duties, will always have to have one eye on the common law and how the courts have interpreted the common law rules.

5.109 At the time of writing, there have not been any actions brought against directors under the new statutory duties and it remains to be seen how the courts will interpret these duties.

Sources

1 Lord Goldsmith, Lords Grand Committee, 6 February 2006, column 254.
2 *Howard Smith v. Ampol Petroleum* [1974] AC 821.
3 [1942] 1 All ER 378.
4 [1967] 2 AC 46.
5 Companies (Tables A to F) Regulations 1985, SI 1985/805.
6 *Industrial Development Consultants Limited v. Cooley* [1972] 2 All ER 162.
7 *Boston Deep Sea Fishing and Ice Co v. Ansell* (1888) LR 39 ChD 339.
8 [1925] CH 407, Romer J.
9 *Re D'Jan of London Limited* [1993] BCC 646.
10 Ss. 170–177, Companies Act 2006.
11 S. 170(3), Companies Act 2006.
12 Companies Act 2006: Explanatory Notes, para. 298
13 S. 172, Companies Act 2006.

14 February 2006, column 249.
15 GC 100: Directors' Duties – Companies Act 2006, 7 February 2007.
16 *Freeman and Lockyer v. Brockhurst Park Properties (Mangal) Limited* [1964] 2 QB 480, CA.
17 [1942] Ch 402.
18 Hansard, column 789, debate, 17 October 2006.
19 www.foe.co.uk/campaigns/corporates/news/orangutan_parliament.html
20 Explanatory Notes, para. 328.
21 Hansard, House of Lords debate, 9 May 2006, column 846.
22 The Insolvency Act 1986, s. 214 – the wrongful trading rules.
23 House of Commons, Hansard, 11 July 2006, column 599.
24 Lord Goldsmith, Lords Grand Committee, 6 February 2006, column 282.
25 *Re City Equitable Fire Insurance Co Ltd* [1925] Ch 407.
26 S. 175(4)(a), Companies Act 2006.
27 GC 100: Companies Act 2006 – Directors' conflicts of interest, 18 January 2008.
28 Grand Committee, 9 February 2006, Hansard, column 326.
29 S. 175(7), Companies Act 2006.
30 S. 177(1), Companies Act 2006.
31 S. 177(2), Companies Act 2006.
32 S. 177(3), Companies Act 2006.
33 S. 173(2)(b), Companies Act 2006.
34 s. 175(4), (5) and (6), Companies Act 2006.
35 s. 170(5), Companies Act 2006.
36 [1985] 3 All ER 52, at 86 per Slade LJ.
37 [1897] AC 22, at 47.
38 S. 170(2), Companies Act 2006.
39 S. 175(3), Companies Act 2006.
40 S. 170(4), Companies Act 2006.
41 House of Commons, 6 July 2006, Hansard, column 531.

6

Directors' transactions with the company requiring shareholder approval

Introduction

6.1 When a company enters into a transaction or arrangement with one of the directors (or certain other persons connected to them) of the company or its holding company, a conflict of interest arises which may result in the director acting in his own rather than the company's interest. This chapter looks more closely at the rules governing a director's conduct when entering into transactions with the company or its holding company contained in the 2006 Act, the Listing Rules, AIM Rules and the Takeover Code.

6.2 Generally, the following statutory and regulatory matters must be considered when directors enter into transactions with their companies or holding companies:

- the company's constitution, i.e. its articles of association and any resolutions and agreements that were made in accordance with, or that affect, the company's constitution;
- the Companies Act 2006 (the 2006 Act), in particular Chapters 2 and 4 of Part 10, which contain a statutory statement of the general directors' duties and require disclosure to shareholders (e.g. with regard to certain interests in transactions with the company and in the case of directors' service contracts) or shareholder approval of certain transactions with directors (e.g. where the company enters into long-term service contracts or substantial property transactions, makes certain payments to a director for loss of office or grants a loan to one of its directors);
- where the company is a UK listed or quoted company, the rules of the relevant regulatory body, i.e. the Financial Services Authority's Listing Rules in the case of UK listed companies and the AIM Rules in the case of companies with shares admitted to trading on AIM;
- in the context of a takeover bid where a bidder enters into a transaction or arrangement with the directors of the target company which falls within the scope of the City Code on Takeovers and Mergers (the Takeover Code), regard must be had to the relevant Takeover Code provisions.

The Companies Act 2006

6.3 The 2006 Act aims to promote fair dealing by directors of private and public companies when entering into transactions with their companies or holding companies by requiring directors to obtain the informed consent of the company's shareholders.

6.4 The 2006 Act sets out four types of transactions that require shareholder approval:

- long-term service contracts;
- substantial property transactions;
- loans, quasi-loans and credit transactions; and
- payments for loss of office.

6.5 The rules governing these types of transactions can be found in Chapter 4 of Part 10 of the 2006 Act (Chapter 4 transactions) and are discussed below.

6.6 Until 1 October 2007, the statutory regulation of Chapter 4 transactions was found in Part X of the Companies Act 1985 (the 1985 Act). The restrictions in ss. 323–329 and Schedule 13 of the 1985 Act on share dealings by directors and their families have been repealed with effect from 6 April 2007. These restrictions have not been replaced in the 2006 Act. Instead, as of 6 April 2007, directors who hold shares in their companies are subject to the disclosure requirements in the Financial Services Authority's Disclosure Rules and Transparency Rules (DTR) sourcebook (see **Chapter 9**). Most of the other provisions of Part 10 of the 2006 Act came into force on 1 October 2007. The new statutory directors' conflict of interest duties dealing with declarations of directors' interests in proposed and existing transactions or arrangements with their companies came into force on 1 October 2008 (see **6.80** below).

6.7 Where a director enters into a Chapter 4 transaction with a company, in addition to any other statutory regulation of such a transaction, both he and the other directors approving the transaction (if they are also shareholders of the company) must comply with their general directors' duties. (See **Chapter 5**.)

6.8 With regard to all of these transactions, according to s. 281(3) of the 2006 Act, the shareholder approval required is an ordinary shareholder resolution, but the company's articles may require a larger majority or even unanimity.[1] Where shareholder approval is required under more than one set of provisions in Chapter 4 of Part 10 the 2006 Act, the requirements of *each* applicable provision must be met (s. 225 of the 2006 Act). Approval may, however, be given by a single resolution making sure that the shareholders give separate consideration to the requirements of each provision.[2]

6.9 It is also important to note that, unless the articles of association provide otherwise, with regard to all Chapter 4 transactions that are discussed in **6.28–6.29** below, the interested directors (where they are also shareholders of the company) and any shareholder(s) connected with them are *not* excluded from the shareholder vote passing the resolution that approves the transaction. However, when approving such a transaction, directors who are also shareholders of the company must comply with their general directors' duties (see **Chapter 5**). So, for example, such a director may approve a loan to a director only if he considers, in good faith, that it would promote the success of the company for the benefit of its members as a whole, having regard to the factors listed in s. 172 of the 2006 Act.[3] Where one of the provisions of Chapter 4 of Part 10 of the 2006 Act (discussed below) or one of the general directors' duties when approving such a Chapter 4 transaction is breached and such a breach ratified by shareholder resolution in accordance with s. 239 of the 2006 Act, votes in favour of the resolution by the relevant director (if a shareholder of the company) and any shareholder connected with him must be disregarded when determining whether the resolution has been passed with the necessary majority (for more on the ratification process, see **Chapter 5**).

6.10 As discussed in **Chapter 1**, there are different types of directors: de jure and de facto directors, executive and non-executive directors, and shadow directors.[4] The 2006 Act does not distinguish between de jure and de facto directors or between executive and non-executive directors, and the duties owed by a de facto or non-executive director are no different from those owed by de jure or executive directors. All the rules in Chapter 4 of Part 10 of the 2006 Act expressly cover shadow directors.

6.11 Special provisions apply to charities that are subject to the Charities Act 1993. These require that charitable companies obtain prior written approval of the Charity Commission before their members can effectively approve any of the transactions mentioned above.

6.12 Unless otherwise stated, references to statutory provisions in this chapter are to the 2006 Act.

Substantial property transactions

6.13 The provisions governing substantial property transactions can be found in ss. 190–196 of the 2006 Act which replace ss. 320–322 of the 1985 Act with effect from 1 October 2007 and apply to transactions entered into on or after that date.

6.14 Section 190 requires that acquisitions involving 'substantial non-cash assets' where the non-cash assets are acquired from, or transferred to, a director of the acquiring or transferring company, be approved by the shareholders. The following transactions fall within the scope of s. 190: acquisitions or sales of non-cash assets by a company from or to:

- a director of the company;
- a director of its holding company;
- a person connected with a director of the company; [5] and
- a person connected with a director of its holding company.[6]

6.15 Shadow directors and de facto directors are treated as directors for the purposes of ss. 190–196.

6.16 Under the 1985 Act, such shareholder approval, by ordinary resolution, had to be obtained *before* the company could enter into the relevant agreement with the director, thus requiring the parties to wait until a shareholders' meeting had been held. As an alternative to obtaining prior shareholder approval, the 2006 Act now offers companies the possibility of entering into such agreements with directors, without prior shareholder approval, provided that the arrangement is *conditional* on such approval being obtained. This offers companies more flexibility and speeds up the acquisition process.

6.17 If, when entering into such a conditional arrangement, the approval is ultimately not forthcoming, the company will incur no liability by reason of that failure (s. 190(3)).

6.18 'Substantial assets' are assets with a value exceeding £100,000 or 10% of the company's net assets, but in any event more than £5,000 (this *de minimis* threshold was raised from £2,000 under the 1985 Act). The company's net asset value must be determined on the basis of its last set of annual accounts or called-up share capital if it has not yet produced accounts (s. 191(3)). The values of non-cash assets of connected transactions – that is, arrangements involving more than one non-cash asset or that are one of a series of arrangements involving non-cash assets – must be aggregated when determining whether the minimum financial thresholds triggering the shareholder approval requirement have been exceeded (s. 190(5)).

6.19 The term 'acquisition' in this context includes the creation or extinction of an estate or interest in or a right over any property, and the discharge of a liability of any person other than a liability for a liquidated sum (s. 1163(2)).

Note, however, that transactions relating to anything to which a director is entitled under his service contract and to payments for loss of office fall outside the scope of s. 190.

6.20 If the director or connected person is a director of the company's holding company, or is a person connected with such a director, the arrangement with the company must be approved by the shareholders of both the company and the holding company or be conditional on their approvals.

Exceptions

6.21 No shareholder approval is required on the part of a shareholder of a wholly-owned subsidiary or the shareholder(s) of overseas companies.

6.22 Shareholder approval is not required for the following transactions:

- a transaction between a company and a director in his character as a shareholder of the company;
- a transaction between a holding company and its wholly-owned subsidiary; and
- a transaction between two wholly-owned subsidiaries of the same holding company (s. 192).

6.23 The 2006 Act also introduces a new exception for companies in administration or winding up (other than members' voluntary winding-up) as the conflict of interest which a director ordinarily faces in substantial property transactions does not arise when an administrator contracts on behalf of the company.[7]

Consequences of a breach of s. 190

Rescission

6.24 The civil consequences which arise from a contravention of s. 190 can be found in s. 195, which states that the arrangement, and any transaction entered into pursuant to the arrangement, is voidable. If rescinded, the arrangement would be avoided as against all parties. Rescission is barred, however, where:

- restitution is no longer possible;
- the company has been indemnified for the loss or damage suffered by it; or
- rights acquired in good faith, for value and without actual notice of the breach by a person who is not a party to the arrangement or transaction would be affected by the rescission.

6.25 If the transaction or arrangement is subsequently affirmed by resolution of the company's or, as the case may be, its holding company's shareholders within a reasonable time, the right of rescission is lost. The resolution can be passed in general meeting or, in the case of a private company, as a written resolution (see **11.48**).

Liability of directors and connected persons

6.26 Regardless of whether the arrangement or transaction has been rescinded, the following persons are liable to account to the company for any profit made, directly or indirectly, by the arrangement or transaction; and to indemnify the company (jointly and severally with any other person so liable) for any loss or damage resulting from the arrangement or transaction:

- any director of the company or its holding company with whom the relevant arrangement was made;
- the connected person with whom the relevant arrangement was made;
- the director with whom that connected person was connected; and
- any other director who authorised the relevant arrangement or transaction.

Service contracts

6.27 The provisions governing directors' service contracts can be found in ss. 188 and 189 and ss. 227–230 of the 2006 Act, which replace ss. 318 and 319 of the 1985 Act with effect from 1 October 2007 and apply to contracts made on or after that date.

6.28 The 2006 Act defines the meaning of service contract in relation to a company for the purposes of Part 10 for the first time. Pursuant to s. 227, a director's service contract means a contract under which:

- a director undertakes personally to perform services (as director or otherwise) for the company or for a subsidiary of the company; or
- services that a director undertakes personally to perform (as director or otherwise) are made available by a third party (e.g. a personal services company) to the company, or to a subsidiary of the company.

6.29 This definition includes contracts of service (e.g. employment contracts), contracts for services and letters of appointment to the office of director. Shadow directors and de facto directors are treated as directors for the purposes of ss. 188 and 189.

Directors' long-term service contracts

6.30 Under s. 188, directors' service contracts with a fixed term (or a fixed or rolling notice period) in excess of two years must be approved by the shareholders. Previously, under the 1985 Act, the requirement for shareholder approval was only triggered by service contracts with a fixed term in excess of five years. The new provision in the 2006 Act brings company law closer to the Combined Code recommendation that contract periods for directors of companies listed on the London Stock Exchange's Official List be no more than one year.[8]

6.31 Where the service contract is between the company and the director of its holding company, resolutions are required from both the company (unless it is a wholly-owned subsidiary) and its holding company.

6.32 No shareholder approval is required on the part of a shareholder of a wholly-owned subsidiary or the shareholder(s) of overseas companies.

6.33 If, more than six months before the end of the guaranteed term of the original service contract, the company enters into a further guaranteed term service contract with that director, the unexpired period of the original service contract must be added to the guaranteed term of the new contract when calculating whether the term exceeds two years and thus requires shareholder approval (s. 188(4)). This does not apply where the new contract is entered into in accordance with a right conferred on the other party to it by or under the original contract. Note, however, that if the original contract may be continued at the instance of the director, this may bring the original contract within the scope of the approval requirement pursuant to s. 188(3)(a)(i).

6.34 Where shareholder approval is required, the company must make available to the shareholders a memorandum setting out the particulars of the proposed contract (s. 188(5)). Where the approval is sought by written resolution, the memorandum must be sent to the shareholders no later than at the time the proposed resolution is sent or submitted to the shareholders. Note, however, that, subject to the company's articles of association, an 'accidental failure' to send the memorandum to the shareholders before the resolution is passed shall not invalidate such approval (s. 224).

6.35 Special rules apply with regard to quoted companies which require such companies to specify certain details of the directors' employment in the directors' remuneration report (see **6.117** below).

Consequences of a breach of s. 188

6.36 Failure to obtain shareholder approval allows the company to terminate the service contract at any time by giving reasonable notice (s. 189). In addition, a service contract that contains a term that made it necessary to obtain such shareholder approval is deemed to have been made for two years. The government states in the Explanatory Notes to the 2006 Act that the purpose of this section is to limit the duration of directors' service contracts, as a long-term contract can make it too expensive for the shareholders to remove a director while preserving the shareholders' ability to approve longer arrangements if they wish.[9]

Inspection of service contracts

6.37 A company must keep available for inspection by the shareholders a copy of every director's service contract (including any variation thereof) with the company or with one of its subsidiaries at its registered office (s. 228). If the contract is not in writing, the company must keep a written memorandum of its terms. The 2006 Act introduces a new requirement that any such contracts, regardless of their term, or memoranda be open to inspection for at least one year after they have expired. The 1985 Act exception for contracts with less than 12 months to run and contracts which were terminable within 12 months has not been retained by the 2006 Act.

6.38 Shareholders may inspect copies of service contracts or memoranda without charge and may request copies thereof on payment of a prescribed fee. Such copies must be provided within seven days following receipt by the company of the request (s. 229(2)). If the company refuses inspection of service contracts or memoranda, or defaults in complying with its obligation to provide copies thereof, the shareholder may apply to the court which may, by order, compel an immediate inspection or direct that the copy be sent to the shareholder (s. 229(5)) (see **Chapter 8**).

Consequences of a breach of s. 228

6.39 Failure to comply with the requirements to keep directors' service contracts in accordance with s. 228 or to provide copies when requested is a criminal offence for which every officer of the company who is in default may be held liable (s. 228(5)). The validity of the relevant service contract is, however, not affected by a breach of s. 228.

6.40 In contrast to the 1985 Act, the 2006 Act does not provide that the company itself be liable under the criminal offence. However, if the company does not comply with a court order for immediate inspection or provision of a copy of the service contract or memorandum, the company (and any director responsible for such non-compliance) will be in contempt of court.

Loans and other credit transactions

6.41 The provisions governing loans to, and other credit transactions with, directors can be found in ss. 197–214 of the 2006 Act which replace ss. 330–341 of the 1985 Act with effect from 1 October 2007 and apply to transactions or arrangements entered into on or after that date.

Most significantly, under the 2006 Act, loans, quasi-loans and credit transactions with directors and connected persons are no longer generally prohibited as was the case under the 1985 Act, subject to exceptions, but are subject to shareholder approval. The separate regimes for private and public companies are, however, maintained. Shadow directors and de facto directors are treated as directors for the purposes of ss. 197–214.

6.42 Under the 2006 Act rules, subject to certain exceptions, a company, whether public or private, may:

- make a loan to a director;
- give a guarantee; or
- provide security in connection with a loan made by any person

to a director of the company or its holding company provided the transaction has been approved by the shareholders (s. 197). The term 'loan' is not defined in the 2006 Act. However, it is likely to be limited to situations where a company advances money on the condition that it is to be repaid rather than the supply of goods or payment of outstanding debt on credit.[10]

6.43 Where the director is a director of the company's holding company, the shareholders of the holding company must also approve the transaction. However, unlike substantial property transactions (see **6.13** above), loans (and, in relation to public companies and private companies associated with a public company, quasi-loans and credit transactions) cannot be entered into conditional on shareholder approval.

6.44 No shareholder approval is required on the part of a shareholder of a wholly-owned subsidiary or the shareholder(s) of overseas companies.

Additional requirements for public companies

6.45 Public companies and private companies associated with a public company (pursuant to s. 256 a holding company is associated with all its subsidiaries, and a subsidiary is associated with its holding company and all the other subsidiaries of its holding company)[11] are subject to additional restrictions as follows:

- The requirement to obtain shareholder approval is extended to include 'quasi-loans' (s. 198) and 'credit transactions' (s. 201).
  - A quasi-loan is defined as a transaction under which the creditor pays or agrees to pay a sum for the borrower, or reimburses or agrees to reimburse expenditure someone incurred on the borrower's behalf on terms that the borrower (or someone on his behalf) will reimburse the creditor; or in circumstances where a liability arises on the borrower to reimburse the creditor.
  - The definition of credit transaction is intended to include transactions where there is credit or deferred consideration.

- The requirement to obtain shareholder approval is extended to apply not only to transactions entered into with or for a director but also with or for a wide circle of persons connected with such a director (s. 200).[12]

Exceptions

6.46 The 2006 Act expands the scope of the exceptions under the 1985 Act and introduces new exceptions to the requirement for shareholder approval. The following exceptions apply with effect from 1 October 2007.

Expenditure on company business (s. 204)

6.47 Shareholder approval is not required where the company provides a director of the company or its holding company, or his connected persons, with funds to meet expenditure incurred by him for the purposes of the company or to enable him to perform his duties as an officer of the company properly. For this exception to apply, the aggregate value of the transactions in question must not exceed £50,000.

Expenditure on defending proceedings, etc. (s. 205)

6.48 Shareholder approval is not required where a company provides one of its directors or a director of its holding company with funds to meet (or avoid) expenditure incurred in defending any criminal or civil proceedings *in connection with* any alleged negligence, default, breach of duty or breach of trust by him in relation to the company or an associated company (companies are associated if one is the subsidiary of the other or both are subsidiaries of the same holding company). If there is no such connection, shareholder approval is required for the loan, quasi-loan, credit transaction or the guarantee or security given in connection with a loan, quasi-loan or credit transaction.

6.49 In the event of a conviction of the director or judgment against him in the proceedings, the loan, quasi-loan or credit must be repaid or the company's liability discharged.

Expenditure in connection with regulatory action of investigation (s. 206)

6.50 The exception from the requirement to obtain shareholder approval in s. 206 was introduced by the 2006 Act. It extends the exception for expenditure on defending proceedings to the provision of funds to meet (or avoid) expenditure incurred by a director of a company or its holding company in defending himself in an investigation by a regulatory authority, or against action proposed to be taken by a regulatory authority in connection with any alleged negligence, default, breach of duty or breach of trust by him in relation to the company or an associated company.

Minor and business transactions (s. 207)

6.51 No shareholder approval is required for minor transactions, i.e. transactions where the loan or quasi-loan, or the guarantee or security given in connection with a loan or quasi-loan, does not exceed £10,000 (raised from £5,000 under the 1985 Act); and the credit transaction, or guarantee or security given in connection with the credit transaction, does not exceed £15,000 (raised from £10,000 under the 1985 Act). In each case, the values of the transaction and any other relevant transaction or arrangement must be aggregated to determine whether the applicable threshold has been reached.

6.52 There is also an exception where the credit transaction, or the giving of a guarantee or security in connection with a credit transaction, is in the ordinary course of the company's business and is not on more favourable terms than would be offered to a person of the same financial standing but unconnected with the company (i.e. at arm's length).

Intra-group transactions (s. 208)

6.53 Where a loan or quasi-loan is made, or a guarantee or security given in connection with a loan or quasi-loan, for the benefit of a company in the same group, no shareholder approval is required. The same applies to intra-group credit transactions, or the giving of a guarantee or security in connection with a credit transaction for the benefit of a company in the same group.

Money-lending companies (s. 209)

6.54 Money-lending companies making loans or quasi-loans, or giving guarantees or security in connection with a loan or quasi-loan, in the ordinary course of the company's business and at arm's length are also exempt from the requirement to obtain shareholder approval. More lenient criteria apply to 'home loans', i.e. loans made to directors of the company or its holding company (or employees) for the purpose of facilitating the purchase or improvement of a main dwelling house.

Consequences of a breach

No criminal penalty

6.55 The 2006 Act abolishes the criminal penalty for a breach of the provisions on loans to directors that existed under the 1985 Act.

Rescission

6.56 Unless one of the exceptions listed above applies, a breach of s. 197, 198, 200 or 201 has only civil consequences (s. 213). Similar to the consequences of a breach of the rules governing substantial property transactions (see **6.13** above), the transaction or arrangement is voidable unless:

- restitution is no longer possible;
- the company has been indemnified for the loss or damage suffered by it; or
- rights acquired in good faith, for value and without actual notice of the breach by a person who is not a party to the arrangement or transaction, would be affected by the rescission.

6.57 If the transaction or arrangement is subsequently affirmed by resolution of the company's or, as the case may be, its holding company's shareholders within a reasonable time, the right of rescission is lost. The resolution affirming the transaction may be passed in general meeting or, in the case of a private company, as a written resolution (see **11.52–11.57**).

Liability of directors and connected persons

6.58 Regardless of whether the arrangement or transaction has been rescinded, the following persons are liable to account to the company for any profit made, directly or indirectly, by the arrangement or transaction, and indemnify the company, jointly and severally with any other person so liable, for any loss or damage resulting from the arrangement or transaction:

- any director of the company or its holding company with whom the relevant arrangement was made;
- the connected person with whom the relevant arrangement was made;
- the director with whom that connected person was connected; and
- any other director who authorised the relevant arrangement or transaction.

Payments for loss of office and retirement

6.59 The provisions governing directors' payments for loss of office and retirement can be found in ss. 215–222 of the 2006 Act, which replace ss. 312–316 of the 1985 Act with effect from 1 October 2007 and apply in relation to payments occurring on or after that date. The new rules are intended to be clearer and easier to follow but are potentially more restrictive.

6.60 For the purposes of ss. 215–222, shadow directors and de facto directors are treated as directors. Note, however, that s. 223(2) provides that references to the 'loss of office as a director' do not apply in relation to the loss of a person's status as a shadow director.[13] (See also **3.52**.)

Payments to directors for loss of office (s. 217)

6.61 The following payments, whether made in cash or the provision of other benefits, by a company to directors or former directors require prior shareholder approval by ordinary resolution (although the company's articles may provide for more stringent requirements):

- compensation for loss of office as director;
- compensation for loss of any other office or employment in connection with the management of the company or its subsidiaries;
- consideration for or in connection with his retirement from office as director; and
- consideration for or in connection with his retirement from any other office or employment in connection with the management of the company or its subsidiaries.

6.62 This includes payments to the nominee of, or otherwise for the benefit of, the director or a connected person, and payments by another person at the direction of, or on behalf of, the director, former director or connected person. The latter would, for example, apply where a transaction between a company and the director of a subsidiary had been entered into at the direction of, or on behalf of, the subsidiary.

6.63 If the payment for loss of office is made to the director of a company's holding company, the transaction must be approved by a resolution of both the company and the holding company. No shareholder approval is, however, required on the part of the member(s) of a company that is a wholly-owned subsidiary or not a UK-registered company.

6.64 Where shareholder approval is required, the company must make available to the shareholders a memorandum setting out the particulars of the proposed payment, including its amount (s. 217(3)). Where the approval is sought by written resolution, the memorandum must be sent to the shareholders no later than at the time the proposed resolution is sent or submitted to the shareholders. Note, however, that, subject to the company's articles of association, an 'accidental failure' to send the memorandum to the shareholders before the resolution is passed shall not invalidate such approval (s. 224).

Payments in connection with a transfer of undertaking and payments in connection with a takeover offer

6.65 In addition, the 2006 Act specifically requires prior shareholder approval with regard to the following payments 'by any person' (including the company) for loss of office to a director of the company:

- in connection with the transfer of the whole or any part of the undertaking or property of the company or its subsidiary (s. 218); and
- in connection with a transfer of shares in the company of its subsidiary resulting from a takeover bid (s. 219).

6.66 Sections 218 and 219 apply to payments made in accordance with an arrangement entered into as part of the asset or share transfer within one year before or two years after the asset or share transfer agreement. With regard to share transfers, the 2006 Act dispenses with the directors' duty previously contained in the 1985 Act to take all reasonable steps to secure that particulars of the proposed payment are brought to the attention of shareholders at the time when they are notified of the offer.

Exceptions

6.67 Shareholder approval is not required for payments made in good faith:

- in discharge of an existing legal obligation;
- by way of damages for breach of such an obligation;
- by way of settlement or compromise of any claim arising in connection with the termination of a person's office or employment; or
- by way of pension in respect of past services.

6.68 In addition, the 2006 Act introduces a new exception for small payments by the company or its subsidiaries (but not, for example, payments made by the offeror in a takeover bid) of amounts up to £200 (or the equivalent value in kind). If there is more than one payment, the value of all relevant payments for loss of office must be aggregated in order to determine whether the small payments exception applies.

Consequences of a breach

6.69 Section 222 clarifies the civil consequences of a breach of ss. 217, 218 and 219 and of a breach of more than one requirement of these provisions.

6.70 An unapproved payment for loss of office by the company in breach of s. 217 constitutes a misapplication of company funds and renders any director who authorised the payment and the director who received it jointly and severally liable to indemnify the company for any loss resulting from it. The payment itself is held by the recipient on trust for the company.

6.71 An unapproved payment in connection with an asset transfer in breach of s. 218 is held by the recipient on trust for the company whose undertaking or property is transferred.

6.72 An unapproved payment in connection with a share transfer in breach of s. 219 is held by the recipient on trust for the persons who have sold their shares as a result of the takeover offer.

6.73 A payment by a company to one of its directors in connection with a takeover bid contravenes both ss. 217 and 219 if none of the required shareholder approvals is obtained. In that case, the payment is held on trust for the persons who have sold their shares as a result of the takeover offer and not on trust for the company making the payment.

Contracts with sole members who are directors

6.74 Special rules apply where contracts are entered into between the company and the sole member who is also a director (whether or not he is the sole director). Section 231 replaces s. 322B of the 1985 Act with effect from 1 October 2007 and applies to contracts entered into on or after that date. Once s. 7 comes into force on 1 October 2009, enabling public as well as private companies to be formed as, or become, single-member companies, s. 231 will apply to both private and public companies. Until then, s. 231 applies to private companies only.

6.75 Contracts entered into by a company with its only shareholder must be recorded in writing if:

- the sole shareholder is also a director, shadow director or de facto director of the company; and
- the contract is not entered into in the ordinary course of the company's business.

6.76 The purpose of s. 231 is to ensure that records are kept in those cases where there is a high risk of the lines becoming blurred between where a person acts in his personal capacity and when he acts on behalf of the company.[14]

6.77 The company must ensure that the terms of the contract are either set out in a written memorandum or recorded in the minutes of the first board meeting following the making of the contract.

Consequences of a breach

6.78 Failure to comply with the requirement to record such contracts in writing in accordance with s. 231 is a criminal offence for every officer in default, punishable by a fine of currently up to £5,000. The company, however, is no longer liable under the criminal offence as used to be the case under s. 322B of the 1985 Act.

6.79 The validity of the contract remains unaffected by a breach of s. 231.

Disclosure of directors' interests

Disclosure of directors' interests in proposed transactions or arrangements

6.80 With effect from 1 October 2008, the equitable rule and s. 317 of the 1985 Act were replaced by ss. 177 and 182 of the 2006 Act. Section 177 codifies one of the general directors' duties and requires directors to disclose the nature and extent of any interest a director has, directly or indirectly, in a *proposed* transaction or arrangement with the company to the other directors. The director does not need to be a party to the transaction for s. 177 to apply; an interest of another person in a contract with the company is sufficient to trigger the disclosure duty if that other person's interest amounts to a direct or indirect interest of the director.[15] Disclosure under s. 177 must be made *before* the company enters into the transaction and must be updated by a further declaration if the original declaration later proves to be, or becomes, inaccurate or incomplete provided, however, that the company has not yet entered into the transaction or arrangement. Disclosure to the shareholders alone is not sufficient. Section 177 is, however, subject to the articles of association, which may, for example, provide that such transactions be approved by shareholder resolution.[16]

6.81 Disclosure may be made by written notice, general notice or disclosure at a board meeting (s. 177(2)).

6.82 There are exceptions to the duty to make a declaration under s. 177. No declaration of interest is required if:

- the director is not aware of his interest or of the transaction or arrangement in question (note, however, that for this purpose directors are treated as being aware of matters of which they ought reasonably to be aware);
- if the director's interest cannot reasonably be regarded as likely to give rise to a conflict of interest (this replaces the materiality test in Regulation 85 of Table A);[17]
- if, or to the extent that, the other directors are already aware of it; or
- if it concerns the terms of his service contract that have been (or are to be) considered at a board meeting or board committee.

6.83 As the duty requires disclosure to be made to the other directors, no disclosure is required where the company has only one director.[18]

6.84 As is the case with regard to the transactions discussed in **6.80** above, conflicted directors may, subject to the company's articles of association, participate in any decision-taking relating to s. 177 transactions with the company[19] (see **Chapter 5**).

Disclosure of directors' interests in existing transactions or arrangements

6.85 A similar duty to disclose the nature and extent of any interest directors may have, whether directly or indirectly, in an *existing* transaction or arrangement with the company can be found in s. 182. A declaration under this section is not required where the interest has already been declared under

s. 177 (see **6.80** above). There is a similar duty to update an incorrect or incomplete declaration and similar exceptions as under s. 177. If and to the extent that the director has previously declared his interest in accordance with s. 177 at the time the transaction was proposed and before it was entered into by the company, he does not need to make another declaration in accordance with s. 182 once the transaction is entered into and becomes an existing transaction (s. 182(1)).

6.86 The most significant difference between s. 177 and s. 182 is that, in contrast to s. 177, a breach of s. 182 constitutes a criminal offence under s. 183, punishable on conviction on indictment by an unlimited fine.

6.87 The new default position codified in ss. 177 and 182 reflects common practice under the 1985 Act. As default rules, they can be modified in the articles of association, for example, by requiring prior shareholder approval instead of disclosure.

Consequences of a breach

6.88 Unless the breach is ratified by ordinary shareholder resolution in accordance with s. 239, a breach of s. 177 may trigger the same consequences as a breach of any other general directors' duty, i.e. damages or compensation where the company has suffered a loss, rescission of the contract and accounting for any profits made by the director (see **Chapter 5**).

6.89 Failure to comply with s. 182 is a criminal offence under s. 183. This section does not, however, affect the validity of the transaction or impose any other civil consequences for a failure to make the declarations of interest required by s. 182.[20] Thus, in contrast to the consequences of a breach of s. 177 (see **6.88** above), the transaction cannot be rescinded and the defaulting director may keep any profits and other benefits derived from the transaction.

Relationship between the general directors' duties and the rules requiring shareholder approval

6.90 Section 180 of the 2006 Act regulates the relationship between the general directors' duties in Chapter 2 of Part 10 of the Act and the provisions in Chapter 4 of Part 10 requiring directors to obtain prior shareholder approval for the types of transactions as follows:

- Compliance with the general directors' duties does not remove the need for shareholder approval of a Chapter 4 transaction (s. 180(3)).
- The general directors' duties apply even if the transaction also falls within the scope of Chapter 4 of Part 10 because the transaction is a substantial property transaction, long-term service contract, loan, quasi-loan, credit transaction, or payment for loss of office (s. 180(2)).

- If the transaction falls within the scope of Chapter 4 of Part 10 because the transaction is a substantial property transaction, long-term service contract, loan, quasi-loan, credit transaction or payment for loss of office and shareholder approval has been obtained, or an exception applies and approval does not need to be obtained under Chapter 4 of Part 10, then the director does *not* need to comply with the duty to avoid conflicts of interest (s. 175) or the duty not to accept benefits from third parties (s. 176) in respect of that transaction (s. 180(2)). All other applicable duties still apply. Thus, for example, a director would not breach his duty to avoid conflicts of interest if he failed to obtain authorisation from the directors or the shareholders for a loan from the company in respect of legal defence costs.[21]

Directors' dealings in shares, debentures and options

6.91 With effect from 6 April 2007, ss. 323–329 of the 1985 Act were repealed without replacement in the 2006 Act. These provisions:

- prohibited directors, including shadow directors, from buying 'put' and 'call' options in listed shares or debentures in the company or another in the same group (s. 327 of the 1985 Act extended this prohibition to spouses and minor children of directors); and
- imposed an obligation on directors, including shadow directors, to disclose to the company their interest in shares in and debentures of the company or any holding or subsidiary company within a group structure, including any interest held by the directors' children or spouse.

6.92 Following the repeal of these sections, directors are now only subject to the general disclosure requirements under the new Disclosure and Transparency Rules (DTR), which came into effect on 20 January 2007, and any applicable exchange rules. DTR 5 requires shareholders of companies whose shares are admitted to trading on a regulated market (such as the London Stock Exchange main market) or a UK prescribed market (such as AIM) to disclose dealings and shareholdings that reach, exceed or fall below 3% and every whole percentage figure thereafter (see **Chapter 9**).

6.93 For directors of companies whose shares are not admitted to trading on a regulated market or a UK prescribed market, there is no statutory requirement in the 2006 Act to disclose their interests in shares held in their companies.

Additional requirements for listed companies

6.94 For companies that have a primary listing of equity securities on the Official List of the Financial Services Authority (FSA), the Listing Rules and the DTR contain additional requirements for shareholder approval of certain transactions with directors. Directors of such companies are also subject to special disclosure rules with regard to their interests in shares in their companies and to restrictions when dealing in the company's securities (see **Chapter 9**).

Related party transactions

6.95 With the aim of preventing a director or shadow director of a listed company, any of its subsidiaries, fellow subsidiaries or its holding company from taking advantage of his position and also to prevent any perception that he may have done so, Listing Rule 11 (LR 11) states, among other things, that transactions with such persons require prior shareholder approval. LR 11 also applies to a person who was a director or shadow director of such a company within 12 months before the date of the relevant transaction or arrangement, or an 'associate' of such a director or shadow director (together referred to as 'related parties'). These requirements apply in addition to the requirements under the 2006 Act (see **6.3–6.12** above).

6.96 The definition of 'associate' in this context is similar to the term 'connected person' in the 2006 Act and includes the director's family (spouse, civil partner or children under 18 years), the trustees (acting as such) of any trust of which the director or any of his family is a beneficiary or discretionary object, and any company in which the director or any member or members of his family (taken together) hold 30% or more of the shares with voting rights or are able to appoint or remove directors holding a majority of voting rights at board meetings.

6.97 LR 11 applies to the following related party transactions:

- a transaction between a listed company, or any of its subsidiaries, and a related party;
- an arrangement pursuant to which the listed company, or any of its subsidiaries, and a related party each invests in, or provides finance to, another undertaking or asset; and
- any other similar transaction or arrangement between a listed company (or any of its subsidiaries) and any other person the purpose or effect of which is to *benefit* a related party; in that case, the related party does not need to be a party to the relevant transaction or arrangement.

6.98 In assessing whether a transaction is in the ordinary course of business under LR 11, the FSA will have regard to the size and incidence of the transaction and also whether the terms of the transaction are unusual in the circumstances (see Guidance LR 11.1.5A–LR 11).

6.99 If an issuer is proposing to enter into a transaction that could be a related party transaction, it must obtain the guidance of a sponsor under LR 8 to assess the potential application of LR 11 (see note to LR 11.1.6).

6.100 If a listed company, or any of its subsidiaries, enters into a related party transaction, it must:

- notify a Regulatory Information System (RIS) of the details of the transaction, including the name of the related party and the details of the nature and extent of the related party's interest in the transaction or arrangement as soon as any form of binding agreement is entered into;
- send an explanatory circular to its shareholders; and
- obtain shareholder approval.

6.101 If the related party is also a shareholder of the company, he should not vote on any relevant resolution.

6.102 The Listing Rules contain specific requirements for related party circulars. Among other things, LR 13.6.1 requires that the circular includes a statement by the board that the transaction or arrangement is fair and reasonable as far as the shareholders of the company are concerned and that the directors have been so advised by an independent adviser.

Exceptions

6.103 Small transactions: Annex 1R to LR 11 provides that none of the related party transaction rules of LR 11 apply to small transactions. A small transaction is a transaction or arrangement where the gross assets of, the profits attributable to the assets of, or the gross capital of the company or business being acquired by, the transaction accounts for 0.25% or less of the company's gross assets, profits or gross capital, or where the consideration for the transaction is equal to or less than 0.25% of the aggregate market value of the company's ordinary shares.

6.104 Smaller transactions: For related party transactions where each of the aforementioned percentage ratios is less than 5% but one or more exceeds 0.25% ('smaller related party transactions'), shareholder approval does not have to be obtained (see LR 11.1.10). Instead, the company must:

- inform the FSA in writing of the details of the proposed transaction or arrangement;
- provide the FSA with written confirmation from an independent adviser that the terms of the proposed related party transaction are fair and reasonable as far as the shareholders of the company are concerned; and
- undertake in writing to the FSA to include details of the transaction in the company's next published annual accounts.

6.105 Other exceptions: LR 11 does not apply to the following types of related party transactions, unless they have any unusual features:

- transactions agreed before the person became a related party;
- new securities or treasury shares taken up by a related party under its entitlement in a pre-emptive offer or made under the exercise of conversion or subscription rights attaching to shares in the company;
- employees' share schemes and long-term incentive schemes;
- certain types of credit (including the lending of money or the guaranteeing of a loan);
- directors' indemnities and loans if permitted by the 2006 Act;
- an underwriting by a related party of an issue of securities by the listed company;
- joint investment arrangements where the investment of the related party is not more than 25% of the amount invested by the company or any of its subsidiaries; and
- insignificant subsidiary undertakings.

6.106 Note that, with regard to all the types of related party transactions, where a company enters into more than one transaction with the same related party within any 12-month period and the transactions or arrangements have not been approved by the shareholders, they must be aggregated.

Additional requirements for AIM companies

6.107 For companies whose shares are admitted to trading on AIM, the AIM Rules contain similar, albeit more lenient, provisions governing related party transactions as LR 11 which apply in addition to the requirements under the 2006 Act (see **6.3–6.12** above).

Related party transactions

6.108 In contrast to the Listing Rules governing related party transactions of listed companies, under the AIM Rules, transactions with a related party which exceed 5% in any of the class tests mentioned above (gross assets, profits, turnover, consideration to market capitalisation, and, in the case of an acquisition of a company or business, gross capital) do *not* require shareholder approval. However, such related party transactions must be notified by the AIM company to a RIS without delay as soon as the terms of the transaction are agreed (AIM Rule 13).

6.109 The AIM Rules define the term 'related party' in a similar way to the Listing Rules. It includes, among others:

- a director or shadow director of the AIM company, any of its subsidiaries, fellow subsidiaries or its parent company (or who was such a director or shadow director within the last 12 months before the date of the relevant transaction or arrangement);

- a 10% shareholder; and
- an 'associate' of such a director or shareholder. The definition of 'associate' in this context includes the director's family (spouse, civil partner or children under 18 years), the trustees (acting as such) of any trust of which the director or any of his family is a beneficiary or discretionary object, and any company in which the director or any member or members of his family (taken together) hold 30% or more of voting rights or are able to appoint or remove directors holding a majority of voting rights at board meetings.

6.110 The following information must be disclosed in the RIS notification:

- the information specified in Schedule Four to the AIM Rules (including, among others, particulars of the transaction; a description of the business carried on by, or using, the assets which are the subject of the transaction; the profits attributable to, and the value of, those assets; the full consideration and how it is being satisfied; the effect on the AIM company; and details of any service contracts of its proposed directors);
- the name of the related party and the nature and extent of their interest in the transaction; and
- a statement that the company's directors (other than the director who is a related party) consider, having consulted with the company's nominated adviser, that the terms of the transaction are fair and reasonable as far as its shareholders are concerned.

Additional requirements in the context of a takeover bid

6.111 In the event of a takeover bid, the directors of the bidder and the target company are subject to particular duties and responsibilities under the Takeover Code in addition to those under the 2006 Act. When receiving a takeover offer, the board of directors of the target company must, among other things, consider whether to recommend it to the target company's shareholders. Takeover Code Rule 25.1 requires the board of directors of the target company to circulate its reasoned opinion on the offer to all target shareholders. However, where a director has a conflict of interest, he should not join the remainder of the board in the expression of its views on the offer. Instead, the nature of the conflict should be clearly explained to the shareholders.[22] If the takeover offer is a management buy-out or similar transaction, a director will normally be regarded as having a conflict of interest where it is intended that he should have a continuing role (whether in an executive or non-executive capacity) in either the bidder or the target company in the event of the offer being successful.[23]

Disclosure in accounts

6.112 Any company must provide certain information concerning directors' remuneration, advances, credit and guarantees in the notes to the company's accounts. The relevant provisions in the 2006 Act are ss. 412 and 413. In addition, large companies must comply with The Large and Medium-sized Companies and Groups (Accounts and Reports) Regulations 2008, which require that certain related party transactions be disclosed in the notes to the accounts.

Disclosure of related party transactions

6.113 Section 412 does not itself require any disclosures in annual accounts. Instead, it gives the Secretary of State a new power to make provision by regulations requiring information about directors' remuneration to be given in notes to a company's annual accounts. To date the following regulations have been made under this provision which came into force on 6 April 2008:

- The Large and Medium-sized Companies and Groups (Accounts and Reports) Regulations 2008; and
- The Small Companies and Groups (Accounts and Directors' Report) Regulations 2008.

6.114 Pursuant to The Large and Medium-sized Companies and Groups (Accounts and Reports) Regulations 2008, only large companies must disclose the particulars of related party transactions in notes to their accounts if such transactions are material and have not been concluded under normal market conditions. Small and medium-sized companies are exempt from this disclosure requirement. Large companies are companies that exceed at least two of the following thresholds:

- annual turnover of £25.9 million;
- balance sheet total of £12.9 million; or
- average number of employees of 250.

6.115 The following information must be disclosed with regard to related party transactions:

- the amount of the transaction;
- the nature of the related party relationship; and
- any other information about the transaction necessary for an understanding of the financial position of the company.

6.116 Directors, and any person who was a director in the last five years, must notify the company of any matters relating to himself that may be necessary for the company to comply with these disclosure requirements.

Disclosure of other transactions with directors

Information about directors' benefits

6.117 Section 413 applies to all companies and contains new disclosure requirements with regard to advances and credits granted by the company to its directors, and guarantees of any kind entered into by the company on behalf of its directors. Such transactions must be disclosed in the notes to the company's individual or group accounts as applicable, regardless of whether such transactions are lawfully entered into in accordance with the provisions in Chapter 4 of Part 10 (see in particular **6.112** above). Note that transactions made between the company and officers other than directors do *not* need to be disclosed in the company's accounts under the 2006 Act.

6.118 Section 413 is supplemented by the relevant accounting standards, in particular, Financial Reporting Standard 8 (FRS 8) and International Accounting Standard 24 (IAS 24) regarding related party transactions. The objective of these accounting standards is to ensure that financial statements contain the disclosures necessary to draw attention to the possibility that the company's reported financial position and results may have been affected by the existence of related parties and by material transactions with them. Thus, typically, these accounting standards aim to regulate the disclosure of the existence of related parties, and of the nature and extent of any transactions with them, rather than the transactions themselves. The scope of persons that are considered to be related parties of the reporting company is much broader under FRS 8 than under the 2006 Act. It includes, among others, directors, shadow directors and members of the key management of the reporting company and its ultimate and intermediate parent companies. In FRS 8 and IAS 24, a related party transaction is broadly defined to include any transfer of assets, liabilities or the performance of services by, to or for a related party irrespective of whether a price is charged.[24]

6.119 Special rules apply with regard to quoted companies (see **6.121** below).

Information about certain forms of indemnity

6.120 As discussed in **Chapter 14**, companies may protect their directors from liability in certain circumstances. In addition to being able to purchase and maintain directors and officers insurance, companies may provide a qualifying third party indemnity (that is, indemnity that may cover liability incurred by a director to any person *other than* the company or an associated company) (s. 234) and, in the case of pension trustee companies, a qualifying pension scheme indemnity (that is, indemnity against liability incurred by a director in connection with the company's activities as trustee of an occupational pension scheme) (s. 235). Section 236 requires that where such indemnities are in force or were in force during the previous year, this must be disclosed in the directors' report. Where the indemnity is provided to the director of one company by an associated company, then it must be disclosed in the directors' reports of both companies.

Disclosure in accounts of quoted companies

6.121 Quoted companies[25] are required to set out a large part of the information concerning directors' remuneration in a directors' remuneration report which forms part of their annual accounts and reports (s. 420), and send a copy of the annual accounts and reports to every shareholder, debenture holder and every other person entitled to received notices of general meetings (including persons nominated pursuant to ss. 145 and 146). The directors' remuneration report requires quoted companies to make much more detailed disclosures in relation to their directors' remuneration than is required of other companies.

6.122 Schedule 8 of The Large and Medium-sized Companies and Groups (Accounts and Reports) Regulations 2008 sets out the content and format requirements of the directors' remuneration report of quoted companies. Among other things, the report must show the amount of each director's emoluments and compensation in the relevant financial year as well as a statement of the company's policy on directors' remuneration for the following financial years. The Large and Medium-sized Companies and Groups (Accounts and Reports) Regulations 2008 also contain a new requirement for quoted companies to state in their directors' remuneration report how they have taken pay and employment conditions elsewhere in the group into account when determining directors' pay. This new requirement must be included in reports for financial years beginning on or after 6 April 2009.

6.123 The remuneration report must be approved by ordinary shareholder resolution. Although the entitlement of a person to remuneration is not conditional on the resolution being passed, the vote gives shareholders a chance to consider the company's remuneration policies and the remuneration actually paid to directors in the previous financial year. The directors must deliver a copy of the directors' remuneration report to the Registrar of Companies, along with the annual accounts and reports, within six months following the end of the company's financial year. Note, however, that, with effect from 20 January 2007, issuers whose securities are trading on a regulated market (excluding exchange-regulated markets such as AIM) must publish their annual financial reports within four months after the end of their financial year (DTR 4.1.3). For issuers whose financial year begins before 20 January 2007, the first time they will need to comply with this new rule is by 2009.

Sources

1 See Explanatory Notes to the Companies Act 2006, para. 393.
2 See Explanatory Notes to the Companies Act 2006, para. 394.

3 See Explanatory Notes to the Companies Act 2006, para. 319.
4 The term 'shadow director' means a person in accordance with whose directions or instructions the directors of the company are accustomed to act (s. 251). This definition is the same as the one used in the 1985 Act.
5 The term 'connected person' is defined in s. 252 of the 2006 Act and includes, among others, certain family members (such as the director's civil partner, his children or step-children, persons with whom the director 'lives as partner in an enduring family relationship'; children or step-children of the director's unmarried partner; and the director's parents); certain companies with which the director is connected and trustees of a trust under which the director or a relative is a beneficiary (see **Chapter 4**).
6 See Explanatory Notes to the Companies Act 2006, para. 402.
7 'Company Directors: Regulating Conflicts of Interests and Formulating a Statement of Duties' (September 1999), The Law Commission and Scottish Law Commission (LAW COM No 261 and SCOT LAW COM No 173), at 10.17–10.19.
8 See Combined Code provision B1.6 (June 2006 version published by the Financial Reporting Council).
9 See Explanatory Notes to the Companies Act 2006, para. 400.
10 Oxford Annotated Companies Acts, para.10.197.04.
11 See Explanatory Notes to the Companies Act 2006, para. 406.
12 See note 1 for a definition of 'connected person'.
13 References can be found in ss. 190(6), 215 and 216–221.
14 Explanatory Notes to the Companies Act 2006, para. 421.
15 See Explanatory Notes to the Companies Act 2006, para. 347.
16 See Explanatory Notes to the Companies Act 2006, para. 348.
17 See Explanatory Notes to the Companies Act 2006, para. 353.
18 See Explanatory Notes to the Companies Act 2006, para. 352; see also s. 186 with regard to the duty to declare an interest in existing transactions under s. 182.
19 See Explanatory Notes to the Companies Act 2006, para. 354.
20 See Explanatory notes to the Companies Act 2006, para. 370.
21 See Explanatory notes to the Companies Act 2006, para. 319.
22 See Note 3 on Takeover Code Rule 25.1.
23 See Note 4 on takeover Code Rule 25.1.
24 See FRS 8 at note 2.6.
25 For the purposes of Part 15 of the 2006 Act, the term 'quoted companies' is defined in s. 385. It means 'a company whose equity share capital (a) has been included in the official list [of the London Stock Exchange] ... (b) is officially listed in an EEA State, or (c) is admitted to dealing on either the New York Stock Exchange or the exchange known as Nasdaq.' This definition does not include AIM companies.

7

Directors' responsibility for accounts and reports

Introduction

7.1 Company law requires all limited liability companies to prepare, circulate and file annual accounts. Subject to certain exemptions on grounds of size, such companies are also required to have those accounts audited. It is the responsibility of the directors to ensure these obligations are complied with and to manage the relationship between the company, its board and the auditors. The provisions governing accounts and audit are derived from a number of EU Directives, including the Accounting Directive and the Directive on Statutory Audit of Annual and Consolidated Accounts.

7.2 The requirements for accounts and audit are well established in UK company law. The Company Law Reform Review in 2001 identified a number of improvements that could be made to the existing regime and some of these were implemented in advance of the Companies Act 2006. For example:

- aligning the small company and audit exemption thresholds;
- allowing all companies subject to audit to provide shareholders with a summary financial statement (previously this was the preserve of listed companies);
- extending the rights of auditors to information and requiring the directors to confirm that they have provided all necessary information to the auditors (The Companies (Audit, Investigations and Community Enterprise) Act 2004);
- expanding narrative reporting (essentially directors' reports) in accounts (The Companies Act 1985 (Operating and Financial Review and Directors' Report) Regulations 2005).

7.3 This chapter looks in detail at the requirements for different types of company in terms of the accounts they produce, the obligation for those accounts to be audited and how the accounts are presented to members and to the general public. It also considers the responsibilities and liability of directors and auditors in respect of annual accounts.

Companies Act 2006: structure of accounting requirements

7.4 The accounts provisions of the Companies Act 2006 are contained in Part 15 (Accounts). Links to the accounts provisions can also be found in Part 23 (Distributions).

7.5 The accounting provisions apply to accounting periods beginning on or after 6 April 2008. Periods beginning before that date will continue to apply the provisions of the Companies Act 1985.

7.6 The accounts provisions are structured to reflect the requirements for different types of company, from the simple ones necessary for small companies (the 'small companies regime' (s. 381)) to those for other private companies, including medium-sized companies and unquoted plcs, to those for quoted companies. A similar structure applies for the audit provisions of the 2006 Act. Private company in this context encompasses companies limited by shares and those limited by guarantee.

Types of company

Quoted companies

7.7 For the purposes of the 2006 Act, quoted companies are those for which the equity share capital is:

- included on the official list under Part 6 of the Financial Services and Markets Act 2000 (essentially those traded on the London Stock Exchange);
- officially listed in a European Economic Area state; or
- admitted to dealing on the New York Stock Exchange or NASDAQ (s. 385(2)).

7.8 This definition effectively means that companies with a listing on AIM or Plus Markets in the UK do not count as quoted for the purposes of the accounting and audit provisions.

Small and medium-sized companies

7.9 Small and medium-sized companies are private companies that meet specific financial criteria and are not ineligible because of regulatory or other restrictions. The relevant financial criteria are turnover, balance sheet total and number of employees. They derive from equivalent EU limits and are periodically reviewed and revised upwards. The limits which apply under the 2006 Act at the date of writing are as follows:

	Turnover	Balance sheet total	Employees
Small company	£6.5m	£3.26m	50
Small group	£6.5m net £7.8m gross	£3.26m net £3.9m gross	50
Medium company	£25.9m	£12.9m	250
Medium group	£25.9m net £31.1 gross	£12.9m net £15.5m gross	250

'Balance sheet total' represents the total assets of the company before deducting its liabilities.

7.10 Number of employees is determined by calculating the number of individuals employed each month (whether for the whole of the month or part of it) under contracts of service and averaging the total number over the number of months. It is therefore a measure of headcount (s. 382(6)).

7.11 As illustrated in the table, the Act also contains equivalent criteria for classifying groups of companies as small or medium-sized. These can be determined on a gross or a net basis.

7.12 The gross limits are calculated by aggregating the turnover or total assets of all the companies that comprise the group. The net limits are calculated by aggregating these figures and then eliminating any amounts which are wholly intra-group. A company or group must meet two out of three of the limits on a rolling two-year basis (s. 382(2)).

7.13 Note that if a company is a parent company (see **Glossary**), its size is determined by the size of the group which it heads and not on the basis of its own financial data. This means that companies which appear to be small on the basis of their own turnover and balance sheet total have to be classified as, for example, large companies if they head a large group. It is essential that the appropriate analysis is applied as, otherwise, a company will produce defective accounts, taking exemptions or using accounting formats to which it is not entitled.

Ineligible companies and groups (s. 384)

7.14 Companies are ineligible to be considered small if they are:

- a public company;
- an authorised insurance company;

- a banking company;
- an e-money issuer;
- a MiFID investment firm;
- a UCITS management company;
- a company carrying on insurance market activity; or
- a member of an ineligible group.

(For explanations of 'e-money issuer', 'MiFID investment firm' and 'UCITS management company', see **Glossary**.)

7.15 An ineligible group is one that contains:

- a public company;
- a body corporate whose shares are admitted to trading on a regulated market in an EEA state;
- a person (other than a small company) who has permission under Part 4 of the Financial Services and Markets Act 2000 to carry on a regulated activity;
- a small company which is a banking company, an e-money issuer, a MiFID investment firm, a UCITS management company or a company carrying on insurance market activity.

7.16 Similar ineligibility criteria apply to companies that would otherwise qualify as medium-sized. Note, however, that in the case of a medium-sized company an ineligible company is one that itself has permission under Part 4 of the Financial Services and Markets Act 2000 to carry on a regulated activity.

Accounting reference periods

7.17 All companies must have a specific accounting reference date. This is usually the end of the month that is the anniversary of the company's incorporation but may be such other date as the directors decide. The first accounting period cannot be less than six months or more than 18 months. Subsequent periods are usually for twelve months, unless the accounting reference date is changed (ss. 390–393).

7.18 A company can change its accounting reference date by notifying the Registrar of Companies. The change can be for the current and future financial years or for the previous year and subsequent years. However, no change can be made if the period for filing the accounts for the previous year has already expired (see **7.86–7.102** below). Companies can lengthen or shorten the accounting period but may not lengthen the period more than once in five years except in very limited circumstances (e.g. when the company is under new ownership and the extension is necessary to coincide with the accounting reference date of its acquiring group.)

7.19 Directors are required to ensure that subsidiaries make their accounts up to the same date as the parent company unless there are good reasons why, in their opinion, the accounting reference dates should not coincide.

7.20 Companies may make their accounts up to a date that is up to seven days either side of the stated accounting reference date. This allows companies to vary their accounting year end so that, for example, it is always the last Friday in the month rather than being on a specific date which falls on a day of the week that may not be administratively convenient.

Accounting records

7.21 Every company must keep adequate accounting records (s. 386). Adequate records are defined in the 2006 Act as being records that are sufficient to show and explain a company's transactions, to disclose with reasonable accuracy at any time the company's financial position and to allow the directors to ensure that the accounts to be prepared comply with the requirements of the 2006 Act or International Accounting Standards (IAS).

7.22 The records must include a day-to-day record of receipts and payments and the matters to which they relate as well as all assets and liabilities. If the company deals in goods, the records must also include a record of the stock. This can be a statement obtained by performing a physical count and valuation of goods held at the year end or a continuously maintained record, for example one automatically updated for all deliveries and despatches.

7.23 The law does not specify that the records must be maintained in hard-copy form or whether electronic records suffice and so it is up to each company to select the format that is more appropriate for it.

7.24 Although directors are unlikely to be directly responsible for making the entries in the records, they bear ultimate responsibility for ensuring that adequate records are maintained. If a company fails to maintain the required records, then every officer of the company who is in default commits an offence. If the company is subject to audit, its auditors will consider whether it has maintained adequate records. They are required to state in their audit report if they consider that the company has *not* done so.

7.25 Accounting records must be maintained at the company's registered office or another appropriate place and must be available for inspection by the directors or company secretary. Private companies must keep their records for three years from the date on which they were made and public companies must keep them for six years. These time limits are simply those for company law purposes. In practice, companies are likely to need to keep them for at least six years to comply with tax legislation requirements.

Preparation of accounts and reports

Overview

7.26 All UK companies are required to prepare annual accounts and a directors' report and to have those accounts audited (subject to certain exemptions on grounds of size, see **7.115–7.124**). Where a company is a parent company (see **Glossary**) it is also required, subject to certain exemptions (see **7.29–7.30** below) to prepare and present accounts which consolidate the results and financial position of itself and its subsidiaries and present them as if they were one entity ('group accounts').

7.27 The accounts of a company or a group can be prepared under one of two regimes:

- Companies Act accounts – these use the form and content requirements of the 2006 Act and are prepared in accordance with generally accepted accounting practice (UK Accounting Standards and associated documents issued by the UK Accounting Standards Board) (s. 396); and
- IAS accounts – these do not apply the form and content requirements of the 2006 Act (except in a very limited sense) as they are prepared in accordance with the International Accounting Standards (IAS) (also known as International Financial Reporting Standards or IFRS) issued by the International Accounting Standards Board which are approved for use in the European Union (s. 397).

7.28 Once a company or group has chosen an accounting regime it should apply it consistently year on year. However, a company may change regimes if, for instance, it is taken over by a group which applies the alternative regime throughout its group or if it leaves a group and becomes an independent entity (s. 403).

7.29 Where group accounts are prepared the directors of the parent company must ensure that the individual accounts of the parent company and those of its subsidiaries are all prepared under the same financial reporting framework unless there are good reasons why this should not be the case (s. 407).

7.30 The annual accounts comprise a balance sheet showing the company's or group's financial position at a point in time and a profit and loss account (called an income statement under IAS) showing its activity for the period ended on the balance sheet date. Where group accounts are prepared and the notes to the parent company's individual balance sheet disclose its profit or loss for the period, the parent company is not required to publish its own separate profit and loss account (s. 408). The directors are required to approve the profit and loss account, however, so one must be prepared.

7.31 The law also specifies certain information that must be disclosed by way of note to the accounts. That information may present data on the balance sheet or in the profit and loss account in greater detail or it may provide additional information about the company's or group's position. Where the 2006 Act refers to a balance sheet or a profit and loss account this also incorporates the related notes.

7.32 Companies Act accounts must give a true and fair view of the company's or group's financial position at a point in time and a true and fair view of its results for the period ended on the balance sheet date and must be prepared in accordance with the requirements of the 2006 Act (s. 396)

7.33 There is no equivalent requirement in the Act for IAS accounts. However, International Accounting Standards require accounts to present the financial performance and position of an entity fairly. Legal opinion obtained from Martin Moore QC by the Financial Reporting Council in the UK (which has delegated authority regarding the setting and monitoring of standards in statutory accounts in the UK) indicates that, in practice, 'fair presentation' and 'a true and fair view' are likely to be interpreted in the same way. Further details can be obtained from www.frc.org.uk

7.34 The detailed form and content of accounts are not set out in the Act itself; instead details are contained in the following regulations:

- The Large and Medium-sized Companies and Groups (Accounts and Reports) Regulations 2008; and
- The Small Companies and Groups (Accounts and Directors' Report) Regulations 2008.

7.35 The Small Companies Regulations are applicable to any company qualifying as small (referred to as the 'small companies' regime'). The Large and Medium-sized Regulations apply to all other companies and any small companies that choose not to adopt the Small Companies' Regulations.

7.36 The Regulations set out the formats that can be adopted for a balance sheet and a profit and loss account in Companies Act accounts of both companies and groups, and the notes that are required to support them. They also set out the contents of the directors' report. Details for the preparation of small group accounts are included to assist groups that voluntarily choose to present group accounts even though they are officially exempt from doing so.

7.37 There are two formats for a balance sheet and four for a profit and loss account. The Format 1 balance sheet and Formats 1 and 2 profit and loss account are probably the most commonly used in the UK. Illustrative formats for a large or medium-sized company balance sheet under Format 1 and for a large or medium-sized company profit and loss account under Formats 1 and 2 are set out at the end of this chapter. There are equivalent but less detailed formats for the balance sheet of small companies. Details are contained in **Table 7.2** at page 167 below.

7.38 Where Companies Act accounts are prepared, the items listed must be in accordance with the specified formats. The same format and classification should be used year on year. If anything changes, the particulars of the change and the reason for it should be explained in the accounts.

Exemptions from preparing group accounts

7.39 All companies are required to prepare annual financial statements for circulation to the shareholders. Companies which are parent companies are also required to prepare group accounts which consolidate the results and position of the company and its subsidiaries, subject to certain exemptions, as follows:

- Small groups are exempt from the requirement to prepare group accounts. The criteria for qualifying as a small group are set out above (see **7.7–7.16** above).
- A parent company does not need to prepare group accounts if all its subsidiaries could be excluded from consolidation on or more of the following grounds:
  - they are immaterial individually and in aggregate; or
  - severe long-term restrictions substantially hinder the ability of the parent company to exercise its rights; or
  - the information for the preparation of group accounts cannot be obtained without disproportionate expense or undue delay; or
  - the interest of the parent company is held exclusively for the purposes of resale.

  (Note that accounting standards provide additional explanations on the application of the exclusions contained in s. 405.)
- Parent companies which are part of a larger group are not required to prepare group accounts for their own group provided that:
  - the company is itself a wholly owned subsidiary of a company incor-

porated in an EEA state or its parent company holds at least 50% of the allotted share capital and no notice has been served by shareholders requesting group accounts (s. 400); and
  - it is included in group accounts of a larger group drawn up and audited to a date the same as or earlier than its accounts date under either the Seventh Directive or International Accounting Standards; and
  - the company's accounts disclose that it is exempt from the requirement to prepare group accounts and state the name and country of incorporation or principal place of business of the parent undertaking preparing group accounts; and
  - the company files a copy of those group accounts (with a certified translation into English, if necessary) within the period for filing accounts (see **7.96** below);
- Parent companies which are in turn part of a larger group and whose parent company is not incorporated in an EEA state are not required to prepare group accounts for their own group provided that:
  - the company is itself a wholly owned subsidiary or its parent company holds at least 50% of the allotted share capital and no notice has been served by shareholders requesting group accounts (s. 401); and
  - it is included in group accounts prepared by a larger group drawn up to a date the same as or earlier than its accounts date under either the Seventh Directive or in a manner equivalent to consolidated accounts drawn up under that Directive; and
  - the group accounts must be audited by a person authorised to do so under the law under which the parent company accounts are drawn up; and
  - the company's accounts disclose that it is exempt from the requirement to prepare group accounts and state the name and country of incorporation or principal place of business of the parent undertaking preparing group accounts; and
  - the company files a copy of those group accounts (with a certified translation into English, if necessary) within the period for filing accounts (see **7.96** below).

7.40 Companies whose securities are admitted to trading on a regulated market in an EEA state are not eligible to use this exemption.

7.41 The 2006 Act does not exempt medium-sized groups from the requirement to prepare group accounts, although the 1985 Act did.

Directors' duties in respect of accounts

7.42 It is the directors' duty to ensure that annual accounts are prepared in accordance with the 2006 Act, although they may delegate the detailed preparation activity to others. Directors retain overall responsibility for ensuring that those annual accounts give a true and fair view as described above and so must be satisfied with the methods and presentation adopted. They are also responsible for approving the accounts for issue to the members.

7.43 The accounts must be approved by the board and signed on behalf of the board by a director. That signature must appear on the company's balance sheet.

7.44 If the accounts are prepared under the small companies regime, the balance sheet must contain a statement above the signature to that effect. A suitable form of words can be found in the Financial Reporting Standard for Smaller Entities (effective April 2008) published by the Accounting Standards Board Limited:

> 'These accounts have been prepared in accordance with the special provisions relating to small companies within Part 15 of the Companies Act 2006.'

7.45 Routines for approving accounts may vary in terms of their detail from company to company, but the basic requirements are the same for all companies, whether private, public, unquoted or quoted.

7.46 It is usual for approval to take place at a board meeting and to be minuted. The accounts must be approved by the board before the audit report is signed (see **7.72**). The law states that directors must not approve the accounts unless they are satisfied they give a true and fair view of the assets, liabilities and financial position of the company or group at the balance sheet date and the profit or loss of the company or group for the period ended on that date (s. 393). This duty applies irrespective of the regime under which the accounts are prepared. Effectively, this enshrines an overarching requirement for accounts to give a true and fair view for all companies, regardless of the regime under which they are prepared. In approving the accounts, directors should consider carefully any differences of opinion between themselves and the auditors regarding the treatment or disclosure of items in the accounts to ensure that they properly understand them and, in particular, to consider their implications for whether the accounts could be said to give a true and fair view.

7.47 If a board of directors approves accounts which do not comply with the requirements of the Companies Act or the IAS Regulation (as appropriate), every director who knew they did not comply, was reckless as to whether they complied or did not take all reasonable steps to ensure they complied commits an offence.

Directors' reports

Overview

7.48 Directors of a company must prepare a directors' report for each financial year (s. 415). If the company is a parent company of a group and prepares group accounts, the directors' report must be a group directors' report. This means it must deal with matters arising in the group as a whole, giving more emphasis to matters that are significant to the whole group than to those that are merely significant in an individual subsidiary. Each subsidiary company will, in any case, be required to produce its own directors' report. Where the term 'company' is used in the remainder of this section, therefore, it should be read as referring to a group where group accounts are prepared.

7.49 The directors' report must be approved by the board of directors and signed on behalf of the board by a director or the company secretary. If the report is prepared in accordance with the small companies' regime there should be a statement to that effect above the signature. An example form of words for such a statement is as follows:

> 'This directors' report has been prepared in accordance with the special provisions relating to small companies within Part 15 of the Companies Act 2006.'

7.50 If a directors' report is not prepared, every person who was a director at the year end and who did not take all reasonable steps to ensure a report was produced is guilty of an offence, which is punishable by a fine.

Statement on disclosure to auditors

7.51 Unless a company has taken advantage of its eligibility for audit exemption, the directors' report must contain a statement (s. 418) to the effect that, in the case of each person who was a director at the date the directors' report was approved:

- so far as each director is aware, there is no relevant audit information of which the auditor is unaware; and
- he has taken all the steps he ought to have taken as a director to make himself aware of relevant audit information and to establish that the company's auditor is aware of that information.

7.52 'Relevant audit information' is information relevant to the auditor in preparing his report. This means that all directors must understand what sort of information is likely to be relevant to the auditor, but must also ensure that they are aware of such information and that they are satisfied it has been duly communicated. Directors will need to make enquiries of their fellows in this respect and take any other steps they consider appropriate in exercising reasonable skill, care and diligence before the directors' report can be signed. It would, therefore, be inappropriate for a director simply to assume that anything relevant had been dealt with by the finance director or person otherwise responsible for dealing with the auditors without discussing the matter. Directors should consider setting aside time to consider the statement formally before the accounts are approved. If the statement is false and the accounts are approved, any director who knew the statement was false or was reckless as to whether it was false and did not take all reasonable steps to prevent approval commits an offence.

Content of directors' reports – companies generally

7.53 The following details must be included in the directors' reports of all companies:

- the names of everyone who was a director during the financial year (s. 416(1) (a));
- the principal activity of the company or, if it is a group directors' report, the principal activities of the undertakings that make up the group (s. 416(1)(b));
- details of donations to political parties or organisations where the aggregate amount of donations exceeds £2,000 in a financial year;
- details of political donations to independent election candidates exceeding £2,000 in aggregate in the financial year;
- details of donations for charitable purposes that exceed £2,000 in aggregate in the financial year;
- details of any purchase of own shares by the company in the financial year;
- all companies, apart from small companies, must also disclose any amount that the directors recommend must be paid by way of dividend (s. 416(3)).

7.54 Any company with more than 250 employees must make additional disclosures concerning the employment of disabled people (Small Company Regulations Schedule 5, Large and medium-sized company Regulations Schedule 7).

Content of directors' reports – large and medium-sized companies

7.55 Large and medium-sized companies must give more information in their directors' reports than small companies (see Schedule 7 to the Large and medium-Sized Company Regulations). For example, the directors' report should include:

- details of any significant difference in the market value of land and buildings compared with the value included on the balance sheet;
- information about the use of financial instruments (cash, loans, debtors and creditors, shares, etc.) by the company, including its risk management

policies and objectives, where financial instruments are material to assessing the company's position or performance;
- important events since the end of the financial year up to the point the directors approve the accounts;
- future developments;
- research and development activities;
- branches outside the UK;
- the policy for payment of creditors.

7.56 Large and medium-sized companies which have more than 250 employees are also required to provide information about employee involvement in the business and the extent of consultations with employees on matters of relevance to them.

Business reviews

7.57 The key requirement for large and medium-sized companies is the business review (s. 417). The business review must include a fair review of the business and a description of the principal risks and uncertainties that the company faces. The review must be balanced and comprehensive, so it must cover both positive and negative factors and address both the development and performance of the business during the year and its position at the year end. Companies are also required to include in the analysis details of the key financial performance indicators and, if they are large companies, the key non-financial performance indictors. A key performance indicator is a factor against which a company's development, performance or position can be measured effectively. By definition, a company will only have a few *key* performance indicators, although the directors may use many different indicators of performance in managing their business. Where appropriate, the review should refer to and explain amounts in the company's accounts.

7.58 The objective of the business review is to inform members and to help them assess how the directors have performed their statutory duty to promote the success of the company. The extent of the information provided in the business review will depend on the size and complexity of the business as this will affect what data are useful to members. Where the company is wholly owned by its directors, the extent of the analysis will probably be less than for a company with non-director shareholders but there is no exemption from the business review requirements except for small companies or companies that would qualify as small but for their membership of an ineligible group (see **7.39** above).

7.59 Nothing in the business review requirements forces companies to disclose information about impending developments or matters in the course of negotiation if to do so would be seriously prejudicial to the company's business.

Additional business review requirements for quoted companies

7.60 Quoted companies are required to provide additional information in their business reviews for any accounting period beginning on or after 1 October 2007. The additional information required is:

- the main trends and factors likely to affect the future development, performance and position of the company;
- details on the following, including the company's policies and the effectiveness of those policies in relation to:
  - environmental matters, which includes but is not limited to the impact of the company's business on the environment;
  - the company's employees;
  - social and community issues.
- Details of persons with whom the company has contractual or other relationships which are essential to the company's business. Information need not be given about a person if the directors believe that to do so would be seriously prejudicial to the person concerned or against the public interest.

Directors' remuneration reports

7.61 All quoted companies must publish a report on directors' remuneration (s. 420). All other companies are required to provide details of directors' remuneration in the notes to the financial statements, but the disclosure is far simpler than for a remuneration report. The remuneration report must be approved by the board of directors and signed on behalf of the board by a director or company secretary.

7.62 If a quoted company fails to produce a directors' remuneration report every person who was a director at the end of the relevant accounting period and who did not attempt to ensure the report was produced commits an offence. Similarly, it is an offence to publish a directors' remuneration report that does not comply with the requirements of the 2006 Act.

7.63 Information contained in a directors' remuneration report can be divided between those parts that are not subject to audit and those that are. As regards the unaudited information, the directors' remuneration report must address the following:

- information about the remuneration committee, including whether one existed, who was on it and whether any outside input was sought;
- information about the company's remuneration policy for the next and future financial years and, in particular, a detailed explanation of any

performance-related conditions on share options or other long-term incentive plans. This includes an analysis of why those conditions were chosen, how they are assessed and the relative balance of performance and non-performance-related elements;
- an explanation as to how the pay and employment conditions elsewhere in the company were taken into account in determining directors' remuneration;
- a comparison in the form of a line graph of the performance of the company's shares against a representative holding across a broad equity index for up to five years. Performance in this context is total shareholder return;
- contract terms, notice periods and compensation rights.

7.64 Where information relates to a particular individual, the report must clearly indicate the name of the individual concerned.

7.65 The information subject to audit must encompass anyone who was a director of the company at any point during the financial year. The analysis required is:

- directors' remuneration, listed by individual and split between emoluments, bonuses and expenses, plus any benefits in kind and any compensation for loss of office or any other kind of termination payment;
- directors' share options, listed by individual and detailing options granted, exercised and lapsed in the period or whose terms were varied;
- directors' interest in long-term incentive schemes;
- directors' pension entitlements, with separate disclosures for money purchase and final salary schemes;
- compensation for loss of office and sums paid to third parties for the services of directors.

7.66 This is referred to as the 'auditable part' of the directors' remuneration report.

7.67 The directors' remuneration report must also be formally approved by the members at the meeting at which the accounts are presented (s. 439).

Directors' liability for false or misleading statements in reports

7.68 A director is liable (s. 463) to compensate the company for any loss suffered by it as a result of an untrue or misleading statement in or an omission from any of the following:

- the directors' report;
- the directors' remuneration report;

- the summary financial statement, to the extent that it contains information derived from either of the above.

7.69 A director is only liable if he knew the statement was untrue or misleading or was reckless as to whether that was the case or if he knew the omission was a dishonest concealment of a material fact.

7.70 Directors are not liable to any other party who relies on the statements in any of the reports mentioned above.

Circulation and publication of accounts and reports

7.71 Once the accounts have been approved by the directors there are two further stages to be completed. First, the accounts must be published by presenting or circulating them to all the shareholders (s. 423). Second, they must be filed with the Registrar of Companies at Companies House (see **7.96** below). In addition, companies may publish their accounts. This means the accounts are circulated, issued, published or otherwise made available to the general public in a way that encourages the general public to read them. A company that places a copy of its accounts on its business website would thus be publishing them.

7.72 The accounts for circulation or presentation to the shareholders must have been approved by the directors and, where appropriate, signed by the auditors. The names of the persons approving the directors' report and balance sheet must be stated on the copies for circulation or presentation (s. 433). They are the company's 'full' financial statements prepared in accordance with the accounting regulations (see **7.26** above) unless the company has agreement to send out a summary financial statement (see below). Copies of the annual accounts and reports must be sent to:

- every member of the company;
- every holder of the company's debentures; and
- every person entitled to receive notice of a general meeting;

unless the company does not have a current address for a person.

7.73 If the accounts are not sent out, the company and every officer commits an offence and is liable to a fine.

Circulation of accounts – private companies

7.74 Subject to anything specific in the company's articles, the requirements for circulation of accounts are the same for all private companies. For accounting periods ending on or after 1 October 2007 the accounts must be circulated to the members (s. 424(2)) by the earlier of:

- the filing deadline for submitting the accounts to the Registrar of Companies; and
- the date on which the accounts are actually filed.

7.75 There does not seem to be anything to prevent the accounts being circulated at an earlier date than the deadlines above, but it is important that companies make a note of when the accounts are circulated as this has implications for the reappointment of auditors (see **7.126** below).

7.76 For accounting periods ending on or before 30 September 2007 the accounts must be circulated in accordance with the requirements of the 1985 Act, which means they should either be laid before the members in general meeting or circulated in accordance with the elective regime.

Circulation of accounts – public companies

7.77 All public companies must lay their annual accounts and reports before members in general meeting. This is usually done at the annual general meeting but in any case must occur before the end of the period for filing the accounts and reports in question (see **7.96**). The accounts must be circulated to members at least 21 days before the relevant accounts meeting (s. 424(3)).

Publication of accounts – quoted companies

7.78 In addition to complying with the requirements for public companies generally, a quoted company must ensure that its annual accounts and reports are made available on a website as soon as reasonably practicable after they have been approved and remain accessible throughout the period until the following year's accounts are made available (s. 430). The website must be maintained by or on behalf of the company and name the company to which it relates. Companies are not allowed to charge for access or for making copies of the accounts and cannot restrict access to certain groups of users. If the accounts are not made available in accordance with the above rules, every officer of the company is deemed to be in default.

Publication of accounts – private and unquoted public companies

7.79 There are specific provisions where a company chooses to publish its statutory accounts. In this context the statutory accounts are those required to be filed with the Registrar of Companies (see **7.86** below).

7.80 If a company decides to publish any part of its statutory accounts they must be accompanied by the auditors' report, unless the company is exempt from audit and the directors have taken advantage of the exemption from audit. A parent company must not publish its own statutory accounts unless it also publishes its statutory group accounts; exemptions from preparing group accounts are outlined above (see **7.39** above)

7.81 Sometimes, companies may decide to publish non-statutory accounts (s. 435). Non-statutory accounts are any balance sheet or profit and loss account other than the statutory accounts for a company or group. If this is done, it must be made absolutely clear that they are not the company's statutory accounts. In addition, it must be stated whether the related statutory accounts have been filed at Companies House, whether an audit report was given on those accounts and, if it was, whether that audit report was qualified. However, companies may not publish the audit report on the statutory accounts with the non-statutory accounts in case this leads to confusion over the accounts to which the auditor report attaches.

Summary financial statements

7.82 Companies subject to audit may provide a copy of a summary financial statement in place of the full annual accounts and reports of the company to any person entitled to receive the full accounts (s. 426). However, they may only do so if the recipient has either indicated a wish to receive a summary financial statement or if the recipient has not responded to an attempt to ascertain any preference. If a recipient indicates that they would prefer to receive the full accounts, these must be supplied.

7.83 A summary financial statement draws information from the full annual accounts and reports. It must be approved by the board and state the name of the person who signed it on behalf of the board. The summary financial statement must make it clear that it does not contain sufficient information to be able to make the same assessment of the company as would be possible with the full accounts. It must also explain how a user can obtain a copy of the full accounts.

7.84 The summary financial statement must contain details of directors' remuneration and otherwise comply with the Companies (Summary Financial Statement) Regulations 2008.

7.85 It must contain a report from the company's auditors confirming that the summary statement is consistent with the annual accounts and information contained in the directors' report.

Filing obligations in respect of accounts

Accounts to be filed

7.86 All UK companies and groups are required to file accounts with the Registrar of Companies. However, the documents to be filed vary depending on the size and nature of the company.

Filing requirements for small companies

7.87 Small companies have three alternatives in terms of the accounts they file (s. 444). These are to file:

1 the company's balance sheet, profit and loss account and directors' report and, where appropriate, the auditors' report (this usually means the accounts as they were circulated to the shareholders); or
2 the company's balance sheet and to omit either or both the profit and loss account and the directors' report. If the company is subject to audit, then the auditors' report must be filed; or
3 an abbreviated balance sheet and, where appropriate, audit report thereon. This option is not available to any small company that chooses to prepare IAS accounts.

7.88 Abbreviated accounts are a more restricted version of the full financial statements and as such are not required to give a true and fair view. There are specific rules for small companies as to what must be included in abbreviated accounts. The restriction takes the form of a reduced disclosure requirement for the notes to the balance sheet; essentially limiting them to the company's accounting policies, total movement on fixed assets and certain information in respect of long-term or secured borrowings. Details are contained in the Small Companies' Regulations. As the form and content are drawn only from what is contained in the law, it is generally accepted that small company abbreviated accounts can exclude any accounting disclosures wholly required by accounting standards.

7.89 The abbreviated accounts must be approved by the board and signed by a director on behalf of the board. The signature on the balance sheet must be accompanied by a statement that it has been prepared in accordance with the small companies' regime.

7.90 Some small companies prefer to file abbreviated accounts as they consider the limited information contained in abbreviated accounts maintains the company's privacy. However, some users of the publicly filed accounts (e.g. some credit reference agencies) dislike abbreviated accounts and may adjust their attitude to the company on the basis of the lack of information available to them.

Filing requirements for medium-sized companies

7.91 Medium-sized companies have two options when it comes to filing accounts with the Registrar of Companies (s. 445). They can choose to file:

1 the company's balance sheet, profit and loss account, directors' report and auditors' report; or
2 abbreviated accounts and the auditors' report thereon.

7.92 The Large and Medium-sized Companies' Regulations state what can be omitted from the full financial statements in preparing abbreviated accounts for a medium-sized company. In practice, it seems that very little can be omitted. The profit and loss account can be shown only from the gross profit line onwards provided that the notes state the company's total turnover. As the Regulations only state what can be omitted from the full financial statements, it is generally accepted that all accounting disclosures required solely by accounting standards should be included in medium-sized abbreviated accounts.

7.93 The requirement for medium-sized abbreviated accounts to disclose total turnover by way of note means that there is very little information in the full financial statements that does not find its way into the abbreviated accounts. Directors should therefore give careful consideration to whether the restrictions in disclosure justify the additional cost of preparing abbreviated accounts and obtaining an auditors' report on them.

7.94 The abbreviated accounts must be approved by the board of directors and signed on their behalf by a director. The signature must be on the balance sheet. It must be accompanied by a statement along the following lines:

> 'These abbreviated accounts have been prepared in accordance with the special provisions relating to medium-sized companies within Part 15 of the Companies Act 2006.'

Filing requirements for large companies

7.95 Large companies must file the financial statements which are laid before the members – the directors' report, auditors' report, balance sheet, profit and loss account and supporting notes (s. 446). Quoted companies must also file the directors' remuneration report (s. 447).

Period for filing accounts

7.96 All limited liability companies are required to file their accounts with the Registrar of Companies by a specified deadline. Private companies (whether limited by shares or guarantee) must do so within nine months of the end of their accounting period; public companies have six months to do so (s. 442(2)). Under the 1985 Act the filing periods were ten months and seven months respectively.

7.97 The filing deadline calculations are slightly different for a company in its first period since incorporation if its accounting period is more than twelve months (s. 442(3)). In such cases the filing deadline is the later of nine (or six) months from the first anniversary of incorporation or three months after the accounting reference period end. For example:

7.98 Accounting reference period 13 months from 1 July 20X0 to 31 August 20X1. Filing deadline is the later of:

Type of company	9/6 months from first anniversary of incorporation	3 months from end of accounting reference period	Filing deadline
Private	1 April 20X2	30 November 20X1	1 April 20X2
Public	1 January 20X2	30 November 20X1	1 January 20X2

Accounting reference period 18 months from 1 July 20X0 to 31 December 20X1. Filing deadline is the later of:

Type of company	9/6 months from first anniversary of incorporation	3 months from end of accounting reference period	Filing deadline
Private	1 April 20X2	31 March 20X2	1 April 20X2
Public	1 January 20X2	31 March 20X2	1 January 20X2

Penalties for late filing of accounts – companies

7.99 Any company that does not file its accounts within the specified period is liable to a penalty fine (s. 453). The penalty fine varies according to the type of company and how overdue the accounts are from the designated filing deadline. Companies that prepare accounts under the 2006 Act and file them late in two successive years will find that the penalty for the second late year is automatically doubled.

7.100 The penalty rates for accounts that are filed late before 1 February 2009 are as follows:

How late?	Private companies	Public companies
Not more than 3 months	£100	£500
3–6 months	£250	£1,000
6–12 months	£500	£2,000
More than 12 months	£1,000	£5,000

7.101 The penalty rates for accounts that are filed late on or after 1 February 2009 are as follows:

How late?	Private companies	Public companies
Not more than 1 month	£150	£750
1–3 months	£375	£1,500
3–6 months	£750	£3,000
More than 6 months	£1,500	£7,500

Penalties for late filing of accounts – directors

7.102 If a company fails to file its accounts by the due date, every person who was an officer of the company immediately before the year end commits an offence (s. 451). There is both a fine on summary conviction and a daily default fine. The defence to late filing is that the person took all reasonable steps to ensure that the accounts would be filed on time. If the directors still fail to ensure the accounts are filed, any member or creditor or the Registrar can apply for a court order to require that accounts are filed within a specified time.

Revision of defective accounts

Voluntary revision of accounts

7.103 If the directors realise that the annual accounts, remuneration report or summary financial statement do not comply with the requirements of the 2006 Act or of the IAS Regulations they may revise them (s. 454).

7.104 The procedure for revising these accounts and reports depends on whether they have been circulated to or laid before the members or filed with the Registrar. If the accounts or reports have been prepared and approved by the directors but not published in any way, then the directors can simply withdraw the accounts or report, correct the defect and approve a corrected version. However, if the accounts or report have already been sent to members and/or the Registrar when the defect is uncovered, then the company must issue revised accounts or a revised report in accordance with the process laid down in the Act. This can be done by issuing a revised version of the accounts, report or statement or by supplementing the defective version with documentation indicating the amendments.

7.105 If the revision is done by replacement, then the directors have to append a statement to the revised accounts which includes the following elements:

- that the revised accounts replace the original accounts;
- that the revised accounts now form the company's statutory accounts; and
- that they have been prepared as at the date of the original accounts and so do not take into account any events occurring since the date of the original accounts;
- the ways in which the original accounts did not comply with the Act; and
- any significant amendments arising as a result of correcting the defect.

7.106 If the revision is done by supplementary note, then the statement must make it clear that the note forms part of the original accounts and that the accounts have been revised as at the date of the original accounts and so do not take into account events occurring since that date.

7.107 In both cases the statement itself is dated with the date on which the revision was approved.

7.108 If the accounts or report have been subject to audit (a summary financial statement is only permitted where the company is subject to audit), then the company's auditors are required to report on the revised version or supplementary documentation. The auditors' report must state whether:

- the revised accounts give a true and fair view of the company's financial position at the year end and its results for the period then ended as at the date of the original accounts;
- the revised accounts have been properly prepared in accordance with the Act; and
- the original accounts failed to comply with the Act in respect of the matters identified by the directors.

7.109 Any revision must relate solely to the matter in which the accounts were originally defective and any consequential adjustments so voluntary revision does not give directors the opportunity to revisit judgements or estimates made elsewhere in the accounts. Indeed, the requirements of the Companies Act 2006 in relation to accounts apply to the revised accounts as if they had been approved as at the date of the original accounts.

Application to court to revise defective accounts

7.110 The Secretary of State or his authorised representatives, the Registrar of Companies and the Financial Reporting Review Panel of the Financial Reporting Council, can apply to the court to require directors to revise the annual accounts or directors' report where it appears that the accounts and/or report do not comply with the requirements of the Act (s. 456).

Companies Act 2006: structure of audit requirements

7.111 The audit provisions of the 2006 Act are primarily contained in Part 16 (Audit). The Act introduced new terminology in respect of auditors to reflect the requirement of EU Directive 2006/43/EC on the statutory audit of annual accounts and consolidated accounts (the Statutory Audit Directive) so that they are now referred to as statutory auditors.

Requirement for auditors

7.112 All companies must be subject to audit of their annual accounts (s. 475) unless they are:

- exempt from audit as a small company; or
- exempt from audit as a dormant company; or
- a non-profit making company subject to public sector audit.

7.113 In all cases, a company is not entitled to exemption from audit unless its balance sheet contains a statement from the directors to that effect immediately above the directors' signatures. That statement must include a reference to members requesting an audit (see **7.123** below) and acknowledge the directors' responsibility for complying with the requirements of the 2006 Act as regards accounting records (see **7.21**) and preparation of accounts.

7.114 Note that audit exemption is an entitlement not an obligation and so if directors consider that it is in the company's best interests for its accounts to be audited, they need not take up the exemption. The procedures for appointing auditors and obtaining an audit report are then the same as for any other company.

Audit exemption for small companies

7.115 A company that qualifies as a small company (see **7.87**) is entitled to exemption from audit provided that it meets certain specified financial criteria for the financial year (s. 477). Those are:

	Turnover less than	Balance sheet total less than
Small company	£6.5m	£3.26m
Small group	£6.5m net £3.26m net	£7.8m gross £3.9m gross

7.116 The small company must be below both the turnover and balance sheet totals in each financial year for which it claims audit exemption. If one limit is breached, then the exemption is lost.

'Balance sheet total' means the total assets of the company before deducting its liabilities as shown in the company's balance sheet.

7.117 If a small company is a member of a group, the entire group must qualify as a small group and that group must be below both the turnover and balance sheet thresholds in each financial year for which audit exemption is claimed. The definition of group encompasses all entities in the group to which the company belongs and so captures the worldwide group.

7.118 The 'gross' limits are calculated by aggregating the turnover or total assets of all the companies that comprise the group. The 'net' limits are calculated by aggregating these figures and then eliminating any amounts that are wholly intra-group.

7.119 Small companies that would otherwise be ineligible companies (see above) are not entitled to audit exemption.

Audit exemption for dormant companies (s. 480)

7.120 A dormant company is one that does not have any transactions during a financial year that would be required to be recorded in the company's accounting records. A company that does not trade but that, for instance, receives dividends or earns interest is, therefore, not a dormant company. Similarly, a company is not dormant if it has issued and made calls on shares during the year.

7.121 A dormant company is not required to have its accounts audited provided that either of the following applies:

- it has been dormant since formation; or
- it has been dormant since the end of the financial year and
  - it is entitled to prepare accounts under the small companies regime or would be if it were not a plc or a member of an ineligible group (see above); and
  - it is not required to prepare group accounts for that year.

7.122 A dormant company which is an authorised insurance company, a bank, an e-money issuer, a MiFID investment firm, a UCITS management company or carries on insurance market activity is not eligible for audit exemption.

Members' entitlement to request an audit

7.123 Members have the right to request an audit even if a small company falls below the audit threshold or claims audit exemption because it is dormant (s. 476). To exercise their right, members holding at least 10% of the shares or any class of shares or, for a guarantee company, holders of at least 10% of the votes, must notify the directors that they wish an audit to be undertaken. Notification must be given within the financial year in question and at least one month before the end of that year.

7.124 As part of the statement on the balance sheet confirming the company's entitlement to audit exemption, the directors must confirm that no members holding 10% or more of the votes, shares or any class of shares have requested an audit.

Appointment of auditors

7.125 All companies not entitled to audit exemption or whose directors decide not to take up an available exemption from audit must appoint auditors annually. However, the process for appointing auditors varies depending on whether the company is private or public.

Appointment by a private company (s. 485)

7.126 In the first period for appointing auditors the audit appointment may be made either by the directors or by the members. Members appoint auditors by ordinary resolution, which can be passed in a general meeting or as a written resolution. The appointment ceases at the end of the next period for appointing auditors unless the auditor is reappointed.

7.127 The period for appointing auditors in any subsequent period is the period ending up to 28 days after the accounts for the previous year have been sent out to members or up to 28 days after the end of the period allowed for sending out the accounts to members for the previous financial year. If no action is taken by the members in this period, then the existing auditor is deemed to be reappointed until the end of the next period for appointing auditors or until the auditor resigns or is removed, if that occurs earlier.

7.128 In practice, therefore, once an audit firm has been formally appointed by the members, a private company need take no further action unless it wishes to remove its auditors or the auditors resign. If members do not wish to reappoint the incumbent auditors, they must give notice to the company before the end of the accounting reference period immediately before the reappointment would take effect. For example, if members do not want to reappoint the auditors for the year ended 31 March 2010 they would have to give notice before the end of the accounting reference period ended 31 March 2009. The notice must be given by members holding at least 5% of the total voting rights (or a lower percentage if the company's articles specify).

7.129 Directors should bear in mind that the 'deemed reappointment' routine only applies where the audit appointment was made by the members in the first place. If the auditors were appointed by the directors to fill a casual vacancy or as a first appointment, then the audit appointment must be confirmed by a simple majority of the members in the period for appointing auditors.

7.130 It should also be noted that if the company's articles require actual reappointment of the auditor in general meeting then the appointment must be formally voted on. This is not a standard article of Table A under the Companies Act 1985 but might arise in a company which has 'bespoke' articles or which was formed under an earlier Act.

7.131 If a company wants to replace its auditor, it is important to remember that the new auditor cannot hold office until his predecessor has ceased to hold office, whether by resignation, removal or simply by not being reappointed. Special notice is required if the company plans to appoint an auditor other than the incumbent.

Appointment and reappointment by a public company (quoted or unquoted) (s. 489)

7.132 In the first period for appointing auditors of a public company the audit appointment may be made either by the directors or by the members. Members appoint auditors by ordinary resolution, via a general meeting. The appointment ceases at the end of the general meeting at which the accounts for the first financial year are laid before the members.

7.133 Ordinarily, the auditors of a public company are appointed or reappointed at the general meeting at which the accounts are laid before the members (the accounts meeting) and the appointment runs until the following meeting unless the auditors resign or are removed in the meantime.

Cessation of the audit appointment

How an audit appointment may cease

7.134 An audit appointment may cease because the auditor resigns, the company votes to remove the auditor or the auditor is not reappointed at the accounts meeting in the case of a public company, or in the period for appointing auditors in the case of a private company.

7.135 If the auditor resigns, a notice to that effect must be deposited with the company. The company must send the notice to the Registrar within 14 days of receiving it.

7.136 Members may remove an auditor at any time in general meeting by means of a simple majority. Special notice is required for the resolution, which is one of the very few decisions a private company is not permitted to deal with as a written resolution. A copy of the special notice must be sent to the auditor. The auditor is allowed to make reasonable written representations regarding his removal, which the company must circulate to the members. If there is no time to circulate the representations, the auditor may ask the company to read out his representations at the meeting. In any case, the auditor has the right to speak at the meeting.

7.137 If the auditor is removed, the company must notify the Registrar within 14 days. An auditor who has been removed has the right to receive notice of, attend and speak at the general meeting that would otherwise have represented the end of his term of office.

Requirements for statements from auditors

7.138 When auditors of unquoted companies cease to hold office for any reason they are required to deposit a statement with the company concerning any circumstances connected with their ceasing to hold office which they consider should be brought to the attention of the members or creditors of the company (a 'statement of circumstances'). If there are no circumstances, the auditor is required to deposit a statement to that effect (a 'statement of no circumstances', also known as a 's. 519 statement' after the relevant section of the Act.

7.139 When auditors of quoted companies cease to hold office for any reason they are required to deposit a statement of the circumstances connected with the cessation of their office. There is no option for a quoted company auditor to deposit a 'statement of no circumstances'.

7.140 If the auditor resigns, the statement is deposited at the same time as the notice of resignation and the resignation is not effective unless the statement is received. If the auditor is removed, the statement is deposited no more than 14 days after he ceased to hold office. If the auditor is not reappointed, the statement is deposited not more than 14 days after the end of the period for reappointing auditors.

7.141 When the company receives a statement of circumstances it has 14 days to send a copy to everyone who is entitled to receive a copy of the accounts or to apply to the court to prevent circulation of the statement. The grounds on which the court would direct that the company need not circulate a statement of circumstances are that the statement gives needless publicity to defamatory matter. Note that it is not enough to argue that the statement is defamatory; the court must be satisfied that circulating the statement would allow the auditor to secure needless publicity for the defamatory matter. If the court finds against the company or the action is discontinued, the company has 14 days to circulate the statement.

7.142 Assuming that there is no court application, the auditor must send a copy of the statement of circumstances to the Registrar between 21 and 28 days after it was sent to the company. If there is an unsuccessful application, the auditor has seven days from the date he is notified that it was unsuccessful to send the statement to the Registrar.

Dual notification to the Appropriate Audit Authority

7.143 In addition to the procedures outlined above, there are additional notification requirements on both companies and their auditors when an audit appointment ends.

7.144 Depending on the circumstances, both the company (s. 523) and the auditor (s. 522) may be required to notify an Appropriate Audit Authority in addition to depositing statements with the company and the Registrar and circulating those statements. Notification is required when:

- an auditor of a 'major audit' ceases to be auditor for any reason;
- the auditor of any other company ceases to be auditor before the end of his term of office.

7.145 For 'major audits' the Appropriate Audit Authority is the Professional Oversight Board of the Financial Reporting Council. For all other audits it is the firm's Recognised Supervisory Body, which could be the Institute of Chartered Accountants in England and Wales, the Institute of Chartered Accountants of Scotland or the Chartered Association of Certified Accountants.

7.146 The Professional Oversight Board has issued guidance on the procedure to be followed, including separate flowcharts for auditors and companies (see: www.frc.org.uk/pob/regulation/auditfirms.cfm and www.frc.org.uk/pob/regulation/companies.cfm). The flowcharts contain details of what is meant by a 'major audit' as follows:

- all UK incorporated companies with equity or debt admitted to the Official List, including Plus listed companies;
- all UK incorporated AIM and Plus quoted companies;
- unquoted companies with a group turnover in excess of £500 million or group long-term debt in excess of £250 million and turnover in excess of £100 million;
- unquoted companies or groups which are subsidiaries of foreign parent

companies where the turnover of the UK group or company is in excess of £1,000 million;
- charitable companies with an income exceeding £100 million;
- subsidiary companies of any of the above.

The auditor is required to submit the following to the Appropriate Audit Authority:

- the fact that they have ceased to be auditors; and
- a copy of any statement of circumstances; or
- a note of why the office ceased.

7.147 The submission must be made at the time the 'statement of circumstances' is sent to the company (for a major audit) or when the appropriate audit authority requires (for any other audit).

7.148 The company must also inform the appropriate audit authority and submit either a copy of the 'statement of circumstances' by the auditor or a statement by the company of the reasons for the auditor ceasing to hold office. The company has no more than 14 days after receipt of the 'statement of circumstances' or 'statement of no circumstances' from the auditor to make the submission.

7.149 Directors of unquoted public and private companies should remember that these dual reporting requirements apply if the audit appointment ceases before the end of the auditor's usual term of office. Therefore, if a company is sold and the new owners want to replace the auditors, it is likely that dual reporting will apply. However, if it is possible to change auditors at the end of the auditor's term of office, no action will be required.

Auditors' duties

7.150 It will be helpful for directors if they understand the duties required of statutory auditors. These can be summarised as follows:

- to form an opinion on the truth and fairness of the financial statements prepared by the directors, whether they have been properly prepared in accordance with the relevant accounting framework and whether they have been prepared in accordance with the Act;
- to form an opinion as to whether the information in the directors' report is consistent with the financial statements;
- to report by exception in the audit report if the company has not kept adequate accounting records, if the accounts are not in agreement with the

underlying books and records and if the auditor has not obtained returns from branches not visited as part of the audit;
- to report by exception if the auditor has not obtained all the information and explanations necessary for the audit;
- as far as they are able, to provide particulars in their report of directors' remuneration, pensions and compensation for loss of office where this is not disclosed in the accounts as required.

7.151 If the directors have prepared accounts under the small companies' regime when the company is not entitled to do so, the auditor must state that fact.

7.152 Quoted company auditors have two further duties in respect of the auditable part of the directors' remuneration report (see **7.60**). These are:

- to state whether the auditable part of the directors ' remuneration report has been properly prepared in accordance with the Act; and
- to report by exception if the auditable part of the report is not in agreement with the company's books and records.

Auditors' rights to information

7.153 Directors should be aware that the auditor has a right of access at all times to the company's books, records and vouchers in whatever form they are held. The auditor also has a right to require a wide range of people to provide information on matters relevant to the audit opinion. Those include any officer or employee of the company, any person holding any of the books, accounts or vouchers, any UK subsidiary of the company, or any officer, employee or auditor of any UK subsidiary.

7.154 Auditors of a parent company also have rights to information from overseas subsidiaries. It is the duty of the parent company (and so, effectively, of the parent company's directors) to ensure that the necessary information is provided.

7.155 It is an offence knowingly or recklessly to provide materially false, misleading or deceptive information to an auditor.

Quoted companies – rights of members to require publication of audit concerns

7.156 Quoted company members can require the company to publish a statement setting out any matter concerning the audit of the accounts to be laid before members at the next accounts meeting which the members wish to raise at that meeting (s. 527). They can also require publication of a statement of any circumstances connected with the auditor ceasing to hold office since the last accounts meeting.

7.157 The request for a statement will be effective if it is made by members holding at least 5% of the total voting rights. It will also be effective if it is made by at least 100 members who each hold shares on which there is an average of £100 paid up.

7.158 The statement must be placed on a website that is maintained by or on behalf of the company and which identifies the company in question. It must be published within three days of the company receiving the request and must remain on the website until the end of the relevant meeting. At the same time as the statement is placed on the website a copy must be sent to the company's auditors.

7.159 Directors should note that while members have a right to raise issues concerning the audit at the accounts meeting this does not oblige the auditor to respond in person. Auditors have a right to attend and be heard at general meetings on relevant matters but they do not have a duty to do so. Similarly, the directors cannot compel the auditors to answer questions from members. Therefore, directors may find that they must assume responsibility for answering any questions which members may have about the audit or the auditors.

Liability limitation agreements

7.160 Under the 2006 Act for the first time it is possible for auditors to negotiate some limitation of their liability in respect of their audit work. This represents a fundamental shift in the position of auditors as previously any provision which purported to exempt an auditor from liability in respect of the audit or which allowed the company to indemnify the auditor for any liability was void. There were several drivers for a change in the law, including the danger of another major audit firm exiting the audit market, the risk of higher fees and the danger that it might become impossible to fill certain high-risk audit appointments.

7.161 The Act therefore gives auditors the right to establish a contractual limitation of the amount of their liability for the audit of a company provided that any agreement complies with the requirements of the Act and the members approve it (s. 534). Such an agreement cannot cover more than one financial year and must specify the year to which it relates. This means that auditors who wish to protect themselves from liability will have to negotiate a separate agreement for each financial year and the directors will have to obtain the approval of the members each year.

7.162 It is immaterial how the limitation of liability is framed and so the 'amount' of the auditor's liability is up to the company and its auditors to agree. It could be a monetary cap, formula or the auditor's proportionate share of any loss so long as it is considered to be fair and reasonable. Indeed, if the company and the auditor agree a limitation that the court decides was not fair and reasonable, it can substitute a limitation which it believes does meet that test.

7.163 Private company members can approve the principle of liability limitation and delegate the detailed negotiation to the directors without any further reference to members. However, private companies can also pass a resolution in advance approving the principal terms or can pass a resolution to approve the agreement in full. This allows considerable flexibility in how the agreement is handled. Approval of the members can be obtained by written resolution.

7.164 Public companies can either approve the principal terms in advance of entering into the agreement or can approve the agreement itself after it has been entered into. In all cases, the relevant resolution is an ordinary resolution at a general meeting.

7.165 For a group of companies it is not sufficient simply to obtain the approval of the members of the holding company; it must also be obtained from all the UK subsidiaries.

7.166 If a liability limitation agreement is entered into, full particulars must be disclosed in the notes to the accounts for the year to which the agreement relates.

7.167 The Financial Reporting Council has published guidance for companies and directors on liability limitation agreements. This can be obtained from www.frc.org.uk/publications. The guidance provides:

- an explanation of what is and is not allowed under the 2006 Act;
- a discussion of some of the issues that directors should consider in relation to an agreement;
- an explanation of what should be included in a liability limitation agreement;
- an explanation of the process to be followed to obtain the agreement of the members;

- draft specimen clauses (including 'proportionate liability', a fixed cap agreement and a 'fair and reasonable' limit); and
- draft specimen resolutions for members.

7.168 The guidance explains that directors will not incur any personal liability as a result of the decision to enter into a limitation of liability agreement provided that they obtain the approval of the members and that 'they act independently with reasonable competence in what they honestly believe to be most likely to promote the success of the company for benefit of the members'.

7.169 Directors have to give careful consideration to whether it is in the best interests of the company to agree to a limitation of the auditors' liability. Many companies agree to limit the liability of other suppliers and in some respects the audit may be considered as just another supply. However, directors will want to consider issues such as whether they will be able to obtain auditors with appropriate expertise if they do not agree to a limitation of the auditors' liability, whether the company will be able to recover its losses from other sources and whether the agreement matches an auditor's responsibility for a loss with his liability. Directors will have to take into account the attitude of investors, especially those from jurisdictions that do not permit liability limitation arrangements with auditors. They should also consider whether any members have established policies with regard to the forms of limitation of liability they are prepared to accept.

Accounts formats

Table 7.1 Illustrative formats for balance sheet and profit and loss account of large and medium-sized companies

Balance sheet – format 1

A. Called-up share capital not paid

B. Fixed assets

  I Intangible assets

    1. Development costs
    2. Concessions, patents, licences, trademarks and similar rights and assets
    3. Goodwill
    4. Payments on account

  II Tangible assets

    1. Land and buildings
    2. Plant and machinery
    3. Fixtures, fittings, tools and equipment

4. Payments on account and assets in the course of construction

III Investments

1. Shares in group undertakings
2. Loans to group undertakings
3. Participating interests
4. Loans to undertakings in which the company has a participating interest
5. Other investments other than loans
6. Other loans
7. Own shares

C. Current assets

I Stocks

1. Raw materials and consumables
2. Work in progress
3. Finished goods and goods for resale
4. Payments on account

II Debtors

1. Trade debtors
2. Amounts owed by group undertakings
3. Amounts owed by undertakings in which the company has a participating interest
4. Other debtors
5. Called-up share capital not paid
6. Prepayments and accrued income

III Investments

1. Shares in group undertakings
2. Own shares
3. Other investments

IV Cash at bank and in hand

D. Prepayments and accrued income

E. Creditors due within one year

1. Debenture loans
2. Bank loans and overdrafts
3. Payments received on account
4. Trade creditors
5. Bills of exchange payable
6. Amounts owed to group undertakings
7. Amounts owed to undertakings in which the company has a participating interest
8. Other creditors including tax and social security
9. Accruals and deferred income

F. Net current assets (liabilities)

G. Total assets less current liabilities
H. Creditors due after one year
 1. Debenture loans
 2. Bank loans and overdrafts
 3. Payments received on account
 4. Trade creditors
 5. Bills of exchange payable
 6. Amounts owed to group undertakings
 7. Amounts owed to undertakings in which the company has a participating interest
 8. Other creditors, including tax and social security
 9. Accruals and deferred income
I. Provisions for liabilities
 1. Pensions and similar obligations
 2. Taxation, including deferred taxation
 3. Other provisions
J. Accruals and deferred income
K. Capital and reserves
 I Called-up share capital
 II Share premium account
 III Revaluation reserve
 IV Other reserves
 1. Capital redemption reserve
 2. Reserve for own shares
 3. Reserves provided for in the articles of association
 4. Other reserves
 V Profit and loss account

Balance sheet – Format 2

Assets

A. Called-up share capital not paid
B. Fixed assets
 I Intangible assets
 1. Development costs
 2. Concessions, patents, licences, trademarks and similar rights and assets
 3. Goodwill
 4. Payments on account
 II Tangible assets
 1. Land and buildings
 2. Plant and machinery
 3. Fixtures, fittings, tools and equipment

4. Payments on account and assets in the course of construction

III Investments

1. Shares in group undertakings
2. Loans to group undertakings
3. Participating interests
4. Loans to undertakings in which the company has a participating interest
5. Other investments other than loans
6. Other loans
7. Own shares

C. Current assets

I Stocks

1. Raw materials and consumables
2. Work in progress
3. Finished goods and goods for resale
4. Payments on account

II Debtors

1. Trade debtors
2. Amounts owed by group undertakings
3. Amounts owed by undertakings in which the company has a participating interest
4. Other debtors
5. Called up share capital not paid
6. Prepayments and accrued income

III Investments

1. Shares in group undertakings
2. Own shares
3. Other investments

IV Cash at bank and in hand

D. Prepayments and accrued income

Liabilities

A. Capital and reserves

I Called-up share capital

II Share premium account

III Revaluation reserve

IV Other reserves

1. Capital redemption reserve
2. Reserve for own shares
3. Reserves provided for in the articles of association
4. Other reserves

V Profit and loss account

B. Provisions for liabilities

1. Pensions and similar obligations
2. Taxation, including deferred taxation
3. Other provisions

C. Creditors

1. Debenture loans
2. Bank loans and overdrafts
3. Payments received on account
4. Trade creditors
5. Bills of exchange payable
6. Amounts owed to group undertakings
7. Amounts owed to undertakings in which the company has a participating interest
8. Other creditors including tax and social security
9. Accruals and deferred income

D. Accruals and deferred income

Profit and loss account – Format 1

1. Turnover
2. Cost of sales
3. Gross profit or loss
4. Distribution costs
5. Administrative expenses
6. Other operating income
7. Income from shares in group undertakings
8. Income from participating interests
9. Income from other fixed asset investments
10. Other interest receivable and similar income
11. Amounts written off investments
12. Interest payable and similar charges
13. Tax on profit or loss on ordinary activities
14. Profit or loss on ordinary activities after taxation
15. Extraordinary income
16. Extraordinary charges
17. Extraordinary profit or loss
18. Tax on extraordinary profit or loss
19. Other taxed not shown under the above items
20. Profit or loss for the financial year

Profit and loss account – Format 2

1. Turnover
2. Change in stocks of finished goods and work in progress

3. Own work capitalised
4. Other operating income
5. a) Raw materials and consumables
   b) Other external charges
6. Staff costs
   a) Wages and salaries
   b) Social securities costs
   c) Other pension costs
7. a) Depreciation and other amounts written off tangible and intangible fixed assets
   b) Exceptional amounts written off current assets
8. Other operating charges
9. Income from shares in group undertakings
10. Income from participating interests
11. Income from other fixed asset investments
12. Other interest receivable and similar income
13. Amounts written off investments
14. Interest payable and similar charges
15. Tax on profit or loss on ordinary activities
16. Profit or loss on ordinary activities after taxation
17. Extraordinary income
18. Extraordinary charges
19. Extraordinary profit or loss
20. Tax on extraordinary profit or loss
21. Other taxes not shown under the above items

Profit or loss for the financial year

Table 7.2 Illustrative formats for balance sheet of small companies
Format 1

A. Called-up share capital not paid
B. Fixed assets
   I Intangible assets
      1. Goodwill
      2. Other intangible assets
   II Tangible assets
      1. Land and buildings
      2. Plant and machinery, etc.
   III Investments
      1. Shares in group undertakings and participating interests
      2. Loans to group undertakings and undertakings in which the company has a participating interest

3. Other investments other than loans
4. Other investments

C. Current assets
 I Stocks
  1. Stocks
  2. Payments on account
 II Debtors
  1. Trade debtors
  2. Amounts owed by group undertakings and undertakings in which the company has a participating interest
  3. Other debtors
 VI Investments
  1. Shares in group undertakings
  2. Other investments
 VII Cash at bank and in hand

D. Prepayments and accrued income
 I Creditors due within one year
  1. Bank loans and overdrafts
  2. Trade creditors
  3. Amounts owed to group undertakings and undertakings in which the company has a participating interest
  4. Other creditors

J. Net current assets (liabilities)

Total assets less current liabilities

K. Creditors due after one year
  1. Bank loans and overdrafts
  2. Trade creditors
  3. Amounts owed to group undertakings and undertakings in which the company has a participating interest
  4. Other creditors

I Provisions for liabilities

J Accruals and deferred income

K Capital and reserves
 I Called up share capital
 II Share premium account
 III Revaluation reserve
 IV Other reserves
 V Profit and loss account

Format 2

Assets

C. Called up share capital not paid

D. Fixed assets

- I Intangible assets
  1. Goodwill
  2. Other intangible assets
- II Tangible assets
  2. Land and buildings
  3. Plant and machinery, etc.
- III Investments
  1. Shares in group undertakings and participating interests
  2. Loans to group undertakings and undertakings in which the company has a participating interest
  3. Other investments other than loans
  4. Other investments

C. Current assets

- I Stocks
  1. Stocks
  2. Payments on account
- II Debtors
  1. Trade debtors
  2. Amounts owed by group undertakings and undertakings in which the company has a participating interest
  3. Other debtors
- III Investments
  1. Shares in group undertakings
  2. Other investments
- IV Cash at bank and in hand

D. Prepayments and accrued income

Liabilities

A. Capital and reserves

- I Called up share capital
- II Share premium account
- III Revaluation reserve
- IV Other reserves
  1. Capital redemption reserve
  2. Reserve for own shares
  3. Reserves provided for in the articles of association

4. Other reserves

V Profit and loss account

B. Provisions for liabilities

1. Pensions and similar obligations
2. Taxation, including deferred taxation
3. Other provisions

C. Creditors

1. Bank loans and overdrafts
2. Trade creditors
3. Amounts owed to group undertakings and undertakings in which the company has a participating interest
4. Other creditors

D. Accruals and deferred income

8

Directors as employees

Introduction

8.1 A director is an office holder and can be an individual or a corporate body (such as a company). Corporate directors are still permitted under the Companies Act 2006 (the 2006 Act) but, from 1 October 2008, a company must have at least one natural person on its board of directors (s. 155 of the 2006 Act). An individual director may be either an employee or be self-employed.

8.2 This chapter focuses on the specific employment and company law issues relevant to directors as employees and briefly highlights the different statutory, contractual and regulatory regime applicable to non-executive directors. In particular, this chapter examines:

- the status of director – employed or self-employed;
- the statutory definition of service contract;
- authorisation of service contracts;
- shareholder approval required for long-term service contracts;
- disclosure of service contracts;
- key provisions in an executive director's service contract;
- key provisions in a non-executive director's letter of appointment;
- the remuneration of directors, including pension, incentive schemes and insured benefits;
- the role of the remuneration committee, requirements of the Combined Code in relation to directors' remuneration and the ABI Guidelines on Executive Remuneration;
- garden leave and restrictive covenants;
- statutory protection for employees;
- compensation for loss of office;
- shareholder approval for payments for loss of office;
- directors and officers' liability insurance and indemnities.

8.3 The most significant recent development is the introduction of the Companies Act 2006, which received royal assent on 8 November 2006 and has been brought into force in stages, with the whole of the Act expected to be in force by 1 October 2009. At the time of writing, eight commencement orders have been published covering provisions of the Act to be brought into force up to 1 October 2009. However, this chapter is written on the basis that the whole of the 2006 Act is in force.

Status of director – employed or self-employed

8.4 The office of director can be independent of any employment relationship that the individual may have with the company. Normally, an executive director will also be an employee of a company employed through a service contract, whereas a non-executive director will be self-employed, providing services pursuant to a letter of appointment. However, it is not always clear whether a director is also an employee, and there is no single definitive test for determining employment status. (**Chapter 1** addresses the question 'what is a director?' and provides a useful commentary on the difference between executive and non-executive directors.)

8.5 The new definition of a director's service contract in the 2006 Act (see **8.13** below) encompasses both executive service contracts and non-executive letters of appointment, thereby blurring the distinction between the two in relation to certain provisions of the 2006 Act. For example, the requirement for shareholder approval to be obtained for long-term directors' service contracts applies to both executive service contracts and non-executive letters of appointment.

8.6 It is important to establish whether a director is an employee as this will impact on his entitlement to various protections and rights under UK employment law (see **8.10** below) and on how he should be taxed.

8.7 A clear statement of intention in relation to employment status and clearly drafted documents (e.g. employment contract or consultancy agreement) consistent with this intention are helpful but not conclusive. In the absence of clear documentation, the parties' intentions may be ascertained from an examination of board minutes, board resolutions or correspondence and a careful consideration of the circumstances in which the services are provided.

8.8 However, a number of factors need to be considered when determining whether an employment relationship exists and no single factor is determinative.

- Mutuality of obligation is fundamental to an employment relationship. This will most commonly be an obligation to provide work or pay during periods of no work and an obligation on the individual to carry out work which the employer requires him to do. However, even an expectation that work will be offered and accepted may crystallise into a legal obligation sufficient to establish an overarching employment contract in circumstances where discrete or ad hoc services are provided over a period of time.
- The right to provide a substitute to carry out duties is often (although not always) seen as inconsistent with the existence of an employment contract.
- The degree of control exercised by the alleged employer is also key. Control includes the power of deciding what is to be done, the way in which it is to be done, the means used and the timing and place where it will be done. Essentially, the more control the company can assert over the manner and form in which the individual must carry out his duties, the more likely it is that an employment relationship exists (the 'control' test).
- The extent to which an individual is integrated into an organisation will be relevant; this encompasses both whether the individual forms an integral part of the company and the extent to which the individual is integrated into the company through adherence to company policies, sick pay and holiday pay provision (the 'integration' test). An employment relationship is more likely to exist where there is a high level of integration.

8.9 The control test is less appropriate than the integration test for directors who, as senior individuals in the organisation, are often in control of the day-to-day running of the company in any event. An executive director who is responsible for managing the business and whose work forms an integral part of the business is likely to be an employee, whereas an individual who provides consultancy or advisory services to the company may not be sufficiently integrated to be an employee. In reality, the courts will look at a variety of factors, including the presence of written documentation, whether the engagement is exclusive, the method of payment, what equipment the individual supplies and the level of risk undertaken to determine employment status. Public policy may also influence the decision of the courts.

8.10 The key factors relevant to determining employment status are shown in the table overleaf.

Key factors relevant to employment status	Self-employed consultant	Employee
Documentary evidence of parties' intentions	Contract for services	Written employment contract or statement of employment particulars.
Mutuality of obligation	Mutuality of obligation unnecessary.	Mutuality of obligation is required.
Control	More freedom to determine time, place and manner in which work is performed.	Control through internal organisational structure or, for senior management, through the board.
Integration	Services are an accessory to the business, rather than integral to it. Little integration through company policies and procedures.	Integral part of the business. Holiday pay, sick pay and benefits and disciplinary and grievance procedures.
Personal service	More likely to be able to provide a substitute.	Personal service usually required (although the ability to appoint a substitute is not fatal to an employment relationship).
Exclusivity of the engagement and typical duration	Freedom to work for other companies whilst carrying out work, save where conflict/ direct competitor. Short-term contracts not unusual but, long-term appointment not inconsistent with contract for services.	Not usually permitted to work for other companies during the course of their employment. Employment contract more likely to be open-ended or permanent.
Method of payment	Monthly or quarterly invoices by reference to number of hours or days spent on tasks. The fee will be gross. The consultant will make his own arrangements for income tax and national insurance. VAT may be charged.	Salary taxed at source through PAYE with income tax and employee's national insurance deducted before payment of salary.

continued on next page

Key factors relevant to employment status	**Self-employed consultant**	**Employee**
	N.B. If an individual pays tax as a consultant but a court then decides he is an employee, the employer may set off tax paid by the contractor against the employer's liability for unpaid PAYE on employment income.	
Equipment	Own equipment and administrative or office support.	Equipment and administrative support provided by the employer.
Level of risk	High degree of personal risk in the vehicle through which services are provided.	Less personal risk, although senior managers' interests may be closely aligned with the success of the company through incentive plans. Further, a controlling shareholder may be an employee (see below).

8.11 A controlling shareholder may also be an employee. The courts will look closely at the true economic relationship between the parties. The fact that a director is a controlling shareholder may be a relevant factor weighing against a conclusion that he is an employee, but it is only one of the factors to be considered and is not determinative. See **Chapter 9** for directors as shareholders.

8.12 Guidance on how to determine whether a controlling shareholder is also an employee (from a recent Employment Appeal Tribunal decision) is set out below:

- Where there is an employment contract ostensibly in place between the company and the shareholder, the onus is on the party seeking to deny its effect to satisfy the court that it is not what it appears to be.
- The mere fact that the individual has a controlling shareholding does not of itself prevent a contract of employment arising. Nor does his ability to exercise real or sole control over what the company does.
- The fact that he is an entrepreneur, or has built the company up, or will

profit from its success, will not be factors militating against a finding that an employment contract is in place.

- If the conduct of the parties is in accordance with the contract that would be a strong pointer to the contract being valid and binding.
- Conversely, if the conduct of the parties is inconsistent with the contract that would be a potentially important factor, militating against a finding that the controlling shareholder is in reality an employee.
- The assertion that there is a genuine contract will be undermined if the terms have not been identified or reduced into writing.
- The fact that the individual takes loans from the company or guarantees its debts could exceptionally have some relevance in analysing the true nature of the relationship, but in most cases such factors are unlikely to carry any weight.
- The degree of control exercised over the company by the shareholder employee will be important, but is not, of itself, determinative. (para. 98) (*Clark v. Clark Construction Initiatives Limited & anr* [2008] UKEAT 0225_07_2902).

Statutory definition of service contract

8.13 The 2006 Act defines directors' service contracts for the first time:

> '(1) For the purposes of this Part [10] a director's "service contract", in relation to a company, means a contract under which –
>
> (a) a director of the company undertakes personally to perform services (as director or otherwise) for the company, or for a subsidiary of the company, or
>
> (b) services (as director or otherwise) that a director of the company undertakes personally to perform are made available by a third party to the company, or to a subsidiary of the company
>
> (2) The provisions of this Part relating to directors' service contracts apply to the terms of a person's appointment as a director of a company. They are not restricted to contracts for the performance of services outside the scope of the ordinary duties of a director.' (s. 227)

8.14 The Explanatory Notes to the 2006 Act confirm that the definition applies to contracts of service (e.g. an executive service contract), contracts for services and non-executive letters of appointment. The definition covers the 'situation' where a director provides services through a third party (e.g. a personal services company). Shadow directors also fall within its scope.

8.15 This definition is relevant to the duty to declare an interest in a proposed transaction or arrangement and to the duty to declare an interest in an existing transaction or arrangement (ss. 177 and 182 of the 2006 Act); to contracts with a guaranteed term of more than two years which require shareholder approval (s. 188); and to substantial property transactions which require members' approval (s. 190).

Authorisation of service contracts – compliance with the company's constitution

8.16 Directors must act within the powers set out in a company's constitution.

8.17 The 2006 Act introduces significant changes to a company's constitution in October 2009. Companies will continue to have a memorandum and articles of association, but the new-style memorandum will simply state that the subscribers wish to form a company, agree to become members of the company and subscribe to at least one share each. All the provisions previously contained in the memorandum of an existing company (other than those mentioned above) will automatically be treated as provisions of that company's articles of association without any need to pass a resolution to this effect.

8.18 The articles of association identify the responsibilities and duties of individual directors and the board as a whole. Any service contract with a director must be authorised in accordance with the company's articles. The articles usually prescribe that vacancies may be filled or additional directors may be appointed by the board of directors as well as by ordinary resolution by the company (subject to the articles' maximum number of directors) and will state the quorum required in order for a board meeting to take place. (See **Chapters 2** and **3** for a discussion of appointment and removal of directors.) The articles of association may also contain relevant provisions relating to directors' powers, directors' remuneration, gratuities and benefits, directors' interests and the ability of a director to vote and count in the quorum at board meetings.

8.19 The articles may authorise the directors to delegate the board's functions to a committee and/or managing director or other executive director. The terms of the service contract may, for example, be determined by a committee of the board of directors. In these circumstances, it is important to ensure that the committee has full authority under the articles to exercise the powers of the directors for these purposes. Without this authority, the committee may only make recommendations to the board and the full board will be required to approve the terms of the contract and authorise entry into the contract.

8.20 The position in relation to a director's obligation to disclose an interest in his own service contract changed with effect from October 2008. Under the Companies Act 1985 Act, s. 317, a director is obliged to disclose an interest in a contract or proposed contract and is obliged to declare his interest in his own service contract or any variation of it at the first board meeting at which the agreement (or variation) is considered. From October 2008, although there is a general duty on directors to declare their interest in a *proposed* transaction or arrangement, breach of which is a civil offence, there is no need for a director to declare an interest if it concerns terms of his service contract that have been or are to be considered by a meeting of the directors, or by a committee of the directors appointed for the purpose under the company's constitution (s. 177(6)(c) of the 2006 Act). However, the articles of association may prescribe that directors do declare their interest in such circumstances.

8.21 There is a separate obligation to declare a direct or indirect interest in an *existing* transaction or arrangement that has been entered into by the company (ss. 182–183 of the 2006 Act), for which a failure to comply would be a criminal offence.

8.22 Directors are under an overriding duty to comply with the new codified directors' duties set out in the 2006 Act. These include:

- a duty to act within powers (s. 171);
- a duty to promote the success of the company (s. 172);
- a duty to exercise independent judgement (s. 173);
- a duty to exercise reasonable care, skill and diligence (s. 174);
- a duty to avoid conflicts of interest (s. 175);
- a duty not to accept benefits from third parties (s. 176); and
- a duty to declare interest in proposed transaction or arrangement (s. 177).

8.23 The first four duties (ss. 171–174) came into force in October 2007 and the latter three (ss. 175–177) in October 2008.

8.24 However, in certain instances, the statutory duties provide for derogation where a director is acting in a way authorised by the company's constitution. Accordingly, it will be important to consider the codified duties and the company's constitution together. See **Chapter 5** for discussion of directors' duties.

Shareholder approval for long-term service contracts

8.25 From 1 October 2007, shareholder approval is required for directors' long-term service contracts where the guaranteed term of a director's employment with the company or any subsidiary is, or may be, longer than two years

(s. 188 of the 2006 Act). Under the 1985 Act (s. 319) approval was only required for directors' service contracts in excess of five years. Further, this new obligation will apply to both executive directors' service contracts and non-executive directors' letters of appointment.

8.26 A guaranteed term is a period during which the director's employment continues, or may be continued, and which cannot be terminated by the company by notice, or can only be terminated in specified circumstances. Alternatively, where the contract can be terminated on notice, the period of notice that is required to be given will be the guaranteed term.

8.27 Further, if more than six months before the end of the guaranteed term of a director's employment the company enters into a further service contract (otherwise than in pursuance of a right conferred by or under the original contract on the other party to it), then this provision will apply as if there were added to the guaranteed term of the new contract the unexpired period of the guaranteed term of the original contract (s. 188(4) of the 2006 Act).

8.28 A resolution of the members of a holding company is required in the case of a director of a holding company. The requirement for shareholder approval does not apply to a contract between a wholly-owned subsidiary and one of its directors. Nor is shareholder approval required if the company is not a UK-registered company.

8.29 The terms of the contract must be made available for inspection for at least 15 days before the meeting to approve it, and at that meeting.

8.30 If a service contract contains such a term and there has been no shareholder approval, the term will be void and the service contract deemed to be terminable on reasonable notice.

8.31 Service contracts – key points

Extending the requirement for shareholder approval to contracts of two or more years' service was intended to encourage the trend towards shorter notice periods to protect shareholders from the expense of paying out the remainder of a contractual term in circumstances where the contract is terminated early or a director is removed from office.

This has led to difficulties in relation to non-executive letters of appointment. Institutional investors have historically expressed concern about the presence of notice provisions in non-executive letters of appointment on the basis that they could make the non-executive director more vulnerable to a termination by the executive directors in the event of a disagreement at board level. However, the purpose of this new provision in the 2006 Act is to ensure that if a company wishes to enter into a contract with either an executive or non-executive director for a term longer than two years then either shareholder approval must be sought or a notice provision should be inserted.

The presence of a notice period has the additional advantage that it should limit the maximum level of damages owed to a departing director to the length of the notice period. In the absence of a notice provision, the company may be left exposed to a claim for the unexpired period of a guaranteed fixed term in circumstances where it is terminated prematurely.

A well-drafted non-executive appointment letter should avoid this kind of difficulty by including a provision in which the non-executive agrees not to bring a claim for compensation on the early termination of his appointment. As a non-executive director will not acquire the statutory protections afforded to employees, this contractual waiver of claims should be effective.

The position will be different in relation to executive directors who are also employees for whom a statutory compromise agreement would be required in cases of premature termination to protect the company from statutory employment claims such as unfair dismissal.

8.32 The revised Combined Code, published by the Financial Reporting Council (FRC) in June 2008, states with regard to public listed companies, at para. B1.6:

> 'Notice or contract periods should be set at one year or less. If it is necessary to offer longer notice or contract periods to new directors recruited from outside, such periods should reduce to one year or less after the initial period.'

8.33 The 'comply or explain' requirement in the Listing Rules in the FSA Handbook refers to the revised Combined Code for reporting periods commencing on or after 29 June 2008.

8.34 The revised Joint Statement on Executive Contracts issued by the Association of British Insurers (ABI) and the National Association of Pension Funds (NAPF) states in relation to notice periods that the one-year notice period referred to in the Combined Code should not be seen as a floor, and boards are strongly encouraged to consider contracts with shorter notice periods.

8.35 The 2007 ABI Guidelines 'Executive Remuneration – ABI guidelines on policies and practices' emphasise that contracts should be drafted to permit companies *not* to pay out where the departing executive is perceived to have failed. Shorter notice periods are one mechanism for avoiding an excessive severance payment on termination. If it is necessary to offer executives longer notice periods, for example for incoming executives at companies in difficulties, the ABI/NAPF Guidelines indicate that the termination provisions and the length of the contract need to be justified and should reduce on a rolling basis (para. 3.6). The ABI Guidelines also suggest that if a director is dismissed following the use of a disciplinary procedure, the contract could provide for termination on a shorter notice period than otherwise (para. 3.7). In reality, this may be difficult to negotiate.

8.36 The Listing Rules do not apply to companies quoted on AIM (the Alternative Investment Market). The three key sources on corporate governance specific to AIM companies reflect much of the best practice guidance outlined in the Combined Code:

- the London Stock Exchange's AIM Rules for Companies;
- the Corporate Governance Guidelines for AIM Companies published by Quoted Companies Alliance (QCA) on 13 July 2005 which is the representative body for small and mid-cap quoted companies (formerly known as CISCO), and
- the voluntary Corporate Governance Policy and Voting Guidelines for AIM Companies published by NAPF in April 2007.

In addition, all companies incorporated in England and Wales are bound by any corporate governance provisions contained in the 2006 Act.

Disclosure of service contracts

8.37 A company must keep copies of every director's service contract (or where there is no written contract, a memorandum of the terms) open to inspection by shareholders without charge. This obligation applies regardless of the length of any service contract and whether or not it is terminable within 12 months. The exception that existed under s. 318(11) of CA 1985 for contracts where the unexpired term of the contract was less than 12 months or where the company could terminate the contract within 12 months without payment of compensation has not been retained. All the copies and memoranda must be available for inspection at the company's registered office or a place specified in regulations under s. 1136 and must be retained by the company for at least one year from the date of termination or expiry of the contract and must be kept available for inspection during that time. These provisions apply equally to variations of a director's service contract and accordingly any documents amending the terms of a service contract must also be open to inspection by shareholders (s. 228 of the 2006 Act).

8.38 The company must give notice in the prescribed form to the Registrar as to the place of inspection and of any change to that place unless they have at all times been kept at the company's registered office (s. 228(4) of the 2006 Act).

8.39 The disclosure requirements apply even where the director's contract requires him to work wholly or mainly outside the UK. The dispensation that existed under s. 318(5) of CA 1985 was not retained under the 2006 Act.

8.40 There are financial penalties for a failure to comply with these requirements. It is a criminal offence for which every officer of the company who is in default may be held liable to pay a fine (currently up to £1,000) (s. 228(6) of the 2006 Act). However, in a change to the position under the 1985 Act, s. 318, the company will no longer be liable under the criminal offence.

8.41 In addition to the right of shareholders to inspect (without charge) the copies of service contracts held by the company mentioned above, a significant new development is that members now have the right, on payment of the prescribed fee, to request a copy of each director's service contract (or, if not in writing, a memorandum of its terms). The copy must be provided within seven days of the company receiving the request. Where a shareholder is denied inspection the court can compel inspection or direct that the copy required be sent to the person requiring it (s. 229 of the 2006 Act).

Best practice guidance on disclosure

8.42 The revised ABI/NAPF Joint Statement 2008 states that companies should clearly disclose key elements of directors' contracts on their website and summarise them in the Remuneration Report.

8.43 The Combined Code requires the terms and conditions of appointment for non-executive directors to be made available for inspection by any person at an annual general meeting for 15 minutes prior to and at the meeting and at the registered office of the company on any business day during normal business hours (para. A4.4).

8.44 Further, the Combined Code requires terms and conditions of appointment of non-executive directors to be made available by placing the information on a website that is maintained by or on behalf of the company (Schedule C: Disclosure of corporate governance arrangements).

8.45 The Combined Code does not contain a comparable requirement to make the terms and conditions of appointment of executive directors available for inspection.

Takeover Code requirements

8.46 The Takeover Code aims to provide a framework within which takeovers of public companies are conducted and to ensure fair and equal treatment of all shareholders. The Code covers both takeovers by contractual offer from the bidder to purchase the target shareholders' shares and schemes of arrangement sanctioned by the court under the 2006 Act.

8.47 Various documents, including all service contracts of offeree company directors, must be on display and available for inspection by the other party, or by any competing offeror or potential offeror, from the time that the offer document or offeree board circular, as appropriate, is published until the end of the offer period (Rule 26 of the Takeover Code). The offer document or offeree board circular must state which documents are available and the place (being a place in the City of London or such other place as the Panel may agree) where inspection can be made. This includes all service contracts of offeree company directors.

8.48 Particulars of service contracts of directors and proposed directors of the target or any of its subsidiaries should be disclosed in the first major circular from the target board advising shareholders on an offer (whether recommending acceptance or rejection of the offer) (Rule 25.4 of the Takeover Code). If any of the contracts have been entered into or amended within six months of the offer document, details of the previous arrangements must be provided (if there has been none, this should be stated).

8.49 The Companies Act 2006 makes it a criminal offence to deliberately or recklessly breach the content requirements of the offer document. This sanction only applies to offers for companies listed on the Official List, and not schemes of arrangement.

Persons entitled to inspect

8.50 As can be seen, different provisions apply to who is entitled to inspect under the Companies Act 2006 and the Combined Code. There are additional disclosure and inspections obligations set out in the Takeover Code which are discussed in more detail above at **8.46**. The table below summarises the position.

Right	Whom it applies to	Statutory reference
Right to inspect directors' service contracts (or, if not in writing, a memorandum of the terms) at no charge	Shareholders	s. 228, CA 2006
Right to a copy of directors' service contracts (or, if not in writing, a memorandum of the terms), contracts for services and letters of appointment upon payment of prescribed fee	Shareholders	s. 229, CA 2006
Right to inspect terms and conditions of appointment of non-executive directors at an AGM, at the registered office of the company during normal business hours and on a website that is maintained by or on behalf of the company	Any member of the public	2006 Combined Code (Schedule C: disclosure of corporate governance arrangements)
Obligation to disclose particulars of service contracts of directors and proposed directors of the target in the first major circular from the target board advising shareholders of an offer (including details of any amendments)	Shareholders of Target on a potential takeover	Rule 25.4 of the Takeover Code
Right to inspect all service contracts of target company directors or proposed directors (together with particulars of any amendments made within the last 6 months) in a takeover situation	The offeror, any competing offeror or potential offeror from when offer document/ circular is published to the end of the offer period	Rules 25.4 and 26 of the Takeover Code

Key provisions contained in an executive director's service contract

8.51 A director's service contract will set out the terms and conditions of employment but will need to be read alongside the company's constitution, the statutory provisions relating to directors, any company handbook setting out policies and procedures, any pension plan, executive incentive plan rules and any other benefits documentation. Section 1 of the Employment Rights Act 1996 (ERA) obliges an employer to provide an employee with a written statement of specified particulars of his employment within two months of commencement of employment. Service contracts for directors must comply with this requirement.

8.52 Checklist – service contracts

Service contracts for directors should comply with s. 1 of ERA and include the following:

- names of employer and employee;
- date when employment began, and date on which the employee's continuous employment began (taking into account any employment with a previous employer which counts towards that period period);
- scale or rate of remuneration or the method of calculating remuneration;
- intervals at which remuneration is paid;
- any terms and conditions relating to hours of work (including any terms and conditions relating to normal working hours);
- any terms and conditions relating to any of the following:
  - entitlement to holidays, including public holidays and holiday pay;
  - incapacity for work due to sickness or injury, including any provisions for sick pay, and
  - pensions and pension schemes
- length of notice period;
- title of the job and a brief description of the work for which he is employed;
- where employment is not intended to be permanent, the period for which it is expected to continue or the expiry date of any fixed term;
- either the place of work or, where the employee is required or permitted to work at various places, an indication of that and of the address of the employer;
- any collective agreements, which directly affect the terms and conditions of the employment including, where the employer is not a party, the persons by whom they were made;
- where the employee is required to work outside the UK information about the terms and conditions, including pay that will operate during that period.

8.53 Details of any disciplinary rules applicable to the employee should also be provided (ERA, s. 3).

8.54 If an employer fails to provide this information, the employee may apply to an Employment Tribunal for a declaration of the terms (or, if they have an additional claim, for compensation of up to £1,400 from 1 February 2009). In practice, most employees, particularly senior employees and executive directors, will be given a fuller employment contract, setting out detailed terms and conditions of employment.

8.55 Other clauses to consider including in a director's service contract:

- Duties and powers: the service agreement may state specific contractual duties relevant to the appointment in addition to the new statutory duties and common law fiduciary duties that all directors (both executive and non-executive) owe to the company;
- Restrictions on interests in other businesses.
- Restrictions on share dealings.
- Intellectual property.
- Confidentiality.
- Restrictive covenants and garden leave (see below).
- Termination provisions (e.g. payment in lieu of notice and/or a liquidated damages) (see below).
- Amalgamation and reconstruction and joint appointment.
- Entire agreement and severability.
- Variation and waiver.
- Third party rights.
- Assignment.
- Data protection.
- Governing law.

8.56 In addition to the express terms of employment, the courts may imply certain fundamental terms into an employment contract, such as the employee's duty of confidentiality, fidelity and good faith, and the duty on both employer and employee not to conduct themselves in a manner calculated and likely to destroy the relationship of trust and confidence between them. Terms may also be implied into a contract through custom and practice (e.g. where an employer has consistently paid an enhanced redundancy package to departing employees).

Key provisions contained in a non-executive director's service contract

8.57 The concept of non-executive directors has been in place for many years; however, the commercial expectations of non-executive directors have recently undergone significant development. The importance of non-executive directors is reflected in the Higgs Report of 2003, in which they are described as 'custodians of the governance process' and in the Combined Code on Corporate Governance.

8.58 Non-executive directors are usually engaged by a company under a letter of appointment which identifies the principal contractual terms between the company and the non-executive director.

8.59 Letter of appointment – key points

The following terms are relatively commonplace in non-executive directors' letters of appointment for listed companies.

- Term of appointment – this will often be for an initial fixed period, but will always be subject to the articles of association.
- Termination provisions – termination provisions will normally be provided for in the articles of association, but are often supplemented in the letter of appointment. Some companies provide for specific notice periods and for payment in lieu of notice in certain circumstances.
- Summary of principal duties – these tend to include attendance at board meetings, meetings with other non-executive directors as well as with institutional investors and other shareholders, attendance at the annual general meeting and any extraordinary general meetings. If the non-executive director is required to sit on or chair any committees, this should be specified in the letter of appointment.
- The letter of appointment will often state expressly that the non-executive director should have particular regard to and comply with the key elements of good corporate governance.
- Restrictions – letters of appointment normally include express confidentiality restrictions and may, depending on the company and the non-executive director's role, include post-termination restrictive covenants.
- External appointments and interests – in addition to statutory conflict obligations, the letter of appointment will normally contain provisions identifying the extent to which the non-executive director may continue with existing and/or accept new external appointments and interests.

- Fees – the letter of appointment should specify the annual fee payable to the non-executive director. The fee will normally be payable by instalments (monthly or quarterly). The fee may be increased if the non-executive director sits on or chairs any committees or has any special additional responsibilities. The letter of appointment may provide for the fee to be increased where the non-executive director has to spend significantly more time carrying out his or her role than originally anticipated (by the company and the non-executive director), for example if the company is involved in a takeover.
- Appendices – it is relatively commonplace for there to be appendices to the letter of appointment that refer expressly to the principles of corporate governance and what is expected of the non-executive director in carrying out his duties and that contain (or refer to) the policies and practices operating within the company that can apply to the non-executive director.

Remuneration of directors

Components of directors' remuneration

Basic salary

8.60 Basic salary is often the most important part of a director's remuneration. However, in some sectors (such as financial services), an executive's basic salary may represent a fairly modest proportion of his overall remuneration, with by far the larger proportion being made up by bonus arrangements and/or other incentive schemes. In listed companies, the remuneration committee will determine the level of executive remuneration in accordance with the principles contained in the Combined Code, the ABI Guidelines on Executive Remuneration and other best practice guidance.

8.61 The prohibition on a company agreeing to pay a director's remuneration free of income tax or agreeing to vary the director's remuneration in line with changes to income tax (CA 1985, s. 311(1)) was repealed by the 2006 Act (s. 1177) with effect from 6 April 2007.

Bonus

8.62 A director may also be entitled to participate in discretionary and/or contractual bonus schemes. Companies often link bonuses to the company's performance in the relevant financial year (or the performance of particular subsidiaries for which a director is responsible) by reference to profits and the individual director's performance. The bonus commonly takes the form of a cash payment, but some companies have adopted deferred share bonus plans whereby a part of the bonus is payable in shares which must be held by the director for a period of time. In many cases, the bonus is only payable on production of an auditor's certificate confirming that the amount is due.

8.63 The ABI/NAPF Joint Statement 2008 states that corporate objectives set for executives by the board should be clear and transparent to make it easier to determine how an executive has performed and therefore to prevent payment for failure. Wherever possible, objectives against which performance will be measured should be made public (para. 3.2). If the bonus scheme is genuinely discretionary, there will be no contractual entitlement to bonus even when individual/company performance targets are met, although the company would be under the general duty not to act in breach of the duty of trust and confidence in the way it operated the scheme (i.e. the company should not exercise its discretion perversely or irrationally). If the scheme is contractual, the director is entitled to be paid a bonus calculated in accordance with the bonus formula and the company cannot refuse to pay it or withhold any part of it. Whether or not the scheme is deemed to be discretionary or contractual will be critical to assessing the level of damages in the event of non-payment or an early termination of the service contract.

8.64 Bonus schemes often provide that an employee must be in employment at the payment date to be eligible for a bonus and a recent decision of the Court of Appeal has confirmed that an employer may rely on such conditions (*Keen v. Commerzbank* [2007] IRLR 132). If the scheme is intended to be discretionary, this should be reflected in the drafting of the scheme rules and any other relevant documentation.

8.65 An employee wishing to challenge the amount of a discretionary bonus has a high evidential hurdle to clear. The fact that the employer may have paid less than a manager's recommendation and less than reflected the success of the employee's team was held in the *Keen* decision to be insufficient, given the employer's wide discretion in fluctuating market and labour conditions. The Court of Appeal in *Keen* suggested that an exceptionally strong case is required to demonstrate a breach of contract on grounds of irrationality or perversity. In a separate decision, an employee who had been on sabbatical for most of the bonus year failed in his claim that the Bank's decision to award him a nil bonus was irrational and perverse (*Ridgway v. JP Morgan Chase Bank National Association* [2007] EWHC 1325 (QB)).

8.66 Perhaps the greater risk facing companies is that a successful case will be brought on grounds of unlawful discrimination or by reference to the 'anti-avoidance' implied term that an employer will not terminate a contract in order to avoid an obligation to make a payment to the employee (a point which was held to be arguable in principle when advanced at a preliminary hearing in the case of *Takacs v. Barclays Services Jersey Ltd* [2007] IRLR 877). The dispute was subsequently settled out of court.

Cash bonus on commencement of employment

8.67 Offer letters may provide for a cash bonus payable when the director commences employment. This is known as a 'golden hello'. Golden hellos often take the form of an immediate cash payment or a guaranteed bonus for the first year/part-year of employment when a discretionary bonus scheme would otherwise operate and are taxable as income in the normal way. Golden hellos often provide that an immediate cash payment would become repayable if the director left within a specified period of commencing employment. Such payments can be justified where they are needed to attract the best recruits.

Pension arrangements

8.68 Pension benefits may be a very significant element of a director's remuneration package. Benefits for directors may be provided through an existing company pension scheme set up for all employees (although often special sections may be appropriate for directors offering a higher scale of benefits, a lower retirement age and special terms on early termination of employment), or through a separate pension scheme for executives, or via contributions to a director's personal pension arrangement.

8.69 There are no limits on employer contributions to registered pension schemes. Employer contributions qualify for tax relief if they are made 'wholly and exclusively for the purposes of the employer's trade'. However, under the new pensions tax regime, the total employer and employee contributions (or the value of the benefit accrual, if the scheme is defined benefit) which can be made to a pension scheme each year and still qualify for tax relief are valued against an 'annual allowance'. An upper rate income tax charge (currently 40%) will be levied on the amount of any excess. HM Revenue & Customs has set the annual allowance at £235,000 for the year 2008/9, rising to £245,000 for the year 2009/10 and to £255,000 for 2010/11.

8.70 With effect from 6 April 2006, the compulsory earnings cap, which set a limit on the amount of earnings in respect of which benefits could be provided under a pension scheme, was abolished. This was replaced by a single lifetime limit on retirement savings for tax purposes. Funds in excess of this 'lifetime allowance' will be subject, on vesting, to a recovery charge of 55%, if taken as a lump sum; and 25% if taken as pension. Transitional protection applies to those individuals whose retirement savings were close to, or in excess of, the lifetime allowance at 6 April 2006. The lifetime allowance is £1.65 million for the tax year 2008/9, £1.75 million for the tax year 2009/10 and will rise to £1.8 million in 2010/11.

8.71 Best practice corporate governance guidance recommends that there should be full disclosure to shareholders of the extent to which actual and potential liabilities, such as pension promises or early retirement arrangements, are funded together with any aggregate outstanding unfunded liabilities. The ABI Guidelines recommend that remuneration committees bear in mind that pension entitlements may represent a significant and potentially costly item of remuneration that is not directly linked to performance. Payments in lieu of pension scheme participation should be clearly disclosed and treated as a separate non-salary benefit and should be excluded from the calculation of bonus entitlements and share scheme grants. Further, changes in pension benefit entitlements or to transfer values reflecting significant changes in actuarial and other relevant assumptions should be fully identified and explained. Where changes to pension benefit entitlements or transfers are of a discretionary nature, the ABI Guidelines state that this should be made clear and justification provided.

Long-term incentive schemes

8.72 Another key component of a director's remuneration can be a long-term incentive scheme which typically offers the director the right to acquire shares in the company or its parent company. Such arrangements will often take the form of a share option, where the director will benefit from any increase in share price, or the grant of a share award, where the director can acquire shares at nil or nominal cost. These awards will generally be dependent on the company's performance, assessed by reference to pre-set targets.

8.73 Alternatively, they may take the form of a deferred and matching bonus award, whereby part of the director's annual cash bonus is taken in the form of shares and, if left with the trustees of the scheme for a certain period, will qualify the director for a matching allocation of additional free shares. Again, the level of the matching award will generally be dependent on the company's performance.

8.74 The main types of schemes for directors are set out below.

8.75 Discretionary share option schemes. This type of scheme normally gives the director the right to buy shares in the company at an exercise price equal to market value at the date of grant of the option. The option will normally be exercisable from the third anniversary of grant until the tenth anniversary of grant (provided the director is still in employment), although some companies will allow a proportion of the option to become exercisable where the director leaves in certain specified circumstances. These type of schemes are usually established in two parts – an approved part (which normally attracts income tax and National Insurance contributions reliefs on options over shares with an aggregate value of up to £30,000 per participant at the original grant price, provided the options are not exercised for at least three years from grant) and an unapproved part (which provides for unapproved options in excess of this limit and which will usually be subject to PAYE and National Insurance contributions).

8.76 Enterprise management incentive (EMI) scheme. EMIs are another type of approved option designed to assist higher-risk trading companies to attract key executives by offering them generous tax reliefs on share options over shares with a value of up to £120,000 at the date of grant. A company, whether quoted or unquoted, can qualify for an EMI provided its gross assets do not exceed £30 million, it has fewer than 250 employees, it is not under the control of another company and it carries on a 'qualifying trade' mainly in the UK. Most trades will qualify, but the following activities, among others, are deemed insufficiently high risk and therefore will not qualify:

- property development;
- shipbuilding;
- coal and steel production;
- hotel management;
- leasing;
- banking; and
- insurance and other financial services.

8.77 There is an aggregate £3 million limit on the total value of shares in the company over which unexercised options under an EMI may exist at any time.

8.78 There is no requirement under an EMI for a minimum period before exercise. Qualifying companies may consequently choose their own exercise periods provided the option can be exercised within ten years of grant. There will normally be no income tax or National Insurance contributions to pay when an EMI option is exercised provided the option was granted at no less than market value (options can be granted at a discount to market value, but any such discount is taxable on exercise). When the shares are sold, capital gains tax will apply to any untaxed gains at the more favourable rate of 18%.

8.79 Share award schemes. Share award schemes, unlike discretionary options, give the right to acquire shares at nil or nominal cost. The awards will generally be structured as a free share award, nil-cost option or as the award of restricted (forfeitable) shares. The extent to which those shares may be received, usually at the end of a three-year period, will depend on the company's performance, assessed by reference to pre-set targets. Share award schemes are unapproved schemes, and so the value of the shares received will be subject to income tax and National Insurance contributions on vesting. Increasingly, companies are requiring their directors to defer part of their annual cash bonus, which is then taken in the form of shares and, if not sold for a certain period, will qualify the director for a matching allocation of additional free shares. Again, the level of the matching award will generally be dependent on the company's performance.

8.80 'Phantom' share schemes. Phantom share schemes are cash bonus schemes made to look like a share option scheme, or other long-term incentive plan, with the amount of the cash bonus mirroring the gain which would have been made on a true share scheme. They are usually used where a share scheme is not possible, but where the company wishes to link part of the director's remuneration to the share price as an incentive.

8.81 Eligibility for participation in any such scheme will be determined by the particular scheme rules which may provide that the board or a board committee, namely the remuneration committee, shall determine whether an individual participates in a scheme in any given year and the extent of that participation. It is therefore advisable not to refer to participation in incentive schemes in the director's service agreement, save to say that the director may be invited to participate in schemes, subject to their rules.

8.82 Share awards for directors usually involve significant numbers of shares and therefore often involve unapproved schemes in addition to schemes approved by HM Revenue & Customs, which benefit from tax advantages but have restrictive grant limits. Unapproved schemes have the benefit of limits set only by shareholders, but do not have the tax advantages of approved schemes.

8.83 Under the Listing Rules, any scheme which may involve the issue of new shares requires shareholder approval (LR 9.4). A scheme which uses existing shares may also require shareholder approval if one or more of the directors is eligible to participate and the scheme involves conditions in respect of service and/or performance to be satisfied over more than one financial year. This principle is reiterated at para. B.2.4 of the Combined Code.

8.84 Listed companies (and companies considering a listing) will be keen to ensure that their share schemes are supported by institutional shareholders. Such companies will also need to take into account the guidelines issued by the ABI when drafting their share schemes. These guidelines provide recommendations on, for example, the maximum amount of new shares which may be used under the schemes and the use of performance targets to link remuneration to performance. The ABI Guidelines provide that share-based incentives should align the interests of executive directors with those of shareholders and link reward to performance over the longer term. Vesting should be based on performance conditions over a period (not less than three years) appropriate to the strategic objectives of the company. Any new share-based incentives should be subject to prior shareholder approval. Where any changes to share incentive award levels or remuneration structures are being proposed or new incentives, disclosures should be made to shareholders of such changes together with the remuneration committee's rationale for the changes and an explanation of the costs.

8.85 The share plan rules will often contain detailed provisions setting out how a departing employee will be treated in relation to share options and awards. Often there will be an 'automatic lapse' provision, which provides that the employee is not entitled to compensation on termination of employment for any loss of any rights and benefits under the scheme (*Micklefield v. SAC Technology Ltd* [1990] IRLR 218). The employer may, in certain circumstances, have a discretion under the terms of the share option scheme itself to allow options to vest. If it does, it will need to show that it has not acted perversely or irrationally in exercising any discretion.

8.86 Jurisdiction and governing law issues may impact on the enforceability of provisions in long-term incentive schemes for global companies. For example, even if such agreements state that they are governed by foreign law and subject to the exclusive jurisdiction of foreign courts, an individual domiciled in the UK may succeed in insisting that any proceedings brought by the employer against him in relation to the agreement are brought in the UK. An important Court of Appeal decision in 2007 illustrated that Council Regulation (EC) 44/2001 could be invoked to obtain an anti-suit injunction in the English courts to restrain overseas proceedings, on the basis that an employee in the European Union can only be sued by the employer in the employee's home country *(Samengo-Turner & ors v. J & H Marsh & McLennan (Services) Ltd and ors* [2007] IRLR 237).

8.87 Further, the High Court recently refused to enforce restrictive covenants contained in an agreement relating to a long-term incentive scheme which was subject to foreign governing law as the covenants were unenforceable under English law (*Duarte v. Black and Decker* [2007] EWHC 2720 (QB)).

Insured benefits

8.88 A well-drafted service agreement will often contain detailed provisions of any contractual benefits, such as private medical insurance, provided by the company. A company handbook may contain details of other contractual and discretionary benefits.

8.89 Where a director is in receipt of ill-health benefits, such as permanent health insurance (PHI), the company should give proper consideration to how such entitlement may be affected by the termination of the contract. Many PHI providers cease to pay out (or continue to pay out) benefits where an individual leaves employment. Case law has established that a term may be implied in the contract that the company may not lawfully dismiss an employee if this would result in their losing their entitlement to PHI cover, save where there is gross misconduct or good cause for dismissal such as redundancy (*Aspden v. Webb Poulty* [1996] IRLR 521; *Jenvey v. Australian Broadcasting Corporation* [2002] IRLR 520). A recent Employment Appeal Tribunal (EAT) decision went further by suggesting that to dismiss an employee who has been on long-term absence on grounds of ill-health without considering the impact on entitlement to ill-health retirement benefits could be an unfair dismissal for which the maximum compensation award is £66,200 from 1 February 2009 (the previous cap was £63,000). In that case, the employer apparently terminated specifically to avoid the possibility of incurring the cost of providing ill-health retirement pension and this was held to be an unfair dismissal (*First West Yorkshire Limited t/a First Leeds v. Haigh* [2008] IRLR 182). Consideration should also be given, before undertaking any process to terminate employment, to whether an employee on long-term sickness absence may have a disability within the meaning of the Disability Discrimination Act 1995.

Role of the remuneration committee, requirements of the Combined Code, and the ABI Guidelines on Executive Remuneration

8.90 The remuneration committee plays a vital role in setting the levels and structure of directors' remuneration. Both the Combined Code and the ABI Guidelines set out best practice guidance on directors' remuneration and the role of the remuneration committee. Non-executive directors should be appointed to the committee to avoid executive directors setting their own remuneration.

Requirements of the Combined Code in relation to directors' remuneration

8.91 The Combined Code contains general guidance as to directors' remuneration policy (see **Appendix 1, paras B1.1–B1.4**). The remuneration committee should provide packages needed to attract, retain and motivate executive directors of the quality required to run the company successfully, but should avoid paying more than is necessary for this purpose. A significant proportion of executive directors' remuneration should be structured to link rewards to corporate and individual performance. Performance-related elements of executive directors' remuneration should be designed to align their interests with those of shareholders and to give directors keen incentives to perform to the highest levels. Executive share options should not be offered at a discount save as permitted by the Listing Rules. Remuneration for non-executive directors should reflect the time commitment and responsibilities of the role and share options should be avoided.

8.92 There should be a formal and transparent procedure for developing policy on executive remuneration and for fixing the remuneration packages of individual directors (Combined Code, para. B.2). No director should be involved in deciding his remuneration. The board should establish a remuneration committee of at least three (in the case of smaller companies, two) independent non-executive directors. The remuneration committee should make its terms of reference available, explaining its role and the authority delegated to it by the board. It should have delegated responsibility for setting remuneration for all executive directors and the chairman, including pension rights and any compensation payments. The board itself or, where required by the articles of association, the shareholders should determine the remuneration of the non-executive directors within the limits set in the articles of association. Shareholders should be invited specifically to approve all new long-term incentive schemes as defined in the Listing Rules, and significant changes to existing schemes, save in the circumstances permitted by the Listing Rules.

8.93 Schedule A to the Combined Code sets out various provisions in relation to performance-related remuneration which the committee should follow. Performance conditions should be relevant, stretching and designed to enhance the business. Upper limits should be set and disclosed. Directors' eligibility for long-term incentive plans should be considered and any new plans should be approved by shareholders. Shares granted or deferred remuneration should not vest, and options should not be exercisable, in less than three years. Grants under executive share options and other long-term incentive schemes should normally be phased rather than awarded in one large block. In general, annual bonuses and benefits in kind should not be pensionable and remuneration committees should consider the pension consequences and associated costs to the company of salary and other increases, especially for directors close to retirement.

The ABI Guidelines on Executive Remuneration

8.94 The revised 2007 ABI Guidelines on Executive Remuneration Policies and Practices were published on 3 December 2007. Boards should demonstrate that performance-based remuneration arrangements are clearly aligned with business strategy and market requirements, and are regularly reviewed. The overall arrangements should be prudent and well communicated, act as an effective incentive and recognise shareholder expectations. Remuneration committees should comprise independent non-executive directors who bring thought and scrutiny to all aspects of remuneration and should maintain a constructive and timely dialogue with their major institutional shareholders on remuneration policy and practice, including issues relating to share incentive schemes. There should be transparency on all matters relating to the remuneration of present and past directors and, where appropriate, other senior executives. Shareholders' attention should be drawn to any special arrangements and significant changes since the previous remuneration report.

8.95 The ABI Guidelines provide that remuneration committees are responsible for ensuring that the mix of incentives reflects the company's needs, establishes an appropriate balance between fixed and variable remuneration, and is based on targets that are stretching, verifiable and relevant. Remuneration committees should satisfy themselves as to the accuracy of performance measures that govern vesting of variable and share-based remuneration and establish effective procedures for disclosure and communication of strategic objectives, which enable shareholders to take an informed and considered view of remuneration policy and its implementation. Where appropriate, account should be taken of the ABI Guidelines on Responsible Investment Disclosure. Remuneration levels should properly reflect the contribution of executives and there should not be unjustified windfalls and inappropriate gains arising from the operation of share incentive schemes and other associated incentives. Effective avenues of redress should be considered where performance achievements are subsequently found to have been significantly mis-stated so that bonuses and other incentives should not have been paid. Particular attention should be paid by remuneration committees to arrangements for senior executives who are not board members but have a significant influence over the company's ability to meet its strategic objectives.

8.96 Further, in relation to pay, bonus provisions, contracts and severance, the ABI Guidelines provide that remuneration committees should ensure that base pay reflects the performance of the executives concerned. Bonuses should reflect actual achievements against carefully chosen and monitored individual and corporate performance targets. Any material *ex gratia* payments should be fully explained, justified and subject to shareholder approval prior to payment. Shareholders are not supportive of transaction bonuses that reward directors and other executives for effecting transactions irrespective of their future financial consequences. Annual bonuses should not be pensionable. Remuneration committees should scrutinise all other benefits, including benefits in kind and other financial arrangements, to ensure they are justified, appropriately valued and suitably disclosed.

Restrictions under the Model Code

8.97 Directors of listed companies are also subject to the restrictions and minimum standard of good practice set out under the Model Code (which forms part of the Listing Rules). The Model Code restricts the ability of directors, senior managers and certain employees of listed companies to deal in their company's securities in addition to those imposed by the market abuse and insider dealing legislation. Directors of listed companies are also subject to restrictions under the Disclosure and Transparency Rules with regard to disclosure of transactions in the company's shares.

Directors' obligations in accounts and reports and audit in relation to directors' remuneration

8.98 The new regime for directors' report and accounts and audit under Parts 15 and 16 of the Companies Act 2006 came into force on 6 April 2008. (The key changes from the 1985 Act and details of the new regime are covered in more detail in **Chapter 7**.) Many of the provisions from the 1985 Act relating to the preparation of a directors' report as referred to in the Directors' Remuneration Report Regulations 2002 are retained, including the requirement for directors to prepare a directors' report for each financial year of the company, which includes the names of the directors and the principal activities of the company in the course of the relevant financial year (ss. 415(1) and 416(1), 2006 Act).

The Listing Rules

8.99 Paragraph 9.8.8R of the Listing Rules (which replaces Listing Rule 12.43A) requires the board of a listed company to include certain information on directors' remuneration in its annual report and accounts to shareholders including, for example:

- a statement of the company's policy on executive directors' remuneration;
- information on the amount of each element in the remuneration package of every director;
- details of any long-term incentive schemes;
- an explanation and justification of any element of a director's remuneration, other than basic salary, which is pensionable;
- details of any director's service contract with a notice period in excess of one year or with provisions for predetermined compensation on termina-

tion which exceeds one year's salary and benefits in kind, giving the reasons for such notice period;

- for money purchase pension schemes, details of the contribution or allowance payable or made by the listed company in respect of each director;
- for defined benefit pension schemes, information on the amount of the increase during the period under review (excluding inflation), and the accumulated total amount at the end of the period, in respect of the accrued benefit to which each director has become entitled over the year, and either the transfer value of the increase (less any contributions made by the director) or sufficient information to assess the transfer value.

Garden leave and post-termination restrictive covenants

Garden leave

8.100 Many service contracts for directors and senior employees contain a provision entitling the employer to require the director to provide no (or limited) services, to stay away from the company's premises and to have no contact with any of the company's employees, customers or suppliers for a certain period ('garden leave'). In the absence of an express garden leave clause, the company should obtain the individual's express consent, preferably in writing, before placing him on garden leave, otherwise imposing such an arrangement is likely to amount to a serious breach of contract and/or constructive dismissal. However, a recent High Court decision held that where the employee is in serious breach of his own contractual duties and so has demonstrated that he is not ready or willing to do the work, the employer may legitimately put him on garden leave even in the absence of an express garden leave clause (*SG & R Valuation Service Co v. Boudrais* [2008] EWHC 1340). It therefore remains best practice to include express garden leave clauses.

8.101 Garden leave is commonly used when a director is serving out a period of notice (while still remaining an employee), but the provision may be drafted to permit garden leave during any period of employment. The company will be obliged to pay salary and benefits during this period. However, garden leave has the advantage of keeping the individual out of the market without having to rely on the enforceability of restrictive covenants. If the garden leave provision has been properly drafted, the director will be prevented from working for a competitor and will remain subject to the duty of fidelity and good faith during the garden leave period. The English courts will only exercise their discretion to enforce garden leave if there is a properly drafted provision and the company has a legitimate business interest to protect. As a broad rule of thumb, it will be difficult to enforce a period of garden leave in excess of 12 months.

8.102 A controversial High Court decision suggested that the implied duty of good faith and fidelity that an employee would normally owe to his employer does not continue during a garden leave period, notwithstanding the continuance of the implied obligation of trust and confidence (*Symbian Ltd v. Christensen* [2001] IRLR 7). Although commentators have expressed doubt about the correctness of this decision, it is advisable to ensure that the contract expressly states that the duty of good faith and fidelity shall continue during this garden leave period.

8.103 The intention and usual effect of a period of garden leave is to keep the executive away from confidential information, employees and customers. Case law has suggested that the courts may set off any period of garden leave against the period of any post-termination restraint. The rationale for this is that if the executive possesses confidential information with a shelf-life of six months, and he is put on garden leave for six months until his employment terminates, then the shelf-life of the confidential information has expired. Given that he has not been at work or exposed to any additional confidential information during the garden leave period, there is no basis for any additional restriction in terms of a non-compete. However, in a robust decision of the High Court in May 2007, an eight-month non-compete clause was upheld without any reduction made for the three-month notice period that the employee had spent on garden leave (*Extec Screens & Crushers Ltd v. David Rice* [2007] EWHC 1043(QB)). In practice, many service agreements do provide for the period of post-termination restrictions to be reduced by any period spent on garden leave to increase the likelihood that the overall period of restraint will be considered to go no further than reasonably necessary to protect the company's legitimate interests.

8.104 In the absence of express provisions, departing executive directors would only be restrained from using or disclosing highly confidential information, such as trade secrets. The basic principle is that for a restraint of trade to be enforceable the covenant must be both reasonable in the interests of the contracting parties and reasonable in the interests of the public. Case law has established that the following are capable of being legitimate business interests:

- confidential information;
- customer connection;
- supplier connection; and
- stability of the workforce.

8.105 The most common examples found in executive directors' service contracts aim to restrain the individual from competing with the company or poaching customers, suppliers or employees. There is an inherent tension between the company's interest in protecting its confidential information, client base and workforce and the interests of departing employees who wish to have the freedom to develop their careers elsewhere.

8.106 If a provision goes beyond reasonable protection of the legitimate business interest, then it will be void and unenforceable as an unlawful restraint of trade, unless the courts consider that they can sever (i.e. cross out or 'blue pencil') the offending words. Blue pencilling is only permitted where the restriction would be enforceable without the offending words and the wording can be read properly from a grammatical perspective. When determining the enforceability of restrictive covenants, the court will also consider the 'balance of convenience' (i.e. the potential impact on the company, the departing director and the new employer or new business) of enforcing the covenant. For example, where upholding a non-competition restriction would result in the employee being unable to work in his field of expertise but the damage to the company would be insignificant, this may influence the court not to enforce the restriction.

Non-compete

8.107 A non-compete will only be enforceable if it goes no further than is reasonably necessary to protect the company's confidential information (or in exceptional cases another legitimate business interest). A court will have regard to several factors when assessing whether a non-compete goes too far. The key factors taken into account are:

- the geographic scope of the restriction; and
- the duration of the restriction.

8.108 Covenant key points

The covenant must be drafted to reflect the geographical scope of the particular company's business. An attempt to restrain an individual from seeking employment in a jurisdiction in which the company does not operate is unlikely to be enforceable.

Similarly, the length of any restraint must correspond to the shelf-life of any truly confidential information that the executive may have. If a company was seeking to enforce a six-month non-compete, it would have to provide evidence to a court that the information in respect of which protection was sought would remain commercially sensitive for the full period of the restraint. Evidence would have to be produced to demonstrate this, including, where necessary, providing to the court (on a confidential basis) details of the nature of the information and an explanation of why it must remain confidential for that period. It is relatively common for companies to allow a carve-out from any non-compete provision to enable a director to hold non-material interests in competing businesses for investment purposes. A common provision will permit the executive to hold up to 3% of shares in listed and 20% of shares non-listed companies.

8.109 Non-compete provisions are typically the hardest to enforce as they impose the most onerous restraint on the departing executive. However, the Court of Appeal recently upheld a non-compete clause in a service contract which restrained an employee from working for a competitor for twelve months (*Thomas v. Farr plc and Hanover Park Commercial Ltd* [2007] IRLR 419). This case demonstrated that, in the right circumstances, the courts are willing to enforce onerous non-competition covenants, even when they last for a relatively long period. The court in *Thomas v. Farr* recognised that it may sometimes be difficult to police lesser restrictions (such as non-dealing or non-solicitation clauses, particularly in relation to senior employees who have people reporting to them) and that this is a factor in favour of enforcing a broader, non-competition restriction. If a company's business interests can be, or could have been, sufficiently protected by one of the restrictions that has less of an impact as a restraint of trade, for example, a non-solicitation of customers provision, then it is likely that the court will hold the non-compete to be unenforceable.

Non-dealing and non-solicitation with customers/prospective customers

8.110 Courts recognise the company's legitimate interest in protecting its customer connections. The courts have upheld covenants restraining a departing executive from contacting a customer or client for a specified period of time, thereby giving the company sufficient time to build up a new relationship with that customer or client. The duration for such provisions should be tied to the company's cycle of dealing with its customers. For example, if the customer is in regular contact with the company (e.g. weekly), then the period of any post-termination restraint should reflect the fact that the company will have an opportunity to build up a new relationship within a few months, and a restraint for twelve months would be unlikely to be enforceable.

8.111 Companies seeking to enforce non-dealing and non-solicitation clauses may take comfort from the pragmatic approach taken by the Court of Appeal in *Beckett Investments Management Group Ltd v. Hall* [2007] IRLR 793. A non-dealing clause which purported to restrain two individuals from dealing with past and present clients with whom they had previously dealt for the purpose of providing specified services was upheld in relation to both the parent company, with whom the individuals had their employment contract, and other group companies for whom the individuals carried out work. The decision may be indicative of a more robust approach to enforcing covenants to ensure they benefit the corporate group that they were intended to protect. Fundamental to this decision was the judge's emphasis on the need to consider the 'practical utility' of the clause. Where a restriction has been carefully drafted to protect a legitimate trade interest, the courts will normally endeavour to construe it in such a way that the restraint is valid and enforceable.

8.112 Key point

Care should be taken at the drafting stage to tailor the covenant to an appropriate temporal and geographical scope to increase the likelihood of enforceability as it cannot be taken for granted that the court will, in any one case, conclude that the parties' intentions are sufficiently clear or that a broad-brush approach will be taken to interpretation.

Non-solicitation of suppliers

8.113 A non-solicitation provision is designed to prevent a departing executive from interfering with the supply of any goods or services to the company by drawing on connections he may have with a supplier.

8.114 The legitimate interest for the company to protect is its connections with the supplier and, to the extent that the supply continues uninterrupted on the same basis, then the interest will have been sufficiently protected. There is no legitimate basis for seeking to prevent the executive from dealing with the supplier completely. The provision is mainly aimed at preventing the executive from trying to influence the supplier to increase charges or to stop or reduce the supply to the company. These provisions are rarely contentious.

Non-solicitation of employees

8.115 These provisions are designed to prevent the executive from drawing on either his internal knowledge of the employees of the company or his influence as a senior member of the team, to encourage the employees to leave the employment of the company (generally to join the executive at his new company).

8.116 The legitimate interest that is protectable here is the stability of the workforce as a whole. Therefore, the restrictions can go no further than this. The restriction generally has to be limited to the solicitation of senior or technically skilled individuals with whom the executive had dealt before leaving his employment (and therefore over whom he could exercise any form of influence) or in relation to whom the executive has confidential information that he would not otherwise have had but for his employment with the company.

8.117 The duration of these provisions should be no longer than is necessary for the departing executive's unfair advantage to be neutralised (e.g. by the information he has about the employees becoming stale or by his influence over them becoming diluted).

Inducing a breach of contract

8.118 A company faced with a situation where a key employee or a team has been poached by a competitor may also consider bringing a claim against the new employer on grounds of inducing a breach of contract. It will be necessary to demonstrate that there was a deliberate intention to induce a breach of contract. Carelessness or negligence about inducing a breach is not considered to be sufficient to establish the tort of inducing a breach of contract (*OBG Ltd and ors v. Allan and ors; Douglas and ors v. Hellos! Ltd and ors; Mainstream Properties Ltd v. Young and ors* [2007] 4 All ER 545).

8.119 A company that obtains an unfair competitive advantage by inducing employees to breach their contract to join a competitor may be restrained from contacting or doing business with the former employer's clients by a springboard injunction (*UBS Wealth Management (UK) Ltd v. Vestra Wealth LLP* [2008] EWHC 1974). This remedy was traditionally granted only to restrain a company that had obtained an unfair competitive advantage through misuse of confidential information.

> **8.120 Key point**
>
> It is important to ensure that the competitor and any recruitment consultants are made fully aware of the existence of the employment contract and key terms which would be breached should the employees join the new employer. The competitor will then find it more difficult to argue that it did not have actual knowledge of the contract or that it did not intend its recruitment of the individual to induce a breach.

Fiduciary duties

8.121 A fiduciary duty imposes a high obligation on the director to act in the best interests of the company, over and above their personal interest. This may include reporting to the company the existence of any competitor activity and also a duty on the director to report his own unlawful activity (*Fassihi and others v. Item Software (UK) Ltd [2004]* EWCA Civ 1244).

8.122 Some fiduciary duties have been codified in chapter 2, Part 10 of the 2006 Act. For example, the statutory duty to avoid conflicts of interest which came into force on 1 October 2008 reflects the fiduciary duty of an employee not to place himself in a position where his interests conflict with the company's. However, existing case law will continue to be relevant to the interpretation of this fiduciary duty.

8.123 Fiduciary duties require the director not to profit from his position at the expense of the company and to have undivided loyalty to the company. There is also a duty of confidentiality which survives the termination of the relationship between the director and the company; there will be a continuing duty to preserve the confidentiality of any information acquired by the director during the course of his appointment. Directors owe fiduciary duties to the company, but employees do not generally owe fiduciary duties.

8.124 However, case law has shown that senior employees may owe fiduciary duties to the company in certain circumstances. For example, an employee who holds a particular position or status within an organisation might be considered by the court to owe fiduciary duties. It is necessary to identify the duties undertaken by the employee and to ask 'whether in all the circumstances he has placed himself in a position where he must act solely in the interest of his employer' (Elias J, in *University of Nottingham v. Fishel* [2000] IRLR 471). A recent case suggested that certain aspects of a role might give rise to a fiduciary obligation even where the position or role of the person as a whole might not be considered sufficiently senior to give rise to fiduciary duties (*Shepherds Investments Ltd v. Walters* [2007] IRLR 110).

8.125 It will be necessary to analyse all the facts, including the responsibilities placed on the individual and the overall commercial context, to determine whether or not a fiduciary duty arises in any particular employment relationship.

8.126 A full analysis of fiduciary duties falls outside the scope of this chapter; however, one important point to note is that the remedies for breach of a fiduciary duty are different from those arising in relation to a breach of contract. In particular, a fiduciary may have to account for profits he has made where he has been unjustly enriched at the company's expense. The company may recover sums for breach of fiduciary duty without having to demonstrate to the court the actual loss suffered.

Statutory protection for employees

8.127 Directors as employees will be covered by the mandatory minimum protections under UK employment legislation. These include the right not to be unfairly dismissed, protection from unlawful discrimination, minimum annual holiday entitlement, statutory sick pay and other basic rights. Brief details of the key rights are set out below.

8.128 Unfair dismissal. After one year of service (which includes any service with a linked, group company) an employee has the statutory right not to be unfairly dismissed. This protection covers both actual dismissals and constructive dismissals. An actual dismissal is where an employer takes steps to terminate the employment relationship by serving notice of the termination or terminating the employment summarily. A constructive dismissal occurs where an employee resigns on the basis of an apparent 'repudiatory breach of contract' by the employer and treats himself as having been dismissed. An Employment Tribunal may award compensation made up of a basic award of up to £10,500 from 1 February 2009 (the previous cap was £9,900), depending on age and length of service and a compensatory award to reflect loss, capped at £66,200 from 1 February 2009 (the previous cap was £63,000). (The caps normally increase on 1 February each year.)

8.129 Redundancy. An employee dismissed for redundancy is entitled to a statutory redundancy payment (capped at £10,500 from 1 February 2009) if he has at least two years' service. Some employers provide enhanced redundancy payments. A fair redundancy procedure involves applying fair selection criteria in a fair way, looking for alternative work and consulting with the employee on an individual basis. A failure to carry out a fair individual redundancy procedure is likely to result in a finding of unfair dismissal. Where 20 or more redundancies are proposed within a period of 90 days or less, there are also obligations to undertake a collective information and consultation process with employee representatives or trade union members. Failure to follow the process in a collective redundancy situation properly can result in awards of up to 90 days' pay to each of the affected employees and can render their dismissals unfair.

8.130 Discrimination. In England, it is unlawful to discriminate on recruitment, during employment and, in certain instances, post-employment on grounds of:

- sex;
- pregnancy;
- marital status/registered civil partner;
- gender reassignment;

- race, ethnic origin, national origin, nationality, colour;
- disability (the legislation includes a duty to make reasonable adjustments to accommodate a disabled employee);
- sexual orientation;
- religion, religious belief or philosophical belief;
- part-time or fixed-term status;
- trade union membership, or
- age.

8.131 The law prohibits direct discrimination (less favourable treatment on one of the above grounds); indirect discrimination (essentially where a practice or policy applied to all staff has a disproportionate adverse effect on a minority group), harassment (where an individual engages in unwanted conduct that has the purpose or effect of violating another's dignity or creating an intimidating, hostile, degrading, humiliating or offensive environment) and victimisation (treating someone less favourably because of their involvement in a tribunal claim or because they intimated a discrimination claim). Employers may raise a defence of justification in relation to any indirect discrimination claims. However, no such defence exists in relation to claims of direct discrimination (save in relation to claims of age discrimination). There are no statutory limits to the compensation awards for discrimination claims. Awards usually reflect future loss of earnings to compensate an individual for the earnings he would have received had he not suffered the unlawful discrimination for the period until they get another job of a similar level. Awards can also be made for injury to feelings and personal injury. Discrimination claims can also bring bad publicity for a company, even if a claim is ultimately unsuccessful. Equality between the sexes is also protected by the Equal Pay Act 1970 which requires that men and women in the same employment receive broadly the same remuneration when employed on like work (work of the same or broadly similar nature), work of equal value, or work rated as equivalent under a job evaluation scheme.

8.132 Whistleblowing. It is unlawful to dismiss an employee or otherwise subject him to any form of detriment on the grounds of his having made a 'protected disclosure'. A protected disclosure is one which, in the reasonable belief of the employee (whether or not actually true), tends to show:

- the commission of a criminal offence;
- a failure to comply with a legal obligations. This is very broad and can include an obligation owed to the whistleblower under his employment contract;
- a miscarriage of justice;
- danger to the health and safety of any individual;

- environmental damage; or
- information tending to show one of the above has been or is likely to be deliberately concealed.

8.133 Complex issues may arise in regulated sectors, such as financial services, because a company must also consider its disclosure obligations to the regulatory authority (e.g. the FSA) in addition to employment law considerations. Damages for a claim for whistleblowing are uncapped and are generally treated on the same basis as the approach taken to unlawful discrimination outlined above.

8.134 Working time. There is legislation in the UK prescribing minimum rest breaks, maximum working hours and minimum annual leave entitlement. Employees are able to opt out of these maximum working hours provisions and there are certain exemptions for senior managers and directors in any event who have unmeasured working time. In basic terms, all employees and other workers have a statutory right to a minimum of 24 days' paid holiday in any year (this will increase to 28 days' paid holiday from April 2009). The eight English public holidays can be included in making up this total. There are also obligations on employers to keep records of this information.

8.135 Business transfers or change of service provider. Employees have significant protection in the event of a business transfer or change of service provider under the Transfer of Undertakings (Protection of Employment) Regulations 2006 (TUPE), which implement the EU Acquired Rights Directive 2001/23/EC. Corporate mergers, out- or in-sourcings, changes of service provider and intra-group transfers can all be covered, depending on the circumstances. When a business (or part of it) or a contract for the provision of services is transferred, the employees engaged wholly or mainly in connection with the business or contract immediately prior to transfer shall automatically transfer to the employment of the purchaser or new service provider on their existing terms and conditions of employment (with limited exceptions) with continuity of service preserved. There are collective consultation obligations to inform and consult representatives of affected employees in relation to the transfer. Any dismissals where the sole or principal reason for the dismissal is the transfer itself or a reason connected with the transfer that is not an economic, technical or organisational reason entailing changes in the workforce of the seller or buyer will be automatically unfair. Liability for transfer-connected dismissals may transfer to the buyer if TUPE applies, even where the dismissal is made by the seller prior to the transfer and there can be significant difficulties changing the terms and conditions of employment where the reason for the change is related to the transfer.

8.136 Domestic/European Works Councils. Some companies have European or domestic works councils which they are required to inform and consult about matters that could significantly affect employment.

8.137 Family-friendly rights and statutory sick pay

- Statutory sick pay. Employers are required to pay statutory sick pay to employees who are off work due to illness or injury. Employees are entitled to statutory sick pay (£79.15 from April 2009) during sick leave for up to 28 weeks during any three-year period. In certain circumstances some of these payments can be recovered by a company from the government. However, in the majority of cases, employers offer sick pay policies which provide for payments in excess of the statutory minimum.
- Maternity leave. A pregnant worker is entitled to 52 weeks' maternity leave and to return to work after her maternity leave. Those with 26 weeks' service at the relevant time are entitled to statutory maternity pay (90% of normal weekly earnings for the first six weeks followed by 33 weeks at a flat rate of £123.06 from April 2009). A pregnant employee is also protected from dismissal or detriment on the grounds of her pregnancy. Pregnant employees must be given time off to attend ante-natal care classes in certain circumstances.
- Paternity leave. Fathers with 26 weeks' service are entitled to two weeks' leave (paid, as a minimum, at the flat rate of £123.06 from April 2009). Paternity leave entitlement may increase from 2010 to enable fathers to take additional paternity leave if the mother returns to work prior to the expiry of her maternity leave entitlement.
- Adoption leave. Adopters can take the equivalent to maternity and paternity leave but are required to have 26 weeks' service at the relevant time.
- Parental leave. Parents with one year's service are entitled to 13 weeks' unpaid parental leave (per child) to be taken before the child is five.
- Compassionate and other authorised absence. Employees have a right to unpaid time off to cope with incidents involving dependants. In addition, companies will often offer a period of paid compassionate leave to employees following the death of a close relative.
- Flexible working. Employees who fulfil the qualifying criteria are able to make a request to change their work patterns (e.g. to work part-time or to work fixed hours in the office). An employer must consider such a request within a timetable specified by statute and can only refuse the request on certain specified grounds.

8.138 Statutory dispute resolution procedures

- Statutory grievance procedure (SGP). An employee has the right to bring a grievance to the attention of the employer who in turn has an obligation to investigate that grievance. Statute sets out a basic grievance procedure which employers are required to adhere to. Essentially, a grievance must be considered at a meeting, the employee must be informed of the outcome of the grievance and given a right of appeal. An employee is required to raise a statutory grievance before pursuing a claim at tribunal. Any failure by the employer to follow the statutory grievance procedures means that compensation payable to the employee can be increased by between 10% and 50%.

- Statutory dismissal and disciplinary procedure (SDDP). Employers must follow minimum statutory procedures when taking disciplinary action against or dismissing employees. As with the SGP, any failure by the employer to follow the statutory disciplinary procedures can give rise to a 10% and 50% increase in compensation payable.

8.139 The statutory dispute resolution procedures are expected to be repealed by the Employment Act 2008 in April 2009. Employers will be encouraged to follow the revised ACAS Code of Practice on discipline and grievance. It is proposed that an unreasonable failure to comply with it could give rise to an increase of up to 25% on any award of compensation.

Compensation for loss of office

Damages for early termination of a service contract

8.140 Where a director's employment is terminated summarily without cause or there is a repudiatory breach of contract, he will be entitled to damages for wrongful dismissal.

8.141 Damages for wrongful dismissal will normally be assessed by reference to the net loss the director has sustained as a result of the breach of contract for the balance of the term of the service contract or the notice period.

8.142 The net loss is calculated by assessing the net basic salary that the director would have received during that period, plus a sum to represent the loss of any other contractual benefits (e.g. a car) for the period. Genuine termination payments which are not taxable under s. 62 of the Income Tax (Earnings and Pensions) Act 2003 (ITEPA) as general earnings or under any other provision may be exempt from tax up to the first £30,000 pursuant to s. 401 of ITEPA. (Section 401 applies to payments made in relation to offices or employment, and so covers termination payments made to non-executive directors.) The balance over £30,000 will be subject to income tax in the normal way and a damages payment will need to be grossed up to take account of the tax that the director will have to pay on the excess over £30,000. Payments under s. 401 ITEPA are not generally liable to Nation Insurance contributions even if they exceed £30,000, as they are not earnings.

8.143 In assessing appropriate damages the board is entitled to make a deduction for accelerated receipt, that is, a deduction to reflect the fact that the director will receive the sum immediately rather than in monthly instalments had he remained in employment. The percentage deduction should be set by reference to what the director might reasonably be expected to earn by way of interest on the total sum.

8.144 Directors are under a duty to attempt to mitigate their loss by seeking suitable alternative employment, thereby reducing the damages payable by the company by the amount that the director might reasonably be expected to earn. The courts will expect the departing director to take reasonable steps to find another job. Initially, the director would be entitled to restrict his search to positions at a similar level, offering equivalent salary and other benefits, but after a reasonable period (usually at least three months) he might be expected to look at a lower level. Clearly, if the director already has another job, this can be taken into account by the company in assessing what it should pay the departing director, provided that the company knows about it. This is why a director may be required to warrant in any settlement documentation that he has not obtained another job or been offered one.

8.145 In deciding the level of damages payable, the board will have to consider carefully the director's prospects of finding alternative employment; it would not be exercising its powers in the best interests of the company if it failed to do so. It may be helpful to take expert advice from, for example, a recruitment consultant experienced in board-level appointments to assist the board in discharging this responsibility. Board minutes should record the board's consideration of the mitigation issue and how and why it reaches its conclusions.

8.146 The director's service contract may contain a liquidated damages provision which sets out an amount (or a formula for calculating the amount) payable in circumstances where the employer has terminated the contract in breach (see **8.165** below).

8.147 The revised 2007 ABI Guidelines place further emphasis on the board's role in approving termination payments. The remuneration committee should ensure that contracts protect the company from being exposed to the risk of payment in the event of failure. In the event of early termination there should be no automatic entitlement to bonuses or share-based payments. If the service contract is simply to include a notice period, damages for breach of which would then be subject to the director's duty to mitigate his loss, shareholders will expect reassurance that the board has taken steps to ensure that the director has mitigated his loss to the fullest extent possible.

8.148 The inclusion of a clause in the service contract providing for phased payments where the company continues to pay the departing executive on the usual basis for the outstanding term of the contract or, if earlier, until the executive finds new employment is supported by the ABI. Continued payment could be stated to be conditional on the executive making reasonable efforts to find other employment (and, possibly, providing the company with proof of this).

Payments in lieu of notice

8.149 Alternatively, a payment in lieu of notice (PILON) clause may be invoked. If a PILON provision is expressly stated in the contract or implied by virtue of custom and practice, the company may terminate the contract with immediate effect and make a payment in lieu of notice. Sums paid under a PILON provision, or sums broadly equivalent to the monies due under such a clause, will normally be fully taxable.

Requirement for shareholder approval for payments for loss of office – ss. 215–222

8.150 The new regime governing the circumstances in which shareholder approval is required for payments made to directors for loss of office is set out in ss. 215–222 of the 2006 Act.

8.151 Section 217(1) of the 2006 Act provides that:

> 'A company may not make a payment for loss of office to a director of the company unless the payment has been approved by a resolution of the members of the company'

made to a director or past director of a company as:

- compensation for loss of office (s. 215(1)(a));
- compensation for loss of any other office or employment in connection with the management of the affairs of the company or of any subsidiary undertaking (s. 215(1)(b));
- consideration for or in connection with his retirement from office as a director (s. 215(1)(c)); or
- consideration for or in connection with retirement from any other office or employment in connection with the management of the affairs of the company or any subsidiary undertaking while a director or in connection with ceasing to be a director (s. 215(1)(d)).

8.152 Extending the scope of the requirement to obtain shareholders' approval to a payment to a director or former director in respect of loss of employment from employment is limited to where the employment relates to the management of the affairs of the company. However, this still represents a significant change.

8.153 It is clear that these provisions cover any payments made to former directors as there is an express reference to past director (s. 215).

8.154 Further, the express inclusion of non-cash benefits has clarified that both cash and non-cash payments fall within the scope of these provisions (s. 215(2)).

8.155 Payments to a person connected with a director, or payments to any person at the direction or for the benefit of a director or a person connected with him will be treated as payments to the director for the purposes of ss. 217–221 and therefore require shareholders' approval (s. 215(3)).

8.156 A company may not make a payment for loss of office to a director of its holding company unless the payment has been approved by a resolution of the members of both the company making the payment and the members of the holding company (s. 217(2)). A memorandum setting out details of the proposed payment, including its amount, must have been made available to members of the company before approval is given. It is now clear that approval will be required from both the holding company and subsidiary where a payment is made in these circumstances (except where the subsidiary is wholly owned, in which case only approval of the members of the holding company is required).

8.157 Members' approval is also required if the company wishes to make a payment for loss of office to a director of the company in connection with the transfer of the whole or any part of the undertaking or the property of the company or of the subsidiary of the company (s. 218).

8.158 In the case of payment for loss of office to a director in connection with the transfer of shares in the company (or in a subsidiary of the company) resulting from a takeover bid, approval is required of the holders of the shares to which the bid relates and of any holders of shares of the same class (s. 219). Persons making the offer for shares in the company (and any associate of them) are excluded from voting on any resolution to approve a payment for loss of office in connection with a share transfer (s. 219(4)).

Exemptions

8.159 Shareholder approval is not required for a payment made in good faith in one of the following situations:

- in discharge of an existing legal obligation (defined as an obligation 'that was not entered into in connection with, or in consequence of, the event giving rise to the payment for loss of office');
- by way of damages for breach of such an obligation;
- by way of settlement or compromise of any claim arising in connection with the termination of a person's office or employment;
- or by way of pension in respect of past services (s. 220(a)–(d)).

8.160 The new provisions in s. 220 replace the exception contained in s. 316(3), CA 1985 for *bona fide* payments made by way of damages for breach of contract. It is likely that for a payment of damages to be made 'in good faith' and to escape the need for shareholder approval, a deduction should be made to take account of mitigation and accelerated receipt. Similarly, in relation to the exception for compensation payable in respect of a settlement or compromise of claims arising from termination of employment, a sensible estimate of the amount of likely compensation for any statutory claims, together with an assessment of likely compensation for breach of contract and a careful consideration of the director's future prospects of employment, will be needed if the proposed compensation is to fall within the exemption and avoid the need to obtain shareholder approval. The final exemption which relates to 'pension for past services' is intended to cover a payment made to a pension scheme on behalf of a director in connection with the loss of office or employment. However, the scope of the exemption is unclear and a cautious approach is advisable, especially given the ABI guidance on ensuring that executives do not depart on special or preferential pension terms (e.g. with limited or no actuarial reduction).

8.161 There is also an exception for small payments. Approval is not required for payments for loss of office made by the company or any subsidiary which are of £200 or less (s. 221).

8.162 The civil consequences of making payments without the requisite shareholder approval in contravention of these provisions is set out at s. 222(1)–(3)).

- s. 217 (payment by company): (a) it is held by the recipient on trust for the company making the payment and (b) any director who authorised the payment is jointly and severally liable to indemnify the company that made the payment for any loss resulting from it;
- s. 218 (payment in connection with transfer of undertaking): it is held by the recipient on trust for the company whose undertaking or property it is or is proposed to be transferred;
- s. 219 (payment in connection with a share transfer): (a) it is held by the recipient on trust for persons who have sold their shares as a result of the

offer made, and (b) the expenses incurred by the recipient in distributing that sum amongst those persons shall be borne by him and not retained out of that sum.

8.163 Clarification is given on the resolution of conflicts between remedies where more than one requirement to these sections is breached (s. 222(4) and (5)). The Explanatory Notes to the 2006 Act give the following example: if the payment contravenes both ss. 217 and 219 because it was a payment by a company to one of its directors and was a payment in connection with a takeover bid, and none of the required member approvals has been obtained, then the payment is held on trust for the persons who have sold their shares as a result of the offer and not on trust for the company making the payment.

Liquidated damages and change of control provisions

8.164 Directors' service contracts sometimes contain a liquidated damages clause which provides for a specific sum to be paid on early termination of the contract. The clause normally sets out a formula as to how the sum is to be calculated. The components of the formula tend to be the number of years/months left to run under the service contract/the length of the notice period and the director's gross basic salary and (usually) a sum (or percentage of basic salary) representing the other contractual benefits. A broadly similar effect can be achieved by including a payment in lieu of notice or PILON clause in the contract. The liquidated damages provision must be a genuine pre-estimate of the director's loss, otherwise it may be unenforceable as a penalty (see the *Murray* decision, **8.167** below).

8.165 Alternatively, the contract may provide that a contingency payment will be made if a particular event occurs, such as a change of control (e.g. where the employing company is taken over or its business is transferred outside the group).

8.166 Such provisions avoid the uncertainties for the company of quantifying the contractual damages for wrongful dismissal which would otherwise be payable. However, where account is taken of the director's duty to mitigate his loss by seeking employment, this can be a significant disadvantage for the employing company. The key advantage to the company of such a provision is the fact that, by paying out under the liquidated damages clause, the company will normally be treated as acting in accordance with the service contract and should therefore be able to rely on any enforceable restrictive covenants in the service contract. By contrast, if it breaches the service contract in dismissing the director unlawfully, it will probably not be able to rely on the restrictive covenants (*General Billposting Company Limited v. Atkinson* [1909] AC 118).

8.167 Liquidated damages clauses now normally provide for a reduction to take account of accelerated receipt and the duty to mitigate. However, the Court of Appeal recently upheld a liquidated damages provision in a chief executive's service contract providing for one year's gross salary, pension contributions and other benefits in kind, notwithstanding that no reduction was made for mitigation (*Murray v. Leisureplay plc* [2005] EWCA Civ 963). In considering whether the liquidated damages provision amounted to a penalty clause (i.e. representing more than a genuine pre-estimate of probable loss arising on termination), the majority of the Court of Appeal held that a clause will only be a penalty if the party seeking to avoid the terms can demonstrate that the sum payable on breach is 'extravagant or unconscionable' compared with the greatest loss that could follow from the breach. Further, the Court of Appeal suggested that the commercial context could be taken into account. The fact that the executive in this case had agreed to significant post-termination restrictive covenants was relevant. Looking at the clause in its commercial context, it was considered appropriate for the employer to pay out the full liquidated damages payment without a reduction for mitigation in return for the executive's agreement to these important restrictions. Companies may now be more likely to be bound by liquidated damages provisions even where the provision permits a departing executive to receive more than they would have obtained in damages at common law.

8.168 Liquidated damages provisions tend to be unattractive from a tax perspective as they are subject to income tax and National Insurance contributions. A liquidated damages payment will not attract the tax-free element of a termination payment referred to above (currently £30,000) as it is construed by the HM Revenue & Customs as a contractual payment and not a payment representing damages for wrongful dismissal.

8.169 A payment made pursuant to a clearly and carefully drafted liquidated damages or change of control provision should not require shareholder approval under the 2006 Act as it should fall within the exemption for payments made in discharge of an existing legal obligation (ss. 215–222).

The Combined Code and ABI Guidelines

8.170 The ABI/NAPF Joint Statement 2008 states that while remuneration committees should have the leeway to design a policy appropriate to the needs and objectives of the company, they must also have a clear understanding of their responsibility to negotiate suitable contracts and be able to justify severance payments to shareholders.

8.171 The Joint Statement 2008 concludes:

> 'It is unacceptable that poor performance by senior executives, which detracts from the value of an enterprise and threatens the livelihood of employees, can result in excessive payments to departing directors. Boards have a responsibility to ensure that this does not occur.'

8.172 In the event of early termination on grounds of poor performance, there should be no automatic entitlement to non-contractual discretionary bonuses or share-based payments, according to the 2007 ABI Guidelines and the 2008 Joint Statement. The liquidated damages approach of agreeing upfront how much a director will receive on severance is not generally supported by shareholder institutions (ABI Guidelines, para. 3.5). Further the ABI/NAPF Joint Statement 2008 states that the ABI and NAPF are not supportive of liquidated damages clauses which involve agreement at the outset on the amount that will be paid in the event of severance. A departing executive will be obliged to mitigate any loss incurred by seeking other employment and reducing the need for compensation. The remuneration committees should ensure that the full benefit of mitigation is obtained (Joint Statement, para. 3.10). Further, contracts should not provide additional compensation for severance as a result of change of control (para. 3.9). Companies should fully disclose in their remuneration report the constituent parts of any severance payments and justify the total level and elements paid (para. 2.8).

8.173 Similarly, the Combined Code (June 2008) sets out remuneration committee's responsibilities in relation to compensation for loss of office:

> 'The remuneration committee should carefully consider what compensation commitments (including pension contributions and other elements) their directors' terms of appointment would entail in the event of early termination. The aim should be to avoid rewarding poor performance. They should take a robust line on reducing compensation to reflect departing directors' obligations to mitigate loss.' (para. B1.5)

Directors' and officers' liability insurance and indemnities

8.174 Companies may not exempt directors from, or indemnify them against, liability in connection with any negligence, default, breach of duty or breach of trust in relation to the company (ss. 232–239). The new provisions under the 2006 Act, which came into force on 1 October 2007, largely mirror the previous regime under the 1985 Act. Any provision by which a company directly or indirectly provides an indemnity for a director of the company or an associated company in respect of such liability will be void, save in relation to certain exemptions:

- A company may purchase and maintain insurance against such liability (s. 233). Indeed, the Combined Code refers to the need to provide appropriate directors' and officers' insurance (Code Provision A.1.5).
- A company may indemnify a director against liability incurred by him to a third party subject to certain conditions, which include that such indemnity must not cover any fines imposed against a director in criminal proceedings, or sums payable to a regulatory authority by way of a penalty in respect of non-compliance with a regulatory requirement, or any liability incurred in defending criminal proceedings in which he is convicted, or in defending civil proceedings in which judgment is given against him (s. 234).
- Directors of pension fund trustees can be indemnified by the pensions trustee company itself or an associated company against any liability incurred in connection with the company's activities as trustee of the scheme. This type of indemnity is wider in scope than may be provided to directors of other types of company, although it cannot extend to liabilities to pay criminal or regulatory fines or to defending criminal proceedings in which the director is convicted.

8.175 See **Chapter 17** for a discussion of indemnities.

Summary

8.176 Key issues for directors as employees in relation to service contracts and remuneration are as follows:

- Directors must act in accordance with the articles of association and the new statutory directors' duties under the 2006 Act.
- Shareholder approval is required for executive and non-executive contracts where the term is, or may be, longer than two years. Failure to obtain this approval will render the term void and the contract will be deemed terminable on reasonable notice.
- The remuneration committee plays a vital role in setting the levels and structure of directors' remuneration. Executive directors' remuneration should be linked to corporate and individual performance to align their interests with those of shareholders.
- Long-term incentive schemes are subject to certain restrictions. These should be taken into consideration when the schemes are designed and implemented.
- It is unacceptable that poor performance can result in excessive payments to departing directors, according to best practice corporate governance guidance issued by the ABI, NAPF and the Combined Code.
- Shareholder approval will, in certain circumstances, be required for

payments for loss of office, retirement, loss of employment or retirement in connection with the management of the affairs of the company.

- Shareholders may inspect copies of directors' service contracts (or a memorandum of their terms) and request copies on payment of a prescribed fee.
- Consider both the contractual documentation and the factual matrix when determining the employment status of a director. The following factors are relevant:
  - the intention of the parties as evidenced in the documentation;
  - the presence or absence of mutuality of obligation;
  - the degree of control which the company exercises over the way in which the work is performed; and
  - the extent to which the individual is integral to the business.
- An employer is obliged to provide an employee with a written statement of specified particulars of employment within two months of commencement of employment.
- Directors who are employees will benefit from statutory protection including:
  - protection against unfair dismissal;
  - the right to a redundancy payments;
  - protection against dismissal or detriment for whistleblowing; and
  - protection against dismissal on a business transfer.

Sources

- Companies Act 2006 (2006 Act)
- Revised Combined Code issued by the Committee on Corporate Governance in June 2008. This replaces the July 2006 version for reporting periods commencing on or after 29 June 2008
- Listing, Prospectus, Disclosure and Transparency Rules which came into force on 20 January 2007. This replaces the previous Listing, Prospectus and Disclosure Rules published in July 2005
- City Code on Takeovers and Mergers (the Takeover Code) issued by the Panel on Takeovers and Mergers on 20 May 2006 (amended by the Takeovers Directive (Interim Implementation) Regulations and the Companies Act 2006)
- Guidelines on Executive Remuneration published on 3 December 2007 by the Association of British Insurers (the ABI Guidelines)
- Revised Joint Statement on Executive Contracts and Severance issued by the ABI and National Association of Pension Funds published in February 2008
- Relevant case law

9

Directors as shareholders

Introduction

9.1 When a director is also a shareholder in the company, or is intending to become a shareholder, he and the company will need to consider any requirements or restrictions associated with that holding, as well as with any dealings in the company's shares. In some cases, these are the same as the requirements that apply to all shareholders, but in a number of respects directors have additional requirements imposed on them, above and beyond those applying to the other shareholders in the company.

9.2 This is an area where the regulatory requirements imposed on directors of listed companies are substantial compared to the requirements imposed on private companies and non-listed PLCs, although in the case of private companies there may be contractual restrictions and requirements in the company's articles of association or in a shareholders' agreement.

9.3 The Companies Act 2006 (2006 Act) introduced deregulation for private companies in relation to disclosure of interests by directors; on the other hand, regulatory developments over the last few years, such as the creation of the Disclosure and Transparency Rules, have created new requirements for listed companies.

9.4 In this chapter the disclosure requirements and restrictions in relation to directors' holdings and dealings in shares (and securities relating to those shares) are considered under the following headings:

- The Companies Act 2006.
- Directors' duties and corporate governance.
- Articles of association and other contractual provisions.
- Disclosure of dealings under the Disclosure Rules.
- Disclosure of dealings under the Transparency Rules.
- The Model Code in the Listing Rules.
- Disclosure of dealings and restrictions under the AIM Rules.
- Market abuse.
- The Takeover Code.

9.5 The provisions and the companies to which they apply are summarised on page 251.

The Companies Act 2006

9.6 Under s. 324 of the Companies Act 1985 (1985 Act), the directors of all UK registered companies were required to disclose their interests and dealings in the shares of the company (and any other companies in the same group) to the company. The company was in turn required under s. 325 of the 1985 Act to maintain a register of those disclosures and to make it available to the public for inspection and copying. In the case of listed companies the company was also required under s. 329 to disclose the interest to the market.

9.7 These provisions were repealed with effect from 6 April 2007 and there is no equivalent or replacement provision in the 2006 Act. So, as a result of this deregulation, there is no longer any UK company law requirement for the disclosure of directors' interests in shares or for the maintenance by companies of a register of directors' interests in shares.

9.8 The corresponding requirement in Schedule 7 of the 1985 Act to disclose the details of directors' interests in shares in the annual accounts was also repealed with effect from 6 April 2007 and has not been replaced by any equivalent provisions in the Regulations setting out the requirements for the content of accounts under the 2006 Act.

9.9 The provision prohibiting directors from dealing in share options (s. 323 of the 1985 Act) was also repealed with effect from 6 April 2007 and has not been replaced in the 2006 Act.

9.10 For directors of listed and AIM companies, there continue to be requirements for disclosure of interests and dealings in shares under the FSA's Disclosure Rules and the AIM Rules respectively (see **9.33** and **9.88** below). For listed companies, there is also a requirement in the Listing Rules for the annual report to disclose the interests in shares of directors and their connected persons based on their Disclosure Rules notifications (see **9.56** below).

9.11 Even for listed and AIM companies, there is no longer any formal requirement for a company to maintain a register of directors' interests. However, listed and AIM companies are recommended to keep a record of interests disclosed by directors, despite there being no formal obligation to do so, in order to show compliance with their Disclosure Rule or AIM Rule obligations (see **9.66** below).

9.12 The interaction between the duties of directors in the 2006 Act and the position of directors as shareholders is discussed below. There are also other provisions in the 2006 Act in relation to which a director's shareholding may be relevant. These are:

- *Transactions with directors*. Section 192 of the 2006 Act expressly provides that approval is not required under s. 190 (substantial property transactions) for a transaction between a company and a person in his character as a member of that company.
- *Right to request information about interests in shares*. As explained in **9.67** below, the provisions requiring the disclosure of material interests in shares previously set out in ss. 198–209 of the 1985 Act are no longer company law provisions, but have become part of the FSA's Transparency Rules. The provisions allowing a public company to require disclosure of interests in its own shares have, however, remained a company law matter and are set out in Part 22 of the 2006 Act, with s. 793 replacing s. 212 of the 1985 Act.

  The tests of interests in shares for the purposes of Part 22 of the 2006 Act are the same as those under the 1985 Act, rather than following the new tests of voting interests in the Transparency Rules. The definition of an interest in shares for the purpose of Part 22 is set out in s. 820. An interest in shares is defined as any interest of any kind. It includes where a person enters into a contract to acquire shares or, not being the registered holder, is entitled to exercise any right, or control the exercise of any right, conferred by the shares (whether or not that right is subject to conditions). It also extends to having a right to call for delivery of the shares or having a right to acquire an interest or being under an obligation to take an interest in shares. Certain family interests and corporate interests are treated as a person's interest for this purpose (ss. 822 and 823 of the 2006 Act).

  This is a power that a public company could use to obtain information from a director about his interests in shares, as it could in relation to any other person who may be interested in shares. Private companies have no equivalent power. It would, of course, be unusual for a public company to need or wish to seek information in this way from one of its own directors, but it is a power that is available if needed. Also as described in **9.58** below, for listed companies, the Disclosure Rules require that any information received from a director and his connected persons in response to a s. 793 notice must be announced, unless the interest has already been disclosed in accordance with DTR 3.
- *Contracts with sole members who are also directors*. Section 231 of the 2006 Act sets out the requirements where the director is the sole member and enters into a contract with the company. Unless the contract is entered into in the ordinary course of business, the contract must be in writing or set out in a written memorandum or recorded in the minutes of the first

board meeting held after it is entered into. Failure to comply is an offence, although it does not affect the validity of the contract.

- *Ratification of breach of director's duties*. Under s. 239 of the 2006 Act, a ratification by shareholders of a breach by a director of his duties can only be passed if the necessary majority is obtained, disregarding any votes in favour of the resolution by the director if he is the member of the company and of any member connected with him (s. 252 as modified by s. 239(5)).
- *Payment for shares in a public company*. Public companies may not accept an undertaking to do work and to perform services in payment of its shares (s. 585 of the 2006 Act, which is the equivalent of s. 99(2) of the 1985 Act). This would therefore include any allotment of shares to a director in consideration of his future services as a director, although an allotment for past services is not prohibited (i.e. the remuneration is paid in arrears so that the shares are issued in respect of services that have already been provided).
- *Schemes of arrangement*. Part 26 of the 2006 Act contains provisions relating to schemes of arrangement between a company and its members or creditors. Under s. 897, the circular convening the scheme meeting must include details of the material interests of the directors, including their interests as members. Any change in the shareholdings of directors after publication of the circular could result in a need to send a further circular to shareholders explaining the nature of the change. Case law suggests that, if the shareholders are not informed of any change in the interests of the directors, then, unless the alteration is minor and therefore would not affect the shareholders' decision-making, the scheme should not be sanctioned (*Re Jessel Trust Limited* [1985] BCLC 119). It is therefore not advisable for directors to deal in the company's shares after the scheme circular is sent to the shareholders.

Directors' duties and corporate governance

Directors' duties

9.13 The directors' statutory duties are set out in Part 10 of the 2006 Act (see **5.34**).

9.14 If a director is a shareholder, his relationship with the company is in two capacities – as a director and as a member. When exercising his powers as a member, a director is not required to comply with his duties as a director because he is not acting in his capacity as a director. He is entitled to exercise his rights as member as he thinks fit, including his voting rights. An example of how this applies in practice is in relation to a takeover offer. In deciding whether or not to recommend a takeover offer to shareholders, directors of the target company must comply with their duties under the Takeover Code and with their duties in the 2006 Act including the duty to promote the success of the company for the benefit of the members as a whole. A director can, however, enter into an irrevocable undertaking to accept an offer without any carve-out for his duties as a director and even if the board decides that the offer should not be recommended, because he is doing so in his capacity as member. What the director cannot do is commit in the irrevocable undertaking to recommending an offer without any carve-out for his duties as director, because by giving such a commitment he is acting in his capacity as a director and not as a member.

9.15 The duties of directors in relation to conflicts of interest are relevant to a director also being a shareholder. An issue that needs to be considered is whether, if a director is also a shareholder, that creates a conflict for the director for the purposes of the duty of directors under s. 175 of the 2006 Act to avoid conflicts, or could trigger a requirement to disclose an interest in a transaction or arrangement as required by ss. 177 and 182 of the 2006 Act.

9.16 Under s. 175, a director must avoid situations in which he has or can have a direct or indirect interest that conflicts, or may conflict, with the interests of the company. The situation is not infringed if the matter has been authorised by the board in accordance with ss. 175(5) and 175(6).

9.17 In principle, the fact that a director holds shares should not of itself create any conflict. The essential duty of directors, as set out in s. 172, is to promote the success of the company for the benefit of the members as a whole. If the director is a member, his interests as a member and the interests of the company are normally aligned, rather than in conflict.

9.18 Furthermore, if the director is to subscribe for shares or enter into another transaction with the company in relation to his shares (such as a buy-back), that is a matter which falls under the rules relating to disclosure of interests in transactions by directors (as described below) and so does not fall within s. 175 (see s. 175(3)).

9.19 Therefore, it should not normally be the case that a director would need to have an authorisation from the board under s. 175(5) simply to hold shares. Nevertheless, the guidance relating to directors' conflicts of interests published by the Association of General Counsel and Company Secretaries of the FTSE 100 in January 2008 (reproduced at **Appendix 3**) does suggest that being a shareholder could create a conflict situation. The guidance cites a director who is a major shareholder in the company as an example of a conflict situation. In the case of a listed company a major shareholder is in a different position from a director with a small holding, particularly if it means that the director has the ability to block shareholder resolutions.

9.20 However, it is still not likely to be the case that the membership alone creates a conflict situation for s. 175 purposes. In practice, a conflict relating to a substantial shareholder and a director is most likely to arise where the substantial shareholder is another company which has appointed one or more directors to the board. The conflict then arises not because the director is a shareholder, but as a result of a conflict between his duty to the corporate shareholder and his duties to the company. A conflict should not arise in relation to a director simply being a shareholder unless there are any other factors which are creating that conflict, such as other interests or duties of the director, in other words going beyond the shareholding itself, for example because the director decides to make a takeover bid for the company. If there is a difference in views or strategy between the various members of the board giving rise, for example, to the possibility that the director who is also a shareholder might vote as a shareholder against a proposal supported by the majority board, then does that create a conflict or is it just a difference of view? Much will depend on the individual circumstances (e.g. the size of the director's holding and why the difference of view has arisen), but again it is likely that the real conflict lies in other factors and not the membership itself.

9.21 If a director has an interest in a proposed transaction as shareholder, then should that be disclosed pursuant to s. 177 or s. 182 of the 2006 Act? Whether the director's interest as shareholder needs to be disclosed depends on the circumstances. Sections 177 and 182 apply only where he is interested in a 'transaction or arrangement' with the company. Therefore, the disclosure requirement should not be triggered just because matters are considered by the board which may have an effect on members (e.g. payment of dividends). But there will be some circumstances in which disclosure is required. For example, if a company proposes to enter into a buy-back agreement with a director in relation to his shares, then that will be a matter that is disclosable under s. 177. However, it should be noted that there is an exception in ss. 177 and 182 for matters of which the other directors should reasonably already be aware and it is also possible under ss. 177 and 182 for directors to make a general disclosure in relation to an interest. It is likely that a director's shareholding will in any event be something the board is already aware of, or which has been subject to a previous general disclosure to the board.

9.22 In addition, there is a separate question to be considered about the disclosure and voting requirements under the articles of association, as described in **9.27** below.

The Combined Code

9.23 The Combined Code on corporate governance issued by the Financial Reporting Council (FRC) is a voluntary code, although listed companies are obliged under the FSA's Listing Rules and Corporate Governance Rules to state whether they comply with it and, if not, to explain why they do not. Many AIM companies also voluntarily comply with the Combined Code, although they have no equivalent obligation to comply or explain under the AIM Rules.

9.24 There is no express statement in the Combined Code in relation to directors holding shares or the issue of shares to directors as remuneration. However, the Combined Code does state that non-executive directors should not be remunerated by being issued with share options and that if options are granted, shareholder approval should be sought in advance. Any shares acquired on exercise of an option should be held until at least one year after the non-executive director leaves the board. Also, the share options could potentially undermine the non-executive director's independence for Combined Code purposes (Paragraph B.1.3 of the Combined Code) (see **Appendix 1** and **8.74**).

Articles of association and other contractual provisions

Enforcement of the articles as a member not as director

9.25 The legal status of the articles of association as a contract between the company and its members (s. 33 of the 2006 Act, replacing s. 14 of the 1985 Act) is, in the case of directors who are also members, interpreted to mean that a director may enforce the contract created by the articles only in his capacity as a member, and not in his capacity as a director. For example, in *Globalink Telecommunications Ltd v. Wilmbury Ltd and Others* [2003] 1 BCLC 145, a director was held to be unable to enforce a provision in the articles relating to directors' indemnities, although the court said that he would have been able to do so if he could have shown that the provision in the articles was expressly or implicitly incorporated into his service contract. However, it does not matter if the director, as a result of enforcing his rights as a member under the articles, is thereby able to enforce a provision in the articles relating to the directors. This was shown in *Quinn & Axtens Ltd v. Salmon* [1909] AC 442 in which the director was able as a member to enforce a requirement in the articles for the consent of two directors in relation to a particular type of transaction. A director who is a shareholder is therefore in a different position as regards enforcing the articles (provided he does so in his capacity as a member) compared to a director who is not a shareholder.

Shareholding qualification for directors

9.26 The traditional concept of a 'shareholding qualification' for directors – that it is a requirement in the articles for each director to hold a minimum number of shares in the company, or for the members to be able to resolve to impose a minimum shareholding qualification for directors – has largely fallen into disuse. The Table A articles issued with the Companies Act 1948 included the concept of a member's resolution setting a minimum shareholding qualification for directors, but in the Table A articles of the 1985 Act, this provision was dropped. In practice it is rare to see any reference to a director's shareholding qualification in articles of association. For private companies with detailed shareholder investment arrangements there are in any event usually detailed provisions in the articles linking a director's shareholding to his position as a director.

Board disclosure and voting requirements

9.27 Articles of association normally include provisions to deal with the disclosure by directors of interests in transactions or arrangements and provisions setting out the circumstances in which directors are not permitted to vote at a meeting of directors. The relevant provisions in the Table A articles are Regulation 85 (requiring disclosure of interests) and Regulation 94 (in relation to voting at board meetings). To what extent will the fact that a director is a shareholder require disclosure or create a voting restriction under these provisions? In relation to the disclosure requirements, the issues are very similar to those raised in relation to disclosure pursuant to ss. 177 and 182 of the 2006 Act (see **9.21** above). A director is required under Regulation 85 to disclose an interest in a transaction, which could include his interest as a shareholder, but a general notice to the directors of the interest is sufficient for these purposes. In relation to voting at board meetings, Regulation 94 of Table A provides that a director shall not vote on any matter at a board meeting in which he has a material interest (subject to limited exceptions). There is no exception in Table A for an interest which he has by virtue of being a shareholder. However, it is unlikely that he will have a 'material' interest in a matter, and therefore be unable to vote, just because he is a shareholder in circumstances in which his interest is the same as any other shareholder (e.g. because it relates to the payment of a dividend). A voting restriction is only likely to apply if he is being treated differently from other shareholders or is entering into a transaction with the company in relation to his shares (e.g. a buy-back contract).

From October 2009, Table A will be replaced by the Model Articles for private companies under the Companies Act 2006. The BERR Model Articles do not contain any equivalent to regulation 85 and instead leave disclosure as a matter for the requirements of the 2006 Act, under ss.177 and 182 (as described above). The equivalent to regulation 94 in the BERR model articles for private companies is article 14, which also states that the director cannot vote or be counted in the quorum, subject to limited exceptions.

Restrictions on transfers – listed and AIM companies

9.28 In the case of companies whose shares are listed on the Official List or traded on AIM or PLUS markets, the articles of association cannot include any restrictions on transfer (except in exceptional cases with the approval of the relevant market, and of the FSA in the case of a listed company). This would include any restrictions on transfer by directors. Therefore, it is very unlikely that there would be any special provisions in the articles of these companies restricting directors' holdings or dealings in shares.

9.29 However, contractual restrictions may be put in place in favour of the company and its financial adviser preventing directors from selling their shares for a certain period (e.g. a year) after the initial admission to listing or trading. These are known as lock-up arrangements. The AIM Rules require a one-year lock-up for directors and others unless at the time of admission the company already has a two-year trading record as an independent, revenue-earning business (AIM Rule 7). This is the only specific requirement for a lock-up arrangement in the AIM Rules, and there are no requirements in the Listing Rules. However, it is common for lock-ups to be put in place for directors following a float, even though it is not required. The period for a lock-up arrangement varies between six months to two years. Any lock-up arrangements need to be disclosed in the prospectus or another document issued as part of the admission to listing or trading.

Restrictions on transfers – other companies

9.30 For non-traded companies, where a shareholder agreement and tailored articles of association have been put in place, these normally include restrictions on the shareholders, including the directors, transferring their shares. In the case of directors, the articles also often include provisions designed to deal with what happens to a director's shares if he ceases to be a director.

9.31 There are normally three types of provisions relating to transfer applicable to a director. It is more common to see these restrictions and arrangements set out in articles of association, but some provisions might be set out in a separate shareholders' agreement. The three relevant provisions are:

- *Permitted transfers.* Setting out the circumstances in which a director is permitted to transfer shares without following the pre-emption procedure. A director would normally be permitted to transfer his shares to family members and family trusts (with the scope of the permission being defined in detail). If such transfers are permitted, then there will need to be a tie-in to the deemed transfer notice (as described below) so that the death or resignation of the director will trigger a transfer notice by the family member or family trust to whom the shares have been transferred.

- *Pre-emption rights on voluntary transfers*. There will normally be a requirement for all shareholders, including directors, to offer their shares to existing shareholders before they can be transferred to a third party and, if a third party buyer has already been found, to offer them to existing shareholders at the price offered by that third party.

  Although a director may be permitted to transfer his shares voluntarily under the pre-emption provisions, there may also be a provision in his service contract which automatically terminates that contract in the event that he ceases to be a shareholder.
- *Deemed transfer notices*. An automatic triggering of the pre-emption rights in favour of the other shareholders on the happening of certain events, which in the case of a director will normally include his death or resignation.

  Typically, particularly where there is an investment by an outside provider of funds, such as a private equity vehicle, the directors are required to transfer their shares if they cease to be a director. The key question is at what price the shares have to be transferred. Often, the concepts of 'good leaver' and 'bad leaver' are built in to the articles of association. When the director is a 'bad leaver' because he has been dismissed for cause or decides to resign, his shares may be required to be offered to the other shareholders at a nominal price. In contrast, when the director is a 'good leaver' because he has been dismissed without cause, the shares are likely to be required to be offered to the other shareholders at a 'fair value' as determined by an expert.

9.32 Where outside corporate investors are also shareholders in a private company, the directors and other senior employees may hold a separate class of shares, with defined rights and defined minority protection provisions. They may have a more limited ability to veto key shareholder decisions than the corporate investors (although the balance of power between the two will always depend on the individual circumstances). Often the corporate investors will have a right to appoint their own directors, but typically these directors will not be subject to the transfer provisions described above because they are not shareholders and are appointed as nominees of the investee companies. A full description of the minority rights provisions and other matters which may be dealt with in articles of association and shareholder agreements is beyond the scope of this chapter. These would normally include drag-along and tag-along provisions so that once the particular percentage of the shareholders have decided to sell to a third party, the other shareholders are 'dragged along' with them, but equally the minority have a right to 'tag-along', and so be bought out when a third party has acquired a particular percentage of the other shares.

Disclosure of dealings under the Disclosure Rules

9.33 The directors of a listed company, and the listed company itself, must comply with the provisions in relation to disclosure of dealings in a company's shares under Chapter 3 of the FSA's Disclosure and Transparency Rules (DTR 3). The Disclosure Rules (Chapters 1–3 of DTR) are made by the FSA under its powers in Part VI of the Financial Services and Markets Act 2000 (FSMA) and were introduced to implement the EU Market Abuse Directive (2003/6/EC). Under DTR 3, directors and other persons discharging managerial responsibilities must 'notify the issuer in writing of the occurrence of all transactions conducted on their own account in the shares of the issuer, or derivatives or any other financial instruments relating to those shares, within four business days of the day on which the transaction occurred' (DTR 3.1.2 R).

9.34 Under DTR 3.1.4 R, a company must notify a Regulatory Information Service (RIS) of any information notified to it by directors, other persons discharging managerial responsibilities and their connected persons under the Disclosure Rules.

The companies to which DTR 3 applies

9.35 The disclosure of dealing obligations in DTR 3 applies to the following companies:

- any company incorporated in the UK (or other legal person or undertaking, including a public sector issuer), any class of whose financial instruments have been admitted, or is the subject of an application for admission, to trading on a EEA regulated market (DTR 1.1.1(2) R); and
- any company incorporated in any non-EEA country which is required to file with the FSA an annual information update in relation to shares in accordance with Article 10 of the EU Prospectus Directive. Article 10 requires filings to be made with the FSA for any company which has the UK as its home member state.

9.36 UK and EEA regulated markets include the Official List but not AIM. DTR 3.1.8 R requires any other company which does not fall within the categories set out above but which has financial instruments admitted to trading on a UK regulated market to notify equivalent information required by DTR 3 to a RIS as soon as possible after the issuer becomes aware of the information. The directors and other persons discharging managerial responsibilities (and their connected persons) of this additional category of companies do not need to comply with DTR 3, but they may be subject to a similar regime under the laws of the place of incorporation of the company which require disclosure to the company.

The remainder of the description below assumes that the relevant company is a UK incorporated company.

Definition of persons discharging managerial responsibilities

9.37 The definition of a person discharging managerial responsibilities (PDMR) is set out in s. 96B of FSMA. This states that they are:

(a) a director of an issuer; and
(b) a senior executive of an issuer who:
  (i) has regular access to inside information relating, directly or indirectly, to the issuer, and
  (ii) has power to make managerial decisions affecting the future development and business prospects of the issuers.

9.38 There is no formal guidance on the definition of 'senior executive' in FSMA or the Disclosure Rules to clarify the extent to which a person who is not a director may be considered to be a person discharging managerial responsibilities. The test is a much narrower one than a list of all senior managers of the company. Companies need to consider only individuals whose decision-making powers extend to matters that can affect the business of the issuer as a whole to be persons discharging managerial responsibilities. In addition, in the test in s. 96B the senior executive must have regular access to inside information. The FSA has stated that the variety and complexity of corporate structures make it difficult to formulate guidance that would be appropriate for all companies. It has, however, given limited informal guidance in its *List!* and *Market Watch* publications. In particular, this informal guidance confirms that persons discharging managerial responsibilities are likely to include senior employees who sit on the executive committee of an issuer, even if they are not board members (*Market Watch* 12, available at www.fsa.gov.uk). It is not necessary for a person discharging managerial responsibilities to make decisions alone. The key test is the substance of an individual's role: if the individual takes decisions which affect the development and business prospects of the issuer (even if the decision is later ratified by the board), he is likely to be a PDMR (*List!* 16). On the other hand, a person who only offers advice or recommendations to the board and does not have any decision-making role himself is unlikely to be a PDMR (*List!* 16).

Definition of a connected person

9.39 The definition of a person connected with a director or any other person discharging managerial responsibilities for the purposes of the DTR 3 is contained in s. 96B(2) of FSMA, where a connected person is defined as follows:

(a) 'a connected person within s. 346 of the Companies Act 1985 (reading that section as if any reference to a director of a company in that section were a reference to a person discharging managerial responsibilities within an issuer);

(b) a relative of a person discharging managerial responsibilities within an issuer, who, on the date of the transaction in question, has shared the same household as that person for at least 12 months;

(c) a body corporate in which:
   - a person discharging managerial responsibilities within an issuer, or
   - any person connected with him by virtue of subsection (a) or (b),

   is a director or a senior executive who has the power to make management decisions affecting the future development and business prospects of that body corporate.'

9.40 Section 346 of the 1985 Act was repealed with effect from 1 October 2007 and replaced with the significantly wider definition of connected person in s. 252 of the 2006 Act. However, the Third Commencement Order (2007/2194) for the Companies Act 2006 expressly provides in paragraph 50 of Schedule 3 that, for the purposes of s. 96B(2) of FSMA, the definition in s. 346 of the 1985 Act is preserved.

9.41 A connected person within s. 346 of the Companies Act 1985 includes:

1 the spouse, civil partner, child or stepchild of a director or any other person discharging managerial responsibilities. For these purposes, the definition of child includes only those under the age of 18 years;

2 a body corporate with which the director or other person discharging managerial responsibilities is associated. A director or other person discharging managerial responsibilities is associated with a body corporate if he and persons connected with him, together are:
   (a) interested in shares comprised in the equity share capital of that body corporate of a nominal value equal to at least 20% of that share capital (excluding treasury shares); or
   (b) entitled to exercise or control the exercise of more than 20% of the voting power at any general meeting of that body corporate (excluding any voting rights attached to any shares in the company held as treasury shares);

3 a person acting in his capacity as trustee of any trust (excluding an employees' share scheme or a pension scheme) the beneficiaries or potential beneficiaries of which include:
   (a) the director or other person discharging managerial responsibilities, his spouse, civil partner or any children or stepchildren of his, or
   (b) a body corporate with which he is associated;

4 a person acting in his capacity as trustee of a trust whose terms confer a power on the trustees that may be exercised for the benefit of the director or other person exercising managerial responsibilities, his spouse, civil partner

or any of his children or stepchildren or any body corporate with which he is associated;

5 a person acting in his capacity as partner of the director or other person discharging managerial responsibilities or of any person who is connected with the director or other person discharging managerial responsibilities.

9.42 There is no detail in FSMA or DTR 3 as to the meaning of 'relative' in the definition in s. 96B(2)(b) of FSMA. Companies could seek guidance from the FSA on their specific case. If they do not seek such guidance, then (until guidance is issued by the FSA to the contrary) they should apply the term widely to cover parents, grandparents and adult children, as well as other members of a family such as siblings. In practice, this should not significantly increase the amount of dealing disclosures an issuer receives and is required to announce via an RIS because the connected person test is only met if the relative has shared the same household as the director or other person discharging managerial responsibilities for at least 12 months prior to the date of the transaction.

9.43 The definition of connected persons in s. 96B(2)(c) of FSMA is very wide. For example, in relation to a non-executive director, on the face of the legislation each company of which he is a director becomes a connected person of the other company. Therefore, a company would potentially be required to disclose any dealings by the company itself in the securities of any other company whose securities are traded on an EEA regulated market and to which DTR 3 applies in which their non-executive directors also hold directorships. However, the FSA stated in *List!* 9 and *Market Watch* 12 that it will give a much narrower interpretation to that definition. In deciding whether a body corporate is connected to a person discharging managerial responsibilities, issuers must consider the level of control that the person discharging managerial responsibilities (or his connected person) has within that body corporate. The FSA will only expect an issuer to announce dealings where the person discharging managerial responsibilities (or one of his connected persons) is the sole director of the body corporate and/or is a director or senior executive who personally has the power to control the body corporate's management decisions affecting its future development and business prospects, rather than merely being able to exert influence over it. This substantially narrows the scope of the test. In particular, if a director is also a non-executive director of another listed company, that other listed company will not be one of his connected persons.

Which types of transactions need to be disclosed under DTR 3?

9.44 Directors and other persons discharging managerial responsibilities must notify the issuer of 'all transactions conducted on their own account in the shares of the issuer, or derivatives or any other financial instruments relating to those shares' (DTR 3.1.2 R).

9.45 The disclosure requirement covers dealings in the listed shares as well as dealings in derivatives and 'any other financial instruments' (whether or not listed) relating to those shares. The definition of 'financial instrument' in the Disclosure Rules includes:

- transferable securities (shares in companies and other securities equivalent to shares in companies, bonds and other forms of securitised debt which are negotiable on the capital market and any other securities normally dealt in giving the right to acquire any such transferable securities by subscription or exchange or giving rise to a cash settlement excluding instruments of payment);
- units in collective investment undertakings;
- money market instruments;
- financial futures contracts, including equivalent cash-settled instruments;
- options to acquire or dispose of any instrument falling into these categories, including equivalent cash-settled instruments; and
- any other instrument admitted to trading on a regulated market in an EEA state or for which a request for admission to trading on such a market has been made.

9.46 The financial instruments must relate to the shares of the relevant issuer in order to be caught by the disclosure requirements in DTR 3. These are equity swaps, share options and share warrants. However, any dealings in debentures or other debt instruments not linked to or convertible into shares do not need to be disclosed under DTR 3.

9.47 The grant or acceptance of options relating to the securities of the issuer (or any other right or obligation to acquire or dispose of any securities of the issuer) and the acquisition, disposal, exercise of or dealings in such options, rights and obligations are transactions which are captured by the disclosure requirements in DTR 3. So share options do need to be disclosed on their grant and exercise.

9.48 The Disclosure Rules do not provide any formal guidance on what transactions will be considered to be conducted on a person's 'own account'. The FSA did, however, give informal guidance in *List!* 11. This states that while it is impossible to set out a definitive 'own account' test which would be applicable to all transactions a person discharging managerial responsibilities may conduct, there are three principles which suggest that a transaction is conducted on a person's 'own account' as follows:

1 a transaction which is the result of an action taken by a person discharging

managerial responsibilities or otherwise undertaken with that person's consent;
2 a transaction whose beneficiaries are mainly persons discharging managerial responsibilities;
3 transactions having a material impact on an interest of a person discharging managerial responsibilities in an issuer.

9.49 The three principles do not apply collectively – a transaction could be an 'own account' dealing even if it falls within only one of the three principles. Also, just because a transaction does not fall within one of the three principles does not automatically mean that the transaction is not conducted on a person's own account. The FSA notes that each transaction has to be assessed on its own facts. In cases of doubt, FSA guidance should be sought.

9.50 In *List!* 11, the FSA also gave informal guidance on which transactions would *not* constitute an 'own account' dealing under DTR 3. This includes transactions for which the person discharging managerial responsibilities has not given any instruction, consent or otherwise had any control over, such as an automatic vesting of an option or dealings by an employee benefit trust for the benefit of all participants, including (but not exclusively) persons discharging managerial responsibilities.

9.51 In relation to dealings made by trustees on behalf of persons discharging managerial responsibilities who are beneficiaries of the trust, it is clear from the second principle that the FSA takes the view that dealings in the beneficial ownership by trustees are caught as 'own account' dealings if the beneficiaries are mainly persons discharging managerial responsibilities (and presumably their connected persons, thereby including e.g. family trusts). This is the case if the dealing is made by non-discretionary or discretionary trustees. Dealings by non-discretionary trustees on behalf of persons discharging managerial responsibilities would in any event also be caught by the first principle, as it is likely that the consent of the person discharging managerial responsibilities would be needed before the dealing took place.

9.52 It would also appear that dealings by a person discharging managerial responsibilities acting as trustee (but not beneficiary) are likely to be an 'own account' dealing as a result of the first principle, where the person discharging managerial responsibilities is acting as a discretionary trustee and takes the investment decisions and actions.

9.53 If a person discharging managerial responsibilities is acting as a non-discretionary trustee, it will be a question of fact whether the dealing results from an action taken by him or with his consent.

9.54 In January 2009, following confusion about the disclosure requirements under DTR 3, the FSA issued a statement confirming that grants of security over shares, by way of a charge or similar arrangement, should be treated as a transaction for the purposes of DTR 3 and should therefore be disclosed (the same would apply to charges over other financial instruments caught by DTR 3). Disclosure would either be at the time of the acquisition if the security is granted at the same time as the acquisition (as part of the details given in the DTR 3 disclosure for the acquisition) or by way of a separate disclosure if the security is granted after the acquisition. By analogy, a release of shares from a security arrangement should also be disclosed under DTR 3.

Timing and contents of the disclosure to the company under DTR 3

9.55 The Disclosure Rules provide that the disclosure must be made by the directors and any other PDMRs and their connected persons to the company within four business days of the day on which the transaction occurred.

9.56 The notification must be made by the director or other person discharging managerial responsibilities to the relevant company and must (DTR 3.1.3 R) contain:

- the name of the director or other person discharging managerial responsibilities within the issuer, or where relevant the connected person;
- the reason for the responsibility to notify;
- the name of the relevant issuer;
- a description of the financial instrument;
- the nature of the transaction (e.g. acquisition or disposal);
- the date and the place of the transaction; and
- the price and volume of the transaction,

9.57 As described below, there is an FSA form for companies to use when notifying the market of relevant dealings via an RIS. For administrative ease, directors and other persons discharging managerial responsibilities should be asked to use this form (or a version of it prepared by the issuer) when disclosing their dealings to the company under DTR 3.1.2 R.

Obligation on the company to announce the information disclosed

9.58 A company must notify an RIS of the information notified to it:

- under DTR 3.1.2 R, by all directors and other persons discharging managerial responsibilities and all persons connected with them (the notification by the company must include the information required by DTR 3.1.3 R);
- s. 793 of the 2006 Act, in relation to the interests of a director or any connected person (unless the information has already been disclosed under DTR 3.1.2 R); and
- in relation to a trading plan entered into under the Model Code.

9.59 The notification by the company must include the date on which the relevant notification was made to the company (DTR 3.1.5 R). A form, 'Notification of Transactions of Directors, Persons Discharging Managerial Responsibility or Connected Persons', is available from the FSA website, which a company may (but is not obliged to) use to make the announcement required by DTR 3.1.4 R.

9.60 Companies are required to make the RIS announcement required by DTR 3.1.4(1) R as soon as possible, and in any event by no later than the end of the business day following receipt of the information by the issuer (DTR 3.1.4(2) R).

9.61 Listing Rule 9.8.6 contains a requirement (which applies to companies with a primary listing of equity securities) for the annual report to contain a statement of the interests in shares of directors and their connected persons which are notifiable under DTR 3 and the changes in those interests over the period covered by the report.

Compliance with the disclosure of dealings requirements in DTR 3

9.62 The responsibility for making the disclosures required from the director, other person discharging managerial responsibilities and their connected person, falls on the individual whose dealings are required to be disclosed.

9.63 The directors and other persons discharging managerial responsibilities are not responsible for the disclosures required to be made by their connected persons under DTR 3. The connected persons are directly responsible. DTR 3 does not expressly impose any responsibility on directors or other persons discharging managerial responsibilities to inform their connected persons of the disclosure obligations, nor do they exonerate any connected person who was not made aware of the obligations from sanctions for breach. However, the Model Code in the Listing Rules (see **9.86**) requires persons discharging managerial responsibilities to inform their connected persons of the need to advise the listed company immediately after any dealing.

9.64 Section 91 of FSMA gives the FSA powers to censure or impose a civil fine on issuers, directors and other persons discharging managerial responsibilities and their connected persons for contravention of the Disclosure Rules. Directors and other persons discharging managerial responsibilities should be made aware that enforcement action may be taken against them personally by the FSA.

9.65 Listing Principle 1 (Chapter 7 of the Listing Rules) requires companies with a primary listing of equity securities on the Official List to take reasonable steps to enable their directors to understand their obligations, including under the Disclosure Rules. If any director fails to disclose dealings in an issuer's securities to the issuer due to a lack of understanding of his duties, the issuer may be held responsible by the FSA for breach of Listing Principle 1, as well as the individual director being liable for failure to make the disclosure.

9.66 Checklist – steps for companies to take to ensure compliance with DTR 3 and Listing Principle 1

- Ensure that directors and persons discharging managerial responsibilities are informed of, and able to understand, their obligations to disclose their dealings in the issuer's securities under DTR 3.
- Persons discharging managerial responsibilities as defined in FSMA should be identified by the company and the list reviewed and updated periodically.
- Draw up a list of the connected persons of directors and other persons discharging managerial responsibilities and update it periodically.
- Consider taking steps to enable the connected persons of directors and other persons discharging managerial responsibilities to be informed of their disclosure obligations and understand the sanctions imposed on them personally for breach of the Disclosure Rules.
- Implement procedures to enable the company to announce dealing information to the market via a RIS within the relevant time frames in DTR 3.
- Keep records to show the dealings that have been disclosed to the company and the RIS announcements made by the company.

Disclosure of interests under the Transparency Rules

9.67 The regime for the disclosure of substantial interests in shares changed from being a company law matter to a requirement in the FSA rules in January 2007. Sections 198–209 of the 1985 Act were repealed and replaced by the FSA's Transparency Rules, which implement the EU Transparency Directive (2004/109/EC). Only the power for a company to investigate interests in its own shares has been left as a company law matter (see **9.12** above).

9.68 The rules on disclosure of substantial interests in shares are set out in DTR 5. The FSA has given guidance on its application in its *List!* publication, particularly *List!* 14 (revised).

9.69 DTR 5 applies not only to listed companies, but also to UK-incorporated PLCs that have their shares admitted to trading on a prescribed market, including AIM and PLUS markets.

9.70 For UK-incorporated issuers, the requirements are to disclose to the company an interest in voting shares that exceeds or falls below 3% and every 1% threshold thereafter (DTR 5.1.2R). Interests in voting rights can arise either directly (as a shareholder) or indirectly (as a result of a voting arrangement with the shareholder, or via financial instruments that give a right to acquire existing shares carrying voting rights). These indirect interests are due to be extended, from May 2009, to include contracts of differences and similar derivatives.

9.71 In the case of UK-incorporated companies, disclosure must be made within two trading days of the person becoming aware (or when he should have been aware) of the disclosable interest (DTR 5.8.3 R). Disclosure is required (DTR 5.8.10 R) to be made to the company on the FSA's prescribed form (available from the FSA's website). In the case of listed companies, this must be filed with the FSA at the same time as it is sent to the company. Listed companies are then required to disclose the information received via an RIS announcement by the end of the trading day following receipt of the information (DTR 5.8.12 R). AIM companies have longer under the Transparency Rules. For those companies the requirement is to make the announcement by the end of the third trading day following receipt of the information (DTR 5.8.12 R). However, as described in **9.98** below, in the case of AIM companies this is effectively replaced by the AIM Rules, which require an announcement without delay.

9.72 Directors are treated in the same way as other shareholders for the purposes of DTR 5. In the case of listed companies, the fact that directors' dealings and shareholdings are disclosed under DTR 3 as well is not relevant. There must be a separate notification by the director under DTR 5 as well if the threshold tests in DTR 5 are met, and there must be compliance with the earlier notification deadlines (two trading days under DTR 5; four business days under DTR 3).

9.73 The only aspect of DTR 5 which may create an additional issue specifically for a chairman, particularly for a chairman who holds shares in his own right, is the treatment of proxies. A person who is appointed as a proxy with the right to exercise voting rights at his discretion gains an indirect interest in shares for the purposes of DTR 5.2.1 R. This means that where the chairman of the meeting holds discretionary proxies which, together with his own interests in shares, amount to more than 3% of the voting rights in the company, he will have a notification obligation under DTR 5. There can be a single notification after the deadline for receiving proxies has passed (DTR 5.8.4 R). There is no requirement to include the names of all the people who have appointed the chairman as proxy, unless the individual holdings amount to a notifiable interest in themselves (see *List!* 14).

The Model Code in the Listing Rules

9.74 The Model Code is set out in Annex 1 of LR 9. The purpose of the Model Code is to ensure that directors and other persons discharging managerial responsibilities do not abuse inside information and do not place themselves under suspicion of abusing inside information, especially in periods leading up to the announcement of the company's results.

9.75 The Model Code prohibits dealings by directors and other persons discharging managerial responsibilities (which has the same meaning as in DTR 3 – see **9.62** above) during certain periods prior to the announcement of results and at any time when there is undisclosed inside information in relation to the company.

9.76 LR 9 only applies to companies that have a primary listing of equity shares and therefore the requirements in relation to the Model Code only apply to those companies.

9.77 LR 9.2.8 R contains an obligation on listed companies to require that its persons discharging managerial responsibilities comply with the Model Code. It must also take reasonable and proper steps to ensure compliance.

9.78 The Model Code sets the minimum standards that a listed company must impose (LR 9.2.8 R). A company may, if it wishes, impose more rigorous dealing obligations than those contained in the Model Code (LR 9.2.9 G). Since August 2007 listed companies are no longer required to impose the restrictions in the Model Code on employee insiders who are not persons discharging managerial responsibilities. They may, however, voluntarily extend their restrictions on dealings to employees who are not required to be covered by the Model Code.

9.79 The company must not carry out any dealings in its own securities (such as a buy-back of shares from its shareholders) at a time when a director of the company would be prohibited from dealing under the terms of the Model Code (LR 9.2.7 R).

9.80 The key element of the Model Code (paragraph 4) is a requirement that a person discharging managerial responsibilities must seek clearance before dealing in any securities of the company, including options and contracts for differences referenced to those securities. Dealing is defined to include acquisitions, disposals, the grant of any security over shares (and other actions creating a change of interest).

9.81 Clearance to deal must not be given (paragraph 8):

- on considerations of a short-term nature (an investment with a maturity of one year or less will always be considered to be of a short-term nature);
- during a close period; or
- during any period when there exists any matter which constitutes inside information in relation to the company.

9.82 A close period is defined in the Model Code as:

- the 60 days immediately preceding a preliminary announcement of the company's annual results (or, if shorter, the period from the end of the relevant financial year up to and including the time of announcement);
- the 60 days immediately preceding the publication of its annual financial report (or, if shorter, the period from the end of the relevant financial period up to and including the time of such publication);
- if the company reports half-yearly, the period from the end of the relevant financial period up to and including the time of publication of its half-yearly report;
- if the company reports quarterly, the 30 days immediately preceding the announcement of the quarterly results, which for these purposes does not include an Interim Management Statement issued pursuant to DTR 4.3 (or, if shorter, the period from the end of the relevant financial period up to and including the time of the announcement).

9.83 Paragraph 4 of the Model Code sets out who can give the clearance to deal. Clearance can be given:

- in the case of the chairman, by the chief executive or, if the chief executive is not present, the senior independent director, or a committee of the board or other officer nominated by the chief executive for that purpose;
- in the case of the chief executive, by the chairman or, if the chairman is not present, the senior independent director, or a committee of the board or other officer nominated by the chairman for that purpose;
- if the roles of chairman and chief executive are combined, by the board as a whole;
- in the case of any other director or the company secretary, by the chairman or a designated director;
- in the case of any other person discharging managerial responsibilities who is not a director, the company secretary or a designated director.

9.84 A response to a request for clearance must be given by the company within five business days of the request being made (paragraph 5). The dealing by the person discharging managerial responsibilities must take place within two business days of clearance being given (paragraph 7).

9.85 The company is required to keep a record of requests and clearances (paragraph 6).

9.86 The Model Code also contains certain obligations on persons discharging managerial responsibilities in relation to their connected persons (paragraphs 20–22). A person discharging managerial responsibilities must take reasonable steps to prevent any dealings by or on behalf of persons connected with him (as defined for the purposes of DTR 3 – see **9.62** above) on considerations of a short-term nature. He must also seek to prohibit any dealings by or on behalf of any person connected with him or by an investment manager on his behalf or on behalf of any other person connected with him (whether or not those funds are managed on a discretionary basis) during a close period. However, the person discharging managerial responsibilities is not required to, and should not, inform his connected persons or investment manager when they are not free to deal as a result of the company having inside information in existence. A person discharging managerial responsibilities must also advise all his connected persons and investment managers acting on his behalf of the name of the listed company of which he is a PDMR, the close periods between which they cannot deal in the securities of that company and the fact that they must advise the listed company immediately after they have dealt in the securities of the company (in other words to ensure that they comply with DTR 3).

9.87 There is a range of limited circumstances in which a dealing may be permitted even though it is in one of the prohibited periods (see paragraphs 9–19 of the Model Code). For the most part, these relate to the grant and exercise options under employee share schemes where the timing of the award of grant has already been fixed or where the company has been in an exceptionally long prohibited period and the final date for exercise will fall within a prohibited period. The FSA has recently amended the Model Code to create an exception so that PDMRs can enter into a trading plan prior to a prohibited period, with dealing then being permitted under the trading plan during a prohibited period. There are strict conditions for qualifying trading plans, including agreeing with a third party prior to the prohibited period the dates, prices and quantities of shares to be dealt in, or giving the third party discretion and not permitting the director to exercise any subsequent influence or discretion over dealings under the plan. Clearance is required to enter into the trading plan, or to cancel or vary the plan, and this could only take place outside a prohibited period. There are also certain other limited exceptions, such as allowing a director to acquire qualification shares on appointment, dealing when a person is in severe financial difficulty and dealing by a person who is acting as a trustee, provided that the decision to deal is taken by the other trustees and the restricted person is not a beneficiary. Just because a person discharging managerial responsibilities falls within one of the exemptions in the Model Code and is therefore permitted to deal pursuant to the Model Code does not mean that the dealing is exempt for the purposes of the market abuse and insider dealing offences (see **9.102** below). The question of whether the dealing could constitute market abuse or insider dealing must be separately considered in each case.

The AIM Rules

9.88 The AIM Rules contain two types of provisions relevant to directors as shareholders: (i) a notification of dealings requirement (the AIM equivalent to DTR 3 for listed companies); (ii) a requirement on AIM companies to ensure that directors do not deal in securities during prohibited periods that are equivalent to those in the Model Code.

Disclosure of directors' dealings

9.89 An AIM company must announce any dealing by a director in AIM securities without delay (AIM Rule 17). The announcement must include:

(a) the director's identity;
(b) the date on which the director disclosed the dealing to AIM company;
(c) the date on which the dealing took place;
(d) the price, amount and class of the relevant AIM securities;
(e) the nature of the transaction;
(f) the nature and extent of the director's interest in the transaction.

9.90 There is no obligation in the AIM Rules on the director to notify the dealing to the company. The AIM Rules cannot be directly enforced against the directors, in contrast to the provisions in DTR 3 for listed company directors. However, the company is required under Rule 31 to ensure that directors disclose to the company without delay all information which company needs in order to comply with Rule 17. This, together with the requirement in AIM Rule 21 for AIM companies to prohibit directors' dealings during certain periods (as described below), means that AIM companies need to ensure that they impose an obligation on their directors to inform the company in advance of any proposed dealings and also to notify the company as soon as any dealing has taken place. The definition of "deal" for the purposes of the disclosure requirement in AIM Rule 17 is the same as that for AIM Rule 21. It is very wide and includes dealings in financial instruments and dealings by certain members of the director's family and other connected persons (see **9.95** below).

Prohibition on dealing during close periods

9.91 Under AIM Rule 21, an AIM company 'must ensure that its directors and applicable employees do not deal in any of its AIM securities during a close period'.

9.92 The restriction on dealings in securities under Rule 21 applies to any securities admitted to AIM.

9.93 Unlike the Model Code in the Listing Rules, the AIM requirement also applies to any employees (defined as 'applicable employees') who are likely to be in possession of price-sensitive information relating to the company as a result of their employment.

9.94 The prohibited periods for AIM Rule purposes are essentially the same as those for listed companies under the Model Code. A 'close period' is defined in the AIM Rules glossary as:

- the two months preceding the publication of annual results (or, if shorter, the period up to the date of publication);
- the two months preceding the announcement of half-yearly results (or, if shorter, the period up to the date of the announcement);
- if the company reports on a quarterly basis, the one month prior to the quarterly results (or, if shorter, the period up to the date of the announcement);
- any other period when the AIM company is in possession of unpublished price-sensitive information; and
- any time when it has become reasonably probable that the announcement of price-sensitive information will be required by the AIM Rules.

9.95 The word "deal" is defined in the AIM rules glossary as including any change whatsoever to the holding of AIM securities, including any sale, purchase or transfer for no consideration and including the grant or disposal of any rights relating to an AIM security or related financial product referenced to an AIM security (for example contracts for differences). It therefore includes the grant or release of any charge or other security over AIM securities or related financial products. It also extends to dealings by the director's family (i.e. his spouse or civil partner and any children under the age of 18) and to any company or trust in which the director or any such a person has an interest of 20% or more.

9.96 There are limited exceptions to the prohibition on dealing during close periods. These include taking up rights in a rights issue and accepting a takeover offer (these are exceptions to the definition of deal), dealing in certain circumstances in accordance with a prior binding commitment and dealing in exceptional cases to alleviate severe personal hardship.

9.97 There is no specific requirement for an AIM company to impose a dealing code on its directors and employees, unlike the requirement for a Model Code for listed companies. However, in practice using such a code, including clearance procedures, is likely to be the most effective way of ensuring compliance with Rule 21, and most AIM companies do adopt such a code.

Disclosure of substantial interests in shares

9.98 As described in **9.67** above, the FSA's Transparency Rules (DTR 5) set out requirements in relation to the disclosure of substantial interests in voting shares of UK-incorporated AIM companies. The AIM Rules also impose, in Rule 17, an obligation on all AIM companies to notify any relevant changes to significant shareholders (defined as 3% or more), setting out the detail specified in Schedule 5 of the AIM Rules. The guidance notes for Rule 17 state that an AIM company subject to DTR 5 will normally comply with its obligation in Rule 17 by complying with DTR 5. There are two exceptions: (i) the company must ensure that the information is disclosed via an RIS rather than just being made public as required for AIM companies in DTR 5; (ii) the AIM Rules require the announcement to be made without delay after receipt of the information, whereas DTR 5 allows three days, and the guidance notes state that the shorter time limit in Rule 17 of the AIM Rules must be complied with.

Compliance with the AIM Rules

9.99 As described above, it is up to the AIM company to impose an obligation on its directors to comply with the obligations in the AIM Rules relating to clearance for and disclosure of dealings.

9.100 Under AIM Rule 31, an AIM company must have in place sufficient procedures, resources and controls to enable it to comply with the AIM Rules.

9.101 If a company breaches the AIM Rules it can be publicly censured or fined by the London Stock Exchange. However, there are no direct rights for the London Stock Exchange to censure or fine a director for breach of the AIM Rules.

Market abuse

9.102 The market abuse offences relating to misuse of information are of particular relevance to directors who are also shareholders because they are the persons most likely to have access to inside information about the company. The FSA has in the last few years emphasised that it intends to be more vigorous in enforcing the insider dealing and market abuse regimes, including pursuing directors and employees who disclose sensitive information or deal in the company's shares or other securities while in possession of price-sensitive information. A director convicted of the criminal offence of insider dealing can be fined and jailed for up to seven years and a director found guilty of the civil offence of market abuse can be subject to a public censure and a fine. It is therefore essential that directors protect themselves against any charge of wrongdoing by adhering to the relevant requirements and restrictions.

The civil offence of market abuse

9.103 Under Part VIII of the Financial Services and Markets Act 2000 (FSMA), the FSA has the power to impose a penalty on any person who has engaged in the civil offence of market abuse. The offences are listed in s. 118 of FSMA. There are seven in all and they fall into the three broad categories: misuse of information, creating a misleading impression and distorting the market. The three types that are relevant to the misuse of information are:

- dealing, or attempting to deal, in a qualifying investment or related investment on the basis of inside information relating to the investment in question;
- disclosing inside information to another person otherwise than in the proper course of the exercise of a person's employment, profession or duties;
- behaviour based on information not generally available but which, if available to a regular user of the market, would be likely to be regarded as relevant by that user when deciding the terms on which transactions in qualifying investments should be effected, if the behaviour is likely to be regarded by a regular user of the market as a failure to observe the standard of behaviour reasonably expected of a person in his position.

9.104 There is also a secondary offence of requiring or encouraging market abuse.

9.105 The market abuse regime is aimed not just at criminal behaviour (in contrast to the criminal offence of insider dealing; see **9.113** below) but also at behaviour that undermines confidence in the market and falls below reasonably expected standards. It is not necessary to show any intent to profit from confidential information or to mislead or deceive.

9.106 Inside information is defined in s. 118C as 'information of a precise nature which:

(a) is not generally available;
(b) relates, directly or indirectly, to one or more issuers of the qualifying investments or to one or more of the qualifying investments; and
(c) would, if generally available, be likely to have a significant effect on the price of the qualifying investments or on the price of related investments'.

9.107 The types of investments and markets to which the market abuse offence applies are set out in The Prescribed Markets and Qualifying Investments Order 2001 (SI 2001/996). The prescribed markets are the UK-recognised investment exchanges and all other EEA markets which are regulated markets. This therefore includes the Official List, AIM and PLUS markets.

9.108 Qualifying investments include all shares, securities and other financial investments. The inside information on which the dealing or attempted dealing is based has to relate to the qualifying investment or related investment which is the subject of the dealing. A related investment for the purposes of the insider dealing offence is one whose price or value depends on the price or value of the qualifying investment.

9.109 Section 118(A)(1) of FSMA provides that behaviour is to be taken into account for the purposes of the market abuse regime only if it occurs:

(a) in the United Kingdom; or
(b) in relation to:
   (i) qualifying investments admitted to trading on a prescribed market, operating in the UK;
   (ii) qualifying investments for which a request for admission to trading on such a prescribed market has been made; or
   (iii) (in relation to the dealing and disclosure offences listed above) investments which are related investments in relation to such qualifying investments.

9.110 The effect is that if the market abuse was committed in respect of a qualifying investment traded or to be traded on a UK prescribed market, the person committing the offence can be anywhere in the world and be caught by s. 118 of FSMA. However, if the market abuse relates to qualifying investments admitted to trading only on an EEA-regulated market outside the UK, then the person committing the offence must be in the UK at the time the offence was committed for the offence to apply. A further complication is that the third type of misuse of information offence listed above only (in any event) applies if the market is a UK market (because it is an offence which goes wider than the market abuse test in the EU Market Abuse Directive and so can only be applied to UK markets).

9.111 The FSA has issued a code providing guidance on market abuse – the Code of Market Conduct (COMC), which is contained in the Market Conduct section of the FSA Handbook (MAR 1). COMC gives examples of the behaviours that may amount to market abuse and also provides certain safe harbours for behaviour that does not amount to market abuse.

9.112 The penalties and remedies available to the FSA against any person who has committed market abuse are: public censure, a fine, an injunction and a restitution order. Penalties may be imposed on a company as well as an individual.

The criminal offence of insider dealing

9.113 The criminal offence of insider dealing is contained in Part V of the Criminal Justice Act 1993 (CJA).

9.114 There are three types of criminal offence in relation to insider dealing:

1 dealing on a regulated market or through a professional intermediary when in possession of inside information (the market abuse offence is wider because it covers all off market dealings as well);
2 encouraging another to deal when in possession of inside information; and
3 disclosing inside information, except in the proper performance of a person's employment.

9.115 For the purposes of the insider dealing offence, inside information is information which:

- relates to particular securities or to a particular issuer or issuers, and not to securities or issuers generally;
- is specific or precise;
- has not been made public; and
- if it were made public, would be likely to have a significant effect on the price of any securities.

9.116 The securities concerned can be any type of shares, debt or other securities, including options and derivatives relating to those securities. The market on which the securities need to be traded in order for the offence to apply are set out in the Insider Dealing (Securities and Regulated Markets) Order 1994 (SI 1994/187). They include the UK Official List, AIM, PLUS markets, a wide range of EEA markets and NASDAQ.

9.117 The securities must either be traded on one of the prescribed markets or be a right to subscribe for (or an option or derivative in relation to) such a security.

9.118 Under s. 62 of the CJA, an individual is not guilty of insider dealing unless he was in the United Kingdom when he did the dealing, or he dealt on a market regulated in the UK (e.g. the London Stock Exchange) or the professional intermediary through which the dealing took place was situated in the UK. In relation to the requiring or encouraging offence there is a narrower scope because it only applies if the person who encourages or requires, or the recipient of the requiring or encouragement, is in the UK.

9.119 An offence can only be committed by an individual, and then only if information is held by him as an insider. Information is held as an insider if the individual knows it to be inside information and it was knowingly acquired from an inside source. This would essentially catch all inside information that a director receives about the company in his capacity as a director.

9.120 There are certain limited defences to the insider dealing offence set out in s. 53 and Schedule 1 of the CJA.

9.121 A director may therefore be guilty of the criminal offence of insider dealing if he discloses the information otherwise than in the proper performance of his employment, office or profession or if he deals in the company's shares or other securities, or encourages another person to deal, at a time when he is in possession of price-sensitive information.

9.122 A person guilty of the criminal offence of insider dealing is liable to a maximum of seven years' imprisonment and a fine.

The Takeover Code – directors' interests and dealings in shares during a takeover bid

9.123 When there is a proposed or actual takeover bid for a company which is subject to the UK Takeover Code, the interests and dealings in the shares of the target and the bidder by any of the directors of the target and the bidder (and their connected persons) are subject to additional requirements and restrictions.

9.124 The UK Takeover Code, issued by the Panel on Takeovers and Mergers pursuant to Part 28 of the 2006 Act, applies to an acquisition or consolidation of control of:

- any public company incorporated in the UK, Channel Islands or Isle of Man which has its shares listed on the UK Official List or admitted to trading on any stock exchange in the Channel Islands or the Isle of Man;
- any other company (including all PLCs, whether or not their shares are traded) incorporated in the UK, Channel Islands or the Isle of Man and which has its place of central management and control in one of those jurisdictions (in the case of a private company only if its securities have been admitted to the Official List, or the subject of a dealing facility or prospectus, in the previous ten years).

9.125 It is the status of the target, rather than that of the bidder, that determines whether or not the Takeover Code applies.

9.126 An offer period starts under the Takeover Code from the time when an announcement of a proposed or possible offer is made until when the offer becomes unconditional as to acceptances or lapses.

9.127 The Takeover Code (Rule 4) prohibits dealings of any kind in the target's securities by any person who is privy to price-sensitive information about a takeover offer or potential offer (there are separate restrictions on dealings by the bidder). This restriction would therefore apply to the target and bidder directors. The prohibition on market abuse and the offence of insider dealing must be considered separately. In the case of listed companies the Model Code, and for AIM companies, AIM Rule 21, will also continue to apply. These offences and provisions in any event prohibit dealings at any time when a director is in possession of inside information.

9.128 The Takeover Code contains requirements for the disclosure of dealings by the bidder, the target and their respective directors and other associates, in the target's shares or interests in target shares (and bidder's shares if it is, or may be, a securities exchange offer) (Rule 8.3). The Takeover Panel takes the view that the interests and dealings of directors include for these purposes the interests and dealings of their spouses civil partner and infant children directors. These dealings must be disclosed via an RIS announcement by noon on the business day following the dealing.

9.129 In addition, dealings in the target's shares (or interests in target shares) by persons who are interested in 1% or more of the target's shares (and bidder's shares if it is, or may be, a securities exchange offer) during the offer period are required to be disclosed during an offer period (Rule 8.1). The 1% threshold is calculated not only by looking at whether the person owns or controls the shares, but also by looking at all of their interests, including options and derivatives. These dealings must be disclosed via an RIS announcement by 3.30 pm on the business day following the day of dealing. A person who has made a disclosure under Rule 8.3 does not need to disclose the same interest under Rule 8.1.

9.130 Rules 24 and 25 of the Takeover Code set out the rules on disclosure of interests and dealings in offer documentation. The interests of the bidder's directors and the target's directors in the target's shares (and, on a securities exchange offer, in the bidder's shares), must be disclosed in the offer document or defence document sent to shareholders from the bidder and the target respectively. The interests and dealings that need to be disclosed include derivatives referenced to, and put or call options in respect of, the relevant shares as well as the shares themselves. Dealings in the target's shares by the target's directors during the offer period and by the bidder's directors during the twelve months prior to the offer period also need to be disclosed in the documents.

9.131 As described in **9.12** above, where a takeover is being effected by way of a scheme of arrangement under Part 26 of the 2006 Act, then the details of the directors' interests need to be disclosed in the scheme circular (s. 897), and any changes in those details between the dispatch of the circular and the scheme meeting, may need to be disclosed in a new circular to shareholders.

9.132 The requirements of the Disclosure and Transparency Rules and the AIM Rules regarding disclosure of dealings by directors and their connected persons and disclosure of significant interests (as described above) continue to apply in the normal way throughout a takeover offer period.

Directors' shareholdings and dealings – regulatory requirements

DISCLOSURE REQUIREMENTS			
Provision	**Types of UK incorporated companies to which it applies**	**Disclosure requirement**	**Paragraph reference in Chapter**
Disclosure Rules (DTR 3)	Companies with securities traded on an EEA regulated market (therefore including the Official List but not AIM)	Disclosure by directors (and other PDMRs) and their connected persons of all transactions conducted on their own account in the shares of the company or financial instruments relating to those shares	**9.33**
Transparency Rules (DTR 5)	Companies with shares traded on an EEA regulated market or on a prescribed market (therefore including the Official List, AIM and PLUS)	Disclosure of interests in voting rights attaching to shares once interests exceed 3% and then every 1% change thereafter	**9.67**
AIM Rules	Companies with shares traded on AIM	Disclosure of any dealings by directors (and certain family members and connected entities) in AIM securities	**9.89**

Directors' shareholdings and dealings – *continued*

Provision	**Types of UK incorporated companies to which it applies**	**Disclosure requirement**	**Paragraph reference in Chapter**
Section 793 Companies Act 2006	Public limited companies	Disclosure (in response to specific request by company) of any interests in company's shares	**9.12**
Takeover Code	(1) Companies with shares listed on the Official List and (2) any other public companies (and private companies that were listed or the subject of a dealing facility or prospectus in the previous ten years) with their place of central management in the UK	Disclosure of any dealings by directors and their families during an offer period and disclosure requirements in offer documentation regarding directors' holdings and dealings	**9.128**
RESTRICTIONS ON SHARE DEALINGS			
Provision	**Types of UK incorporated companies to which it applies**	**Dealing restriction**	**Paragraph reference in Chapter**
Market abuse (Part VIII Financial Services and Markets Act 2000)	Companies with any securities traded on an EEA regulated market or a UK recognised investment exchange (including therefore the Official List, AIM and PLUS markets)	Civil offence to deal whilst in possession of, or base behaviour on, inside information or encourage another to do so	**9.103**

Provision	Types of UK incorporated companies to which it applies	Dealing restriction	Paragraph reference in Chapter
Insider dealing (Part V Criminal Justice Act 1993)	Companies with securities traded on one of the markets prescribed for that purpose, including the Official List, AIM and certain EEA markets	Criminal offence to deal, or encourage another to deal, on a market or relying on a professional intermediary whilst in possession of inside information	9.113
Model Code in the Listing Rules	Companies with a primary listing of equity securities on the Official List	Prohibition on dealing during 'close periods' – certain periods prior to the announcement of results and at any time whilst inside information exists in relation to the company	9.74
AIM Rules	Companies with shares traded on AIM	Prohibition on dealing during 'close periods' – certain periods prior to the announcement of results and at any time whilst inside information exists in relation to the company	9.91
Takeover Code	(1) Companies with shares listed on the Official List and (2) any other public companies (and private companies that were listed or the subject of a dealing facility or prospectus in previous ten years) with their place of central management in the UK	Restriction on dealings in target securities by any person who is privy to price sensitive information about a takeover offer or potential offer	9.127

10

Board meetings

Introduction

10.1 Whilst the Companies Act 2006 (the 2006 Act) represents a fundamental review of the law relating to companies, the conduct of board meetings for companies will, to a large extent, be unaffected. The new legislation will, however, inevitably lead to changes in practice, particularly given the new statutory statement of directors' duties in Chapter 2 of Part 10 of the 2006 Act.

10.2 In addition, companies that adopt (or in the case of companies incorporated after 1 October 2009 that retain) the relevant provisions of the new Model Articles will be subject to more prescriptive provisions in connection with the conduct of board meetings, albeit that these generally reflect accepted best practice.

10.3 For the purposes of this chapter it should be noted that:

- the different versions of the Model Articles (for private companies limited by shares, private companies limited by guarantee and public companies) are generally the same in respect of the provisions referred to, but to the extent that there are significant differences they are highlighted; and
- references to the Model Articles for private companies are references to both the Model Articles for private companies limited by shares and those limited by guarantee, such Model Articles being essentially the same in respect of the matters referred to in this chapter.

10.4 The Model Articles referred to in this chapter are those published by BERR in December 2008.

The board's authority

10.5 The directors derive their authority to conduct the affairs of the company by delegation from the company's shareholders usually through the articles of association. Under Table A of the Companies Act 1985 (The 1985 Act, Table

A) power is delegated to the directors by Regulation 70. The first sentence of which provides that:

> 'Subject to the provisions of the Act, the memorandum and articles and to any directions given by special resolution, the business of the company shall be managed by the directors who may exercise all the powers of the company.'

Regulation 88 further provide that:

> 'Subject to the provisions of the articles, the directors may regulate their proceedings as they think fit.'

10.6 Thus within the confines of this general authority the directors have freedom to manage their affairs in exercising the powers of the company as they see fit.

10.7 This position is preserved under Article 3 of the Model Articles, which provides that:

> 'Subject to the articles, the directors are responsible for the management of the company's business, for which purpose they may exercise all the powers of the company.'

10.8 This power is expressly made subject to any directions of the shareholders by special resolution, directing the directors to take (or refrain from taking) any specified action (article 4 of the Model Articles).

10.9 The Model Articles also provide (article 16 for private companies; article 19 for public companies) that subject to the articles, the directors may make such additional rules as they think fit about how they take decisions and about how such rules are to be recorded or communicated to directors.

Convening board meetings

Who may convene a board meeting?

10.10 The company's articles of association usually contain a power to convene board meetings. Regulation 88 of Table A provides that: 'A director may and the secretary, at the request of a director shall, call a meeting of the directors.'

10.11 Under the Model Articles (article 9(1) for private companies, article 8(1) for public companies), any director may call a directors' meeting and request or authorise the company secretary to do so.

10.12 In practice, what often happens is that public companies and larger private companies timetable board meetings to be held at regular times and dates. In such circumstances and subject always to the company's articles of association, provided that the dates, times and location of the meeting have been sent to the directors, there is no obligation to give further notice, although best practice would dictate that reminders are issued in any event.

What form should the notice convening a board meeting take?

10.13 The provisions of most companies' articles of association are not prescriptive as to the form or content of the notice convening a board meeting and this is the case under Table A. It would be unusual for there to be any requirement for notice to be in writing, for example, or that an agenda be provided. Each company's approach will develop based on a combination of past practice, the constitution of the board and the nature of the business to be considered at the relevant meeting.

10.14 Under the Model Articles the flexibility of the current position under Table A has been retained. The Model Articles are, however, more prescriptive as article 9(2) (article 8(4) for public companies) provide that notice convening a board meeting must indicate:

(1) the proposed date and time of the meeting,
(2) where the meeting is to take place, and
(3) where it is anticipated that the directors participating in the meeting will not be in the same place, how it is proposed that they should communicate with each other during the meeting.

10.15 The Model Articles also expressly state (article 9(3) for private companies, article 8(5) for public companies) that notice of a board meeting need not be in writing.

10.16 For companies where formal board meetings are held at regular intervals, and particularly where there are non-executive directors, it is advisable that notice should be given in writing (or, where the meeting is being held in accordance with a pre-arranged timetable, that a reminder is given). In these circumstances, to the extent that it is possible, the notice should be accompanied or followed by an agenda.

10.17 It is advisable to circulate prior to the meeting, in sufficient time to allow the directors to review them, any supporting papers which need to be considered at or in advance of the meeting and the drafting of any specific resolutions which it is proposed that the directors adopt.

10.18 There is usually no prescribed method by which notice needs to be given, and again established practice and what is reasonable in the circumstances (such as the urgency of the matter in question, the location of the directors and the nature of the matter being considered) will determine the most appropriate method by which notice should be given.

10.19 For many smaller private companies, board meetings, to the extent that formal board meetings are held, are often convened on an ad hoc basis. This is often done at very short notice/without formal notice being given. For larger companies, formal written notice will be given, with the method of delivery being determined by the company's established practice. In either case, it is important that it is clear that a board meeting is being convened.

What length of notice is required?

10.20 It is unusual to have prescribed periods in the articles of association for notice convening board meetings and Table A is silent on this. The general rule is that meetings need to be convened on notice which, taking into account the circumstances, allows each of the directors reasonable opportunity to attend or participate at the meeting.

10.21 The flexibility in Table A is retained by the Model Articles, which do not contain any provisions as to the length of notice required to convene a board meeting.

To whom should notice be given?

10.22 Notice should be given to each of the directors. Any alternate directors who have been appointed have the same right to receive notice of board meetings as their appointers and should therefore be sent notice at the same time as the other directors. The one fairly common qualification to this is that Regulation 88 of Table A provides that it is not necessary to give notice to any director who (at the time the notice is given) is absent from the UK.

10.23 This default provision is replaced by article 9(3) of the Model Articles for private companies (and article 8(5) for public companies), which provides that notice must be given to all directors without exception (including directors outside the UK).

10.24 Previously, it had been thought that a director could not waive his entitlement to notice of a board meeting. However, the Model Articles (article 9(4) for private companies, article 8(6) for public companies) provide that directors have the capacity to waive their entitlement to receive notice of a particular meeting by giving notice to the company to that effect before or not more than seven days after the date on which the meeting is held. To the extent that the right to receive notice of a meeting is waived after the relevant meeting this does not affect the validity of a meeting or any business conducted at it.

Effect of failure to give notice to all directors

10.25 The effect in law of a failure to give notice of a board meeting to all the directors remains unclear. While it could be argued that such failure invalidates the resolutions passed at the relevant meeting (notwithstanding that a valid quorum may have been present) this needs to be considered in light of the statutory protections in the 2006 Act.

10.26 Section 40 of the 2006 Act (which comes into force on 1 October 2009) provides that a person dealing with the company in good faith can assume that the directors have the power to bind the company or authorise others to do so, free of any limitation under the company's constitution. Section 40(2)(b) makes it clear that dealing in good faith does not put the third party under an obligation to enquire as to any limitation on the directors' powers to bind the company and that there is a presumption that a third party is acting in good faith unless the contrary is proved. Further, a third party is not to be deemed to be acting in bad faith only because it knew that an act was beyond the scope of the directors' authority.

10.27 Case law suggests that failure to give notice to a director entitles that director to request that a second meeting is convened to reconsider the matters decided at the first meeting, although this does not affect the underlying validity of the resolutions passed at the original meeting. The right to call a second meeting should to be exercised within a reasonable time after the relevant director becomes aware of the first meeting as otherwise he may be deemed to have waived his right to call a second meeting.

Persons entitled to attend

10.28 All the directors, including alternates in the absence of their appointor(s), are entitled to attend board meetings.

10.29 There is no right for anyone other than the directors of the company concerned to attend board meetings. However, others may be invited to board meetings, such as managers and possibly professional advisers, usually for specific parts of the meeting where they are required to report to the board. In addition, the company secretary (to the extent that the company has one) will usually be in attendance.

Quorum

General

10.30 In order for resolutions to be passed at a board meeting a quorum must be present. The articles of association will usually set out the number of directors who need to be present to constitute a quorum. This is often two, but it will depend on the circumstances of the particular company concerned.

10.31 Table A provides in Regulation 89 that the quorum for the transaction of business of the directors may be fixed by the directors but in the absence of such determination the quorum is two.

10.32 The Model Articles provide (at article 11(1) for private companies, article 10(1) for public companies) that unless a quorum is participating no proposal is to be voted on at a directors' meeting except a proposal to call another meeting.

10.33 In addition, the Model Articles (at article 11(2) for private companies, article 10(2) for public companies) provide that the quorum for directors' meetings may be fixed by the directors, but must never be less than two, and unless the directors determine otherwise, shall be two.

10.34 Many companies disapply the Table A provisions (and will, it should be anticipated, disapply the Model Articles provisions) by removing the directors' discretion on determining the quorum and fixing it at the level agreed by the shareholders. These companies will often extend the provisions by setting out not only the number of directors required to be in attendance, but also that those persons need to include representatives of certain shareholders or classes of shares.

10.35 For the purposes of determining whether a quorum exists, alternate directors are counted, provided that their appointer is not also present.

Prohibitions on counting in quorum and voting

10.36 Directors (including alternate directors) may be prohibited from voting and counting in the quorum at a board meeting if they (or persons connected with them) have an interest in the matter(s) being considered at the relevant meeting.

10.37 Table A provides at Regulation 94 that

> 'a director shall not vote at any meeting of the directors or committee of directors on any resolution concerning a matter in which he has, directly or indirectly, an interest or duty which is material and which conflicts or may conflict with the interests of the company'

save in the limited circumstances set out in Regulation 94 in respect of resolutions relating to:

> '(i) the giving to such director of a guarantee, security or indemnity in respect of money lent to, or an obligation incurred by him for the benefit of, the company or any of its subsidiaries,

(ii) the giving to a third party of a guarantee, security or indemnity in respect of an obligation of the company or one of its subsidiaries and in respect of which the director has assumed some form of personal responsibility under a guarantee or indemnity or form of security;

(iii) the relevant director subscribing or agreeing to subscribe for shares, debentures or other securities in the company or its subsidiaries or by such director participating in an underwriting or sub-underwriting of an offer of any such securities; or

(iv) a retirement benefits scheme which has been approved, or is conditional upon approval by, the Board of Inland Revenue for tax purposes.'

10.38 Regulation 94 provides that the interests of directors for these purposes include the interests of any person connected with them (as determined by the relevant provisions of the relevant Companies Act). Interests of directors are considered to be interests of any alternates they may appoint, in addition to any interests such alternates (or persons connected with them) may themselves have.

10.39 Where such an interest exists Regulation 95 of Table A states that a 'director shall not be counted in the quorum present at a meeting in relation to a resolution on which he is not entitled to vote'.

10.40 Whilst this prohibition can usually be suspended or relaxed by the shareholders by ordinary resolution under Regulation 96 of Table A, the prohibition can cause practical difficulties, particularly where more than one director has an interest in the matters under consideration with the result that a quorum does not exist. As a consequence, articles of association often disapply the provisions of Regulations 94 and 95 and provide that, notwithstanding any interest that a director may have in the matters before the meeting, he may vote on and be counted in the quorum in the meeting considering the particular matter.

10.41 Under the Model Articles similar provisions have been included, albeit that they vary slightly depending on the type of company concerned.

10.42 In the Model Articles for a private company limited by shares, article 14 provides that:

'14(1) If a proposed decision of the directors is concerned with an actual or proposed transaction or arrangement with the company in which a director is interested, that director is not to be counted as participating in the decision making process for quorum or voting purposes.

14(2) But if paragraph (3) applies, a director who is interested in an actual or proposed transaction or arrangement with the company is to be counted as participating in the decision making process for quorum and voting purposes.

14(3) This paragraph applies when –

(a) the company by ordinary resolution disapplies the provisions of the articles which would otherwise prevent a director from being counted as participating in the decision making process;

(b) the director's interest cannot reasonably be regarded as likely give rise to a conflict of interest; or

(c) the director's conflict of interest arises from a permitted cause.'

Permitted cause is defined under article 14(4) and covers:

(a) a guarantee given, or to be given by or to a director in respect of an obligation incurred by or on behalf of the company or any of its subsidiaries;

(b) subscription, or an agreement to subscribe, for shares or other securities of the company or any of its subsidiaries, or to underwrite, sub-underwrite or guarantee subscription for any such shares or securities; and

(c) arrangements pursuant to which benefits are made available to employees and directors or former employees and directors of the company or any of its subsidiaries which do not provide special benefits for directors or former directors.

10.43 The provisions are therefore broadly the same as the current position under Table A. However, the Model Articles do not expressly refer to the interests of connected persons of a director for these purposes, although arguably they would in any event still potentially be caught.

10.44 In addition, the concept of interests being discounted to the extent that they cannot reasonably be regarded as giving rise to a conflict is introduced (this effectively replaces the Table A test of materiality in Regulation 94) and the permitted purpose language in relation to employee benefits has been made more specific whilst removing the need for 'Board of Inland Revenue consent for tax purposes', as required under Table A.

10.45 Article 14(5) makes it clear that, for the purposes of article 14, 'references to proposed decisions and decision-making processes include any directors' meeting or part of a directors' meeting'.

10.46 For companies limited by guarantee, the provisions are essentially the same, save that the references to shares in the capital of the company have been omitted.

10.47 For public companies the equivalent provisions are set out in article 16. These differ from the private company Model Articles in that they refer only to a 'directors' meeting' rather than 'proposed decisions of the directors', which are concerned with actual or proposed transactions or arrangements with the company in article 16(1). There is no equivalent to article 14(5) for private companies. There is also a prohibition in article 13(3) on any director and his alternates from voting on any proposal relating to an actual or proposed transaction or arrangement in regard of which the director has an interest.

10.48 To the extent that any question arises as to a director's ability to vote on a matter either at a meeting of the board or a committee, Regulation 98 of Table A provides that the question may, before the conclusion of the meeting, be referred to the chairman of the meeting, and his ruling in relation to any director other than himself shall be final and conclusive.

10.49 The ability of the chairman to determine whether a director has the right to vote and also count in the quorum on a matter is preserved in article 14(6) (article 16(5) for public companies).

10.50 The provisions of Table A do not address the issue of how questions relating to whether the chairman is entitled to vote at the meeting may be resolved. The Model Articles, however, cover this at article 14(7) (article 16(6) for public companies), which provides that:

> 'If any question as to the right to participate in the meeting (or part of the meeting) should arise in respect of the chairman, the question is to be decided by a decision of the directors at that meeting, for which purpose the chairman is not to be counted as participating in the meeting (or that part of the meeting) for voting or quorum purposes.'

10.51 The fact that directors may not be entitled to attend a board meeting (e.g. because they are out of the country at the time it is convened) does not obviate the need to satisfy the requirement to have a quorum at the meeting.

Lack of quorum

10.52 If a quorum is not present at a meeting or any part of it, then the resolutions passed at the meeting (or any part of it where a quorum is not present) will not be valid save in the limited circumstances permitted by the articles (see below).

10.53 In addition, where a quorum is present at the beginning of a meeting care should be taken to avoid a quorum ceasing to be present because, for example, one or more directors leave the meeting or become unable to count in the quorum because they have an interest, directly or indirectly, in the matter under consideration.

10.54 Another potential issue and one that often arises is the situation where the number of directors in office in the particular company falls below the number required to constitute a quorum.

10.55 Regulation 90 of Table A provides that in such circumstances,

> 'the continuing or a sole continuing director may act notwithstanding any vacancies in their number, but, if the number of directors is less than the number fixed as the quorum, the continuing directors or director may act only for the purposes of filling vacancies or of calling a general meeting.'

10.56 The Model Articles (article 11(3) for private companies) similarly provide that if the number of directors for the time being in office is less than the number required to constitute a quorum, the remaining director(s) may only take decisions to appoint further directors or call a general meeting to appoint further directors. Further, article 11(3) provides that if there is more than one director the remaining directors can call a board meeting to appoint additional directors or call a general meeting to enable the shareholders to do so and that if a directors' meeting is called in these circumstances, but only one director attends, that director may appoint sufficient numbers of directors to make up a quorum or call a general meeting in order to make such appointments. Article 11 of the public company Model Articles contains different provisions which provide that if there is only one director, that director can appoint additional directors to make up a quorum or call a general meeting to do so.

10.57 However, unlike Table A, the Model Articles do not otherwise expressly permit the continuing directors to continue to act where there is a vacancy in their number.

10.58 Where a company's articles provide that the attendance of specific directors is required for a quorum to be present (usually as representatives of particular shareholders or classes of shareholders) an issue can arise where such directors are unable or unwilling to attend meetings. In these circumstances, the lack of quorum may prevent the directors from passing resolutions and running the company. In order to avoid this situation arising some companies provide in their articles that to the extent a quorum is not present at any duly convened board meeting the meeting be reconvened at a stated place and at a stated time (for example the same time and place two business days later). At the reconvened meeting the quorum requirement is relaxed often providing that any two directors or the directors who attend the reconvened meeting shall constitute a quorum. The alternative would be to remove a director from office if he fails on a regular basis to attend board meetings although this may not be possible where his appointment is made by the holders of a particular class of shares (and in any event commercially this may not be an option).

Use of electronic means to hold board meetings

10.59 The law as to whether a board meeting may be held by some form of electronic communication (telephone conference, video conference or webcast) remains unclear. As a consequence many articles of association contain a specific authority for the directors to hold board meetings in any way where each of the participants can hear the proceedings and may be heard by the other participants.

10.60 The use of electronic means to conduct board meetings is recognised in the Model Articles which provide (article 10 for private companies, article 9 for public companies) that:

> '(1) Subject to the articles, directors participate in a directors' meeting, or part of a directors' meeting, when –
> (a) the meeting has been called and takes place in accordance with the articles, and
> (b) they can each communicate to the others any information or opinions they have on any particular item of the business of the meeting.

10.61 The Model Articles provide that in determining whether directors are participating in a directors' meeting, it is irrelevant where any director is or how they communicate with each other. Therefore, board meetings may be held by any means where any form of two-way communication is possible between participants.

10.62 One practical point to consider where board meetings are held by electronic means is the deemed location of the meeting, which should be recorded in the minutes. Many articles of association provide either that the location of the meeting is where the chairman is situated or where the majority of the directors participating at the meeting are present. This point is addressed in the Model Articles which provide (in article 10(3) for private companies and article 9(3) for public companies) that:

> 'If all the directors participating in a meeting are not in the same place, they may decide that the meeting is to be treated as taking place wherever any of them is.'

Disclosure of interests

General provisions

10.63 As noted above, the articles of association often require directors to disclose any interest they may have in actual or proposed transactions or arrangements with the company (for example Regulation 85 of Table A although this provision has not been carried over into the Model Articles). Directors are also subject to statutory duties to disclose interests in proposed or actual contracts or arrangements with the company under ss. 177 and 182 of the 2006 Act.

10.64 Section 177(1) of the 2006 Act provides that:

> 'If a director of a company is in any way, directly or indirectly, interested in a proposed transaction or arrangement with the company, he must declare the nature and extent of that interest to the other directors.'

10.65 This extends the previous requirement in s. 317 of the 1985 Act as the declaration must cover both the nature and extent of the interest reflecting Regulation 85 of Table A, whereas s. 317 required disclosure only of the nature of the interest.

10.66 Any declaration may be made either at a meeting of the directors or by written notice to the directors in accordance with s. 184 of the 2006 Act, or may be covered by a general notice pursuant to s. 185 and must be made before the company enters into the proposed transaction or arrangement.

10.67 Further, if a declaration of interest made under s. 177 becomes inaccurate or incomplete, it must be updated to ensure that it is complete before the proposed transaction or arrangement is entered into.

10.68 Declarations of interests are not required where the director concerned is not aware of the particular interest, the transaction or arrangement in question, although directors are deemed to be aware of matters they ought reasonably to be aware of.

10.69 An interest does not need to be declared to the extent that such interest cannot reasonably be regarded as likely to give rise to a conflict of interest. However, prudence will dictate that all interests of which a director is aware should be formally declared in any event to avoid any debate as to what may or may not be reasonably likely to give rise to a conflict.

10.70 In addition, there is no duty to declare interests of which the other directors are already aware (for this purpose other directors are treated as being aware of anything of which they ought reasonably to be aware) or if the interest derives from the director's service agreement which has been or is to be considered by the board or a committee of the board. This is a useful change to the old rules and should protect directors from inadvertent breaches of the requirements for matters of which the other directors are aware but in respect of which no formal declaration of interest has been made.

10.71 Whilst s. 177 deals with proposed transactions or arrangements, s. 182 of the 2006 Act deals with the situation where a director of a company is interested in a transaction or arrangement that has been entered into by the company. The provisions mirror those in s. 177 (including the same requirements for declaring the nature and extent of interests and the same exclusions) and provide that they do not apply to the extent that the interest has been declared under s. 177. There is a similar obligation to update any declarations made to the extent that they become inaccurate or need to be updated.

10.72 One important difference between the sections is that breach of s. 177 is treated as a breach of a director's duties and is therefore capable of being ratified by the shareholders, whereas breach of s. 182 is an offence under CA 2006.

10.73 The provisions of s. 182 are extended to shadow directors pursuant to s. 187 of the 2006 Act, although a shadow director cannot make a declaration in a meeting and so must do so in writing pursuant to s. 184.

10.74 Any notice in writing needs to comply with the provisions of s. 184 of the 2006 Act and must be sent to the other directors in hard copy form or by electronic means if agreed by the recipient. Section 184(5) provides that should a director declare his interest in writing, then the making of a declaration is deemed to form part of the proceedings at the next meeting of the directors after the notice is given and should be minuted accordingly.

10.75 A general notice of interest may be given under s. 185 of the 2006 Act, which constitutes sufficient declaration of interest in relation to the matters to which such notice relates for the purposes of ss. 177 and 182. Such notice may be given to the effect that the director has an interest (as a member, officer, employee or otherwise) in a specified body corporate or firm and is to be regarded as interested in any transaction or arrangement that may, after the date of the notice, be made with that body corporate or firm. A general notice may also specify that a director is connected with a specified person and is accordingly to be regarded as interested in any transaction or arrangement that may, after the date of the notice, be made with that person by the company. Consistent with the requirements in ss. 177 and 182, a general notice given under s. 185 must state the nature and extent of the director's interest in the body corporate or firm or, as the case may be, the nature of his connection with the relevant person. To be effective, a general notice must be given at a meeting of the directors, or the director must take reasonable steps to secure that it is brought up and read at the next meeting of the directors after it is given.

10.76 Directors must declare matters where they have a direct interest (which may arise even where the relevant director is not party to the transaction or arrangement) and also indirect interests. Whilst this is not defined, standard practice under s. 317 of the 1985 Act has been to look to see if the contract is made with someone who is considered to be a connected person to the director within the meaning of the Companies Act. The definition of connected persons for these purposes is set out in ss. 252–256 of the 2006 Act and includes:

- a director's spouse, children or stepchildren, parents, partner or civil partner (but not the director's siblings);
- any body corporate with which the director is 'associated' (s. 254);
- the trustees of a trust of which the beneficiaries or potential beneficiaries include the director or any person connected with the director or which is a discretionary trust under which the director or persons connected with him could benefit (but excluding a trust for the purposes of an employer's share scheme or pension scheme);
- persons with whom the director lives as partner in an enduring family relationship;
- children or stepchildren under the age of 18 of the director's unmarried partner;
- a partner of the director of any person or entity connected with such director; and
- a firm of which the director is a partner or one of the partners of which is connected with the director or one of the partners of which is a firm of which the director is a partner (or the director is connected with one of the partners of such firm).

10.77 The definition of connected persons has therefore been extended beyond the rules in the 1985 Act to include the director's parents, children and stepchildren over the age of 18, children and stepchildren of a partner who are under the age of 18 and live with the director, civil partners and partners with whom the director lives as part of 'an enduring family relationship' (this expression is not defined in the 2006 Act).

10.78 For each of these interests every director should make the requisite declaration at the earliest opportunity, which in the case of a new director should be no later than the first board meeting which follows his appointment (assuming he has not given notice of his interests previously under s. 184).

Companies with sole directors

10.79 The provisions in s. 317 of the 1985 Act relating to the disclosure of directors' interests required that each such declaration had to be made at a meeting of the directors. For companies with a single director this meant that director holding a meeting on his own to make the relevant declaration.

10.80 Under the provisions of ss. 177 and 182 of the 2006 Act, as declarations under these sections are required to be made to the other directors, there is, by implication, no requirement on a sole director to comply with either section. However, for companies with a sole director but which are required to have more than one director (e.g. public companies), s. 186 of the 2006 Act requires the sole director to make a declaration of interest under s. 182. Any such declaration must be recorded in writing and form part of the proceedings at the next board meeting of the company after the notice is given.

10.81 As a practical point, for companies which have a sole director and to which s. 182 does not apply but where additional directors may be appointed, compliance with the principles of s. 186 is recommended to assist with making s. 182 declarations following the appointment of an additional director. One other point that should be noted is that, in respect of companies with a sole director who is also the only member of the company, section 231 of the 2006 Act requires any contract outside of the ordinary course of business between the company and the director to be either in writing or reduced to writing in a memorandum or in the minutes of the first board meeting following the making of the contract. Failure to comply with the section is an offence but does not invalidate the contract.

Directors' Resolutions

10.82 Directors' decisions made either at a board meeting or by written resolution. In summary, decisions at board meetings are, subject to anything to the contrary in the articles of association, made by a vote of the directors present at the meeting, with each director having a single vote and the majority view prevailing. Written resolutions are subject to the requirements set out in the articles and typically require the approval of all the directors who would be entitled to vote on the matter in question.

Voting at directors' meetings

General provisions

10.83 Usually, each director present has one vote (subject to any prohibitions on voting in the articles on matters in which the director or any person connected with him has a personal interest) and matters are decided by majority vote. However, the articles may provide for special voting arrangements for certain directors on particular matters. This is more usual for companies which have outside investors or which are joint venture companies and where directors are appointed by particular investors/shareholders. In these situations the articles may provide that certain matters may only be approved with the sanction of a particular director's vote in favour.

10.84 Table A provides at Regulation 88 that 'questions arising at a meeting shall be determined by a majority of votes'. Directors will usually have a single vote and any director who is an alternate shall, in addition to his own vote, have a separate vote for each director who has appointed him as his alternate and who is not present at the meeting.

10.85 In the Model Articles for private companies the voting provisions are set out in articles 7 and 8. Article 7 provides that:

> '(1) The general rule about decision-making by directors is that any decision of the directors must be either a majority decision at a meeting or a decision taken in accordance with Article 8.'

10.86 For private companies which have only one director (public companies are required always to have at least two directors) article 7(2) of the Model Articles stipulates that if there is no provision in the articles requiring the company to have more than one director the general rule is that article 7(1) does not apply. The sole director is accordingly authorised to take decisions without regard to any of the provisions of the articles relating to directors' decision-making.

10.87 For public companies, article 7 of the Model Articles provides that:

> '7 Decisions of the directors may be taken –
> (a) at a directors' meeting, or
> (b) in the form of a directors' written resolution.'

Article 13 of the public company Model Articles goes on to provide that:

> '(1) Subject to the articles, a decision is taken at a directors' meeting by a majority of the votes of the participating directors.
> (2) Subject to the articles, each director participating in a directors' meeting has one vote.

(3) Subject to the articles, if a director has an interest in an actual or proposed transaction or arrangement with the company-
  (a) that director and that director's alternate may not vote on any proposal relating to it, but
  (b) this does not preclude the alternate from voting in relation to that transaction or arrangement on behalf of another appointer who does not have such an interest.'

10.88 This last point clarifies that an alternate director of a company which has adopted the Model Articles, to the extent that he is appointed to that role by more than one director, may not be entitled to vote on a matter for one of his appointors (because of that person's interest in the matter under consideration), but may still vote on the matter on behalf of his other appointor(s) (to the extent that they are not interested and therefore prohibited from voting). Similarly, if the alternate is also a director of the company otherwise than as an alternate, the interests of his appointor will not preclude him from voting on matters on his own behalf where he himself does not have a personal interest in the matter in question.

10.89 The public company Model Articles also confirm (article 15) that a director who is also an alternate director has an additional vote on behalf of each appointor who is not participating at the meeting and would have been entitled to vote had they been participating at the meeting.

10.90 It should be noted that the private company Model Articles do not refer to the appointment of alternate directors or their rights to participate at directors' meetings or decision-making processes. These points would therefore need to be addressed by specific amendments to the Model Articles.

Chairman's casting vote

10.91 If there is an equal number of votes for and against a resolution, articles of association often provide that the chairman has a second or casting vote (in addition to any other vote(s) he may have as a director) and this is the default position under Regulation 88 of Table A.

10.92 The Model Articles provide (article 13(1) for private companies, article 14(1) for public companies) that the chairman or other director chairing the relevant board meeting shall have a casting vote. However, any such casting vote will not be effective in the event that relevant person holding the casting vote is not, in accordance with the articles, to be counted as participating in the decision-making process for quorum or voting purposes (articles 13(2), article 14(2)).

10.93 To the extent that the chairman does have a casting vote he will have discretion as to how he uses it, although prudence would dictate that the chairman should vote against any proposal where a majority of the directors are not in favour.

Directors' resolutions in writing

10.94 The directors are usually authorised under the articles to pass resolutions in writing without the need to have a meeting.

10.95 Regulation 93 of Table A provides authority for the directors to pass resolutions in writing without a meeting. In order to be effective, the resolution should be signed by all the directors entitled to receive notice of the board or committee meeting (e.g. to the extent that notice of a meeting need not be given to directors outside the UK such persons do not need to sign the written resolution in order for it to be effective provided that a quorum of directors does sign the resolution in any event) and such resolution may be validly passed by the directors signing more than one document, provided it is in the same form. In addition, Regulation 93 provides that alternates may sign in place of their appointors and are not required to sign if their appointors have already signed the resolution (unless they themselves are directors).

10.96 The basic principle that resolutions in writing may be passed by directors is retained in the Model Articles.

10.97 For private companies decisions of the directors may be taken in accordance with article 8 when all eligible directors indicate to each other by means that they share a common view on a matter and that such a decision may take the form of a resolution in writing, copies of which have been signed by each eligible director or to which each such director has otherwise indicated agreement in writing (article 8(2). For these purposes an eligible director is a director who would have been entitled to vote on the matter in question if it had been proposed at a board meeting (article 8(3)). In addition, for a resolution to be passed pursuant to article 8, the eligible directors saying it must constitute a quorum. For private companies there is a greater degree of flexibility in passing written resolutions as signature is not required and could, therefore, by way of example, be passed by an exchange of emails.

10.98 For public companies more formal provisions apply. Article 17 sets out the process for passing a directors' written resolution. Each director is authorised to propose a written resolution and has the power to require the company secretary to propose a written resolution if the director so requests. Any such proposal is made by giving notice in writing to each of the directors, which must indicate the proposed resolution and the time by which it is proposed that the directors should adopt it. Article 17(6) obliges the director and company secretary, in giving notice of a directors' written resolution, to act reasonably and in good faith in taking any decision in connection with the process of adopting that resolution.

10.99 Article 18 of the public company Model Articles goes on to provide that:

> '(1) A proposed directors' written resolution is adopted when all the directors who would have been entitled to vote on the resolution of a directors' meeting have signed one or more copies of it, provided that those directors would have formed a quorum at such a meeting.
> (2) It is immaterial whether any director signs the resolution before or after the time by which the notice proposed that it should be adopted.
> (3) Once a directors' written resolution has been adopted, it must be treated as if it had been a decision taken at a directors' meeting in accordance with the articles.
> (4) The company secretary must ensure that the company keeps a record, in writing, of all directors' written resolutions for at least ten years from the date of their adoption.'

10.100 Signature of each of the directors entitled to vote on the resolution if it had been proposed at a board meeting is therefore essential under the public company Model Articles. In order for a written resolution to be validly proposed, the directors agreeing the resolution must constitute a quorum.

10.101 Note that there is no equivalent to s. 248 of the 2006 Act (which requires minutes of directors' meetings to be kept) for directors' written resolutions and therefore no statutory requirement that they be retained. To the extent that written resolutions are permitted under the company's articles there is often a specific requirement to maintain a record of such resolutions. The Model Articles for private companies (article 15) provide that records must be kept in writing of every unanimous or majority decision for at least ten years from the date the decision is 'recorded' (the meaning of which is not defined). For public companies article 18(4) provides that the company secretary must ensure that the company keeps a record in writing of all directors' written resolutions for at least 10 years from the date the resolution is adopted (within the meaning of article 18(1) being the date when all of the directors have signed it).

10.102 Best practice, however, should be to retain any such resolutions with the board minutes of the company and for as long as the board minutes are retained.

Chairman

10.103 It is usual for a chairman be appointed to preside over the meetings of the directors. This appointment is either for a fixed period or made on a case-by-case basis. The authority of the directors to appoint a chairman is derived from the articles of association.

10.104 Regulation 91 of Table A provides that the directors may appoint one of their number to act as chairman and also gives them the power to remove the chairman. The chairman is appointed to preside over every meeting of the board at which he is present. To the extent that there is no person holding the position of chairman or the incumbent is unwilling to act or is not present within five minutes of the start of the relevant meeting, Regulation 91 provides that the directors present may appoint one of their number to act as chairman.

10.105 In the Model Articles, article 12 provides that the directors may appoint a director to chair meetings and that any such appointment may be terminated at any time by the directors.

10.106 For public companies, article 12(3) provides that the directors may appoint other directors as deputy or assistant chairmen to chair directors' meetings in the chairman's absence. Again such appointments may be terminated at any time by the directors.

10.107 If the chairman is not present at a directors' meeting (or any director appointed generally to chair board meetings in the chairman's absence in the case of public companies) within ten minutes of the time at which it was due to start, the participating directors must (as opposed to 'may' in Table A and note that the power to appoint a chairman is permissive in any event) appoint one of their number to chair it (article 12(4) for private companies, article 12(5) for public companies).

Committees

10.108 It is common for the directors to delegate some of their powers to committees. This is done for a variety of reasons, particularly where full board meetings are deemed inappropriate to deal with particular matters, for example, final approval of the terms of a business sale or acquisition which has been agreed in principle by the board may be delegated to a committee and committees may also be established for particular purposes such as audit, remuneration or nomination committees. Many larger companies also have executive committees which meet on a regular basis in between full board meetings.

10.109 The ability of the directors to delegate their powers to committees is usually set out in the articles, and Regulation 72 of Table A provides the directors with authority to delegate any of their powers to a committee consisting of one or more directors. Regulation 72 also provides that, subject to any conditions imposed by the directors, the proceedings of any committee consisting of two or more directors shall be governed by the same provisions of the articles relating to board meetings to the extent applicable. The provisions in Regulation 93 relating to the passing of directors' written resolutions also extend to resolutions of committees.

10.110 This approach is followed in the Model Articles, which provide at article 5 that the directors may, subject to the other provisions of the articles, delegate the powers conferred on them under the articles to committees on such terms and conditions as they think fit.

10.111 Article 6 of the Model Articles goes on to provide that:

> '(1) Committees to which the directors delegate any of their powers must follow procedures which are based as far as they are applicable on those provisions of the articles which govern the taking of decisions by directors.
>
> (2) The directors may make rules of procedure for all or any committees, which prevail over rules derived from the articles if they are not consistent with them.'

10.112 Therefore, the same rules relating to the passing of directors' resolutions, both in meetings and in writing, will apply to committees.

10.113 In practice, many companies draw up specific terms of reference for committees setting out, among other matters, the composition of the committee, the quorum requirements and the basis on which it makes its decisions.

10.114 Without such provisions, either in the articles or in separate terms of reference, the proceedings of any committee require the attendance of all the directors appointed to it and the committee does not have the ability to approve changes to its composition without reverting to the full board.

Minutes

General

10.115 It is a statutory requirement that every company must maintain a record of the decisions taken by its board of directors.

10.116 The old provisions set out in s. 382 of the 1985 Act have been replaced by s. 248 of the 2006 Act, which provides that minutes must be taken of all proceedings at directors' meetings and that records of such proceedings must be kept for at least ten years from the date of the meeting. Failure to comply is an offence on the part of each of the officers of the company in default.

10.117 In addition to the statutory obligation to keep minutes, there is often an obligation in the company's articles to maintain records of meetings of directors and of committees.

10.118 Regulation 100 of Table A provides that the directors will cause minutes to be kept in books kept for the purpose of all appointments of officers made by the directors and of all proceedings of meetings of the directors and of committees of the directors and to include the names of all directors present at such meeting.

10.119 Similarly, article 15 of the private company Model Articles provides that the directors must ensure that the company keeps a written record for at least ten years from the date of the decision recorded of every unanimous or majority decision taken by the directors.

10.120 Once the minutes have been drawn up, best practice would be to circulate them to the directors who participated in the relevant meeting for any comments before being submitted to the chairman of the relevant meeting (or the chairman of the next board meeting) for approval and, once finalised, signature.

10.121 Section 249 of the 2006 Act provides that minutes authenticated by the chairman of the meeting or by the chairman of the next directors' meeting are evidence (in Scotland, sufficient evidence) of the proceedings at that meeting.

10.122 Preparation of the minutes of a directors' meeting are also deemed under s. 249 to create presumptions that, unless the contrary is proved, the meeting was duly held and convened and that all proceedings at the meeting have duly taken place and all appointments made at the meeting are valid.

10.123 Once minutes have been signed by the chairman they should not be amended or altered in any way. To the extent that minutes of a meeting are found to be incorrect after they have been signed, the correct procedure is to add a further minute or note correcting the error or mistake, which should be signed by the chairman.

10.124 In relation to the requirement to keep records of board meetings, it should be noted that the records may be stored electronically pursuant to

s. 1135 of the 2006 Act provided that they are capable of being reproduced in hard copy. However, the benefits of having the minutes signed by the chairman (as the signed version is deemed to be evidence under section 249(1) of the 2006 Act of the matters considered at the meeting) mean that it is advisable in any event to keep the hard copy bearing the chairman's original signature rather than having to rely on a copy should the minutes ever need to be produced in evidence.

10.125 Matters to be covered by board minutes are dealt with more fully at **10.127**, but in summary they include:

- Sequential number of board minute.
- Name of the company.
- Date, time and place of meeting.
- Note of the directors present and any other persons in attendance.
- Note of how directors participate in the meeting to the extent not in person.
- Note of the identity of the chairman.
- Note that notice has been given to all the directors entitled to receive the same and confirm that a quorum is present.
- Note the declaration of any interests of the directors (or persons connected with them) that are required to be disclosed and minute any declarations of interests made under s. 184 or s. 186 of the 2006 Act.
- The text of each resolution passed by the directors.
- The text of any instruction to others, including the company secretary, in relation to matters decided at the meeting.

Form and content

10.126 It is usually down to the company secretary to take notes of the discussions and resolutions at board meetings and to draft the minutes accordingly. The exact form and content of the minutes will vary depending on the matters under consideration and the company's past practice.

10.127 Generally speaking, board minutes for companies fall into one of two categories:

1. those prepared for a particular corporate matter or transaction which are often prepared by the company's solicitors and therefore follow a fairly rigid legal formula and are usually prepared in advance of the relevant meeting; and
2. those prepared for everyday business which often contain general updates in relation to a number of areas of the company's business and updates on ongoing matters which are usually prepared by the company secretary (or the person designated to prepare them following the relevant meeting).

In either case, best practice dictates that the board minutes should cover the following:

- A record of those directors present. The board minutes should record which directors were present and any apologies received from absent directors. The record should also specify if the director was physically present or participated by telephone or other method of electronic communication. To the extent that directors are present for part of the meeting only, this should be recorded in the minutes, with notes specifying the parts of the meeting where such persons entered or left the meeting.
- Anybody else 'in attendance' at the meeting, such as the company secretary, should have their presence noted.
- Note of quorum. The company secretary will need to ensure that a quorum is present throughout the meeting and this should be noted in the minutes.

  The company secretary will need to have particular regard to the quorum as directors arrive and leave during the course of the meeting. In addition, the company secretary will need to keep in mind any prohibitions on voting or counting in the quorum where directors have declared interests in the matters under consideration and for these purposes it is useful if the company secretary has a record of the previous declarations of interests made by the directors.
- Declaration of any directors' interests in the business to be conducted at the meeting. Any personal interests declared by the directors either pursuant to the Companies Act or the articles of association should be minuted. To the extent that such interests prohibit a director from forming part of the quorum or voting on any matter, this should be reflected in the minutes (e.g. that the relevant director abstained from voting on the matter in which he had an interest).

  The minutes should also include reference to any declarations of interests made under s. 184 of the 2006 Act.
- Business of the meeting. The minutes should contain summaries of the matters considered by the directors at the meeting, including details of any contracts or other documents produced to the meeting which were considered by the directors, and clear statements of any resolutions passed.
- The minutes should include details of any directions given by the directors which need to be followed up.
- It is recommended that board minutes are numbered sequentially to enable ease of reference at a later date.

10.128 It is not necessary for the minutes to set out a verbatim account of everything that was said at the meeting or indeed the reasoning or arguments behind the decisions reached by the directors at the meeting. There may, however, be circumstances where the directors will want the record to reflect the reasons why they reached a particular decision particularly if there is uncertainty over the company's solvency or to demonstrate that in reaching their decision they are complying with their duties.

10.129 As there is no requirement to record arguments put forward in the meeting for or against a particular proposal, dissenting comments or views do not need to be set out in the minutes. While the minutes should record how the directors voted if a decision is not reached unanimously, dissenting directors may also request that their comments or views be included in the minutes. If a dissenting director requests that his views are minuted, the matter should be referred to the chairman for determination. If necessary, the chairman may raise the matter at the next meeting for resolution.

10.130 The codification of directors' duties in Part 10 of the 2006 Act has led to a considerable debate as to what extent directors will modify the way in which they reach decisions and what impact this will have on the record of their proceedings. This is particularly relevant to the general duty to promote the success of the company under s. 172(1) of the 2006 Act, which requires directors to consider certain factors set out in the section in exercising this duty.

10.131 In the same way that there is no need to set out the arguments for and against each resolution made by the directors, the general view (and one taken by the GC100) is that there is no need to restate the factors set out in section 172(1) irrespective of the matters being considered by the directors. To the extent that any of the factors are specifically considered, it may be appropriate that this is recorded in the minutes particularly where the matter under consideration is of importance but this will depend on the prevailing circumstances. Ultimately, it is a question for each director as to whether he has complied with his duties. The minutes may assist with establishing whether a particular matter was considered by the directors at the relevant meeting but should not be seen as being definitive on the point. As such they and the supporting papers may provide useful evidence of the directors deliberations and accordingly the secretary should ensure that a complete pack of the minutes and all of the supporting papers are stored securely for possible future reference.

Role of company secretary

10.132 One of the key changes brought in by the 2006 Act is to allow private companies to dispense with appointing a secretary should they so choose. Section 270 provides that 'a private company is not required to have a company secretary'.

10.133 Where companies do not appoint a company secretary, s. 270(3) provides that anything required or authorised to be done by the secretary may be done by a director of the company or a person authorised generally or specifically by the directors of the company for that purpose. It is anticipated that many private companies, particularly small owner-managed businesses, will take advantage of this exemption and dispense with formally appointing a company secretary.

10.134 Public companies must continue to have a company secretary (s. 271) and, in the event that they fail to appoint one, can be directed to do so by the Secretary of State. In addition, most larger private companies are also likely to retain a company secretary.

10.135 Irrespective of whether a company has a company secretary, the role traditionally performed by the company secretary in relation to the convening and conduct of board meetings still needs to be performed.

10.136 This role can be split into three areas:

- pre-meeting responsibilities;
- responsibilities during the meeting;
- post-meeting responsibilities.

Pre-meeting responsibilities

10.137 The company secretary is likely to be responsible for convening board meetings, at the request of the chairman or one of the other directors of the company.

10.138 The exact nature and extent of the preparations for the board meeting will be dictated by the business to be considered at the meeting and the company's usual practice. Larger companies typically adopt more formal procedures for convening board meetings, particularly where the company has a large board which includes both executive and non-executive directors.

10.139 The company secretary may be required to prepare formal board packs of papers prior to the board meeting and, to the extent that it is necessary, these will need to be circulated in sufficient time to allow for their consideration prior to the board meeting. These papers may accompany the agenda for the meeting and may include copies of any reports or documents. The board packs may include the text of any resolutions that the directors will be asked to consider at the meeting to the extent that they have been prepared beforehand. For smaller private companies the approach is likely to be less formal, with meetings often being convened with the minimum of ceremony often without written notice or a pre-circulated agenda or papers.

10.140 In either case the company secretary needs to ensure that the meeting is properly convened and that notice is given of the board meeting to all of the directors entitled to receive notice. It is also advisable that appropriate reminders are given where the meeting has already been notified or diarised.

10.141 The company secretary is also likely to be responsible for ensuring that the facilities required for the meeting, including to the extent applicable, effective telephone conference, video conference, webcasting or presentation facilities are available for the meeting and that an appropriate room is booked.

10.142 Checklist for preparation for board meeting:

- Circulate notice of meeting setting out date, time and place of meeting, together with arrangements for video conference, telephone conference or webcasting facilities to the extent necessary.
- Notify any persons (managers, professional advisers, for example) who are invited to attend the meeting or part of it of the date, time and location of the meeting.
- Notify any persons (e.g. managers, professional advisers) who are preparing written materials for the board meeting as to the proposed date of the meeting and the date on which the materials they are providing need to be available for circulation to the board.
- Ensure minutes for previous meeting have been circulated to the directors and any suggested changes have been incorporated into the draft and/or discussed with the chairman.
- Circulate reminders of the meeting.
- Ascertain:
  - whether any board members are out of the UK (at the time that notice is given or at the time of the meeting) or are otherwise unable to attend; and
  - whether any of such persons to the extent entitled to notice of the meeting wish to participate either through video conference, telephone conference or webcasting facilities or wish to appoint an alternate.
- Prepare and circulate to the extent applicable:
  - board packs of papers together with any relevant supporting papers;
  - the agenda; and
  - text of any specific resolutions proposed to be passed.
- ensure appropriate board or meeting room is booked and properly resourced and that appropriate video conference, telephone conference or webcasting facilities are available and have been tested and appropriate audio visual facilities are available and have been tested for any presentation.
- For listed companies, ensure schedules of any transfers of securities made since the preceding board meeting are available for inspection to the extent required.

- Ensure copies of the agenda, board packs and resolutions are available at the meeting.
- Ensure that copies of the board minutes for previous meetings of the directors to the extent required to be signed by the chairman are available.
- Ensure that copies of the company's procedural manual on the holding of board meetings are available for reference.
- Ensure that copies of the company's memorandum and articles of association, Table A or the Model Articles (to the extent incorporated into the company's articles) and a copy of the Companies Acts are available for reference.
- Ensure that any third parties who are to attend the board meeting in whole or in part are ready to join the meeting at the relevant time

During the meeting

10.143 The company secretary is usually responsible for taking notes during the meeting for the purposes of subsequently preparing the board minutes. In addition, the secretary may be asked to advise on procedural matters during the meeting, such as the rules as to voting or quorum and the declaration of directors' interests. For this reason it is recommended that copies of the company's memorandum and articles of association, Table A or the Model Articles to the extent adopted and the Companies Act are available at the meeting.

10.144 The company secretary should also ensure that additional copies of the papers sent to the directors prior to the meeting are available and that the minutes from the previous meeting, to the extent not already signed by the chairman, are available at the meeting for approval and signing.

Post-meeting

10.145 The company secretary will usually be charged with a number of obligations following the meeting. These may include:

- making appropriate filings at Companies House – e.g. to reflect any appointments or resignations made of officers of the company approved at the meeting;
- overseeing the distribution of resolutions to shareholders together with any supporting papers;
- implementing any other resolutions with which the directors have charged the company secretary; and
- preparing the minutes of the meeting, circulating the minutes for comments by the directors and preparing a final version of the minutes for signature by the chairman.

10.146 Checklist for post-board meeting:

- Ensure any regulatory announcements or filings required to be made following the resolution of the matters at the board meeting are promptly made.
- Ensure Companies Act forms are prepared and filed within the statutory deadlines for matters arising from the meeting.
- Ensure that any documents that have been approved by the directors for distribution to shareholders are sent.
- Notify any managers or other third parties of any actions that the directors have requested that they take.
- Prepare minutes and circulate an initial draft to the directors as soon as reasonably practicable following the end of the meeting.
- Ensure minutes are finalised with the chairman prior to the next meeting and that a final draft is presented at the next meeting for approval and signature.
- Update the company's statutory registers, including minute books, to the extent required in connection with any of the matters resolved at the meeting.
- Update the register of details of directors' conflicts of interests, including the extent of any authorisations given by the directors under the 2006 Act or the shareholders of the company in respect of any such conflict.
- Ensure that all confidential papers are taken from the meeting room and not left behind following the meeting.

Recommended procedures

10.147 It is recommended that companies that hold formal board meetings on a regular basis, and particularly where they have a large board with executive and non-executive directors, establish formal rules and procedures for the convening and conduct or board and committee meetings. This is particularly the case for listed companies.

10.148 As noted at the start of this chapter the directors have a great deal of flexibility as to how they conduct their proceedings subject only to the specific requirements in the articles and the 2006 Act. Written rules of procedure are useful for ensuring that the directors understand the company's standard practices in respect of the convening and conduct of board meetings as well as being a reminder of the directors' duties and the specific rules on conflicts of interest, alternates and directors' written resolutions and the duties of directors under the Model Code appended to Chapter 9 of the Listing Rules and the Combined Code on Corporate Governance (see **Appendix 1**). A manual can also deal with other areas of corporate governance that the directors need to be mindful of such as company policy in respect of benefits which directors may accept from third parties.

10.149 The procedural manual should be made available to all directors each time it is updated and should be issued to new directors on appointment. Copies should be available at all board meetings.

10.150 The manual should also cover the function, powers and constitution of committees and sub-committees of the main board (and if not incorporated in the manual identify where the terms of reference for the committees of the board may be found).

10.151 In addition to establishing a procedural manual, companies should ensure that those responsible for preparing briefing papers or reports for the board are made aware of the factors that the directors need to consider under s. 172(1) so that, to the extent relevant, they can be addressed in the papers presented to the board.

10.152 Formal schedule of matters specifically reserved for the decision of the board:

Checklist of possible matters to be included in procedural manual

- Final schedule of matters specifically reserved for the decision of the board.
- Formal schedule of matters specifically reserved for each of the committees of the board of directors.
- Terms of reference for each committee of the board.
- Summaries of the company's rules relating to:
  - conflicts of interest;
  - the rules on voting on matters in which directors (or persons connected with them) have a personal interest (including a summary of the meaning of connected persons for these purposes);
  - the company's share dealing rules and, to the extent applicable, the provisions of the Model Code;
  - duties of directors of the company including those set out in the 2006 Act;
  - the company's policy in respect of benefits received from third parties.

Additional requirements for listed companies

10.153 There are no specific provisions in the 2006 Act or the Model Articles which particularly relate to conduct or procedure of board meetings of listed companies other than those that relate to companies generally and which are highlighted above.

10.154 However, in addition to the company's articles of association and the requirements of the 2006 Act, directors of listed companies need to have regard to the requirements of the Combined Code.

10.155 While the Combined Code is not legally binding, directors of companies admitted to the Official List of the UKLA must either comply with the Code or explain why they have not done so.

10.156 The key parts of the Code which relate to the conduct and holding of board meetings (and leaving aside the provisions of the Code which deal with composition and independence of the board) are:

(a) Main Principle A.1: Every listed company should be headed by an effective board which is collectively responsible for the success of the company.
The supplemental Code Provisions provide that:
   (i) The board should meet sufficiently regularly to discharge its duties effectively and that there should be a formal schedule of matters specifically reserved for its decision.
   (ii) The company's annual report should contain a high-level statement as to which decisions are reserved to the board and which are delegated to management.
   (iii) The number of meetings of the board and its main committees and individual attendance should be identified in the annual report.
   (iv) The chairman should meet with the non-executive directors without the executive directors present and the non-executive directors should meet without the chairman and the executive directors present at least once a year.
   (v) If a director has concerns about the running of the company or a proposed action which are not resolved he or she should ensure that these concerns are recorded in the board minutes.

(b) Main Principle A.5: The board should be supplied in a timely manner with information in a form and of a quality appropriate to enable it to discharge its duties. All directors should receive induction on joining the board and should regularly update and refresh their skills and knowledge.

The Supporting Principles to Main Principle A.5 provide that:

(i) Management has an obligation to provide the board with appropriate, timely and clear information but that the directors should make further enquiries where necessary. It is a responsibility of the chairman to ensure that this occurs.

(ii) Under the chairman's direction, the company secretary is responsible for ensuring good information flows within the board and its committees and between senior management and non-executive directors and also facilitating inductions and assisting with professional development.

(iii) The company secretary is also responsible for advising the board on all governance matters.

11

Shareholder meetings

Introduction

11.1 The issues to be considered when organising and holding a meeting will vary depending on the size of the company, the number of members it has, the business to be conducted and the resolutions to be proposed. In the case of large, usually publicly quoted companies, general meetings, especially the annual general meeting, are large public meetings and will be used to both conduct regular formal business and inform the members of matters such as the successes of the previous financial year. Of course, if success is limited, the members are likely to take this opportunity to ask difficult questions and hold boards to account. There may even be votes against the resolutions proposed, especially in relation to the appointment or reappointment of directors and the approval of their remuneration packages.

11.2 In the case of smaller companies, a shareholder meeting can be a much more relaxed affair, especially if there are only a handful of members. Although formal procedures must be followed in order for the necessary resolutions to be approved, difficult questions are unlikely and meetings can even be held at very short notice. In the case of private companies, resolutions can be agreed in writing so that a formal meeting, as such, does not even take place.

11.3 The law on company meetings and resolutions was re-enacted and, in some cases, amended by Part 13 of the Companies Act 2006 (the 2006 Act) which came into force on 1 October 2007. In some areas the 2006 Act has provided a useful confirmation of the previous common law position. Much of the law and regulation on company meetings is, in any event, not contained in statute but is set out in a company's constitutional document, known as its articles of association. This is the key document to be consulted when organising a shareholder meeting since it will set out most of the formal meeting procedures and deal with other relevant matters such as who will chair the meeting and who may attend and vote.

11.4 Companies can either be incorporated with their own articles or can simply adopt government-approved articles (Table A). The form of Table A applicable to companies incorporated between 1 October 2007 and 30 September 2009 is an interim version – which is basically the original Table A, amended to reflect the 2006 Act. There are two versions of the interim Table A, one for private companies and one for public companies. Companies incorporated prior to 1 October 2007 do not need to amend their articles to reflect the interim Table A, although some have chosen to do so. After 1 October 2009 companies will be incorporated either using their own articles or government-approved Model Articles. Different versions of these Model Articles will apply depending on whether the company is a private company limited by shares, a private company limited by guarantee or a public company. In this chapter reference is made to both Table A and the Model Articles because, for the time being, many existing companies will retain their Table A-based articles.

11.5 Another important change in the running of shareholder meetings has been the growing use of electronic communications to publicise meetings and to circulate documents, such as the notice of the meeting and a company's annual report and accounts. In the context of the 2006 Act provisions on meetings and resolutions, the term electronic communications encompasses sending out notices of meetings in electronic form such as by e-mail and via a website, as well as by disc or even text message. The ICSA published a Guidance Note on electronic communications with shareholders in 2007.[1]

11.6 The 2006 Act provides greater powers for indirect investors to exercise membership rights, even though the shares are held via a nominee who is the legal owner of the shares and whose name is actually entered on the share register. See **11.143** below for an explanation of these changes.

11.7 The Combined Code, with which companies listed on the Official List are required to comply (see **Chapter 12**), requires listed companies to enter into a dialogue with their institutional shareholders and to make constructive use of their annual general meeting. The government and bodies such as the ABI and the NAPF are keen to use shareholder meetings to their full effect and to encourage investors to vote their shares. There is also a growing number of activist shareholders in listed companies who use their rights as members to call meetings, propose resolutions and question the board.

Shareholder powers

11.8 On a day-to-day level, it is usually the directors and not the shareholders who run companies. The Model Articles for private and public companies begin with a statement of the directors' general authority – 'Subject to the articles, the directors are responsible for the management of the company's business, for which purpose they may exercise all the powers of the company'. This means that shareholders cannot generally force the directors to take a particular course of action unless they override the general authority by means of a special resolution. In spite of this widely accepted general power for directors to manage a company there are, however, some actions which the Companies Acts (as defined in s. 2(1) of the 2006 Act) require must be approved by the shareholders. For this reason, any examination of the role of directors would be incomplete without an understanding of the powers of a company's shareholders. Actions which must be approved by the members of a company include:

- amending the company's constitutional documents;
- altering the company's share capital;
- approving a reduction of capital or share buy-back;
- converting the company from one form into another, e.g. from a private company to a public company;
- approving the payment of a political donation;
- changing a company's name;
- approving a loan to or a substantial property transaction involving a director;
- approving a payment for loss of office to a director;
- removing an auditor from office; and
- approving a liability limitation agreement between an auditor and the company.

11.9 In addition, listed companies are required to seek shareholder approval for certain transactions (see **11.170** below). Shareholder resolutions may, in the case of a private company, be passed at a general meeting or by written resolution (s. 281(1)). Resolutions of the shareholders of a public company must be passed in a meeting (s. 281(2)). The required resolution will be either an ordinary resolution, requiring approval by a simple majority (i.e. over 50%) of the members, or a special resolution, requiring approval by at least 75% of the members. See **11.48–11.72** for a further explanation of resolutions and the thresholds needed for approval.

11.10 In the context of shareholder meetings other significant thresholds are:

Shareholding	All companies	Additional requirements for public companies
5%	Holders of 5% of voting rights of a company have the right to have an item placed on agenda of a general meeting and the right to circulate a written statement of not more than 1,000 words to members of the company before a general meeting.	Directors of a quoted company (see **glossary**) are required to obtain an independent report on a poll taken at a general meeting if they receive requests from members representing not less than 5% of the total voting rights of all the members who have a right to vote on the matter to which a poll relates. Members representing not less than 5% of the voting rights may also require a quoted company to publish on the website a statement of concerns about audit matters (see **11.6**).
10%	Holders of 10% of the voting rights of a company have the right to requisition a general meeting.[2]	
25%	Holders of more than 25% of the voting rights at a general or class meeting can prevent the passing of a special resolution at a meeting or as a written resolution.	
More than 50%	Holders of more than 50% of the voting rights can ensure that ordinary resolutions are passed and can defeat ordinary resolutions (including those proposed as a written resolution) proposed by others.	
75%	Holders of 75% or more of the voting rights will normally be able to ensure that a special resolution or a special written resolution is passed.	

continued overlead

Shareholding	All companies	Additional requirements for public companies
90% or more	A general meeting of a private company can be called on short notice with the approval of 90% of members who have a right to attend and vote at the meeting (subject to the articles not imposing a higher threshold).[3]	
95%		A general meeting of a public company (other than an AGM) can be called on short notice with the approval of 95% of members who have a right to attend and vote at the meeting.

11.11 All shareholders are entitled to receive notices of general meetings of the company and to receive a copy of the company's annual report and accounts.

Requisitioning meetings and resolutions

Members' power to require directors to call general meeting

11.12 A general meeting will usually be called by the directors of a company. However, the members of a company may require the directors to call a general meeting (s. 303). Generally, this right can be exercised by members holding 10% of the rights to vote at a general meeting. However, in the case of a private company, this threshold will be reduced to 5% (s. 303(3)) where more than 12 months have elapsed since the end of:

- the last general meeting called pursuant to s. 303 of the 2006 Act; or
- the last general meeting in advance of which members had a right to circulate resolutions.[4]

11.13 Members can include the text of the resolution to be moved (s. 303(4)(b)). A request in electronic form is permitted (s. 303(6)).

11.14 The directors who are required to call a general meeting must do so within 21 days from the date on which they become subject to the requirements and the meeting must be held no more than 28 days after the date of the notice convening the meeting (s. 304(1)). This statutory requirement will override Regulation 37 of the original Table A, which states that directors must call a meeting not later than eight weeks after the receipt of the requisition. Regulation 37 has been amended in the interim versions of Table A to reflect the change introduced by the 2006 Act.

11.15 If the directors do not comply with the procedure set out in the 2006 Act, the members who requested the meeting (or any of them representing more than half of the total voting rights of all of them) may themselves call a general meeting (s. 305).

Members' power to require circulation of statements

11.16 Members of a company who represent at least 5% of the voting rights or comprise at least 100 members who have a right to vote and who hold £100 each on average of paid-up capital have the right to require the company to circulate a statement with respect to a matter referred to in a proposed resolution or other business to be dealt with at a meeting (s. 314). Where the statement relates to a matter referred to in a proposed resolution, the shares which trigger this right must carry rights to vote on the relevant resolution, rather than just to vote at the meeting.

11.17 The expenses of circulating a members' statement must be paid by the members unless:

- the meeting in question is a public company AGM and requests to circulate the statement are received before the end of the financial year preceding the meeting; or
- the company resolves otherwise.

11.18 Unless the company has previously resolved to do so, it is not bound to comply with the request to circulate a statement unless it has received a sum sufficient for its expenses no later than a week before the meeting (s. 316(2)).

Public companies – circulation of resolutions at AGMs

11.19 Members of a public company who represent 5% of the voting rights or comprise at least 100 members who have a right to vote and who hold £100 each on average of paid-up share capital have the right to propose, and require the company to circulate, a resolution for an AGM (s. 338). The 2006 Act requires that their shares must, in each case, carry rights to vote on the resolution to which the request relates. (Under the 1985 Act, the 5% threshold was linked to the right to vote at the meeting to which the requisition related.)

11.20 If the request is received before the financial year end preceding the meeting (which may be several months in advance of the meeting), then the members are not required to cover the costs of circulation (s. 340). If this is not the case, the expenses of circulating the resolution must be paid by the members making the request, unless the company resolves otherwise. The 2006 Act also provides that, unless the company has previously resolved to do so, it is not bound to circulate a resolution unless it receives money sufficient to meet its expenses six weeks before the AGM to which the request relates, or, if later, the time at which notice of the AGM is given.

11.21 Under the 2006 Act, members of private companies no longer have rights to requisition resolutions without also requisitioning a general meeting, although such rights could be conferred by the articles. However, they do have the right to require the circulation of written resolutions (see **11.52** below).

Shareholder ratification

11.22 The 2006 Act includes an express provision which permits the shareholders to ratify conduct by a director which amounts to negligence, default, breach of duty or breach of trust in relation to the company (s. 239).

11.23 Although this power was previously available at common law, the statutory process in the 2006 Act is a useful confirmation of the previous position. However, any decision to ratify such conduct must now be taken without reliance on the votes of the relevant director or any of his connected persons. Connected persons may include fellow directors (see s. 252(2)(d)). In practice this means:

- if the ratification decision is taken by way of written resolution, then the director and his connected persons may not take part in the written resolution procedure; and
- if the decision is taken at a meeting, then the members whose votes are to be disregarded may still attend and take part in the meeting and count towards the quorum for the meeting (if their membership gives them the right to do so).

11.24 The ability to ratify under this section does not affect the common law principle known as the *Re Duomatic* principle; see **11.141** below.

Shareholder activism

11.25 Recent years have seen a growth in activist shareholders who may acquire sufficient shares in a company (usually a listed company) to give them the power to take the actions mentioned above. Shareholder meetings will often provide an opportunity for activists to challenge the board by asking questions or voting down key resolutions.

Institutional shareholders

11.26 In large quoted companies many of the shareholders might not be individuals but large corporates such as insurance companies or pension funds. At the end of 2006 approximately 41% of shares in companies listed on the London Stock Exchange were owned by UK institutional shareholders[5]. Both the government and the EU would like to see such shareholders take a more active and engaged role in the companies in which they invest; voting on resolutions at company general meetings is one of the areas where such shareholders are being encouraged to do so.

11.27 In the UK the government has reserved powers in the 2006 Act to pass regulations in the future which would compel institutional shareholders to disclose how they vote at shareholder meetings. The hope is that, in the meantime, such shareholders will, of their own volition, vote their shares at general meetings and publicly disclose how they intend to vote.

11.28 The EU Shareholder Rights Directive is aimed at encouraging institutions that hold shares in companies in different member states to exercise their rights as shareholders.

11.29 There has been comment and concern in recent years that even if shareholders try to engage in shareholder meetings by appointing proxies or corporate representatives, their voting instructions are often lost and therefore not exercised. Electronic voting and appointment of proxies is designed to assist here and most large listed companies now enable their shareholders to appoint proxies and vote electronically. The 2006 Act has also introduced provisions enabling persons with underlying interests in shares held through custodians or nominees to obtain information directly and to exercise rights directly as if they were shareholders.

11.30 Investor bodies, such as the ABI, PIRC and NAPF, monitor the notices and conduct of shareholder meetings of listed companies and report back to their clients on the resolutions being proposed, advising them on whether to support, abstain or vote against them. The bodies publish general guidance on items routinely considered at shareholder meetings which the relevant companies should bear in mind when preparing for their meetings. (See **Chapter 12**.)

Notice of shareholder meetings

11.31 In order for a shareholder meeting to be held, notice of the meeting must first be sent to the members.

Contents of notice

11.32 Notice of a general meeting must state the time, date and place of the meeting and the general nature of the business to be transacted (s. 311).

However, this is subject to the company's articles, which should be checked for any surplus or contrary requirements. The notice must also contain a statement informing members of their rights to appoint proxies (s. 325), and, in the case of a quoted company, the AGM notice should refer to the possibility of a statement about any audit concerns being published on its website under s. 527 of the 2006 Act (see **11.143** below). For the impact of the provisions relating to members' rights on the contents of notices see **11.142** below.

Minimum notice period

11.33 Generally, the minimum notice period for a shareholders' meeting is 14 clear days (*not* working days), regardless of the type of resolution proposed (s. 307(1) and (2)). The only exception is public company annual general meetings, which still require at least 21 clear days' notice (s. 307(2)). However, companies may provide in their articles for a longer period of notice than that set out in the 2006 Act (s. 307(3)) and companies should consider whether or not they wish to amend their articles to do this (or to retain any existing provisions requiring a longer notice period). It should be noted that the Combined Code, paragraph D.2.4, which should be complied with by all fully listed companies, recommends a notice period for AGMs of at least 20 working days.

11.34 The implementation of the Directive on the exercise of certain rights of shareholders in listed companies (the 'Shareholder Rights Directive') in August 2009 will impose restrictions on the use of the 14 day notice period by companies whose shares are admitted to trading on a regulated market (see **Glossary**). Such companies will be able to call a general meeting on 14 days' notice only if:

- they offer the facility for shareholders to vote by electronic means accessible to all shareholders (at the time of writing, the Government is consulting on exactly what this will mean); and
- they have passed a shareholders' separate resolution approving the 14 day notice period. Pending the outcome of the Government's consultation on the implementation of the Shareholder Rights Directive, it is recommended that this is a special resolution. The resolution will be required even if the company's articles already contemplate general meetings being held on 14 days' notice.

11.35 The 2006 Act has introduced a 'clear day rule', which states that any reference in certain specified provisions to a period of notice, or to a period before a meeting by which a request must be received or a sum deposited or tendered, excludes both the day of the meeting and the day on which the notice is given, the request received or the sum deposited or tendered, as appropriate (s. 360). This rule applies, *inter alia*, to notice required of a general meeting, resolutions requiring special notice and members' requests to circulate resolutions or statements.

Short notice

11.36 Meetings may be held at short notice if this is agreed to:

- in the case of private companies, by 90% of the shareholders (or any higher percentage, not exceeding 95%, set by the articles (s.307(6)(a)); and
- in the case of a public company, by 95% of the shareholders (s.307(6)(b)) or, in the case of a public company's annual general meeting, *all* of the shareholders (s. 337(2)). This cannot be varied by the articles.

Persons entitled to receive notice

11.37 Notice of a general meeting must be sent to every member and every director (s. 310(1)). However, this is subject to any provision of the company's articles so that, as is commonly the case, the articles may provide that no notice need be sent to shareholders with registered addresses outside the UK. The auditors are entitled to receive notice of general meetings under s. 502, but unless Regulation 38 of Table A (or a similar provision) is included in the articles, there is no specific requirement to serve notice on the auditors.

Means of giving notice

11.38 Notice of a general meeting can be given in hard copy form, electronic form or by means of a website (s. 308). 'Electronic form' encompasses electronic means (e.g. e-mail or fax) or any other means while in an electronic form (e.g. sending a disk by post) (s. 1168). Notice of a meeting can be sent to a member by e-mail if the member has supplied an e-mail address for that purpose (Sched 5, Part 3 CA 2006). It may be sent via a website if the company has complied with the procedure specified in the 2006 Act for obtaining shareholders' consent or being able to deem consent in relation to website communications (Sched 5, Part 4 CA 2006).

Quorum

11.39 In order for a meeting to be valid there must be a sufficient number of shareholders present. The minimum number, usually set out in the company's articles, is known as the quorum.

11.40 The statutory quorum requirement depends on the number of shareholders a company has. In the case of a company with one member the quorum is satisfied by one qualifying person being present. In any other case, and subject to any other provision in the company's articles, two qualifying persons present at a meeting will constitute a quorum.

11.41 Section 318(3) states that a 'qualifying person' means:

- an individual who is a member of the company;
- a corporate representative; or
- a person appointed as a proxy of a member in relation to the meeting.

11.42 It is worth noting that two corporate representatives appointed by the same corporation or two proxies appointed by the same member do not satisfy the two qualifying person test mentioned above, unless the articles provide otherwise.

What if a meeting is inquorate?

11.43 The articles will generally provide what happens if a quorum is not present. The Model Articles provide that if, at the appointed time for the meeting, there are insufficient members present, then no business other than the appointment of the chairman of the meeting is to be transacted at such a meeting. The chairman of the meeting would then adjourn the meeting until a quorum could be found. Similarly, if a meeting ceases to be quorate at any time after it has been commenced, then the chairman will adjourn the meeting until a quorum can be reached.

11.44 Table A provides that if a quorum is not present within half an hour of the start of the meeting, or if during a meeting such a quorum ceases to be present, the meeting shall stand adjourned to the same day in the next week at the same time and place or to such time and place as the directors may determine.

11.45 See **11.129** for the consequences of a meeting being held despite the quorum requirements not being satisfied.

Quorum at class meetings

11.46 Where the rights of a class of shareholders are being varied and therefore a separate meeting of a class of shareholders is to take place, s. 334(4) provides that the quorum for such a meeting is:

- for a meeting other than an adjourned meeting, two persons present holding at least one-third in nominal value of the issued shares of the relevant class (excluding any treasury shares); and
- for an adjourned meeting, one person present holding shares of the relevant class.

This requirement cannot be varied by the company's articles.

11.47 Where a person is present by proxy or proxies he is treated, for the purposes of assessing whether the thresholds mentioned above are satisfied, as holding only the shares in respect of which those proxies are authorised to exercise voting rights (s. 334(5)).

Shareholder resolutions

11.48 The primary reason for holding a shareholder meeting is to approve resolutions to authorise actions such as those mentioned above. In respect of most matters the Companies Acts stipulate whether the necessary resolutions are to be passed as ordinary or special resolutions. The 2006 Act provides that, where any of its provisions require a resolution of a company or its members without specifying the kind of resolution, an ordinary resolution will be required, unless the articles require a higher majority or unanimity (s. 281(3)).

Ordinary resolutions

11.49 An ordinary resolution is defined by the 2006 Act as 'a resolution that is passed by a simple majority' (s. 282(1)). Ordinary resolutions can be passed either at a meeting (s. 282(3)) or, in the case of a private company, by way of a written resolution (s. 282(2)).

11.50 The 2006 Act provides that a simple majority means a simple majority of the members who are entitled to vote and do so in person or by proxy (s. 282(3) and (4)). Although this potentially means that the chairman of a general meeting cannot have a casting vote in the event of an equality of votes, any provision for a chairman's casting vote contained in a company's articles immediately prior to 1 October 2007 will continue to have effect.[6] The Government has indicated that from 3 August 2009, this saving provision will be disapplied for traded companies, meaning that any provision in a traded company's articles which allows the Chairman to have a casting vote at a general meeting will not have any effect (regardless of whether the company was incorporated pre or post 1 October 2007). The Government has addressed this issue in its consultation on the implementation of the Shareholder Rights Directive.

Special resolutions

11.51 A special resolution is defined as 'a resolution passed by a majority of not less than 75%' (s. 283(1)). A special resolution can be passed either at a meeting (s. 283(4)) or, in respect of private companies, by way of a written resolution (s. 282(3)). A majority of not less than 75% means not less than 75% of the members who are entitled to vote and do so in person or by proxy (s. 283(4) and (5)). Anything that can be done by ordinary resolution may also be done by special resolution (s. 282(5)).

Written resolutions

11.52 The statutory written resolution regime applies only to private companies; resolutions of a public company can only be passed at a meeting (s. 281(2)).

11.53 Under the 2006 Act, written resolutions of shareholders no longer require unanimity; they can be passed either as ordinary resolutions or special resolutions (ss. 283(2) and 283(3)) although the majorities required relate to all eligible members (see **11.59** below) and not just those who actually vote. In order to be passed as a special resolution, a written resolution must state that it is a special resolution. The simplified regime should be advantageous as it avoids the difficulties involved in obtaining signatures of all the shareholders. For smaller private companies, it may eliminate the need for holding a meeting in most cases.

11.54 Any proposed written resolution must be 'sent or submitted' to each 'eligible member'. Eligible members are the persons entitled to vote on the resolution on the 'circulation date of the resolution', i.e. the date on which copies of the resolution are sent or submitted to members (or, if copies are sent or submitted on different days, the first of those days) (ss. 289 and 290). (This is different from the position under the 1985 Act, which provided that members must have the right to vote 'at the date of the resolution', i.e. the date on which the resolution was signed by the last member.)

11.55 A written resolution is passed when the requisite majority of eligible members have signified their agreement to the resolution in accordance with the Act (s. 296(4)).

11.56 Companies can send copies of the resolution to members by:

- sending the resolution to all members at the same time (by hard copy, e-mail or by means of a website);
- sending the same copy of the resolution to members in turn; or
- using a combination of these methods (s. 291(3)).

11.57 The resolution must be accompanied by a statement informing the member:

- how to signify his agreement to the resolution – the 'authenticated' (i.e. signed) document must be sent to the company in hard copy or electronic form (since the document must be signed, it is implied that if the document is returned by e-mail, the signed version must be scanned and attached to the e-mail); and
- the date by which the resolution is to lapse if it has not been passed. If no period is specified in the company's articles for this purpose, this period will be 28 days from the circulation date of the resolution (s. 297(1)). Companies wanting the resolution to be passed before the end of this 28-day period will have to encourage shareholders to signify their agreement as soon as possible. If notice of the resolution is given on a website, the notice must be available on the website throughout the relevant period.

11.58 The 2006 Act does not state where this information may be included; it could be contained in notes to the resolution or in a cover letter.

Practical issues

Eligible member

11.59 The definition of an eligible member excludes:

- somebody who has lost the right to attend and vote at a meeting of the company (e.g. in a public company context this could apply where shares are subject to restrictions under s. 794 for failure to supply information about interests in the shares; in a private equity context, this could apply to a 'bad leaver'); and
- someone who has purchased shares of the company between the period of time from when the first copy of the resolution is sent or submitted to a member to the passing of the resolution.

11.60 Under the 2006 Act written resolution procedure, such persons would not be entitled to receive a copy of, or to vote on, the resolution.

Sending a resolution to all eligible members

11.61 The new requirement to send or submit a proposed written resolution to all eligible members means that even if somebody else actually signs the resolution on a member's behalf (e.g. under a power of attorney), the member must still receive a copy. Sending or submitting a document in hard copy includes handing the communication to a recipient, so a resolution could be handed to a member (Sched 5, Part 2, para 3 CA 2006).

11.62 There is some uncertainty as to whether a resolution can be passed if the requisite majority is reached before a member is deemed to have received a copy. The Act does not expressly state that all members must be deemed to have received copies of the resolution in order for it to be passed, only that the resolution must be sent to them.

11.63 If all of the members are present or represented at a meeting where the resolution will be signed, the company could rely on the common law *Re Duomatic* principle. (See **11.141** below.)

Timing of passing resolution

11.64 Since a written resolution is passed when the requisite majority is reached, ordinary and special resolutions proposed at the same time as written resolutions may be passed at different times. If it is important that the resolutions are passed at the same time, one way to ensure this is to bundle the resolutions together as a special resolution.

Exceptions to using statutory procedure

11.65 Written resolutions under the statutory regime cannot be used for the purpose of removing a director or an auditor (s. 288(2)) or for revoking, varying or renewing the authority of directors under s. 80 of the Companies Act 1985 to allot securities.[7]

Notification to auditors

11.66 In contrast to the requirements of the statutory written resolution procedure under the 1985 Act, there is now no longer a *duty* to notify a company's auditors of a proposed written resolution (and it will no longer be an offence if this is not done). However, auditors are still *entitled* to receive all communications relating to a written resolution as are required to be supplied to members of the company under s. 502.

Members' power to require circulation of written resolution

11.67 As well as providing for written resolutions proposed by directors, the 2006 Act contains provisions which enable members of a private company to circulate a resolution that is proposed to be moved as a written resolution (s. 292). The requisite percentage is 5% of the voting rights or such lower percentage as is specified in the articles. The members may require the company to circulate an accompanying statement of not more than 1,000 words on the subject matter of the resolution.

11.68 The cost of circulating a resolution proposed by the members is paid by the members who requested the resolution, unless the company resolves otherwise (s. 294). The company can require a deposit to meet the cost before it circulates the resolution, subject to any resolution to the contrary.

Effect of articles on written resolution procedure

11.69 Regulation 53 of Table A, which allowed a company to pass a resolution in writing signed by all the members, has been deleted from the interim versions of Table A. There is some debate as to whether existing companies can still rely on Regulation 53 if their articles incorporate this regulation. One view is that companies could do this as the 2006 Act simply provides that 'a provision of the articles of a private company is void if it would have the effect that a resolution that is required by or otherwise provided for in an enactment could not be proposed and passed as a written resolution [under the Act]' (s. 300). A company's articles cannot therefore exclude the statutory procedure, but the Act does not say that the articles cannot provide for an alternative means of passing a resolution. However, there may be contrary views as to the validity of Regulation 53 or another procedure in the articles for passing a resolution in writing.

Extraordinary resolutions

11.70 The 2006 Act has not carried forward the concept of extraordinary resolutions. However, any references to an extraordinary resolution in a company's articles or a contract will continue to have effect and be construed in accordance with s. 378 of the 1985 Act, notwithstanding that that provision of the 1985 Act will have been repealed[8]. Such extraordinary resolutions must be filed with the Registrar of Companies under Chapter 3 of Part 3 of the Act[9].

Resolutions requiring special notice

11.71 Where special notice is required of a resolution, the company must be given notice of the resolution at least 28 days before the meeting (s. 312). However, where it is not practicable for the company to give its members notice at the same time and in the same manner, at least 14 days' notice must be given to the members either by newspaper advertisement or in any other manner allowed by the company's articles (s. 379(2)).

11.72 Special notice is required of a resolution to remove a director (s. 168). Whereas s. 303 of the 1985 Act applied notwithstanding anything in the articles, this saving was not carried over into the 2006 Act. However, this omission should not change the meaning of the section in practice. Companies should be able to provide in their articles for another removal mechanism (e.g. removal by a majority shareholder on written notice). Section 168 does not provide that removal by resolution is the only permissible method, but that companies may use this method.

Voting

11.73 Unless a resolution is to be passed by a private company as a written resolution it will be voted on at the relevant meeting.

Taking the vote

11.74 Votes may be taken on a show of hands or on a poll. On a show of hands the vote will be decided by reference to the number of people raising their hands for and against the resolution, whereas on a poll the votes will be determined by reference to the number of shares represented by those voting. Because a poll will be likely to reflect the relative voting strengths of the shareholders present (both in person and by proxy or corporate representative) more accurately than a vote on a show of hands, many companies now automatically conduct polls on all resolutions. In the light of changes introduced by the 2006 Act this practice may become more widespread. If a vote is taken on a show of hands but the chairman considers that the outcome of that vote is unrepresentative of the views of all shareholders (as evidenced by proxy directions received), he should call for a poll.

Demanding a poll

11.75 If the chairman does not call a poll, a poll may be demanded:

- by not less than five members entitled to vote;
- by members representing not less than 10% of the total voting rights of members entitled to vote on the resolution; or
- by members holding shares conferring a right to vote on the resolution which are paid up to an extent of not less than 10% of the total amount paid up on all of the shares conferring such rights;

Any provision of the articles requiring a more stringent qualification to demand a poll will be invalid (except in relation to a poll on the election of the chairman of the meeting or on an adjournment of the meeting) (s. 321).

Voting rights

11.76 Votes may be cast at meetings by the registered shareholders, by proxies appointed on their behalf, or by representatives authorised by corporate shareholders.

Proxies

11.77 A member of a company may appoint one or more proxies to exercise all or any of his rights to attend and speak and vote at a meeting of the company. As a result of a change introduced by the 2006 Act, the right for a proxy to vote now extends to a vote on a show of hands as well as on a poll. If more than one proxy is appointed by a shareholder, each proxy must be appointed to exercise the rights attached to a different share or shares held by the appointer.

11.78 The default position under the 2006 Act is that each proxy will have one vote on a vote taken on a show of hands. This rule applies regardless of the number of shareholders for whom he is acting as proxy (s. 284(2)). The rule may be varied by the company's articles, but the proxies collectively may not have fewer votes than the member would have if he attended the meeting in person. Whilst in theory it would be possible, to avoid a vote on a show of hands potentially being swamped by multiple proxies, for the articles to provide that the proxies between them had only one vote, this is not recommended since it would give rise to considerable difficulties in determining which one of conflicting votes should be counted. The better course, if such swamping were to occur, would be for the chairman of the meeting to call a poll.

11.79 The rule that a proxy has one vote gives rise to certain practical difficulties:

- If the proxy is given conflicting instructions by different shareholders, how should he vote? Whatever he does he will be going against instructions of at least one of his appointers. There is not clear authority on the point, but it may be prudent, as a minimum, for the notice of meeting, which will contain notes about the appointment of proxies, to make clear that where the same person is appointed proxy by two or more members, or is himself a member, he will only be able to cast one vote on a show of hands. The Companies Act 2006 will be amended in August 2009 to deal with this issue. The Government is addressing this as part of its consultation on the implementation of Shareholder Rights Directive.

- Customarily the default position on proxy appointment forms is for the chairman of the meeting to be appointed unless somebody else is specifically named. This means that if the vote is taken on a show of hands, the chairman would have only one vote and therefore the votes of all his appointers would not be counted, unless the articles provided otherwise. It may be sensible for the articles to provide that where a chairman is appointed proxy for more than one shareholder with conflicting instructions he may abstain from voting on a show of hands. The chairman would have to decide whether the result of the vote would be different if the votes of all his appointers were cast and would have to use his discretion as to whether or not to call a poll. In practice this is likely to result in more companies taking votes on a poll as a matter of course.
- If the articles were to provide that a proxy had more than one vote on a show of hands, there would be likely to be considerable difficulties in establishing how the votes should actually be cast and how the result of the vote would be determined.

Corporate representatives

11.80 Corporate shareholders may, instead of appointing proxies, authorise representatives to attend meetings on their behalf. Now that proxies have the same rights as members attending in person it may be that corporate representatives will be less frequently appointed, although unlike proxies representatives can be appointed right up to the time of the meeting, which allows greater flexibility.

11.81 A corporate shareholder holding shares on behalf of a number of different beneficial holders may wish to exercise votes in different ways. A single corporate representative appointed by it could vote some of the shares one way and some the other way (although this could only be done on a poll) since a single representative has the same powers as the corporation itself (s. 323(3)). However, where multiple representatives are appointed, their ability to vote in different ways is less certain in consequence of s. 323(4) of the Act which provides that if more than one representative purports to exercise a power in different ways, the power will be treated as not having been exercised. Views currently differ as to whether this is subject to an implied exception under s. 152, which allows a shareholder to vote in different ways (see **11.165** below). Until the matter is tested in the courts, or the legislation is amended, the safe course would be to appoint multiple proxies in these circumstances or to adopt a procedure which has been formulated by the ICSA in conjunction with a number of leading law firms and representatives of registrars, custodians and institutional shareholders.[10] This procedure involves the chairman of the meeting, or one of the corporate representatives, being appointed as the designated corporate representative of the relevant shareholder with authority to vote in a poll as directed by all the other corporate representatives of that shareholder at the meeting. This would require the company to make directions cards available at the meeting in addition to poll cards. The ICSA guidance sets out the recommended procedures and specimen wording for meeting notices, and proxy and directions forms. The Companies Act 2006 will be amended in August 2009 to clarify that corporate representatives will be able to vote in different ways from one another in respect of different blocks of shares. The Government is addressing this issue as part of its consultation on implementation of the Shareholder Rights Directive.

Appointing proxies

11.82 The procedure for appointing proxies will normally be set out in the company's articles. Proxy appointment forms may be submitted in hard copy form by post or in electronic form.

11.83 Proxy appointments must be delivered by a deadline set by the company. Section 327 of the 2006 Act provides that this deadline may not be set more than 48 hours before the time fixed for the meeting (but for these purposes weekends and bank holidays may be excluded from the calculation of the 48-hour period). In the case of polls taken more than 48 hours after they are demanded, the deadline for proxy appointments cannot be set earlier than 24 hours before the time set for taking the poll. Similar timing constraints apply to provisions in the articles relating to the termination of proxy authorities (s. 330). If a proxy authority is terminated, the proxy's vote may nevertheless be treated as valid unless notice of the termination is received by the company before the meeting at which the vote is cast, or, in the case of a poll taken more than 48 hours after it is demanded, before the time for taking the poll.

Conduct of meetings

11.84 The aim of most companies is to conduct any shareholder meetings in the most orderly and efficient manner, while allowing members the opportunity to comment and vote on the business of the meeting. Most meetings will be held for a specific purpose either to pass resolutions to enable the company to proceed with its business (see **11.8** above for examples of when shareholder approval is needed) or because, for example, the annual report and accounts of a public company are required to be laid before a meeting.

Chairman of the meeting

11.85 The company's articles will normally provide for the chairman of the board to chair a shareholder meeting. This is the position in article 42 of Table A and also the Model Articles, which also state that if the chairman of the board is not present, then another director may be appointed in his place. If no directors are present, then the meeting will appoint a chairman from among those present. Sections 319 and 328 of the 2006 Act permits, subject to any provision in the company's articles, a member or a proxy to be elected as chairman of a general meeting by a resolution of the company passed at that meeting.

11.86 It is the chairman's responsibility to ensure the orderly conduct of the meeting. Some articles include a specific provision which requires the directors and, particularly the chairman, to ensure all meetings are conducted in an orderly fashion. A company's articles will usually include a provision that the chairman's decision on matters relating to eligibility to vote is final. Such a provision is included in Table A and in the Model Articles.

11.87 The chairman's other duties include:

- establishing that a quorum is present;
- chairing the proceedings, including facilitating discussion to ensure a fair hearing is given to all views and moving to a vote;
- ruling on points of order;
- permitting persons who are neither shareholders nor proxies to attend and speak;
- dealing with any amendments proposed to resolutions;
- making arrangements for a vote to be taken on a show of hands or on a poll and explaining such arrangements to the meeting;
- declaring the results of any votes; and
- adjourning the meeting.

11.88 Depending on the complexity of the issues to be covered a script may be prepared for the chairman by the company secretary (perhaps in conjunction with the company's legal advisers) to guide the chairman through the business of the meeting.

Who may attend the meeting?

Directors

11.89 If the meeting is a significant, formal meeting, such as the company's annual general meeting, then it would be usual for all the directors to attend.

Both Table A and the Model Articles state that directors, even if they are not shareholders, may attend and speak at general meetings.

11.90 In listed companies, where there may be separate board committees to look at audit, remuneration and nomination and appointment issues (see **Chapter 12**), the Combined Code recommends that the chairmen of those committees, who will usually in any case be directors of the company, should attend the annual general meeting and be prepared to answer questions about the work of their committee.

Auditors

11.91 The company's auditors would usually attend the company's annual general meeting. Section 502 permits them to attend any general meeting. However, they are entitled to speak only on business which concerns them as auditors. They are never entitled to vote.

Other advisers

11.92 Depending on the nature of the meeting the board may ask other advisers to attend. This may include the company's legal advisers, particularly if the matters to be discussed or resolutions to be approved require further detailed explanation to the shareholders present.

11.93 For large companies, particularly quoted companies, the company's registrars will probably be an essential part of the meeting as they will assist in ensuring the right members, proxies and corporate representatives are admitted and will organise any votes on the matters to be considered at the meeting.

Proxies and corporate representatives

11.94 Shareholders are entitled under the 2006 Act to appoint proxies to exercise all their rights at any meeting. This includes the rights to attend and speak, as well as to vote (see **11.77** above).

11.95 Shareholders who are corporate bodies may wish to appoint a corporate representative to exercise their rights to attend and speak, as well as to vote on their behalf.

11.96 Most companies' articles set out the process for appointing proxies and corporate representatives. Depending on the number of shareholders and the type of company, it is the responsibility of the company secretary or the company's registrars to check the validity of any appointment. (See **11.137** below for the consequences of invalidly appointed proxies or corporate representatives voting on a resolution.)

Speaking and questions

11.97 As mentioned above, people attending most meetings will be there in different roles. Depending on the purpose of the meeting some of them may be required (or wish) to speak. The chairman must coordinate this and also ensure that the members present, in person or by proxy or corporate representative, have sufficient time and opportunity to speak, ask questions and give their views on the business of the meeting. While being careful not to bring an end to discussions prematurely, the chairman may wish to do one or more of the following to control the debate:

- ask for questions in writing in advance of the meeting (although oral questions should not be excluded);
- limit discussion only to the resolution under consideration;
- limit the number of questions from any one shareholder; and
- if necessary, ask for a vote that the debate be brought to an end.

11.98 The chairman should explain at the start of the proceedings how he intends to conduct the meeting.

Voting

11.99 See **11.73–11.76** above.

Issues which might arise at the meeting

Points of order

11.100 A shareholder may raise a point of order about the conduct of the meeting. No notice is needed of a point of order and the chairman should deal with it immediately. The chairman's ruling on the point is final but he may wish to give others present, such as the company secretary, the registrars or the company's legal advisers, as well as other shareholders, the opportunity to respond to the point being raised.

Logistics and security

11.101 Before a meeting is called, careful consideration will need to be given to the suitability of the venue and whether any additional security measures may be needed. The annual general meetings of public quoted companies are often held in large conference venues, while a meeting of a small private company may be comfortably held at the company's offices or the offices of an adviser.

11.102 The important points to consider are that the venue is accessible, there is sufficient space and that all those attending can participate as necessary – being able to see and hear the chairman and all other speakers, and being able to speak to the meeting, are vital. It may be necessary to book additional rooms if the company is unsure how many members (or their proxies or corporate representatives) will attend and ensure that anyone in such a room is able, by means of audio-visual links, to see, hear and participate in the proceedings in the main venue. Anyone unable to fit into the main room should be clearly directed to the additional venue. The chairman of the meeting should refer to the additional venue in his opening remarks and ensure that anyone seated there can and does participate as fully as he wishes.

11.103 If the business of the meeting (or the business conducted by the company generally) is contentious, the company would be well advised make additional security arrangements to ensure the orderly conduct of the meeting. Excluding members who refuse to comply with any reasonable arrangements is easier to do if there is provision in the company's articles giving the company power to make all arrangements deemed necessary for the security and safety of those attending the meeting and to exclude anyone who does not comply with such reasonable arrangements. Any specific security arrangements should be detailed in the notice of the meeting so that those wishing to attend are fully aware of any particular arrangements that will apply to them.

Adjourning or postponing the meeting

Adjournment

11.104 It may be necessary for the meeting to be adjourned or postponed. This may occur because the meeting is inquorate at the time fixed for the start of the meeting (see **11.43** above) or for some other reason, such as a problem affecting the venue or because the business proposed to be conducted has changed due to events which have taken place since the meeting was called.

11.105 The chairman may adjourn a meeting:

- in accordance with the company's articles. Adjournment is permitted by both Table A and the Model Articles;
- with the consent of the meeting – an ordinary resolution would need to be passed consenting to the adjournment; or
- if it is necessary to establish order or to facilitate the conduct or business of the meeting.

11.106 The chairman must adjourn the meeting if directed to do so by the meeting.

11.107 The articles will normally state whether notice of an adjourned meeting is required to be given. However, good practice is to announce the date of any adjourned meeting in any event.

11.108 Only business which could properly be conducted at the original meeting can be conducted at the adjourned meeting.

Postponement

11.109 Once a meeting has been called it is not possible to postpone a meeting unless a provision dealing with this is included in a company's articles. If the company desires to postpone the meeting, the usual course is to hold the meeting but adjourn it and to give notice of the intended adjournment as widely as possible to try to ensure that members do not turn up to an adjourned meeting. However, if the members disagree with the reason for the proposed adjournment they may turn up anyway and vote against the adjournment resolution.

Delay in starting

11.110 The chairman will usually wish to start a shareholder meeting as promptly as possible. However, this may be impossible if the meeting being held is inquorate (see **11.43** above) or because of some other issue, such as problems with the venue or unexpectedly high attendance and everyone not having been admitted on time. It is in the chairman's discretion to wait until all those wishing to attend could do so. The chairman should certainly avoid any votes being taken until everyone has been admitted, although any preliminary business may be dealt with.

Disorderly conduct

11.111 If a person who is not a shareholder makes trouble, then he can be asked to leave and, if he refuses, ejected from the meeting.

11.112 If a member's conduct is disorderly, then it is the chairman's role to deal with him as fairly and efficiently as possible, while ensuring that the meeting is not unduly disrupted. This may involve asking the member to refrain from any actions, offering a separate meeting or adjourning the meeting for a short period to allow order to be restored. The member may be asked to leave and, if he refuses, may be expelled from the meeting at the direction of the chairman.

Amendments to resolutions proposed at the meeting

11.113 Depending on the business to be conducted at the meeting, amendments to the proposed resolutions or even additional resolutions may be put to the meeting. The chairman will need to deal with these proposals.

11.114 The Model Articles suggest that an ordinary resolution to be proposed at a general meeting may be amended by ordinary resolution if:

- notice of the proposed amendment is given to the company in writing by a person entitled to vote at the meeting at which it is to be proposed not less than 48 hours before the meeting is to take place, or such later time as the chairman of the meeting may determine; and

- the proposed amendment does not, in the reasonable opinion of the chairman of the meeting, materially alter the scope of the resolution.

11.115 In the case of a special resolution the Model Articles provide that such a resolution may be amended by ordinary resolution if:

- the chairman of the meeting proposes the amendment at the general meeting at which the resolution is to be proposed; and
- the amendment does not go beyond what is necessary to correct a grammatical or other non-substantive error in the resolution.

11.116 If the company's articles are silent on whether amendments to resolutions can be proposed, then the position at common law is that an amendment to an ordinary resolution is only admissible if:

- it is within the scope of the notice of the meeting (where the notice sets out the resolution, the test will be what a reasonable shareholder would consider the business set out in the resolution to be);
- it is no more onerous on the company than the existing resolution; and
- it does not have the effect of negating the substantive resolution.

11.117 The chairman of the meeting might also reject amendments if they are, for example, obstructive, vexatious or irrelevant.

11.118 At common law a special resolution can be amended to correct grammar or typographical errors provided there is no departure from the substance of the resolution set out in the notice of the meeting. An amendment may also be made if, having agreed to the amendment, all the members or the relevant class of members agree to waive the notice required of a special resolution (*Re Moorgate Mercantile Holdings Limited* [1986] All ER 40).

11.119 Where an amendment is validly proposed there should first be a vote on whether or not to accept it. If the amendment is accepted, there must then be a second vote on whether to accept or reject the amended resolution. If the amendment is not accepted, the meeting will then vote on whether to accept or reject the original resolution.

Amendments to resolutions appointing or re-electing directors

11.120 Additional considerations apply if the resolution in question relates to the appointment of a new director or a resolution to approve the re-election of an existing director.

11.121 If the resolution proposes appointing or re-electing one or more named persons as directors, then the members could propose an amendment which substitutes another person for someone named in the notice of the meeting. Whether or not such a proposal would negate the substance of the original resolution will depend on how the proposal is dealt with. The proper way to deal with such a proposal is to put the resolution in the form: 'If Mr X is not appointed, that Mr Y be appointed as a director'. Members would then vote on the original resolution and, if that was not passed, the new resolution. Companies should check their articles in such a case to make sure any applicable requirements have been complied with (e.g. a requirement that notice of intention to propose as a director anybody other than those recommended for appointment by the board, and the consent of the proposed director, must be given to the company ahead of the meeting), otherwise there is a risk that the chairman may reject the proposal.

Minutes

11.122 Section 355 requires companies to keep records comprising:

- copies of all resolutions of members passed otherwise than at general meetings;
- minutes of all proceedings at general meetings; and
- where the company has only one member, any decisions made by that member.

11.123 The records must be kept for at least ten years from the date of the meeting, resolution or decision. It is an offence to fail to comply with this requirement and every officer of a company in default would be liable to a fine.

11.124 The records must be kept available for inspection either at the company's registered office or at a place permitted by supplementary regulations made under the 2006 Act. In practice, companies will usually keep such records and minutes at the company's registered office. Records must be open to inspection, without charge, by any member of the company who may request a copy of the record, on payment of a fee. Failure to comply with these requirements is an offence and every officer of a company in default would be liable to a fine.

11.125 The minutes will usually be taken and records maintained by the secretary or an assistant secretary or by any other person, such as the company's legal advisers. Provided that the substance of the meeting and details of the resolutions passed are contained in the minutes there is no need to minute every detail of the discussions.

11.126 The records of resolutions and meetings are important because they provide evidence that the resolution was passed or the meeting was held. Section 356 provides that:

- a record of a resolution passed otherwise than at a general meeting, if it purports to be signed by a director or by the company secretary, is evidence of the passing of the resolution;
- where there is a record of a written resolution of a private company, the requirements of the 2006 Act about the passing of the resolution are deemed to be complied with unless the contrary is proved;
- the minutes of proceedings of a general meeting, if purporting to be signed by the chairman of that meeting (or by the chairman of the next general meeting) are evidence of the proceedings at the meeting; and
- where there is a record of proceedings of a general meeting of a company then, until the contrary is proved, the meeting is deemed to be duly held and convened, all proceedings at the meeting are deemed to have taken place and all appointments at the meeting are deemed valid.

11.127 In any legal proceedings involving an examination of the records of a meeting then the 2006 Act's Explanatory Notes state that 'a litigant will have to accept that the records are accurate unless he can prove that they are not'.[11]

11.128 The provisions of the 2006 Act on records and minutes apply to the resolutions and meetings of any class of shareholders of a company.

Effects of irregularities in conduct and documentation

11.129 A defect may be discovered after a meeting has taken place, which could render the decisions taken at the meeting invalid. Such a problem may arise for a number of reasons.

Accidental failure to give notice of the meeting

11.130 Section 313 provides that where a company gives notice of a general meeting or a resolution intended to be moved at a general meeting, any accidental failure to give notice to one or more persons shall be disregarded for the purpose of determining whether notice of the meeting or resolution is duly given. Except in relation to notices of meetings required or called by members or notices of resolutions at annual general meetings proposed by members of a public company, this section is subject to any contrary provision in the company's articles.

11.131 A company's articles usually contain a similar provision. Table A provides that 'the accidental omission to give notice of a meeting to, or the non-receipt of notice of a meeting by, any person entitled to receive notice shall not invalidate the proceedings at that meeting'.

11.132 If the failure to give notice is due to some intervening event, such as a postal strike, then often a company's articles will provide that notice may be given by some other means such as a national newspaper.

11.133 The 2006 Act and Table A deal with accidental failure to give notice of a meeting. (The Model Articles do not contain such a provision since the general approach taken was not to repeat matters addressed in the 2006 Act.) A deliberate failure to give notice to a member would invalidate proceedings since all members are entitled to receive notice of all meetings.

Insufficient notice given

11.134 If the notice given is insufficient, then, unless the members consent to the meeting being held at short notice, the meeting cannot validly be held. In practice, if the error is discovered before the meeting, then the company will normally send out a new notice explaining the error and giving the correct number of days' notice for a new meeting. The original meeting will be opened and immediately adjourned until the new date.

11.135 If the error is discovered after the meeting, and if *all* the members have attended the meeting, the company could rely on the *Re Duomatic* principle (see **11.141** below).

Inquorate meeting

11.136 If the quorum requirements are not met, and the meeting is therefore inquorate, any resolutions passed at the meeting will be invalid.

Proxies or corporate representatives who are not validly appointed

11.137 The company's articles will usually set out the process for appointing a proxy or corporate representative. If, however, that process is not followed or a query arises over the validity of an appointment, then Table A provides that 'no objection shall be raised to the qualification of any voter except at the meeting or adjourned meeting at which the vote objected to is tendered, and every vote not disallowed at the meeting shall be valid. Any objection made in due time shall be referred to the chairman whose decision shall be final and conclusive'. The Model Articles include an almost identical provision. If no objection is raised at the meeting and it later becomes clear that a proxy or corporate representative was not validly appointed, then the resolution or vote is not affected.

Amendments of resolutions

11.138 The manner in which resolutions can be amended, or new resolutions proposed, is dealt with above (see **11.113–11.121**). The Model Articles state that if the chairman of the meeting, acting in good faith, wrongly decides that an amendment to a resolution is out of order, his error does not invalidate the vote on that resolution.

11.139 Prior to this the common law position (in the absence of a contrary provision in the articles) was that if the chairman had wrongly rejected a valid amendment, then the resolution as passed would be invalidated, even if he was acting in good faith.

Problems with the minutes or records

11.140 As mentioned above, the burden of proof is on the person seeking to prove that any minutes or records do not provide evidence of a meeting having been held or a resolution having been passed.

Unanimous consent – the *Re Duomatic* principle

11.141 The common law principle, the *Re Duomatic* principle named after the case of *Re Duomatic* [1969] 2 Ch 365, provides that if all the members of the company entitled to vote on a matter unanimously reached agreement on a course of action then they could not later purport to disagree even if it was established that a formal procedure, such as that required by the company's articles, had not been followed.

11.142 The 2006 Act has confirmed and preserved this common law principle in section 281(4), which deals generally with company resolutions. In practice, this principle is only available to companies with a small enough shareholder base to ensure that all the members are able to consent whether at a meeting or in writing.

Exercise of members' rights

11.143 The growing numbers of institutional shareholders in companies, many of whom will hold their shares through an intermediary or a chain of intermediaries, led the review of company law which preceded the introduction of the 2006 Act to recommend that indirect investors should be given greater powers to exercise rights as members. Until now investors have had to rely on contractual arrangements with the intermediaries to deal with issues such as obtaining information from the company and to give instructions about how their shares should be voted.

11.144 The exercise of members' rights by non-members is likely to be of particular relevance in the context of shareholder meetings. This is because 'rights' in this context include not only the right to be told about and receive information about the meeting but also rights such as the ability to vote and to propose resolutions.

11.145 Chapter 9 of the 2006 Act therefore introduced rights for members to nominate other persons to enjoy or exercise all or any specified rights of the member in relation to the company. This nomination process differs according to the type of rights which are to be exercised by someone other than the registered member (i.e. the legal owner).

11.146 The ICSA has prepared a Guidance Note on Part 9 of the 2006 Act.[12]

Information rights – traded companies

11.147 Part 9 of the Act includes specific powers to enable persons who are not direct members of a company whose shares are admitted to trading on a regulated market[13] to enjoy 'information rights' (s. 146). The legal member may nominate such persons on whose behalf he holds the shares to enjoy such rights. The right to nominate such a person exists regardless of whether this is reflected in the company's articles.

11.148 Information rights are defined in s. 146(3) as:

- the right to receive a copy of all communications that the company sends to its members generally or to any class of its members that includes the person making the nomination; and
- the rights specifically conferred to require copies of accounts and reports and to require hard copy versions of documents or information provided in another form.

11.149 A company does not need to act on a nomination which purports to relate to certain information rights only (s. 146(5)).

11.150 If a person to be nominated wishes to receive information in hard copy, then, before the nomination is made, he must request that the person making the nomination notifies the company of that fact and provides an address to which the information is to be sent. Once the person making the nomination has received such a request he must notify the company of the nominated person's wishes and their address. The nominated person will then be entitled to receive hard copies of any information sent.

11.151 If no such notification is given (or no address is provided) then the nominated person is taken to have agreed that documents or information may be sent or supplied to him only by means of a website. However, this agreement may be revoked by the nominated person and he may, in the future, require a hard copy of any information supplied to him via a website.

11.152 It would appear that the government's intention under these sections was to provide an outline framework for appointing someone else to receive information but much of the detail which would have been useful to companies in deciding how members should make nominations and the form of those nominations is not included in the 2006 Act. Therefore, companies whose shares are admitted to trading on a regulated market and who may therefore be subject to nomination notices may choose to include additional details in their articles. There remain, however, practical difficulties, such as keeping the register of nominations up to date. The ICSA Guidance Note explores these issues. Companies should discuss how to manage nominations with their registrars.

11.153 Keeping track of nominations made, particularly when shares may be traded frequently and the underlying members change often, is a particular challenge. The Act provides that a nomination may be terminated at the request of the member or the nominated person. The nomination will also cease to have effect in the event of the member's or the nominated person's death or bankruptcy in the case of an individual or dissolution or winding up, otherwise than for the purposes of reconstruction, in the case of a corporate body.

11.154 There are two other situations when a nomination may be suspended:

- if there are more nominated persons than the member has shares in the company; and
- where the company has enquired of a person whether he wishes to retain information rights and has not received a response within 28 days of the enquiry. The nomination then ceases to have effect at the end of that period. Such an enquiry can only be made once in any twelve-month period.

11.155 The termination or suspension of a nomination means that the company is not required to act on it, but it does not prevent the company from continuing to do so for as long as it thinks fit.

Status of information rights

11.156 Although the intention of the new information rights provisions was clearly to allow indirect shareholders to receive information about the companies in which they have invested, the 2006 Act does not envisage that such persons should have a direct relationship with the company. It therefore provides that enjoyment of the rights conferred by the nomination is enforceable against the company only by the member as if they were rights conferred by the company's articles.

11.157 However, to facilitate these provisions the 2006 Act also provides that any enactment, and any provision of the company's articles, which deals with communications with members, has a corresponding effect (subject to any necessary adaptations) in relation to communications with a nominated person. In particular, provisions relating to the date and time by which persons are determined to be entitled to receive documents and provisions relating to addresses apply to both members and nominated persons.

11.158 A failure by the company to give effect to a nomination notice does not affect the validity of anything done by or on behalf of the company (s. 150(6)).

Notices of meetings

11.159 One of the items of information likely to be sent to nominated persons will be notices of shareholder meetings. Where a notice is sent to a nominated person it must be accompanied by a statement that:

- the person may have a right under an agreement between him and the member by whom he was nominated to be appointed, or to have someone else appointed, as a proxy for the meeting; and
- if he has no such right or does not wish to exercise it, he may have a right under such an agreement to give instructions to the member as to the exercise of voting rights.

11.160 The emphasis in these statements is on the agreement between the member and nominated person and this does not involve the company.

11.161 The usual statement that a member has rights in relation to the appointment of proxies should be omitted from any notice sent to a nominated person. Alternatively, the notice could include such a statement but state that it does not apply to nominated persons (s. 149(3)). Companies must decide whether they will have one form of notice which will be sent to both members and nominated persons and which contains appropriate wording for both or separate forms of notices.

Other rights for non-members in a company's articles

11.162 If someone other than the legal owner wishes to exercise all or any of the member's specified rights, then the company's articles must be amended to enable this (s. 145). For example, provisions in a company's articles relating to appointing proxies, the right to be sent written resolutions and the right to receive notice of general meetings would need to be drafted so that they contemplate a person who has been nominated by the member receiving notice of meetings or resolutions or appointing a proxy. Any company, whether private or public, whose articles have been amended may take advantage of these provisions.

11.163 Section 145 of the Act sets out a non-exhaustive list of the following rights which may be exercised by someone other than the registered member provided that the articles so provide:

- the right to be sent proposed written resolution;
- the right to require circulation of written resolution;
- the right to require directors to call general meeting;
- the right to notice of general meeting;
- the right to require circulation of a statement;
- the right to appoint proxy to act at meeting;
- the right to require circulation of resolution for annual general meeting of public company; and
- the right to be sent a copy of the annual accounts and reports.

11.164 The 2006 Act makes it clear that the ability to exercise these rights does not confer any rights which are enforceable against the company by anyone other than the member. Whoever has been nominated, the legal ownership remains with the registered member and the legal relationship remains between the company and its registered member.

Rights where shares are held on behalf of others

11.165 Where a member holds shares on behalf of more than one person, then the rights attached to those shares and the rights under any enactment which are exercisable by virtue of holding the shares do not all need to be exercised. If they are exercised, they do not all need to be exercised in the same way. The terms 'rights attached to the shares' and 'rights under any enactment exercisable by virtue of holding the shares' are not defined and are not particularly clear. It seems that voting rights would be caught by these terms and clearly they could, in theory, be exercised in different ways (see **11.77** above for problems which could arise if a proxy appointed by several members is instructed to vote in different ways).

11.166 A member who exercises such rights but does not exercise all his rights is under an obligation to inform the company to what extent he is exercising the rights. A member who exercises such rights in different ways must inform the company of the ways in which he is exercising them and to what extent they are exercised in each way.

11.167 Section 152(4) states that if a member exercises such rights without informing the company that he is not exercising all his rights or he is exercising his rights in different ways then the company is entitled to assume that he is exercising all his rights and is exercising them in the same way.

Shareholder requests exercised by indirect members

11.168 The Companies Acts require companies to carry out certain actions, such as circulating a statement or resolution before a meeting if requested to do so by a certain number of shareholders (see **11.67** above). Part 9 of the Act envisages circumstances where such requests could be exercised by indirect members. Section 153 sets out four situations where the threshold required to trigger a right is 100 persons holding, or being the indirect holders of, £100 each on average of paid-up share capital. These situations are the power to require:

- circulation of a statement about a resolution or matter to be dealt with in a general meeting;
- circulation of a resolution for an annual general meeting (public companies only);
- an independent report on a poll (quoted companies only); and
- website publication of members' audit concerns (quoted companies only).

11.169 Indirect shareholders submitting such requests must also submit a statement (s.153) which sets out:

- the full name and address of the member who holds shares on behalf of that person;
- that the member is holding those shares on behalf of that person in the course of a business;
- the number of shares in the company that the member holds on behalf of that person;
- the total amount paid up on those shares;
- that those shares are not held on behalf of anyone else, or if they are, that the other person(s) are not among the persons making the request;
- that some or all of those shares confer voting rights that are relevant for the purposes of making a request under the relevant section; and
- that the person has the right to instruct the member how to exercise those rights.

Additional requirements for listed companies

Requirements for shareholder approval

11.170 Under the Listing Rules listed companies are required to obtain shareholder approval to transactions which are classified by the rules as Class 1 transactions. The classification is made by reference to the relative size of the gross assets, gross capital or profits attributable to the undertaking or assets the subject of the transaction or the consideration for the transaction when compared with the gross assets, gross capital, profits or market value of the listed company. Shareholder approval will be required where any of the ratios is equal to or more than 25%. (See **Chapter 10**.)

11.171 Any transaction with a related party (which includes directors, substantial shareholders, persons exercising a significant influence over the listed company and associates of any of them) also requires shareholder approval unless all the ratios referred to above are less than 5%.[14]

Notice of AGM

11.172 Although the 2006 Act requires 21 clear days' notice to be given for annual general meetings, the Combined Code, which should be complied with by all fully listed companies, recommends a notice period of 20 working days.

Disclosure of proxy appointments

11.173 The Combined Code recommends that listed companies should for each resolution, except where a poll is taken, disclose at the meeting after the vote has been taken and make available on the company website the number of shares:

- in respect of which proxy appointments have been made;
- for and against the resolution; and
- in respect of which the vote was directed to be withheld.[15]

Website publication of poll results

11.174 Quoted companies must publish details of poll votes on their website, including the number of votes cast in favour and against (s. 341). The 2006 Act imposes a fine on every officer who is in default. Failure to comply with this requirement does not affect the validity of the poll or the resolution or other business to which the poll relates.

Independent report on poll

11.175 The 2006 Act gives members of a quoted company the right to require an independent report of any poll taken or to be taken at a general meeting. The minimum threshold required for the demand is the same as that for requiring the circulation of a resolution, i.e. shareholders holding 5% of the voting rights or at least 100 members who have a right to vote on the relevant matter and hold shares on which an average sum, per member, of at least £100 has been paid up. The members may use this procedure on a controversial resolution or where there appears to be a problem relating to voting procedures. The request must be made within one week of the meeting at which the poll was taken. Alternatively, requests may be made in advance, although, in such a case, unless the articles already require all votes to be taken on a poll, members will have to ensure that a poll is called.

11.176 Directors who are required to prepare an independent report must appoint an independent assessor to prepare the report. The appointment must be made within one week after the company is required to obtain the report. An independent assessor must fulfil the independence criteria set out in s. 344, which correspond to the independence requirements for a statutory auditor. The assessor must not be somebody already involved in the voting process of the company. An auditor can be appointed as an independent assessor and the report must contain the matters set out in s. 347 of the 2006 Act. Where an independent assessor has been appointed, the company must make available on its website:

- the fact of the appointment;
- the identity of the independent assessor;
- the text of the resolution or subject matter of the poll; and
- a copy of the report (s. 351).

11.177 A penalty is imposed on every officer in default for non-compliance. Failure to comply with the requirement does not, however, invalidate the poll or the resolution or other business to which the poll relates. The 2006 Act does not specify what the effect is of a report disclosing some irregularity in the poll procedure but if the articles provide that the chairman's decision on matters relating to eligibility is final and binding, it may be appropriate to make this provision subject to any irregularity revealed by the report.

11.178 Those preparing the chairman's script and other AGM papers may wish to contemplate how such a request, and the appointment of the independent assessor, would be dealt with if requested prior to the meeting.

Audit concerns

11.179 Members of quoted companies who represent 5% of the voting rights, or comprise at least 100 members who have the right to vote and who hold shares on which an average sum per member of at least £100 has been paid, have the right to require the company, at no expense to the relevant members, to publish on a website maintained by the company a statement setting out members' concerns about any matter which:

- relates to the audit of the company's annual accounts (including the auditors' report and the conduct of the audit) which are to be laid before the next accounts meeting; or
- any circumstance connected with the auditor ceasing to hold office since the previous accounts meeting, that the members propose to raise at the next accounts meeting (s. 527).

11.180 The request must be received by the company at least one week before the meeting to which it relates, be made available within three working days of the company being required to publish it and be available until after the meeting to which it relates. The company must draw attention in the notice of the accounts meeting to the possibility of a statement being included on a website (s. 529(1)). The company must forward the statement to its auditor not later than the time when it makes the statement available on the website.

Sources

1 The guidance note is available at www.icsa.org.uk
2 For private companies this may reduce to 5% in certain circumstances (s. 303(3)).
3 The company's articles may provide for a higher percentage, not exceeding 95% (s. 307(6)).
4 Explanatory Note 548 to the 2006 Act. The only type of meeting at which members of a private company could have the right to circulate a resolution would appear to be one in respect of which a specific right is contained in the articles since, unlike members of public companies, private company members do not have rights under the 2006 Act to requisition resolutions without also requisitioning a general meeting.
5 www.statistics.gov.uk/pdfdir/share0707.pdf
6 See saving provision in Sched 5, para 2 of the Fifth Commencement Order.
7 Schedule 1, para. 13 of the Third Commencement Order.
8 Schedule 3, para. 23 of the Third Commencement Order.
9 Schedule 5, para. 2(4) of the Fifth Commencement Order, which inserts a new sub-para. 23(2) into Schedule 3 of the Third Commencement Order.
10 ICSA guidance on proxies and corporate representatives at general meetings, January 2008. www.icsa.org.uk
11 Explanatory Note 605.
12 The guidance note is available at www.icsa.org.uk
13 For a list of regulated markets, see the list of Exchanges on the FSA Register page at www.fsa.gov.uk. This includes the Main Market of the LSE but AIM is not a regulated market.
14 LR11.
15 Provision D.2.2.

12

Corporate governance

Introduction

12.1 Corporate governance is principally a means of safeguarding shareholders' interests. It centres on the way in which companies are managed and controlled, ensuring that those persons responsible for the management of the company – the directors – account to shareholders in relation to matters where transparency, fairness, independence, integrity and responsibility are required.

12.2 With heightened awareness of the wide social impact that businesses have on the environment and society as a whole, it has also come to encompass how the health, safety, social and environmental aspects of a business are addressed by the management of the company.

12.3 Issues of corporate governance tend to be a far greater focus for companies whose securities are publicly traded. When a company is listed on either the Main Market or AIM, it is taking a step which means that its actions and corporate strategy will be subject to far greater public scrutiny than it would as a private company. Private companies often have a restricted number of shareholders who often control the board of directors, making the board more directly accountable to the shareholders. In larger private companies, particularly those seeking external investment from private equity or individuals, or companies considering listing in the future, instigating corporate governance procedures can assist these processes. By contrast, public companies tend to have a far greater number and more diverse groups of shareholders than private companies and so the issue of safeguarding shareholder interests is of particular concern. Accordingly, publicly listed companies will be the focus of this guide to corporate governance, although larger private companies should take note of the key principles and guidelines as none have been developed specifically for private companies.

12.4 This chapter focuses on:

- the sources of corporate governance rules;
- the Combined Code, which is the cornerstone of corporate governance in the UK;

- Main Market companies – market rules;
- AIM companies – corporate governance;
- other guidelines; and
- future changes.

Sources of corporate governance rules

12.5 Given the diverse nature of shareholder and other interests which corporate governance seeks to safeguard, its sources are equally diverse and range from statutory obligations to guidelines laid down by supranational organisations such as the Organisation for Economic Co–operation and Development (OECD) and specific organisations such as the National Association of Pension Funds (NAPF).

12.6 The cornerstone of corporate governance in the UK is the Combined Code, which has evolved from a number of independent reports carried out in the UK in relation to corporate governance. The first, the Cadbury Report, was published in 1992 and was followed, three years later, by the Greenbury Report. In 1998, the Hampel Report resulted in the publication of the Combined Code. Following a number of high-profile corporate failures, most notably the collapse of Enron and Worldcom in April 2002, Derek Higgs was appointed by the then Department of Trade and Industry (DTI) to review the role and effectiveness of non-executive directors in the UK. At the same time, a review of audit committees was carried out by a group led by Sir Robin Smith. As a result of the Higgs Review and the Smith Report, both completed in early 2003, a revised consolidated version of the Combined Code was published. In July 2006, the Financial Reporting Council published an amended version of the Combined Code (see **Appendix 1**) and in June 2008 it was again amended. This latest version applies to reporting years beginning on or after 29 June 2008. The provisions of the Combined Code are considered further in **12.19–12.40**.

Other sources of corporate governance

Statute

12.7 A number of statutes aim to safeguard the interests of shareholders. The most notable of these is the Companies Act 2006 (the 2006 Act), pursuant to which directors' duties have been codified. The Act sets out a statutory statement of directors' duties, comprising seven general duties, which cannot be excluded or varied by a company except as specifically permitted by the the 2006 Act.

12.8 Four of the seven general duties came into effect on 1 October 2007:

- the duty to act within the company's powers;
- the duty to promote the success of the company;
- the duty to exercise independent judgment; and
- the duty to exercise reasonable care, skill and diligence.

12.9 The remaining three general duties came into effect on 1 October 2008:

- the duty to avoid conflicts of interest;
- the duty not to accept benefits from third parties; and
- the duty to declare interests in a proposed transaction or arrangement.

However, it should be noted though that these duties already existed under common law.

12.10 From a corporate governance standpoint, the most important is the duty to promote the success of the company as this states that a director must act in the way the director considers, in good faith, would be most likely to promote the success of the company for the benefit of its members as a whole. In doing so, the director should have regard to:

- the likely consequences of any decision in the long term;
- the interests of the company's employees;
- the need to foster the company's business relationships with suppliers, customers and others;
- the impact of the company's operations on the community and the environment;
- the desirability of the company maintaining a reputation for high standards of business conduct; and
- the need to act fairly as between shareholders of the company.

12.11 The 2006 Act also contains provisions detailing the information that is to be included in the business review section of directors' reports. The stated purpose of the business review is to inform members and help them to assess how the directors have performed their new statutory duty to promote the company's success. There are more stringent disclosure requirements for Main Market companies in relation to the business review which include the need for certain forward-looking statements.

12.12 As will be seen these duties encompass a number of principles which the various codes on corporate governance seek to safeguard.

12.13 The Takeover Code has also been given a statutory footing under the 2006 Act for offers for companies which have their registered offices in the UK, Channel Islands or the Isle of Man and whose securities are admitted to trading on a regulated market, such as the Main Market. The Takeover Code operates on a non-statutory footing for other companies which have their registered office in the UK, the Channel Islands or Isle or Man and whose place of central management and control is in the UK, the Channel Islands or Isle of Man where the company's shares have been publicly marketed or traded. The Takeover Code contains rules and general principles which govern how takeovers of companies to which it applies are governed so that the following key principles are maintained:

- all shareholders are treated equally;
- shareholders have sufficient time and information to reach a properly informed decision; and
- the board of the target company acts in the best interests of the company as a whole.

12.14 Other statutes such as the Financial Services and Markets Act 2000 (FSMA) also seek to safeguard shareholders' interests by regulating the way in which information is communicated to investors and the market as a whole and on what basis and how dealings in the company's securities are transacted.

Common law rules

12.15 The way in which directors are expected to act has also evolved under a set of common law principles which have been judicially applied. These are often referred to as fiduciary duties and include duties of the directors to act in the best interests of the company, to avoid conflicts and not to make a secret profit. Many of these duties have been incorporated in the statutory duties under the 2006 Act.

Market rules

12.16 The rules of, and applicable to, the market or stock exchange on which the company's securities are traded also help to safeguard shareholders' interests. These include the Listing Rules and the Disclosure Rules and Transparency Rules. Market Rules are considered below (**12.41–12.54**).

Other guidance

12.17 There are a wide range of other, non-legal guidelines on a variety of topics from systems and controls to health, safety and environmental issues, all of which should be taken into account from a corporate governance standpoint. Such guidelines include those which are published by the OECD, the ABI, the NAPF, the Institute of Chartered Secretaries and Administrators (ICSA) and the Association of General Counsel and Company Secretaries of the FTSE 100 (GC100). These and other guidelines are considered further below (**12.90–12.118**).

Memorandum and articles of association

12.18 The company's own constitutional documents will also govern how the directors act and seek to safeguard shareholders' interests. The memorandum and articles of association usually include provisions on how the directors are to conduct the affairs of the company, deal with conflicts of interests and interact with the shareholders.

Combined Code

12.19 The Listing Rules require companies registered in the UK and whose securities are admitted to the Official List and to trading on the Main Market of the London Stock Exchange by way of a primary listing to adhere to the Combined Code (see **Appendix 1**) by way of a 'comply or explain' approach. This requirement has led to the Combined Code becoming the cornerstone of corporate governance in the UK and, accordingly, the standard expected of companies which are publicly traded in the UK, whether or not they are formally required to.

12.20 The Combined Code is structured as a series of 17 main principles. Each main principle is supported by a number of supporting principles and then a number of Combined Code provisions, which are effectively guidelines on how a company can meet the objectives of the main principle.

12.21 A summary of the principal areas of the Combined Code is set out below. The principal areas fall within the following categories: Directors; Remuneration; Financial Reporting; Relations with Shareholders; and Institutional Shareholders.

Directors

12.22 Every company should be headed by an effective board of directors which is collectively responsible for the success of the company (Principle A.1). This includes regular meetings for the board and at least annual meetings of non-executive directors; without the executive directors present.

12.23 There should be a clear division of responsibilities at the head of the company between the running of the board of directors and the executives responsible for the running of the company's business. No one individual should have unfettered powers of decision (Principle A.2). The roles of chairman and chief executive should not be held by the same individual; where this is not possible, the board should consult major shareholders and explain its reasons for combining these roles.

12.24 The board of directors should include a balance of executive and non-executive directors (and, in particular, independent non-executive directors) such that no individual or small group of individuals can dominate the board. Provision A.3.1 states examples of situations where a director may not be considered to be independent which include those set out in Table 12.1.

Table 12.1 Relationships or circumstances which should be taken into account when determining independence

	Combined Code	**QCA Corporate Governance Guidelines for AIM Companies (see 12.109–12.123)**	**NAPF Corporate Governance Policy and Voting Guidelines for AIM Companies (see 12.125–12.138)**
Non-executive director should not have been an employee in the group within last five years	✔	✔	
Non-executive director should not have had a material business relationship with the company in the last three years (whether directly or as a partner, shareholder, director, senior employee)	✔	✔	
Non-executive director should not receive or have received additional remuneration (other than a non-executive director's fee)	✔	✔ if fee paid in securities this does impair independence	
Non-executive directors should not participate in the company's share option or a performance-related pay scheme, or be a member of the company's pension scheme	✔	✔	✔ previously issued options to non-executive directors in the form of a one-off grant acceptable, provided the quantum is not considered to be material

Table 12.1 *continued*

	Combined Code	**QCA Corporate Governance Guidelines for AIM Companies (see 12.109–12.123)**	**NAPF Corporate Governance Policy and Voting Guidelines for AIM Companies (see 12.125–12.138)**
Non-executive director should not have close family ties with any of the company's advisers, non-executive directors or senior employees	✔	✔	
Non-executive directors should not hold cross-non-executive directorships or have significant links with other non-executive directors through involvement in other companies	✔	✔	
Non-executive director should not be or represent a significant shareholder	✔	✔	✔ independence may be compromised if a director has a beneficial or non-beneficial shareholding of more than 3 per cent of the company's issued share capital
Non-executive director should not have served on the board for more than 9 years	✔	✔	✔ but 9 to 12 years acceptable if this is the only factor affecting independence

12.25 At least half of the board should be independent non-executive directors; however, smaller companies (those outside the FTSE 350) may have at least two independent non–executive directors. A nomination committee should be established to ensure a rigorous and transparent procedure for the appointment of new directors. The key role and responsibility of the nomination committee are set out in **Table 12.2** overleaf.

Table 12.2 Key corporate governance committees

	Nomination Committee	Remuneration Committee	Audit Committee
Function	To ensure rigorous and transparent procedure for appointment of new directors to the board – Principle A.4	To develop formal and transparent policy on executive remuneration and fix individual remuneration packages, ensuring that no director is involved in deciding his own remuneration	• Financial reporting • Internal controls and risk management • Whistle-blowing and fraud • Internal audit • External audit
Established by	Board of directors with formal terms of reference	Board of directors with formal terms of reference	Board of directors with formal terms of reference
Make-up	Majority should be independent non-executive directors	All should be independent non-executive directors	All should be independent non-executive directors
Number of members	• Three • Two for AIM companies/main market companies below FTSE 350	• Three (plus chairman) • Two for AIM companies/main market companies below FTSE 350	• Three • Two for AIM companies/main market companies below FTSE 350 • At least one member should have recent and relevant financial experience
Chairman	Ideally not chairman of board. Acceptable in small companies provided chairman does not deal with appointment of own successor	Chairman can sit on committee if considered independent on appointment, but should not chair it	Chairman can sit on committee if considered independent on appointment, but should not chair it
Duration of appointments to the committee	Three years. Extended for two further three-year periods providing majority remain independent	Three years. Extended for two further three-year periods providing majority remain independent	Three years. Extended for two further three-year periods providing majority remain independent
Meetings	Twice a year minimum; once a year to appraise own performance	Recommended twice yearly	Recommended three times a year

Table 12.2 *continued*

	Nomination Committee	Remuneration Committee	Audit Committee
Source of rule guidance	• Combined Code • ICSA Guidance on Terms of Reference – Nomination Committee • Higgs Review/ Related Guidance and Good Practice Suggestions of the Combined Code	• Combined Code • ICSA Guidance on Terms of Reference – Remuneration Committee • Higgs Review/Related Guidance and Good Practice Suggestions of the Combined Code	• Combined Code • Guidance on Audit Committees • Disclosure and Transparency Rule 7 • ICSA Guidance on Terms of Reference – Audit Committee
Authorisations	• To seek any information from any employee • To obtain outside legal or other advice at the company's expense	• To seek any information from any employee • To obtain outside legal or other advice at the company's expense • To commission any reports or surveys	• The management of the company should ensure that the audit committee is kept properly informed and is regularly supplied with information • To seek any information from any employee • To obtain outside legal or other advice at the company's expense • To obtain training
Statement in annual report?	Yes including the process used to make appointments and, if external advice or open advertising has not been used, an explanation of why not.	Yes	Yes That the business is a going concern with supporting assumptions or qualifications as necessary If the directors do not accept the audit committee's recommendation, explaining the recommendation and then setting out the reasons why the board of directors has taken a different approach Explaining to shareholders how, if the auditor provides non audit services, auditor objectivity and independence is safeguarded

Table 12.2 *continued*

	Nomination Committee	Remuneration Committee	Audit Committee
Availability of terms of reference	On website	On website	On website
Key duties and remit	• Reviewing composition and balance of board • Succession planning • Identifying and nominating candidates for board vacancies • Preparing job descriptions for board vacancies • Reviewing (annually) the time required from non-executive directors • Ensuring new non-executive directors receive formal letter of appointment with clear terms and time commitment • Making recommendations on membership of audit and remuneration committees • Making recommendations on appointments; re-appointments; and re-elections by shareholders under 'retirement by rotation' • Reviewing matters relating to the continuation in office of any director at any time, including the suspension or termination of service of an executive director • Reporting formally to the Board after each committee meeting	• Agreeing fair and responsible policy on remuneration for executive management to incentivise them and encourage enhanced performance • Ensuring no director sets his own remuneration • Determining targets for performance related pay schemes and approving payouts • Reviewing share incentive plans and determining whether awards will be made • Setting policy for pension arrangements • Ensuring fair contractual terms on termination, and mitigating loss • Agreeing individual remuneration packages • Agreeing policy on expense claims • Obtaining information on remuneration in other companies; • Reporting formally to the Board after each committee meeting	• *Financial reporting* Monitoring integrity of company's financial statements • Reviewing accounting policies, standards and disclosure *Internal controls/risks* • Reviewing internal controls and risk management systems *Whistleblowing/fraud* • Reviewing arrangements for employees to raise concerns, and facilitate whistle-blowing • Reviewing fraud detection procedures • Ensuring investigations are proportionate and independent *Internal audit* • Approving appointment/removal of head of internal audit Monitoring internal audit function • Reviewing internal audit plans and reports, and meeting with head of internal audit at least once per year *External audit* • Overseeing selection of, and relationship with, external auditors • Monitoring external auditors' compliance and performance, meeting with them at least once a year • Reviewing findings and reports of external auditors • Reporting to the Board after each committee meeting

Table 12.2 *continued*

	Nomination Committee	Remuneration Committee	Audit Committee
Key duties and remit *contd*			• Considering the risk of the withdrawal of the auditor from the market • Considering the auditor's annual transparency report • Providing information on the appointment, reappointment or removal of the auditor

12.26 For reporting periods beginning on or after 29 June 2008 Provision A.4.3 has been relaxed to permit an individual to chair more than one FTSE 100 company.

12.27 The board should be supplied, in a timely manner, with information in a form and of a quality appropriate to enable it to discharge its duties.

12.28 All directors should submit themselves for re-election at regular intervals, and, in particular, the re-election of a non-executive director for a term which would exceed six years service should be subject to particularly rigorous review. It should be noted that in recent months there has been a trend for all directors in some of the larger companies to be submitted for re-election annually to ensure that the composition of the board is acceptable to the shareholders.

Remuneration

12.29 Levels of remuneration should be sufficient to attract, retain and motivate directors of the quality required to run the company successfully, but a company should avoid paying more than is necessary for this purpose. A significant proportion of executive directors' remuneration should be structured to link rewards to corporate and individual performance (Principle B.1). Increased shareholder activism has, for some companies, led to queries by shareholders as to why some non-executives do not have interests in the company once they have joined the board. Some shareholders appear to prefer all directors to have an interest in the company and in some cases share options have been awarded to non-executive directors to address shareholder confidence even though this may impair independence from a corporate governance standpoint. As to the test for independence, see Table 12.1.

12.30 There should be a formal and transparent procedure for developing policy on executive remuneration and for fixing the remuneration packages of individual directors led by a remuneration committee. No director should be involved in deciding his or her own remuneration (Principle B.2). The remuneration of the non-executive directors, including members of the remuneration committee should be determined by the board of directors, or where required by the articles of association of the company, the shareholders. In practice, a maximum amount payable to all non-executive directors is set out in the articles of association of a public company and the sponsor or nominated adviser is involved in setting this amount at an appropriate level. The key role and responsibilities of the remuneration committee are set out in Table 12.2.

Financial reporting

12.31 The board should present a balanced and understandable assessment of the company's position and prospects (Principle C.1).

12.32 The board should maintain a sound system of internal control to safeguard shareholders' investment and the company's assets (Principle C.2).

12.33 The board should establish formal and transparent arrangements for considering how they should apply the financial reporting and internal control principles and for maintaining an appropriate relationship with the company's auditors through an audit committee of at least three non-executive directors, with written terms of reference. A summary of the key role and responsibilities of the audit committee is set out in Table 12.2. The board of directors should, at least annually, conduct a review of the effectiveness of the group's system of internal controls and should report to shareholders that they have done so. The board should also establish formal and transparent arrangements for considering how they should apply the financial reporting and internal control principles and for maintaining an appropriate relationship with the company's auditors.

Relations with shareholders

12.34 The board of directors as a whole has responsibility for ensuring that a satisfactory dialogue with shareholders takes place (Principle D.1). The senior independent director should attend meetings with management and a range of major shareholders (Provision D.1.1). In addition, it is a requirement to state in the annual report the steps which the board has taken to ensure that members of the board have developed an understanding of the views of these major shareholders (Provision D.1.2).

12.35 The board of directors should use the AGM to communicate with shareholders and to encourage their participation (Principle D.2).

Institutional shareholders

12.36 The Combined Code contains three main principles of good governance in relation to institutional shareholders. The first, Principle E.1, requires institutional shareholders to participate in a dialogue with companies based on the mutual understanding of objectives.

12.37 Principle E.2, provides that institutional shareholders should carefully consider any explanations given for departure from the Combined Code. On some occasions the institutional investors will require a detailed explanation and guidance on governance structures.

12.38 Principle E.3 deals with shareholder voting, and provides that institutional shareholders should ensure their voting intentions are being carried out in practice, and should attend AGMs when appropriate and practicable.

Disclosure of corporate governance information

12.39 In addition to the disclosure required under Listing Rule 9.8.6R (see **12.41**), Schedule C to the Combined Code has been amended for reporting periods beginning on or after 29 June 2008. These amendments reflect disclosure requirements imposed by the Disclosure Rules and Transparency Rules. A comparison of the disclosure required by the Combined Code and the Disclosure Rules and Transparency Rules is set out in Table 12.3.

12.40 In addition, the company can satisfy its obligation to make information available to shareholders by publishing it on the website. This is typically how companies will make available the terms of reference for the board committees.

Main Market Companies – market rules

The Listing Rules

12.41 Listing Rule 9.8.6 R requires companies incorporated in the UK and whose securities are admitted to the Official List and to trading on the Main Market of the London Stock Exchange by way of a primary listing to adhere to the Combined Code by way of a 'comply or explain' approach. Accordingly, a company must detail in its annual report how it has applied the main principles of the Combined Code and whether it has complied with all of the Combined Code provisions. Where a company has not complied with the Combined Code it should, in its annual report, identify those provisions it has not complied with, the period in which it did not comply and explain why it did not comply.

12.42 For companies incorporated outside the UK but whose securities are admitted to the Official List and to trading on the Main Market by way of a primary listing, Listing Rule 9.8.7 R requires a statement to be included in its annual report as to whether or not it complies with the corporate governance regime in its country of incorporation. Listing Rule 9.8.7 R also requires these companies to give details of the significant ways that their corporate governance regime differs from the Combined Code and why such differences are appropriate for that particular company. This detailed explanation affects the ABI rating of the company and the likely levels of shareholder activism. The question of whether overseas companies with a primary listing on the Main Market should adopt a higher standard and adhere to the Combined Code by way of a 'comply or explain' approach has been the subject of much discussion and is under review by the Financial Services Authority. These companies may well need to comply more fully in the future (see **12.119** below). If implemented, these changes will increase the pressure on such companies to constitute the various corporate governance committees regardless of whether or not they were required under the corporate governance regime in their countries of incorporation.

12.43 In addition, under Listing Rule 9.8.10 R the auditors need to review the 'comply or explain' statements in the annual report of companies which are incorporated in the UK, but only in relation to those which are objectively verifiable, i.e. Combined Code Provisions C.1.1, C.2.1, C.3.1–C.3.7 (see **Appendix 1**).

12.44 There has also been discussion as to whether smaller companies (those outside the FTSE 350) should have a reduced version of the Combined Code or only have to comply with certain principles or provisions of the Code. These approaches have been resisted, amongst others by the ABI, which would prefer companies to give fuller explanations of any non-compliance.

12.45 Under Listing Rule 9.2 a company must instigate provisions, in accordance with the Model Code, to regulate the way in which directors deal in the company's securities.

12.46 A company must also take all proper and reasonable steps to ensure compliance with the Model Code of dealing which it has adopted and it should take appropriate disciplinary action in the event of a breach of the Model Code.

12.47 The purpose of the Model Code is to ensure that directors and persons discharging managerial responsibilities (being directors and senior executives who have regular access to inside information and have power to make managerial decisions – PDMRs) do not abuse, and do not place themselves under suspicion of abusing, inside information that they may have or be thought to have, especially in periods leading up to an announcement of results. Accordingly, a company must require every PDMR (including its directors) who has access to inside information in relation to the company to comply with the Model Code which is set out in Annex 1 to Chapter 9 of the Listing Rules. If they wish, companies may impose more rigorous restrictions upon dealings by PDMRs than those set out in the Model Code.

12.48 The principal elements of the Model Code include:

- a PDMR must not deal in any securities on considerations of a short-term nature;
- a PDMR must not deal during a 'close period', i.e.:
  - the period of 60 days immediately preceding a preliminary announcement of the listed company's annual results or, if shorter, the period from the end of the relevant financial year up to and including the time of announcement; or
  - the period of 60 days immediately preceding the publication of its annual financial report or, if shorter, the period from the end of the relevant financial year up to and including the time of such publication; and
  - if the listed company reports on a half-yearly basis, the period from the end of the relevant financial period up to and including the time of such publication; and
  - if the listed company reports on a quarterly basis, the period of 30 days immediately preceding the announcement of the quarterly results or, if shorter, the period from the end of the relevant financial period up to and including the time of the announcement;
- a PDMR must not deal at any time when there exists any matter which constitutes inside information in relation to the company nor must a PDMR deal where clearance has not been given by the chairman (or one or more other directors designated for this purpose); and
- a PDMR must also take reasonable steps to prevent any dealings by or on behalf of persons connected with him (within the meaning of s. 96B(2) of FSMA) on considerations of a short-term nature, and must (so far as is consistent with his duties of confidentiality to the company) seek to prohibit any dealings by or on behalf of any person connected with him or by an investment manager on his behalf or on behalf of any other person connected with him (whether or not those funds are managed on a discretionary basis) during a close period.

Figure 12.1 sets out the close period for a Main Market company:

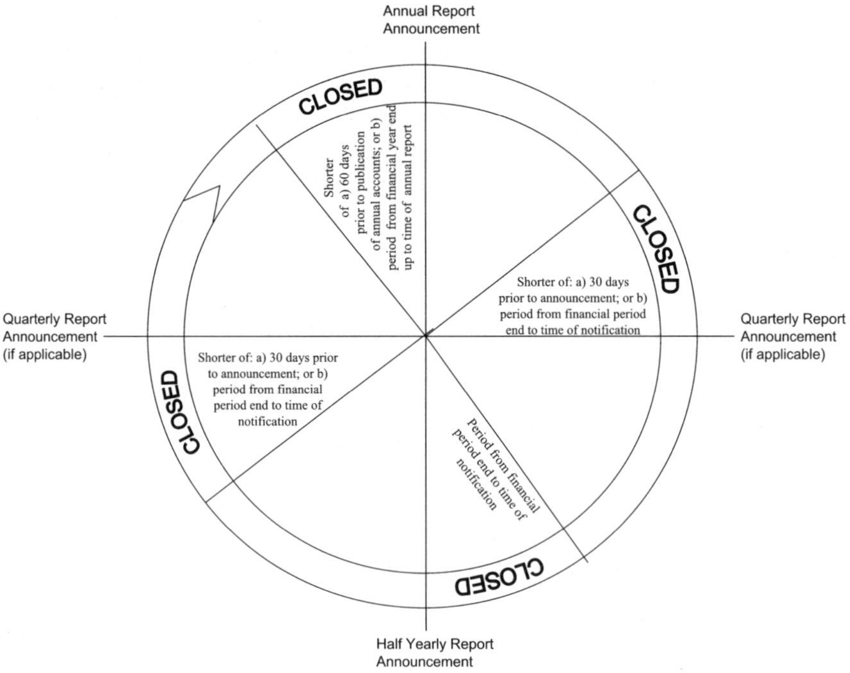

Figure 12.1 Close periods for a Main Market company.

12.49 The requirements imposed by the Model Code in some respects go beyond those imposed by law. However, conversely, just because a director falls within one of the exemptions in the Model Code, and is thus permitted to deal pursuant to the Model Code, does not mean that the dealing cannot constitute market abuse or insider dealing.

Disclosure Rules and Transparency Rules

12.50 In addition to the Listing Rules, the other key market rules for Main Market companies are the Disclosure Rules and Transparency Rules (DTR). In accordance with the statutory audit directive and the company reporting directive, the DTR have been amended with effect from 29 June 2008 to include DTR7, applying to financial periods commencing on or after 29 June 2008. There is a certain degree of overlap between DTR7 and the Combined Code. The main requirements of DTR7 are:

- to have a body responsible for carrying out the audit functions;
- to issue a statement identifying the body which carries out the audit functions and to summarise how that body is composed;
- to issue a statement that refers to the corporate governance code that the company applies and explains whether, and to what extent, it complies with such a code to include a description of the main features of the issuers'

internal control and risk management features for the financial reporting process and the composition of the various administrative, management and supervisory bodies and their committees (DTR7.2).

12.51 Companies that do not fall within the definition of a company under s. 1(1) of the 2006 Act do not have to comply with the provisions of DTR7 (which in practice is UK companies only) and DTR7 applies only to companies that have shares admitted to trading on a regulated market, unless shares are also traded on a multilateral trading facility. This means that DTR7 only applies to customers listed on the Main Market of the LSE and not those listed on AIM.

12.52 The June 2008 version of the Combined Code acknowledges that there is a certain degree of overlap between it and the DTR. Appendix 2 of Schedule C to the Combined Code highlights where provisions of the Combined Code will also satisfy the DTR7 requirements and is set out in Table 12.3.

Table 12.3 A comparison between the DTR and the Combined Code

DTR	Code provision
DTR 7.1.1 R Sets out minimum requirements on composition of the audit committee or equivalent body.	**Provision C.3.1** Sets out recommended composition of the audit committee.
DTR 7.1.3 R Sets out minimum functions of the audit committee or equivalent body.	**Provision C.3.2** Sets out the recommended minimum terms of reference for the audit committee.
DTR 7.1.5 R The composition and function of the audit committee or equivalent body must be disclosed in the annual report. DTR 7.1.7 R states that compliance with Code provisions A.1.2, C.3.1, C.3.2 and C.3.3 will result in compliance with DTR 7.1.1 R to DTR 7.1.5 R.	**Provision A.1.2** The annual report should identify members of the board committees. **Provision C.3.3** The annual report should describe the work of the audit committee. Further recommendations on the content of the audit committee report are set out in the Smith Guidance.
DTR 7.2.5 R The corporate governance statement must include a description of the main features of the company's internal control and risk management systems in relation to the financial reporting process. While this requirement differs from the requirement in the Code, it is envisaged that both could be met by a single internal control statement.	**Provision C.2.1** The board must report that a review of the effectiveness of the internal control system has been carried out. Further recommendations on the content of the internal control statement are set out in the Turnbull Guidance.

Table 12.3 *continued*

DTR	Code provision
DTR 7.2.7 R The corporate governance statement must include a description of the composition and operation of the administrative, management and supervisory bodies and their committees. DTR 7.2.8 R states that compliance with Code provisions A.1.1, A.1.2, A.4.6, B.2.1 and C.3.3 will result in compliance with DTR 7.2.7 R.	This requirement overlaps with a number of different provisions of the Code: **A.1.1** the annual report should include a statement on how the board operates. **A.1.2** the annual report should identify members of the board and board committees. **A.4.6** the annual report should describe the work of the nomination committee. **B.2.1** a description of the work of the remuneration committee should be made available. Note: in order to comply with DTR 7.2.7 R this information will need to be included in the corporate governance statement. **C.3.3** the annual report should describe the work of the audit committee.

NAPF Policy

12.53 In November 2007 NAPF published 'Corporate Governance Policy and Voting Guidelines' (the NAPF Policy), which apply to companies whose securities are admitted to the Official List and to trading on the Main Market of the London Stock Exchange by way of a primary listing. The NAPF Policy effectively supports the OECD Corporate Governance principles (see **12.90–12.91** below). The NAPF Policy is designed to assist shareholders and others in interpreting the Combined Code. The NAPF Policy gives voting guidelines to its members when a company is not adhering to any of the Combined Code provisions. It also supports and expands on various principles relating to directors, remuneration, accountability and audit as set out in the Combined Code.

12.54 In addition, NAPF endorses the UN principles for responsible investment to provide a framework for incorporating environmental, social and governance issues into investment decisions (see **12.100–12.108** below).

AIM companies – corporate governance

AIM Rules

12.55 There is no formal requirement for AIM companies to comply with the Combined Code, however the principal provisions and recommendations set out in the Combined Code are generally followed by companies traded on AIM as a matter of good practice. In addition, in recognition of the size and stage of development of many AIM companies, two sets of guidelines, the QCA Guidelines for AIM Companies and the NAPF Corporate Governance Policy and Voting Guidelines for AIM Companies, have been specifically drafted for AIM companies, but most of their principles are derived from the Combined Code. Practice as to which guidelines are followed by AIM companies is determined, in part, in consultation with a company's nominated adviser. However, a significant number of AIM companies continue to base their corporate governance regime on the full provisions of the Combined Code.

12.56 In order to address corporate governance requirements, as well as seeking to ensure compliance with Rule 21 of the AIM Rules for Companies, the board of directors of an AIM company will adopt a code on dealings in securities by directors and employees and their families, related companies and related trusts. Rule 21 states that an AIM company must ensure that its directors and applicable employees and their families, related companies and related trusts do not deal in any of its AIM securities during a close period. Details of close periods are set out in Figure 12.2. In addition, the purchase or early redemption by an AIM company of its AIM securities or sale of any AIM securities held as treasury shares must not be made during a close period.

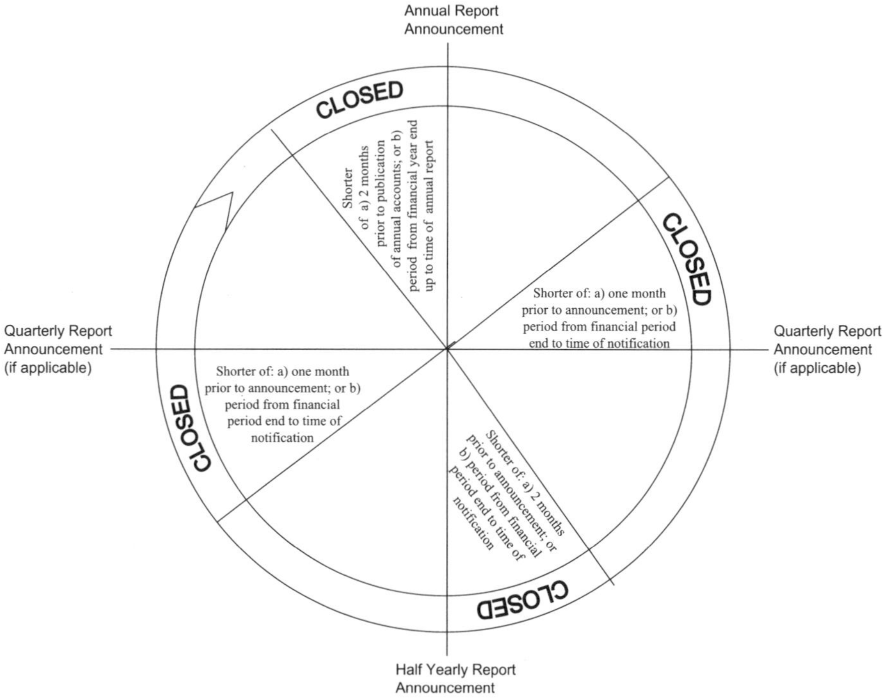

Figure 12.2 Close periods for AIM companies.

12.57 Rule 21 will not apply, however, where such persons have entered into a binding commitment prior to the AIM company being in such a close period where it was not reasonably foreseeable at the time the commitment was made that a close period was likely, and provided that the commitment was notified at the time it was made.

12.58 The company's code for dealing in securities incorporates and builds on the restrictions set out in the AIM Rules for Companies. Its purpose is to ensure that the directors, applicable employees and their families, related companies and related trusts do not abuse, or place themselves under suspicion of abusing, price-sensitive information that they may or may be thought to have, especially in periods leading up to the announcements of results.

12.59 A company's code on dealings in securities applies to any person who acts as a director of the company, whether or not officially appointed, and so catches shadow directors. The company's code on dealing in securities also applies to applicable employees, being any employee who is likely to be in the possession of unpublished, price-sensitive information in relation to the company because of their employment in the company and/or any of its subsidiaries. The company's code on dealing in securities also applies to the family of the directors and employees likely to be in possession of price-sensitive information.

12.60 It should be noted that, whilst it is usually best practice for AIM companies to follow guidance and procedures for companies whose securities are admitted to trading on the Main Market, dealings in AIM securities in circumstances permitted under the Model Code on Directors Dealings as set out in the Appendix to Chapter 9 of the Listing Rules is one exception to this rule. The AIM Rules for Companies are very narrowly drafted in order to protect investor confidence, and the circumstances in which dealings are permitted under the AIM Rules for Companies are more restrictive than those permitted under the Model Code. Accordingly, the dealings which are permitted by an AIM company's code for dealing in securities are usually limited to:

- undertakings or elections to take up entitlements under a rights issue or other pre-emptive offer, including an offer of securities in lieu of a cash dividend;
- the take-up of entitlements under a rights issue or other pre-emptive offer, including an offer of securities in lieu of a cash dividend;
- allowing entitlements to lapse under a rights issue or other pre-emptive offer, including an offer of securities in lieu of a cash dividend;
- the sale of sufficient entitlements nil paid to allow take-up of the balance of the entitlements under a rights issue;
- undertakings to accept, or the acceptance of, a takeover offer.

12.61 While it is not a requirement for an AIM company to establish a code on dealing in securities as Rule 21 applies in any event, virtually all AIM companies do so as a matter of good corporate governance in order to monitor and control dealings by directors, senior employees and their related persons and to assist the company with its disclosure requirements related thereto.

QCA Guidelines

12.62 Insofar as AIM companies are not formally required to comply with the Combined Code, in July 2005, the Quoted Companies Alliance (QCA) published a set of corporate governance guidelines entitled 'Corporate Governance Guidelines for AIM Companies' (the QCA Guidelines). The QCA is an organisation which seeks to promote the interests of smaller quoted companies (companies outside the FTSE 350). The QCA Guidelines are a simple set of guidelines which are largely based on standards set out in the Combined Code and which are intended to provide a minimum standard for AIM companies to follow.

Audit committees

12.63 It is best practice for AIM companies to establish an audit committee to deal with financial reporting, audit and internal control issues. Virtually all AIM companies establish an audit committee either voluntarily or at the request of their nominated adviser. Following the introduction of Rule 26 of the AIM Rules for Companies and the QCA AIM Website Guidance – Rule 26, it is best practice to set out the terms of reference of the audit committee on the AIM company's website. Under Rule 26, composition of the audit committee must be set out on the website.

12.64 The establishment of an audit committee as an independent body monitoring financial reporting procedures ensures investor confidence, and an audit committee is regarded by shareholders, in particular institutional shareholders, as an integral part of the management of the company.

Remuneration committees

12.65 It is best practice for AIM companies to establish a remuneration committee to check the remuneration of individual directors and senior executives. Many nominated advisers also require AIM companies to establish a remuneration committee and summarise the constitution of the committee and its role in any AIM admission document. There would be concern among shareholders, in particular any institutional shareholders, if a company did not have a properly constituted remuneration committee with clear, predetermined terms of reference. In addition, following the introduction of Rule 26 and the QCA AIM Website Guide – Rule 26, it is best practice to set out the terms of reference of the remuneration committee on the AIM company's website. Under Rule 26, composition of the relevant committees must be set out on the website.

Nomination committees

12.66 Again, while AIM companies are not required to comply with the Combined Code, it is best practice for AIM companies to establish a nomination committee which will be responsible for the appointment and reappointment of directors and senior executive officers. However, due to their size and stage of development, it might not be appropriate for all AIM companies to have a nomination committee, although this is a matter to be discussed with the nominated adviser. Where it is felt that it is not appropriate to have a nomination committee the reasons should be set out in any AIM admission document. Even though it is not a formal requirement, many large AIM companies now establish a nomination committee alongside the remuneration and audit committees, resulting in the procedure for selection and recruitment of directors and senior executives being streamlined in a formal, systematic manner.

12.67 Where there is a formal nomination committee, the nominated adviser will require the constitution of the nomination committee to be set out in any AIM admission document and on the website pursuant to Rule 26. In addition, following the introduction of Rule 26 and the QCA Website Guide – Rule 26, it is best practice to set out the terms of reference of the nomination committee on the AIM company's website.

Reporting procedures

12.68 The recommended minimum reporting procedures in relation to corporate governance for AIM companies are set out in the QCA Guidelines.

12.69 The QCA Guidelines state that an AIM company should have a corporate governance statement on its website. The statement should be updated annually and describe how the company has achieved good corporate governance. As an alternative to publication on the company's website, the statement could be included in the company's annual report and accounts but where such report is published on the company's website, the directors' report should identify where the corporate governance statement can be found and confirm the date at which it was reviewed and updated. The corporate governance statement should, as a minimum, describe how each of the QCA Guidelines is put into practice by the company, together with a description of any additional corporate governance standards and procedures that the company applies beyond this basic level. Where a company is not able to apply all the QCA Guidelines (although there is an expectation that each company will be able to) the statement should describe how the features of good corporate governance are being achieved. This is effectively applying the 'comply or explain' approach to corporate governance taken by the Listing Rules in relation to companies whose securities are traded on the Main Market.

12.70 Where an AIM company complies with the Combined Code as opposed to the QCA Guidelines, similar statements should be included in respect of the Combined Code.

12.71 The QCA Guidelines also recommend that each AIM company's annual report include the following basic disclosures:

- a statement of how the board operates, including a high-level statement on which types of decisions are taken by the board and which are delegated to management;
- the identity of the chairman, the deputy chairman (if there is one), the chief executive, the senior independent director and the chairman and members of the nomination, audit and remuneration committees. This is a requirement under Rule 26;
- the identity of those directors the board considers to be independent and the reasons why it has determined a director to be independent notwithstanding factors that may appear to impair that status;
- the board should describe any performance evaluation procedures it applies;
- the names of directors, accompanied by sufficient biographical details and any other relevant information to enable shareholders to take an informed decision on the balance of the board and the re-election of certain of them;
- the number of meetings of the board and of the committees and individual directors' attendance at them;
- an explanation of directors' responsibility for preparing the accounts and a statement by the auditors about their reporting responsibilities;
- a statement by the board that the business is a going concern, with supporting assumptions or qualifications as necessary; and
- an explanation to shareholders of how, if the auditors provide significant non-audit services, auditor objectivity and independence is safeguarded.

12.72 Many of these disclosure requirements are derived from the provisions of the Combined Code, which should be the first point of reference for corporate governance requirements.

12.73 Finally, the QCA Guidelines recommend that the following items are available for inspection on the company's website (this is now embodied in the QCA AIM Website Guidance – Rule 26) or made available to shareholders on request:

- the terms and conditions of appointment of non-executive directors; and
- the terms of reference for each of the audit, remuneration and nomination committees, together with an explanation of each committee's role and the authority delegated to it by the board of directors.

12.74 Where an AIM company has not appointed a nomination committee, the board should explain its processes in relation to matters normally dealt with by such a committee.

QCA Guidelines and Combined Code compared

12.75 The QCA Guidelines set out the minimum standard of corporate governance which should be followed by AIM companies. Table 12.4 details the relevant QCA Guidelines and its nearest equivalent principle/provision of the Combined Code.

Table 12.4 Relevant QCA Guidelines and Combined Code provisions

QCA Guideline	Equivalent Combined Code Reference
There should be a formal schedule of matters specifically reserved for the board's decision	Provision A.1.1
The board should be supplied in a timely manner with information, including regular management financial information, to enable it to discharge its duties	Main principle A.5
The board should review the effectiveness of the group's system of internal controls (including financial, operational and compliance controls and risk management systems) at least annually and report to shareholders that they have done so	Provision C.2.1
The roles of chairman and chief executive should not be exercised by the same individual. If they are, there should be a clear explanation of how other board procedures provide protection against the risk of concentration of power within the company	Provisions A.2.1/A.2.2
A company should have at least two independent non-executive directors, one of whom may be the chairman, and the board should not be dominated by one person or group of people	Principle A.3 – Provision A.3.2
All directors should be submitted for re-election at regular intervals, subject to continued satisfactory performance, and the board should ensure planned and progressive refreshing of the board	Principle A.7

Table 12.4 *continued*

QCA Guideline	Equivalent Combined Code Reference
The board should establish an audit committee of at least two members who should be independent non-executive directors. There should be formal terms of reference for the committee	Provision C.3.1
The board should establish a remuneration committee of at least two members who should be independent non-executive directors	Provision B.2.1
Recommendations for appointments to the board should be made by a nomination committee after due evaluation	Provision A.4.1
There should be a dialogue with shareholders based on the mutual understanding of objectives. The board as a whole has responsibility for ensuring that a satisfactory dialogue with shareholders takes place	Principle D.1

National Association of Pension Funds Guidelines

12.76 In March 2007, the National Association of Pension Funds (NAPF) also published a set of guidelines entitled 'The Corporate Governance Policy and Voting Guidelines for AIM Companies' (NAPF AIM Guidelines). Once again, the NAPF AIM Guidelines are principally derived from the Combined Code and the introduction to the NAPF AIM Guidelines states that 'boards of directors of AIM companies should be familiar with the main principles of the Combined Code and should seek to apply them as appropriate to each company's circumstances'.

12.77 The NAPF AIM Guidelines consider certain key matters covered by the requirements of the Combined Code and the QCA Guidelines and address how smaller AIM companies in particular should apply these.

12.78 Matters covered include the following.

Combined roles of the chairman and chief executive

12.79 In relation to the combined roles of the chairman and chief executive, the NAPF AIM Guidelines follow the NAPF Policy, which applies to companies whose securities are admitted to the Official List and to trading on the Main Market of the London Stock Exchange by way of a primary listing (see **12.53**). The NAPF Policy reiterates the Combined Code and QCA Guidelines provision that the functions of chairman and chief executive are different and should be clearly distinguished and not confused or compromised by being combined. If these roles of chairman and chief executive are combined, the company should provide details of the exceptional circumstances which explain this and make a forward-looking statement explaining the company's intentions to separate the roles.

Chief executive becoming chairman

12.80 In relation to the chief executive becoming chairman, NAPF Policy states that the chief executive should not become chairman of the same company. Should this happen, the company must disclose in its annual report the reasons for the appointment and describe the selection process.

Appointment of a senior independent director

12.81 Whilst it is a Combined Code requirement that a senior independent director be appointed, the QCA Guidelines do not specifically consider this requirement. However, NAPF Policy suggests a senior independent director should be appointed where the role of chairman and chief executive has been combined, primarily to ensure that there is an independent voice on the board that can provide a communication channel for shareholders if needed. Where the roles of chairman and chief executive have not been combined, a senior independent director is encouraged but not required.

Balance of the board of directors

12.82 The NAPF AIM Guidelines relating to the balance of the board of directors are that larger boards of directors should follow the NAPF Policy, which requires a smaller company to have at least two independent directors, excluding the chairman. Smaller companies should have at least two independent non-executive directors to comprise not less than one third of the board, one of whom may be the chairman. (See Table 12.1 for more information regarding the test of independence for NAPF purposes.) This less stringent requirement is appropriate for AIM companies that have boards of directors comprising no more than four directors. NAPF Policy suggests such boards might consist of the chairman, chief executive and, at the most, two non-executive directors, of whom one should be independent. Most nominated advisers apply this guidance to smaller AIM companies and seek to ensure that an AIM company has at least one independent non-executive director. For larger AIM companies, the nominated adviser may require it to have two independent non-executive directors who should comprise not less than one third of the board of directors. This position should be contrasted with the QCA Guidelines set out in Table 12.4, which recommend that there be at least two non-executive directors.

Composition of the audit, remuneration and nomination committees

12.83 Where possible, the NAPF AIM Guidelines support the Combined Code provisions in relation to the composition of the audit, remuneration and nomination committees. However, it recognises that in some AIM companies the lack of independent membership and too few non-executive directors on the board make compliance with the Combined Code provisions unachievable. Where this is the case, NAPF AIM Guidelines recommend that each of the three committees should ideally comprise only independent non-executive directors, with a majority of independent directors on the board of directors committees, at the very least. Again, this should be contrasted with the QCA Guidelines set out in Table 12.4, which recommend that for the audit and remuneration committees there should be at least two members, both of whom are independent. For smaller AIM companies, it is not unusual for nominated advisers to accept the NAPF position of a majority of the committee being independent. Notwithstanding the NAPF AIM Guidelines and QCA Guidelines some AIM companies do not have nomination committees.

Remuneration arrangements

12.84 The NAPF AIM Guidelines suggest AIM companies adhere to current best practice guidelines (ABI and NAPF Remuneration Guidelines) and state that a significant component of senior management's remuneration should be linked to performance and that there should be disclosure of the performance conditions attaching to any bonuses or long-term incentive plans. AIM companies are also strongly encouraged to put remuneration reports to a vote at the annual general meeting.

Director independence

12.85 NAPF believes that some of the independence criteria specified in the Combined Code may need to be applied more flexibly for AIM companies as they may be subject to significant shareholders, option grants and tenure. Table 12.1 shows the factors that could compromise a director's independence, according to each of the Combined Code, QCA Guidelines and NAPF AIM Guidelines.

Pre-emption rights

12.86 NAPF recommends that AIM companies seek annual approval from shareholders to issue securities on a non pre-emptive basis, following the Pre-emption Group's Statement of Principles (see **12.92–12.99**). It goes on to state that there may be good reasons for smaller AIM companies wanting to waive pre-emption rights (e.g. cost, shareholder structure or speed). Where this is the case, companies should consult with their leading shareholders in advance and give them a full justification for a decision to seek authority to issue more than 5% of the annual limit, as well as accounting for usage in the company's annual report.

12.87 In practice, it is not unusual for an AIM company to exceed this limit, following consultation with its nominated adviser, but in any event the increase should be justified to shareholders either in the AIM admission document or shareholder circular accompanying the notice of general meeting at which such approval is to be sought. Even when increases are agreed, unless it is being obtained for a specific purpose, it is unusual for such an increase to be beyond 10% of the issued share capital.

12.88 Given the minimum standards set out in the QCA Guidelines, the NAPF AIM Guidelines are only likely to have a bearing on a particularly small AIM company.

12.89 In addition to the requirements of the Combined Code and NAPF AIM Guidelines outlined above, AIM companies are required to comply with the continuing obligations contained in the AIM Rules for Companies as well as any specific corporate governance provisions contained within the company legislation of its country of incorporation.

Other guidelines

OECD

12.90 The key international influence on corporate governance in the UK has been provided by the OECD. The key OECD initiatives in recent years have focused on publishing a revised version of its principles of corporate governance in 2004, the launch of a business sector group to give practical guidance to board members trying to improve corporate governance in April 2005 and a methodology for assessing implementation of the OECD principles in December 2006.

12.91 The OECD Principles of Corporate Governance cover six main areas:

- call on governments to have in place an effective institutional and legal framework to support good corporate governance practices (Chapter I);
- call for a corporate governance framework that protects and facilitates the exercise of shareholders' rights (Chapter II);
- strongly support the equal treatment of all shareholders, including minority and foreign shareholders (Chapter III);
- recognise the importance of the role of stakeholders in corporate governance (Chapter IV);
- look at the importance of timely, accurate and transparent disclosure mechanisms (Chapter V); and
- deal with board structures, responsibilities and procedures (Chapter VI).

Pre-emption Group – Statement of Principles

12.92 On 15 May 2006 the Pre-emption Group published its Statement of Principles, which provides guidance on disapplication of pre-emption rights and some clarity on authority for a non-pre-emptive share issue.

12.93 Although the principles set out in the Statement of Principles apply to issues of equity securities for cash by companies listed on the Main Market of the London Stock Exchange, AIM-traded companies are also encouraged to adhere to these principles. These principles are supported by ABI and NAPF.

12.94 The Statement of Principles is aimed to promote flexibility in circumstances 'where new equity issuance on a non-pre-emptive basis would be in the interest of companies and their owners'. The Statement of Principles then goes further and identifies four main criteria for establishing the effective and flexible application of the guidance. These criteria are:

- companies have to signal an intention to seek a non-pre-emptive issue as soon as possible;
- companies must 'establish a dialogue' with the company's shareholders;
- shareholders must communicate with companies and, if necessary, ask for companies' help with understanding all aspects of the proposed issue; and
- companies must consult with their main shareholders.

12.95 The Pre-emption Group recognised that there will be occasions where the disapplication is likely to be considered non-controversial by shareholders. For this reason the Pre-Emption Group established a concept of routine disapplication that would ease the process of granting the authority. Requests are likely to be routine when the company is seeking authority to issue non-pre-emptively no more than 5% of issued ordinary share capital in a year and no more than 7½% of the company's issued ordinary share capital in a rolling three-year period. In both cases shares should be offered at a discount of not more than 5% to the market price.

12.96 However, it is important to remember that requests for routine disapplication do not reduce the importance of the flexibility criteria listed above, but rather reduce the need for in-depth discussion. The requests which might cause the company to exceed the levels mentioned above should be considered by shareholders on an individual basis.

12.97 A routine request would normally be made at an AGM; however, a non-routine request would be made at an AGM only when the company is in a position to justify this approach by providing relevant information to shareholders.

12.98 Once a request to disapply pre-emption rights has been approved, any subsequent annual report should include information on discount achieved, the amount raised and how it was used, and the percentage of shares issued on a non-pre-emptive basis over the last year and over the last three years.

12.99 On 7 July 2008, the Pre-Emption Group published an updated version of the Statement of Principles. These introduced three changes:

- clarified that convertible instruments are covered by the Statement of Principles;
- acknowledged that shareholders would not normally have concerns if there is no dilution of value as a result of the proposed issue; and
- recommended that companies should not seek authorisation for more than a maximum of 15 months, in line with current practice.

ABI Guidelines on Responsible Investment Disclosure

12.100 Public debate on the role of companies in the wider social setting and their responsibility to society has increased dramatically over recent years. Publicly traded companies may attract adverse publicity if they do not take adequate steps to mitigate the impact their business may have on the environment or community and for there to be corresponding levels of shareholder activism. When an applicant company is listing on the Main Market or AIM, it is taking a step which means that its actions and corporate strategy will be subject to far greater public scrutiny than it would as a private company. As a result, many companies may choose to establish a committee to deal with health, safety, social and environmental issues (often referred to as the HSE or HSSE committee). In addition, many institutional shareholders will require evidence of minimum standards of corporate social responsibility before they consider making an investment in the company.

12.101 Mining, oil and gas companies have a much greater exposure in this area. Therefore, a sponsor or nominated adviser may, in any event, request that an HSSE committee is established in order to ensure that the company has appropriate procedures in place to deal with the management of health, safety, environment and community relations risks.

12.102 The principal role of the HSSE committee is to provide an administrative framework by which a company can identify and manage the environmental and social risks to the long- and short-term value of the company. It has responsibility for formulating and recommending to the board the company's policy for HSSE issues as they affect the company's operations. The HSSE committee is also responsible for reviewing management investigations of incidents or accidents that occur in order to assess whether policy improvements are required.

12.103 The ABI's 'Guidelines on Responsible Investment Disclosure' (ABI Guidelines) set out recommendations regarding the disclosures in connection with HSSE matters which institutional shareholders expect to see in the annual report. The ABI Guidelines recommend that the annual report should make disclosures stating whether the board takes HSSE matters into account in its regular risk assessment procedures, whether the board has identified and assessed the significant HSSE risks to the company's long- and short-term value and the corresponding opportunities to enhance value, whether the board receives adequate information to make these assessments, whether directors receive training in HSSE matters and whether the board has effective systems for managing and mitigating significant HSSE risks which are likely to arise.

12.104 In addition to the statements concerning the board's level of involvement in HSSE matters, the ABI Guidelines recommend that the annual report should contain disclosure of the following items:

- information on the HSSE risks and opportunities that may significantly affect the company's short- and long-term value, and how they might impact on the future of the business;
- in the description of the company's policies and procedures for managing risks, include the possible impact on short- and long-term value arising from HSSE matters;
- using key performance indicators where appropriate, include information about the extent to which the company has complied with its policies and procedures for managing material risks arising from HSSE matters and about the role of the board in providing oversight;
- where performance falls short of the objectives, describe the measures the board has taken to put it back on track; and
- describe the procedures for verification of HSSE disclosures.

12.105 The ABI Guidelines state that if the annual report includes a statement that the company has no such policies and procedures, the board should provide reasons for this.

12.106 The ABI Guidelines envisage that in aiming to meet these disclosure requirements, a company will develop its internal procedures and policies on corporate responsibility. By setting up an HSSE committee, the company creates a forum in which these issues can be managed and decisions recorded.

12.107 The principal duties of an HSSE committee should include the following:

- formulating the company's policies and systems for identifying and managing HSSE risks in the company's operations;

- evaluating the effectiveness of the company's policies and systems;
- assessing the policies and systems in the company for ensuring compliance with HSSE regulatory requirements;
- assess the performance of the company with regard to the impact of HSSE decisions and actions on employees, communities and other third parties, and the impact of such decisions and actions on the reputation of the company;
- receive reports from management concerning all fatalities and serious accidents in the company and any action to be taken; and
- review the results of independent audits of the company's performance in regard to HSSE matters, review any strategies and action plans developed by management in response to issues raised and, where appropriate, make recommendations to the board.

12.108 There are no recommended guidelines for the practicalities of implementing an HSSE committee, so in terms of practical detail of the terms of reference, the HSSE committee's are likely to track the terms of reference of the company's other committees. It is common for an HSSE committee to meet four times a year; however, this will depend on the size of the company and the scale of its operations. The composition requirements will vary according to the size of the company and the size of the board, but it is not uncommon to require that, of the minimum number of individuals on the committee, only one needs to be a board director.

Turnbull Guidance

12.109 The Combined Code sets out the principle that the board should maintain a sound system of internal control to safeguard shareholders' investment in the company's assets and this should be reviewed at least annually. The requirements for systems of internal controls are further explained in the Turnbull Report on internal control – guidance to the directors on the Combined Code (the Turnbull Guidance) which was last reviewed in October 2005 and applies to all accounting periods ending on or after 1 January 2006.

12.110 The Turnbull Guidance focuses on the identification, management and control of risks to which the company is, or may potentially be, subject. It further recommends that the systems for internal risk management are frequently monitored and reviewed.

Institute of Chartered Secretaries and Administrators

12.111 The Institute of Chartered Secretaries and Administrators (ICSA) has published guidance on the terms of reference of nomination, remuneration and audit committees in its publications entitled:

- ICSA Guidance on Terms of Reference – Nomination Committee;
- ICSA Guidance on Terms of Reference – Remuneration Committee; and
- ICSA Guidance on Terms of Reference – Audit Committee.

12.112 ICSA also produces guidance on matters which should be reserved for the full board (as opposed to a committee or any one director) in their publication ICSA Guidance on Matters Reserved for the Board.

GC100

12.113 The directors should also bear in mind the guidelines on the practical implementation of certain aspects of the Listing Rules and the Disclosure Rules and Transparency Rules published by the Association of General Counsel and Company Secretaries of the FTSE 100 (GC100 Guidelines). The GC100 Guidelines (reproduced at Appendix 4) are divided into three sections and cover:

- guidelines for establishing procedures, systems and controls to ensure compliance with the Listing Rules;
- guidelines on the requirement to maintain Insider Lists; and
- guidelines on obligations to notify dealings and Model Code compliance.

Pensions & Investment Research Consultants

12.114 The PIRC Shareholder Voting Guidelines 2008 (PIRC Guidelines) are non-legal guidelines issued by the Pensions & Investment Research Consultants (PIRC). PIRC is an independent body which represents institutional investors, especially pension funds. The guidelines, now in their twelfth edition, give guidance to listed companies and in some cases go further than the Combined Code. PIRC produces detailed corporate governance reports for institutional investor clients on large listed company meetings, giving advice on how they should vote on resolutions to be tabled at the general meeting. In coming to its voting recommendations, PIRC considers the PIRC Guidelines its shareholder voting guidelines as well as other factors such as the board's explanation of a proposal and any market implications resulting from it.

12.115 The PIRC Guidelines cover areas including directors, directors' remuneration, audit and reporting, share capital and shareholder relations, and environmental management and reporting. The PIRC Guidelines take account of the Combined Code governance policies and indicate where their best practice goes further than the Combined Code as well as other existing legal or regulatory requirements.

International Corporate Governance Network

12.116 The International Corporate Governance Network (ICGN) was set up in 1995 to further the corporate governance endeavours of investment committees and other bodies. It has four primary purposes:

- to provide an investor-led network for the exchange of views and information about corporate governance issues internationally;
- to examine corporate governance principles and practices;
- to develop and encourage adherence to corporate governance standards and guidelines; and
- to generally promote good corporate governance.

12.117 In 2003 ICGN published its first Statement on Institutional Shareholder Responsibilities. This statement sets out a framework of best practice on the implementation of fiduciary responsibilities in relation to equity shareholdings. On 15 August 2007 ICGN published its revised Statement on Institutional Shareholder Responsibilities. The revised Statement sets out its view of the responsibilities of institutional shareholders in relation to their external roles as owner of company equity and in relation to their internal governance.

12.118 Both statements were designed to address the entirety of relations between institutional shareholders and their agents around the world. They make it clear that these are general guidelines only and that institutional shareholders and their agents should determine the implications for them and consider the suggestions made on how to implement these responsibilities.

Future changes

12.119 In addition to the changes introduced by DTR7 (see **12.50**) and the changes to the 2008 Combined Code (see **12.20–12.22**), the European Commission has published the Shareholder Rights Directive (Directive 2007/36/EC of the European Parliament and of the Council on the exercise of certain shareholder rights in listed companies) which must be implemented by EU member states by 3 August 2009. The key recommendations of the Directive not currently embodied in UK best corporate governance practice are:

- extending the period of notice for the general meeting (other than the annual general meeting where shareholder consent has been given and electronic voting is permitted);
- the right of shareholders to put items on the agenda of the general meeting;
- reducing the rules restricting the eligibility of proxy holders' rights; and
- the disclosure of voting results on the company's website.

12.120 The implementation of this Directive should further codify the key principles in corporate governance, safeguard shareholder interests, promote greater interaction between companies and shareholders and increase the accountability of the directors.

Sources

1 Combined Code 2006 and 2008; www.frc.org.uk/corporate/combinedcode.cfm
2 Listing Rules; fsahandbook.info/fsa/html/handbook/lr
3 Disclosure Rules and the Transparency Rules; fsahandbook.info/fsa/html/handbook/dtr
4 Organisation for Economic Co-operation and Development Principles of Corporate Governance; www.oecd.org
5 National Association of Pension Funds (NAPF) AIM Guidance; www.napf.co.uk
6 Greenbury Report; www.frc.org.uk
7 Cadbury Report; www.ecgi.org
8 Hampel Report; www.ecgi.org
9 Higgs Review; www.frc.org.uk
10 Smith Report; www.frc.org.uk
11 Smith Guidance; www.frc.org.uk
12 Guidance on Audit Committees; www.frc.org.uk
13 Companies Act 2006; www.opsi.gov.uk/acts
14 Financial Services and Market Act 2000; www.opsi.gov.uk/acts
15 Takeover Code; www.thetakeoverpanel.org.uk
16 ICSA Guidance on Terms of Reference – Remuneration Committee; www.icsa.org.uk
17 ICSA Guidance on Terms of Reference – Nomination Committee; www.icsa.org.uk
18 ICSA Guidance on Terms of Reference – Audit Committee; www.icsa.org.uk
19 AIM Rules for Companies; www.londonstockexchange.com
20 QCA Corporate Guidance Guidelines for AIM Companies; www.quotedcompaniesalliance.co.uk
21 QCA AIM Website Guidance, Rule 26; www.quotedcompaniesalliance.co.uk
22 Executive Contracts and Severance (ABI/NAPF Joint Statement); www.napf.co.uk
23 ABI Guidelines on Responsible Investment Disclosure; www.abi.org.uk
24 NAPF Corporate Governance Policy and Voting Guidelines for AIM Companies; www.napf.co.uk
25 NAPF Corporate Governance Policy and Voting Guidelines 2007; www.napf.co.uk
26 ABI and NAPF Remuneration Guidelines; www.ivis.co.uk
27 Pre-Emption Group's Statement of Principles; www.ivis.co.uk
28 Turnbull Guidance; www.frc.org.uk
29 Association of General Counsel and Company Secretaries of FTSE 100 Guidelines
30 Pension & Investment Research Consultants 2008 Shareholder Voting Guidelines; www.pirc.co.uk
31 ICGN Statement on Institutional Shareholder Responsibilities; www.icgn.org
32 EU Directive 2007/36/EC of the European Parliament and of the Council; www.eur-lex.europa.eu

13

Relations with stakeholders

Introduction

13.1 A stakeholder is best described as someone who can be affected by or affect a company's actions. Stakeholders may be individuals, groups, corporate bodies or organisations. But from a company perspective, it may be helpful to relate this responsibility to the forthright definition of one stakeholder as recorded in *The Financial Times*.[1] Stakeholders are '*Anyone that can bugger up your company.*'

13.2 Typically, stakeholders include:

- employees;
- customers or clients;
- suppliers;
- communities;
- government;
- non-governmental organisations (NGOs);
- the media.

13.3 In addition, from a company perspective, the list includes financial stakeholders such as shareholders, lenders and creditors. However, for some NGOs such inclusions are unacceptable, since they see the company and financial stakeholders as being one and the same.

13.4 Nevertheless, as the list shows, some of these are direct stakeholders (e.g. employees), whilst others are indirect stakeholders (e.g. the media and NGOs, who consider their views to be representative of direct stakeholders such as local communities).

Stakeholders and directors' duties

13.5 Relations with stakeholders are effectively encompassed within directors' duties following the introduction of the Companies Act 2006. This new set of responsibilities challenges directors to fulfil their duties without transgressing the realms of executive management with direct responsibility for engagement with stakeholders.

13.6 The full range of a director's duties introduced under the 2006 Act is discussed in **Chapter 5**. Directors of all companies, whether large or small, have seven general duties to their company, including those of which they are a shadow director.[2] These are in addition to the other duties set out in other statutes and regulations. Of the seven the most significant change comes with the second – the duty 'to promote the success of the company'. The full wording is as follows:

> 'A director of a company must act in the way he considers, in good faith, would be most likely to promote the success of the company for the benefit of its members as a whole, and in doing so have regard (amongst other matters) to –
> a) The likely consequences of any decision in the long term,
> b) The interests of the company's employees,
> c) The need to foster the company's relationship with suppliers, customers and others,
> d) The impact of the company's operations on the community and the environment,
> e) The desirability of the company maintaining a reputation for high standards of business conduct, and
> f) The need to act fairly between members of the company.'[3]

13.7 This duty identifies stakeholders directly impacted by the company's activities, but in addition covers aspects such as the environment and reputation, which too may impact on direct stakeholders. This is particularly the case as regards such indirect stakeholders as the government or NGOs whose actions in relation to a company's activities may affect the company's own reputation. When first introduced, many experts, including company secretaries and lawyers, considered that this reflected existing legal responsibilities, such as a director's duty of care with regard to health and safety, and the new definition was assumed to be a codification of existing laws. As a consequence, its introduction did not attract much attention or cause any degree of concern among practitioners, observers or advisers.

13.8 However, this attitude altered when consideration was given to the detailed wording of the enhanced requirements for the Business Review in the Act. The Business Review is a formal part of a company's annual report and accounts. As a consequence, a company's directors have a responsibility (and liability) to ensure that the Business Review conforms to legal requirements.

In the section of the Companies Act that sets out the required content of the Business Review[4] a statutory purpose for the Business Review was declared for the first time. This stated that:

> 'The purpose of the Business Review is to inform members of the company and help them assess how the directors have performed their duty under section 172 (duty to promote the success of the company).'

13.9 This statutory purpose was not available at the time of the introduction of the original Business Review regulations,[5] leaving it open to subjective interpretation. The result of the creation of the statutory purpose is to give greater legal weight to the Business Review as a means of assessing the quality of directors' actions with regard to wider stakeholder audiences. This new duty applies to all directors, regardless of the size of company in which they hold office.

13.10 Now, for the first time, directors have a legal responsibility to consider their company's stakeholders as part of their overall company law duties. To whom does this duty apply and how is it reported?

13.11 The Business Review has a statutory purpose as the means of reporting on stakeholder matters and, as a consequence, assesses the board's actions in relation to them. There are two requirements for non-financial information. The Companies Act 2006[6] introduces enhanced levels of reporting for quoted companies. The term 'quoted companies' applies specifically to those listed on the London Stock Exchange (regardless of size) but excludes companies listed on alternative markets such as AIM, which are treated in the same way as private and subsidiary companies. For the purpose of this chapter, these companies are called 'other companies'.

13.12 For other companies, there is an exclusion for small companies producing a Business Review. Medium-sized companies are also excluded from the requirement to include key performance indicators in respect of non-financial matters.

13.13 The distinction between quoted and other companies is not always straightforward. Some business sectors are adopting similar standards to those for the quoted regime (even where not legally required to do so), as in the private equity market. Most members of the British Venture Capital Association have signed up to a code of practice[7] developed after accusations of a lack of transparency. This requires private equity companies of a significant size to publish a Business Review to the same standards as if they were a quoted company.

13.14 Whatever form of reporting the company adopts, the underlying requirement for the company's directors is that 'The Business Review must, *to the extent necessary*, for an understanding of the development, performance or position of the company's business, include ...' This gives the board the option to consider whether or not particular information should be included. Table 13.1 covers the different levels of reporting for quoted companies and others, with the bold type in each section showing the differences between the two sets of reporting requirements:

Table 13.1 Different levels of reporting for quoted companies and others

Quoted company reporting	Other companies' reporting
The main trends and factors likely to affect the future development, performance and position of the company's business (**including providing forward looking statements, with a safe harbour if provided in the Directors' Report**)	The main trends and factors likely to affect the future development, performance and position of the company's business
Information about environmental matters (including the impact of the company's business on the environment), with key performance indicators, **including information about any policies of the company in relation to these matters and the effectiveness of those policies**	Information relating to environmental matters, with key performance indicators
Information about the company's employees with key performance indicators, **including information about any policies of the company in relation to these matters and the effectiveness of those policies**	Information relating to employee matters, with key performance indicators
Information about social and community issues, including about any policies of the company in relation to these matters and the effectiveness of those policies	Nothing specified
Information about persons with whom there are contractual or other arrangements	Nothing specified
If the Review does not contain information on the four areas immediately above, it must state which of those kinds of information it does not contain	Nothing specified

13.15 There are several points to make about the differences between the requirements for quoted companies and others.

13.16 First, the inclusion of 'persons with whom there are contractual or other arrangements' caused concern at the outset. Such persons could include suppliers, major customers and joint ventures. It was thought that provision of such information could represent a potential security risk to directors. This was particularly of concern to companies involved in pharmaceutical research. Their view was that this could require reporting on contractual arrangements with companies involved in animal testing. As a consequence, it was felt that the provision of such information could result in the targeting of directors by animal rights activists. To address these concerns, there is a safeguard that information does not require to be provided if it is considered by the board to be 'prejudicial to company and contrary to public interest'.

13.17 Second, the requirement to report on 'policies and their effectiveness' related to non-financial matters is far more arduous than may have been expected. Few companies have group-wide policies (e.g. health and safety policies tend to be local to the country of operation because of variations in legislative requirements). More importantly, where there are such policies, companies are unlikely to have systems in place that enable their effectiveness to be assessed across the whole group. As this is part of the statutory purpose to assess a director's fulfilment of his/her duty, this is even more onerous on non-executive directors, who would not have a regular, in-depth understanding of the operational effectiveness of a company.

13.18 Third, the requirement to 'state which of those kinds of information it does not contain' has added strength when perceived from the perspective of professional investors as well as interested NGOs (although the latter have less legal power for change, unless they are also shareholders). Any companies choosing to take the route of exclusion of information would need to explain why such information is not included, and this would be closely inspected by investors. To avoid incurring the potential wrath of investors, in practice, directors may be more likely to err on the side of inclusion, rather than exclusion.

13.19 Furthermore, a provision was introduced into the Climate Change Act (which received Royal Assent at the end of November 2008), which may impact on companies' Business Reviews. This provision 'requires the Secretary of State to "make regulations under section 416(4) of the Companies Act 2006 (c. 46) requiring the directors' report of a company to contain such information as may be specified in the regulations about emissions of greenhouse gases from activities for which the company is responsible" by 6th April 2012'. At this stage, until Statutory Instruments are laid down, it is not clear whether this will be only for quoted companies (and therefore private equity companies due to the Walker Guidelines) to report on their greenhouse gas emissions as part of their Business Review or whether it would extend to **all** companies. This would change this area of reporting from a 'to the extent necessary' basis to a mandatory one. The detail of such reporting is still to be defined, but it is likely to be demanding for those companies that have not previously reported on such non-financial areas. This requirement will build on another aspect of the Climate Change Act which will require large companies (as well as similar sized public sector organisations) to enter into 'cap and trade' schemes for their greenhouse gas emissions, under the Carbon Reduction Commitment. This scheme includes the publication of league tables of organisation's performance in this area. Clearly, directors need to anticipate there will be far more public information about their companies' environmental performance in the future.

13.20 It is important to see the Business Review in the context of a board's reporting on relations with its company's stakeholders. In the past, when the focus was only on shareholders, the annual report and accounts were the formal element of the board's relationship with the shareholders.

13.21 Now that the board has to consider a wider range of stakeholders as part of its audience, the Business Review (as part of an enhanced Directors' Report within the annual report and accounts) takes on the role of a formal communication of activities impacting on company stakeholders. It is based on this change that the need to relate to stakeholders is considered.

How can other aspects of the Companies Act 2006 affect this duty?

13.22 The list of factors to which a director should give consideration as part of the duty to promote the success of the company is not exhaustive, and it should be remembered that the duty is owed to the company and not to individual shareholders or external stakeholders. In this respect a new element introduced[8] under the Act is the ability of members to bring derivative claims against directors on behalf of the company if the directors are held to be in breach of their duties. Such claims represent the potential for increased litigation against directors.

13.23 The GC100 (a group representing the senior general council and company secretaries within the UK's largest companies, based on the FTSE 100) have produced a paper on how they consider directors' duties should be addressed in terms of boardroom process management (see **Appendix 4**).

13.24 As well as suggesting how executive management can give guidance to the board on their relations with stakeholders, the GC100 state that it 'is of the view that directors are not currently, and should not be, as a result of this legislative codification, be forced to evidence their thought processes whether that is with regard to the stated factors or any other matter influencing their thinking'.

How directors might relate with stakeholders

13.25 Table 13.1 describes how directors should report in the various areas affecting stakeholders, but an annual report alone does not make a relationship. We now look at how relationships with stakeholders can be developed.

13.26 At this stage, it is important to consider the role of the board. The Combined Code[9] states that the board is 'collectively responsible for the success of the company'. The Code states that the board is responsible *inter alia* for having a framework of prudent and effective risk management, setting the strategic aims, ensuring that necessary resources are in place to achieve its objectives and reviewing management performance. In this context, the board has the responsibility for corporate governance and reviewing and agreeing strategic direction, while executive management has responsibility for implementing the strategy and delivering performance.

13.27 With these responsibilities, the extension of the role of directors to include consideration of stakeholders does not require these directors to take operational responsibility for stakeholder activities. Instead, directors should consider how they can move to a position where they are aware of the needs and interests of stakeholders so they can efficiently undertake their role of providing 'a framework of prudent and effective risk management'.

13.28 However, consideration of risks relating to stakeholders does not require directors to usurp the role of those executive managers accountable for stakeholder responsibilities. As stated in the supporting principle to the Combined Code, the role of non-executive directors of a board is to 'constructively challenge and to help develop proposals on strategy'.

13.29 To do this effectively, it is necessary to consider how to prioritise stakeholders in terms of their impact on the company's longer-term performance. For this purpose, stakeholders can be considered in terms of their role and contribution as business drivers and reputation influencers. This enables executive management to prioritise stakeholders and allow the board to consider how to allocate responsibilities within the board for considering their needs and interests. Such actions should take account of the issue of derivative claims. In this chapter, directors are assumed to be quoted company directors, who now have additional responsibilities for ensuring satisfactory stakeholder relations. Directors of other companies have less onerous responsibilities and should decide on the extent to which they wish to attain similar standards.

13.30 The range of stakeholders typically includes shareholders as well as other financial stakeholders (such as lenders and creditors), employees, customers, suppliers and the community, including governmental organisations (as non-financial stakeholders). Later in this chapter, the environment and business conduct are considered, not as stakeholders in their own right, but as represented by policies which may or may not impact on stakeholders.

Relations with shareholders as financial stakeholders

13.31 The Business Review regulations refer to 'members', i.e. current shareholders. But relations with shareholders or investors for most companies cover both existing and potential investors. In this context, the role of developing shareholder relations has the objectives of encouraging investors to consider buying the company's shares and/or encouraging existing shareholders to retain ownership. For many companies these activities cover other financial stakeholders, such as holders of preference shares and bonds, together with major lenders.

13.32 For most companies, investor relations activity undertaken on behalf of the board is probably finely tuned. Investor relations executives are often employed as part of the corporate affairs team, backed up by financial communications advisers. Their role is to support the board in the company's relationship with investors (both current and potential shareholders) by:

- understanding the profile of investors – the extent to which they are institutional, quasi-institutional (acting on behalf of high net worth clients) or retail investors;
- understanding the needs and expectations of the investor base; and
- communicating with investors.

13.33 The activity is similar to segmentation and communication exercises that might be undertaken by a company's marketing department, which leads to a detailed understanding of the needs and interests of the target audience. In the case of investors, the investor relations' programmes:

- enable investors to have sufficient knowledge of the company and its business performance to make informed investment decisions;
- encourage a realistic market value to be established for the company (bringing with it potential protection from takeovers and a lower weighted average cost of capital);

- listen to and understand investor sentiment that may be damaging to the company's financial reputation; and
- identify the potential for shareholder activism (e.g. NGOs buying shares to enable them to request resolutions at AGMs) and develop strategies to manage activists.

13.34 Many tools are available for investor relations; their use depends on the circumstances.

13.35 A starting point for investor relations' teams is often a research study into the perceptions of different groups of investors. The study may be undertaken on a rolling basis. Such studies are a form of opinion research and cover both current major investors and also potential institutional investors. The research attempts to ascertain attitudes towards the company, its performance, directors and management. It enables investors' experiences with the company to be better understood and to understand the range of investor expectations.

13.36 Such studies may also help develop the basis for continuing dialogue with investor groups, and as such is a form of stakeholder engagement. These dialogues include communication tools such as:

- Market announcements – to be issued immediately, whenever the board believes there is news material on the performance of the company. These announcements are issued via one of the Regulatory Information Services (RIS) and distributed electronically.
- Investor relations websites – usually found as part of the corporate website, these include information relevant to shareholders, including a financial calendar of dates of announcements and meetings, and of dividend payments. They also typically include an archive of presentations to investor meetings (including investment analysts), together with presentations made at media briefings. These presentations will have been made by company executives, usually as part of a team including one or more board directors. They will be made available over the web to ensure that presentations are not construed as insider information.
- Webcasts and conference calls – these are usually organised immediately after major announcements have been made, typically at times of annual results, but also could include briefings during takeovers, major acquisitions or divestments. These will be organised by financial media communications agencies on behalf of the company. They will either comprise a pre-recorded interview with senior directors, who will provide their interpretations of the announcement – for example, explaining the reasons behind the company's annual results performance – or a live conference

call over the web. In the case of the latter, the audience is able to submit questions, typically by email, to the communications agency, who will then put them to the company executives.

13.37 These tools supplement and enhance regular relationship activities with shareholders.

13.38 The latter usually involve a limited number of directors, typically the chairman, the chief executive and the finance director, although other directors, with specific operational or business responsibility are sometimes involved.

13.39 These regular, often face-to-face, activities include:

- Quarterly and preliminary statements – typically in the form of written communications, although, especially for half-yearly and preliminary statements, webcasts are used, usually involving the chief executive and the finance director.
- Annual general meetings – a statutory requirement, at which the full board is expected to attend, although presentations are typically made by the chairman, the chief executive and the finance director.
- Analysts' presentations and investor conferences – also known as investor road shows, these tend to be limited to selected investors and/or analysts. They help to give investors greater insight into the company's strategy and performance. The presenters are some or all of the executive directors, as well as some of the company's management with specific business responsibilities. The presentations made at these events should be provided on the investor section of the corporate website to ensure they are available to all investor groups.

13.40 Non-executive directors are not usually involved directly in developing relationships with investors. An obvious exception is the chairman, but in this case, he acts on behalf of the board. Another exception is that of formal documents such as the annual report and accounts, in which the Business Review is the report of the full board of directors and for which they are legally responsible. It is worth noting in this respect that an Annual Review[10] (which may be provided in hard copy or electronically) does not have to include a Business Review, and thus these summary reports are more typically the responsibility of the executive team.

13.41 As can be seen, the role of the directors in developing relationships with shareholders of their company is typically done at arm's length, i.e. via professionals specialising in this area, or directors of the board who are effectively delegated to undertake this task.

13.42 This is a feature that arises with all aspects of a director's relationships with stakeholders. It is essential from a corporate governance perspective that directors undertake some form of review with these individuals to ensure that their duty to promote the success of the company is carried out in a manner with which they are satisfied.

13.43 Directors should decide how they can best address relations with shareholders. This can be achieved in several ways; examples include greater involvement by other directors in observing analysts' presentations or by participating in the presentation of findings of investor perception studies. Non-executive directors must make efforts to ensure they are more aware of shareholders' attitudes as a means of fulfilling their obligations under the duty to promote the success of the company.

Relationships with other financial stakeholders

13.44 It is important to recognise that shareholders are not the only financial stakeholders. There are creditors (i.e. organisations that provide short-term loans, long-term bonds and mortgages) as well as suppliers that make credit available for a company's purchases. (See **13.71** below on suppliers as persons with whom there are contractual arrangements.) Such financial arrangements are handled in large companies by the treasury function, which will have regular discussions with financial institutions that make credit available. The information provided to these institutions may be broader than that available to shareholders.

13.45 Most companies treat creditors in the same way as shareholders. Regular presentations will be made to institutions that are bond holders in the same way as there are investment analysts' presentations. For this purpose, the board representative is typically the finance director, supported by executives that manage the treasury function. Other members of the board are unlikely to be closely involved, although they should adopt the approach recommended for shareholders of understanding the issues and attitudes of creditors.

Relationships with non-financial stakeholders

13.46 The introduction of the new directors' duty means that directors have an obligation to consider also the interests of stakeholders other than the company's shareholders. While directors have had an obligation to consider the interests of employees since 1985,[11] this is the first time such a wide-ranging requirement has existed.

13.47 However, this is only in so far as any stakeholder may impact on the directors' duty to promote the success of the company – there is no requirement for any director to be philanthropic or altruistic in their actions towards these other stakeholders.

13.48 It is also important to emphasise that any consideration of stakeholders' interests should be set against the requirement for directors to take into account the likely consequences of any business decision in the long term.

13.49 In this respect, the criterion by which to evaluate any decision to consider stakeholders' interests is the extent to which decisions will reinforce or detract from the company's strategic direction. This requires that directors evaluate the extent to which other stakeholders can be seen as business drivers (in terms of business performance and risk) or influencers on a company's reputation (in terms of the longer-term development of shareholder value).

13.50 In order to consider how directors should develop relationships with other stakeholders, each stakeholder group is considered and the extent to which it could be considered a business driver or reputation influencer reviewed. This helps directors set priorities. Some suggestions on subsequent actions relating to each group are made. At the end of the section on non-financial stakeholders, the way in which directors could manage relationships with non-financial stakeholders is considered.

Employees

13.51 The director's duty requires that attention is paid to the interests of the company's employees. Before this can be achieved, it is necessary to consider how employees affect the long-term success of the company, in order to consider the extent to which employees represent a priority stakeholder group.

Employees – business driver or reputation influencer?

13.52 Employees are often described in companies' annual reports as 'our most important asset'. Yet, rarely is there supporting evidence that directors act to ensure that they pay attention to the interests of their employees as a means of safeguarding or developing their company's 'most important asset'.

13.53 Employees can be considered to be business drivers in terms of their:

- ability to perform their job productively, both as individuals and as part of a team;
- motivation to consider new ideas and approaches to deliver added value in their job;

- proficiency in their job to ensure that their employer is not faced with any unexpected risks or liabilities;
- approach to personal health and safety – this may be in terms of inadequate behaviour that could potentially affect their own well-being, as well as the safety of others;
- approach to the safety and security of the company's assets – for example, in the case of a fire caused by employee negligence, or negligent use of computer equipment or electronic data records.

13.54 As regards employees as reputation influencers, their representation of the company means they can affect its reputation through the quality of their communication with:

- commercial third parties, such as customers and suppliers;
- friends and relatives (the 'grapevine effect');
- media representatives (including via telephone enquiries, interviews or even phone-in chat shows);
- central and local government representatives.

13.55 Based on a board's evaluation of the extent to which employees represent a business driver and/or reputation influencer, a judgement can be made on the scope of activities necessary to ensure that directors fulfil their role of taking account of the interests of employees.

Developing relationships with employees

13.56 As with shareholders, relationships with employees are usually delegated to members of the board with direct and executive responsibilities. This is likely to be at chief executive level, but it could also be at human resources director level, if that individual is a member of the main board.

13.57 However, arguing that this responsibility is delegated is insufficient excuse for not considering the interests of employees, given the new wording of the director's duty. What should a director do to ensure that he or she can justifiably argue that their work as a director takes into account the interests of employees, (particularly a non-executive director whose responsibilities include the need to challenge and help develop and deliver proposals on strategy)?

13.58 There are several courses of action open to some or all directors. The most direct is to undertake a series of plant or site visits to meet employees and get to know their interests. If the company has staff representatives, is unionised or has a European or national works council, then a more focused approach is to have a series of regular (six-monthly or annual) meetings with these representatives to achieve the same level of insight into employees' interests and concerns but alongside line managers with executive responsibility.

13.59 Indirect action involves a director being more proactive in discussion with functions responsible for considering employees' interests (e.g. human resources, line managers). Such activities include some or all of the following:

- review employee survey results;
- review internal communications programmes, including employee 'speak up' (whistleblowing), feedback and complaints systems;
- participate in staff and management conferences, as well as other events and employee get-togethers;
- participate in health and safety review programmes;
- review outcomes of staff recruitment programmes.

What could be the results of these actions?

13.60 Gaining an understanding of employees' interests and concerns is one thing, but the real question is what a director should do with the benefit of such knowledge.

13.61 The director has to consider to what extent acting on employees' interests can be considered to be within the normal running of the company (in which case, the responsibility lies with executive management) or whether the issues could affect the long-term performance of the company. The director should consider his understanding of employees' interests or concerns against the following:

- Will these concerns affect the long-term performance of employees?
- To what extent could these concerns derail any of the key company strategic initiatives?
- Will employees' concerns (if realised) have a significant impact on the cost structure of the business?
- Could employees' concerns result in a long-term deterioration in the reputation of the company?

13.62 If the answer to any of these questions is a possible or definite 'yes', then the director should review his understanding of employee interests with the chief executive and, if required, with the board as a whole. Then a policy addressing these interests or concerns should be formulated by executive management and reviewed and agreed by the board.

Customers

13.63 Typically, a director may have little involvement with customers because the role is delegated from the board to individuals within the executive with customer responsibility. These may be individuals with sales or marketing responsibilities, operational responsibility (typically when there is a branch network) or customer service responsibility. This is even more likely where there is a group structure with customer contact via operational companies, with a result that the main board director is one step further removed.

13.64 However, the director has a duty to have regard to the need to foster the company's relationship with customers. For most well-run companies this should be a normal part of everyday business life, but does not mean there is no role for a director to support the activity. Again, given the long-term aspect of the director's duty, the starting point is the extent to which customers can be instrumental in affecting the long-term success of the company.

Customers – business driver or reputation influencer?

13.65 In the 1980s a slogan often used by companies was 'the customer is king' and this was occasionally symbolised on posters showing a lion roaring. That such a statement was necessary indicated how customers had been treated in the past, but it is not necessarily so different 20 years on.

13.66 Customers should be considered in their different groups (consumers, key accounts, strategic business partners) to obtain a clear view of their relative importance to the company's overall business strategy. Each will be a business driver for a company in different ways. In this capacity this includes their ability to:

- deliver ongoing revenue streams – perhaps a statement of the obvious, but for major customers, it is important to be able to work with them to identify changes in market trends and modify the approach to ensure any changing demands are met;
- contribute to product and/or service development, such as customers contributing to research into their changing needs;
- improve systems to reduce direct costs, such as those associated with delivery logistic systems, e.g. supermarkets taking delivery from food manufacturers in the form of palletised systems.

13.67 Customers can have a significant role to play as reputation influencers, particularly when the company fails to address some of the customers' interests adequately. These may be in the form of poor service, poor quality of delivery or because a company's behaviour is perceived by customers to be inappropriate. The latter can lead to customer boycotts, as with Shell and its attempt to scrap its Brent Spar oil platform in the North Sea. Customers (led by NGOs) regarded this as unacceptable environmental behaviour and boycotted Shell's petrol stations in Germany. A similar example is Nike, which was criticised for using child labour at suppliers' factories. Customers led a boycott against the company's products which did considerable damage to its reputation. It has since made significant strides to overcome these allegations and restore its reputation.

A review of customers as business drivers or reputation influencers helps determine priority areas and focus the nature of activities in which a director should be involved as part of his duty to foster relationships with customers.

Developing relationships with customers

13.68 The role of directors to foster relationship with customers means they must have a good knowledge of the needs of different customer groups, as well as understanding issues that relate to them. This can be done via two routes:

- Indirectly – by having an in-depth review of the results of customer surveys, the nature of customer complaints and proposals for product and service development approaches. This should take place as part of a formal review with management of these areas. In addition, where there are key accounts or strategic partners within customer groups, this review represents an opportunity to understand in more detail the needs of specific customers and the actions proposed to address these needs. As a result, the director will be in a better position to develop relevant strategies within the board.
- Directly – the challenge for directors is how they can create a direct relationship with customers. Not every director is in the favourable position of directors of retail companies such as supermarkets who can visit stores at weekends to meet staff, and speak with and listen to their customers. But similar opportunities exist in each industrial sector. There is great benefit in accompanying an account manager at least one day in a year to visit a key account to understand their issues and expectations of your company. The effort will be repaid handsomely by being able to have a more considered debate with the individuals responsible for customer management and its development. It will also enable the director to participate more effectively in board reviews of customer strategy, surveys and complaint reports.

Taking actions to foster customer relationships

13.69 It is important for a director not to usurp the role of those directly responsible for customer management. However, helping to foster relationships can be achieved by identifying areas where:

- customer needs or concerns are not addressed adequately;
- product development could be better focused to meet potential customer needs;
- potential cost savings can be achieved without detriment to quality or service to the customer.

13.70 In this respect, the approach should be to develop strategic questions to put to individuals responsible for customer management. They should focus on long-term development and/or policy rather than short-term tactical issues. The result of a discussion on these issues will challenge customer management teams to develop appropriate customer relationship strategies to provide for long-term success. In this respect, the board director may be able to contribute useful insights based on knowledge gained of customers' interests.

Suppliers

13.71 As with customers, the director's duty is to have regard to the need to foster the company's relationship with suppliers. Unlike customers, there have not been posters advocating that 'suppliers are king'. In contrast, for some companies, there is an attitude that suppliers should be 'beaten up rather than partnered'.

13.72 Why is it necessary to consider supplier relationships? Again, it is useful to consider the business drivers and reputation influencers relating to suppliers as a means of establishing the priority of suppliers as a stakeholder group, and to determine the appropriate level of activity required of directors.

Suppliers – business driver or reputation influencer?

13.73 When considering how to develop relationships with suppliers, follow the same approach as with customers and consider them by category. Increasingly management responsible for a company's supply chain strives to reduce the number of suppliers – for cost reasons and to develop mutually beneficial partnerships. Often the Pareto rule applies to suppliers as much as to customers – 80% of purchases come from only 20% of suppliers.

13.74 By categorising suppliers, the areas in which each group can be a business driver can be considered. Examples of business drivers relating to suppliers include:

- improved product or service efficiency, leading to improved prices or quality for your company as the customer;
- acquiring different operational approaches, based on understanding the ways in which the supplier deals with its wider customer base;
- identifying product development opportunities based on having a research and development partnership with the supplier.

13.75 Suppliers also play a significant role in the reputation of the customer company. This includes suppliers' ability to demonstrate good environmental and social practices in providing products and services. Examples where this can be seen include:

- Process – suppliers deal with customers through a number of processes, including fulfilling order requests, as well as the overall business practices required to deal with customers. Where suppliers are seen to have inappropriate business practices in their dealings with their customers, both suppliers and customers will suffer reputation loss. Examples include bribery or poor treatment of staff by supplier management. The most severe example of the latter has occurred in timber plantations in the Far East, where slave labour has been exposed by human rights NGOs. In such cases, they traced the supply chain from the timber plantations to the distributors in the West. They promoted a highly visible media campaign against these companies. This was on the grounds that they believed these companies would be easier to influence in terms of the impact on their reputation, and would encourage them to put pressure on their suppliers to rectify the practices. The result is that major timber distributors in Europe have taken action to ensure their products come from responsible sources.
- Product – as western industrial activity, including both product manufacturing and support services such as call centres, is increasingly outsourced to developing countries, so there is perceived to be a risk of poor product or service quality (including product safety). Unless the company has watertight quality control procedures for its supply chain, it may suffer loss of reputation if the products or services provided fail to measure up to the standards expected by its customers. However, it is very risky to blame outsourced suppliers for poor quality if this is found not to be the case. Mattel, the toy manufacturer, issued several product recalls in 2007, and blamed its Chinese suppliers for poor quality. The general manager of one of its suppliers committed suicide. Based on its own enquiries (due to public outcry, particularly from the Chinese government) Mattel had to make a public apology to the Chinese government in which it admitted that the problem was not the quality of its Chinese suppliers, but its own design faults. The result was that the company's reputation suffered on a highly visible, worldwide basis.

13.76 By undertaking evaluation of suppliers, the board can determine the extent to which each group of suppliers is a priority as a business driver or reputation influencer. As a result it will be able to set relevant and appropriate levels of activity for its board members to undertake in relation to the role of fostering relationships with suppliers.

Developing relationships with suppliers

13.77 Because of the nature of relationships with suppliers – often based on price, quality and delivery times – taking actions to foster relationships with suppliers will be a more challenging action for a director. To do so, there are indirect and direct courses of action:

- The indirect course is to request the procurement department to provide a review to the board of its supplier profile, categorised by the nature of the supplier relationships – e.g. as 'partners', 'fulfilling basic supply requirements' and 'suppliers of last resort'. This review would include suppliers' social and environmental credentials. It should enable the board to establish an overall approach to supplier relationships. As a result, it enables directors to question plans with a view to improving the quality of supplier relationships from the perspective of promoting the success of the company over the longer term.
- The direct course would be to have meetings with strategic partner suppliers to ascertain how well they believe their views and plans are taken on board by the company and as a result determine the extent to which they believe they have a sound commercial relationship with the company – one that is mutually beneficial for long-term development.

Taking actions to foster supplier relationships

13.78 It is probably in a company's best interests to improve commercial relationships with suppliers, although the need to focus on key short-term factors such as price, quality and delivery times continue to be important priorities.

13.79 However, if, as a result of either indirect or direct actions, it is apparent that there is any relationship breakdown, this may lead to the company not benefiting from gaining insights into market developments or receiving product or service initiatives.

13.80 The procurement teams should be asked how they intend to build suppliers into longer-term strategic developments, identifying programmes, such as jointly to improve service or quality, or deliver product development activities. At all times, this questioning should not be to change the commercial short-term objectives of these teams, but rather ensure they additionally take into account a range of possible longer-term objectives.

The community

13.81 A director's duty is to have regard to the need to consider the impact of the company's operations on the community. This is a far less proactive requirement than those for either customers or suppliers, where the requirement is to foster relationships. Indeed, in some companies, community relationships are seen as low-level activities, often linked to charitable donations.

13.82 So why is there a need to consider a company's impact on its community? The answer is that, in some circumstances, the community can be influential in terms of a company's 'licence to operate'. Again, it is of use to consider the business drivers and reputation influencers relating to areas of the community as a means of establishing the priority of community matters to the company's long-term success.

Community – business driver or reputation influencer?

13.83 The community should be considered as being made up of several distinct groups, some or all of which may be linked to employees (e.g. as relatives). It can include representative groups, made up of individuals living close at hand to company locations. It can also include government bodies (both local and central) whose role is to oversee certain behaviours of companies in respect of the community in their locations. Then there are local charitable and voluntary bodies, whose role is to provide support to local groups of needy or disadvantaged individuals. Lastly, there can be people – individuals or very small groups – that have local issues relating to the company. Any of the above could also be prospective employees.

13.84 In terms of business drivers, the community is unlikely to feature high on any company's agenda, unless it requires a licence to operate. Such examples include the need to secure planning permission for new sites or extensions to an existing one. The need to be seen to be active in the community is often a key measure in gaining local government support for a planning request. This is typically the case with retailers seeking to secure new store outlets. The same requirement for a licence to operate applies to companies working in the developing world, especially those in extractive industries, where community support can be a critical factor in gaining central government agreement for extension of activities outside the current sites, as well as motivating the workforce.

13.85 Examples chosen as business drivers can also be seen as reputation influencers within the community. Relationships with local charitable or voluntary bodies can also be reputation influencers if combined with employee volunteering, whereby the employees choose the local bodies they wish to support. Such activities can be motivating to the employees, and, if structured properly, deliver training in key skills such as leadership.

13.86 By reviewing the range of community activities in terms of whether they are business drivers or reputation influencers, the board can determine the extent to which they take part in activities to review the impact of their company's impacts on the community.

Considering the impact of the company's operations on the community

13.87 Distinct from seeing the community as a business driver or reputation influencer, the requirement on directors is to consider the impact of the company's operation on its communities.

13.88 To do this there needs to be some form of review of areas in which the company may impact. This includes consideration of environmental matters (e.g. noise pollution or spills and leakages of toxic substances into local water courses), health and safety issues (including road traffic accidents) and employment issues (especially when there may be risks of staff cutbacks or plant closures affecting the local community).

13.89 For the most part, these follow local legislative requirements, but it is advisable to ask questions of management to ensure that common practices are in place on a company-wide basis.

13.90 An alternative approach is to request a review of the numbers and types of complaints and other feedback made to the company from community sources. An analysis of these will identify the extent to which the company is at risk and has due regard to its impact on its communities.

Taking actions with regard to community activities

13.91 When a director considers what actions can or should be taken with regard to the community, the focus should be on how community relations play a part as one of the company's business drivers, as well as mitigate the company's potential impacts on the community.

13.92 The approach should be to consider the community from a reputation and risk perspective. The intention should be to develop a strategic approach that ensures the company can continue to operate local sites with the minimum of interference from local groups, while maintaining a position as an admired and respected business partner in its communities.

The environment and high standards of business conduct

13.93 These last two areas have been grouped together because they are not stakeholders in themselves, but a company's approach towards them can impact on a wide range of stakeholders. They are in fact based on a series of policies, including:

- environmental policies – relating to areas such as carbon emissions, resource usage and causes of pollution;
- business conduct policies – including policies such as codes of ethics, 'speak-up' programmes and compliance training.

13.94 As such, there are often formal structures in place, reporting to the board, which takes account of these policies and their implementation. These go some way to meeting a director's duty. For example, ethical behaviour and business conduct are typically subjects of review by a company's audit committee. For many companies, there is a similar formal health, safety and environment committee that will report to the board on these issues. In terms of ensuring the company's reputation is maintained, it is not only necessary to have such committee reports, but also to ensure that the outcomes of reports are visible and available to a wider stakeholder audience.

13.95 A director has to consider the extent to which the company is maintaining its reputation for both environmental matters and standards of business conduct, and to understand the extent to which the policies are in place, and the level of effectiveness associated with them.

13.96 In this context, probably the most important task for a director is to be familiar with the range of policies in place and how widespread these policies are across the company's operations. Weaknesses in the scope of the policies in terms of their geographic scope or the areas covered need to be addressed from a governance perspective. In addition, levels of effectiveness should be evaluated.

13.97 One measure for scope and effectiveness can be undertaken at an operational level, by asking whether group policies are in place at a local level, and the extent to which local management considers they are observed throughout their operation. This can be the subject for some form of internal audit if it is felt there needs to be a tighter review of effectiveness. In the environmental area, the review can be supplemented with benchmarking environmental data such as fuel efficiency or energy usage – and the need for the larger companies to provide data for their Carbon Reduction Commitments will mean that such data will be readily available in the future. These aspects can be significant business drivers in some circumstances, such as in the transport sector. Such benchmarking highlights areas of policy ineffectiveness.

13.98 Another measure is the extent to which there have been breaches to policies. This can be in the form of legal prosecutions – e.g. environmental pollution – or by internal evaluation. Of the latter, the strongest and most visible measure is the extent to which there has been disciplinary action over breaches of the code of conduct.

13.99 As an example, BAE reported that, in 2007, 260 of its employees were sacked because of unethical behaviour[12] that breached its code of business conduct. Included within this overall number were individuals dismissed for fraud, inaccurate labour charging, misuse of company IT and threatening behaviour. Given the media focus on this company's ethical behaviour, its openness indicated that the company was serious in its intent to address this area. It also reflected awareness on the part of the board of its need to build reputation in this area of its relationship with stakeholders.

Managing relationships with stakeholders

13.100 As can now be appreciated, managing relationships with stakeholders would be very demanding for a director if every course of action were to be undertaken. This is not necessary if stakeholder groups have been prioritised and courses of action agreed to improve the quality of relationships. Not all stakeholder groups require the same degree of intensity. The choice depends on the extent to which a company perceives each stakeholder group's significance as a business driver or reputation influencer.

13.101 Once prioritisation of stakeholders and actions is achieved, there needs to be some allocation of responsibility within the board, unless there is agreement that every director considers every stakeholder group – something that is inadvisable. The alternative is for individual directors as stakeholder champions within the board to adopt specific categories of stakeholders as their area of responsibility. The requirement is then on each director to report back to the board about their findings and views on areas for long-term improvement. As such individual directors become champions for specific stakeholders within board discussions and have responsibility for continuing dialogue with executive management responsible for relevant stakeholder strategic activities. As a result they can confidently report on these matters in the Business Review.

13.102 The value and potential business opportunity in better understanding stakeholders and working to improve the quality of relationships with them should now be apparent. The key message is that a company's relationships with its stakeholders – both financial and non-financial – should be firmly placed in the longer-term commercial and profit and loss context. Directors should always be aware and consider the fact that stakeholders can both drive a company's performance and affect its reputation on both the up- and downside!

Sources

1 This explicit definition of a stakeholder came from a City conference, and was quoted in the media column of *The Financial Times* on 14 September 2004.
2 See **Chapter 1** for definition and detail regarding shadow directors.
3 Companies Act 2006, s. 172.
4 Companies Act 2006, s. 417(2).
5 Companies Act 1985 (Operating and Financial Review and Directors' Report, etc.) Regulations 2005 (SI 2005/1011) and Companies Act 1985 (Operating and Financial Review) (Repeal) Regulations 2005 (SI 2005/3442).
6 Companies Act 2006, s. 417(5).
7 The code of practice is based on the Walker Report undertaken for BVCA. The

consultation document and final recommendation can be found on the Walker Working Group website: www.walkerworkinggroup.com

8 Companies Act 2006, ss. 260–264.

9 Code principle A1.

10 Also known as a summary financial statement. The rules regulating such statements for quoted companies are in Companies Act 2006, s. 428.

11 Companies Act 1985, s. 309.

12 *Personnel Today* (14 April 2008). Report based on a statement from BAE's 2007 Corporate Responsibility Report.

14

Directors' liabilities

Introduction

14.1 Directors discharge their roles subject to duties and obligations that are legally imposed on them. In some cases a breach of these obligations may give rise to personal liability on the part of the director, notwithstanding that he acts as an agent of the company and is thereby commonly protected against claims brought by third parties. This chapter analyses the major areas in relation to which directors are exposed to personal liability.

Breach of duty

14.2 Directors owe general duties to the company and will be liable for breaches of those duties. It is important in the context of this chapter that directors are aware that breaches of those duties are a source of potential liability.

14.3 Until the introduction of the Companies Act 2006 (the 2006 Act), the duties which directors owed to their company were found in case law rather than in legislation. Some of these general duties were codified under ss. 171–177 of the 2006 Act under the following headings:

- duty to act within powers (s. 171);
- duty to promote the success of the company (s. 172);
- duty to exercise independent judgement (s. 173);
- duty to exercise reasonable care, skill and diligence (s. 174);
- duty to avoid conflicts of interest (s. 175);
- duty not to accept benefits from third parties (s. 176); and
- duty to declare interest in proposed transaction or arrangement (s. 177).

14.4 Sections 171–174 came into force on 1 October 2007 and ss. 175–177 came into force on 1 October 2008. Other duties, such as the duty of confidentiality, remain uncodified or are set out by other provisions in the legislation.

14.5 These general duties could formerly only be enforced against the director by the company. Now, under Part 11 of the 2006 CA, members of the company can enforce them on behalf of the company by bringing a derivative claim (see **Chapter 15**).

14.6 A director in the context of general duties is any person occupying the position of a director, whether validly appointed or simply acting as a *de facto* director without having been appointed (s. 250).

Duty to act within powers

14.7 A director must act in accordance with a company's constitution and only exercise powers for the purposes for which they are conferred (s. 171). Under s. 257, a company's constitution is defined broadly to include resolutions or decisions reached in accordance with the constitution. The definition of constitution includes decisions by the members of the company, or a class of members, that are treated by virtue of any enactment or rule of law as equivalent to a decision by the company as well as any resolutions and agreements listed under s. 29 of the Act. As a result, the director must be aware of all the decisions and agreements that comprise the company's constitution in order to ensure that he complies with it.

14.8 What a proper purpose will comprise depends on the specific situation. Where directors act for their own benefit rather than that of the company this is clearly unacceptable,[1] but conversely if the directors' interests are advanced while acting for the purpose of the company, then that is acceptable.[2] The director must therefore have the purpose of the company foremost in mind when making decisions.

Duty to promote the success of the company

14.9 A director has a duty to promote the success of the company by acting in a way he considers, in good faith, would most likely promote the success of the company for the benefit of the members as a whole (or for whatever other purpose the company has in addition to or instead of the benefit of the members), having regard to such factors as the long-term consequences of the decision, the interests of the company's employees, the company's business relationships and reputation, the need to act fairly as between members, and the impact on the company's business relationships with suppliers, customers and others (s. 172).

14.10 The duty to promote success is subject to other circumstances, such as insolvency, which may require the director by law to act in the interest of the creditors (s. 172). However, apart from this exception, the director must always act in the interest of the company.

Duty to exercise independent judgement

14.11 A director of a company must exercise independent judgement, although this duty is not infringed by the director's acting in accordance with an agreement entered into by the company that restricts the future exercise or discretion by its directors or acting in a way authorised by the company's constitution (s. 173). A director must not delegate his discretion unless authorised to do so under the constitution (which, in the broad definition under the 2006 Act, includes company resolutions).

14.12 Case law shows that a director may not, for instance, fetter his discretion by agreeing to vote in a certain way, although the directors may cause the company to enter into a contract and undertake to exercise their powers to ensure the proper fulfilment of a contract that is in the best interests of the company.[3] Directors should thus not give undertakings to fulfil obligations in relation to contracts or to recommend to shareholders courses of actions they feel may not be in the best interests of the company in the future.

Duty to exercise reasonable care, skill and diligence

14.13 A director must exercise reasonable care, skill and diligence. This is defined under s. 174(2) as the care, skill and diligence that would be exercised by a reasonably diligent person with:

- the general knowledge, skill and experience that may reasonably be expected of a person carrying out the functions carried out by the director in relation to the company; and
- the general knowledge, skill and experience that the director has.

14.14 Section 174(a) sets out the minimum standard required by the directors, whereas those directors with a higher set of knowledge and skills will be required to meet s. 174(b). For instance, a non-executive's experience of working as a banker was taken into account when considering his breach of duty by failing to exercise the appropriate level of competence by allowing the company to accept an upstream loan from a subsidiary.[4]

14.15 A director must therefore be wary of accepting a directorship for which he is under-qualified (e.g. if he has no knowledge of the relevant industry) and similarly must continue to use his skills when acting as a director for the company. A negligible involvement in the company is not a valid excuse to a breach of directors' duties.[5] While directors cannot absolve themselves entirely of responsibility by delegation to others,[6] they are entitled in the absence of suspicious circumstances to rely on the expertise of their co-directors or other officers of the company and on the opinion of outside experts. The extent of this reliance depends on the circumstances and the experience of the directors as well as the functions that he carries out for the company.

Duty to avoid conflict of interest

14.16 Under s. 175(1), 'a director must avoid a situation in which he has, or can have, a direct or indirect interest that conflicts, or possibly may conflict, with the interests of the company'. The 'indirect interest' may include the interest of any person or legal entity connected with a director (s. 252). It is stated explicitly in s. 175(2) that s. 175(1) applies in particular to the exploitation of any property, information or opportunity, whether or not the company could take advantage of the property, information or opportunity.

14.17 The duty of conflicts applies to potential conflicts as well as actual conflicts, which means that the conflicts will need to be addressed at an earlier stage than they did under the previous law.

14.18 Conflict of interest is taken to mean conflict of duties, and the only conflicts of interest not covered under s. 175 – those in relation to a transaction or arrangement with the company – are covered by different provisions in the 2006 Act.[7]

14.19 The conflict of interest duty is not infringed if the situation cannot be regarded as likely to give rise to a conflict of interest or the matter has been authorised by the directors (s. 175(4)). Non-conflicted directors of a private company incorporated on or after 1 October 2008 can authorise such an action if it is not expressly prohibited in the constitution. By contrast, non-conflicted directors of private companies incorporated before this date can give such authorisation only if it is permitted by ordinary resolution of the company. Non-conflicted directors of a public company can provide such authorisation only if there is a provision which expressly allows them to do so in the constitution. Shareholders may authorise conflicts and prevent a breach of duty under s. 180(4)(a).

14.20 If a conflict of interest between an interest of the company and another interest of the director exists, the director must account for any benefit he has received from the transaction, unless he received informed approval from the shareholders or the company's constitution allowed it. Also, if the company suffered a loss by virtue of the conflict, the director will be liable to account for the loss even if he did not benefit personally.

Duty not to accept benefits from third parties

14.21 A director must not accept a benefit from a third party conferred by reason of his being a director or his doing (or not doing) anything as director, unless the acceptance of such benefit could not reasonably be regarded as giving rise to a conflict of interest. However, it would be wise for a director to obtain shareholder authorisation.[8] A conflict of interest includes a conflict of duty.

14.22 Under common law, directors must account for the profit they have made even if the company could not have made the profit itself.[9]

Duty to declare interest in proposed transaction or arrangement

14.23 From 1 October 2008, if a director of a company is in any way, directly or indirectly, interested in a proposed transaction or arrangement with the company, he must declare the nature and extent of that interest to the other directors.[10] The director's indirect interest may arise as a result of the interest of a person connected with him.

14.24 The director's declaration of interest must be made before the company enters into this transaction. It can be made at a meeting of the directors or by notice to the directors. Section 176 does not require a declaration of interest of which the director is not aware or where he is not aware of the transaction or arrangement in question. A director does not have to declare an interest if it is not likely to give rise to a conflict of interest, if the other directors are already aware of it (or should reasonably be aware of it) or it concerns the terms of his service contract that are considered at a meeting of directors or by a committee of directors.

14.25 Where a company's articles contain provisions for dealing with conflicts of interest, the general duties are not infringed by anything done (or omitted) by the directors in accordance with those provisions.[11]

14.26 A breach of s. 177 is not a criminal offence, unlike a breach of s. 182, which deals with declarations of interest in existing transactions or arrangements.[12]

Consequences of breach of duties

14.27 The consequences of breach of general duties are not codified and the same remedies apply for breach of general duties under the 2006 Act as for those under common law rules and equitable principles. Breach of duty may thus give rise to remedies such as damages, compensation, restoration and rescission of a transaction. The director will be personally liable and will be ordered to account for any personal profit. If a breach has been threatened but has not yet taken place, an injunction or declaration may be granted.

14.28 However, the director may escape liability for breach of duty by having his breach of duty ratified by a resolution of the members of the company (s. 239). In addition, a director may be entitled to statutory relief in respect of his conduct amounting to negligence, default, breach of duty or breach of trust.

Liability for contracts of the company

14.29 In certain circumstances a director may be liable for contracts made in the company's name, although the general position is that he is not.

14.30 Companies do not exist prior to their incorporation and for this reason, pre-incorporation contracts are null and void and are unenforceable by or against the company.[13] They cannot be ratified.[14] A director will be personally liable under the pre-incorporation contract if he intended to be a party to the contract himself, regardless of whether he represented that he was signing on behalf of the company. The English courts are inclined to find that directors contracted as principals in such circumstances in order to give effect to the pre-incorporation contract.[15]

14.31 Section 36C of the 1985 Act[16] provides that a director is personally liable if he enters into a pre-incorporation contract purportedly on behalf of the company prior to its incorporation. This section applies even if all parties to the contract knew that the company had not been formed at the date of the contract.[17] Section 36C of the 2006 Act applies 'subject to any agreement to the contrary'. This allows for the possibility that the pre-incorporation contract may be novated to the company once it is formed.[18] If the director is personally liable, he can sue as well as be sued on the pre-incorporation contract.[19] These principles do not apply to a company which contracts in a new name prior to its change of name becoming effective.[20]

14.32 Directors also need to be aware of the Bills of Exchange Act 1882, s. 26 of which provides that:

(a) Where a person signs a bill as drawer, endorser, or acceptor, and adds words to his signature, indicating that he signs for or on behalf of a principal, or in a representative character, he is not personally liable thereon; but the mere addition to his signature of words describing him as an agent, or as filling a representative character, does not exempt him from personal liability.
(b) In determining whether a signature on a bill is that of the principal or that of the agent by whose hand it is written, the construction most favourable to the validity of the instrument shall be adopted.

14.33 In practice, a cheque expressed to be drawn on the company's account at its bank will avoid a director signatory being personally liable on it.[21] However, in the case of other bills of exchange, a director signing on behalf of the company should include words expressly stating that he signs in this capacity. This is affirmed by s. 37 of the 1985 Act,[22] which sets out that:

'[a] bill of exchange or promissory note is deemed to have been made, accepted or endorsed on behalf of a company if made, accepted or endorsed in the name of, or by or on behalf or on account of, the company by a person acting under its authority.'

14.34 In order to avoid personal liability for the company's contracts when signing documents, directors should ensure that they are acting within their authority and in the course of the company's business.[23]

14.35 It is an offence for a public company to transact business or borrow money without a trading certificate issued under s. 761(1) of the 2006 Act.[24] The conduct will not render the transaction invalid,[25] but the directors will be jointly and severally liable to indemnify the counter-party in respect of any loss or damage that arises as a result of the company's failure to comply with its obligations under the transaction within 21 days of being called upon to do so. Both the company and the directors at the time the company entered into the transaction may be liable under s. 767 to a fine on indictment or to a fine not exceeding the statutory maximum on summary conviction.

Liability for torts by the company

14.36 Directors may be liable for the torts of a company in certain circumstances but they are not automatically to be identified with the company's tortious acts. In imposing personal liability on directors, English law seeks to strike a balance between ensuring that a tortfeasor answers for his wrongs while also respecting and upholding the principle of the company as a separate legal entity with limited liability. English judges are also conscious of discouraging parties to join directors to actions in tort against companies where it is inappropriate to do so and this also influences how the English courts analyse the issue of directors' personal liability for torts.[26]

14.37 There are many circumstances in which directors, including a small number of them, will have full control of the business of the company, exercise a large amount of power over its affairs and be involved in authorising the company's conduct. The very fact of being a director will mean that the director is involved in the decisions that may give rise to tortious acts, may instruct agents, servants and employees of the company to implement them and may vote on them at board meetings. If those factors alone resulted in directors' personal liability for torts, the principle of limited liability would be substantially eroded. Accordingly, English law shies away from imposing personal liability on directors merely because those factors are present.[27]

14.38 Conduct that attracts personal liability is qualitatively different from the above and requires the director to have committed, directed, authorised or procured the relevant tortious act.[28] Equally, if a director assumes responsibility for the company's tortious act, he may be personally liable. The issue of whether a director's conduct meets such criteria gives rise to 'difficult questions of degree' that will be decided on the basis of a thorough examination of the director's conduct.[29] The test cannot be simply formulated, but in each case the court considers whether the director has in some way made the company's wrongdoing his own. That quality may arise because of a director's state of mind – knowledge or recklessness as to the wrongfulness of an act. Alternatively, there may be an element of independence in the director's conduct that makes the tortious act his own albeit the company is involved.

14.39 Where a director commits a tortious act the question of his mental state is irrelevant, except to the extent that it is an element of the tort alleged. If a director personally commits a tort he cannot hide behind the company or his directorship.[30] A director may not be liable if he is simply carrying out his constitutional role in the governance of the company, by, for example, voting at board meetings. If, however, a director exercises control outside the constitutional organs of the company, and if his conduct would have been culpable even if he were not a director, it will attract personal liability.[31] If a director forms a company for the express purpose of committing a tortious act, he will be personally liable for its conduct.[32]

14.40 Such direct conduct is not a necessary element of personal liability. A director may also be personally liable if he, expressly or impliedly, directs or procures the commission of a tortious act.[33] Historically, there have been attempts to distinguish a director's and the company's liability for torts by imposing in all circumstances a test of knowledge or recklessness on the director, but the English courts have not accepted such a high test.

14.41 It will not always be the case that a mental element needs to be established in order to found personal liability. This depends on the nature of the tort in question. If the claimant has to prove a particular state of mind or knowledge as a necessary element of the tort alleged, a mental state may have to be alleged and established against the director.[34] However, if no such state of mind is an element of the tort, it may not be a precondition of liability that there be a 'knowing, deliberate, wilful quality' to the director's actions in order for liability to attach.[35] The courts have preferred to state the test as an open-textured one and no definitive guidance can be given on what will or will not amount to direction or procuration in all circumstances. Rather, the test is developed on application to the particular circumstances at hand. The court can take into account broad policy considerations in order to determine on which side of the line the conduct falls.[36] The court may be reluctant to go behind the veil of incorporation.[37]

14.42 A director who merely 'facilitates' a tort is not personally responsible for it. His conduct must at least amount to conduct that would render him liable as a joint tortfeasor if the company had not existed.[38] For example, selling materials for the purpose of infringing a patent to the man who is going to infringe it, even knowing that the buyer is going to do so, may not amount to procuring a tort. The fact that a director has participated in 'authorising' the company's tortious act will also not necessarily result in personal liability. Voting at a board meeting may be characterised as a form of authorisation, but without more, it will probably not amount to authorisation of the standard required for direction or procuration. [39]

14.43 A director will be jointly liable with the company where he, expressly or impliedly, assumes responsibility to the victim for the tort.[40] This will usually require the director to put himself into a special relationship with the victim, for example, corresponding or dealing with the victim in a way that suggests that the director was personally answerable for services owed by the company in the particular circumstances.[41] This applies, for example, to the tort of negligent misstatement. A director will not be personally liable merely because he is an officer of the company. In a small company, the director will almost inevitably have qualities and skills that are core to the advice or services offered by the company but that does not mean that the director will have assumed personal responsibility to the customers of the company. However, where the director, or someone on his behalf, conveys, directly or indirectly, to the claimant that the director has assumed personal responsibility towards the victim, personal liability may arise provided it was also reasonable for the claimant to have relied on an assumption of personal responsibility by the individual director. The director, and not just the company, must have a special relationship with the claimant.

Contempt of court and breaches of injunctions and undertakings

14.44 Directors can also be held personally liable for breaches of undertakings and injunctions served on the company. Undertakings are promises made to a court of law. Injunctions are orders of a court requiring a company to refrain from certain actions or, less commonly, requiring them to take certain actions. Breach of an injunction or an undertaking is contempt of court. The court has power to deal with contempt as if it were a criminal offence and individual directors found to be in contempt may be committed to prison.

14.45 The courts will not commit a director for contempt simply because he holds office and has knowledge of the order. The director must be in contempt[42] or otherwise responsible for the company's breach of the order, whether by his actions or wilful failure to ensure the company's compliance with its obligations.[43] Nonetheless, directors cannot be passive in the face of orders made, or undertakings given, restraining a company from doing certain acts. A director who is aware of such an order or undertaking must take reasonable care to secure the company's compliance with it. Even if he has not participated in the company's breach, he may be guilty of contempt if the company breaches the order in circumstances where he wilfully failed to take adequate and continuing steps to ensure that those to whom compliance had been delegated had not misunderstood or overlooked the obligations.[44]

Liability for crimes by the company

14.46 Actions and decisions made by directors can also expose them to personal criminal, regulatory and civil sanctions. It is important for directors to be aware of the specific offences that can be committed by directors in the course of commercial activities and to take steps to reduce the likelihood of an incident likely to lead to an investigation occurring, for example, by consulting professional advisers as appropriate and observing good corporate governance standards. Investigations can be time-consuming and distracting. Investigations into directors' conduct may take several years. Even in the event of an investigation being discontinued, there may be substantial reputational damage. (See **14.154–14.196** for further information on investigations.)

14.47 Criminal offences committed by directors will result in a criminal record and may be punished by imprisonment and fines. There may also be prohibitions placed on a director's ability to continue as a director of a company.

14.48 Other personal liabilities, known as regulatory or civil penalties, are circumstances in which a director may be ordered to pay a fine for a breach of a regulation or requirement but which does not amount to a criminal offence, or where a director may be required to pay compensation or damages personally for the consequences of his actions.

14.49 As discussed above, directors have general duties that must be observed when acting on behalf of the company. The codification of the general duties in the 2006 Act was intended to encourage directors to focus on their core obligations and simplify the bringing of actions against those who act improperly. The 2006 Act has also expanded the exposures of directors to derivative claims brought against them by shareholders for negligence, breach of duty, breach of trust and default. However, the 2006 Act codification was not exhaustive and directors must comply with all other applicable laws and regulations.

14.50 Directors may be held to be personally liable under, among others, environmental and health and safety legislation, the Financial Services and Markets Act 2002, the Anti-Terrorism, Crime and Security Act 2001 and the Enterprise Act 2002, as well as the 2006 Act. There are new offences of dishonesty contained in the Fraud Act 2006 which was enacted as part of a review of fraud in the commercial context following the collapse of several very high-profile fraud trials. The Fraud Act is intended to remove some of the difficulties faced by prosecutors when bringing prosecutions for fraud and to increase the conviction rate particularly in sophisticated and document heavy cases.

14.51 In addition, directors of a company admitted to the Official List of the FSA and to trading on the London Stock Exchange (LSE) have to comply with the further requirements imposed by the Listing Rules, the Prospectus Rules and the Disclosure and Transparency Rules of the FSA (the Listing Rules or LRs, the Prospectus Rules or PRs and Disclosure and Transparency Rules or DTRs respectively). These continuing obligations apply as long as a company remains admitted to the Official List of the FSA irrespective of whether the shares are being traded.

Basis for criminal liability

14.52 There are two elements to most criminal conduct – conducting the prohibited act or behaviour and *at the time of doing so* possessing the requisite state of mind – most commonly a dishonest state of mind or a reckless state of mind. There is a significant distinction made in the criminal law and in sentencing between acts done deliberately, knowingly and intentionally and those done recklessly.

Dishonesty, recklessness and intention

14.53 A magistrate or jury will assess *intention* to commit an offence by considering what the defendant (an accused person in a criminal trial) did or did not do and the effect of his actions or inaction and by what he said or did not say. Assessment must be made of the defendant's actions before, at the time of and after the alleged offence. All these things may shed light on his intention.

The prosecution only has to prove that the defendant had the necessary intention at the time of the alleged offence. It does not need to have been a long-standing intent it is sufficient for it to have been formed in a matter of seconds, for example, in a sudden decision or reaction.

A person can be convicted on the basis of *recklessness* if the prosecution can prove:

(a) that he was aware of a risk that circumstances or an eventuality would occur; and

(b) that in the circumstances which were known to him it was unreasonable for him to take that risk.

Recklessness is not the same as negligence. *Dishonesty* is the essential element of most acquisitive or breach of trust offences. Before convicting a defendant of an offence involving dishonesty, the magistrate or jury must consider:

(a) Was what the defendant did dishonest by the ordinary standards of reasonable and honest people?
(b) Did the defendant himself realise that what he was doing would be regarded as dishonest by those standards?

Fraud Act 2006

14.54 Under the Fraud Act 2006, it is an offence to:

- make a false representation (by words or conduct) as to fact, law or the state of mind of any person. The victim of the representation need not actually rely on it. Doubts as to the accuracy of any representation or assertion could lead to a criminal charge if accompanied by the appropriate dishonest intent;
- fail to disclose information where there is a legal duty to do so;[45]
- abuse a position where the person occupying that position is expected to safeguard, or not act against, the financial interests of another person.[46] The types of relationship which may lead to the expectation are the relationship between a director and the company. Such an abuse is capable of being committed by omission.

14.55 Each of these offences requires dishonesty and an intention to make a gain (either for the offender or another), or to cause loss to another or to expose another to a risk of loss.

14.56 The Fraud Act does not require an actual gain or loss for an offence to be committed. There were no cases at the time of writing.

14.57 A company officer (including a director, manager, secretary or other similar officer) may be criminally liable with the company if any of these offences is proved to be committed by the company with the consent or connivance of that company officer.[47] This leads to the risk of prosecution for those who merely acquiesce in, as opposed to positively promote, dishonest conduct by the company.

14.58 A person guilty of an offence under the Fraud Act may be liable to imprisonment (up to a maximum of ten years) or to an unlimited fine, or to both.[48]

Misleading statements under s. 397 of the Financial Services and Markets Act 2000 (FSMA)

14.59 It is an offence for a person to:

- make a statement, promise or forecast knowing it to be misleading, false or deceptive;
- dishonestly conceal any material facts whether in connection with a statement, promise or forecast made by him or otherwise; or
- recklessly make (dishonestly or otherwise) a statement, promise or forecast which is misleading, false or deceptive

for the purpose of inducing (or being reckless as to whether it may induce) another person (whether or not the person to whom the statement, promise or forecast is made) to:

- enter into a 'relevant agreement' or refrain from doing so; or
- exercise, or refrain from exercising, any rights conferred by a 'relevant investment'.

14.60 'Relevant agreement' means an agreement the entering into or performance of which by either party constitutes a specified activity[49] and which relates to a relevant investment. 'Specified activities' include (among others) accepting deposits in certain circumstances, effecting and carrying out contracts of insurance, dealing in securities and contractually-based investments, managing, safeguarding, administering, advising on and arranging deals in investments and agreeing to carry on certain of these activities.[50]

14.61 Examples of a 'relevant investment' include (among others) a deposit, rights under a contract of insurance, shares or stock in the share capital of a body corporate (wherever incorporated) or any unincorporated body constituted under the law of a territory outside the UK, instruments creating or acknowledging indebtedness, government and public securities and options, futures and contracts for differences.[51]

14.62 By way of example, any misleading statement, promise or forecast which induces or is likely to induce a shareholder to sell or refrain from selling shares could constitute an offence if the person making the statement knew or was reckless as to whether it was misleading, false or deceptive or if he dishonestly concealed any material facts.

14.63 A person who is found guilty of making a misleading statement or engaging in a misleading practice may be liable to an unlimited fine or to imprisonment (up to a maximum of seven years), or to both.[52] There has been only one prosecution under this section brought by the Financial Services Authority.

Offering of securities to the public

14.64 It is a criminal offence to offer transferable securities to the public in the UK or request admission of transferable securities to trading on a UK-regulated market (which includes the Official List), unless an approved prospectus has been made available to the public before the offer or request has been made. This criminal offence may be committed by the directors of the company if they contravene these provisions of the FSMA.

14.65 If the company does not issue an approved prospectus when required to do so under the FSMA and the Prospectus Rules, the offence is punishable on summary conviction by imprisonment for up to three months or on indictment by imprisonment for up to two years, or a fine.

14.66 The LR, PR and DTR govern behaviour in relation to the treatment of the company's inside information and release of information to the market. Failure to comply with the rules could lead to prosecution for certain offences. While these offences are more likely to arise within a listed company, their scope includes any director, especially in relation to activities where they are privy to material non-public information. Offences include:

- the civil prohibited behaviour of market abuse set out in Part VIII of FSMA;
- the criminal offence of making a false statement to induce a person to enter into an investment agreement or the creation of a false or misleading impression as to the market in or the value or price of investments, set out in s. 397 of FSMA;
- the criminal offence of insider dealing under Part v. of the Criminal Justice Act 1993; and
- the criminal offence of fraud under the Fraud Act 2006.

Market abuse under Part VIII of FSMA

14.67 There are seven civil prohibited behaviours relating to market abuse. These behaviours, set out in s. 118, FSMA, are:

- insider dealing;
- improper disclosure;
- misuse of information;
- manipulating transactions;
- manipulating devices;
- dissemination of misleading information; and
- distortion.

14.68 It is also a prohibited behaviour for a person (A) to require or encourage another person (B) to carry out behaviour which would be market abuse if A himself had carried out that behaviour.[53]

14.69 Market abuse may be committed by an individual or by a company, whether or not the person concerned is regulated by the FSA. In order to constitute market abuse, there must be:

- behaviour in relation to
- qualifying investments (and in some cases, related investments) admitted to
- trading (or for which a request for admission to trading has been made) and on a
- prescribed market.

14.70 Exemptions to and safe harbours from these prohibited behaviours are available. Professional advisors should be consulted before a director relies on one of the exemptions.

14.71 FSMA does not generally require the person engaging in the behaviour to have actually intended to commit market abuse.[54]

14.72 'Behaviour' is defined in s. 130A of FSMA to include action or inaction.

14.73 'Qualifying investments' include transferable securities (e.g. shares), money market instruments, forward interest rate agreements, currency and equity swaps, commodity derivatives and any other instrument admitted to trading on a regulated market in the EEA.[55]

14.74 'Related investments' under the first and second offences (insider dealing and improper disclosure), behaviour in relation to investments which are related to qualifying investments, will also be caught.[56]

14.75 These 'related investments' are investments whose price or value depends on the price or value of qualifying investments (s. 130A, FSMA). For example, a spread bet priced or valued by reference to shares traded on the London Stock Exchange is a 'related investment' for these purposes.[57]

14.76 In connection with the third prohibited behaviour (misuse of information) and the seventh prohibited behaviour (distortion), the two 'super-equivalent' provisions, the net is spread wider. Behaviour can be caught if it relates to:

- anything that is the subject matter, or whose price or value is expressed by reference to the price or value, of the qualifying investments; or
- any investment whose subject matter is the qualifying investments.[58]

14.77 For example, the purchase or sale of a commodity will be caught under this definition where there is a link between its price and the price of the on-exchange contract.

14.78 'Prescribed markets'. These markets include all markets established under the rules of a UK-recognised investment exchange (i.e. London Stock Exchange, AIM, IPE, LIFFE, LME, EDX London and virt-x Exchange) and Plus Markets (formerly OFEX), and all other markets which are EEA-regulated markets.[59]

14.79 The EEA-regulated markets are not, however, relevant for the third offence (misuse of information) and the seventh offence (distortion).

14.80 Penalties. A penalty may take the form of an unlimited fine or the publication of a statement that the person in question has engaged in market abuse (s. 12, FSMA). These penalties may be imposed on a company as well as an individual.

14.81 In addition, an injunction may be granted to restrain threatened or continued market abuse and a restitution order may be made in respect of any profits made or losses suffered as a result of the market abuse.

14.82 If approved persons are involved, the FSA may also seek to obtain a prohibition order against them.

14.83 The market abuse regime is aimed not just at criminal behaviour (in contrast to the offence of insider dealing and the offence of making false statements or encouraging in false conduct), but also at behaviour which undermines confidence in the market and which falls below reasonably expected standards. It is not necessary to show any intent to profit from confidential information or to mislead or deceive.

14.84 The company and the directors need to consider market abuse issues both when the company is acting as a market participant in relation to securities other than its own (e.g. when it has any confidential information which might result in a dealing being regarded as insider dealing or a misuse of information), and when behaviour is in relation to the company's own securities or information.

14.85 The FSA has issued a code providing guidance on market abuse, the Code of Market Conduct (the Code), which is contained in the FSA Handbook and available from the FSA website at www.fsa.gov.uk. The Code provides certain safe harbours for behaviour so that it does not amount to market abuse. Some of these safe harbours prevent market abuse arising from behaviour required or permitted by the LR, PR and DTR (as well as the Takeover Code) in relation to disclosure, announcement, communication or release of information. The detail of the safe harbours is set out in the Code and in the

LR and the DTR. However, it is only to the extent that the behaviour complies with those specific rules that a safe harbour is available and this does not mean that the behaviour could not constitute market abuse in some other respects.

14.86 An example is that, when the directors are considering whether or not to issue a profits warning, they will have to consider whether failing to do so could constitute market abuse by the creation of a false or misleading impression as well as whether it would be in breach of the DTRs. Similarly, the disclosure of information about trading performance to the press or analysts prior to an announcement being issued could be treated as an encouragement to commit market abuse.

14.87 One key aspect in relation to which no specific safe harbour is given is compliance with the Model Code. If a director falls within one of the exemptions in the Model Code, and is thus permitted to deal pursuant to the Model Code, this does not mean that the dealing cannot constitute market abuse or insider dealing. The question of whether the dealing could constitute market abuse or the criminal offence of insider dealing must be separately considered in each case.

14.88 Market abuse is also relevant in relation to the buy-back of the company's shares. Under the LR, a buy-back cannot occur at a time when the Model Code would prevent the directors from dealing in the company's shares, but a purchase of the company's own shares at a time permitted by the Model Code could still constitute market abuse and this should be considered in each case. Compliance by the company with the EU Buy-back and Stabilisation Regulations would constitute a safe harbour from market abuse (as contained within those Regulations). This would require additional notifications to be made to the UK market via a RIS and consulted on by the FSA in advance.

Insider dealing under the Criminal Justice Act 1993 (CJA)

14.89 There are three distinct offences under s. 52 of CJA:

- dealing as an insider;
- encouraging another person to deal; and
- disclosing inside information.

14.90 These offences are only capable of being committed by an individual and not by a company.

14.91 Insider. An insider[60] is a person who has (and knows he has) inside information from an inside source, that is:

- through his being a director, employee or shareholder of an issuer of securities (not necessarily being the company to which the information relates); or
- by virtue of his employment, office or profession (not necessarily in relation to the company to which the information relates); or
- directly or indirectly from one of the above.

14.92 Insiders need not have any direct or indirect connection with the company and can include a person such as a research analyst who does not derive any information from a truly 'inside' source.

14.93 Inside information. Inside information[61] is defined as information that:

- relates to particular securities, or to a particular issuer of securities or to particular issuers of securities (and not to securities generally, or to issuers of securities generally);[62]
- is specific or precise;
- has not been made public (see **14.97** below); and
- is price-sensitive, that is, if it were made public, would be likely to have a significant effect on the price or value of any securities.

14.94 Information ceases to be inside information if it has been made public. The definition of 'made public' in s. 58 of CJA is non-exhaustive but it does provide considerable guidance. There are two categories of information: those where the information must be treated as made public and those where it may be so treated. The provisions are complex, and specific advice should be sought in relation to these matters.

14.95 The CJA applies to:

- a dealing in
- securities effected on
- a regulated market or through or by
- a professional intermediary.

(i) 'Dealing'[63] means the acquisition or disposal of securities (whether as principal or agent). Acquisition in this context includes agreeing to acquire or entering into a contract which creates the security and disposal includes agreeing to dispose of or bringing to an end a contract which created the security. A person also deals if he procures, directly or indirectly, an acquisition or disposal of securities by any other person.

(ii) 'Securities'[64] include shares, debt securities, warrants, depositary receipts, options, futures and contracts for differences and which satisfy the conditions of the Insider Dealing (Securities and Regulated Markets) Order 1994, as amended. The Order includes any security which is officially listed within the EEA or is admitted to dealing on, or has its price quoted on or under the rules of, a regulated market. Warrants to subscribe for a share or debt security which is so listed, dealt in or quoted and depositary receipts for any such share or debt security are also included. The securities must be price-affected securities in relation to the inside information, that is, the information would, if made public, be likely to have a significant effect on the price of the securities.

(iii) 'Regulated market'.[65] The definition of 'regulated market' is very broad. The Order provides that the definition of a regulated market includes any market established under the rules of the London Stock Exchange Limited (e.g. AIM), NASDAQ, EASDAQ and the listed EEA stock exchanges, including second-tier markets. It also extends to LIFFE Administration and Management, OMLX (the London Securities and Derivatives Exchange Limited), virt-X Exchange Limited, COREDEALMTS and Plus Markets.

(iv) 'Professional intermediaries'.[66] The CJA catches all off-market transactions involving a professional intermediary. For this purpose, a professional intermediary is a person who carries on a business, or who is employed in a business, consisting of the following activities:
- acquiring or disposing of securities, whether as principal or agent; or
- acting as an intermediary between persons taking part in any dealings in securities.

However, a person is not treated as carrying on a business consisting of one of the above activities if this is merely incidental to some other activity or if he conducts one of those activities only occasionally. This means that accountants and solicitors will not normally be regarded as professional intermediaries.

14.96 Encouraging another person to deal. Where an individual has information as an insider he is also guilty of insider dealing if he encourages another person to deal in the securities, knowing or having reasonable cause to believe that dealing will take place on a regulated market or by or through a professional intermediary. The offence is committed whether or not the person so encouraged knows that the securities are 'price-affected'.[67]

14.97 Disclosing inside information. It is also an offence for an individual to disclose inside information to another person except where the disclosure is made in the proper performance of the functions of his employment, office or profession.[68]

14.98 Defences. The CJA contains a number of defences, some general and some specific, which are designed to protect legitimate activities. In all cases, the burden of proof is placed on the individual to establish that he is entitled to the benefit of the defence. This is a complex area and specific advice should be sought in relation to these matters.

14.99 Penalties. An individual guilty of insider dealing may be liable to an unlimited fine or to imprisonment (up to a maximum of seven years), or to both (s. 61 of CJA).

Fair dealing provisions in the Companies Act 2006 – transactions with directors

14.100 Companies are not, in most circumstances, permitted to enter into arrangements under which a director (of the company or any holding company) or a connected person is to acquire from, or to dispose to, the company or any of its subsidiaries, a non-cash asset worth in excess of £100,000 or 10% of the company's net assets (subject to, in the latter case, a £5,000 limit) unless the arrangement is first approved at a general meeting or if the arrangement is made conditional on obtaining such approval. If it is not, the contract can be set aside and the director who was party to the arrangement and any director who authorised it are liable to account for any gain made as a result of the arrangement and to indemnify the company against any resulting loss.

14.101 Companies may grant loans or provide security or other financial accommodation to directors (of the company or any holding company) and their connected persons only so long as approval has been obtained from members at a general meeting.

Distributions and share capital

14.102 A company may only make a distribution out of accumulated net realised profits and only if the net assets of the company are not less (and would not be less following the distribution) than the aggregate of its called-up share capital and undistributable reserves, in each case judged on the last accounts laid before the general meeting and in each case based on the company's own accounts.

14.103 There is a general rule, subject to certain exceptions, prohibiting a company from acquiring its own shares or otherwise reducing capital.

14.104 Under s. 142 of the Companies Act 1985, if the net assets of a company are half or less of its called-up share capital, the directors must, not later than 28 days from the earliest date on which that fact is known to a director, convene an extraordinary meeting of the company for a date not later than 56 days from that day for the purpose of considering what, if any, steps should be taken to deal with the situation. A breach of these requirements can lead to the directors being liable to a fine. Section 656 of the 2006 Act contains equivalent provisions which will replace s. 142 with no significant changes on 1 October 2009.

Political donations

14.105 Section 366 of the 2006 Act requires a company to obtain prior shareholder approval for any donation (of money or benefits in kind) to any political organisation, EU political party, or (from 1 October 2008) independent election candidate, or for any political expenditure to be incurred by the company. No shareholder authorisation is required for political donations if all donations made by group companies do not exceed £5,000 in aggregate over 12 months.

14.106 If prior shareholder approval is not obtained, each director is jointly and severally liable to the company for the amount of the unauthorised donation or expenditure, plus interest and any damages which the company suffers as a result of the unauthorised donation or expenditure.

14.107 Directors of the ultimate UK holding company may also be jointly and severally liable for unauthorised donations or expenditure of a subsidiary if they fail to take all reasonable steps to prevent the donation or expenditure.

14.108 There are also requirements to disclose any such political donations and expenditure in the directors' report and in the annual accounts. Multiple small donations to UK political parties must also be disclosed to the Electoral Commission. If these disclosures are not made, the company and its directors may be fined or, in the case of the directors, they may be found criminally liable.

Benefits from third parties

14.109 Directors must not accept any benefit from a third party conferred by reason of their being a director or their doing, or not doing, anything as director. This duty is not infringed if the acceptance of the benefit could not reasonably be regarded as likely to give rise to a conflict of interest. Directors will be liable to pay to the company any benefit which they receive in breach of this duty. It is immaterial that the company itself could not have obtained the benefit.

14.110 The 2006 Act provisions setting out this duty came into force on 1 October 2008. Until that date, the existing general law duty required that directors should not misuse their powers or the opportunities of their position to benefit themselves.

Insolvency

14.111 A director may in certain circumstances become liable to contribute to any deficiency suffered by the creditors of the company if the company becomes insolvent. Directors' duties in respect of insolvency are discussed in **Chapter 18** and the key issues for directors to consider are set out below only in brief.

Fraudulent trading

14.112 A director may be held liable to contribute to the company's assets on its winding up if it is shown that he has knowingly carried on the company's business with the intention of defrauding creditors of the company or any other person, or for any fraudulent purpose. This also constitutes a criminal offence.

Wrongful trading

14.113 A director of the company may be personally liable to contribute to its assets if at any time before the company went into insolvent liquidation:

- the director knew, or ought to have concluded, that there was no reasonable prospect that the company would avoid going into insolvent liquidation; and
- he then failed to take 'every step' to minimise the potential loss to the creditors of the company.

14.114 The standard required as to what the director ought to know, the conclusions he ought to reach and steps he ought to take is that which would be known, reached or taken by a reasonable diligent person with the general knowledge, skill and expertise that may reasonably be expected of a person carrying out the same functions as those of the directors in relation to the company and with the general knowledge, skill and experience that the director has.

Transactions at an undervalue and preferences

14.115 A liquidator (or administrator) can obtain a court order setting aside certain transactions made when the company was insolvent, or which caused the insolvency and which were made at an undervalue. A transaction is at an undervalue if the company receives no consideration for it, or significantly less consideration than it provides itself. The liquidator (or administrator) may also set aside transactions which 'prefer' any creditor of the company.

Disqualification

14.116 Apart from personal liability, where a director engages in fraudulent or wrongful trading or has been found guilty of other misconduct in connection with a company and is held to be unfit by the court, he may under the Company Directors Disqualification Act 1986 be disqualified by court order for up to 15 years from acting as a director or from having any involvement in the promotion, formation or management of a company.

Competition laws

14.117 Under the Enterprise Act 2002 criminal penalties may be imposed on individuals who dishonestly engage in what are considered to be the most serious types of cartels such as horizontal price-fixing, limiting supply or production, market shares or bid-rigging. Prosecution by the OFT and the Serious Fraud Office could lead to five years' imprisonment and an unlimited fine on conviction.

Health and safety

14.118 The general obligations on a director discussed above, in particular the duty under the 2006 Act to promote the success of the company, extend to health, safety and environmental (HSE) matters.

14.119 HSE matters have, however, been singled out for special attention in the context of directors' duties and potential liabilities. This is principally because most HSE statutes include provisions for personal liability of directors where an HSE incident is due to their consent, connivance or neglect. The provisions result in a number of prosecutions of individual directors each year.

14.120 In addition to criminal penalties, a director may also be disqualified if found criminally liable under HSE legislation.

14.121 A director cannot safely assume that HSE matters are the responsibility of a nominated head of HSE within the company, even if that person is a senior employee. Each director should satisfy itself that a proper HSE management system is in place which reports to the board and that sufficient resources are provided for HSE matters to be dealt with in accordance with legal obligations and company HSE policy.

Additional exposure for directors of listed companies

Persons discharging managerial responsibilities

14.122 Certain obligations under the Disclosure and Transparency Rules apply to persons discharging managerial responsibilities (PDMRs). PDMRs include directors and senior executives who have:

- regular access to inside information relating, directly or indirectly, to the company; and
- the power to make managerial decisions affecting the future development and business prospects of the company.

14.123 The FSA has clarified that the following persons could fall within the category of PDMRs:

- senior employees who sit on the executive committee of a company even if they are not also board members; and
- directors/senior executives of a subsidiary company who regularly have access to inside information and make decisions affecting the development and business prospects of the company.

What are the Listing Principles?

14.124 The Listing Principles are set out in Chapter 7 of the Listing Rules, which are enforced by the FSA, in its capacity as the UK Listing Authority (UKLA). These principles apply to every listed company with a primary listing of equity securities in respect of all its obligations arising from the Listing Rules and the Disclosure and Transparency Rules and are designed to ensure adherence to the spirit as well as the letter of such obligations. Directors of a listed company must ensure that due regard is paid to the Listing Principles, which are as follows:

Principle 1	A listed company must take reasonable steps to enable its directors to understand their responsibilities and obligations as directors.
Principle 2	A listed company must take reasonable steps to establish and maintain adequate procedures, systems and controls to enable it to comply with its obligations.
Principle 3	A listed company must act with integrity towards holders and potential holders of its listed equity securities.
Principle 4	A listed company must communicate information to holders and potential holders or its listed equity securities in such a way as to avoid the creation or continuation of a false market in such listed equity securities.

Principle 5	A listed company must ensure that it treats all holders of the same class of its listed equity securities that are in the same position equally in respect of the rights attaching to such listed equity securities.
Principle 6	A listed company must deal with the FSA in an open and co-operative manner.

14.125 UKLA guidance to Listing Principle 2 makes it clear that the aim is to ensure timely and accurate disclosure of information to the market. In doing so, a company's systems and controls must enable it properly to identify inside information in a timely manner. This means that it needs adequate reporting lines and a flow of management information to its board to ensure that information is escalated within the organisation and to allow directors properly to consider whether any information needs to be disclosed to the market.

14.126 Also, a listed company must at all times comply with various continuing obligations contained in Chapters 9–13 of the Listing Rules, Chapters 4–6 of the Disclosure and Transparency Rules, and PR 5.2 of the Prospectus Rules.

Specific liabilities arising for listed companies

14.127 The FSA, in its capacity as the UK Listing Authority (UKLA), has a number of powers if it is not satisfied that these rules are being adhered to. Aside from penalties against the company which can ultimately lead to the suspension of listing, the UKLA may censure or impose penalties on any director 'knowingly concerned' in the company's breach of a rule, or on any director who breaches a personal obligation under the Disclosure and Transparency Rules, e.g. to disclose their share dealings.

Code for dealing in the company's securities[69]

14.128 Listed companies must adopt the Model Code, and must require every PDMR (including directors) to comply with the Model Code and take all proper and reasonable steps to secure their compliance. However, companies may also impose more rigorous dealing obligations than those required by the Model Code. The Model Code applies in addition to the insider dealing statutory restrictions in Part V of the Criminal Justice Act 1993, and the market abuse offences under the Financial Services and Markets Act 2000 (FSMA).

14.129 The purpose of the Model Code is to ensure that such PDMRs do not even place themselves in a position where they could be suspected of taking advantage of inside information. The Model Code prohibits dealing in certain circumstances, establishes a clearance procedure for dealing where permissible and requires companies to keep records of any clearance given. In particular, the Model Code prohibits dealing during a 'close period' (i.e. the 60 days immediately preceding a preliminary announcement of the company's annual results or the 60 days immediately preceding the publication of its annual financial report, and, if the company reports on a half-yearly basis, the period from the end of the relevant financial period up to and including the time of such publication, and, if the company reports on a quarterly basis, the 30 days immediately preceding the announcement of the quarterly results) and at any time when a relevant person is in possession of inside information in relation to the company's securities.

14.130 Directors and company secretaries must seek clearance from the chairman (or a designated director). The chief executive and the chairman must seek clearance from each other or, if the other is not present, the senior independent director, a committee of the board or other officer nominated for that purpose. Any other person subject to the Model Code should seek clearance from the company secretary or a designated director.

14.131 A response to a request for clearance must be given by the company within five business days of the request being made and dealing by the person discharging managerial responsibilities must take place as soon as possible after clearance is received and in any event within two business days of clearance being given.

14.132 A PDMR must also take reasonable steps to prevent any dealings by or on behalf of persons connected with him[70] on considerations of a short-term nature, and must seek to prohibit any dealings by or on behalf of any person connected with him or by an investment manager on his behalf or on behalf of any other person connected with him (whether or not those funds are managed on a discretionary basis) during a close period. However, a PDMR should not inform his connected persons or investment manager when they are not free to deal as a result of the company having inside information in existence.

Companies Act 2006 statutory liability regime for listed companies

14.133 Section 1270 introduces a new statutory liability regime under which a listed public company is liable to compensate a person who has acquired shares and suffered loss in respect of those shares as a result of any untrue or misleading statement in, or omission from, any periodic financial report or any preliminary announcement. A company will only be liable if a director:

- knew that the statement was untrue or misleading, or was reckless as to whether it was; or

- knew that omission was a dishonest concealment of a material fact. The company (and not the directors) will be liable to third parties, although the directors concerned may be liable to the company.

14.134 Under s. 463, directors are liable to compensate a company for any loss suffered as a result of false or misleading statements or omissions of required information from the annual directors' report, directors' remuneration report and any summary financial statement so far as it is derived from such reports. However, liability only arises if the relevant director:

- knows that, or is reckless as to whether, the statement is untrue or misleading, or
- knows that the omission is a dishonest concealment of a material fact. A director will not be liable to any person other than the company which may rely on information in such reports.

Sanctions for LR and DTR breaches[71]

14.135 If the FSA considers that an issuer has contravened any provision of the Listing Rules and that a person who was at the material time a director was knowingly concerned in that breach, it may take disciplinary action against that director or former director. The FSA may impose on a director a financial penalty of any such amount it considers appropriate, or may publish a statement censuring him. Similar, but slightly different, provisions apply in relation to a breach of the DTR. If a PDMR (including a director) or a connected person has breached the DTR, the FSA may either impose a financial penalty or publish a statement censuring that person. Also, if the FSA considers that a former director was knowingly concerned in a breach by the issuer, it may impose a financial penalty on him.[72]

14.136 The disciplinary action taken against the director or former director or PDMR may be in addition to any action taken against the issuer, or where the FSA does not consider it appropriate to seek a disciplinary sanction against the issuer, it may nonetheless seek a disciplinary sanction against any director or former director or PDMR. An issuer may also be subject to a financial penalty.

14.137 In determining the amount of any financial penalty, the FSA will take into account the seriousness of the breach, the extent to which the contravention was deliberate or reckless and whether the person on whom the penalty is to be imposed is an individual. Chapter 6 of the FSA's Decision Procedure and Penalties Manual (DEPP) also sets out a number of factors that the FSA may consider when determining the amount of the penalty to be imposed.

14.138 Where the FSA has cause for concern regarding the behaviour of the issuer, director or former director or PDMR, but does not consider formal disciplinary action to be necessary, it may issue a private warning. The response by the issuer, director or former director or PDMR to the private warning, together with the warning itself, will form part of their compliance history and may be taken into account in deciding whether the FSA brings disciplinary action against them in the future.

14.139 Other action available to the FSA where it considers it necessary to take protective or remedial action, may include the suspension of the listing of any securities, a public statement censuring the issuer or where the FSA is satisfied that there are special circumstances which preclude normal regular dealings in any listed securities, it may cancel the listing of any security.[73]

14.140 Under LR 9.8 and DTR 4.1, directors must ensure that proper accounting records are kept which are sufficiently comprehensive to reveal reasonably accurately the state of the company's finances at any time and enable the directors to publish annual accounts giving a true and fair view. Directors are also obliged to prepare interim profit and loss accounts. Accounting records must be kept for six years.

Directors' liabilities accruing directly from breach of the Model Code

14.141 As all PDMRs are required to comply with the Model Code, relevant listed companies must take proper and reasonable steps to secure that there is compliance.[74] Directors should not only review the provisions of the Code, contained in LR 9 Annex 1, but also ensure that they comply with any other more rigorous obligations that may have been imposed by the company. Breaches of the Model Code will be treated as breaches by the company, to whom enforcement action will normally be targeted. However, if the breach is attributable to a PDMR (such as a director) then the FSA has power to impose financial penalties directly against the relevant PDMR. Section 91 of FSMA states that where the FSA finds that a PDMR within such a relevant issuer has contravened any provision of the disclosure rules, it may impose on him a penalty 'of such amount as it considers appropriate'.

Ratification and statutory relief from liability

Ratification

14.142 In certain circumstances a director's conduct may be authorised or ratified thus relieving the director from potential liability arising from his conduct. Directors' conduct amounting to negligence, default, breach of duty or breach of trust can be ratified under the provisions of the 2006 Act.

14.143 Section 239 of the 2006 Act effectively provides for ratification by way of ordinary resolution, although a requirement for a special resolution may be imposed by the articles of association and the section does not affect any general law requirement for a special resolution.

14.144 Section 239 provides:

Ratification of acts of directors

(1) This section applies to the ratification by a company of conduct by a director amounting to negligence, default, breach of duty or breach of trust in relation to the company.

(2) The decision of the company to ratify such conduct must be made by resolution of the members of the company.

(3) Where the resolution is proposed as a written resolution neither the director (if a member of the company) nor any member connected with him is an eligible member.

(4) Where the resolution is proposed at a meeting, it is passed only if the necessary majority is obtained disregarding votes in favour of the resolution by the director (if a member of the company) and any member connected with him. This does not prevent the director or any such member from attending, being counted towards the quorum and taking part in the proceedings at any meeting at which the decision is considered.

(5) For the purposes of this section –
  (a) 'conduct' includes acts and omissions;
  (b) 'director' includes a former director;
  (c) a shadow director is treated as a director; and
  (d) in s. 252 (meaning of 'connected person'), subsection (3) does not apply (exclusion of person who is himself a director).

(6) Nothing in this section affects –
  (a) the validity of a decision taken by unanimous consent of the members of the company, or
  (b) any power of the directors to agree not to sue, or to settle or release a claim made by them on behalf of the company.

(7) This section does not affect any other enactment or rule of law imposing additional requirements for valid ratification or any rule of law as to acts that are incapable of being ratified by the company.

14.145 The section provides that votes cast in favour of the resolution by the director and the votes of any member connected with him must be disregarded in determining whether the resolution is passed. The definition of a connected person in the 2006 Act is wider than it was in the 1985 Act and is set out in s. 252 as follows:

Persons connected with a director

(1) This section defines what is meant by references in this part to a person being 'connected' with a director of a company (or a director being 'connected' with a person).

(2) The following persons (and only those persons) are connected with a director of a company –

  (a) members of the director's family (see s. 253);

  (b) a body corporate with which the director is connected (as defined in s. 254);

  (c) a person acting in his capacity as trustee of a trust –

    (i) the beneficiaries of which include the director or a person who by virtue of paragraph (a) or (b) is connected with him, or

    (ii) the terms of which confer a power on the trustees that may be exercised for the benefit of the director or any such person,

  other than a trust for the purposes of an employees' share scheme or a pension scheme;

  (d) a person acting in his capacity as partner –

    (i) of the director, or

    (ii) of a person who, by virtue of paragraph (a), (b) or (c), is connected with that director;

  (e) a firm that is a legal person under the law by which it is governed and in which –

    (i) the director is a partner,

    (ii) a partner is a person who, by virtue of paragraph (a), (b) or (c) is connected with the director, or

    (iii) a partner is a firm in which the director is a partner or in which there is a partner who, by virtue of paragraph (a), (b) or (c), is connected with the director.

(3) References in this part to a person connected with a director of a company do not include a person who is himself a director of the company.

14.146 Sections 288–300 of the 2006 Act provide for ratification by way of written resolutions insofar as private companies are concerned.

14.147 Although related votes cannot be counted towards ratification, they may be counted towards authorisation of conduct relating to a director's duty to avoid conflicts of interest (s. 175). Section 175(5) provides that such authorisation may be given by the directors in the case or a private company by the matter being proposed to and authorised by the directors (provided nothing in the company's constitution invalidates such authorisation) and, in a public company, by the matter being proposed to and authorised by the directors in accordance with the constitution (provided that constitution so enables the directors). The authorisation is effective only if any requirement as to the quorum at the meeting at which the matter is considered is met, without counting the director in question or any other interested director, and the matter was agreed to without their voting or would have been agreed to if their votes had not been counted. (See also s. 180.)

14.148 Not all types of conduct can be ratified, however, so the absolute bar of ratification may not always be available to the director. In particular, the following conduct cannot be ratified:

- fraud on the minority and wrongdoer control (although this issue primarily arose in relation to derivative actions which are now governed by Part 11 of the 2006 Act);
- fraud on creditors;
- misappropriation of property in bad faith;
- if the shareholders did not know all the relevant circumstances;
- if the company is insolvent (or near-insolvent), in which case the interests of creditors will prevail (see **Chapter 18**);
- unlawful acts, such as acts in breach of statute or general law, such as directors making an unlawful dividend or an unlawful return of capital.

Statutory relief from liability

14.149 It may be the case that the director's conduct is not authorised by the directors or ratified by the members and that proceedings are commenced against the director by the company. In these circumstances, a director may also be relieved from liability for negligence, default, breach of duty or breach of trust by the court. Section 1157 provides:

Power of court to grant relief in certain cases

(1) If in proceedings for negligence, default, breach of duty or breach of trust against –
  (a) an officer of a company, or
  (b) a person employed by a company as auditor (whether he is or is not an officer of the company),

  it appears to the court hearing the case that the officer or person is or may be liable but that he acted honestly and reasonably, and that having regard to all the circumstances of the case (including those connected with his appointment) he ought fairly to be excused, the court may relieve him, either wholly or in part, from his liability on such terms as it thinks fit.

(2) If any such officer or person has reason to apprehend that a claim will or might be made against him in respect of negligence, default, breach of duty or breach of trust –
  (a) he may apply to the court for relief, and
  (b) the court has the same power to relieve him as it would have had if it

had been a court before which proceedings against him for negligence, default, breach of duty or breach of trust had been brought.

Section 1157(3) extends the provision to cases before a jury.

14.150 The section can be used to excuse a director from liability for negligence.[75] For conduct that is *ultra vires* the company may also be excused depending on the circumstances because the provision is designed to protect honest directors.[76] The section applies whether a company has elected to claim damages or an account of profits against the director.[77] The section also applies to some penal proceedings that may arise under the Companies Acts.[78]

14.151 Under s. 1157(2), a director may apply for relief in anticipation of proceedings. If, however, a court is already seised in respect of proceedings, only the court seised may grant s. 1157(2) relief.[79]

14.152 In order to be entitled to relief, a director has to satisfy the court that:

- he acted honestly,
- he acted reasonably, and
- having regard to all the circumstances of the case (including those connected with his appointment) he ought fairly to be excused.[80]

14.153 The test for honesty is essentially subjective, whereas the test for reasonableness is, by its nature, an objective one. The standard of reasonableness is that of 'a man of affairs dealing with his own affairs with reasonable care and circumspection'; the company's past conduct may be taken into account.[81] Given the scope of the analysis that has to be undertaken in order to determine whether relief will be granted, an application for summary judgment is unlikely to succeed.[82]

Investigations

14.154 The last few years have been marked by an increase in the criminalisation of regulatory and commercial misconduct. The criminal law is now affecting many of those it would previously have not. There has been a substantial increase in the number of criminal offences in the last 15 years which directly affect those who become company directors. The threat of criminal penalties is being used to change behaviour.

14.155 There is an increased public appetite to see directors held to account in the criminal courts for offences committed by the companies under their direction. There is enhanced international (particularly trans-Atlantic) co-operation between investigation agencies and an increased willingness on the part of the US Department of Justice to seek the extradition of British citizens to face trial in US courts. There has been an increase in the number of bodies with statutory prosecution powers such as the Financial Services Authority (FSA) and the Office of Fair Trading (OFT).

14.156 Concurrent regulatory and criminal investigations are now common as this means that investigators can pursue a regulatory sanction if there is insufficient evidence or resolve to pursue a criminal prosecution.

14.157 Directors should be aware that criminal and regulatory investigations are highly specialised areas of law and there can be extremely serious ramifications for defendants of decisions made at the early stages of an investigation, for example, choosing whether or not to answer investigators' questions or to provide evidence on a voluntary basis. It is important to have expert legal advice immediately upon becoming aware of an investigation affecting the company or its directors.

14.158 In the United Kingdom, most criminal offences likely to involve company directors are tried by a jury of twelve lay people (this however may be limited in future in cases concerning allegations of serious fraud).

The initiation of an investigation

14.159 Investigations can be initiated by a variety of means. Some are initiated as a result of a company self-reporting an incident or circumstances which have come to light to an investigatory body. Occasionally, employee whistleblowers report unsafe working conditions, compliance or governance concerns or fraudulent conduct. Suspicious activity reports made to the Serious Organised Crime Agency (SOCA) by financial services institutions or others in the regulated sector may lead to the initiation of an investigation against a company and its directors.

14.160 You will not necessarily be informed if you are being investigated. There is the potential for simultaneous investigations in a number of jurisdictions by different regulators or criminal prosecutors into the same conduct. Some investigation agencies are notoriously bad at maintaining confidentiality and it is not unknown for directors to learn from a media source that they are under investigation. Not infrequently, investigative bodies will refuse to confirm or deny the existence of an investigation.

Search warrants

14.161 The execution of a search warrant at the company's offices or the private homes of its directors is sometimes the first indication that an investigation has been initiated. The execution of a search warrant is colloquially known as a *dawn raid* largely due to their often taking place in the early morning.

14.162 There is a trend towards an increasing number of agencies having powers to enter and search premises, either alone or in conjunction with the police, and technological developments mean that it is now rare for a criminal investigation into markets, cartels, corruption or fraud to concern only one location or jurisdiction. Enhanced co-operation between international criminal investigative bodies often means that search warrants must be executed simultaneously in several countries to avoid tipping off the suspects and to limit the opportunities for the destruction of evidence. It is increasingly common for search warrants to be obtained by UK authorities at the behest of foreign regulatory or government bodies under mutual co-operation treaties. Firms which hold a large amount of data on IT systems, including trading data or recorded telephone lines, will be targeted by investigators early on in an investigation to avoid the risk that evidence will be destroyed, whether inadvertently, by the application of overwriting policies or by deliberate intervention. Material obtained from IT systems is often the most incriminating form of evidence, and investigators have become increasingly adept at identifying likely sources.

14.163 In most cases it will not be possible to prevent a search taking place but there is a great deal that can be done to minimise the fallout from a raid, particularly in areas where trust is an important factor in the relationship with clients and suppliers, to avoid the loss of clients or employees and, most importantly, to avoid prejudicing the position should the company and its directors be charged with an offence.

Who may enter without my consent?

14.164 A company director is most likely to be subject to the exercise of search and seizure powers by the following bodies:

- the police;
- the Serious Fraud Office (SFO);
- the Department of Business, Enterprise and Regulatory Reform (BERR);
- the Competition Commission (CC);
- the Office of Fair Trading (OFT);
- HM Revenue & Customs (HMRC);
- the Financial Services Authority (FSA) (for companies in the regulated sector).

They have wide-ranging statutory powers to search premises and seize material and, in addition, have the ability to apply to a magistrate or judge for a search warrant. Some of these bodies will use their powers in support of an overseas police force, regulator or prosecuting authority.

Why do public bodies use powers to search and seize evidence?

14.165 Many public bodies, like the SFO and the FSA, have the power to compel the provision of information from financial institutions without the need to obtain a warrant. The reason why public bodies that have statutory powers of compulsion choose to obtain search warrants is usually to maintain an element of surprise. This is important if they suspect that, were an individual or a firm to be aware that they were under investigation, they would destroy evidence which might be deployed against them or tip off an accomplice.

14.166 A search is likely only where the investigative body believes that material would not be provided voluntarily or where there is a risk that evidence (including documents and electronically stored material) will be destroyed or the risk that assets will be moved or dissipated. It is not uncommon for whistle-blowers to allege that documents have been removed from premises or that their destruction is imminent. In most investigations involving companies, investigators gather evidence by way of compulsory notice served on the company to deliver specified documents.

Coming under investigation

14.167 Once an investigation has commenced there are a number of practical steps which should be taken:

(a) Remember that *any* information given to the investigators is likely to be used as evidence.
(b) Immediately stop *all* email communications on the subject of the investigation.
(c) Suspend the routine destruction of records.
(d) Secure all potentially relevant contemporaneous material taking particular care in respect of tape-recorded telephone lines and electronically stored communications.
(e) Ensure any newly created material is covered by legal professional privilege (see below) and consider which jurisdiction material may end up in.
(f) Minimise the number of individuals who are aware of the investigation.
(g) Anticipate that the investigation may become public knowledge and prepare a reactive press response.
(h) Consider whether there are likely to be conflicts of interest between the company and its directors.
(i) Consider whether the company should conduct an internal investigation.

(j) Consider whether directors should receive separate legal advice independent from that received by the company.
(k) Inform the insurers of the investigation if the director has Directors' and Officers' Insurance cover for legal costs incurred during the course of an investigation.
(l) Become familiar with any limitations on the insurance cover, in particular, whether making admissions or accepting a limited sanction would have ramifications for insurance cover.

Legal Professional Privilege

14.168 It is important not to create any unnecessary non-privileged documents or emails discussing the issue under investigation as these may have to be disclosed later to another party to litigation, or to an investigator. The most damaging emails are invariably sent immediately after an incident has occurred and are often very difficult to explain away should an investigation result. Legal professional privilege includes:

(a) Communications between a professional legal adviser and his client or any person representing his client made in connection with the giving of legal advice to the client.
(b) Communications between a professional legal adviser and his client or any person representing his client or between such an adviser or his client or any such representative and any other person made in connection with or in contemplation of legal proceedings and for the purposes of such proceedings.
(c) Items enclosed with or referred to in such communications and made:
    (i) in connection with the giving of legal advice; or
    (ii) in connection with or in contemplation of legal proceedings and for the purposes of such proceedings.

Searches

14.169 If you are the subject of a search, identify the investigating authority and the legislative basis for their right of entry, search and seizure. Ascertain if they have the right to search in all circumstances or only in respect of certain investigations or potential offences. Ask to see the investigator's warrant or any other document authorising the investigation. Investigators or police officers exercising powers of search and seizure will normally produce identification without being requested to do so. Investigators can be accompanied by other persons with specific expertise in, for example, IT, market abuse, data retrieval, forensic recovery and privilege. The expertise of the individuals accompanying the investigation team will be a good indication of the type of misconduct which is being alleged. If you are in any doubt as to the authority of the investigators, telephone the relevant authority for confirmation of their identity.

14.170 Do not volunteer documents or information which have not been requested. Only identify and locate those documents that have been requested by the investigators. Do not be tempted to provide documents which you believe may present your actions or that of the company in a positive light. You are unlikely to have sufficient information available to you to enable you to properly assess the allegations you face. Further material can be supplied later should your lawyers believe it is in your interest to do so.

14.171 Documents which are commercially sensitive will have to be provided to the investigators. The investigators are unlikely to accept arguments relating to confidentiality. It is very unlikely that any of the material will be in the public domain for some time after the search and points relating to sensitive material can be made at a later stage.

14.172 Investigators are likely to want to access electronic documents and files by removing laptop computers, imaging other computer systems or seizing back-up tapes.

14.173 The investigators are entitled to use the powers given to them by law. Nothing should be done to impede the search. You may be arrested if you obstruct a search. Under no circumstances hide, destroy or tamper with documents or other material.

Interviews

14.174 It is normal for investigators to seek to interview both witnesses and suspects. It is essential to clarify the basis on which you are being interviewed before the the interview commences. Directors may not have a choice as to whether or not to answer questions as several investigation agencies have the power to compel directors to answer questions or provide information. Failure to comply may be treated as if it were a contempt of court (see above).

14.175 Directors may be invited to provide information on a voluntary basis. Care should be taken before information which might be covered by confidentiality obligations. In the event that the information requested does relate to confidential material belonging to another party it is preferable to be compelled to provide it to investigators.

Being interviewed as a witness

14.176 It is important to appreciate why you are being interviewed. Some of the most common reasons include:

(a) to explain documents;
(b) because there are gaps in the evidence seen by the investigators;
(c) because there are complex IT systems or products which the investigators do not fully understand;
(d) because the investigators hope the director will incriminate others; and
(e) so the investigators can determine whether appropriate compliance/risk management systems and controls were implemented and understood by key employees.

14.177 Extensive and strategic preparation is essential. Directors should anticipate which documents, questions and themes may be discussed and which defences might be raised. Advance disclosure (advance notice of topics and documents which will be discussed) may also be provided. Information provided to an investigator or regulator may be subsequently deployed against you by a litigant bringing proceedings against the company or shareholders bringing an action against the directors of a company. Material created during the course of an investigation (probably by the use of powers to compel the provision of information) which would not otherwise have existed but for the investigation may be used by an affected investor or shareholder following the conclusion of the investigation irrespective of whether there were prosecutions or adverse regulatory findings.

Interviews as a suspect

14.178 In almost all circumstances an investigator body is not entitled to interview you regarding a criminal offence unless you are under caution. The Code to the Police and Criminal Evidence Act 1984 requires that where there are grounds to suspect a person has committed a criminal offence, he must be cautioned before any questions about it (or any further questions if it is answers to previous questions that have given rise to the grounds for suspicion) are put to him regarding his involvement in that offence, if his answers or his silence (i.e. his failure or refusal to answer questions satisfactorily) are to be admissible as evidence against him by the prosecution in court. An individual does not need to be cautioned to establish matters of fact – for example, his identity, his ownership of a business or a document or a mobile telephone.

14.179 The making by a suspect of a *significant statement* is the trigger for the investigating officer to issue the caution. A *significant statement* is a phrase which puts the officer on immediate notice that the individual may be involved in some way in the commission of the offence under investigation. This is not a subjective but an objective test. It is common for investigators to administer a caution as soon as there is any indication, even a remote one, that an individual may be involved in an offence.

14.180 A caution is a warning which is given by an investigator making the following statement to you:

> 'You do not have to say anything. But it may harm your defence if you do not mention when questioned something you later rely on in court. Anything you say may be given in evidence. Do you understand the caution?'

This means that the answers given to the investigating officer will be used in court. If you plead not guilty, the court can ask whether anything you say in court could have been said by you to the investigating officer. If you mention something new in court that you do not mention to the investigating officer, the jury may be directed by the judge that they can hold it against you as some additional support for the prosecution case but that you do not have any obligation to say anything. The investigating officers and the prosecution must prove all the elements of the case against you and there is no obligation on you to give them more evidence which might assist them.

14.181 If you are being questioned about a criminal offence you have a right to be represented by a lawyer. If you are questioned about misconduct which is not a criminal offence, for example, market abuse, you will not be cautioned. You will not have an absolute right to have a lawyer present but most investigating authorities are content to allow a lawyer to be present during questioning. It is very unusual for a lawyer to be excluded.

14.182 Adverse inference may be drawn against an accused from a failure to mention a fact when questioned which he later relies upon in court. *Fact* means any fact which is in issue and is put forward by the defence at trial.

14.183 The judge's direction to the jury (see www.jsboard.co.uk) informs the jury that where there has been a failure to mention a fact the jury may draw the conclusion that the defendant:

(a) had no answer that he then believed would stand up in interview; and/or
(b) has since invented his account; and/or
(c) has since tailored his account to fit the prosecution's case.

The jury will be warned that they must not convict wholly or mainly on the strength of the defendant's failure to mention a fact in interview, but that it may be taken into account as some additional support for the prosecution case and when deciding whether the defendant's evidence about these facts is true.

14.184 Legal advice to remain silent does not prevent an inference being drawn as the judge will warn the jury that they may bear in mind that a person given legal advice has a choice whether to accept or reject it and that the defendant was warned that any failure to mention facts which he relied upon at trial might harm his defence.

14.185 Directors are especially vulnerable to adverse inferences being drawn as a jury may expect that they will be very familiar with the day-to-day running of the company including, for example, its governance, its accounting policies, what products it sold and that there is simply no good reason for not answering questions relating to issues well within the directors knowledge and experience.

14.186 A director who chooses to answer questions will not have had full disclosure of the entirety of the prosecution case at the time of interview. It is likely that further information will come to light which might undermine the answers given in interview. The director will not know what co-defendants or witnesses (who will probably include other directors of the company) have said about the events and his involvement in them. There is the possibility that investigators will encourage 'cut-throat' defences whereby each director incriminates the other(s).

14.187 Providing a written statement in interview is rarely advisable as it is very unlikely that it will be possible to anticipate every positive fact which will be mentioned in trial if advancing a positive defence. A full risk assessment should be conducted of the relative merits of pursuing this route. Not being able to remember is also seldom a sensible tactic, especially if your memory recovers during trial, as this will undermine your credibility as a witness. If you are questioned, it is imperative to seek expert advice and to think carefully through the implications of each available course of action.

Powers to grant immunity from prosecution to an assisting offender – statutory framework

14.188 The Serious Organised Crime and Police Act 2005 (SOCPA) creates a statutory mechanism for immunity from prosecution in return for incriminating an accomplice.

14.189 Section 71 of SOCPA provides that a specified prosecutor may offer any person immunity from prosecution by means of a written notice where it is appropriate to do so for the purposes of the investigation or prosecution of any offence. If evoked, s. 71 specifies that an immunity notice must be drawn up by the prosecuting agency confirming the conditions that must be adhered to in return for immunity. If the prosecution considers that the conditions have not been met, you can be prosecuted alongside the individuals against whom you produced evidence and for the offences you have admitted during the course of producing that evidence.

14.190 Section 72 provides that if a specified prosecutor thinks that, for the purposes of an investigation or prosecution of any offence, it is appropriate to offer any person an undertaking that information of any description will not be used against the person in any proceedings a written 'restricted use undertaking' notice may be given.

14.191 Section 73 provides for a reduction in sentence when a defendant has made a written agreement with a specified prosecutor to assist the investigator or prosecutor.

Who can offer immunity?

14.192 The power to grant immunity under SOCPA applies to:

- the Director of Public Prosecutions (DPP);
- the Director of the Serious Fraud Office;
- the Director of the Revenue and Customs Prosecutions Office.

The OFT has similar powers under the Enterprise Act 2002. The FSA is not currently a designated prosecutor. However, plans have recently been announced to give these powers to the FSA to assist them in prosecuting insider dealing and other market abuse cases.

Why now?

14.193 Historically, the UK criminal courts have been reluctant to rely on accomplice evidence. However, the past few years has seen the re-emergence of evidence of this kind. This shift in attitude towards accomplice evidence is partly due to the influence and initiative of US provisions. For example, the US Securities and Exchange Commission (SEC) has the power to grant immunity and this has been perceived as a highly effective tool in securing insider trading convictions. Indeed, since 2001, the SEC has filed more than 300 insider trading cases as compared to one in the UK in that period. Further, US antitrust prosecutions, where the success in cracking cartels has been seen to be largely attributable to immunity, have exerted considerable influence. Similar immunity provisions have been in operation in the UK since 2003 in an antitrust context. Under the Enterprise Act 2002, immunity can be granted to the *first* person to inform the OFT about cartel activity in which he is involved. SOCPA therefore represents an attempt to apply the same principles to *all* corporate crime and suggests that there is an increasing trend towards immunity for cooperation. Indeed, within two or three years it is likely to be normal in all forms of corporate offending – fraud, cartels, corporate manslaughter, corruption, environmental offences – to agree formal co-operation with a prosecutor in exchange for immunity.

Will it work?

14.194 For the powers to be effective there needs to be a clear framework established for the way in which the powers are applied and decisions taken – for example, at what stage in the investigation will decisions on immunity have to be taken? Will decisions on whom to grant immunity have to be taken when the prosecution imperfectly understand their case? What happens if, after absolute immunity is offered, information subsequently comes to light which demonstrates the greater culpability of the immune witness *vis-à-vis* the defendants? Further, there is also an issue of what happens if the deal falls through – what is the impact on sentencing in that case?

14.195 Moreover, for the objective of the powers to be met, there needs to be clear guidance as to how immunity is to be applied as, without such guidance, those who assist the prosecutors are unlikely to come forward for fear of simply helping the authorities to build a case against them. There will also need to be clear guidance on how the decision of who will be offered immunity and who will be tried will be made as the immunity provisions must be applied in a consistent manner for their purpose to be served.

14.196 It should be noted that, even if the relevant guidance is put in place, a number of drawbacks remain to the usefulness of evidence provided by an immunised witness. First, it must be considered whether the information provided in soliciting immunity will distort the investigation, if, for example, the party seeking immunity may lead the prosecutor to evidence which is helpful to the individual assisting, but not necessarily to all relevant material. Immunity can also be an incentive to provide exaggerated or untruthful evidence, which in turn can lead to a larger issue of credibility problems for immunised witnesses before the jury.

Acknowledgement

Thanks to Alexander Garcia-Deleito and Mirea Lyton-Grotz for their research and drafting assistance.

Sources

1 *MacPherson v. European Strategic Bureau* [2002] BCC 39.
2 *CAS (Nominees) Ltd v. Nottingham Forest FC Plc* [2002] BCC 145.
3 *Fulham Football Club Ltd v. Cabra Estates plc* [1994] 1 BCLC 363.
4 *Re Continental Assurance Co of London plc (In Liquidation) (No. 1)* [1997] 1 BCLC 48.

5 *Re Galeforce Pleating Co* [1999] 2 BCLC 704.
6 *Re Bradcrown Ltd* [2001] 1 BCLC 547.
7 Ss. 177 and 180, CA 2006.
8 S. 180(4)(a), CA 2006.
9 *Regal (Hastings) Ltd v. Gulliver* [1942] 1 All ER 378.
10 S. 177, CA 2006. Until 1 October 2008, s. 317, CA 1985 continues to apply.
11 S. 180(4)(b), CA 2006.
12 S. 182, CA 2006 replaced s. 317, CA 1985.
13 *Newborne v. Sensolid (GB) Ltd* [1954] 1 QB 45.
14 *Kelner v. Baxter* (1867) LR 2 CP 174; *Natal Land and Colonisation Co v. Pauline Syndicate* [1904] AC 120.
15 *Newborne v. Sensolid (GB) Ltd* [1954] 1 QB 45.
16 The provision is replicated by s. 51, CA 2006, which comes into force on 1 October 2009.
17 *Phonogram Ltd* v. *Lane* [1982] QB 938.
18 *Howard v. Patent Ivory Mf. Co* (1888) 38 Ch D 156.
19 *Braymist Ltd and others v. Wise Finance Co Ltd* [2002] EWCA Civ 127 [2002] 1 BCLC 415.
20 *Oshkosh B'Gosh Incorporated Ltd v. Dan Marbel Inc Ltd and another* [1989] BCLC 507.
21 *Bondina Ltd v. Rollaway Shower Blinds Ltd* [1986] 1 WLR 517.
22 This is replicated by s. 52 CA 1985, which comes in force on 1 October 2009.
23 *UBAF Ltd v. European American Banking Corporation* [1984] QB 713.
24 The relevant CA 2006 provisions came into force on 6 April 2008.
25 S. 767(3), CA 2006; cf. the position at common law: *Re Otto Electrical Manufacturing Company (1905) Limited, Jenkins's Claim* [1906] 2 Ch 390).
26 *Evans (C.) and Sons Ltd v. Spritebrand Ltd* [1985] 1 WLR 317 at 329.
27 *Rainham Chemical Works Ltd v. Belvedere Fish Guano Co Ltd* [1921] 2 AC 465; *British Thomson-Houston Co Ltd* v. *Sterling Accessories Ltd* (1924) 41 RPC 311, referred to in *Evans (C.) and Sons Ltd v. Spritebrand Ltd* [1985] 1 WLR 317, at 325.
28 *Rainham Chemical Works Ltd v. Belvedere Fish Guano Co Ltd* [1921] 2 AC 465, at 476.
29 *Evans (C.) and Sons Ltd v. Spritebrand Ltd* [1985] 1 WLR 317, at 330.
30 *Evans (C) and Sons Ltd v. Spritebrand Ltd* [1985] 1 WLR 317, at 323.
31 *MCA Records Inc v. Charly Records Ltd* [2001] EWCA Civ 1441.
32 *Rainham Chemical Works Ltd v. Belvedere Fish Guano Co Ld* [1921] 2 AC 465.
33 *Performing Right Society Ltd v. Ciryl Theatrical Syndicate Ltd* [1924] 1 KB 1, at 14–15, quoted in *Evans (C) and Sons Ltd v. Spritebrand Ltd* [1985] 1 WLR 317, at 328.
34 *Evans (C) and Sons Ltd v. Spritebrand Ltd* [1985] 1 WLR 317, at 329–330.
35 *Evans (C) and Sons Ltd v. Spritebrand Ltd* [1985] 1 WLR 317, at 330.
36 *Evans (C) and Sons Ltd v. Spritebrand Lt/d* [1985] 1 WLR 317, at 330. See *Mancetter Developments Ltd v. Garmanson Ltd* [1986] 1 All ER 449 and *AP Besson Ltd v. Fulleon Ltd* [1986] FSR 319.
37 *Williams v. Natural Life Health Foods* [1998] 2 All ER 577.
38 *PLG Research Ltd. v. Ardon International Ltd* [1993] FSR 197, at 238–239.
39 *MCA Records Inc v. Charly Records Ltd* [2001] EWCA Civ 1441.

40 *Fairline Shipping Corporation v. Adamson* [1975] QB 180.
41 See also *Yuille v. B&B Fisheries (Leigh) Ltd, The Radiant* [1958] 2 Lloyd's Rep 596, at 619–620.
42 *Director General of Fair Trading v. Buckland* [1990] 1 WLR 920.
43 *Re British Concrete Pipe Association's Agreement* [1982] ICR 182, at 195.
44 *AG for Tuvalu v. Philatelic Distribution Corp* [1990] 1 WLR 926.
45 S. 3, Fraud Act 2006.
46 S. 4, Fraud Act 2006.
47 S. 12, Fraud Act 2006.
48 S. 1(3), Fraud Act 2006.
49 These specified activities are defined in the FSMA (Misleading Statements and Practices) Order 2001: SI 2001/3645.
50 Part I of Schedule 1 to the FSMA (Financial Promotion) Order 2001: SI 2001/1335.
51 Part II of Schedule 1 to the FSMA (Financial Promotion) Order 2001: SI 2001/1335.
52 S. 397(8), FSMA.
53 S. 123(1)(b), FSMA.
54 Para 1.2.3G of the FSA's Code of Market Conduct, as amended by the Market Abuse Directive Instrument 2005 (FSA 2005/15).
55 Qualifying investments defined in article 5 of the Financial Services and Markets Act 2000 (Prescribed Markets and Qualifying Investments) Order 2001, as amended by The Financial Services and Markets Act 2000 (Market Abuse) Regulations 2005. EEA-regulated markets are defined under the Investment Services Directive and include: Euronext, Deutsche Borse and the Irish Stock Exchange. For a complete list, see www.europa.eu.int.
56 Ss. 118(1)(a)(iii), 118(2) and 118(3) FSMA.
57 See para.1.3.20G of the Code of Market Conduct.
58 Ss. 118(4), 118(8) and 118A(3) FSMA.
59 Article 4 of the Financial Services and Markets Act 2000 (Prescribed Markets and Qualifying Investments) Order 2001, as amended by The Financial Services and Markets Act 2000 (Market Abuse) 2005.
60 S. 57, CJA.
61 S. 56, CJA.
62 Information shall be treated as relating to an issuer of securities which is a company (as distinct from a public sector body) not only where it is about the company but also where it may affect the company's business prospects (s. 60(4)).
63 S. 55, CJA.
64 S. 54 and Schedule 2, CJA.
65 The Insider Dealing (Securities and Regulated Markets) Order 1994 (SI 1994/187), the Insider Dealing (Securities and Regulated Markets) (Amendment) Order 1996 (SI 1996/1561), the Insider Dealing (Securities and Regulated Markets) (Amendment Order) 2000 (SI 2000/1923) and the Insider Dealing (Securities and Regulated Markets) (Amendment) Order 2002 (SI 2002/1874).
66 S. 59, CJA.
67 S. 52, CJA.
68 S. 52, CJA.
69 LR 9.2.7–9.2.10.

70 S. 96B(2), FSMA.
71 S. 91, FSMA, section 7 of the FSA's Enforcement Guide (EG).
72 S. 91, FSMA and DTR 1.5.3G.
73 DTR 1.5.3G and LR 5.1 and 5.2.
74 LR 9.2.8
75 *Re D'Jan of London Ltd* [1994] 1 BCLC 561; *Barings plc (in liquidation)* v. *Coopers & Lybrand (a firm), Barings Futures (Singapore) Pte Ltd (in liquidation)* v. *Marra* [2003] All ER (D) 294 (October).
76 *Claridge's Patent Asphalte Co Ltd* [1921] 1 Ch 543.
77 *Coleman Taymar Ltd* v. *Oakes* [2001] 2 BCLC 749.
78 *Customs and Excise Commissioners* v. *Hedon Alpha Ltd and others* [1981] 2 All ER 697.
79 *Coleman Taymar Ltd* v. *Oakes* [2001] 2 BCLC 749.
80 *Coleman Taymar Ltd* v. *Oakes* [2001] 2 BCLC 749.
81 *Re Duomatic Ltd* [1969] 2 Ch 365.
82 *Equitable Life Assurance Society* v. *Bowley and others* [2004] 1 BCLC 180.

15

Shareholder remedies

Introduction

15.1 The focus of this chapter is the risks faced by directors of being sued by shareholders. Directors are vulnerable to being removed from office if they lose the confidence of a majority of shareholders voting in a general meeting of the company. However, directors are liable to be sued by individual shareholders in exceptional circumstances, whether or not they enjoy the confidence of the majority. Directors need to be aware of these risks and to act accordingly. The UK does not, however, have the rabid shareholder litigation culture which is a feature of many US jurisdictions.

15.2 It is a fundamental principle of English law that a director owes no duty *in general* directly to the shareholders or any individual shareholder or any group of shareholders (see **Chapter 5**). This is because *in general* the duties owed by directors, such as the duty to act to promote the success of the company, are owed to the company itself. And only the company can *in general* bring proceedings against a director for breaching the duties owed to the company.

The rule in *Foss v. Harbottle*[1] and the exceptions to it

15.3 The above general principles form the core of the well-known rule in *Foss v. Harbottle*.

15.4 They are a product of the fact that the company is a legal entity in its own right separate from its members.

15.5 However, the above principles do not tell the whole story: there are exceptions and qualifications to them. The purpose of this chapter is to examine these exceptions and qualifications, which may be grouped under the following headings:

(1) The derivative claim – the 'fraud on the minority' exception to the rule. In exceptional circumstances amounting to a 'fraud on the minority' a share-

holder may be permitted by the court to bring an action for the benefit of the company so as to enforce duties owed by a director to the company. Such an action is called a 'derivative claim', because it derives from and is brought to vindicate the rights of the company.

(2) Breach of the company's constitution. Where a director acts in breach of his duty to act in accordance with the company's constitution, the breach is ordinarily capable of ratification by a simple majority of members and therefore no individual shareholder can complain of the breach. There are, however, special cases in which the breach is not capable of ratification in this way, and accordingly a shareholder may be able to bring an action to enforce the terms of the constitution.

(3) Duties owed by a director to all or some of the shareholders personally. A director may in special cases owe duties directly to individual shareholders, either in tort (e.g. where misrepresentations are made which are foreseeably relied on by shareholders resulting in loss to them) or in contract (e.g. where a director is a party to a contract with a shareholder) or in equity (e.g. where a fiduciary relationship of trust and confidence is shown to exist between a director and a shareholder). In such cases, the shareholder, having a personal cause of action, can bring a claim based on that cause of action without involving the company as a party.

(4) Statutory remedies for relief against oppression of minority shareholders. The actions of the controlling directors of a company may have such an oppressive effect on minority shareholders that the latter may have a claim either for relief against the oppressors on the statutory unfair prejudice ground (now s. 994 of the Companies Act 2006) or for the winding up of the company on the just and equitable basis (s. 122(1)(g) of the Insolvency Act 1986).

15.6 The Companies Act 2006 (the 2006 Act) has not made major changes to the substantive law in this area. So far as derivative claims are concerned, they have been put on a statutory footing (ss. 260–269),[2] but this is intended largely to effect a change in procedure as opposed to substance.

Derivative claims – the 'fraud on the minority' exception

The problem in practice

15.7 While a director owes a wide range of duties to the company, only the company can bring proceedings to enforce these duties or to claim compensation and restitution from the wrongdoer for loss suffered by the company or profits wrongly made. Furthermore, because of the expense and uncertainty of litigation, the bad publicity and the waste of management time, it may well be a proper commercial decision for a board of directors to decide not to bring proceedings in respect of the breach of duty even if there is a case of wrongdoing.

15.8 The problem, and potential injustice, arise where the alleged wrongdoing director is in a position to influence the board's decision whether or not to bring proceedings in respect of the breach of duty in question. This problem is particularly acute where the director is also the controlling shareholder of the company and accordingly controls the composition of the board. It is the law that only the company can in general sue in respect of a wrong done to it by a director, but it sticks in the throat, so to speak, to carry this to the extreme of allowing the wrongdoing director to stifle any claim against him, to the obvious detriment of a minority shareholder. In such an extreme case there exists a glaring conflict between the personal interest of the director/shareholder in question (i.e. his interest in not being sued by the company) and his duty as a director to act so as to promote the success of the company.

The 'fraud on the minority' exception to the rule in *Foss v. Harbottle*

15.9 In order to meet the obvious injustice thrown up by that extreme case, the courts, without any statutory basis and in the exercise of their inherent jurisdiction, fashioned a remedy to prevent what the courts called a 'fraud on the minority'. This was the derivative claim. The remedy allows a shareholder to pursue a claim for a wrong done to the company: the shareholder is the claimant and the company is a defendant. Because a derivative claim was for the benefit of the company, the court retained a strict control over the proceedings and its permission was needed for it to proceed through its various stages, with its future progress being open to re-evaluation at each stage. The general principle was that a court would, by way of the 'fraud on the minority' exception to the rule in *Foss v. Harbottle*, permit a derivative claim if the wrongdoers had control[3] of the company and were unjustly stifling a claim by the company against them.[4] However, the case law that developed was quite confused.

The provisions of the 2006 Act

15.10 The derivative claim has now been put on a statutory footing. However, the new statutory provisions do not formulate a substantive rule to replace the rule in *Foss v. Harbottle*[5] but provide a new procedure with more modern, flexible and accessible criteria for determining whether a shareholder can pursue an action.[6] Basically,[7] the existing law as to what falls within the 'fraud on the minority' exception to the rule in *Foss v. Harbottle* continues to apply.

15.11 Any shareholder wishing to pursue a derivative claim must obtain the permission of the court.

15.12 It is proposed to deal with the new statutory procedure under the following headings:

- the cause of action upon which the claim is based;
- the criteria to be applied by the court in exercising its discretion whether or not to grant permission for the claim to continue;
- a costs indemnity order;
- the procedural safeguards built in for the protection of the defendant and the company.

The cause of action on which the claim is based

15.13 The claim is brought by and in the name of an existing shareholder, but it is to enforce a cause of action vested in the company and for the benefit of the company. The main defendant will usually be a director, but third parties can be joined as co-defendants (s. 260(3)). The cause of action may have arisen before the shareholder became a shareholder, but the claimant must be a current member[8] (s. 260(4)). After the court has granted permission to continue, it can make an order that the claim not be settled without the leave of the court: Civil Procedure Rules (CPR) 19.9F.

15.14 A derivative claim may only be brought in respect of a breach of duty or trust by a director (s. 260(3)). Breach of duty covers negligence and the breach of the duty of care. A director includes a former director, and a shadow director is treated as a director (s. 260(5)).

15.15 It is not necessary to plead or show that the director benefited personally from the breach of duty.[9]

15.16 It is also not necessary to plead or show that the defendant director controls the majority of the shares in the company.[10]

The criteria to be applied by the court in exercising its discretion whether or not to grant permission for the claim to continue

15.17 The 2006 Act provides at the outset[11] that, if the court is satisfied on either of the following two issues, the court *must refuse* permission to continue with the action:

(i) A person acting in accordance with the general duty of directors (s. 172) to promote the success of the company would not seek to continue with the claim (s. 263(2)(a)).[12]

The difficulty with this 'knock-out' criterion is that there will often be disputed questions of fact at the permission stage of the proceedings, on which this criterion will ultimately turn. Its importance as a 'knock-out' criterion is in any event much diminished by the fact that it is one of the particular criteria set out in s. 263(3)(b) as going to the discretion of the court. This criterion is likely to be useful in cases where the company has made a decision not to sue, based on the votes of independent directors and/or shareholders, and on independent professional advice. In such circumstances, the court may be satisfied that the claim was not being brought to promote the success of the company. Another type of case where this criterion may be useful is where there is evidence that the claimant shareholder is acting to advance his own personal interests and to secure an advantage for himself rather than the company.

(ii) The act or omission of the director has been authorised or ratified by the company (s. 263(2)(b) and (c)).

On a superficial reading, this would suggest that a director who controlled the composition of the board could simply procure ratification of his alleged misdemeanours by the exercise of his voting power in general meeting. However, this is not what this criterion is intended to allow. First, s. 239 provides that any decision by a company to ratify any breach of duty on the part of a director is only valid if taken without reliance upon the votes by the director or any connected person. Second, to be authorised or ratified for the purposes of s. 263(2)(b) and (c) presumably means *validly* authorised and ratified, and s. 239(7) preserves existing case law as to the whether an act or omission is capable of being validly ratified.[13] So, in effect the existing law continues to apply: if under existing case law an act or omission falls within the 'fraud on the minority' exception to the rule in *Foss v. Harbottle*, then the court has a discretion whether or not to allow the action to proceed.

15.18 The 2006 Act sets out the criteria to be applied by the courts in particular in the exercise of its discretion on whether or not to grant permission for the claim to continue. The criteria are:

(2) Whether the claimant is acting in good faith in seeking to continue with the claim (s. 263(3)(a)).
(3) The importance that a person acting in accordance with the director's general duty to promote the success of the company (s. 172) would attach to continuing it.
(4) Ratification of the act or omission in question (s. 263(3)(c) and (d)).
(5) Whether the company has decided not to pursue the claim (s. 263(3)(e)).
(6) Whether the claimant has another remedy in his own right (s. 263(3)(f)).
(7) The views of members who have no interest, direct or indirect, in the matter (s. 263(4)).[14]

15.19 The factors were applied in *Mission Capital v. Sinclair* [2008] BCC 866. The court refused permission to continue a speculative derivative claim where the claimant had a remedy under s. 994 (see **15.32** below). Permission to continue was also refused in *Franbar Holdings v. Patel* [2008] BCC 885 on the ground of availability of alternative remedies. The overriding question to be addressed in the exercise of the court's discretion to grant permission to continue is whether a claim is being improperly stifled. Since it is always difficult to challenge on appeal the exercise by a court of a discretion vested in it, the hearing in the court of first instance is crucial to the success of a derivative claim. Directors who feel unjustly accused of wrongdoing by certain shareholders should ascertain the views of independent directors and other shareholders and, depending on the circumstances, invite them to obtain independent professional advice on the merits of the claim.

A costs indemnity order

15.20 Not only did the courts fashion a remedy for the case where a claim against a director was being improperly stifled, but they also fashioned a procedure for enabling the claimant shareholder to apply for an order that the company, for whose benefit the claim was being pursued, should fund the claim and be responsible for any adverse costs. For obvious reasons, with such costs protection, this is a potent weapon in the hands of the claimant shareholder, who would otherwise have to bear all the usual financial burdens and risks arising out of the litigation. The protection is known as a Wallersteiner order, after the case in which it was recognised: *Wallersteiner v. Moir (No. 2)* [1975] QB 373.

15.21 A claimant will not be granted a Wallersteiner order automatically, on the assumption that permission to continue with the derivative claim has been granted. Under existing case law, there is a 'need for caution'.[15] It is not necessary to show that the claimant is unable to fund the proceedings himself.[16] A relevant factor is whether there has been an independent investigation which supports continuing proceedings.[17] A Wallersteiner order is unlikely to be granted where the claimant and the defendant director hold all the shares in the company so that it would be unfair for the defendant director, if ultimately successful, to bear the burden of the costs of the proceedings.[18]

The procedural safeguards for the protection of the defendant and the company

15.22 As stated, a derivative claim may not be pursued without permission of the court.

15.23 If minded at the first hearing to grant permission, the court will nevertheless seek to retain close supervision of the proceedings throughout their life in order to review their continuation at key stages, such as after the exchange of witness statements and disclosure, or if there is a material change in circumstances.[19]

15.24 The procedure is governed by CPR 19.9–19.9F, as supplemented by the Practice Direction – Group Litigation. The rules provide that:

(1) The claimant must lodge, together with the claim form,[20] the application for permission to continue and the evidence relied on in support of that application.[21] The claim form must be headed 'Derivative Claim'.[22]

(2) The company must not be made a respondent to that application,[23] but must in general be sent copies of all the documents lodged, together with a notice in the prescribed form. The court can, on the claimant's application, direct that serving the documents on the company be delayed if it is likely to frustrate any part of the remedy sought.[24]

(3) After the claim form is issued, the claimant must not take any further step in the proceedings other than applying for permission to continue or making an urgent application for interim relief.[25]

(4) The claimant should include in the application for permission any claim for a Wallersteiner order.[26]

(5) As stated in that notice to be served on the company, the company does not need to take any action immediately[27] and the court[28] will make its initial decision as to whether a *prima facie* case is made on the basis of the documents filed. This reflects s. 261(2), which requires the court in every case to filter out claims where a *prima facie* case is not made. At this preliminary, filter stage the court is not concerned with making a Wallersteiner order.

(6) If the court is not satisfied at this filter stage that a *prima facie* case has been made out, the claimant has the right to a hearing.[29]

(7) If the court decides to dismiss the application for permission for any reason at this filter stage, that is an end of the claim, subject to any appeal. The court is under a duty at this stage to dismiss the application and dismiss the claim if it is satisfied that the claimant has not shown a *prima facie* case.[30]

(8) If the court decides not to dismiss the application for permission at this filter stage, with or without a hearing attended by the claimant, then the company becomes a respondent to the application.[31] Directions will be given for the determination of the application at a hearing before a judge,[32] assuming that it is resisted by the company. There may only be a dispute over the making of a Wallersteiner order.

(9) If the court decides to grant permission to continue with the claim, terms may be imposed.[33] Invariably, terms will be imposed which enable the court to review the progress of the proceedings and the grant of permission to continue at various key stages or if circumstances change.

(10) The court can also impose a condition that the claim not be settled or discontinued without the leave of the court. This may be appropriate where any future proposal to settle does not come to the attention of members who may wish to take over the action.[34] Derivative claims can be abused by a claimant shareholder to put pressure on directors to buy off the claimant, rather than make recompense to the shareholders as a whole, and the court will be aware of this and impose such a condition, even if it were opposed by all the parties before it.

(11) There are also provisions dealing with cases where a shareholder wishes to take over control of proceedings commenced by the company or another shareholder for breach of duty against a director.[35]

Breach of the company's constitution

15.25 This is a narrow category and includes instances where directors exercise their powers in circumstances where the material provisions of the company's articles of association have not been complied with and where the breach cannot be ratified by a simple majority of shareholders in general meeting.

15.26 An example of a breach which is capable of ratification is where insufficient notice has been given to shareholders of a meeting to consider passing an ordinary resolution: it would be pointless for the court to intervene at the suit of a minority shareholder if it is clear that the majority of shareholders support the resolution in question.

15.27 It would be otherwise if the resolution in question were a special resolution or any other resolution requiring a special majority. In this case, an individual shareholder may obtain relief from the court to stop the directors acting on a resolution where the rules have not been followed in the procedure leading to it.

Duties owed by a director to all or some of the shareholders personally

15.28 The general principle is that directors owe their duties to the company, not to individual shareholders. This is why it is necessary for a shareholder, seeking redress for the benefit of the company for breach of the duties owed by directors, to apply to the court for permission to bring a derivative claim (see **15.6–15.23** above). However, there are exceptions to this principle; these fall into three categories.

15.29 The first category is where the directors' ordinary fiduciary duties are held to be owed in reality and substance primarily to shareholders personally, if also to the company itself. The shareholder is recognised to have a personal cause of action because he suffers loss distinct from any loss suffered by the company[36] and a wrong to the shareholder would go unremedied if a personal cause of action were not recognised. An example is where, in the course of a contested takeover bid, the directors of the target company (and majority shareholders) accept proposals that reduce the value of the company's assets and induce the minority shareholders to accept the lower of two rival bids. The minority shareholders are then held to have a personal cause of action because they have been deprived of a personal right – the opportunity of accepting the higher bid.[37] Similarly, where the directors issue new shares in the company for the improper purpose of destroying an existing majority or creating a new majority, shareholders may have a personal cause of action in circumstances where it would be unrealistic to regard the company as the wronged party.[38] In a takeover directors should:

- refrain from issuing shares in order to influence the outcome of a bid;
- attempt to obtain the best price for all shareholders equally; and
- give advice to shareholders if they need to, but only to enable the shareholders to make a fully informed decision for themselves.[39]

15.30 The second category of exceptional case is where a director allows himself to be brought into a special relationship with a particular shareholder with regard to a transaction and thereby assumes a responsibility to that shareholder. The result may be that the director assumes a duty of care or a fiduciary duty to that shareholder, in addition to the duties he owes to the company. Thus, because there is no special relationship between the board and the shareholders, the mere supply of information by directors in the course of a takeover pursuant to the provisions of the City Code is not sufficient to give rise to a duty of care owed to shareholders (*Partco Group v. Wragg* [2002] 2 BCLC 323).[40] In contrast, where the directors and majority shareholders in a family company persuade the minority to sell their shares to them, a fiduciary relationship may be held to exist between the directors and the minority (*Platt v. Platt* [1999] 2 BCLC 745).[41]

15.31 The third category is where a director makes a misrepresentation of fact to a shareholder – the director is liable in deceit if he knew the statement to be false, whether or not a special relationship existed between himself and the shareholder in question (*Noel v. Poland* [2001] 2 BCLC 645). The director is not, however, liable in negligence, i.e. if he did not know but ought to have known the statement to be false, unless a special relationship existed.

Statutory remedies for relief against oppression of minority shareholders

15.32 There are two statutory remedies: s. 994 of the 2006 Act (unfair prejudice) and s. 122(1)(g) of the Insolvency Act 1986 (winding up on the just and equitable basis). The first is the more important and has all but eclipsed the latter.[42]

The unfair prejudice remedy

15.33 Sections 994 (grounds of unfair prejudice) and 996 (the relief that may be granted by the court) are drafted in extremely wide terms.

15.34 In order to establish unfair prejudice[43] the member has to establish that:

- the requisite standing to bring a petition;
- the affairs of the company in question have been conducted in the material manner, that is to say:
  - (a) unfairly; and
  - (b) prejudicial to the interests as a shareholder of the petitioner or the members generally.

15.35 If these conditions are established, then the court has the widest discretion to 'make such order as it thinks fit for giving relief in respect of the matters complained of'.[44] The principles on which the court exercises wide discretion are set out in **15.76–15.84** below.

Standing to petition

15.36 The petitioner has to be a current member[45] or a person to whom shares have been transferred (by means of an instrument of transfer in writing) or transmitted by operation of law (e.g. on the death or bankruptcy of the registered shareholder).[46]

15.37 If a person claims to be entitled to be registered as a member but has not been so registered, he cannot present a petition but must first obtain his registration by bringing proceedings for rectification of the register or otherwise.

15.38 If a person is registered as a member but his entitlement to be registered is disputed, the issue may be resolved in the petition, or the court may require it to be resolved in separate proceedings before any petition is pursued by that shareholder.

15.39 Although it is a general requirement that the petitioner be a current member, the petitioner can rely on conduct of the company's affairs which occurred before he became a member,[47] although it is still necessary to establish unfair prejudice to the petitioner's interests as a shareholder.

15.40 Even though only the registered shareholder has in general standing to petition, as opposed to any person with a beneficial interest in the shares, the registered shareholder can, in appropriate circumstances, rely on prejudice to the interests of the beneficial owners,[48] e.g. where there has been some breach of an agreement or understanding between those in control of the affairs of the company and those beneficial owners.[49]

Conduct of the affairs of the company

15.41 The conduct complained of by the member must be the conduct of the affairs of the company in question or some act or omission of the company (including an act or omission on its behalf).[50]

15.42 It follows that a member cannot complain about the conduct of the affairs of some other business or company. However, the courts take a broad view of a company's affairs: they look at the business realities and have held that a company's affairs extend to the affairs of other companies under the effective control of the company.[51]

Interests as a shareholder

15.43 It is well established that the unfair prejudice remedy exists for the protection only of a member's interests as a shareholder. So, a member cannot complain about prejudice to his interests as the company's landlord, for example.[52] But the policy of the courts is to construe a member's interests liberally and widely so as to recognise that in special cases no real distinction can be drawn between a member's interests in one capacity and his interests in another. So, where a member has made an investment in a company by means of both equity and loan capital investment, the whole investment, including the loan capital, will be regarded as part of the member's interests as a shareholder. It is not necessary in such a case to show that the company is solvent.[53] So, if a company is in substance, if not in form, a partnership and the joint venturers make their investment in the company on the basis that they will be entitled to participate actively in the business as executive directors, their interests as shareholders include their right to participate actively in the business.[54] However, where there is no close personal relationship between shareholders and their relationship is a purely commercial one, a strict line may be drawn between an investor's rights as a shareholder and any rights that he may happen to have as a director.

Prejudice

15.44 It is essential that the complaining member establishes real prejudice to his interests. For example, if the member is complaining about an advantage having been obtained by the majority in circumstances where he personally is in no worse position than he was before that advantage was obtained, it may be held that no prejudice has been suffered by the minority shareholder.[55]

15.45 Prejudice, however, may be established in a wide variety of forms. Actual financial loss and diminution in the value of shares are good examples of prejudice, but are by no means the only ones. If directors act in breach of their fiduciary duties but the minority shareholders suffer no prejudice in the form of a diminution in value of their shares or otherwise, the petition may fail.[56]

15.46 In the case of companies where the relationship between the shareholders is a purely commercial one, the courts will be astute to prevent the use of the unfair prejudice remedy for improper collateral purposes where the petitioner has suffered no real prejudice.[57]

Unfairness

15.47 This is the core ingredient, but also the most difficult to define. It is not enough simply to persuade a court that the majority's conduct was 'unfair' in some general subjective sense. What has to be established can be summarised[58] as follows.

The bargain between shareholders

(i) There has been a breach of the 'bargain' between shareholders.

(ii) The starting point in ascertaining the bargain between the shareholders is the *legal* bargain represented by the articles of association and any supplemental shareholders' agreement.

Breach of duty by directors

(iii) The bargain between shareholders includes the duties owed by the directors to the company. However, not every breach of duty by a director will amount to unfair prejudice. First, no prejudice to the complainant shareholder may flow from a particular breach of duty by a director (see **15.44–15.46** above). Second, the principles (see **15.7–15.24** above) governing when a court will grant permission for a derivative claim to be pursued must be taken into account: the court will not allow an unfair prejudice petition to be used to outflank those principles, i.e. where the remedy sought is essentially the same as would be available in a derivative claim.[59]

Relief in equity

(iv) Relief may also be granted where, applying settled equitable principles, the majority are acting contrary to promises or understandings which are enforceable *in equity*. Equity will, in appropriate circumstances, look to the spirit rather than the letter of the agreement between shareholders.

(v) In appropriate and exceptional circumstances relief may be also granted, where, under settled equitable principles, the majority are insisting on maintaining the association in circumstances outside the contemplation of the parties when they entered into the association.

(vi) It should be emphasised that, where the court grants relief under (iv) and (v) above, it does so under *settled* equitable principles only, i.e. principles developed independently of the unfair prejudice remedy (e.g. the law of partnership or estoppel) and not by applying any general concept of 'fairness'.

The bargain between shareholders

15.48 The starting point in determining whether there has been unfair prejudice is to see whether the majority have acted in breach of the agreement reached between the shareholders that governs their relationship. The agreement between shareholders will usually be set out in the company's articles of association. By s. 33 of the 2006 Act the provisions of the articles of association bind the company and its members as if they were covenants on the part of the company and of each member to observe their provisions. It is not uncommon, however, for shareholders to supplement the articles of association with a collateral written contractual agreement among themselves. Such an agreement is on general principles binding in contract on the parties to it.

15.49 An example of unfair prejudice flowing from breach of the bargain between shareholders is a case where the majority shareholders refuse to recognise a director nominated by the minority shareholders pursuant to a right to nominate a director contained in the company's articles of association.[60] In such a case the minority shareholders had a personal right to nominate a director, which was fundamental to their entry into a business association with the majority shareholders, and it is clear that breach of such a right is a fundamental breach of the agreement among the shareholders, giving the court jurisdiction to grant appropriate relief under the unfair prejudice remedy.

15.50 However, not every breach of the articles of association will amount to unfair prejudice. Many such breaches of a purely procedural nature can be cured by a bare majority vote in general meeting and do not amount to a serious breach of the personal rights of individual shareholders.

15.51 Since the starting point of the exercise of the court's powers under the unfair prejudice remedy is the enforcement of the bargain between shareholders, it follows that, in circumstances where the agreement among the shareholders makes provision for the events which are complained of by the aggrieved minority, the court will in general enforce the terms of the agreement. Thus, where the company's articles of association provided that a member was obliged to offer his shares to the other shareholders where he ceased to be 'employed for whatever reason', the court enforced that term even though it was alleged that the dismissal was wrongful (*Holt v. Faulks* [2000] 2 BCLC 816).[61]

Breach of duty by directors

15.52 A breach of duty by directors, even if the duty is owed to the company alone, is a *prima facie* ground of unfair prejudice.[62] However, the aggrieved shareholder must still establish that the company or he has suffered real prejudice in fact as a result of the breach of duty.

15.53 As has been seen (**15.6–15.23** above), a minority shareholder cannot bring a derivative claim in respect of every breach of duty owed by directors to the company; in order to obtain permission to bring such a claim, he has to bring himself within the exceptions to the rule in *Foss v. Harbottle*, enshrined in ss. 260–264 of the 2006 Act. It would appear, therefore, to be paradoxical that a minority shareholder can obtain relief under the unfair prejudice remedy in circumstances where he would not be granted permission to bring a derivative claim in respect of the same breach. The solution is to be found by analysing the nature of the relief being sought by the aggrieved shareholder: if the aggrieved shareholder is in reality using the unfair prejudice remedy to circumvent the rule in *Foss v. Harbottle*, the court will prevent this abuse.[63]

15.54 Whether a minority shareholder can obtain relief under the unfair prejudice remedy for many of the classic cases of minority oppression where equitable considerations do not come into play, such as excessive remuneration paid to directors who are the majority shareholders,[64] non-payment of dividends,[65] dealings between the company and other persons associated with the majority,[66] rights or other share issues,[67] commercial mismanagement or takeover bids, will generally turn on whether the aggrieved minority shareholder can show that the majority have acted in breach of their fiduciary duties as directors.

Relief in equity

15.55 Where the relationship among shareholders is purely commercial and at arm's length, it is most unlikely that the court will grant relief under the unfair prejudice remedy where there has been no breach of the legal bargain among the shareholders (i.e. including a breach of fiduciary duty by the directors), applying ordinary canons of construction in the interpretation of that bargain. In other words, the parties have entered into the association with each other on the basis of contract and it would not be right to grant relief under the unfair prejudice remedy unless there has been a breach of that contract.

15.56 Exceptionally, equitable principles of estoppel may provide the basis of a remedy to a minority shareholder. Even parties in a purely commercial relationship can make promises to each other which are enforceable in equity under settled principles of the law of estoppel, i.e. a promise of sufficient certainty on which another party has relied to his detriment.[68] If a shareholder has broken such a promise and the aggrieved shareholder has suffered real prejudice as a result, the court may grant relief on the unfair prejudice ground.[69]

15.57 However, principles derived from the law of equity, including the law of estoppel, are far more likely to come to the aid of a minority shareholder where the relationship among shareholders is not a purely commercial one but is a closer relationship based on trust and confidence, akin in other words to a partnership. Such a relationship is often described for short-hand purposes as a 'quasi-relationship', but this term can be excusing. It is no more than a label to describe those circumstances which

> 'as equity always does, enable the court to subject the exercise of legal rights to equitable considerations; considerations, that is, of a personal character arising between one individual and another, which may make it unjust, or inequitable, to insist on legal rights, to exercise them in a particular way.' (per Lord Wilberforce in his seminal speech in *Re Westbourne Galleries Ltd* [1973] AC 360)

That was a case dealing with the just and equitable winding-up remedy, but the same principles have been held to apply in the unfair prejudice remedy (*O'Neill v. Phillips* [1999] 1 WLR 1092).

15.58 The unfair prejudice remedy was introduced in order to widen the protection afforded to minority shareholders, but in case it be thought that the new remedy had enabled a court to grant relief whenever it considered the conduct of the majority to have been 'unfair', it has been held by the House of Lords in *O'Neill v. Phillips* that under the new remedy reliance has to be placed exclusively on settled (or traditional) equitable principles, not general notions of fairness.

15.59 It is, however, difficult to state what those settled equitable principles are. Prior to the *Westbourne Galleries* case it had been customary to analyse the cases as falling into four categories:

- loss of substratum (i.e. circumstances akin to frustration in the law of contract);
- deadlock;
- justifiable loss of confidence in management; or
- exclusion of the minority from management.

That categorisation, although still illuminating, was rejected by the House of Lords in the *Westbourne Galleries* case.

15.60 It is convenient to analyse the relevant equitable principles by first determining the circumstances giving rise to the intervention of equity (i.e. quasi-partnerships), and then looking at the most common examples of minority oppression to see how the equitable principles are applied.

15.61 If there is a common theme to the application of equitable principles in this context, it is that the majority will not be allowed to use their powers in circumstances 'entirely outside what can fairly be regarded as having been in the contemplation of the parties when they became members of the company' (per Smith J. in *Re Wendoflex Textiles Pty Ltd* [1951] VLR 458, at 467).[70]

Quasi-partnerships

15.62 There must be something special about the relationship between the shareholders to enable the court to apply equitable principles of good faith. The three key factors are:[71]

(1) an association based on a personal relationship involving mutual confidence;
(2) an agreement or understanding that all or some of the members shall participate in the conduct of the business;
(3) a restriction upon the transfer of shares.

15.63 So far as (3) is concerned, this will exclude almost every company whose shares are listed on a public exchange or are otherwise readily marketable. Almost every unlisted company will be included, but this factor alone will not make the company a 'quasi-partnership', since most such companies are based on a purely commercial relationship between the shareholders.

15.64 So far as (1) and (2) are concerned, these usually go together. A classic example is a partnership business which decides to incorporate itself for fiscal or other business reasons. Another classic example is where two parties do not give any detailed thought at the outset to the terms of their relationship generally, or more particularly the circumstances in which and the terms on which one party is entitled to leave the association: it is an informal association based on trust and confidence, rather like a marriage (i.e. begun in a spirit of optimism and good faith), which encounters difficulties as soon as the parties' expectations diverge and cannot be reconciled, or for any other reason they lose confidence in each other.

15.65 A company can begin as a quasi-partnership and cease to be one;[72] equally it can begin as a purely commercial relationship and become a quasi-partnership.[73]

15.66 A company can be a quasi-partnership even though the aggrieved shareholder does not participate in the day-to-day running of the business. It is not uncommon for minority shareholders to establish an agreement or understanding that they shall be consulted on important policy decisions.[74]

Application of equitable principles to common examples of minority oppression

15.67 Common examples are:

- breakdown of trust and confidence;
- exclusion;
- breach of specific promises;
- deadlock;
- frustration.

Breakdown of trust and confidence

15.68 Breakdown of trust and confidence is not of itself a ground of unfair prejudice.[75] Even where the company is *ex hypothesi* a quasi-partnership, and one based on an understanding that the minority shareholder shall participate in management, it is necessary to go further and show that the aggrieved shareholder has been excluded or forced out by the majority. If the aggrieved shareholder, following a breakdown of trust and confidence, voluntarily leaves the company, he will not have a remedy.

Exclusion

15.69 Where the company is a quasi-partnership based on an understanding that the minority shall be entitled to participate in the management (whether the day-to-day conduct of the business or policy decision-making), the minority shareholder will be entitled to relief under the unfair prejudice remedy if he is excluded from the promised participation by the majority. In many cases there may be a very thin line[76] between a mere breakdown in the relationship of trust and confidence on the one hand (which is not of itself a sufficient basis for an unfair prejudice claim) and actual exclusion of the minority shareholder (which is a sufficient basis) on the other.

15.70 If the exclusion of the minority *prima facie* gives the minority a remedy on the unfair prejudice basis, this gives rise to the obvious question: what if the exclusion was justified for good commercial reasons, such as misconduct? Exclusion cannot be justified in this context by good commercial reasons generally,[77] such as redundancy. In no case has any justification, other than actual misconduct on the part of the minority, justifying his exclusion, been held to suffice (see e.g. *Grace v. Biagioli* [2006] BCC 85). The rationale for this is that the minority's right to participate in the business was fundamental to his agreement to enter into the association with the majority, so that if circumstances were to change it would generally be right that the association should come to an end, with the majority buying out the minority at a fair value. However, if the minority brought his exclusion on his own head by his serious misconduct, then equity, applying by analogy the principle that he who seeks equitable relief must come to court with clean hands, would not grant him relief.[78]

Breach of specific promises

15.71 In the case of a quasi-partnership the court is more likely to recognise specific promises enforceable in equity, although not having contractual force. A promise of management participation is not the only promise capable of being enforced in this context in equity.[79]

Deadlock

15.72 In the case of a company with two equal shareholders, where there is in practice deadlock between the two even though it is still technically possible for one side to carry on the business of the company, it is likely that the court will grant to the aggrieved side relief under the unfair prejudice remedy.[80]

Frustration

15.73 It is well-recognised in principle that a court may grant relief to an aggrieved minority shareholder where the majority is using its powers to maintain the association in circumstances to which the minority can reasonably say it did not agree.[81]

15.74 This appears to be a very broad principle, but, given the analogy that is being drawn in this context with frustration in the law of contract, it may be applied narrowly. A modern example[82] is the case of *Virdi v. Abbey Leisure* [1990] BCLC 342, where a company was the vehicle for the sole purpose of the acquisition and management of a nightclub, so that, when the nightclub was sold, it was right to bring the association to an end.

Defences available to majority shareholders

15.75 Two common factors which may defeat a claim of unfair prejudice are misconduct[83] and delay and/or acquiescence,[84] i.e. on the part of the aggrieved minority shareholder.

Remedies

15.76 As noted, if unfair prejudice is established, then the court has the widest discretion to 'make such order as it thinks fit for giving relief in respect of the matters complained of'.[85] The court is acting as if it were a GP, remedying the malady from which the patient is suffering during the life of the patient (in contrast to the remedy of winding up on the just and equitable basis).[86]

15.77 In fact, it is not accurate to suggest that relief under the unfair prejudice remedy is likely to be painless and to be contrasted with the drastic remedy of winding up. On the contrary, the most common and useful remedy is an order that the majority buy out the minority at a fair value, which is likely to be just as onerous on the majority and just as final as a winding up order. In exceptional circumstances, the court may make an order in favour of the aggrieved minority that the majority sell its shares to the minority. The court will almost never grant relief to a majority shareholder, ordering the minority to sell its shares.[87]

15.78 Where a share purchase order has been made, it will become necessary to arrive at a fair value for the shares being purchased. Valuation of shares is far from an exact science. They will be valued ignoring any unfairly prejudicial conduct which has been established and which has diminished the value of the shares in question. Share valuers will usually begin with a valuation of the shares based on applying an appropriate multiplier to the maintainable profits of the company. In some cases it may also be appropriate to consider a net assets basis of valuation.

15.79 Where it makes a share purchase order, the court will have to determine the date at which the shares should be valued. If that date precedes the date of trial, it will also have to consider whether to grant any compensation (akin to interest) for the passage of time.[88]

15.80 A crucial issue will often be whether or not to apply a discount for a minority shareholding. The general principle is that such a discount should be applied unless the company has the characteristics of a quasi-partnership.[89] This may be extremely important in practice, since the majority may be more than happy and the minority most unhappy at the prospect of the majority buying out the minority with a full and substantial discount to reflect the minority status of the shareholding.

15.81 The valuation will not necessarily be carried out by the court; it has power to delegate this task (but generally not issues raising points of law or principle) to an independent expert appointed by the court.[90]

15.82 A share purchase order is by no means the only remedy available to the court. In some, relatively unusual, cases, the court will make orders for the future regulation of the company's affairs, leaving the warring parties to continue in association with each other but removing the causes of friction or deadlock.[91]

15.83 The court also has power under the unfair prejudice remedy to grant similar relief to that obtainable in a derivative claim, namely relief by way of compensation of the company for wrongs done to it, including relief against third parties involved in the wrongdoing.[92] However, an unfair prejudice petition cannot be used to outflank the principles which govern whether a minority shareholder can bring a derivative claim[93] (see **15.53** above).

15.84 When faced with a threat of proceedings under the unfair prejudice remedy by an aggrieved minority, the majority should give urgent consideration (in the interests of saving the costs and trouble of litigation) to making an offer to address the legitimate concerns of the minority, particularly making an offer for the purchase of the minority's shares at a fair value to be determined by an independent expert. If such an offer gives the minority all that it could reasonably expect to receive at trial, the court may strike out the petition as an abuse of the process of the court.[94]

Winding up on the just and equitable ground

15.85 This power of winding up, at the instance of an aggrieved minority shareholder, is given to the court under s. 122(1)(g) of the Insolvency Act 1986.

15.86 The grounds on which the court may make a winding up order on the just and equitable ground are however no wider than those on which relief may be granted under the unfair prejudice remedy (*Re Guidezone Ltd.* [2000] 2 BCLC 321), although doubts have recently been expressed about this by some judges. Given the far wider powers of the court as to the form of relief under the latter remedy, and the reluctance of the court to make a winding up order where a less drastic remedy is available, the unfair prejudice remedy has all but superseded the winding up remedy. That does not mean that it will never be appropriate to claim winding up on the just and equitable basis in the alternative to relief under the unfair prejudice remedy; there may well be tactical advantages in doing so.[95] So it is not unusual for a petition to claim winding up on the just and equitable ground in the alternative to relief on the unfair prejudice ground.

15.87 In one important respect, the winding up remedy is narrower than the unfair prejudice remedy, namely the need to show that the company is solvent. In general, a petitioner seeking winding up must plead and prove that there would be a surplus in a liquidation of the company, otherwise the petitioner would have no sufficient interest in such a remedy.[96]

15.88 Furthermore, in order to have standing to present a winding up petition, the aggrieved minority shareholder in general has either to be the original allottee of his shares or to have acquired the shares by devolution from the deceased former holder or to have been registered as the holder of the shares for at least six months during the preceding 18 months.[97]

The prohibition against the use of company funds in shareholder disputes

15.89 It is a well-established general principle that the majority shareholders may not lawfully use company funds to assist in paying the legal costs involved in shareholder disputes to which they are parties.[98] It may, however, be appropriate for the company (through its independent directors) to resist permission being granted for what is either in form or in substance a derivative claim brought ostensibly for the benefit of the company.

Sources

1 This 'rule' has been described by Lord Hoffmann in an extrajudicial capacity as 'a fire-breathing and multi-headed dragon'.

2 As have directors' duties; see **Chapter 5**.

3 A broad spectrum extending from overall absolute majority to effective control by reason of influence over or apathy of others: *Prudential v. Newman Industries* [1982] Ch. 204, at p. 219; *Smith v. Croft (No. 2)* [1988] Ch. 114, at 184–5.

4 The leading cases are *Prudential v. Newman Industries (No. 2)* [1982] Ch. 204, at 210–211; *Daniels v. Daniels* [1978] Ch. 406, at 413, and *Barrett v. Duckett* [1995] 1 BCLC 243, at 249–250.

5 See **15.3** above.

6 Explanatory Note to the 2006 Act (EN) No. 491.

7 One uncertainty has been resolved: a claim in negligence against a director can now be pursued by way of a derivative claim.

8 A member is defined in s. 112. Section 112(5) provides that references to a member include a person to whom shares have been transferred or transmitted by operation of law. These are the same as the rules that govern the standing of a shareholder to bring a claim for relief under the statutory unfair prejudice remedy.

9 EN No. 491. However, the fact that the director did derive personal benefit may be relevant in persuading a court to grant permission to continue, this being a relevant factor under existing case law: see e.g. *Daniels v. Daniels* [1978] Ch. 406, at 413.

10 EN No. 491. Again, however, the fact that the director did control a majority of

the shares will be a highly material factor in persuading a court to grant permission to continue, this being a relevant factor under existing case law: see *Barrett v. Duckett* [1995] 1 BCLC 243, at 249–250.

11 S. 263(2).

12 This echoes dicta in existing case law, e.g. per Walton J in *Smith v. Croft (No. 1)* [1986] 1 WLR 580, at 559.

13 As confirmed by EN Nos. 441, 445 and 499(b).

14 Under existing law this criterion has been held to be decisive: *Smith v. Croft (No. 2)* [1988] Ch. 114.

15 Per Hoffmann L.J. in *McDonald v. Horn* [1995] 1 All ER 961, at 974–5.

16 *Jaybird Group v. Greenwood* [1986] BCLC 319.

17 See note 15.

18 *Halle v. Trax* [2000] BCC 1020, at 1023.

19 *Fraser v. Oystertec* [2004] EWHC 2225 (Ch) at paras. 29–33.

20 In the vast majority of cases it would be appropriate to include Particulars of Claim with the claim form. CPR 19.9A(4)(b) seems to assume that Particulars of Claim will exist from the outset.

21 CPR 19.9A(2).

22 19CPD para. 2(1).

23 CPR 19.9A(3).

24 CPR 19.9A(7) and (8) and 19CPD para. 4. For such circumstances, see per Walton J in *Smith v. Croft (No. 1)* [1986] 1 WLR 580, at 558–9.

25 CPR 19.9(4). An example of such urgent interim relief is an interim injunction to stop an irreversible step threatened by the alleged wrongdoers.

26 19CPD para. 2(2).

27 Rather like a respondent in an application for permission to appeal, the company is discouraged from taking any active part at thie filter stage by any costs normally being disallowed: 19CPD para. 5.

28 It seems that even at this filter stage the application will be determined by a judge: 19CPD para. 6.

29 CPR 19.9A(10).

30 Section 261(2).

31 CPR 19.9A(12).

32 19CPD para. 6.

33 S. 261(4).

34 19CPD para. 7.

35 Ss. 262 and 264; CPR 19.9B.

36 See *Johnson v. Gore Wood (No. 1)* [2002] 2 AC 1 (a case concerning whether a duty of care was owed to a shareholder, as distinct from the company, by a non-director outsider).

37 *Heron International Ltd v. Grade* [1983] BCLC 244, approved and explained in *Johnson v. Gore Wood (No. 1)* [2002] 2 AC 1. See also *Hunter v. Senate Support Services* [2005] 1 BCLC 175.

38 *Re Sherborne Park Residents Co Ltd* [1987] BCLC 82. Contrast *Bamford v. Bamford* [1970] Ch. 212, where the court held that the duty owed by the directors was owed to the company alone and could be ratified by a bare majority of the members.

39 But see *Partco Group v. Wragg* [2002] 2 BCLC 323.

40 Applying *Williams v. Natural Life Health Foods Ltd* [1998] 1 WLR 830, per Lord Steyn, at pp. 834–835.
41 Contrast the majority of cases where no fiduciary relationship is found to exist, e.g. *Peskin v. Anderson* [2001] 1 BCLC 372; *Sinclair Investments v. Versailles Trade Finance* [2006] 1 BCLC 60; *Halton International Inc (Holding) v. Kaddoura* [2006] 1 BCLC 78, [2006] EWCA Civ 801.
42 See **15.86** below.
43 S. 994(1).
44 S. 996(1).
45 Ss. 112 and 994(1).
46 S. 994(2). It is not enough to be the beneficial owner of the shares.
47 *Lloyd v. Casey* [2002] 1 BCLC 454.
48 *Re Brightview Ltd.* [2004] BCC 671; *Baker v. Potter* [2005] BCC 855.
49 See e.g. *Hawkes v. Cuddy, Re Neath Rugby Ltd* [2007] EWHC 2999 (Ch).
50 S. 994(1).
51 *Gross v. Rackind* [2005] 1 WLR 3505; contrast *Hawkes v. Cuddy, Re Neath Rugby Ltd* [2007] EWHC 2999 (Ch), where the affairs of two interlocking deadlock companies were held to be distinct.
52 *Re J. E. Cade & Son Ltd* [1992] 2 BCLC 213.
53 *Gamlestaden v. Baltic Partners* [2007] BCC 272. In this case the court was considering an application to strike out a petition on the ground that it was obviously hopeless, so it is not a complete guide as to what factors the court may take into account at the final trial.
54 See e.g. *O'Neill v. Phillips* [1999] 1 WLR 1092 (HL).
55 See e.g. *Greenhalgh v. Arderne Cinemas* [1951] Ch. 286, at 292; *Re A Company (No. 001761 of 1986)* [1987] BCLC 141.
56 *Re Blackwood Hodge* [1997] 2 BCLC 650; *Wilkinson v. West Coast Capital* [2005] EWHC 3009 (Ch).
57 *Rock Nominees v. RCO* [2004] 1 BCLC 439; *Re Astec (BSR) plc* [1998] 2 BCLC 556.
58 This is a summary of the leading cases of *Re Saul D. Harrison & Sons plc* [1995] 1 BCLC 14; *O'Neill v. Phillips* [1999] 1 WLR 1092; *Re Guidezone Ltd* [2000] 2 BCLC 321.
59 *Re Chime Corp Ltd* [2004] HKCFA 85.
60 *Re A & B C Chewing Gum* [1975] 1 WLR 579.
61 Contrast *Isaacs v. Benfield* [2006] 2 BCLC 705.
62 Per Hoffmann L.J. in *Re Saul D. Harrison* [1995] 1 BCLC 14.
63 *Re Chime Corp Ltd.* [2004] HKCFA 85, per Lord Scott (sitting as a Judge of the Hong Kong Court of Final Appeal).
64 E.g. *Re Campbell Irvine (Holdings) Ltd* [2007] 1 BCLC 349.
65 E.g. *Re Sam Weller & Sons Ltd* [1990] Ch. 682.
66 E.g. *Nicholas v. Soundcraft Ltd* [1993] BCLC 360.
67 See *Smith v. Ampol* [1974] AC 821; *Re Cumana* (1986) 2 BCC 99,453.
68 See per Oliver L.J. in *Taylor Fashions v. Liverpool Victoria Trustees* [1981] 2 WLR 576.
69 Per Jonathan Parker J. in *Re Guidezone Ltd* [2000] 2 BCLC 321, para. 175.
70 Approved by Lord Wilberforce in *Re Westbourne Galleries* and by Lord Hoffmann in *O'Neill v. Phillips*.

71 Per Lord Wilberforce in *Re Westbourne Galleries*, at p. 380
72 E.g. *Re D R Chemicals Ltd* (1989) 5 BCC 39.
73 E.g. *O'Neill v. Phillips.*
74 E.g. *Re Metropolis Motorcycles Ltd.* [2007] 1 BCLC 520.
75 E.g. per Lord Hoffmann in *O'Neill v. Phillips.*
76 Compare e.g. *Symington's* (1905) 8 F. (Ct of Sess) 121, approved by Lord Wilberforce in the *Westbourne Galleries* case, and *Larvin v. Phoenix* [2003] 1 BCLC 76.
77 See Lord Wilberforce in the *Westbourne Galleries* case.
78 E.g. *Blackmore v. Richardson* [2006] BCC 276.
79 E.g. *Re Regional Airports Ltd* [1999] 2 BCLC 30.
80 *Hawkes v. Cuddy* [2007] EWHC 2999 (Ch); appeal pending to Court of Appeal.
81 Per Lord Hoffmann in *O'Neill v. Phillips*.
82 For older cases, see e.g. *Re German Date Coffee* (1882) 20 Ch. D. 169.
83 E.g. *Blackmore v. Richardson* [2006] BCC 276.
84 E.g. *Re Grandactual Ltd.* [2006] B.C.C. 73.
85 S. 996(1).
86 Per Mummery J in *Re Estate Acquisition and Development Ltd* [1991] BCLC 154.
87 *Re Baltic Real Estate Ltd (No. 2)* [1993] BCLC 503.
88 See *Profinance Trust SA v. Gladstone* [2002] 1 BCLC 141.
89 *Re Campbell Irvine (Holdings) Ltd (No 2)* [2007] 1 BCLC 445.
90 See *North Holdings v. Southern Tropics* [1999] 2 BCLC 625.
91 A recent example is *Hawkes v. Cuddy* [2007] EWHC 2999 (Ch).
92 *Clark v. Cutland* [2003] 2 BCLC 393.
93 *Re Chime Corp Ltd* [2004] HKCFA 85.
94 As to what amounts to a fair offer, see per Lord Hoffmann in *O'Neill v. Phillips*, at pp. 1106–1108; *Fuller v. Cyracuse* [2001] 1 BCLC 187; *CVC v. Demarco* [2002] 2 BCLC 108.
95 *Re A Company (No. 001363 of 1988)* (1989) 5 B.C.C. 18; *Re Copeland & Craddock Ltd* [1997] BCC 294.
96 *Re Martin Coulter* [1988] BCLC 12. Contrast **15.43** above in the case of the unfair prejudice remedy.
97 Insolvency Act 1986, s. 124(2).
98 E.g. *Re a company (No. 001126 of 1992)* [1993] BCC 325.

16

Directors' and officers' liability insurance

Introduction

16.1 This chapter describes the options available to companies to protect their directors against the consequences of becoming embroiled in civil, regulatory or criminal action against them. The principal options involve the purchase of directors' and officers' liability insurance (D&O insurance), a promise to fund their defence of such litigation, and the provision of a qualifying third party liability indemnity under ss. 232–235 of the Companies Act 2006 (the 2006 Act). In practice these options tend to be offered together as a package to directors.

16.2 This chapter explains how D&O insurance works and ends with a check-list of key points. See also **Chapter 17**, which explains the interrelationship between the scope of protection available under D&O insurance policies and typical director indemnity arrangements.

16.3 Note that the scope of D&O insurance policies and corporate indemnities differ case by case, so the language of each must be considered on its own terms and merits.

16.4 One other warning: the word 'claim' is used liberally in the context of liability insurance with two entirely different meanings: sometimes it refers to the legal or other claim brought against the insured person; at other times it refers to the claim that the insured person himself makes under his insurance policy. In an attempt to clarify this, here we capitalise Claim when it refers to the claim *against the insured party*, and use claim with a lower case c when referring to the claim under the policy.

16.5 We start with a background note explaining why directors are exposed to the risk of being sued and to regulatory and criminal charges – risks that lead most directors to expect companies to insure them against. This background summarises points made more fully in **Chapters 14** and **15**. We also:

- explain what cover a typical D&O insurance policy provides and how the policy works;
- introduce the concepts of sides A, B and C cover and refers to typical policy extensions and exclusions (**16.15–16.59**);
- mention other insurance coverages that directors may be able to benefit from (**16.60**); and
- provide a checklist of key D&O insurance issues (**16.65**).

Background – why insure?

16.6 In the UK, civil claims against directors are relatively rare. Those that are brought can be very expensive to pursue, and their success rate is relatively low. Many of the cases that the courts have considered have involved claims arising by reason of the company having become insolvent, where the liquidator has a statutory obligation to consider whether or not the directors have allowed the company to continue trading while insolvent and whether they have otherwise acted in accordance with their duties (see **Chapter 18**); or disputes between joint venture companies between two individuals or groups that have fallen out amid mutual recriminations (often as a result of the company itself failing).

16.7 Nonetheless there is no doubt that directors, especially directors of listed companies, are vulnerable to being sued. The risk may be increased slightly as a result of the lowering of the bar for the pursuit of shareholder derivative claims under Part 11of the Act (see **15.7**).

16.8 Directors and senior executives, at both holding company level and below, are often made personally accountable for corporate as well as personal compliance with laws and regulations. So they also run the risk of regulatory or criminal proceedings if they breach those laws or regulations.

16.9 Increasing corporate governance demands on boards serve to highlight the onus on directors to 'get it right' and the risks to them personally of being perceived to have failed to do so. Factors that increase litigation potential include:

- weak corporate governance controls;
- where the company operates in a regulated environment, such as financial services;
- where the company or its subsidiaries sell technologically advanced products, or ones associated with a perceived health hazard;
- companies in a position to abuse a strong market position;
- a public listing, and especially a listing on a US stock exchange, since US

federal and state securities laws, and litigation procedures, enable shareholders who deal in the company's shares on a US stock exchange rights and a freedom to sue that exceed those generally available elsewhere.

16.10 In the case of UK listed companies the increasing litigation risk for directors was recognised in a review by Sir Derek Higgs (published in January 2003) of the role and effectiveness of non-executive directors. One key point made by Higgs in relation to UK listed companies was that the perceived litigation risk was a deterrent to potential non-executive directors accepting board appointments, and that it was important that if companies' are to recruit high-calibre directors they should be in a position to assure them from the outset that they have in place effective protection against the risk of becoming embroiled in lawsuits that could threaten their personal wealth. For this reason, Higgs was keen to ensure that these protections were addressed as part of a director's recruitment process and in his engagement letter or (in the case of executive directors) service contract.

16.11 The Higgs principles of good corporate governance are now incorporated in the Combined Code on Corporate Governance. Paragraph A.1.5 of the Combined Code provides that companies should 'arrange appropriate insurance cover in respect of legal action against its directors', and enshrines as good practice the principle that appointment letters for directors of listed companies should include information on those arrangements and make a copy of the policy available to the directors (see **Chapter 12**).

16.12 This is important for another reason: in the case of civil proceedings the most likely claimant against a director will be the company itself, whether acting at the initiative of the board itself, or one or more shareholders via a derivative action or, in the case of a company that has become insolvent, at the behest of its liquidator or administrator (see **14.112**). This creates a conflict of interest between the company and the director. That is no time for a director to try to negotiate the terms of an indemnity or other protection! So addressing the potential for future conflict at the outset of the relationship is important for any director, as well as for good practice.

16.13 There are now few, if any, UK listed companies which do not buy D&O insurance for their directors. Many other public and private companies do so too. Section 233 of the 2006 Act empowers companies to buy D&O insurance on behalf of their directors. So current discussion of D&O insurance cover tends to revolve around the limits and scope of its cover rather than on whether it is needed. As the dynamics of the D&O insurance market are volatile, the terms and limits on offer are liable to change year by year.

16.14 By the same token, a relaxation in 2005 of the restrictions governing the scope of what a company can do to indemnify directors, and to fund their defence of actual and threatened litigation, has led to most listed and many other companies entering into indemnity arrangements for the benefit of their directors. This aspect is explained in **Chapter 17**.

D&O insurance – its general nature and scope

Sides A, B and C cover

16.15 A typical D&O insurance policy provides insurance for:

- directors and officers (and often other senior executives) of the insured company or group of companies where they are accused of a wrongful act in civil, regulatory or criminal proceedings, and where the allegations against them relate to their directorial, officer or management functions. This is known as Side A, or management liability, cover, and is explained in more detail at **16.22** below;
- the insured company or group of companies for the cost incurred by the company in indemnifying a director or officer who faces actual or potential litigation in his or her capacity as a director or officer. This is known as Side B, or corporate reimbursement, cover. It is explained in more detail at **16.35** below.

16.16 Some companies also buy so-called Side C cover. This insures the company (or group) against the company's own liability to a civil third party claimant (usually a shareholder or group of shareholders) who bring a claim against the company alleging breach of laws relating to disclosure obligations to shareholders and/or the purchase or sale of the company's publicly listed securities. Side C cover is not really relevant to unlisted companies and is most commonly brought by companies whose securities are listed on a US stock exchange, where the perceived risk is greatest. Side C cover is explained in more detail at **16.42**.

A D&O insurance policy is a claims made policy

16.17 D&O insurance policies are always structured as 'claims made' policies. This means that the policy responds to wrongful act Claims and allegations that are made against an insured director or officer during the policy period, provided that the Claim or threat is promptly notified to the D&O insurers during the policy period, or any available discovery period provided for in the policy. As the cover under a claims made policy is triggered by the notification to insurers of a Claim made against a director or officer during the policy period, it does not matter when the alleged wrongful act occurred. The only proviso occurs in those policies which specifically provide insurers with the protection of a backstop date (a 'retro-inception date'), in which case liability for wrongful acts which are alleged to have occurred before that date will be excluded.

16.18 It is an inherent consequence of a claims made policy that it does *not* cover liability for a wrongful act which was committed during the policy period, but which only come to light after the policy has expired. For this reason D&O insurance needs to be renewed annually in order to provide continuing protection for a director in respect of future Claims for past wrongful acts. For example, a retired director will still be exposed for some years to being sued for mistakes that he is alleged to have made during his time on the board; indeed, he may still owe continuing duties of e.g. confidence after retiring. So, even after retiring, he will need D&O insurance cover to be renewed annually to protect him against ongoing litigation risk.

D&O insurance policy limits

16.19 D&O insurance policy limits will invariably impose an aggregate limit on the amount that can be claimed under the policy during the policy period. That overall limit applies irrespective of both the number of claims made under the policy and of the number of insureds making claims. It is an inherent risk with D&O insurance that the aggregate limit of cover will be insufficient to satisfy in full all the claims made against the insurers during the policy period. In that event, English law does not provide that the insurance money should be allocated pro rata among all valid claimants: rather, in the absence of any contractual agreement to the contrary, the first in the queue scoops the pool. The implications are further discussed at **16.45**.

Some recent policies have offered a small additional aggregate limit of cover. This is designed to provide the directors of listed companies with some defence costs cover to fight a second Claim in circumstances where the main policy cover has been exhausted by a large single Claim. Sometimes that additional cover is limited to non-executive directors, though the logic of that limitation is questionable.

D&O insurance policy wordings

16.20 All insurers writing D&O insurance have their individual wordings. They may have different wordings (or special clauses) for different types of insured according to their perception of the risk involved. The wording offered to a given insured tends to be based on the preferred standard wording of the leading primary insurer. Typically, but not always, the primary policy wording is adopted by any excess layer insurers (even where they would be using a different wording if they were leading the primary layer).

16.21 D&O insurance policy wordings are not straightforward, and by their nature often require bespoke negotiation. While the basic cover offered by insurers of D&O risks is substantially the same, the wording differences between different insurers' policies, and their willingness (or otherwise) to negotiate individually tailored coverage, can make a material difference to the overall cover obtained. As the market itself is relatively volatile in terms of claims experience, and hence pricing, the scope of detailed coverage available is liable to differ from one year to the next according to market conditions. So, reviewing the scope and limits of one's D&O insurance cover annually, obtaining regular expert broking and legal advice on it, can make a real difference. The following paragraphs on what a D&O insurance policy covers, and how it works, are necessarily a generalisation.

Management liability Side A cover

The scope of Side A cover

16.22 This is the main cover provided by a D&O insurance policy directly to directors and officers. Cover is based on providing an indemnity to an insured individual for Loss[1] that he incurs in respect of any Claim made against him during the policy period which alleges a wrongful act by the individual in his capacity as a director or officer. This cover will normally be provided to the insured individual without the individual having to fund any deductible or excess.

16.23 'Loss', 'Claim' and 'wrongful act' will all be defined terms within the policy. Different insurers use subtly different definitions.

16.24 Claim will typically be defined to cover:

- written demands making an allegation of a wrongful act;
- the initiation of civil litigation (including securities Claims) or arbitration proceedings against an insured individual by the company or a third party seeking monetary compensation for an alleged wrongful act;
- the initiation of criminal or regulatory proceedings against an insured individual in respect of an alleged wrongful act;
- the initiation of a regulatory or other formal investigation into the conduct of the insured individual or (sometimes) his company.

16.25 'Loss' definitions commonly:

- cover defence costs incurred with the insurer's prior consent;
- include damages and arbitral awards (including claimant costs and interest);
- allow for insurer-approved compromise payments and settlements to be treated as an insured Loss;

- may extend to multiple damages awards where insurable (as they are under English law);
- exclude criminal and civil fines and penalties, and taxes.

16.26 Some Loss definition wordings leave ambiguous the extent to which the term includes restitutionary and compensatory payment obligations that do not arise from civil damages awards (e.g. wrongful trading orders made by a court under s. 214 of the Insolvency Act 1986).

16.27 'Wrongful act' definitions also vary among insurers (and policies). One leading insurer uses the following definition:

> 'any actual or alleged breach of duty, breach of trust, neglect, misrepresentation, misleading statement, defamatory statement, libel, slander, beach of warrant of authority, act, error, default or omission by an insured person acting in an insured capacity'.

A definition in these terms would, in principle, cover breaches of those director duties which are now codified in Part 10 of the Act.

Who is insured under the Side A cover?

16.28 The cover is typically provided to all past and present directors of the insured company, and to anyone appointed to the board during the policy period, to the company's officers (other than the external auditors) and to other senior executives, but only where the Claim arises from their exercise of managerial or supervisory functions or, in the case of FSA-regulated entities, where they are performing certain FSA Approved Person functions (see Financial Services and Markets Act 2000 s. 59 and FSA Handbook SUP, Chapter 10).

16.29 Where the company is the parent company of a group, it would be normal for the 'company' to be defined to extend to the company's subsidiaries as well as the parent, in order to extend the benefit of the Side A protection to directors, officers, managers and Approved Persons of those subsidiary companies. Note that cover is not normally provided automatically for Wrongful Acts committed by an individual at a time before a company joined the insured group, or after it left the group.

Coverage extensions

16.30 The scope of available coverage extensions tends to vary from one policy to another and according to changing market conditions and trends. Currently, the following extensions are commonly available within the premium quoted for standard cover:

- the cost of fighting extradition and of buying a bail bond where the courts are willing to grant bail against such security (as in the US);
- the cost of resisting a claimant's attempts to attach or sequester the assets of the insured individual and/or his partner;
- the cost of participating in investigations into the affairs of a company in circumstances that may lead to future wrongful act allegations against the insured individual;
- Loss attributable to alleged wrongful employment practice violations;
- outside entity cover extensions: i.e. cover for an insured individual who sits on the board of a non-subsidiary entity (e.g. a joint venture company, or trade body) at the written request of the company. This extension is often subject to a condition that the cover is only excess of any D&O insurance arranged by that outside entity for its own directors;
- a six-year extended reporting period available to retired directors to notify Claims against them during six years after the end of the policy period, but only if D&O insurance cover is not renewed with the same or other insurers at the end of the policy period. The language of this extension is often such as to make its application of very limited practical value unless the company has become insolvent during the policy period.

The concepts of indemnifiable and non-indemnifiable Loss

16.31 All D&O policies distinguish between losses and liabilities of an insured individual that their company could indemnify the individual against, and those losses and liabilities that it cannot by law indemnify him against. The Side A insuring cover clauses of some policies only cover an insured individual in cases of non-indemnifiable Loss. Such policies effectively require the individual to seek indemnity from his company first in circumstances where the Loss is one in respect of which the individual would have a legal right to indemnity from the company. (As a fall-back, such policies usually state that the policy will respond to a claim if the company does not in fact provide an indemnity.)

16.32 Such policies define 'Non-indemnifiable Loss'. However, they tend to do so in very narrow terms which ignore practical constraints on a company's ability or willingness to provide indemnity in practice. Policies which only insure non-indemnifiable Loss also require insured individuals to seek protection from their companies instead of the D&O insurers where their Loss is indemnifiable, rather than giving the individual an equal choice of recovery route. Their language often begs legal questions as to when defence costs, for example, become indemnifiable.

16.33 Policies whose insuring clauses do not limit an insured individual's right to cover to Non-indemnifiable Loss situations are preferable from the point of view of the individual. From the company's standpoint the difference is less material because of the so-called presumptive indemnity clause, which is almost invariably included in D&O insurance policies.

Corporate reimbursement Side B cover

What does this cover provide?

16.34 Side B cover reimburses the company for the cost of satisfying any indemnity promise that the company has made to the insured individual. It applies therefore in circumstances where there has been a wrongful act Claim against an insured individual, and the individual's Loss is one that is insured under the Side A cover provided by the D&O insurance, but the individual has been indemnified in respect of his defence costs and and/or other Loss by the company rather than directly by the D&O insurers.

16.35 Side B cover is always subject to a deductible or retention, which requires the company to bear the first portion of each Loss that it incurs and which would otherwise be insured under Side B cover. Levels of retentions accepted by companies vary widely, reflecting companies' differing risk appetite to accept liability on their own balance sheet and the premium saving involved.

16.36 Side B cover provides a company with additional protection against subrogated and other claims against it from the D&O insurers. When a D&O insurer pays a Side A claim he will assume whatever legal or contractual rights (if any) the individual has to be indemnified for the Loss concerned, including rights against the company of which he was a director. In addition to subrogation rights, which arise as a general matter of insurance law, D&O insurance policies typically give insurers a direct contractual right, via a so-called presumptive indemnity clause, to recover from the company any amounts paid out by the insurers to an insured individual unless the payment is in respect of a non-indemnifiable Loss (see **16.31**) for an explanation of non-indemnifiable Loss.

16.37 Side B cover restricts the amount that the D&O insurers can recover from the company in respect of indemnifiable Loss to the amount of the company's retention: there is no point in the insurers seeking to recover more as the company is insured under the same policy via the Side B cover for the amount that it would otherwise have to reimburse to the insurers.

Risk allocation between the D&O insurers and the company

16.38 There has been a recent trend for some companies not to buy Side B insurance, though the amount of the premium saving achieved may be questionable. Where Side B cover is purchased, the allocation of risk between the company and the D&O insurers is that the buck stops with:

- the D&O insurers for all non-indemnifiable Loss and for indemnifiable Loss excess of the company's Side B retention; and
- the company up to the level of the company's retention, but only in respect of indemnifiable Loss.

16.39 If Side B cover is not purchased, that risk allocation shifts significantly because of the insurers' subrogation and presumptive indemnity clause rights:

- the D&O insurers only bear the ultimate risk if the Loss is non-indemnifiable Loss;
- in all other cases the company bears all the risk.

16.40 From a legal perspective there is a further downside for a company in not purchasing Side B cover, namely that the consequences of the different risk allocation between the company and insurers make it far more likely that there will be a dispute with the insurers as to whether or not a large Loss is indemnifiable (i.e. for the company's account) or non-indemnifiable Loss (i.e. for the D&O insurers' account).

16.41 It should go without saying that any issue between the D&O insurers and the company as to whether an insured individual's rights are indemnifiable or not should not affect the individual's rights to claim on the D&O policy. There is some risk though that a policy whose Side A insuring cover clause only applies to non-indemnifiable Loss may get dragged into such an argument and be left out of pocket in the interim.

Company's security claim Side C cover

16.42 Side C cover insures a company for its own Loss (including defence costs) where the company is sued in a shareholders' securities action. Contrast this with Side B cover, where the Loss for which the company is being indemnified is a Loss of the director or other insured individual for which the company has made him whole.

16.43 While it is possible to bring shareholder actions against a company and/or its directors in the UK (e.g. for misleading statements in a prospectus) and a number of other countries, the main driver for companies to buy Side C cover is the fear of US shareholder class action Claims under US securities laws. In cases brought under the US Federal Securities Act 1933 or the Securities Exchange Act 1934, it is common for the listed company and some or all of its directors to be named as co-defendants. Side C cover recognises the likelihood that the defendant company and directors will have a common interest in fighting the allegations by insuring the liability of all.

16.44 US federal securities legislation only applies to securities traded on a public US exchange; companies without US listing do not carry the same degree of risk. So it is more common (though far from universal) for companies with a US listing to buy Side C cover than for those without a US listing.

16.45 The purchase of Side C cover has one significant drawback from the point of view of insured individuals. Its existence inevitably creates the potential for a conflict of interest between the individuals and the company, who could find themselves competing for a potentially inadequate cover limit. Companies buying Side C cover should consider whether it is appropriate for them to address that potential conflict by providing within the policy that policy claims by individuals will always be settled ahead of company claims if there is a risk of the policy limit being exhausted. The corporate downside of a payment prioritisation clause of this kind is that it leaves the value of Side C cover uncertain, and hence the degree of protection to the corporate balance sheet that Side C cover provides. That uncertainty has led some companies to conclude that the cost of buying Side C cover is not worthwhile.

D&O policy exclusions

16.46 D&O policy exclusions vary in scope and detail, making generalisations dangerous. Common exclusions include Loss attributable to:

(a) Directors' dishonest, fraudulent and criminal conduct (where public policy would probably render the cover unenforceable even in the absence of an exclusion clause), or based on a director making an improper personal profit from his actions. With this exclusion it is important to ensure that:

- the policy will pay defence costs up to the point when the improper conduct is admitted or proved in a court or other tribunal; and
- one individual's improper conduct cannot be attributed to another individual.

Public policy precludes a person from having a right to be indemnified against the financial consequences of his own dishonest or criminal conduct. So insurers may have a right at law to recover from the dishonest director (and, in some policies, the company) advanced defence costs that insurers have paid as a Side A or Side B claim if improper conduct is proved in court or admitted by the individual concerned.

(b) Bodily injury and professional negligence claims. A D&O policy is not designed to protect an executive from negligent errors in the course of his client/customer facing work, but only in his capacity as a director, officer or manager.
(c) Some so-called insured v. insured Claims: i.e. civil claims brought by the company or another insured individual. At worst this can be a very broad exclusion because the most likely person to be suing a director in a civil claim is the company itself. This is the consequence of the rule of English law that (with very few exceptions) a director owes his duties to the company rather than to shareholders, creditors, customers, etc.; it is therefore the company, rather than anyone else, that is damaged by his wrongful acts. However, in practice this exclusion is usually subject to important carve-outs, not least for defence costs. Many policies also currently limit this exclusion to Claims brought by the company or other insured party in North America. So whilst insured v. insured exclusions need to be looked out for with special care, and advice sought on their scope, they are usually not as broad as they at first appear.
(d) Claims brought by large shareholders.
(e) Claims based on prospectus liability (unless specifically negotiated in respect of a particular transaction and, usually, an additional premium is paid).
(f) Pension trustee liability Claims.
(g) Matters that were, or should have been, notified in an earlier policy period, or which were not properly disclosed to insurers when the current policy was negotiated.
(h) Wrongful acts committed before a company joined, or after it left, the group.
(i) Wrongful acts committed after a change of control of the parent insured company.

16.47 Not all D&O policies include all these exclusions. Other policies may include other exclusions not mentioned above. Companies should generally be seeking to limit exclusions to those that are relevant to the business and which are really essential to their insurers' willingness to underwrite the risk.

Other D&O insurance policy points to watch out for

16.48 This section does not attempt to summarise all the residual policy provisions. It does, though, highlight some of the more important practical ones.

Severability

16.49 Most good D&O policies offer a degree of protection to insured individuals against the risk that their cover will be avoided by insurers by reason of a failure by someone else to make fair disclosure of the risk to insurers in the course of negotiating the cover. The optimal position for any individual is that his right to cover should only be prejudicially affected if either he is personally guilty of a deliberate misrepresentation of the risk; or if a notification of a policy claim is made by him or on his behalf outside the policy period (or any applicable discovery period). As this is a crucial protection for insured individuals, and as standard D&O policy wordings do not necessarily provide that optimal protection, legal advice should be taken if there is any uncertainty.

Notification of claims[2]

16.50 As D&O policies are invariably claims made policies (see **16.15** above), it is vital that Claims against an insured party be reported to insurers within the policy period (or any applicable discovery period). Some policies impose a tighter requirement by also making it a condition precedent that the Claim against the insured party be notified to insurers as soon as possible. It may be possible to negotiate arrangements as to which individuals within the company need to have the requisite knowledge before a Claim against the individual has to be notified in order to satisfy that condition precedent.

16.51 Most D&O insurance policies allow notification of circumstances that the company or insured individual reasonably considers could give rise to a future Claim against them, and deem any policy claim based on a notified circumstance to be insured even if the Claim itself against the insured party is only made after the end of the policy period. Careful drafting of any circumstance notification is essential, especially if the policy itself imposes requirements on the level of information required to support a circumstance notification.

16.52 It is important that the policy provision governing the basis on which a circumstance can be notified under the current policy should not be more restrictive than the obligation to disclosure information at the next renewal: otherwise the law may impose on the company and its directors a duty to disclose information about a matter at renewal which leads to cover being excluded for that matter at renewal, whilst the current policy terms preclude that matter from being validly notified as one that could lead to a future Claim, leaving the directors, etc. uninsured for that potential Claim. Some standard D&O policy wordings create that hazard via the restrictive conditions that they impose on notification of circumstances that might lead to future claims.

Defence of third party Claims against insured individuals

16.53 This is a crucial clause as it bears directly on a key purpose of the insurance, namely to provide a fund for the defence and resolution of Claims against directors. It therefore should be considered very carefully, preferably with in-house or external lawyers who would be involved in the handling of the defence of a Claim if one arose. The key thing is to ensure that it is practical and effective from the standpoint of the insured individuals, and provides them, as well as the insurers, with reasonable comfort as to the manner in which a Claim could be defended and, if appropriate, settled.

Allocation

16.54 This is an issue which arises when:

(a) Claims against an insured individual include wrongful act allegations that are covered under the D&O insurance, and other allegations that are not insured under the policy; and/or
(b) a number of parties are facing wrongful act allegations, but one or more of the defendants is not insured under the D&O insurance.

16.55 In both these situations the question will arise as to the extent to which the cost of defending the allegations should be met out of the D&O insurance, particularly where co-defendants share the same defence lawyers.

16.56 The current position of the English courts is that the indemnity should cover all legal costs that reasonably relate to the insured parties' defence of the insured Claim, even if some of that cost has also at the same time benefited the uninsured element of the allegations, or uninsured parties.[3] D&O insurance policies typically seek to water down this principle by requiring coverage payments be allocated on a rather fuzzier basis.

Resolution of policy disputes

16.57 Do you want coverage disputes with insurers resolved through the English courts – a public process – or via confidential arbitration? Such disputes may well involve the washing of dirty linen. If that is a substantial concern, it argues in favour of arbitration. Probably the most effective arbitral body to deal with such disputes, with the most flexible rules, is the London Court of International Arbitration, though there are alternatives. Not all D&O policies provide for arbitration of disputes. A possible clause to ask to have inserted into each policy, to replace any alternative dispute resolution provision that the policy may contain, is:

> 'All disputes arising under, out of or in connection with this policy, including as to its existence or validity, shall be resolved by arbitration in the London Court of International Arbitration (LCIA), whose rules shall be deemed incorporated by reference into this clause. The number of arbitrators shall be [one/three]. The seat or legal place of arbitration shall be England. The language to be used in connection with the arbitral

proceedings shall be English. The arbitrators shall apply the governing law of this policy.

In the event that a substantially similar dispute exists between any Insured and one or more insurer on other layers of insurance underlying or excess of the cover provided by this policy, and such other disputes be resolved in the same LCIA proceedings as those with the Insurer, in which event the same panel of arbitrators shall handle all such disputes in a single arbitration process.'

16.58 It is important to ensure that all co-insurance and excess layer policies contain the same arbitration clause and that a dispute which may affect co-insurers and/or excess layers is capable of being resolved in the same arbitration forum and proceedings.

Other potential insurance coverage for directors

Individual portable D&O policies

16.59 Many listed company directors sit on two or more company boards in an executive or non-executive capacity. One might have thought that it would be more effective for a director in that position to have his own individual D&O insurance policy covering all his directorship and management positions. In practice, that does not happen; whilst individual policies are available in principle, the limits of cover are low and the cost to the individual is high. It is a market that has not developed.

Trustee liability insurance

16.60 It is common for D&O policies to exclude coverage for an individual's loss or liability arising from the operation and management of company (and other) pension schemes. Separate trustee liability policies are available to cover this risk. It is essential that the trustee liability policy and the D&O insurance should dovetail effectively. For instance, if your pension trustee is an incorporated company, are its directors covered for their D&O exposure under the D&O insurance or the trustee liability policy – or neither? If the cover is provided under the trustee liability policy, is their protection as broad, and is the limit of cover as high, as it would be under the D&O insurance policy?

Professional indemnity insurance

16.61 As mentioned in **16.46(b)** above, D&O policies do not normally cover the liability of a senior executive where he is accused of making a mistake in the course of providing non-directorship professional services on behalf of the company to one of its clients or customers. It is the function of professional indemnity insurance to provide that insurance protection. It is far more common for professional negligence claims to be made against the company involved and not against the individual executive or employee who was involved in giving the advice. However, there may be circumstances where a valid Claim could be pursued against the individual as well as, or instead of, the company. A good professional indemnity policy will provide protection for employees as well as the company. The main problems tend to be the high level of deductible or excess required by insurers, and the fact that any such deductible normally applies to Claims against employees as well as to the company.

Prospectus liability insurance

16.62 We have seen (**16.48(e)**) that a normal D&O policy will not automatically protect directors in respect of their personal liability for misstatements in offering circulars and prospectuses on which shareholders are invited to rely in deciding whether to invest (or divest) in an offering of the company's securities, or other transaction which requires the issue of a public circular. Prospectus liability is the main exception to the rule of English law that directors do not owe a duty of care to a company's members.

16.63 While it will often be possible to negotiate (for an additional premium) an extension of a D&O insurance policy to cover the directors' prospectus liability exposure for a particular circular, it may not necessarily be the most prudent course to cover this additional risk. The insurance market offers a tailored prospectus liability insurance policy product. The main advantages of these standalone policies are usually seen to be:

(a) the fact that they offer at least a six-year assured coverage period, thus eliminating the risk that the prospectus liability cover extension cannot be renewed (a real risk if there is a threat of future prospectus liability Claims),
(b) the potentially broader scope of cover and range of insurable persons on offer; and
(c) the fact that the general D&O policy limit is not exposed to erosion by Claims relating to this additional one off prospectus risk.

If the company is considering issuing a prospectus, it is worth taking advice on whether there is an additional risk worth insuring and, if so, what the most suitable policy would be in the circumstances.

16.64 Tax advice should also be taken before purchasing a long-term policy, as the concession in the Income Tax (Earnings & Pensions) Act 2003, s. 346 which exonerates insurance benefits from being treated as taxable benefits in kind in the hands of the director/executive is not available where policies taken out for the benefit of a director have a policy period of two years or more. There may be a policy structuring solution to overcome this problem.

D&O insurance checklist

- Do you check annually that your D&O policy provides the broadest available cover?
- Does your D&O policy limit Side A cover to non-indemnifiable Loss?
- Does the wrongful act definition cover the full range of statutory and common law duties owed by directors?
- Is the definition of insured subsidiaries sufficiently broad to encompass any non-standard structured entities in the group, such as limited liability partnerships and their directors or partners?
- Do you need Side C cover?
- Do you need to provide outside directors with outside directors' cover extension? And do you require directors on outside boards to ensure that the company concerned maintains adequate D&O insurance of its own for all its directors?
- Do you want to include a clause giving directors payment priority ahead of company claims in the event that the aggregate limit may not be enough to satisfy all claims? If so, what should the wording of the clause be?
- Are you satisfied with the way that your D&O insurance programme interrelates with your trustee liability insurance and other insurance covers to avoid unintended cover gaps, and that the terms and limits of cover are adequate for directors of incorporated pension trustee subsidiaries?
- Do your directors have a contractual right of access to the D&O policy, as required by the Combined Code?

Sources

1 In this chapter the word 'Loss' is capitalised where the sense requires it to refer to a loss that is covered within the policy definition of insured loss.
2 On the use of the word 'claim' in different contexts, see **Introduction** above.
3 *Thornton Springer v. NEM Insurance Co Ltd and others* [2000] 2 All ER 489, at paras 224–226. See also the Privy Council case of *New Zealand Forest Products Ltd. v. New Zealand Insurance Co. Ltd* [1997] 1 WLR 1237.

17

Corporate indemnification of directors

Introduction

17.1 In this chapter we explain the typical indemnity arrangements, and the interrelationship between these and the scope of protection available under D&O insurance policies (see **Chapter 16**). This chapter summarises:

- what the Companies Act 2006 does, and does not, allow a company to do by way of funding a director's defence of Claims[1] against him and indemnifying a director against liabilities incurred in the course of his directorship (**17.6–17.14**);
- identifies the main corporate considerations to be borne in mind: articles of association power to indemnify; the form of the indemnity contract; UKLA Listing Rules and UK tax considerations; and public disclosure requirements (**17.15–17.32**);
- offers detailed comments on the issues to be addressed by the board in considering indemnities, and on voting procedures to address the fact of directors' personal interests in the decision (**17.33–17.41**); and
- provides a checklist of issues that should be considered in scoping and approving director indemnity arrangements (**17.43**).

Background

17.2 Many companies now supplement the D&O insurance arrangements that they put in place for their directors' benefit by additionally offering directors an indemnity against liabilities which they incur in the course of their duties and to fund their defence costs.

17.3 This chapter explains what a company incorporated under the Act (or one of its predecessors) can and cannot do under the Act to assist a director by way of funding his liability for paying for his defence of a Claim against him, and indemnifying him against any liability that he incurs as a result of an adverse judgment against him, or any compromise payment that he agrees to make to settle a Claim that he faces. The relevant sections of the Act are ss. 205 (defence costs loan), 232 and 234–235 (director indemnities) and

236–238 (public disclosure). These came into force in October 2007. They substantially re-enact provisions inserted into the Companies Act 1985 with effect from April 2005 by ss. 19 and 20 of the Companies (Audit, Investigations & Community Enterprise) Act 2004. Apart from the position of directors of corporate pension trustee companies mentioned at **17.13–17.14** below, the Act does not make any substantive change to the law from that which has been in effect since 1 April 2005.

17.4 The administrative and procedural requirements that a company must undertake before granting any such indemnity are addressed at **17.33–17.41** below.

17.5 The restrictions in the Act apply to indemnities provided to directors of companies incorporated under the Act or any of its predecessors. The Act does not restrict the scope of any indemnity that may be offered to:

(i) employees and other individuals who are not directors of UK companies in the group; or
(ii) directors of non-UK companies. However, in this case, the UK Listing Rules impose a broader restriction covering directors of all companies in the group where the holding company has its primary listing on the London Stock Exchange (see **17.22** below).

What the Act permits by way of a director indemnity

Defence costs

17.6 By virtue of s. 205 of the 2006 Act, a company is now allowed to lend money to a director to finance his legal and other costs involved in defending himself against any civil regulatory or criminal proceedings brought against him alleging breach of duty, breach of trust or negligence in relation to the company or any associated company.[2] The loan may also cover the cost of an application for relief from liability under s. 661(3) or (4) or s. 1157 of the 2006 Act. The funding must be by way of a loan because the Act requires that in some circumstances when the director is found to have acted in breach of duty, or where is convicted of a criminal offence, he must repay what the company has funded on his behalf.

17.7 The Act requires the funding arrangement to be such that, subject to two exceptions, the loan involved is repayable immediately in the event that the final outcome of the proceedings is that the director is not exonerated. There are two exceptions to the statutory requirement that the director must repay a company loan if he is not exonerated of wrongdoing, namely if the director is found guilty in a third party civil action (i.e. one not brought by or on behalf of the company or any of its UK-incorporated associated companies), and a regulatory proceeding against him. In these two exceptional cases, the company has a discretion as to whether or not to indemnify a director for his defence costs and (if so) whether to do so via a loan or direct indemnity arrangement.

17.8 In a case where the director is exonerated of wrongdoing, or is not otherwise required by the Act and the company to repay the loan, it may be written off by way of indemnity, unless the indemnity contract itself provides otherwise. The obligation to impose a contingent repayment obligation necessitates the loan arrangement being documented in a formal contract.

17.9 Often the primary source of funds for the fulfilment of the director's loan repayment obligation will be the D&O insurance policy involved. So it is important to ensure that the D&O insurance policy provides expressly that the insurers will repay the director's loan in any circumstance in which the insurers would been required to indemnify the director for his defence costs if the director had requested that indemnity rather than borrowing money from the company. In many cases a director may be better advised to look to his D&O insurers to fund his defence rather than borrowing from the company, as no loan is involved as between the director and insurers, and the only circumstance in which insurers can recover defence costs that they have paid on the director's behalf is if the director is convicted of, or admits, deliberately dishonest or criminal behaviour.

Other liabilities (QTPIPs)

17.10 Section 234 of the 2006 Act allows a company incorporated under the Act or any of its predecessors to provide a director of the company or of any of its UK associated companies (i.e. other UK-incorporated companies in the same group) with an indemnity against certain liabilities via a qualifying third party indemnity provision (QTPIP). Any broader indemnity to a director is rendered void by virtue of the Act.

17.11 A QTPIP permits a company to indemnify a director against any liability that he may incur (in any capacity) in connection with any negligence, default, breach of duty or breach of trust in relation to the company of which he is a director or any associated company if, but only if, the liability arose out of third party civil proceedings. A QTPIP cannot provide the director with an indemnity in respect of a liability:

(i) owed to the company or any of its UK associated companies, as that would render the remedy obtained by the company in the breach of duty proceedings against the director valueless, and so would be contrary to public policy; or

(ii) imposed in criminal or regulatory proceedings by way of a fine or penalty for wrongdoing. In the case of FSA fines, this is supplemented by a specific regulatory prohibition under the Financial Services & Markets Act 2000.

17.12 Any indemnity provided in respect of liabilities mentioned in (i) or (ii) is rendered void by s. 232(2) of the 2006 Act. Section 232(1) makes void any provision which purports to exempt a director from any liability that would otherwise attach to him in connection with his negligence, default, breach of duty or breach of trust in relation to the company.

Indemnification of directors of pension trustee companies (QPSIPs)

17.13 Section 235 of the 2006 Act, a new provision, allows a company to provide a slightly wider form of indemnity (a so-called qualifying pension scheme indemnity provision, or QPSIP) to directors of a UK-incorporated pension trustee company in the group than that described above. The additional protection that may be offered to a director of such a company is an indemnity that extends to the costs of an unsuccessful defence of civil and regulatory (but not criminal) proceedings against a pensions trustee company director.

17.14 Pension schemes often already include a company indemnity in favour of trustees and directors of corporate pension scheme companies. So it will not always be clear what, if any, additional QPSIP comfort is required or appropriate, or which company in a group should give QPSIP indemnity. Advice should be taken on a case-by-case basis.

Corporate considerations

Indemnification powers in articles of association

17.15 As a decision to grant an indemnity contract to a director, and/or to lend him money to fund his defence, involves a fiduciary relationship between the company and the director(s) concerned, it is necessary for the board to be given the express power to do so within the company's articles of association. The same applies to the purchase of D&O insurance for the company's directors.

17.16 An example of a suitable indemnity and insurance article is as follows:

> 'As far as the legislation allows, the Company may:
> (i) indemnify any director of the Company (or of an associated body corporate) against any liability;
> (ii) indemnify a director of a company that is a trustee of an occupational pension scheme for employees (or former employees) of the

Company (or of an associated body corporate) against liability incurred in connection with the company's activities as trustee of the scheme;

(iii) purchase and maintain insurance against any liability for any director referred to in (i) or (ii) above; and

(iv) provide any such director with funds (whether by way of loan or otherwise) to meet expenditure incurred or to be incurred by him in defending any criminal, regulatory or civil proceedings or in connection with an application for relief (or to enable any such director to avoid incurring such expenditure).

The powers given by this article shall not limit any general powers of the Company to grant indemnities, purchase and maintain insurance or provide funds (whether by way of loan or otherwise) to any person in connection with any legal or regulatory proceedings or applications for relief.'

17.17 Neither the Association of British Insurers nor the National Association of Pension Funds has issued any guidance as to their expectation of the form of indemnity articles. The only guidance they have issued which affects the scope of indemnity contracts comes indirectly via a recent joint statement on executive contracts and severance (see **17.34** below).

The form of the indemnity contract

17.18 Any indemnity will need to be documented by contract, as will any defence costs loan arrangement. It has been held by the courts that directors cannot rely on an indemnification provision in the company's articles of association, even where the article expresses the directors' indemnity rights in mandatory form (i.e. 'the directors shall be indemnified ...').[3] That is because the articles constitute a contract between the company and its members, not between the company and its directors. A director's right to be indemnified therefore derives from his contractual relationship with the company.

17.19 In any case the requirements of the Act governing what type of indemnification qualifies as a QTPIP or QPSIP, and the requirements in s. 205 of the 2006 Act regarding permissible funding and required repayment arrangements, are such that carefully drafted indemnity deed and loan contract agreements are essential if the corporate purpose is to be achieved and risk of their being unenforceable is to be avoided.

17.20 Indemnity contracts can be effected by deed or by deed poll. In cases where the company wishes all directors to have the automatic benefit of a similar form of indemnity on appointment, the easiest way of implementing the indemnity arrangement may be by way of deed poll. The main advantage of a deed poll is that it is only executed once, and protects automatically everyone who falls within the scope of the definition of beneficiary to whom it is intended to apply. Thus it removes the need to prepare and negotiate individual contracts with each beneficiary. The use of a deed poll does not fetter the board's discretion to change indemnification arrangements prospectively at any time.

17.21 The checklist (**17.42**) sets out a non-exhaustive list of provisions that companies may want to consider incorporating into an indemnity deed or deed poll (not all those provisions will be appropriate in all cases).

UKLA Listing Rules considerations

17.22 Whilst the Act itself only regulates the scope of permissible indemnities for directors of UK-incorporated companies, for companies with a primary listing on the London Stock Exchange the Listing Rules effectively extend the application of the Act to all non-UK companies in the group and their directors.

17.23 This comes about because an indemnity contract between any company in the listed group, and any director of any such company, is a related party transaction for the purpose of the Listing Rules (see Listing Rules, Chapter 11). Related party transactions are class 1 transactions which require prior public shareholder approval before they can be effected, unless one of the limited exemptions set out in the Appendix to chapter 11 of the Listing Rules applies. The principal relevant exemption relates to director indemnity contracts, but this applies only where the scope of the indemnity is no broader than would be permitted under the 2006 Act.

17.24 UK listed companies with non-UK subsidiaries therefore need to be careful to monitor the scope of any indemnity proposed to be granted by their non-UK subsidiaries to ensure that they do not require prior public shareholder approval that has not been granted.

UK tax considerations

17.25 Neither the cost of the premium paid by the company for D&O insurance for the benefit of directors or employees, nor claim payments made under a D&O insurance, normally constitute taxable benefits in their hands under English law (Income Tax (Earnings & Pensions) Act 2003, ss. 346–349), provided the policy is for less than two years.

17.26 The grant of an indefinite indemnity to a director or employee is not in itself a taxable benefit. However, benefits received under it may be taxable in the hands of the individual. That applies to both indemnity payments made to or on behalf of a director and to any beneficial loan arrangements where the interest charged on the loan is less than the Official Rate from time to time prescribed under s. 178 of the Finance Act 1989.

17.27 The taxable nature of benefits derived by a director or employee from an indemnity therefore raises the question of whether the company should gross up indemnity payments, or whether the director should be expected to meet his tax liability on the benefits himself. In practice most companies who consider the point do agree to gross up.

17.28 Consideration should be given in appropriate cases to possible non-UK tax implications.

Disclosure requirements

17.29 Section 236 of the 2006 Act requires disclosure of the existence of QTPIPs and QPSIPs from which any director of the company benefits. That disclosure must be made in the directors' report and must make reference to any qualifying indemnity which was in force at the date when the directors' report was approved or during the financial year to which the directors' report refers. Typical language for such disclosure might be in the following form:

> 'The Company has entered into qualifying third party indemnity arrangements for the benefit of [all its directors or X] in a form and scope which comply with the requirements of the Companies Act 2006.'

17.30 Where a company has given a qualifying indemnity for the benefit of a director of an associated company disclosure is required in the directors' reports of both the company granting the indemnity and of the associated company involved.

17.31 In addition, under ss. 237 and 238 of the 2006 Act, the company is required to keep available for inspection a copy of every QTPIP and QPSIP in force whose existence it is required to disclose in its directors' report (or a memorandum setting out its terms). The copy or memorandum must be made available at the company's registered office or, if it is not kept at the registered office, at another location notified to the Registrar of Companies under s. 1136 of the 2006 Act. Note that a failure to notify the Registrar of a different location at which the indemnity is available for inspection is an offence. Members of the company are entitled to inspect the qualifying indemnity or the memorandum setting out its terms without charge and (on payment of a prescribed fee) to be provided with a copy.

Ratification of director negligence

17.32 Section 239 of the 2006 Act allows a company to ratify a director's or former director's negligent conduct and his breach of duty. Ratification requires either a shareholder resolution or the unanimous consent of all the company's members. The votes of the director and of persons connected with him are not to be counted in determining whether the requisite majority of votes has been obtained at a shareholder meeting.

Board approval and voting considerations

Board approval considerations

17.33 Any decision taken by the board to offer some or all of its members indemnification against liabilities incurred in the course of their duties in relation to the company or any associated company is a decision that must be taken by the board in good faith and with a view to promoting the company's success.

17.34 The Act specifies matters that can and cannot be the subject matter of an indemnity granted by a UK company to one of its directors, or to a director of one of its associated companies. It does not automatically follow that, because a QTPIP or QPSIP is permitted by the Act, it is necessarily beneficial to the company's success to grant such an indemnity against a liability to a third party. The ABI and the NAPF have, for example, issued a joint statement on executive contracts and severance issued on 18 February 2008. This states (para. 3.4) that, in negotiating employment contract terms, 'boards should consider and avoid the reputational risk of being obliged to make large payments to executives who have failed to perform'. It is therefore important that any board considers the particular circumstances that apply to it in deciding the scope of any indemnity that it is appropriate to offer, and any limitations or conditions that it may be proper to impose on any such QTPIP or QPSIP.

17.35 For the director(s) due to benefit from an indemnity there is a clear conflict of interest. That conflict is all the more obvious where it is proposed that all directors should benefit. That conflict makes it important that the decisions taken should be objectively justifiable. That means that the relevant key issues should be set out clearly in a written briefing paper to the board, and that the board's reasoning, and the process by which the decision was reached, are clearly recorded in the board minutes. In addition, the formalities of compliance with the requirements of the company's articles must be observed which deal with attendance and voting on matters in which a director has a personal interest (see **17.38**).

17.36 The board briefing paper should, at a minimum:

(i) summarise in reasonable detail the key terms of the proposed indemnity, and their rationale;
(ii) explain the reasoning as to why it would promote the company's success to offer an indemnity in the form proposed to the director(s) concerned. If the indemnity is intended to extend to cover any liability of a director arising out of a breach of a duty owed by the director to a third party, it is particularly important to explain the rationale for that proposal and any conditions, limitations and other protections built into the indemnity to protect the company from abusive calls on the indemnity;
(iii) provide any available information to the board about whether the proposed indemnity is in line with arrangements effected by the company's pier group;
(iv) explain the public disclosure requirements (see **17.29** above);
(v) refer to the interrelationship between the proposed indemnity and the company's D&O insurance arrangements;
(vi) refer to whatever professional advice has been obtained and any shareholder or other consultation undertaken, and confirm that the board has the power to enter into the proposed arrangements under the company's articles; and
(vii) explain the proposed voting process.

17.37 Depending on individual circumstances, there may be other factors that will be relevant to the board's consideration and which should be mentioned in the board paper.

Board voting and conflict of interest disclosure issues

17.38 The article in the company's articles of association which deals with voting on matters in which a director has a conflict of interest should be considered and followed carefully. Check:

- what the articles and s. 177[4] require by way of formal disclosure to the board of the nature of his personal interest before the indemnity arrangements are to be discussed;
- whether the director is aware of particular circumstances that might lead to him making a claim on the indemnity, if granted to him;
- whether a director is allowed to attend the part of any board meeting which is considering a matter in which he has a personal interest and, if so, whether he is allowed to participate in the discussion; and
- whether the director is allowed to vote on a contract between him and the company where the contract may involve lending money to the director, indemnifying him against liability to third parties and/or arranging insurance for the director's benefit.

17.39 In addressing conflict disclosure to the board by a director to whom an indemnity is to be offered, that director should disclose not only the obvious fact that he would be a party to the contract with the company, but also the separate question of whether he is aware of any circumstances that could involve him in expense or other liability that would be covered by the indemnity, if granted to him. If so, the nature of those circumstances also needs to be openly disclosed to the board. Directors should have that requirement drawn to their attention so that they make a positive or negative statement as to the existence of matters known to them which could lead to a call on their indemnity. Any such disclosure should be clearly minuted.

17.40 The conflict of interest issue becomes more problematic if the board is to be faced with a proposal to grant indemnities to all its members. It is very unlikely to be possible under the terms of the company's articles for the board as a whole to vote itself indemnities in these circumstances; and even if this is technically permissible under the company's articles, it is not consistent with sound corporate governance.

17.41 The appropriate solution will depend on the facts of the individual case. One possibility may be to split the decision into two: one under which the executive members of the board consider and vote on an indemnity for the chairman and non-executive directors, with the non-executive directors absenting themselves from the discussion and taking no part in the vote; and a second separate resolution involving only the non-executive directors in which they consider the proposal to grant indemnities to the executive directors on the board and any other officer or employee who it is suggested should benefit from an indemnity.

17.42 The minutes of the meeting should be drawn up in a way that identifies:

- all required personal interest disclosures in a form complying with the requirements of the company's articles of association, including the positive or negative statement as to the existence of matters known to them which could lead to a call on their indemnity;
- the number of resolutions involved (e.g. whether there were separate resolutions to consider indemnities to executive and non-executive directors), who participated in the discussion on each resolution, and who absented themselves from the discussion on each resolution;
- any important points raised by any director in discussion;
- the resolution actually considered, the outcome of the vote and who voted;
- any follow-up action required as a result of the discussion and voting.

17.43 This section flags up some key points to bear in mind when considering the scope of a director's indemnity. As decisions taken on issues mentioned in this checklist have a number of ramifications, legal advice should be taken on the structuring and terms of proposed indemnity arrangements.

Director indemnification checklist

1 Has the board got the power to grant the indemnity? Check the director indemnity and lending powers in the memorandum and articles.

2 Who should benefit from an indemnity:

- (i) Just directors of the holding company?
- (ii) In what capacities should individuals be indemnified: just as a director? also as an employee? also as a director of subsidiary companies? also as a director representing the company on outside boards?
- (iii) Should subsidiary company directors be indemnified, even though the risk that they run is different, and if so, which company in the group should indemnify them? (Note the potential for non-UK laws/tax to be relevant if non-UK subsidiaries or non-UK resident directors are involved).
- (iv) Should already retired directors be offered an indemnity?
- (v) Should non-director officers and senior executives, e.g. the company secretary; heads of internal audit and/or legal affairs; FSA-authorised persons, be offered indemnities and, if so, in what form? (Note that s. 232 of the Act does not restrict the scope of indemnities that can be offered to individuals who are not directors).
- (vi) How broad an indemnity will it be appropriate to offer that is consistent with the directors' duty to promote the company's success? That question is particularly relevant *vis-à-vis* any liability for a proven breach of a duty owed to a third party.

3 What should be the scope of the indemnity? Does it cover:

- (i) Defence costs in civil, regulatory and criminal proceedings. If so, have you got a s. 205-compliant loan agreement in place, and will you require a loan arrangement where the Act provides discretion to a company on whether or not to require repayment of defence costs)? (See **17.6**.)
- (ii) Extradition avoidance and bail bond funding costs?
- (iii) Costs involved in seeking relief from liability under s. 1157 of the 2006 Act, and costs of appealing against an adverse judgment? If so, is it subject to suitable protections for the company against the possibility of having to fund an unmeritorious appeal or application?
- (iv) Contribution proceedings brought by or against a director in respect of a liability shared jointly with the company or someone else?
- (v) Third party civil liability and third party Claim settlements/compro-

mises; and, if so, is the company's obligation subject to any good faith, honesty or other condition?

4 What, if any, carve-outs or limitations should the company impose on the individual's right to indemnity? Options include:
   (i) where indemnity is prohibited by law (essential for a valid QTPIP/QPSIP);
   (ii) matters which the individual improperly failed to disclose to the board at the time when the indemnity was offered to him;
   (iii) where the claimant is a non-UK company in the group, and so not an 'associated company' within the meaning of the Act;
   (iv) where the individual has not acted in good faith, or has acted wilfully or recklessly (or some other formulation);
   (v) for costs incurred, or settlements effected, without the company's prior consent (but with a carve-out where the company is the claimant);
   (vi) appeal and relief from liability costs where the appeal or relief application is unlikely to succeed;
   (vii) costs of defending disqualification proceedings under the Company Directors Disqualification Act 1986;
   (viii) a monetary cap.

5 Other possible provisions to include:
   (i) tax gross-up;
   (ii) requirement for the individual to keep the company informed of Claims and (where required) to co-operate with the company in their defence;
   (iii) requirement for the individual to comply with the D&O insurance policy terms;
   (iv) assignment to the company of the individual's rights under the D&O insurance policy and/or policy proceeds;
   (v) company promise to maintain D&O insurance cover for the individual indefinitely after he leaves the company;
   (vi) right for the individual to take independent legal advice at the company's expense where a conflict arises;
   (vii) right of access to relevant company documents to assist the individual's defence;
   (viii) LCIA arbitration of disputes.

6 What procedures do the articles require for the approval of indemnities given the director's conflict of interest?

7 Is there an advantage in constituting the indemnity by way of a deed poll?

8 Do the indemnification and D&O insurance policy arrangements tie together effectively?

9 What information needs to be included in the directors' report to comply with the disclosure obligations in s. 236 of the 2006 Act?

10 Will the details of the indemnity arrangement be maintained at the company's registered office and, if not, has the requisite notification been made to the Registrar of Companies of the location where they are available for inspection?
11 Do your directors have a contractual right of access to the D&O policy, as required by the Combined Code?

The interrelation between D&O insurance and director indemnities

17.44 An explanation of the way in which a typical D&O insurance policy and director indemnity interrelate in terms of the scope of protection that each offers is best illustrated by way of a Venn diagram:

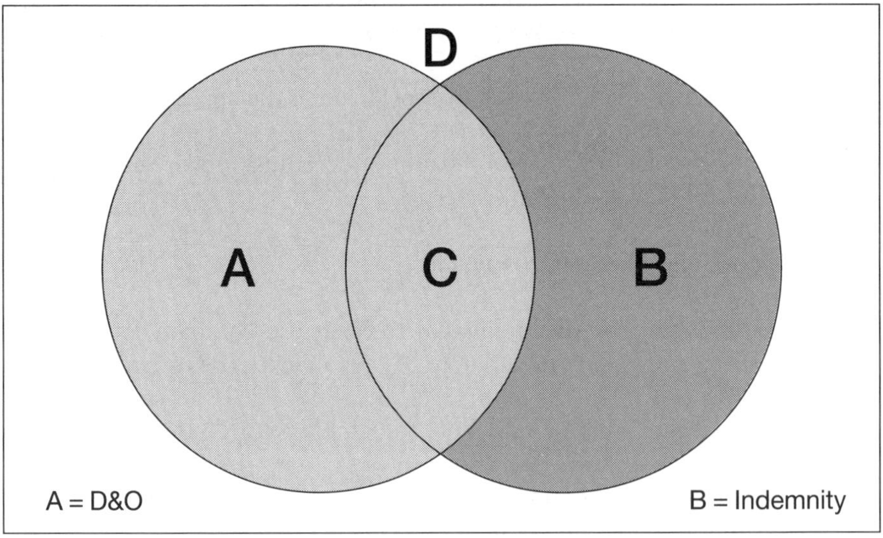

What only a D&O insurance policy can do for you

17.45 Only the D&O insurance policy (circle A) can provide protection in the form of:

(i) defence costs cover (civil, regulatory and criminal proceedings), with no repayment risk in the event of the director or officer[5] being held to have acted wrongfully unless the director or officer is found to have acted dishonestly or fraudulently;
(ii) cover for director's liability to the company or an associated company, subject to any limitations within the insured v. insured exclusion. The Act precludes a company from providing a director with indemnity protection in respect of liability to the company itself. A combination of (i) and (ii) means that, speaking in general terms, a D&O insurance policy can

provide a broader range of indemnity protection than a company indemnity can do;

(iii) a source of indemnity protection that is independent of the company; thus removing the conflict problems that arise when the company is involved in the Claim against the director/officer;

(iv) a source of indemnity that is available to respond even if the company has become insolvent (rendering any corporate indemnity valueless).

17.46 But a D&O insurance policy will be subject to policy exclusions and an aggregate policy limit which do not appear in typical indemnity arrangements, and a D&O policy is subject to an annual renewal and renegotiation process.

What only an indemnity contract with the company can do for you

17.47 Only an indemnity agreement (circle B) can, subject to its terms, provide protection in the form of:

(i) an uncapped indemnity;

(ii) no policy exclusions (though most indemnities do include a number of conditions);

(iii) no insurer payment refusal/default/insolvency risk;

(iv) a long-term indemnity assurance, which is not subject to annual renegotiation, and thus to the risk of change or cancellation.

17.48 But restrictions imposed by the Act on the scope that is permitted by way of indemnification to a director means that an indemnity contract for a director is likely to be more limited in its scope, and that defence costs are often only available as incurred on the basis of a loan: one which would potentially have to be repaid if the director's defence fails.

17.49 By means of Side B cover the D&O insurance can also protect the company in respect of amounts paid by the company under any indemnity agreement to or on behalf of the director or officer to meet the individual's liabilities (so long as the liability of the individual concerned is not excluded by the terms of the policy).

What both a D&O insurance policy and a company indemnity can do for you

17.50 Both a D&O insurance policy and a corporate indemnity have the ability to provide protection for directors and officers against:

(i) liability arising from civil proceedings brought against the individual by third parties (i.e. by parties other than the company or an associated company); and

(ii) defence costs payments for which the director or officer is entitled to be indemnified, e.g. by reason of his being exonerated from wrongdoing. However, in the case of a company indemnity to a director, unlike the D&O insurance protection, this protection is, in most cases, only available once the outcome of the proceedings is known and is dependent on a successful outcome.

What neither a D&O insurance policy nor a company indemnity can do for you

17.51 By reason of a combination of general legal constraints imposed as a matter of public policy, statutory and regulatory provisions, and D&O insurance policy terms, neither a D&O insurance policy nor a corporate indemnity will provide a director or officer with indemnity protection against:

(i) liability arising by reason of the director's dishonest, fraudulent or criminal conduct;
(ii) criminal fines or regulatory penalties.

Sources

1 The word 'claim' arises liberally in the context of liability insurance with two entirely different meanings: sometimes it refers to the legal or other claim brought against the insured person; at other times it refers to the claim that the insured person himself makes under his insurance policy. This chapter capitalises Claim, when it refers to the claim against the insured party, and uses claim (with a small c) when referring to the claim under the policy
2 'Associated company' is defined in s. 256(b) the 2006 Act. In effect, any company incorporated under that Act or any of its predecessors and which is a holding company or subsidiary of the company is an associated company. The term is used in that defined meaning in this chapter. It should be noted that companies in a group which are not incorporated in the United Kingdom are not associated companies for the purposes of the definition, and the provisions of the 2006 Act dealing with director liabilities and indemnities do not apply to those companies (subject to the comments above regarding the application of UK Listing Rules to all subsidiaries of a UK listed company).
3 *Globalink Telecoms Ltd v. Wilmbury* (2002) BCC 958.
4 Section 177 came into force on 1 October 2008. Before that s. 317 of the Companies Act 1985 applies.
5 In this section references to an 'officer' include any senior executive insured under a D&O insurance policy whilst acting in a management or supervisory capacity.

18

Duties of directors of a company facing insolvency

Introduction

18.1 This chapter looks at the duties directors have when the company is in financial difficulty and the possibility of insolvency arises. There comes a point in the deterioration of a company's financial position where the interests of shareholders become secondary to the interests of creditors. The key questions that arise in this context are exactly when a director needs to consider the additional duties that arise for the directors of a company facing insolvency, what these duties require and to whom they are owed. The context in which these issues are most commonly considered is after a company has been placed into a formal insolvency procedure and the insolvency professional put in charge of that process reviews the actions of directors in the period leading up to that event. It is therefore necessary to consider three stages:

1 when a company becomes insolvent;
2 when a company enters into a formal insolvency procedure; and
3 the period between these stages.

The tests for insolvency

18.2 To determine when a company becomes insolvent, one must look to how the courts determine whether a company is insolvent at any given point in time. The key definition of insolvency is set out in s. 122 of the Insolvency Act 1986 (IA 1986) as a ground for the court to order the liquidation of the company: 'the company is unable to pay its debts'. This is commonly divided into two separate tests, though it is not always necessary for both to be satisfied for a company to be considered insolvent. The two tests are the cash-flow test and the balance sheet test.

The cash-flow test

18.3 A company is cash-flow insolvent if it is unable to pay its debts as they fall due.

This test is set out in s. 123 of IA 1986 and is reasonably self-explanatory.

The only question that sometimes arises is how far into the future directors should look when seeking to ascertain whether the company will be unable to pay its debts as they fall due. Construing this test to involve looking far into the future blurs the line between this and the balance sheet test, but to interpret it in a way that would not include a large debt due in a few weeks' time would clearly be unrealistic. The court has recently considered this question in the context of a contract that defined an 'Insolvency Event' as a determination by a receiver that the company was, or was about to become, unable to pay its debts: effectively the cash-flow test. The court held that when assessing whether a company is unable to pay debts as they fall due, it is possible to take into account known future events, even where these would not occur for more than a year.[1] The nature of future events that can be taken into account and how far into the future will be highly fact-sensitive and the circumstances in which a company will be held to be cash-flow insolvent because of future events as far as a year away are likely to be very rare. In this case the company was an investment vehicle that had future liabilities and a pool of assets both of which were fixed. As the company had no ability to trade and improve its position, it was possible to say with certainty that it would not be able to pay its debts beyond a certain point. In most cases no such certainty will exist and a trading company is entitled to make reasonable assumptions as to its ability to improve its financial position over a longer period.[2]

The balance sheet test

18.4 A company is balance sheet insolvent if its liabilities exceed the value of its assets.

18.5 While the value of the company's assets and liabilities shown in its accounts will be the starting point for applying this test, if there are reasonable grounds to look at other evidence it may not be determinative and the court will consider all the evidence. In the case of a company dealing in assets whose value is very volatile, such as financial instruments, the court may take the view that any valuation of the company's assets needed to be made with a wider view than the value on any particular day.

18.6 In the context of wrongful and fraudulent trading (see **18.39–18.70** below) the test applied as to whether a company was insolvent at its liquidation includes the costs of the liquidation as a liability of the company, though this is rarely likely to be determinative.

Formal insolvency procedures

18.7 A full description of the insolvency procedures available to a company and its creditors is beyond the scope of this chapter. However, before discussing the role of the directors in the period before insolvency, it is necessary to outline what constitutes formal insolvency and the forms it may take. A company formally becomes insolvent when it enters into an insolvency procedure either at its own instigation or on the action of a creditor. There are four forms of formal insolvency for English companies:

(a) voluntary arrangements with creditors;
(b) receivership;
(c) administration;
(d) liquidation (or winding up).

Voluntary arrangements

18.8 A voluntary arrangement can simply be a renegotiation of contracts between a company and its creditors in order to allow a company that has a viable business to continue trading where its debt burden may otherwise drive it into insolvency. There are also statutory schemes under Part 1 of IA 1986 and s. 895 of the Companies Act 2006 (the 2006 Act) that involve the appointment of a nominee or supervisor to oversee such arrangements.

Receivership

18.9 Receivership was once the most common form of insolvency procedure and involves the appointment of a receiver by a creditor to take control of the company's assets, or a part of them, pursuant to a contractual right of security. The most common situation in this context is for a bank to appoint a receiver under a loan agreement giving it this power if the company is in breach of the terms of that agreement. A receiver may be appointed to take control of either a class of assets that the company has offered as security for the loan or, where the company has granted a 'floating charge', all its assets, in which case the receiver will be an administrative receiver. Where an administrative receiver is appointed by a creditor, no administrator can be appointed without that creditor's consent. Receivership is no longer common however as, under the Enterprise Act 2002,[3] the holder of a floating charge created on or after 15 September 2003 cannot appoint an administrative receiver other than in limited circumstances, mostly relating to capital markets transactions or project finance agreements.

Administration

18.10 Administration involves the appointment of an administrator to take control of the company from the directors, while at the same time imposing a moratorium on creditors enforcing their rights against the company. The purpose of administration is to allow the company to survive and its business to be revived, or otherwise to enable a better outcome for its creditors than if it was simply liquidated. Where the company itself will not survive, administration may therefore be appropriate where a business can be sold as a going concern and this would lead to a greater value being available to the company's creditors than simply selling its assets. Since the Enterprise Act 2002 came into force, it has become easier for either the company itself or a creditor holding a floating charge to appoint an administrator and it is no longer necessary to involve the court. The court can still appoint an administrator upon the application of any creditor, the company or its directors, where a company is insolvent or is likely to become so and the court is satisfied that the administration is likely to achieve its aims of reviving the company or giving a better outcome to the creditors than a liquidation.

Liquidation

18.11 Liquidation is the default option for insolvent companies in England. It involves the appointment of a liquidator to take control of the company's assets and to distribute them to creditors and, if sufficient, to members. A liquidation can either be voluntary, by way of a shareholders' resolution to dissolve the company, or compulsory, where the company is insolvent and a creditor petitions the court for its winding up. Where a company is insolvent and the members vote for a liquidation, there must also be a meeting of creditors to agree the identity of the liquidator to be appointed. The appointment of a liquidator does not prevent secured creditors from enforcing their security against the assets of the company.

The twilight period

18.12 Of these four formal insolvency procedures, it is the latter two that form the backdrop for the issues discussed in this chapter. This is because a voluntary arrangement between a company and its creditors is a contractual arrangement (though in some cases requiring the consent of the court), which does not give rise to a formal examination of the directors' conduct in the preceding period and receivership is now increasingly uncommon. When a company goes into administration or liquidation, the role of the directors in managing the company is effectively at an end. It is therefore not the period of formal insolvency itself that is relevant as much as the period before it. This is sometimes referred to as the 'twilight period'. The directors' conduct in this period may be considered to determine whether they have breached their fiduciary duties, whether certain transactions can be undone as preferences or transactions at an undervalue and, most seriously for the directors, whether they have engaged in wrongful or fraudulent trading.

18.13 The point at which the twilight period ends is easily identifiable as when:

(a) a petition is presented to the court for the liquidation or administration of the company;
(b) a notice of appointment or intent to appoint an administrator is filed at court where the appointment is made out of court; or
(c) a resolution is passed by the company's members to wind the company up, if the liquidation is voluntary.

18.14 The twilight period begins for most purposes when the company becomes insolvent, though for wrongful trading it begins when the director in question should have concluded that there was no reasonable prospect of the company avoiding insolvent liquidation. This may occur before the company actually becomes insolvent for the first time.

Recent developments and the Companies Act 2006

18.15 The majority of the duties imposed on the directors of companies facing insolvency arise under IA 1986 and not under Companies Act 2006 (the 2006 Act). The newly codified duties set out in ss. 171–177 of the 2006 Act are owed solely to the company. No new rights of action accrue to creditors from these provisions and nothing in them enables creditors to sue directors directly for breaches of duty. In this respect, the 2006 Act has less of an impact on this area of directors' responsibilities than elsewhere. The new Act acknowledges this at s. 172(3), where the new duty to promote the success of the company set out in s. 172 is expressly made subject to:

> 'any enactment or rule of law requiring directors, in certain circumstances, to consider or act in the interests of creditors of the company'.[4]

18.16 This effectively preserves the existing body of law relating to the twilight period when a company is either insolvent or facing insolvency and the interests of the creditors take precedence over those of the members. The rationale behind this long-standing principle is that if a company is insolvent, the equity in it has been expended and the members have no further interest in it, whereas the creditors' contractual rights against the company remain intact. In this context it is clear that the new duties set out in the 2006 Act to consider, for example, the likely consequences of any decision in the long term (s. 172(1)(a)) or the need to foster the company's relations with suppliers and customers (s 172(1)(c)), will effectively fall away where the company's financial situation is such that the directors should properly be considering the interests of the company's creditors.

Impact on directors' conduct

18.17 It is possible that, as court decisions start to shape the application of these new provisions, some of the newly codified directors' duties may be relevant to some of the considerations of directors' conduct in the twilight period. A liquidator bringing an action against a director for breach of fiduciary duty, for example, will be able to compare the director's conduct against the factors set out in s. 172(1) that the director should have regard to in considering how best to promote the success of the company. The duty of directors to have regard to the likely consequences of any decision in the long term and to foster the company's business relationships with suppliers and customers may be relevant when assessing the director's conduct. Essentially, there is nothing new here, however, and the courts have always looked at such factors when assessing a director's liability for breach of duty. The courts have also historically been very wary of second-guessing the commercial judgement of directors where there is no indication of improper motive.

18.18 There has been much discussion of the extent to which the codification of the factors which directors must consider in their decision-making requires additional recording and minuting of such consideration. This subject is dealt with in more detail in **Chapter 5**, but in the context of insolvency directors have long been advised that the more precarious a company's financial situation, the more important it is to keep records of the information available to the directors and the reasons for the decisions taken. This will include consideration of the interests of creditors where there is any chance of the company becoming insolvent.

18.19 The following sections examine some of the circumstances commonly considered in the context of a corporate insolvency. Many of these revolve around the powers of insolvency practitioners to unwind transactions that the company has entered into in the twilight period, though the definition of this varies depending on the particular statutory provision that is being relied on. For the directors of a company potentially facing insolvency, it is necessary to know what duties are imposed on them in such circumstances and how the courts will assess their actions should they later be called into question by a liquidator or administrator.

Personal guarantees

Introduction

18.20 It is common for directors, particularly those of smaller companies, to be required by lenders to the company to provide personal guarantees of the company's debts. In this way banks and other lenders can get comfort that the limited liability status of the company is not being used by the directors to enable them to run a business without financial consequences for them should it not succeed. Whenever a company enters into a transaction that involves a personal guarantee by a director, including the repayment of a debt guaranteed by a director, that director will need to declare an interest in the transaction before it is entered into in accordance with ss. 177 and 182 of the 2006 Act (see **Chapter 5**).

Personal guarantees and insolvency

18.21 Should the company be unable to pay its debts to the lender as they fall due, the lender will be entitled to call on the director to pay instead. Under English law there is no requirement for the lender to take steps to seek payment from the company first, such as taking legal action or awaiting the outcome of any insolvency process. Where a company is in a formal insolvency process such as administration or liquidation, the lender will be able to submit a claim against the company while simultaneously claiming from the director under the guarantee. Only where an amount is ultimately paid out from the insolvent company to the lender that leads to the lender having recovered more than it was owed by the company will the lender then have to account to the director who has paid under the guarantee for the excess.

18.22 A director who has paid a lender to the company under a personal guarantee is entitled to claim back from the company what he has paid in its place. Where the company is insolvent, the director will simply be an unsecured creditor of the company and his claim against the company will rank alongside all other creditors such as trade suppliers. Where there are funds available to be distributed to unsecured creditors in the liquidation, but these are insufficient to pay them in full, each creditor will be paid the same percentage of what he is owed. A director who has personally guaranteed certain debts of the company and has paid out under such a guarantee may therefore ultimately recover a proportion of what he has paid in the liquidation.

Treatment of guaranteed creditors in the twilight period

18.23 When a company's financial situation starts to look precarious, it is natural that any directors who have given personal guarantees of the company's debt will start to consider their personal exposure should the company become insolvent. Great care is needed in such situations, because the fact that a director has given a personal guarantee does not alter his duties to the company and its creditors in any way. Wherever a company enters into administration or insolvent liquidation, any director who has given personal guarantees can expect the administrator or liquidator to pay careful attention to how the creditor whose debt was guaranteed was treated in the twilight period.

18.24 Any repayment of a debt that was guaranteed by a director may be void as a preference under s. 239 of IA 1986 if it is shown that it was influenced by a desire to put the director in question in a better position in the event of the company's insolvency. A director's relationship with the company obviously makes him a connected party and this has the effect of creating an assumption that such a desire existed. It will be for the director to show that the transaction was not motivated by such a desire and this will not usually be easy to prove. More is said about preferences at **18.91** below.

18.25 The repayment of a guaranteed debt when the company faces the prospect of insolvency may also call into question a director's conduct in relation to his fiduciary duties to the company. Unless the repayment of the debt is commercially sensible for the company at that time, for example because the creditor has additional security that needs to be released to enable an asset to be sold,[5] it is unlikely to be considered bona fide. If the court finds that the director put his own interests first to the detriment of the company or its creditors as a whole, he may be liable for breach of fiduciary duty or for entering into a transaction defrauding creditors (see **18.102** below). A director who acts in his own interests in such a situation is very likely to be disqualified from acting as a director. The disqualification of directors is dealt with in more detail in **Chapter 19**.

Misfeasance or breach of fiduciary duty

Are fiduciary duties owed to creditors?

18.26 As discussed in **Chapter 5**, directors owe fiduciary duties, now predominantly set out in the 2006 Act, to the company at all times. The company in this context is distinct from its shareholders and its creditors, and any action against a director for a breach of those duties or for misfeasance such as negligence must be brought by the company (see **Chapter 15**). It is an important principle of English company law, however, that when a company is insolvent, or in danger of becoming so, directors must take account of the interests of its creditors. This is expressly recognised in s. 172(3), where it makes clear that the duties owed by a director to the company are subject to 'any enactment or rule of law requiring directors, in certain circumstances, to consider or act in the interests of creditors of the company'.

18.27 Defining the circumstances in which the law requires directors to consider or act in the interests of creditors is not always easy. In recent years, the courts have considered the application of directors' fiduciary duties in the context of insolvency and, more specifically, whether such duties are owed to creditors. The result is that it is now clear that directors owe fiduciary duties to creditors when a company is insolvent. This is because once a company is insolvent, its assets effectively belong to its creditors rather than its shareholders and it is therefore the interests of the creditors that the directors must consider when dealing with the company's assets.

Ratifying breaches of duty

18.28 In the usual case of a breach of fiduciary duties by a director, it is possible for the shareholders to ratify the actions of that director by ordinary resolution. However, where the shareholders no longer have any interest in the company due to its insolvency, it is obviously illogical that the shareholders should have the power to ratify an act in breach of the director's fiduciary duties owed to the company's creditors. There is no direct authority of an English court on this point, but it has been considered by the Australian courts and held that a breach of duty owed to creditors could not be ratified by the company's shareholders.[6] This has been considered and approved by the English court[7] and should be considered to be the legal position in England as well.

When do duties start to be owed to creditors?

18.29 The position when a company is insolvent is therefore reasonably clear. The interests of creditors supersede those of the shareholders and the director's duties become owed to the creditors as well as the company. The situation is more complex when one considers whether a director owes fiduciary duties to creditors before the company is actually insolvent, but when such insolvency becomes a possibility. The fortunes of most companies that become insolvent do not change overnight. Instead, there is a gradual worsening of the financial position. This makes the identification of a point in time when directors should start considering the interests of creditors very difficult in practice. The courts have held that it is not necessary for a company to be insolvent before duties are owed to creditors, in a case where the company was 'in a very dangerous financial position' and requiring refinancing arrangements in order to survive.[8] While drawing a definitive line in this area is impossible, therefore, it is sensible to assume that wherever a company faces a possibility of insolvency that is anything other than remote, the directors should consider the interest of creditors in any transaction they approve. Directors who ignore the interest of creditors may be subject to claims of misfeasance or breach of fiduciary duty by an administrator or liquidator at a later date.

The applicable standard

18.30 The key fiduciary duty that a director will owe to creditors will be the duty under s. 174 to exercise due care and skill in fulfilling his functions. The standard is set by reference to both an objective and a subjective test. The objective level of competence is that expected of a person carrying out the functions carried out by that director, while the subjective level considers the actual experience and skills that the director in question has. The applicable standard will be the higher of the objective and subjective tests, meaning that while no director will be excused for conduct falling below reasonable expectations for someone carrying out that role, the more experienced and skilled a director is, the higher the standard by which his behaviour will be judged. In the case of listed companies, the Combined Code on Corporate Governance provides further detail on what is expected of directors in particular roles (see **Appendix 1** and also **Chapter 12**).

Transactions that might constitute a breach of fiduciary duty

18.31 It is common that in company group structures where the whole group faces financial difficulty the different companies in the group will become insolvent at different points in time. It is in such situations that transactions are often entered into that potentially breach the fiduciary duties of the directors. Any transaction that is entered into for the benefit of another company in the group (and therefore to the detriment of the contracting company) is likely to be in breach of fiduciary duty. If both companies later become insolvent, the creditors of the company that acted to its own detriment in order to assist another group company will have been denied recourse to assets they should rightfully have. In such a case the creditors are not able to bring an action against the directors themselves, but an insolvency practitioner could bring an action against the directors for breach of fiduciary duty, as well as applying to set aside such transactions as having been at an undervalue (see **18.71** below).

18.32 There may be circumstances where directors can legitimately allow the company to enter into a transaction for the benefit of another company in the group, such as making an unsecured loan to ease its cash flow. However, the circumstances in which this will not be a breach of fiduciary duty are very narrow. It is necessary that:

(a) there is an objectively justifiable benefit for the company giving the assistance so as to make the transaction commercially rational. This will in practice always be the interdependency of the companies giving and receiving the assistance, so that if the beneficiary company becomes insolvent it will inevitably lead to the collapse of the company offering the assistance; and
(b) there is a real prospect that, by entering into the transaction, the insolvency of both companies might be avoided. This will require there to be circumstances leading to a justifiable conclusion that the financial circumstances of the group may shortly be revived and are not merely unrealistic optimism.

18.33 In the absence of circumstances such as these, a director who authorises the use of company assets to benefit a separate company can expect a claim by an administrator or liquidator for breach of fiduciary duty. Even in these circumstances it is likely that an insolvency practitioner would seek to attack the transaction for having been at an undervalue, with potential consequences for the directors involved (see **18.34–18.35**). It is imperative, therefore, that directors at all times consider the company for which they act as a separate and distinct legal entity. However closely knitted the management of a group of companies may be, they remain separate entities and the creditors of one are entitled not to see its assets diverted to another.

The consequences of misfeasance or breach of fiduciary duty

18.34 The 2006 Act does not set out the remedies for misfeasance or breach of a director's duties but states at s. 178 that a breach of the duties set out in ss. 171–177 will have the same consequences as under the common law for breach of the previous corresponding duties. Where the court finds that a director has breached his fiduciary duties or is guilty of misfeasance, it may order the director to pay damages or compensation, or to contribute personally to the assets of the company in order to rectify the consequences of the breach. The court has a very broad discretion and will consider all the circumstances of each case in deciding the extent of the director's culpability. The amount that a director may have to pay if found guilty of misfeasance or breach of fiduciary duty may exceed the loss he caused to the company as he may have to pay interest and legal costs as well as making good the original loss.

Court examination of director

18.35 As well as the ability to bring an ordinary action for breach of fiduciary duty or misfeasance, s. 212 of IA 1986 provides a summary remedy in such circumstances for the use of liquidators, but also creditors and those required to contribute to the assets of the company. This provision does not create any separate form of liability, but entitles the applicant to summon an officer of the company to be examined before the court as to his conduct. Upon the application of a liquidator or creditor under this provision, the court may conduct an examination of the actions of the director in the manner of a summary trial and, if it finds him in breach of any fiduciary or other duty in relation to the company, can order him to contribute an amount to the company's assets in compensation of this misfeasance or breach of duty in an amount to be decided by the court.

Duty to co-operate with insolvency practitioner

18.36 It should also be noted that in the context of an administration or liquidation of a company, any director or former director of the company is in any event under a duty to cooperate with the liquidator or administrator under s. 235 of IA 1986. This imposes a duty to provide such information about the company and its affairs as that insolvency practitioner may reasonably require. Directors and former directors are also under an obligation to attend meetings with such insolvency practitioner as he reasonably requires. Administrators and liquidators further have the power to apply to the court to summon a director or former director to appear before the court and answer questions relating to his dealings with the company. The court can also order that any books, papers or other records in his possession be produced to the court at such a hearing. The court is then empowered, under s. 236 of IA 1986, to require the director to submit an affidavit to the court containing an account of his involvement in the matter specified in the application. This gives a liquidator or administrator a very broad power to obtain evidence from the director as to his actions where misfeasance or breach of fiduciary duty is suspected. Failure to appear in response to such a summons can lead to a warrant for the director's arrest under s. 236(5) of IA 1986, while failure to answer questions during the examination is a contempt of court, which is punishable by imprisonment. The powers of insolvency practitioners to obtain evidence from directors as to events in the twilight period are therefore formidable.

Court discretion to relieve directors of liability

18.37 Where a director is found to have breached his fiduciary duties the court has discretion under s. 1157 of the 2006 Act to relieve him of liability to the extent it sees fit if it finds that he acted honestly and reasonably and ought fairly to be excused from liability in all the circumstances. This restates the position under the Companies Act 1985.

Disqualification

18.38 Beyond the possibility of being ordered to contribute personally to the company's assets, any director found to have committed a misfeasance or breach of fiduciary duty will almost inevitably be the subject of an order disqualifying him from acting as a company director. The Company Directors Disqualification Act 1986 lists 'any misfeasance or breach of any fiduciary or other duty by the director in relation to the company' as the first matter to be considered in determining the unfitness of a director.[9] A disqualification order can prevent the director from acting as a company director for up to 15 years.

Wrongful trading

18.39 In simple terms, wrongful trading is to continue to trade when there is no reasonable prospect that a company will avoid insolvent liquidation. Where a company enters into a formal insolvency procedure, the conduct of the company's directors in the period preceding that insolvency can be scrutinised by the liquidator or administrator. If it is concluded that any director did not comply with their duties so as to be guilty of wrongful trading, that director can be held liable to make a contribution to the company's assets at the discretion of the court.

The test for wrongful trading

18.40 Under s. 214 of IA 1986, a director or shadow director of a company may be held liable to make a contribution to the company's assets if:

(a) the company has gone into insolvent liquidation;
(b) at some time before the commencement of the winding up of the company the director or shadow director knew, or ought to have concluded, that there was no reasonable prospect that the company would avoid going into insolvent liquidation; and
(c) the court is not satisfied that the director took every step with a view to minimising the potential loss to the company's creditors as he ought to have taken from the moment he knew, or ought to have concluded, that insolvent liquidation was inevitable.

18.41 In deciding whether a director is guilty of wrongful trading, the court therefore looks to two tests: (1) when the director should have concluded that there was no reasonable prospect that the company would avoid liquidation; and (2) whether he took every step to minimise potential loss to creditors after that point. The assessment of the director's conduct for each of these tests is both objective and subjective. The objective part is that the director is assumed to have had the general knowledge, skill and experience that may reasonably be expected of a person carrying out the functions that he carried out in relation to the company. This sets a minimum objective standard for a director's competency. The subjective part allows the standard to be raised, but not lowered, to reflect the actual knowledge, skill and experience that the director in question has. This is the same as the test in s. 174 of the 2006 Act.

18.42 In practice, this dual objective–subjective test means that a director's inability to recognise that insolvency of the company was unavoidable, or his inability to determine all the steps necessary to minimise the potential loss to creditors, is no defence to an accusation of wrongful trading if the court believes that a higher standard could reasonably be expected of a person carrying out that director's role. However, where a director does have a high level of experience, relevant professional qualifications or other particular skills, his conduct will be judged with this in mind. A typical scenario is where a company director is, for example, a chartered accountant, and the court therefore expects a greater level of understanding of the company's accounts than would otherwise be the case.[10]

The first test: when should the director have concluded insolvency was inevitable?

18.43 In the case of every company that ends up in insolvent liquidation there will have come a moment when the directors realised, or should have realised, that the company would ultimately face insolvent liquidation. The longer the period between this moment and the commencement of an insolvency procedure such as administration or liquidation, the more likely it is that an allegation of wrongful trading will be made. In seeking a declaration of wrongful trading from the court, the liquidator will need to show the date of this moment, usually by reference to the information available to the director in question and the conclusions that he should have drawn from it.

18.44 The court will consider the financial prospects of the relevant company over a period of time preceding the insolvent liquidation and what should reasonably have been expected by the director, applying the objective and subjective tests referred to above. Judges are generally reluctant to decide, with the benefit of hindsight, that a given decision of the director fell below the requisite standard if it was a genuine commercial decision that was reasonable in the circumstances. The conduct of business necessarily involves risk. Directors are not expected to be clairvoyant and the mere fact that a company is trading at a loss in a given period is not sufficient to show that there was no reasonable prospect of avoiding insolvent liquidation at that time. The question of whether a company is insolvent is a different question from whether it will inevitably face insolvent liquidation.[11] Whether a director should have concluded that insolvent liquidation was inevitable does not depend on a snapshot of the company's financial position at any given time, but on the rational expectations of what the future might hold.[12] If a company was balance sheet insolvent and trading at a loss at the relevant time, however, a director would need to show evidence of grounds for a reasonable belief at that time that the company faced a brighter future. These might include fairly advanced arrangements for a further injection of equity capital, a predicted increase in income as the company became more established or the payment of a particularly significant receivable, such as on the forthcoming completion of a contract. It could also include plans to sell the business or parts of it that would restore the company to solvency.

The second test: did the director take 'every step' to minimise potential losses to creditors?

18.45 The second test is to establish whether a director has a defence to a charge of wrongful trading if, under the first test, it has been established that he knew or should have known that there was no reasonable prospect of the company escaping insolvent liquidation and allowed the company to continue to trade. The only defence available is set out at s. 214(3) of IA 1986 and sets a very high threshold. The director must show that he took 'every step' that he ought to have taken with a view to minimising the loss to the company's creditors. The drafting of the Act in this respect is deliberate and intended to afford a defence only to those who have acted with the highest level of care and diligence. Indeed, the wording of this section was debated in the House of Lords before the Act was passed and a proposed amendment that the wording read 'all **reasonable** steps' was rejected.

18.46 In order to avail himself of this defence, therefore, a director has the burden of proving that he took every possible step to minimise the risk of loss to creditors. In practice this will be extremely difficult to prove if the court has already concluded that the director should have foreseen that insolvent liquidation was inevitable and the company did not cease to trade immediately, though it will depend entirely on the circumstances. There may be situations where a delay to the liquidation of the company will allow the realisation of receipts that would not be possible if it ceased to trade. Continuing to trade to enable the sale of the business or a part of it as a going concern might also be justifiable where this will reduce the shortfall in what is available to creditors. It should be noted, however, that continued trading in order to realise the highest value from the company's assets is the purpose of administration and in these circumstances there is little incentive for a director to impose on himself the burden of later proving that he took every step to minimise loss to creditors. Once a director realises that insolvent liquidation is inevitable, he should seek the appointment of a liquidator or administrator as soon as possible. It is perhaps for this reason that the majority of cases brought for wrongful trading turn on the question of the director's assessment of when insolvent liquidation became unavoidable, rather than whether the defence of having taken all reasonable steps is made out.

Avoiding wrongful trading

18.47 The steps that a director must take to ensure that he does not become liable for wrongful trading fall into two categories: steps to ensure that he becomes aware of any likelihood of insolvent liquidation at the earliest possible stage and steps he must take as soon as that appears to be a realistic possibility. These are considered in turn.

Awareness

18.48 The most important steps that any director can take to avoid the risk of being held liable for wrongful trading are to keep himself well appraised of the company's financial position and to act on that information. Directors need to:

1 ensure that adequate financial records are kept and that they are complete and up to date;
2 monitor key financial indicators such as turnover, profitability, cash reserves, cash-flow forecasts and positions with creditors, even if this is outside the scope of the director's immediate duties;

3 be wary of any delay in producing either management accounts or statutory accounts and make appropriate enquiries if there appears to be any information missing relating to the financial performance and balance sheet position of the company;
4 consider information outside the company's accounts in order to ascertain the best possible picture of the company's financial health and business prospects;
5 look out for obvious danger signs such as a fall in turnover, an increase in short-term trade debt, receivables remaining outstanding for longer than normal periods and overexposure to the credit of a small number of customers; and
6 investigate the circumstances of any situation in which the company's creditors take steps such as threatening proceedings or engaging debt collection agencies.

If insolvent liquidation appears possible

18.49 As soon as anything in the financial or other day-to-day business information raises any prospect of the company having financial difficulties, a director must bear in mind the possibility of his conduct later being tested in the context of an allegation of wrongful trading. In this context the following steps should be taken:

1 ensure that the fullest possible picture of the company's financial situation is available to the board, if necessary requiring special reports from relevant staff to set out the situation in full;
2 identify the terms of any covenants in loan agreements or major supply agreements that the company may breach due to its financial position and seek legal advice on this;
3 raise any concerns as to the company's financial viability, either short term or long term, as soon as possible and ensure that it is minuted at the next board meeting. If a board meeting is not scheduled in the near future, the director should call an extraordinary board meeting at which to discuss his concerns;
4 if other directors disagree, or seek to downplay the risk for reasons that do not satisfy the director in question, he must ensure that his view is recorded, even if he is in a minority of one;
5 seek external, independent advice from an accounting or insolvency professional. This will enable the director to put the company's performance and financial situation in context with advice from someone with experience of similar situations and thereby better be able to judge the seriousness of the situation;
6 if the company's prospects depend on the outlook for a certain market, seek external professional advice on market conditions and forecasts; and

7 consider the prospects of selling the business or a part of it if the best outcome for creditors might be the solvent liquidation of the company after the sale of its business.

18.50 It may be that, having taken these steps, the only logical conclusion is that the company cannot escape insolvent liquidation, in which case the only proper step a director can take is to table a motion that the company cease to trade with immediate effect or call in an insolvency professional. It is difficult to see that any other steps will satisfy the second test of s. 214 of IA 1986, unless trading is continued in order to sell the business as a going concern and thereby maximise the return to creditors in a subsequent liquidation. This should ordinarily be done through placing the company under the protection of administration.

18.51 In many cases, the situation will not be so clear-cut and the directors will be placed in the unenviable position of having to decide whether to pull the plug or attempt to trade out of the difficulties. Ceasing to trade too early may lead to claims that the director put his personal interests above those of the company, though a claim for breach of his fiduciary duties would be unlikely to succeed where the company was insolvent, as the collective body of shareholders effectively has no further interest in the company and the directors' duties are to the creditors. Nonetheless, criticism will undoubtedly be levelled at a director who is felt to throw in the towel too early. Trade creditors will often believe that continued trading would have allowed them to be paid (and the problems passed on to later creditors), while all creditors will see any repayment reduced by the substantial costs of liquidation. On the other hand, bravely deciding to attempt a turnaround of the company may later be seen as foolhardiness and the director accused of wrongful trading.

Continuing to trade

18.52 While the greatest of care is needed in these situations, the courts have at least recognised that it is not desirable for directors simply to place a company into liquidation at the first sign of financial difficulty out of fear of personal liability.[13] If, having considered all the relevant information at board level, it is decided to continue to trade, a director should consider the following steps:

1 Record the reasons in full in the board minutes and establish a formal turnaround plan with input from external accountants.
2 Create cash-flow forecasts that will enable the performance of the company to be constantly measured against the turnaround plan and for the decision to continue to trade to be revisited in the event of any failure to meet those targets.

3 Inform creditors such as banks and major suppliers and seek their support for the recovery plan.
4 Consult an insolvency practitioner as to the realistic prospects of the business surviving under the recovery plan, ensuring that such an adviser has prompt and full access to the company's records as the basis of his advice, which should be in writing.
5 Ensure board meetings are held regularly to consider the position of the company and continually assess its prospects.
6 Consider placing deposits by new customers into a trust account held completely separately from the other accounts of the company and given a suitable name to ensure that its purpose is clear. This will enable these customers to be repaid in full if the company goes into insolvent liquidation before they receive what they have ordered and avoids the possibility of the directors later being accused of continuing to trade at the risk of new creditors.
7 If the purpose of continuing to trade is to preserve the value of a business or assets that can be sold, ensure that this intention is recorded and a time limit put on efforts to find a buyer and negotiate the sale. However, it is likely that in this situation it will be far more sensible to place the company into administration than to continue to trade without this protection.

Resignation

18.53 Faced with responsibility for a failing company and the difficult decision of whether there is a reasonable prospect of avoiding liquidation by continuing to trade, it is perhaps unsurprising that resignation crosses the minds of many directors. This is particularly the case where there is disagreement among directors of the company as to whether the company's fortunes can be turned around. Resignation from the board will not necessarily release a director from his duties, however[14] and s. 214 of IA 1986 expressly applies to any person 'who is **or has been** a director'. A director who faces disagreement from his fellow directors over his assessment of the company's ability to avoid insolvent liquidation is less likely to face criticism by the court, and ultimately liability for wrongful trading, if he remains in post and seeks to persuade the board to take appropriate steps. In such a position the director should seek independent advice from both a lawyer and an accountant.

The consequences of wrongful trading

Order to make financial contribution

18.54 Wrongful trading is not a criminal offence and the liability attaching to a finding of wrongful trading is limited to being ordered to make a financial contribution to compensate creditors. The court has a wide discretion to determine the amount of such liability, but it is important to note that it will be determined by the loss caused by the director's conduct and will not simply be the whole of the shortfall in the company's assets as against its debts. It has been established that the purpose of an order under s. 214 is compensatory rather than penal and that the amount should generally relate to the amount by which the company's assets have been reduced due to the director's conduct.[15] The shortfall caused by the director's conduct may, for example, be the total of the company's debts outstanding that were accrued after the point at which the court decides that a reasonable director would have concluded there was no hope of avoiding insolvent liquidation.[16] Following this rationale, recent decisions of the courts have suggested that cases of wrongful trading should not be pursued against directors unless the company was in a worse position at liquidation than it would have been had it been liquidated at the point in time that the liquidator contends it should.[17]

Disqualification

18.55 Where an order is made that a director is guilty of wrongful trading, the court can impose a disqualification order preventing the director from acting as a company director for up to 15 years, even if no separate application has been made for a disqualification order.[18] The disqualification of directors is discussed in **Chapter 19**.

Companies Act 2006, s. 1157

18.56 As discussed in the context of misfeasance or breach of fiduciary duty at **18.37**, s. 1157 provides that the court has the power to relieve an officer of a company, including directors, of liability for negligence, default, breach of duty or breach of trust where, having regard to all the circumstances of the case, he ought fairly to be excused. This restates the position in CA 1985. This is a broad discretionary power, but it has been held that it is not applicable to actions against directors for wrongful trading, as the test set out in s. 214 of the Insolvency Act 1986 is purposefully more stringent than to behave reasonably in all the circumstances.[19]

Fraudulent trading

18.57 Unlike wrongful trading, fraudulent trading is both a civil and a criminal offence. The scope of fraudulent trading is in some ways wider than wrongful trading, covering every person who is knowingly a party to the fraudulent trading and conduct that will defraud not just creditors of the company but anyone. Civil actions against directors or other parties for fraudulent trading are less common than actions for wrongful trading, however, because of the requirement for an intention to defraud in order for liability to be established. Indeed, the offence of wrongful trading was introduced because fraudulent trading is so difficult to prove. It is perhaps for this reason that some cases brought for wrongful trading involve abuses of the company by a director that might arguably constitute fraudulent trading.[20]

Criminal liability

18.58 Under s. 993 of the 2006 Act:

> 'If any business of a company is carried on with intent to defraud creditors of the company or creditors of any other person, or for any fraudulent purpose, every person who is knowingly a party to the carrying on of the business in that manner commits an offence.'

18.59 The criminal liability can be established at any time and does not require the business to be in liquidation. The test for liability is subjective and requires proof that the defendant was dishonest, meaning that there was either an intent to defraud or a reckless indifference whether or not people were defrauded. The fact that criminal liability attaches to anyone 'knowingly a party' to the fraudulent trading makes clear that the offence is not limited to directors.

18.60 The criminal penalties for fraudulent trading depend on whether the conviction is summary or on indictment. On a summary conviction a person is liable to up to 12 months' imprisonment in England or Wales, (six months in Scotland or Northern Ireland) and/or a fine. On conviction on indictment, a person guilty of fraudulent trading is liable to a term of imprisonment of up to ten years and/or a fine. This period of imprisonment has been raised from the previous seven-year limit under CA 1985. It should be noted that fraudulent trading is taken very seriously by the courts and these limits are for each count of such behaviour. Where a director has been involved in the carrying on of business by a number of companies with the necessary intent to defraud, separate terms of imprisonment can be imposed in respect of each company, to run consecutively should the judge think it appropriate.[21] A charge of fraudulent trading has also been used by the authorities in cases where companies have been used to defraud HM Revenue & Customs, but the person responsible is domiciled in a country that will not extradite people for fiscal offences. Such countries will extradite people charged with fraudulent trading pursuant to the 2006 Act.[22]

18.61 Where a company is in liquidation and it appears that a person is liable for fraudulent trading under s. 993, the court can impose a disqualification order preventing the director from acting as a company director for up to 15 years, even where the person has not been convicted of this offence and no separate application has been made for a disqualification order.[23] The disqualification of directors is dealt with in more detail in **Chapter 19**.

Civil liability

18.62 Civil liability for fraudulent trading arises under s. 213 of IA 1986. This provides that:

'1 If in the course of the winding up of a company, it appears that any business of the company has been carried on with intent to defraud creditors of the company or creditors of any other person, or for any fraudulent purpose, the following has effect
2 The court on the application of the liquidator may declare that any persons who were knowingly parties to the carrying on of the business in the manner mentioned above are to be liable to make such contributions (if any) to the company's assets as the court thinks proper.'

Other than the requirement that the company be in liquidation, the test for fraudulent trading under IA 1986 is the same as that under the 2006 Act. This includes that intent is proved to the criminal standard. The three key elements of the offence are therefore that:

1 the business has been carried on;
2 with intent to defraud; and
3 the accused person was knowingly a party to that carrying on of the business for fraudulent purposes.

18.63 There is no period within which the fraudulent trading has to have occurred and it is not necessary that insolvent liquidation was in prospect at the time.

Carrying on a business

18.64 The requirement for carrying on of business does not mean that the company has to be actively trading. The collection of assets or Crown revenue can constitute fraudulent trading.[24] However, a company cannot be treated as carrying on business for the purpose of s. 213 of IA 1986 once a winding up petition has been presented against it, on which a winding up order is subsequently made. The only exception to this is if the business of the company continued after the making of the winding up order on the instructions of the liquidator or with his consent.[25] Where a company is dissolved but subsequently restored to the register and in the interim its assets are dealt with by its former officers, it is open to the court to hold that the company has carried on business with intent to defraud creditors if the conduct would fulfil this criterion but for the dissolution.[26] The fraudulent trading does not have to be the dominant purpose for which the business was conducted, nor does there have to be a continuous course of fraudulent conduct. While individual examples of frauds on customers are perhaps unlikely to be held to constitute fraudulent trading, there have been examples where a single significant transaction has been held to be sufficient.[27]

Intent to defraud

18.65 The courts have interpreted this requirement broadly and with some flexibility. There must be an element of dishonesty, though not necessarily an intention to cause harm to the victim of the fraud. Deliberately and dishonestly exposing them to risk is sufficient. For a transaction to be intentionally fraudulent it is not necessary that there be an intent never to perform, i.e. supply the goods, pay the amount due or provide the services in question. It is enough if the person in question knows that these things will not be done at the time that had been promised and knows that this may disadvantage the other party.[28] In reality, the court is very unlikely to find fraudulent trading where the promise was made in the knowledge that performance would be slightly late and that this would inconvenience the counterparty. Knowledge that performance would not be possible until substantially later and that this might cause real loss to the other party may be sufficient however, even where there is no intent to cause that loss.[29] A common situation in which this question arises is when a company already in financial difficulty borrows more funds in order to continue to trade. This illustrates the line between wrongful and fraudulent trading. If the directors lack real belief that the borrowed amount will be repaid substantially in accordance with the terms of the loan, this is likely to constitute fraudulent trading. If they honestly believe that such repayment will be made, but it is later found that this was an unreasonable belief in the circumstances and the company was already doomed to insolvent liquidation, they might instead be held liable for wrongful trading.

Knowingly being a party

18.66 The scope of s. 213 allows liability to be imposed on people beyond the prime mover, or even the person with the actual intent to defraud. Participation is required for liability for fraudulent trading, however, and a person will not be guilty of fraudulent trading simply by being involved in the carrying on of a business that is subsequently shown to have been conducted with fraudulent intent. To be liable, a person involved in the running of a business must realise that they are involved with a transaction or line of business that is being conducted for fraudulent purposes and must have continued their involvement after such realisation. Not asking questions is no defence if the court finds that the reason for not asking was because the person had an actual appreciation that the answers to those questions would disclose the existence of fraud.[30] However, it is not sufficient to show that the person negligently failed to realise that this was the case or only realised after the event.

Avoiding fraudulent trading

18.67 The steps that a director should take to avoid later being accused of fraudulent trading are basically the same as those that should be taken to avoid allegations of wrongful trading (see **18.47** above). Of particular relevance will be the consideration of whether to continue to trade when it appears possible, but not certain, that the company will face insolvent liquidation. If a company continues to trade when in financial difficulties, the position of new creditors, commonly suppliers and customers, needs to be carefully considered. It may be legitimate to continue to trade where the survival of the company is contingent on a future event, such as a major contract being won or an anticipated injection of capital, so long as this is genuinely a realistic prospect and not mere optimism. However, no new contracts should be entered into that the directors do not honestly believe the company can perform, or they may face liability for fraudulent trading. If supplies or deposits for new orders are received while the future of the company is in the balance, arrangements should be made to ensure no loss is suffered by those new creditors should the company not survive. In the case of customer deposits this will best be achieved by opening a separate bank account that is clearly designated as an account for funds held by the company on trust for customers placing orders after that date. In the event of the company then going into insolvent liquidation those deposits could be returned to the customers who placed them. In the case of suppliers it is more difficult, but could, for example, be achieved by contracting on the basis that title passes only upon payment, where this is practical.

The consequences of fraudulent trading

Order to make financial contribution

18.68 A person found guilty of fraudulent trading under IA 1986 is liable to make such contributions to the company's assets as the court thinks proper. This gives a very broad discretion to the court, but the section is designed to be compensatory and the sum ordered will normally be linked to the amount by which creditors or other persons have been defrauded by the conduct in question. There should be no scope for a penal element to be added to the amount the guilty person is ordered to contribute, as any punishment is properly dealt with by a criminal prosecution for fraudulent trading under s. 993 of the 2006 Act.[31] Any contribution to the company's assets for fraudulent trading is payable to the liquidator and will be applied for the benefit of the body of creditors generally, not just those who are the victims of the fraudulent trading.

Personal liability for deceit

18.69 It should be noted that a director who signs a document on behalf of a company that makes an implicit representation that the company will be able to pay for something when he knows that that is not the case will be liable personally to the recipient in deceit as well as being guilty of fraudulent trading. The fact that a director signs on behalf of the company does not alleviate his liability for deceit if he knows that the company will be unable to meet its obligations at the time he puts his name to the document.[32] This may allow a defrauded creditor to pursue a director personally if a contribution ordered against the director for wrongful trading is dissipated among other creditors and does not make the defrauded party whole.

Disqualification

18.70 Where an order is made that the director is guilty of a civil claim of fraudulent trading, the court can impose a disqualification order preventing the director from acting as a company director for up to 15 years, even if no separate application has been made for a disqualification order.[33] Disqualification is dealt with in more detail in **Chapter 19**.

Undervalue transactions

18.71 A company enters into a transaction at an undervalue if it provides something to another party, either without receiving anything in return or where what is received in return is worth significantly less than what the company provides. Where such a transaction occurs, in specific circumstances, the court can intervene to make any order necessary to put the parties to the transaction back into the position they would have been had it not taken place.

The test for transactions at an undervalue

18.72 Under ss. 238 and 240 of IA 1986 a company enters into a transaction with a person at an undervalue if:

(a) the company makes a gift to that person or otherwise enters into a transaction with that person on terms that provide for the company to receive no consideration; or
(b) the company enters into a transaction with that person for a consideration the value of which, in money or money's worth, is significantly less than the value, in money or money's worth, of the consideration provided by the company.

18.73 The court has power to make an order in respect of a transaction at an undervalue only where that transaction has taken place at 'a relevant time'. This is defined in s. 240 of IA 1986 as:

(a) in the period of two years ending with the onset of insolvency;
(b) at a time between the making of an administration application in respect of the company and the making of an administration order on that application; or
(c) at a time between the filing with the court of a copy of notice of intention to appoint an administrator and the making of that appointment.

18.74 If the relevant time in question is the period of two years ending with the onset of insolvency, it is necessary that at the time of the transaction, the company was unable to pay its debts on either the cash-flow or the balance sheet test as set out in s. 123 of IA 1986 (see **18.3** above for these tests) or becomes unable to pay its debts under those tests as a consequence of the transaction in question. The 'onset of insolvency' means one of the steps that triggers a formal insolvency procedure, being:

(a) the date on which an application for an administration order is made;
(b) the date on which a copy of a notice of intention to appoint an administrator is filed with the court;
(c) if neither of the steps of (a) or (b) is taken, the date on which an administrator or liquidator is appointed; or
(d) the date on which a resolution is passed by the company's members to wind the company up.

Identifying an undervalue

18.75 Clearly, where a company makes a gift to another entity or person, this is liable to be held to be a transaction at an undervalue. Where a transaction involves mutual passing of consideration between the parties however, the question of whether the transaction is at an undervalue is more difficult. It will be for an administrator or liquidator of the company in the subsequent insolvency procedure to prove that the transaction was at an undervalue. However, where the evidence clearly points to a transaction being at an undervalue, the burden of proof may switch to the party that appears to have benefited to show that it was not at an undervalue.

18.76 The starting point for assessing the transaction will be whether the value received by the company matches the value of what it has provided. The value of an asset will be taken to be the amount a reasonably well-informed purchaser would be prepared, in an arm's length transaction, to pay for it. The value will always be considered at the date of the relevant transaction.[34] The court will consider all the relevant facts in determining the proper value of what the company has provided under the transaction. This can take into account:

(a) what is provided under a matrix of agreements that are entered into together;
(b) the likelihood of non-performance of any obligation undertaken by the parties;
(c) any relevant future event that was foreseeable at the time of the transaction; and
(d) the availability of similar goods or services in the market at the time of the transaction.

18.77 Any fact that a commercial person would take into account to arrive at the value of what the company provided and received can therefore be considered. The court will consider expert evidence on the issue of valuation as appropriate. It is important to note that the court does not have to arrive at a precise valuation of what the company provided and what it received in return. As long as the court is satisfied that the incoming value is significantly less than the outgoing value, it is able to make an order.[35]

Transactions with connected persons

18.78 Where the transaction at an undervalue is entered into with a person who is connected with the company it is presumed that at the time that transaction occurred, the company was unable to pay its debts as they fell due until the contrary is shown.

18.79 Connected persons are effectively directors, shadow directors or an associate of the company, its directors or shadow directors. A person is an associate of another person or a company if they have an employer–employee relationship, a trustee–beneficiary relationship or are relatives or partners. Companies are associates where they are under common control as in a group structure.

The defence to a claim of a transaction at an undervalue

18.80 Section 238(5) of IA 1986 provides a defence for a party that has contracted with a company where that transaction is later claimed to be at an undervalue. This provides that the court shall not make an order restoring the status quo if it is satisfied that:

(a) the company which entered into the transaction did so in good faith and for the purpose of carrying on its business; and
(b) at the time it did so there were reasonable grounds for believing that the transaction would benefit the company.

18.81 This test provides both a subjective and an objective element, meaning that it is necessary to show that the company acted in good faith without any intention to advantage the counterparty and that it was reasonable for the company's directors to believe that the transaction was to the benefit of the company. If the company enters into a transaction that is later challenged as a transaction at an undervalue, it may be possible for the directors to show that the transaction was commercially sensible in their view and that such a view was reasonable in the circumstances.

The consequences of a transaction at an undervalue

Court order

18.82 Where a liquidator or administrator successfully challenges a transaction as being a transaction at an undervalue, the court may make:

'Such order as it thinks fit for restoring the position to what it would have been if the company had not entered into that transaction.'

18.83 It should be noted that the court has no jurisdiction to rewrite the transaction on terms that it believes would have been reasonable and reflect the proper value of what was provided by the company. The court can only make such an order as it believes will restore the position to one as if the transaction never took place, not to impose the transaction that it believes should have taken place.[36]

18.84 Nevertheless, the court enjoys a very wide discretion in terms of the orders that it may make. Among other possibilities, the court may order that property be transferred back to the company, that security be discharged or released, that any person who has benefited from the transaction pay an amount to the liquidator or administrator as the court directs, or vary the amount by which a party is entitled to prove in the insolvency of the company. Where a party who was not connected with the company and did not have notice of the surrounding circumstances has, in good faith and for value, acquired an interest in property from the counterparty to the transaction at an undervalue, the court will not deprive such person of that interest.[37]

Disqualification

18.85 The extent of a director's responsibility for the company entering into a transaction at an undervalue is specifically listed as a matter for determining the unfitness of a director in Schedule 1 of the Company Directors Disqualification Act 1986. A disqualification order is likely to be made in any case where a director has been shown to be responsible for the company entering into a transaction at an undervalue and this can prevent the director from acting as a company director for up to 15 years.

Issues for company directors

18.86 Any transaction entered into by a company when it is insolvent under the cash-flow or balance sheet test, or which will render it so, should necessarily be treated with the utmost care and scrutiny. Likewise, any transaction with a connected person needs to be looked at carefully. This is particularly true in the context of groups of companies where a director may be a director of more than one company. While it can seem artificial, a director must always consider transactions from the perspective of the company for whom he is acting at the time. One of the most common forms of transaction at an undervalue is where one company in a group assists another by giving a guarantee to a bank of the liabilities of the parent or sister company. Interest-free loans between companies or the purchase of a non-performing asset are other common examples. Whenever one company in a group faces financial difficulties and it is proposed that another company should assist it in some way, it is necessary to analyse carefully the benefit arising to the company that is giving the assistance. If it is insufficient to justify the transaction, the transaction should not be entered into.

Continuing to trade

18.87 Where a company is in financial difficulties and it is intended to attempt to trade out of the situation, any proposed transactions need to be considered with the interest of all creditors in mind. One situation in which it is not entirely clear whether a transaction will be considered to be a transaction at an undervalue is where a company offers security over its assets in respect of already existing debts. It is not uncommon where a company is in financial difficulty for its lenders to seek increased protection against the risk of insolvency. For a long time it was considered that the mere creation of security over the company's assets does not deplete them or diminish their value.[38] On this basis the granting of security for an existing debt could not be a transaction at an undervalue. A more recent Court of Appeal case has questioned this reasoning, but did not overturn it.[39] Until the courts further consider this issue, the position in relation to such transactions will unfortunately be unclear and likely to be specific to the facts of each case. It is possible that even if granting security is acknowledged to give value to the recipient, it might not be a transaction at an undervalue if a real commercial benefit is obtained in return by extending the availability of an essential line of credit.

Personal liability and disqualification

18.88 While it is the counterparty to the transaction at an undervalue who is made subject to an order by the court on an application by a liquidator or administrator under s. 238 of IA 1986, where the court finds that a transaction at an undervalue has occurred it may also have consequences for directors personally. A transaction at an undervalue that is shown to defraud another party by reducing the assets available to the company may constitute fraudulent trading by the director. Likewise, if at the time of the transaction the director realised, or should have realised, that the company had no reasonable prospect of avoiding insolvent liquidation, the transaction may constitute wrongful trading. In either case, the director in question could be pursued by a liquidator to contribute personally to the assets of the company. As already noted, a transaction at an undervalue can also be sufficient grounds to disqualify a director from acting as a company director.

Preferences

18.89 Put briefly, a preference is anything that a company does, or allows to be done, at a time when it is insolvent or which makes it insolvent, that puts a particular creditor in a better position than if the company had gone into liquidation at that moment instead. A liquidator or administrator can challenge a preference if he can show that the transaction was influenced by a desire by those controlling the company to prefer the creditor in question. This is done by application to the court for an order to restore the situation to that as if the preference had not been made.

18.90 There are, therefore, three essential elements to a preference:

1 The transaction must improve the position of the creditor on insolvent liquidation.
2 There must be some element of a desire on the part of the company to prefer the creditor.
3 The transaction must take place within a designated period relating to the company's solvency.

The test for a preference

Changing the position of creditors

18.91 Under ss. 239 and 240 of IA 1986 a company gives a preference to a person (including a company) if:

(a) that person is one of the company's creditors or a surety or guarantor for any of the company's debts or other liabilities; and
(b) the company does anything or suffers anything to be done which (in either case) has the effect of putting that person in a position which, in the event of the company going into insolvent liquidation, will be better than the position he would have been in if that thing had not been done.

18.92 The test is therefore whether the alleged preference changed the positions of creditors relative to each other. If the debt of one creditor is repaid in full when the company is unable to pay all its debts, that creditor may have been preferred. However, if that creditor had security over sufficient assets to make good the debt, the repayment of the debt will not have changed its position as a creditor and no preference will have occurred.[40] This is because its position on an insolvent liquidation would have been no different from the position following the repayment: in effect it would always have been repaid before other creditors.

Desire to prefer

18.93 The second element that needs to be shown is that the decision to commit or allow the relevant action was influenced by a desire to benefit the creditor in question. This test replaced the old one, under the now defunct law of fraudulent preference, of a dominant intention to prefer and it is no longer necessary to show that the desire to prefer was the dominant factor in the thinking of the directors in question. It may be that there were several factors that caused directors to allow the company to enter into a transaction, but if a desire to prefer that creditor in question was one of them, this will be sufficient. The counterpoint is that directors shall not be taken to desire the inevitable results of everything that they do and even where it is clear that a transaction will put the creditor in a better position, the court will not necessarily infer a desire for that result. The court has expressly recognised that a man can choose the lesser of two evils without desiring either of them.[41] Where, for example, a company offers security over its assets to an existing creditor (often its bank in respect of its overdraft), this will necessarily improve the position of that creditor on insolvent liquidation. This will not be a preference, however, if there is no desire to prefer that creditor and the reason for granting the security is to prevent the withdrawal of credit necessary to enable the company to continue to trade.

Connected persons

18.94 Where the creditor who is alleged to be preferred is a connected person, the desire to prefer is presumed and it is for the directors to show that no such desire existed. The meaning of connected persons is the same as in the test for a transaction at an undervalue (see **18.79** above). It should be noted that the scope of creditors covered by s. 239 includes guarantors and sureties. One potential situation is that a creditor is repaid in preference to other creditors because the debt is personally guaranteed by a director of the company and by ensuring the company repays it the director hopes to avoid personal liability. In this situation it is the position of the director that is improved and it is therefore the desire to prefer the guarantor that is relevant rather than the desire to prefer the primary creditor.

18.95 A court can only make an order to unwind the preference if the preference was made during a period prior to the onset of insolvency, which has the same meaning as in the test for a transaction at an undervalue (see **18.73** above), namely:

1 in the case of a preference given to a connected person other than an employee, two years; and
2 in the case of a preference given to anyone else, six months.

18.96 It is also necessary that the company was unable to pay its debts at the time of the preference or became so as a consequence of making the preference. It should be noted that, unlike in the case of a transaction at an undervalue, there is no presumption that the company was insolvent at the relevant time by virtue of the preference being in favour of a connected party.

Preferences and transactions at an undervalue

18.97 In practice a transaction may be considered as both a preference and a transaction at an undervalue and it is common for liquidators and administrators to challenge transactions as being either one or the other to maximise their chances of obtaining an order. In this context, it has been held by the court that in a transaction involving three parties, if consideration for a transaction given by one party is a preference, it has no value. This means that whatever was given in return was given in a transaction at an undervalue.[42]

The consequences of a preference

Court order

18.98 The scope of order that the court can make where it finds that a preference has occurred is similarly broad as in the finding of a transaction at an undervalue. The order will be sought by a liquidator or administrator of the company that granted the preference and the purpose of the provision is to enable the general body of creditors who were disadvantaged by the preference to be put in the position that they would have been in had it not occurred. The court may therefore order the preferred creditor to repay the company, transfer assets or release or discharge security. The same protections for a third party who has subsequently acquired for value assets which might otherwise be the subject of an order arising from a preference exist as in an order relating to a transaction at an undervalue (see **18.84** above).

Disqualification

18.99 Those affected by an order of the court under s. 239 of IA 1986 will ordinarily be the creditor who benefited from the preference. It should not be thought, however, that those directors that sanctioned the preference will escape the attention of the court. The extent of a director's responsibility for the company entering into a transaction that is later deemed to be a preference is specifically listed as a matter for determining the unfitness of a director in Schedule 1 of the Company Directors Disqualification Act 1986. A disqualification order is likely to be made in any case where a director has been shown to be responsible for the company entering into a transaction held to be a preference and this can prevent the director from acting as a company director for up to 15 years.[43]

Avoiding preferences

18.100 Where a company is insolvent or there is a real prospect that it will become so, the company directors need to be careful not to do anything that would change the relative position of creditors upon liquidation. Where the company deals with an existing creditor in a way that might later be seen to have advantaged them, it would be necessary for the directors to ensure that they are not motivated by any desire to benefit that creditor. Transactions with connected parties, particularly directors and their families, will inevitably be subject to close scrutiny by an administrator or liquidator should the company subsequently enter into a formal insolvency procedure. Where such transactions are contemplated, the starting point for the directors will be the board minutes of the meeting at which the transaction is considered. These should record the commercial rationale behind any transaction that might later be questioned and set out the benefits for the company of the proposed course of action.

Granting security

18.101 It is common where a company's financial viability is starting to be called into question for financial creditors to seek security for their debts. The granting of security for an existing debt will clearly benefit the creditor in question to the detriment of the other unsecured creditors. The key question, however, will be whether the motivation for granting security includes any element of desire to benefit that creditor. It is quite possible that granting the security is commercially rational or necessary in order to avoid the creditor withdrawing credit from the company and causing it to cease trading immediately. If the reason for the granting of security is to prevent the withdrawal of credit and there is no desire to prefer that creditor, the transaction will not be a preference. In this context, any decision may later be examined by an insolvency practitioner and should therefore be recorded meticulously with a full explanation of the reasoning behind it.

Transactions defrauding creditors

18.102 IA 1986 contains a further provision relating to transactions at an undervalue that provides a liquidator or administrator of a company an additional means of unravelling such a transaction where it was not within the 'relevant time' defined in s. 240 of IA 1986 (see **18.73** above). This allows a director to be held to account for any dispersal of the company's assets, regardless of whether this occurred within the two years before the company became insolvent, but where it was carried out specifically for the purpose of putting assets beyond the reach of a potential creditor. As well as providing a route for insolvency practitioners to recoup assets for the creditors of the company, it is open for anyone who is the 'victim' of such a transaction to apply for an order under s. 240, though they require leave of the court to do so. The court has the same discretion in the orders it may make as where it has found a transaction at an undervalue or a preference under ss. 238–240 of IA 1986. The provision applies to the acts of individuals as well as companies, but this section will deal only with its application to companies.

The test for transactions defrauding creditors

18.103 Under s. 423 of IA 1986 a company enters into a transaction defrauding creditors if:

(a) the company makes a gift to a person or otherwise enters into a transaction with a person on terms that provide for the company to receive no consideration; or
(b) the company enters into a transaction with a person for a consideration, the value of which, in money or money's worth, is significantly less than the value, in money or money's worth, of the consideration provided by the company; and
(c) the purpose of the transaction was to put assets beyond the reach of a person who is making, or may at some time make, a claim against the company, or otherwise prejudicing the interests of such a person in relation to such a claim.

18.104 The test for whether the transaction is at an undervalue at (a) and (b) above is therefore the same as for transactions at an undervalue under s. 238 of IA 1986. The additional consideration is the necessary intent behind the transaction. It is necessary for the applicant who is seeking an order to show that the purpose of the transaction was to put assets beyond the reach of a creditor (or potential creditor) or otherwise to prejudice their position as against the company. The courts have held that it is not necessary for such prejudice to be the sole purpose of the transaction, or even the dominant purpose, but it does have to be one of the real reasons behind the transaction rather than simply a consequence.[44] The test is therefore subjective and requires the court to consider the state of mind of those who authorised the transaction, rather than just a consideration of the results.[45] There is no requirement for an intention that the general body of creditors be prejudiced by the transaction. It is sufficient that one particular creditor is intended to be prejudiced.[46]

Who can use s. 423?

18.105 Section 424 of IA 1986 sets out who may apply for an order under s. 423. Insolvency practitioners may apply in respect of a company that is being wound up or is in administration in the same way that they can apply under ss. 238 and 239. The provisions relating to transactions defrauding creditors also refer to a 'victim' of such an arrangement, who is able to apply to the court under s. 423, provided they first obtain leave to do so from the court. This requirement essentially ensures that there is sufficient substance in the application before allowing it to progress.

18.106 Where the application is brought by the victim, it is not necessary for the company to be insolvent or in administration or liquidation. A person who believes that a transaction has been entered into in order to frustrate a claim they have against the company can therefore seek to have this transaction unwound as soon as they are aware of it. It is not necessary for the victim to have proved their claim against the company, nor even to have made such a claim, but they will need to convince the court that the claim they might bring is a genuine one. The victim can be anyone who proves to be prejudiced by the transaction, even if this person was not the person whose claim the transaction was designed to frustrate.[47]

When would ss. 423 and 424 Insolvency Act 1986 be used?

18.107 Because of the necessity to prove that the transaction was entered into with the intention, on the part of the relevant directors of the company, that it would prejudice a creditor or potential creditor, s. 423 is not widely used in the context of companies. In the absence of some written evidence that the transaction was designed to put assets beyond the reach of creditors, such intent might be hard to prove, though the courts are willing to draw inferences where the circumstantial evidence is sufficient to show a deliberate and dishonest course of conduct.[48] Nevertheless, if the transaction took place within two years of the company becoming insolvent, the liquidator or administrator would normally take the easier route of attacking it as a transaction at an undervalue under s. 238 of IA 1986. In the context of litigation, any claimant who learns that assets are likely to be moved out of the company in order to reduce what he can recover would ordinarily apply for a freezing injunction before such a transaction could take place. Only where such a transaction has already occurred might a claimant apply to the court to reverse a transaction defrauding creditors.

18.108 Circumstances in which s. 423 has been used tend to revolve around company group structures, where the assets of one company are depleted to prejudice the creditors of that company to the advantage of those of another in the group. Such rearranging of financial affairs sometimes starts at an earlier and less desperate stage of the companies' difficulties than other transactions set aside by insolvency practitioners, where directors organise matters 'just in case' the worst should happen. The transfer by a company of assets to another entity within the group before embarking on a risky venture in order to minimise the impact should it go wrong will constitute a transaction defrauding creditors. Where insolvency follows more than two years later, s. 423 may be the only route available to an insolvency practitioner to undo such a transaction.

Consequences of a transaction defrauding creditors

Court order

18.109 Where the court is satisfied that a transaction defrauding creditors has occurred, it is able to make any order it thinks fit for:

(a) restoring the position to what it would have been if the transaction had not been entered into; and
(b) protecting the interests of persons who are victims of the transaction.

18.110 The scope of an order that the court can make where it finds that a preference has occurred is similarly broad as in the finding of a transaction at an undervalue or a preference. The court may order that the beneficiary of the transaction repay the company, transfer assets or release or discharge security. The court is at liberty to order that the directors who authorised the transaction for the purpose of defrauding creditors contribute to the company's assets or to the victim of the transaction and an order of this kind is more likely where the reversal of the original transaction is not possible. The same protections for a third party who has subsequently acquired for value assets which might otherwise be the subject of an order arising from a preference exist as in an order relating to a transaction at an undervalue (see **18.84** above).

Disqualification

18.111 As well as the possibility of being ordered to contribute personally to the company or victim, any director found to have authorised a transaction defrauding creditors will face the possibility of an order disqualifying them from acting as a company director. While a director's responsibility for the company entering into a transaction that is later deemed to be a transaction defrauding creditors under s. 423 of IA 1986 is not listed as a matter for determining the unfitness of a director in Schedule 1 of the Company Directors Disqualification Act 1986, it is obvious that any finding that a director acted to defraud creditors is likely to lead to a disqualification order. This can prevent the director from acting as a company director for up to 15 years.

Additional considerations for public and listed companies

18.112 Directors of listed companies facing the deterioration of a company's financial position must remain alert to their obligations to shareholders and prospective shareholders which remain while the company's shares are listed. Directors face personal liability if they fail to comply with the Disclosure and Transparency Rules (DTR) or Listing Rules (LR).

Financial Services and Markets Act 2000

18.113 Under s. 91 of the Financial Services and Markets Act 2000 (FSMA), the Financial Services Authority (FSA) in its capacity as the United Kingdom Listing Authority (UKLA) has the power to impose an unlimited financial penalty of such amount as it considers appropriate and a public censure where it considers there has been a contravention of the DTR or LR by a 'person discharging managerial responsibilities'. A 'person discharging managerial responsibilities' will include a director:

(a) of a company registered in the UK; or
(b) which is not registered in the UK or any other EEA state but is required to file annual information in relation to shares in the UK in accordance with Article 10 of the Prospectus Directive;

where it has requested or approved the admission of a financial instrument on a regulated market.

18.114 Investigations are often lengthy and extremely costly, in terms of disruption and the diversion of resources. A high-quality audit trail documenting the reasons why actions were taken may lead to an investigation terminating at an early stage.

18.115 Potential liability under the DTR and LR is dealt with in more detail at **14.52.**

Misleading statements and practices

18.116 It is a criminal offence for any person to make a misleading statement, promise or forecast or to engage in a course of conduct that creates a false or misleading impression to the market in, or price or value of, any relevant investment. Directors of listed companies should be extremely careful in respect of trading updates and forecasts released to the market as to the company's expectations of its performance and as to reporting its actual performance. In the event that there is a substantial movement in the price of the company's listed securities as the result of an announcement, the circumstances of that announcement will be scrutinised by the UKLA and the timeliness and accuracy of the announcement will be considered. Particular attention is likely to be paid to the accuracy of revenue recognition and the plausibility of overoptimistic statements regarding expectations as to performance, especially given that investigations tend to be precipitated by substantial share price movements.

18.117 Under s. 397, FSMA, a person may be prosecuted for knowingly or recklessly making a statement, promise or forecast which is misleading, false or deceptive in a material particular. For the offence to be made out, it is necessary for the prosecution to show that the statement was made for the purpose of inducing, or being reckless as to whether it would induce, another person to exercise any rights conferred by a relevant investment or from entering into or refraining from entering into an agreement.

18.118 It is an offence for a person to dishonestly conceal a material fact, whether in connection with a statement, promise or forecast made by him or otherwise. This offence is very wide and covers both deliberate and reckless acts and omissions. It is particularly relevant to circumstances in which the deteriorating financial condition of the company is not known to the market and the failure to update market expectations may constitute a criminal offence.

Creating a false or misleading impression

18.119 It is also an offence for a person to engage in any course of conduct which creates a false or misleading impression as to the market in or price or value of any 'relevant investment'.

18.120 It is a defence to a charge of having made a misleading, false or deceptive statement for a director to demonstrate that he reasonably believed that his actions would not create a false or misleading impression. The penalty for making a misleading statement is up to seven years' imprisonment or a financial penalty. Company directors have been imprisoned for recklessly misleading the market.

18.121 It is important that announcements made to the market are demonstrably accurate and do not omit any information which an investor would expect to be made available to him when making investment decisions. Full and well-documented compliance with the rules of the exchange on which an issuer's securities are listed will minimise the risk of being found to have recklessly committed the offence, as will consulting advisers in respect of a company's obligations where there is uncertainty.

18.122 Directors should note that these offences are drafted very widely and cover both deliberate and reckless actions and omissions. Investigators will have the benefit of hindsight and for this reason contemporaneous materials such as emails, draft announcements and consultation with the company's advisers are often essential in establishing a defence.

Market abuse

18.123 Directors of listed companies facing insolvency should also consider their position if, as a result of the deterioration of the company's financial position, information in their possession constitutes insider information. Inside information is defined by s. 118C of FSMA. This is dealt with in greater depth at **14.67**. Inside information is information of a precise nature which is not generally available and would, if generally available, be likely to have a significant effect on the price of a relevant investment.

18.124 The following constitutes market abuse:

(1) dealing or attempting to deal on the basis of inside information (insider dealing);
(2) disclosing inside information other than in the context of employment, profession or duties (improper disclosure);
(3) misusing information which is not generally available (misuse of information);
(4) trading which gives a false or misleading impression (manipulating transactions);
(5) trading which employs fictitious devices, deception or contrivance (manipulating devices);
(6) dissemination of information which gives a false or misleading impression (dissemination); and
(7) behaviour giving a false or misleading impression or distorting the market (false and misleading impressions and distortion).

18.125 The regime covering the conduct described in (1)–(2) and (4)–(6) above was introduced in the UK by the EU Market Abuse Directive, whilst the conduct described in (3) and (7) relates to the previous market abuse regime introduced by FSMA. These offences are subject to a 'sunset provision', meaning they will cease to have effect on 31 December 2009 unless specific provisions are introduced to permit their continued existence. Market abuse is not a criminal offence and will not lead to imprisonment or a criminal record but an unlimited fine may be imposed by the FSA.

Sources

1 *Cheyne Finance plc (in receivership)* [2007] EWHC 2116.
2 See, for example, *Highberry Ltd v. Colt Telecom* [2003] BPIR 324 where the applicant's attempt to rely on future events to show insolvency on the cash-flow basis was rejected by the court when considering an ordinary trading company as 'tentative and shaky peering into the middle distance'.
3 This Act created s. 72A of IA 1986 which became effective on 15 September 2003.
4 Companies Act 2006, s. 172(3).
5 *Re Hawkes Hill Publishing Co Ltd (in liquidation) Ward v. Perks and another* [2007] All ER (D) 422.

6 *Kinsella v. Russell Kinsella Pty Ltd (in liq)* (1986) 4 NSWLR 722.
7 *Liquidator of West Mercia Safetywear Ltd v. Dodd* [1988] BCLC 250.
8 *Facia Footwear Limited 'in administration' and another v. Hinchliffe and another* (1998) 1 BCLC 218.
9 Company Director's Act 1986, Schedule 1, Part 1.
10 The defendant's education and professional qualifications were considered in *Re Living Images Ltd* [1996] BCC 112.
11 *Secretary of State for Trade and Industry v. Gash* [1997] 1 BCLC 341.
12 *Re Hawkes Hill Publishing Co Ltd (in liquidation) Ward v. Perks and another* [2007] All ER (D) 422.
13 *Re Continental Assurance Company of London plc* [2001] All ER (D) 299.
14 *Re DKG Contractors Ltd* [1990] BCC 903.
15 *Re Produce Marketing Consortium Ltd* (1989) 5 BCC 569.
16 *Re Purpoint Ltd* [1991] BCC 121.
17 In the matter of Marini limited, Chancery Division, unreported, 3 March 2003.
18 See Company Directors Disqualification Act 1986, s. 10.
19 *Re Produce Marketing Consortium Ltd, Halls v. David & Anor* (1989) 5 BCC 399. This case referred to the same provision in Companies Act 1985, s. 727.
20 See, for example, *Re Purpoint Ltd* [1991] BCC 121.
21 *Re Leaf* [2007] All ER (D) 52 (April).
22 *Re Leaf* [2007] All ER (D) 52 (April).
23 See Company Directors Disqualification Act 1986, s. 4.
24 *Re Sarflex Limited* [1979] Ch 592.
25 *Carman v. The Cronos Group SA* [2005] WL 3067026 (4 November 2005) (Ch D).
26 *Carman v. The Cronos Group SA* [2005] WL 3067026 (4 November 2005) (Ch D).
27 *Morphitis v. Bernasconi & ors* [2003] Ch 552.
28 *R v. Grantham* [1984]1 QB 675 CA.
29 *Welham v. DPP* [1961] AC103.
30 *Morris & Ors v. Bank of India* [2004] All ER (D) 378 (MAR) (19 March 2004) (Ch D).
31 *Morphitis v. Bernasconi* [2003] Ch 552, though note that this principle is not as clearly established as it could be, due to the judgment in *Re a Company No. 001418 of 1988* [1990] BCC 526.
32 *Context Drouzhba Limited v. Wiseman and Another* [2007] EWCA Civ 1201.
33 See Company Directors Disqualification Act 1986, s. 10.
34 *Reid v. Ramlort Ltd* [2002] All ER (D) 235.
35 *Reid v. Ramlort Ltd* [2002] All ER (D) 235.
36 *Reid MDA Investment Management Limited* [2003] All ER (D) 128.
37 IA 1986, s. 241(2)(a).
38 This was taken from the judgment in *Re M C Bacon Limited (No. 1)* [1990] BCC 78.
39 *Hill v. Spread Trustee Company Limited and Warr* [2006] EWCA Civ 542.
40 *Re Hawkes Hill Publishing Co Ltd (in liquidation) Ward v. Perks and another* [2007] All ER (D) 422.
41 *Re MC Bacon Ltd* [1990] BCC 78.
42 *Hill v. Spread Trustee Company and another*, Case no. 1242 of 2005, Manchester District Registry, 8 June 2006.

43 See *Re Living Images Ltd* [1996] BCC 112 where the giving of a preference was grounds for the making of a disqualification order.
44 *Commissioners of Inland Revenue v. Hashmi and another* [2002] All ER (D) 71 (3 May 2002) (CA).
45 *Pagemanor Limited v. Ryan & ors* [2002] All ER (D) 50 (5 February 2002) (ChD).
46 *National Westminster Bank plc v. Jones* [2000] All ER (D) 857 (22 June 2000) (ChD).
47 *Sands v. Clitheroe* [2006] BPIR 1000.
48 *Commissioners of Inland Revenue v. Hashmi and another* [2002] All ER (D) 71 (3 May 2002) (CA).

19 Disqualification

Introduction

19.1 The Company Directors Disqualification Act 1986 (CDDA 1986)[1] sets out a number of circumstances in which persons concerned in the management of companies may be disqualified, either by court order or voluntarily (by giving an undertaking to the appropriate governmental entity, in most cases the Secretary of State for Business Enterprise and Regulatory Reform – BERR). For these purposes, a disqualification order or undertaking results in a wide prohibition on being involved in a company's management, unless the court has given specific permission, and an absolute prohibition on being or acting as an insolvency practitioner. In addition, once a person is subject to disqualification, there are various other impediments and disabilities on holding certain offices and positions. Disqualification is effectively a statutory injunction, breach of which results in a criminal offence. In addition, breach of a disqualification may result in civil liability for the debts of the company or other entity in relation to which the disqualified person has acted in breach of the statutory injunction. As such the model for disqualification by statutory injunction is one that has been utilised in other areas of the law.[2] As at 2005–6 the number of disqualifications, as a result of court order or voluntary undertaking, was running at some 1,197 per year.

19.2 Disqualification will follow on from certain types of past misconduct. However, the jurisdiction to disqualify is not at large. The CDDA 1986 sets out a number of defined circumstances in which disqualification may be imposed or defined gateways to disqualification. In order to ascertain when disqualification may be imposed it is necessary to identify the relevant defined type of past misconduct by a defined category of person and, usually, a further connecting event. As regards the types of misconduct involved these include, among others, criminal offences connected with the management of companies, filing defaults and conduct which falls so short of required standards as to be such as to make the person unfit to be concerned in the management of a company.

19.3 The persons who may be disqualified are not in all cases restricted to company directors or those involved with companies, and the effect of disqualification is not limited to a prohibition on being a company director or being involved in companies. The jurisdiction to disqualify has been extended beyond companies to other entities, including limited partnerships, partnerships and other bodies, such as building societies, friendly societies and NHS foundation trusts. However, this chapter concentrates solely on the company ramifications of the legislation. The most common connecting events are the entry of a company into a formal insolvency regime and an investigation into a company's affairs.

19.4 In addition to misconduct in the management of a company forming the basis of disqualification, automatic disqualification applies during the currency of a bankruptcy and during any period while a person is subject to bankruptcy restrictions.[3] The form of automatic disqualification is in slightly different terms from a disqualification order or undertaking but is similar in the wide extent of the prohibition which applies. A form of automatic disqualification also applies where a court revokes a personal administration order made under the County Courts Act 1984.[4]

19.5 As regards the territoriality of the CDDA it should be noted that it primarily applies across Scotland, and England and Wales. Northern Ireland disqualifications (whether by court order or as a result of voluntary undertaking) are given effect to within Scotland and England and Wales by treating them as carrying the consequences of disqualification imposed under the CDDA, ss. 12A, 12B and 13–15. However, the power to grant leave notwithstanding disqualification in such cases is reserved to the High Court of Northern Ireland. Where a company incorporated outside the UK has sufficient connection with Scotland or England and Wales such that it would be subject to winding up by those courts, then conduct in relation to such company may ground jurisdiction to disqualify under the CDDA. Similarly, the prohibition on acting in relation to companies under the CDDA will extend to such companies. More recently, the Companies Act 2006 (the 2006 Act) introduces new provisions whereby those who are subject to prohibitions or restrictions, similar in effect to a UK disqualification, in overseas jurisdictions may be made subject to disqualification under the laws of England and Wales, Scotland and Northern Ireland.

19.6 Although the Office of Fair Trading (OFT) and a number of specified regulators have responsibility for competition disqualifications, the main responsibility for disqualification lies with BERR. The Secretary of State for these purposes effectively operates primarily through the Insolvency Service, an executive agency which has particular responsibility for insolvency-related cases under s. 6 of CDDA. In addition, the Companies Investigation Branch, now located within the Insolvency Service, although not limited in its responsibilities to insolvent companies, has particular responsibility for s. 8 CDDA cases.

Historical background

19.7 The CDDA brings together certain provisions that were formerly introduced by, and contained in, various Companies Acts and Insolvency Acts. The earliest provision, the automatic disqualification of bankrupts, dates back to recommendations of the Greene Committee and was first enacted as s. 84 of the Companies Act 1928. The rationale of this provision was to block an easy way round the direct prohibition on a bankrupt incurring credit by doing so through a limited company. Also, disqualification became an available response to fraudulent trading (Companies Act 1928, s. 75). The essential rationale of this power was to avoid security filling. It also became an available response to fraudulent conduct (Companies Act 1928, s. 76). The scope of these provisions was widened under the Companies Act 1948.

19.8 Under the Insolvency Act 1985 the new civil wrong of wrongful trading became a basis for disqualification. A separate jurisdictional basis for disqualification – persistent failure to comply with filing requirements under companies legislation – first appeared in the Companies Act 1976, s. 28, following recommendations of the Jenkins Committee. The first jurisdiction to disqualify based on past misconduct which was such as to make the director unfit to be concerned in the management of a company was s. 9 of the Insolvency Act 1986. Originally limited to cases where two companies had become insolvent within a set period, the power was widened to permit disqualification on the grounds of 'unfit conduct' following a relevant investigation under the Companies Acts.

19.9 The Insolvency Act 1985 made significant changes to the jurisdiction to disqualify. At about this time, significant government resources were devoted to the use of insolvency-based jurisdiction to disqualify and it is from the mid-1980s that the civil jurisdiction to disqualify became used to a significant extent and played a key role in the legal development of standards of conduct to be expected of company directors. The Insolvency Act 2000 introduced a new power in the Secretary of State to accept the offer of a disqualification undertaking which, once accepted, has the same effects as a disqualification order. The rationale of this new power was to withdraw cases from the courts where agreement was possible.

19.10 The Enterprise Act 2002 introduced a specific power to disqualify based on a breach of competition law where the relevant director's conduct was such as to make him unfit to be concerned in the management of a company; it also introduced the new bankruptcy restrictions regime.

19.11 The latest legislative development is Part 40 of the Companies Act 2006. The provisions contained in that Part are designed to enable the Secretary of State to 'close the gap' where persons are subject to disqualification or 'restrictions' by reason of overseas laws but not subject to restrictions under the CDDA. Regulations will be capable of being made which will provide a basis for subjecting such persons to the UK restrictions currently applying under the CDDA.

The jurisdiction to disqualify – overview

19.12 There are now ten jurisdictional bases for disqualification:

1. discretionary disqualification for up to 15 years by the civil or criminal court following conviction for an indictable offence in connection with the promotion, formation, management, liquidation or striking off of a company, with receivership of a company's property or with being an administrative receiver (CDDA, s. 2);
2. discretionary disqualification for up to five years by the civil or criminal court for persistent default in relation to filing of returns and other documents under Companies legislation (CDDA, ss. 3 and 5);
3. discretionary disqualification for up to 15 years for fraudulent trading, fraud or breach of duty whilst acting as an officer or liquidator of a company, receiver of a company's property or administrative receiver of a company (CDDA, s. 4);
4. mandatory disqualification for between 2 and 15 years where the person has been a director of a company which has become insolvent (within the defined meaning of that term) and where that person's conduct makes him unfit to be concerned in the management of a company (CDDA, ss. 6 and 7);
5. discretionary disqualification for up to 15 years following receipt of a report or information by the Secretary of State, under various statutory investigation provisions, about a director of a company on the basis that that person's conduct is such as to make them unfit to be concerned in the management of a company (CDDA, s. 8);
6. mandatory disqualification for up to 15 years where a company has committed a breach of competition law, the person concerned was a director at the relevant time and that person's conduct as director makes him unfit to be concerned in the management of a company (CDDA, s. 9A);
7. discretionary disqualification for up to 15 years where the civil court makes an order that a person contribute to a company's assets under

either the fraudulent trading (s. 213) or wrongful trading provisions (s. 214) of the Insolvency Act 1986 (CDDA 1986, s. 10);

8 automatic disqualification during the period of any bankruptcy or the existence of bankruptcy restrictions (CDDA 1986, s. 11);

9 automatic disqualification for up to two years where a personal administration order made under Part VI of the County Courts Act 1984 is (as an exercise of discretion) revoked (CDDA, s. 12);

10 disqualification following on from equivalent restrictions applied under overseas law (Companies Act 2006, Part 40, ss. 1182–1191).[5]

19.13 These provisions have different historical antecedents and, in many cases, different immediate drivers. By far the greatest judicial examination of the disqualification regime has focused on the unfit conduct provisions of s. 6. However, over recent years it has been possible to see the courts seeking to apply the CDDA as a cohesive whole with an overall rationale underlying it. This makes perfect sense. On any given factual situation there may be jurisdiction to disqualify under more than one provision of the CDDA and by both criminal and civil courts. The effect of disqualification is in all cases (save ss. 11 and 12) identical. In each case where disqualification is not automatic the ground for disqualification is identified past misconduct. Accordingly, it is suggested that the underlying purpose of the jurisdiction to disqualify is the same in all cases, namely the protection of all members of the public (including, without limitation, shareholders, creditors, investors, employees, consumers and customers). That protection is achieved by keeping the disqualified person 'off the road' and away from companies for a limited period, by deterring that person and others from future misconduct and thus raising standards of probity, competence and commercial morality in the context of the management of companies.[6]

Section 6: unfit conduct of directors of insolvent companies

19.14 By far the largest number of disqualifications that arise each year result from the jurisdiction to disqualify under CDDA, s. 6. The jurisdiction is conferred solely on the civil courts. Under s. 6 the court is compelled to make an order for between 2 and 15 years if three conditions are met in relation to any person, that is:

- the person (who may be an individual or a body corporate) is or was a director of a company;
- the company has become 'insolvent' within the specific statutory definition of that term under s. 6; and
- that person's conduct as a director of that company, either taken alone or taken together with his conduct as a director of another company, is such as to make him unfit to be concerned in the management of a company.

Directors of a company

19.15 Turning to these preconditions in more detail, it should be noted that CDDA, s. 6 bites not just on those properly and lawfully constituted directors of a company but also those who, although not appointed, act as directors (that is, de facto directors) or are shadow directors. The reason that s. 6 bites on de facto directors is not the definitional section CDDA, s. 22 (which provides that 'director' includes any person occupying that position, by whatever name called) but by reason of a process of statutory construction of s. 6 itself.[7] Shadow directors are included in the definition by reason of s. 6(3C). A de facto director is essentially a person who, while not properly and lawfully appointed as a director, acts as a director by assuming the role and functions of a director. A shadow director is a person in accordance with whose directions or instructions the directors of a company are accustomed to act (but so that a person is not deemed a shadow director by reason only that the directors act on advice given by him in a professional capacity) (see CDDA, s. 22(5)). Many of the cases which discuss and decide the scope of de facto and shadow directors have been decided in the disqualification sphere, see **Chapter 1**.

19.16 The 'companies' to which s. 6 extends include not only companies incorporated within England and Wales or Scotland but also companies incorporated overseas which are liable to be wound up[8] in England and Wales.

19.17 The CDDA extends the definition of 'director' and 'company' in a number of important respects. For present purposes it is sufficient to say that disqualification under s. 6 is potentially available against not only directors of companies but also those holding equivalent office or positions in a wide range of organisations, including[9] LLPs, partnerships, building societies, incorporated friendly societies, NHS Foundation Trusts, open-ended investment companies, European Economic Interest Groupings, European Companies and Community Interest Companies.

'Insolvent' company

19.18 The second requirement under s. 6 is that the relevant company must have 'become insolvent'. For these purposes this means that the company must have entered administration, had an administrative receiver appointed or gone into liquidation at a time when its assets are insufficient to pay its debts and other liabilities and the expenses of the winding up (CDDA, s. 6(1)(a)). The time when this condition is first met is relevant in determining the two-year period after which s. 6 proceedings can only be commenced with the court's permission.[10] The first two of the circumstances which will satisfy the insolvency condition are fairly straightforward. Normally, it is not appropriate to use disqualification proceedings themselves as the forum for challenging the validity of the appointment of an administrator or administrative receiver (or, it would seem, the company going into liquidation). Instead, separate proceedings may be necessary, though any disqualification proceedings may be stayed in the interim.[11]

19.19 Where the issue is whether the company's assets were sufficient for the payment of its debts and other liabilities and the expenses of the winding up will usually be an issue appropriate to be heard within the disqualification proceedings themselves. It can be a much more difficult issue to resolve.[12] The test is not one of cash-flow insolvency as at that date but, in effect, a refined balance sheet test. In most cases, insolvency will be obvious, but there have been cases where the position has been far from straightforward. The test is slightly odd as it involves an element of futurity: the need to bring into the equation costs and expenses of the liquidation which have not been incurred as at the date of the company going into liquidation. The Statement of Affairs is likely to be very important, as an admission by the directors who make it. So far as assets and liabilities are concerned, it is fairly clear that, for s. 6 purposes, the assets and liabilities are to be valued as at the date of liquidation. Interest and other gains accruing after liquidation are to be ignored in calculating the assets of the company. However, it appears that assets in existence at the date of liquidation but which were left out of the Statement of Affairs in error will be included. Similarly, interest in respect of periods preceding the liquidation are taken into account. Statutory interest payable on liabilities of the company under the Insolvency Act 1986, s. 189 is similarly to be left out of account. So far as the expenses of the winding up are concerned, it appears that these are to be limited to 'reasonable costs'. What remains unclear is whether these costs and expenses are simply the actual costs and expenses incurred at the date that the court considers the s. 6 test or whether future estimated costs and expenses are also to be taken into account.

Conduct as director regarding one or more companies making the director unfit to be concerned in the management of companies

19.20 The test involves consideration of a number of elements:

- the companies in relation to which conduct as a director is relevant;
- the relevant conduct that can be considered;
- the test of 'unfit conduct'.

Relevant companies

19.21 The first issue is the extent to which conduct in relation to more than one company may be taken into account. Section 6(1)(b) speaks of conduct as a director of a company which has become insolvent either alone or taken together with conduct as a director of 'another' company being such as to make the director 'unfit' to be concerned in the management of a company. In this context, it has become common to speak of 'lead' and 'collateral' companies. For these purposes the 'lead' company is a reference to the company that has become insolvent within the meaning of CDDA, s. 6 and in relation to which proceedings have been commenced within the two-year period of insolvency (or, if outside that period, with the permission of the court) as required by CDDA, s. 7(2). There may be more than one lead company. All lead companies should be identified in the title to the proceedings. A collateral company is a reference to any 'other' company in relation to which the director's conduct is taken into account, together with his conduct in relation to the lead company. There is no requirement that such 'other' company should have become insolvent or that, if it has become insolvent, the proceedings should have been commenced within two years of the insolvency (or with leave of the court if outside that period). There must be some misconduct in relation to the lead company. If there is none then the condition under s. 6 is not met.[13] If there is some misconduct in relation to the lead company then s. 6 will be satisfied if either that conduct by itself is sufficient to make the director 'unfit to be concerned in management' or if that misconduct, together with misconduct in relation to any 'other' company, taken together, is such as to make him so unfit. There is no requirement that there be any factual or other nexus between the types of misconduct in relation to the lead company and any collateral company.[14]

Relevant conduct

19.22 Under CDDA, s. 6, the court focuses solely on the past conduct alleged to constitute misconduct. It is not concerned with the question of whether the director is, at the time of the hearing, 'now' unfit to be concerned in the management of a company. The court, in determining whether the director's conduct is such as to make him unfit to be concerned in the management of a company, considers solely whether the specified past conduct that is alleged and proved by the claimant is such as to make the director unfit to be concerned in the management of a company. It does not take into account whether the director has since learned his lesson so that he may be said, at the time of the hearing, to be 'fit' to be concerned in the management of a company.[15]

Conduct which makes the director 'unfit to be concerned in the management of as company'

19.23 The test of whether the conduct makes the director unfit to be concerned in the management of a company involves the court embarking on a question of mixed fact and law. The court has to consider whether the conduct that is proved, both separately and cumulatively,[16] and taking into account any extenuating circumstances, falls below the standards established by the courts as appropriate for persons fit to be directors of companies.[17] In carrying out that task, the court is given various statutory pointers and further pointers are laid down by relevant case law:

- The test for the court is not whether or not it is in the public interest for the person to be disqualified. The decision whether or not it is in the public interest to institute proceedings under s. 6 is one for the Secretary of State. The court's function is limited to finding what conduct is made out and evaluating that conduct.[18]
- Under s. 6, the conduct that is in question is conduct as a director, not conduct relating to the company more generally.[19]
- The test is whether the particular conduct falls below the standards fixed by the court. Although the test is whether his past misconduct makes him unfit to be concerned in the management of 'a' company, a defendant cannot escape a finding of unfit conduct by demonstrating that it is possible to conceive of a management role in some other company, real or imagined, in which he would have the competence and integrity to be involved without risk to the public.[20]
- The test of 'unfit conduct' under s. 6 requires the application of ordinary words of the English language which should be applied as such. Described circumstances in other cases in which unfit conduct has been found should not be taken as judicial paraphrases of the section but only an indication of circumstances where unfit conduct has been held to be established in the past.[21]
- Although unfit conduct will often arise where there has been incompetence, dishonesty or a lack of proper discipline (in the sense of regard to statutory and other duties), these concepts are useful tools of categorisation only and do not form a self-standing test of unfit conduct.[22] The test is whether the relevant conduct falls below the standards of probity and competence fixed by the courts as being appropriate for those who manage companies.
- Where the company has become insolvent, the court will have regard to conduct in relation to any matter connected with or arising out of the insolvency of the company.[23] This could include, for example, a failure to co-operate as a former director under s. 235 of the Insolvency Act 1986.[24]
- The court is to have regard to the matters set out in Schedule 1 of the CDDA.[25] Those matters are not an exhaustive list of the matters which, if established, may be such as to make the director 'unfit' within the meaning of s. 6.[26] The better view is that each matter of conduct is to be considered on its own merits and that the fact that it may fall within or outside Schedule 1 is not of itself a factor going to its weight in the particular case.[27] Accordingly, a finding of breach of duty (a factor under Schedule 1) is neither necessary nor of itself sufficient for a finding of unfitness.[28]

- The focus is on individual responsibility not 'collective responsibility'. It is necessary to show that the individual director's individual conduct fell below applicable standards.
- However, it has to be borne in mind that each director owes duties to the company to inform himself about its affairs and to join with his co-directors in supervising and controlling them; a proper degree of delegation and division of responsibility is permissible and often necessary, but not total abrogation of responsibility, and a board of directors must not permit one individual to dominate them and use them.[29]
- Where the misconduct in question is, effectively, incompetence the level of incompetence required must be demonstrated to a very marked degree or a high degree.[30] However, the degree of 'incompetence' that will satisfy a finding of unfit conduct should not be exaggerated.[31]
- The fact that a director had professional advisers who failed to draw attention to the impropriety of transactions may (but not necessarily will) be a negative finding of unfitness or be a mitigating factor in the period of disqualification to be imposed.[32]
- The court must guard against being too wise after the event.[33]

Section 8: Disqualification based on unfit conduct as a director as disclosed following investigation of a company

19.24 Broadly speaking, CDDA, s. 8 is very similar to s. 6 in focusing on the conduct of directors of companies and whether their past conduct is such as to make them unfit to be concerned in management. However, the gateway to proceedings in s. 8 cases is not that the company has become insolvent but that there has been a relevant type of statutory investigation. Again, jurisdiction to disqualify under this section is conferred solely on the civil courts.

19.25 Under s. 8, if the Secretary of State considers from certain investigatory material that it is in the public interest that a disqualification order should be made against a person who is or was a director of a company, then he may apply to the court. On such an application the court, if satisfied that that person's conduct makes him unfit to be concerned in the management of a company, may make a disqualification order. A number of points arise.

19.26 First, it is to be noted that, as in the case of s. 6 proceedings, the persons liable to disqualification under s. 8 include de facto and shadow directors. Further, the entities to which the section applies are not limited to companies or to companies formed in England and Wales. In these respects the position is very similar to that under s. 6.

19.27 Second, 'investigative material' includes certain types of statutory reports, as provided for under CA 1985, s. 437, the Financial Services and

Markets Act 2000[34] or regulations made in relation to open-ended investment companies.[35] In addition, 'investigative material' encompasses documents or information obtained pursuant to certain sections of the Companies Act 1985,[36] the Criminal Justice Act 1987,[37] the Criminal Law (Consolidation) (Scotland) Act 1995,[38] the Companies Act 1989[39] or the FSMA 2000.[40]

19.28 Third, although the court has a discretion to disqualify when the statutory criteria are made out (in contrast to the mandatory position under s. 6), in reality the court is unlikely to act very differently whether the proceedings are brought under s. 6 or s. 8.[41] If the policy grounds are the same throughout the CDDA 1986, and the purposes of disqualification are indeed to protect the public by keeping unfit directors 'off the road', to discourage misconduct and thereby to raise standards, then this comes as no great surprise.

19.29 Finally, it should be noted that the maximum period of disqualification that can be imposed is 15 years (CCDA, s. 9(a)(9)). There is no minimum.

Section 9A: Disqualification based on unfit conduct relating to breaches of competition law

19.30 The Enterprise Act 2002 introduced a new statutory regime empowering the Office of Fair Trading (OFT)[42] and other specified regulators to apply to the civil courts for a disqualification order against a director of a company where that company has committed a relevant breach of competition law.

19.31 Under CDDA, s. 9A the court is obliged to make a disqualification order against a person on the application of the OFT or a specified regulator (a phrase hereafter abbreviated to 'the regulator' for ease) if two conditions are satisfied in relation to him:

- that an undertaking which is a company of which he is a director commits a breach of competition law (s. 9A (2));
- that the court considers that his conduct as a director makes him unfit to be concerned in the management of a company (s. 9A (3)).

The maximum period of disqualification that can be imposed is 15 years.[43] There is no minimum.

19.32 The term 'director' in s. 9A clearly includes de jure directors and is expressly extended to include shadow directors by s. 9E (5). In guidance issued just before the competition disqualification regime came into force, the OFT expressed the view that 'director' for section 9A purposes includes a de facto director.[44] It is suggested that this is correct and in line with the authorities under s. 6.

19.33 Under s. 9A(4) an undertaking 'commits a breach of competition law' for the purposes of the first condition if it engages in conduct which infringes any of the following:

1 The Chapter I prohibition in the Competition Act 1998. This prohibition bites on agreements between undertakings, decisions by associations of undertakings or concerted practices which may affect trade within the UK, and which have as their object or effect the prevention, restriction or distortion of competition within the UK.[45]
2 The Chapter II prohibition in the Competition Act 1998. This prohibition bites on any conduct on the part of one or more undertakings which amounts to the abuse of a dominant position in so far as it may affect trade within the UK.[46]
3 Article 81 of the EC Treaty. This prohibits agreements between undertakings, decisions by associations of undertakings or concerted practices which may affect trade between member states, and which have as their object or effect the prevention, restriction or distortion of competition within the common market.
4 Article 82 of the EC Treaty. This prohibits abuse by one or more undertakings of a dominant position within the common market or in a substantial part of it in so far as the abuse may affect trade between member states.

19.34 Thus, the Chapter I prohibition and Article 81 regulate anti-competitive agreements whereas the Chapter II prohibition and Article 82 regulate the abuse of market power.[47] In relation to conduct infringing the Chapter I prohibition or Article 81, s. 9A(8) provides that 'references to the conduct of an undertaking are references to its conduct taken with the conduct of one or more other undertakings'. This simply reflects the fact that the anti-competitive conduct targeted by these provisions – agreements between competitors and other forms of concerted practice – by definition involves more than one party.

19.35 For the purpose of deciding whether a person is unfit to be concerned in the management of a company, CDDA, s. 9A(5) provides that the court:

- must have regard to whether CDDA, s. 9A(6) applies to him;
- may have regard to his conduct as a director of a company in connection with any other breach of competition law;
- must not have regard to the matters mentioned in Schedule 1.

19.36 CDDA 1986, s. 9A(6) applies to a person if as a director of the company:

1 his conduct contributed to a relevant breach of competition law;
2 his conduct did not contribute to the breach but he had reasonable grounds

to suspect that the conduct of the undertaking constituted the breach and took no steps to prevent it;

3 he did not know but ought to have known that the conduct of the undertaking constituted the breach.

19.37 For the purposes of the first alternative (direct contribution to the breach), s. 9A (7) further provides that it is immaterial whether the person knew that the conduct of the undertaking constituted the breach. Section 9A (6) establishes what appears to be a sliding scale of culpability to which the court must have regard. However, it does not give the court clear guidance as to where the line between fit conduct and unfit conduct should be drawn. The provision gives nothing more than a general indication that a person's direct participation in a relevant breach of competition law could make that person unfit while suggesting, at the same time, that something less than direct involvement may be enough. Moreover, section 9E provides that 'conduct' includes omission. Thus, in cases where the defendant was not directly involved in the breach, there is scope for the court to fashion standards of conduct and further develop the positive, non-delegable obligation on directors to keep themselves informed of the company's affairs and to supervise its activities,[48] albeit with particular reference to compliance with competition law. As with ss. 6 and 8, the issue of whether or not a director's conduct makes him unfit will ultimately boil down to a question of judgement in individual cases. In practice, it is suggested that the courts are likely to refine and apply the broad test of probity and competence that has emerged in cases under ss. 6 and 8.[49]

Section 2 – disqualification based on conviction of an indictable offence

19.38 Jurisdiction to disqualify under s. 2 of CDDA is given to both the civil and the criminal courts. The prerequisite is that the person in question has actually been convicted of a relevant indictable offence, that is an offence which is capable of being tried on indictment. If the convicting court is one exercising summary criminal jurisdiction the maximum period of disqualification is five years, otherwise the maximum period of disqualification is 15 years. Offences that will trigger the s. 2 jurisdiction are ones which are 'in connection with' the promotion, formation management, liquidation or striking off of a company, with the receivership of a company's property or with the defendant's being an administrative receiver. It will be noted that the disqualification jurisdiction under this section extends beyond directors to a much wider category of persons (including, among others, employees, managers, company secretaries and, in certain circumstances, insolvency practitioners). Promotion and formation usually provide little problem, but 'management' has given rise to a certain amount of case law. What is required is that there be some factual connection with the management of a company. It is not necessary that the conviction is of those who actually manage the company (though that may be common).[50] Thus, in *R v. Creggy*[51] a solicitor was disqualified under s. 2, having been convicted of money-laundering offences which involved assisting the retention of criminal property through the use of his solicitor client account. The argument that this was not an offence in connection with the management of a company: that the defendant was not the manager of the company; was not convicted of operating either that company or any other company for the purpose of the fraud; that he had done no more than to receive sums of money and to shelter them; and that it was immaterial to that offence whether he received them from a company or from an individual criminal were all rejected.

Sections 3 and 5 – persistent breach of companies legislation

19.39 Sections 3 and 5 of CDDA cover much the same ground. The difference between them is that s. 3 confers jurisdiction on the civil court to disqualify for persistent default with regard to the making of returns to the Registrar of Companies, while s. 5 confers jurisdiction on the criminal court which convicts of a relevant summary offence, again relating to filing defaults under companies legislation. In each case the maximum period of disqualification is five years.

Under s. 3 the requirement is that there has been 'persistent default' by the relevant person in relation to provisions of companies legislation (i.e. the Companies Act 1985, the Companies Act 2006 and the Insolvency Act 1985) requiring any return, account or other document to be filed with, delivered or sent, or notice of any matter to be given to, the Registrar of Companies. The section is not limited to directors. Under s. 3(2) 'persistent default' may conclusively be proved by showing that in the five years ending with the date of the application for the making of a disqualification order, an individual has been adjudged guilty of three or more relevant defaults. For these purposes 'adjudged guilty' amounts to conviction of a relevant non-filing offence or having been ordered under specifically identified provisions, to have been required to remedy some such default (a default order). In the absence of reliance on the conclusive presumption the onus is on the applicant to demonstrate 'persistent default' which connotes a degree of continuance or repetition and this may involve persistence in the same default or persistent commission of a series of defaults.[52]

Under s. 5 the criminal court can disqualify on the occasion of a summary conviction for a relevant filing default provided that, on a totting up basis, there has been a relevant number of convictions or default orders over the previous five years. Unlike the civil jurisdiction, there must have been this criminal record. For these purposes the person must have had made against him, or been convicted of, not less than three default orders and offences counting for the purposes of s. 5 (including the current conviction and any other relevant filing conviction on the same occasion).

Section 4 – disqualification for fraud, etc. in winding up

19.40 Section 4 of CDDA confers jurisdiction on the civil court to disqualify where it appears in the course of a winding up that a person has been guilty of the offence of fraudulent trading under the Companies Act 1985, s. 458 (whether or not convicted) or has otherwise been guilty, while an officer or liquidator or receiver of the company's property or administrative receiver of the company, of any fraud in relation to the company or of any breach of his duty in such capacity. The maximum period of disqualification is 15 years. There is no minimum period.

The relevant misconduct must be discovered during the course of liquidation. On particular facts there may be an overlap of jurisdiction to disqualify under this section and that under s. 6 and/or s. 2.[53]

Section 10 – disqualification for fraudulent or wrongful trading

19.41 Section 10 of CDDA confers jurisdiction on the civil court, when making a declaration of liability to contribute to the company's assets under either s. 213 of the Insolvency Act 1986 (fraudulent trading) or s. 214 of the Insolvency Act 1986 (wrongful trading) to make a disqualification order against the person to whom the declaration relates. Although the court acts on its own initiative, better practice is to join or at least notify the Secretary of State so that he can assist the court.[54]

Procedure in civil cases

19.42 Where the criminal court has jurisdiction to disqualify it does so as a matter of sentencing. In a related sense the same is true of the civil courts in cases where jurisdiction is conferred under s. 10 of CDDA. Otherwise, however, civil proceedings for disqualification are governed by the Insolvency Companies (Disqualification of Unfit Directors) Proceedings Rules 1987 (the Disqualification Rules 1987) and/or the Disqualification Practice Direction made under the Civil Procedure Rules. The former are being reviewed as part of the Insolvency Service's general review of insolvency-related rules. Under the current provisions, civil disqualification proceedings are brought by way of a Part 8 Claim Form and the substantive evidence has to be in affidavit form.

19.43 Despite judicial urgings[55] that cases should be kept simple and that a broad-brush approach should be taken, not surprisingly, given the important effects of disqualification for an individual, where proceedings are fought these urgings have proved optimistic.

Notice prior to issue of proceedings

19.44 Prior to issue of most types of civil proceedings seeking a disqualification order, there is a statutory requirement to give at least ten days' notice of intention to bring the proceedings (CDDA, s. 16). However, failure to adhere to this requirement does not automatically result in the proceedings being void.[56] Further, and in practice, where a governmental body is a potential claimant, it is usual for contact to be made well in advance of the issue of proceedings and, subject to conditions as to use and confidentiality, for draft evidence to be made available prior to issue so that a prospective defendant will have an opportunity to answer the allegations being made with a view to persuading the Secretary of State not to bring proceedings and/or to consider whether or not to offer an undertaking prior to issue of proceedings. In part this assists the relevant governmental arm in complying with its duty to conduct disqualification proceedings fairly.[57] In s. 6 cases it will be usual for there to be an officeholder's report to the Secretary of State as required by s. 7(3). This report will also usually be made available in advance of proceedings subject to undertakings as to use and confidentiality. The views of the relevant officeholder will, however, generally be irrelevant, and cannot be used for or against the claimant.[58] The Secretary of State or Official Receiver has power to require certain officeholders to provide information and books, papers and documents as may reasonably be required to exercise relevant functions under s.7(4).[59]

The claimant

19.45 In civil cases brought under ss. 2–4 of CDDA the application may be brought by the Secretary of State, the Official Receiver, the liquidator or any past or present member or creditor of a company in relation to which it is alleged that the relevant defendant committed, or is alleged to have committed, the offence or default. There is doubt as to the circumstances in which it would be appropriate for a liquidator to bring proceedings given the responsibilities of government in this field. As regards creditors and members, the position appears to be that they will not have standing to make an application unless they have a relevant financial interest.[60]

Applications under ss. 6 and 8 may only be made by the Secretary of State or, under s. 6, if the Secretary of State so directs in the case of a person who is or was a director of a company which is being or has been wound up by the court, by the Official Receiver.

19.46 Applications under s. 9A may be made by the OFT or a 'specific regulator'[61] for the purposes of a breach of competition law in relation to which he or it has a function.

The court

19.47 In ss.8 and 9A cases the relevant court with jurisdiction is, in England and Wales, the High Court.

19.48 In cases brought pursuant to ss. 2–4 the court with jurisdiction is the court having jurisdiction to wind up any of the companies with the relevant connection to that section. That will be the High Court or, where the paid-up share capital does not exceed £120,000, the relevant county court with insolvency jurisdiction within the jurisdiction of which the company's registered office has been in for the longest period within the six months immediately preceding the application.[62]

19.49 In s. 6 cases[63] the court will be:

- where the company is being, or has been, wound up by the court, that court;
- where the court is or has been wound up voluntarily, any court which has (or had) jurisdiction to wind it up;
- in any other case, any court with jurisdiction to wind up the company.

Time to commence proceedings

19.50 Other than in s. 6 cases there is no express time limit under the CDDA within which disqualification proceedings must be brought. However, proceedings seeking a disqualification order under s. 6 must be brought within two years of the relevant insolvent event and outside that period they may only be brought with the court's permission (s. 7(2)). In deciding whether to grant permission to bring proceedings outside the two-year period, the court considers all the circumstance, including the length of the delay, the reasons for it, the strength of the case against the director and the degree of prejudice caused to the director by the delay.[64]

The evidence and directions

19.51 Evidence in disqualification proceedings is currently by affidavit. The claimant sets out in the affidavit not only the facts relied on, but also the inferences that the court is asked to draw. A summary of the allegations is also required to be set out.[65] The claimant is responsible for service of the Part 8 Claim Form and the evidence in support. Where the defendant is out of the jurisdiction there may be a need to seek an order for service out of the jurisdiction. It should be noted that the regime for service out of the jurisdiction is a separate one from that under CPR rr. 6.17–6.31.

19.52 Under the Disqualification Rules 1987 and the Practice Direction a timetable is set out under which the defendant is to serve an acknowledgement of service within 14 days of service of the Claim Form and affidavit evidence in opposition to the claim within 28 days of service of the Claim Form. Each defendant is required to serve his evidence on any other defendant unless the court otherwise orders. The Claim Form usually sets out the first hearing day for the matter, which is usually a directions hearing. As matters currently stand a disqualification order for more than five years cannot be made on the first hearing of the Claim Form. It is quite common for there to be a number of directions hearings as the prescribed timetable is rarely appropriate.

Disclosure

19.53 Disclosure is rare. Unless ordered it does not take place, though there may be voluntary disclosure. In most s. 6 cases there will be limited documentation within the control of the Secretary of State.[66] The bulk of the documentation is likely to be with the company or, if the company is in a relevant insolvency regime, the office holder. It will be to the office holder that requests for disclosure will often be directed. The position will be different in, for example, s. 8 cases. In disqualification proceedings third party disclosure orders are potentially very important.[67]

Standard and burden of proof

19.54 The burden of proof in a disqualification application lies on the claimant. The standard is the civil standard of the balance of probabilities.[68]

Appeals and review

19.55 In cases governed by the Disqualification Rules 1987 the general review power of the Insolvency Rules 7.47 applies.

19.56 Appeals in cases governed by the Disqualification Rules 1987 are subject to the Insolvency Rules procedures. Appeals from the county court (whether Judge or District Judge) or from the Registrar or District Judge sitting in the High Court lie to the High Court Judge with permission and from there, with permission of the Court of Appeal, to the Court of Appeal. Appeals from the High Court Judge sitting at first instance lie to the Court of Appeal with permission of either the High Court Judge or the Court of Appeal.

19.57 Appeals in other cases lie according to the usual rules in civil proceedings under the CPR.

Disqualification orders

19.58 A disqualification order by its terms prohibits an individual or a company from acting in certain capacities or in certain ways in relation to companies. A disqualification order takes effect in the full terms of the order as defined by s. 1 of CDDA and the court cannot narrow the scope of that order by deciding to disqualify only as regards certain of the capacities or matters set out in the definition. Thus, it is not, for example, possible to disqualify a person only from being a director or being involved in management or to disqualify only in relation to public companies but not to disqualify in respect of the other matters set out in s. 1 of CDDA.[69]

19.59 In the case of all orders made after 2 April 2002,[70] the period of disqualification, as set by the court, will commence when the court orders and if it makes no express provision the period of disqualification will commence at the end of the period of 21 days beginning with the date of the order (see CDDA, s. 1).

When two or more disqualifications apply to the same person, then such periods run consecutively rather than concurrently.[71]

19.60 The period of disqualification is set by the court, subject to any maximum or minimum period laid down by the CDDA itself. Generally speaking, the guidance given by the Court of Appeal (Civil Division) in *Re Sevenoaks Stationers (Retail) Limited*[72] and in *Re Westmid Packing Services Limited, Secretary of State for Trade and Industry v. Griffiths*[73] both of which were s. 6 cases, has been adopted and utilised (with necessary amendments) as guidance in all disqualification cases, including those in the criminal courts.[74] In the first case the court identified three brackets in s. 6 cases: 2–5 years (relatively speaking, not very serious cases); 6–10 years (serious cases not meriting the top bracket) and 10–15 years (for particularly serious cases, such as where the director is disqualified for a second time). In the *Westmid* case the Court of Appeal identified that even in s. 6 cases the court, once the conditions of s. 6 were found to be met, was engaged in effect in a sentencing exercise. The period of disqualification must reflect the gravity of the misconduct and must contain deterrent elements. However, allowance should be made for mitigating factors and the period reduced accordingly.

19.61 Once made the disqualification order is to be recorded on the register of disqualification orders and undertakings, maintained by the Secretary of State (in fact through the Registrar of Companies) pursuant to s. 18 of CDDA. This register is open to public inspection.

Disqualification undertakings

19.62 Prior to 2 April 2001, the CDDA did not permit the claimant and defendant in civil disqualification proceedings to obtain a disqualification order by consent.[75] In each case the court had to be satisfied that there was jurisdiction to make the order and that the period of disqualification to be imposed was appropriate on the facts of the case. The lack of any mechanism for the parties to reach a settlement by consent led to the development of a procedure, sanctioned by Ferris J. in *Re Carecraft Construction Co Ltd*[76] and approved by the Court of Appeal in *Secretary of State for Trade and Industry v. Rogers*,[77] whereby civil disqualification proceedings could be disposed of on a summary basis.

19.63 Under the *Carecraft* procedure, the parties may put a statement of agreed or non-contested facts before the court on the basis that the facts stated warrant disqualification and invite the court to make a disqualification order for an agreed period or a period falling within an agreed range. The court is asked to make findings based on the agreed statement and dispose of the matter without the necessity of a full trial. It is the essence of the *Carecraft* procedure that the court is not strictly bound by the parties' agreement. Strictly speaking, the court must make its own findings based on the *Carecraft* statement. In theory, the court could hold that the conduct described in the *Carecraft* statement is of insufficient gravity to merit a finding of unfitness. Alternatively, the court might be satisfied that the agreed conduct makes the director unfit but disagree with the parties' assessment of the appropriate period of disqualification. If the court disagrees with the parties on either question, the case would have to be adjourned to a full hearing with both sides able to adduce evidence in the normal way. Before 2 April 2001 the *Carecraft* procedure was used widely in s. 6 cases and had also been used to dispose of s. 8 cases.[78] Since then a scheme of statutory undertakings, which can be offered to and accepted by the relevant arm of government, has been enacted. However, the undertaking regime does not apply to all civil bases for disqualification and the *Carecraft* summary procedure may still have a residual role to play in such cases.

19.64 The main features of the undertakings regime are as follows:

1. The statutory undertakings regime applies only to cases where disqualification under CDDA, s. 6, 8 or 9A is being or would otherwise be sought. It does not apply to civil disqualification cases under CDDA 1986, ss. 2, 3, 4 and 10.
2. A disqualification case under CDDA, s. 6 or 8 can be compromised by the Secretary of State accepting an undertaking from a person in terms that, for a period specified in the undertaking, that person: (a) will not be a director of a company, act as receiver of a company's property or in any way, whether directly or indirectly, be concerned or take part in the promotion, formation or management of a company unless (in each case) he has the permission of the court; and (b) will not act as an insolvency practitioner (CDDA, s. 1A).
3. A disqualification case under CDDA, s. 9A can be compromised by the OFT or specified regulator accepting an undertaking in similar terms to

those defined by CDDA, s. 1A. The form of undertaking is defined in s. 9B(3) and (4). There is an argument that it is possible to agree to a prohibition that is absolute and does not provide for court permission to act in certain otherwise prohibited capacities in relation to a company.

4 The decision to accept an undertaking is exclusively a matter within the administrative discretion of what would otherwise by the relevant claimant, that is, the Secretary of State, the OFT or the specified regulator depending on the case being compromised. As regards the Secretary of State, before an undertaking can be accepted, two criteria must be satisfied. First, it must appear to the Secretary of State from the material available that the conditions for the making of an order under s. 6 or s. 8 are satisfied. Second, the Secretary of State must consider that it is expedient in the public interest to accept an undertaking instead of applying for, or proceeding with, an application, for a disqualification order (ss. 7(2A) and 8(2A)). In the case of competition disqualification undertakings, the OFT or specified regulator must, in broad terms, consider that the conditions of s. 9A for the making of a disqualification order against a person are met before accepting the offer of an undertaking (s. 9B(1)).

5 The refusal of an offer of an undertaking and a decision to press on with proceedings is susceptible to judicial review in the normal way.

6 It is clear from the wording of ss. 7(2A), 8(2A) and 9B(2) that the Secretary of State, OFT or specified regulator can accept undertakings either before or after formal court proceedings have been commenced. In practice, the acceptance of an offer of an undertaking will usually not be made before the point at which a decision would ordinarily be made to bring proceedings. This is because of the requirement to form a view on the merits.

7 The courts have effectively approved the operation of a policy by the Secretary of State where an offer of an undertaking will only be accepted where the director is prepared to admit (or at least not dispute) the factual basis of the disqualification, short details of which will then be recorded in a schedule annexed to the undertaking.[79]

8 An undertaking has the same legal effect as a disqualification order. The scope of the prohibition, the period of disqualification that can be agreed, the sanctions for breach and the provisions on registration are now the same in all respects.

9 In cases where an undertaking has been accepted, the court has power under s. 8A to vary the undertaking, by reducing the period for which it is to be in force, or to discharge the undertaking altogether. The circumstances in which this power will be exercised appear to be quite limited.[80]

10 Once accepted and in force, a disqualification undertaking is recorded on the Register of Disqualification Orders and Undertakings maintained by the Secretary of State (through the Registrar of Companies) pursuant to CDDA, s. 18.

Effect of disqualification

19.65 As noted, disqualification under the CDDA 1986 acts as a civil injunction, backed by specific civil and criminal sanctions applying in the event of breach. In addition to the specific consequences of disqualification as provided for under CDDA (as amplified in various respects by various statutory instruments which apply the Act in other contexts, for example with regard to limited liability partnerships), other statutory provisions provide for specific consequences flowing from disqualification which stretch from disqualifying a person disqualified under CDDA from holding certain offices or positions to making such disqualification a ground for removal from offices or positions. In addition to the statutory consequences of disqualification, there may be other consequences, for example, with regard to professional rules and regulations.

Prohibitions under CDDA

19.66 The basic prohibition, whether the disqualification is based on an order or an undertaking, is that the disqualified person is prevented:

- from being a director of a company, acting as a receiver of a company's property or in any way, directly or indirectly, being concerned with or taking part in the promotion, formation or management of a company unless, in each case, he has the leave of the court; and
- from acting as an insolvency practitioner.

Effect of breach of prohibition

19.67 If the prohibition is breached, then there are both criminal and civil consequences.

19.68 The criminal consequences are that the person who contravenes the disqualification order or undertaking (or of the automatic disqualifications under CDDA flowing from e.g. bankruptcy) will be liable on conviction on indictment to maximum term of imprisonment of three years, a fine or both. On a summary conviction the maximum imprisonment is six months and the fine cannot exceed the statutory maximum.[81] In addition, where a body corporate acts in contravention of a disqualification order, any director, manager, secretary or other officer or any person purporting to act in such capacity will also be guilty of an offence if the breach by the company occurred with his consent or connivance or is attributable to any neglect on his part (CDDA, s. 14).[82]

19.69 The direct civil consequences of a breach of a disqualification are that the person who is in breach will be personally liable for the 'relevant debts' of the company. The 'relevant debts' are the debts and liabilities the company incurs at a time when the breach takes place. In addition, a person who is involved in the management of a company and who acts, or is willing to act, on instructions given, in breach of a disqualification, by a person whom he knows to be disqualified or to be disqualified, for example by reason of the bankruptcy provisions, is similarly personally liable for the debts and liabilities of the company as are incurred at that time (s. 15).

Indirect effects

19.70 In addition to the direct consequences of disqualification provided expressly under CDDA, there are indirect consequences arising under other statutory provisions. The precise position needs checking in each case as the further disqualifications which flow under other statutes do not always match or flow on from each of the different forms of disqualification under CDDA. The following is a broad summary of some of the relevant provisions.

Charities Act 1993

19.71 A person who is the subject of a disqualification order or undertaking is automatically disqualified by the Charities Act 1993, s. 72(1)(f) from acting as a charity trustee. The Charity Commissioners have the power to waive this automatic disqualification in individual cases but cannot exercise this power to allow the disqualified person to remain as a trustee of a charity which is an incorporated body.[83] Equally, it is clear that s. 72(1)(f) does not apply where the court has granted the disqualified person permission to act under the CDDA in relation to a corporate charity.[84] Section 73(1) makes it an offence for a person to act as a charity trustee while disqualified under section 72. However, the effect of section 73(2) is that a person who continues to act as a director of a corporate charity in breach of the s. 1 prohibition only commits an offence under CDDA.[85]

Pensions Act 1995

19.72 A person who is disqualified under CDDA is automatically disqualified by the Pensions Act 1995, s. 29(1)(f) from acting as a trustee of an occupational pension scheme established under a trust. A corporate trustee is similarly disqualified by s. 29(1)(c) from so acting where any of its directors is the subject of a disqualification falling within s. 29. The Occupational Pensions Regulatory Authority established by the Act has the power to waive this automatic disqualification.[86] Section 30 of the Pensions Act makes it an offence for a person to act as a trustee while disqualified. The Authority also has the power to suspend a trustee where CDDA proceedings against him are pending.[87] A person the subject of an order under the Insolvency Act 1986, s. 429(2)(b) (which encompasses a person disqualified under CDDA, s. 12) is also disqualified by s. 29(1)(f) of the Pensions Act.

Police bodies

19.73 By the Police Act 1996, Schedule 2, para. 11(1)(c) a person who is disqualified under CDDA is automatically disqualified from being a member, or from being appointed as a member, of a police authority. The position is the same in respect of persons who are the subject of an order under the Insolvency Act 1986, s. 429(2)(b) and therefore disqualified in the terms of CDDA, s. 12. Similar disqualifications or circumstances where disqualification can found a ground for removal, apply in relation to the Metropolitan Police Authority,[88] the British Transport Police Authority,[89] the office of Commissioner under the Police Act 1997,[90] the Central Police Training and Development Authority[91] and the Independent Police Complaints Commission.[92]

Housing Act 1996

19.74 By the Housing Act 1996, Schedule 1, Part II, para. 4(2)(b), a local housing authority or, where appropriate, a social services authority may make an order removing a director, trustee or committee member of a housing association (now termed a registered social landlord) where he is the subject of a disqualification order under the CDDA.[93] A person disqualified under CDDA who is a director of a housing association constituted as a company limited by guarantee would have to resign anyway, unless the court gives him permission to act. This is also true of a trustee of a housing association constituted as a registered charitable trust by virtue of the automatic disqualification provisions in the Charities Act 1993 (see **19.71** above). Otherwise, a disqualification order under CDDA does not automatically trigger disqualification under the Housing Act. The onus is on the appropriate authority to take steps to remove the person. The position is the same in relation to persons who are the subject of an order under the Insolvency Act 1986, s. 429(2).

Education bodies

19.75 Disqualification under CDDA may also affect appointments as a member of a school company,[94] school PFI companies,[95] Foundation bodies,[96] school governor of a maintained school[97] or school governor of a 'new school'.[98]

Health and social care bodies

19.76 Disqualification under CDDA also affects the ability to be appointed to a number of positions with regard to health and social care bodies[99] and affects the ability to enter into general medical service contracts.[100]

Regulatory and other consequences

19.77 CDDA disqualification may have regulatory consequences for a disqualified person who is a member of a professional body, for example, the Institute of Chartered Accountants in England and Wales. Similarly, where a person is someone who is carrying on a regulated activity for the purposes of the Financial Services and Markets Act 2000 (FSMA), authorised business under financial services or related legislation, the disqualification could prompt the Financial Services Authority (FSA) to withdraw his authorisation on the ground that he is no longer a fit and proper person.[101] These are both matters of discretion for the appropriate professional body or regulator. In the context of securities regulation, it is a requirement of the United Kingdom Listing Authority's (UKLA) Listing Rules that the directors of an issuer disclose details of any bankruptcies or CDDA disqualifications in the prospectus or listing particulars. On a different note, it is likely that a CDDA disqualification will have an adverse effect on the disqualified person's individual credit rating.

Permission to act notwithstanding disqualification

19.78 Disqualification under of CDDA, ss 1 and 1A is absolute as regards the prohibition on being an insolvency practitioner. However, the prohibition on acting as a director, or in the promotion, formation or management, of companies (which need not be limited companies) is subject to the court's power to grant leave.[102] Exercise of that power is effectively a privilege or indulgence.[103] The same is broadly true of the prohibitions in s. 9B(3) (competition undertakings), s. 11 (undischarged bankrupts and bankruptcy restrictions) and s. 12 (where a county court administration order is revoked). It is to be noted that the power to grant leave is confined to the civil courts. If a criminal court makes a disqualification order, it is not able to grant leave or restrict the scope of the disqualification by reference to any grant of leave that it might wish to grant.[104] Similarly, while the Secretary of State and certain others are given powers to 'agree' a disqualification under CDDA, ss. 7(2A), 8(2A) and 9B, there is no power in any entity other than the court to grant permission to act notwithstanding disqualification. CDDA, s. 17 sets out the relevant courts with jurisdiction to hear applications for leave notwithstanding disqualification and relevant procedure. In the case of bankruptcy and bankruptcy restrictions, the procedure is laid down by the Insolvency Rules 1986.

19.79 The power to grant leave to act is, as a matter of jurisdiction, an unfettered one, though of course it has to be applied judicially and in accordance with principle. The starting point is that the burden to show that leave should be granted lies on the person disqualified, his past conduct, in ss. 6, 8, 9A and 9B cases, having been such as to ground a finding that makes him unfit to be concerned in the management of a company. That burden is the standard civil one.[105] Furthermore, usually the applicant will have to produce an up-to-date and substantial account of a company in respect of which a leave application is made.[106] Any application for leave must be approached against the background of the purposes of CDDA, and, if the disqualification is under s. 6, the purposes of a mandatory disqualification under that section.[107] The purposes of disqualification can be summarised as being to protect the public by (a) keeping the director 'off the road'; (b) deterring the director and others from future misconduct; and thereby (c) raising corporate standards of management.[108] Leave must not be granted too freely, otherwise these objectives will be undermined.[109]

19.80 The court may make the grant of leave subject to conditions. Conditions rather than undertakings to the court are usually the preferred course. However, caution should be exercised in granting conditional leave. 'If it is felt that leave should not be unconditional this may suggest that the better view is that it should not be granted at all.'[110] Conditions need to be considered carefully to ensure that they cannot being too easily disregarded and almost impossible to police. Breaches may come to light only when a second company has come to grief, by which time it is too late to do anything.[111]

19.81 In considering whether or not to grant leave the court is required to carry out an 'in all the circumstances test', balancing factors pointing in favour of the grant of leave against factors pointing against it. There is no gateway or threshold condition of establishing 'need' to act, followed by a consideration of whether the purposes of the disqualification order will be unduly damaged in that either the public will not be protected if leave is granted or the deterrent purposes of the order will be undermined. Rather, it is necessary to balance all relevant factors. Among these, and of particular importance, are the strength of the reasonable requirements for, or legitimate interest in, the applicant acting in the position from which he would otherwise be disqualified from acting in, and the risk to the public and any undermining of the deterrent aspects of the disqualification if leave is given.[112]

19.82 There are different types of interest which may point in favour of the granting of leave and different weights to be attached to them.[113] As regards public protection there is no restriction on the different public interest groups whose interests are relevant.[114] As regards past misconduct and the risk to the public in the future, the court should not narrowly concentrate on the risk to the public from the precise repetition of the matters of misconduct on which the disqualification is based.[115]

19.83 The role of the Secretary of State (or the Official Receiver in cases where bankruptcy is involved or the specified regulator who secured the competition disqualification in such cases) is to draw attention to relevant matters. On some occasions the Secretary of State has formally opposed, on others he has not. In the final analysis the question is whether the court is persuaded that leave should be granted in light of all the evidence. It is usual for the Secretary of State to be awarded his costs of a leave application, even if leave is granted.[116]

19.84 It is best practice for the same judge who made any disqualification order also to deal with the application for leave and for any such application to be dealt with immediately after the hearing at which the director is disqualified. Interim leave may be granted but this tends to be exceptional and for a limited period only.[117]

Sources

1 This chapter deals solely with the position in England and Wales. CDDA 1986 also applies to Scotland. Northern Ireland has its own regime, which is very similar.

2 See discussion in *R (on the application of McCann) v. Crown Court at Manchester* [2003] 1 A.C. 787 at paras 17–18.

3 Company Directors Disqualification Act 1986, s. 11.

4 Company Directors Disqualification Act 1986, s. 12.

5 These provisions are due to come into force in October 2009 but will not be effective until secondary legislation is also in force.

6 See in the context of CDDA, s. 6: *Re Swift 736 Limited, Secretary of State for Trade and Industry v. Ettinger* [1993] BCLC 896; Re *Grayan Building Services Limited, Secretary of State for Trade and Industry v. Gray* [19954] Ch 241.

7 See *Re Lo-Line Electric Motors Limited* [1988] Ch. 477.

8 Under the Insolvency Act 1986, Part V, usually on the basis that there is sufficient connection with the jurisdiction

9 This list is not exhaustive.

10 See **19.50–1957**.

11 *Secretary of State for Trade and Industry v. Jabble* [1998] 1 BCLC 598; *Re Kaytech International plc, Secretary of State for Trade and Industry v. Kaczer* [199] 2 BCLC 351 at 396A; *In the Matter of Brampton Manor (Leisure) Ltd, Secretary of State for Trade and Industry v. Woolf* [2005] EWHC 3074 (Ch).

12 See *Re Gower Enterprises Limited, Official Receiver v. Moore* [1995] BCC 293 and on the subsequent enquiry, [1995] 2 BCLC 107; and *Secretary of State for Trade and Industry v. Glover* (21 October 2005, unreported).

13 *Re Surrey Leisure Ltd, Official Receiver v. Keam* [1999] 1 BCLC 731.

14 *Re Country Farms Inn Ltd, Secretary of State for Trade and Industry v. Ivens* [1997] 2 BCLC 334.

15 *Re Grayan Building Services Limited, Secretary of State for Trade and Industry v. Gray* [1995] Ch. 241.

16 *Re Copecrest Limited. Secretary of State for Trade and Industry v. McTighe (No 2)* [1996] 2 BCLC 477.

17 *Re Grayan Building Services Limited, Secretary of State for Trade and Industry v. Gray* [1995] Ch. 241.

18 *Re Barings plc, Secretary of State for Trade and Industry v. Baker* [1999] 1 WLR 1985.

19 *Secretary of State for Trade and Industry v. Goldberg* [2004] 1 BCLC 597.
20 *Re Barings plc (No 5)* [2000] 1 BCLC 523.
21 *Re Sevenoaks Stationers (Retail) Limited* [1991] Ch 164.
22 *Secretary of State for Trade and Industry v. Goldberg* [2004] 1 BCLC 597.
23 CDDA 1986, s. 6(2).
24 As regards conduct in disqualification proceedings themselves see *Re Howglen Limited, Secretary of State for Trade and Industry v. Reynard* [2002] EWCA Civ 947; [2002] 2 BCLC 625.
25 CDDA 1986, s. 9.
26 *Re Bath Glass Limited* [1988] BCLC 329.
27 *Re Amaron Limited* [2001] 1 BCLC 562. To contrary effect, see *Secretary of State for Trade and Industry v. Goldberg* [2004] 12 BCLC 597.
28 *Re Barings plc (No 5)* [2000] 1 BCLC 523.
29 *Re Westmid Packing Services Ltd* [1998] 2 All ER 124; *Re Barings plc (No 5)*[2000] 1 BCLC 523 *Bishopsgate Investment Management Ltd v. Maxwell (No 2)* [1994] 1 All ER 261.
30 *Re Sevenoaks Stationers (Retail) Ltd* [1991] Ch 164; *Re Barings plc (No 5)* [2000] 1 BCLC 523.
31 *Re Barings plc (No 5), Secretary of State for Trade and Industry-v-Baker* [1999] 1 BCLC 523.
32 see e.g. *Re Bath Glass Ltd* [1988] BCLC 329; *Re McNulty's Interchange Ltd* [1989] BCLC 709; *Re Aldermanbury Trust plc* [1993] BCLC 598; *Re Bradcrown Limited; Official Receiver v. Ireland* [2001] 1 BCLC 547.
33 *Re Living Images Ltd* [1996] BCC 112.
34 S. 167, 168, 169 or 284.
35 Under Financial Services and Markets Act 2000, s. 262(2)(k).
36 S. 437, 446E, 447, 448, 451A or 453A.
37 S. 2.
38 S. 28.
39 S. 93.
40 S. 165, 171, 172, 173 or 175.
41 See *Re Atlantic Computers plc, Secretary of State for Trade and Industry v. Ashman* (unreported: June 15 1998); *Re J.A. Chapman & Co. Limited, Secretary of State for Trade and Industry v. Amiss* [2003] EWHC 523 (ch); [2003] 2 BCLC 206.
42 The OFT is the corporate body established to take over the functions of the former Director General of Fair Trading the Enterprise Act 2002, Part 1.
43 CDDA, s. 9A(9).
44 Office of Fair Trading, *Competition Disqualification Orders – Guidance* (May 2003) at para. 2.3.
45 Competition Act 1998, s. 2(1).
46 Competition Act 1998, s. 18(1).
47 The Chapters I and II prohibitions are closely modelled on Articles 81–82 of the EC Treaty. This reflects a policy of deliberate alignment designed to improve the effectiveness of UK competition law and reduce the regulatory burden on businesses affected potentially by two sets of rules: see M. Coleman and M. Grenfell, *The Competition Act 1998* (Oxford, 1999), pp. 4–13.

48 See, e.g., *Re Barings plc, Secretary of State for Trade and Industry v. Baker (No. 5)* [1999] 1 BCLC 433 and discussion in paras 4.16–4.17, 5.70–5.74.
49 See **19.23** above.
50 See e.g. *R v. Goodman* [1993] 2 All ER 789 (offence of insider dealing); *R v. Corbin* (1984) 6 Cr. App.R(S) 17 (offences of obtaining property by deception using the company); *R v. Austin* (1985) 7 Cr. App.R.(S) 214 (offence of obtaining property be deception); *R v. Georgiou* (1988) 87 Cr. App.R 207 (carrying on unlawful insurance business through a company).
51 [2008] EWCA Crim 394, (2008) 3 All ER 91.
52 *Re Arctic Engineering Limited* [1986] 1 WLR 686.
53 See e.g. *Re Dennis Hilton Limited* [2002] 1 BCLC 302.
54 See e.g. *Re Brian D Pierson (Contractors) Limited* [1999] BCC 26 at 58.
55 See e.g. *Re Westmid Packing Services Limited, Secretary of State for Trade and Industry v. Griffiths* [1998] 2 All ER 124.
56 *Re Cedac Limited, Secrteray of State for Trade and Industry v. Langridge* [1991] Ch 402.
57 See e.g. *Re Moonlight Foods (UK) Limited, Secretary of State for Trade and Industry v. Hickling* [1996] BCC 678; *Re Finelist Limited, Secretary of State for Trade and Industry v. Swan* [2003] EWHC 1780 (ch), [2004] BCC 877.
58 *Re Park House Properties Limited* [1998] BCC 847.
59 As regards the office holder's own investigatory powers and the extent to which they may be used in furtherance of disqualification purposes, see *Re Pantmaenog Timber Co Limited, Official Receiver v. Meade-King* [2003] UKHL 49, [2004] 1 AC 158.
60 *Re Adbury Park Estates Limited, Juer v. Lomas* (Unrep. Ch D 28 June 2001; (CofApp) [2001] EWCA Civ 1568.
61 As set out in s. 9E.
62 See Insolvency Act 1986, s. 117.
63 See CDDA, ss. 6(3),6(3A) and 6(3B).
64 *Re Prove Data Systems Limited (No 3), Secretary of State for Trade and Industry v. Desai* [1992] BCC 110; *Re Blackspur Group plc, Secrteray of State for Trade and Industry v. Davies* [1996] 4 All ER 289.
65 *Kappler v. Secretary of State for Trade and Industry* (2008) 1 BCLC 120.
66 See e.g. *Re Lombard Shipping and Forwarding Limited* [1992] BCC 700.
67 See e.g. *Re Howglen Limited* [2001] 1 ALL ER 376, *Re Skyward Builders plc* [2002] EWHC 1788 (ch), [2002] 2 BCLC 750.
68 *Re Living Images Limited* [1996] BCC 112. See also *Re B (Children)* [2008] UKHL 35, [2008] 3 WLR 1 and *Re D* [2008] UKHL 33, [2008] 1 WLR 1499.
69 See *Re Gower Enterprises Limited (No 2)* [1995] 2 BCLC 201; *Re Seagull Manufacturing Limited (No 3)* [1995] BCC 1088; *Re Cannonquest Limited, Official Receiver v. Hannan* [1997] 2 BCLC 473; *R v. Cole, Lees & Birch* [1998] BCC 87; *R v. Ward* [2001] EWCA Crim 1648; [2002] BCC 953.
70 When a new s. 1 of CDDA was inserted. Prior to that, rule 9 of the Disqualification Rules 1986 applied.
71 See CDDA 1986, ss. 1(3) and 1A(3).
72 [1991] Ch 164.
73 [1998] 2 ALL ER 124.
74 In the criminal courts, see e.g. *R v. Edwards* [1998] 2 Cr. App. R(s) 213.

75 See e.g. *Re Carecraft Construction Co. Ltd* [1994] 1 WLR 172; *Re Blackspur Group plc* [1998] 1 WLR 422.
76 [1994] 1 WLR 172.
77 [1996] 1 WLR 1569.
78 *Re Aldermanbury Trust plc* [1993] BCC 598 is an example of a s. 8 case in which the procedure was successfully invoked.
79 *Re Blackspur Group plc, Secretary of State for Trade and Industry v. Eastaway* [2001] EWCA Civ 1595; [2002] 2 BCLC 263.
80 *Re Ins Realisations Ltd, Secretary of State for Trade and Industry v. Jonkler* [2006] EWHC 135 (Ch), [2006] 1 WLR 3433.
81 CDDA 1986, s. 13.
82 CDDA 1986, s. 14.
83 Charities Act 1993, s. 72(4).
84 Charities Act 1993, s. 72(3)(a).
85 Note that ss. 72–73 of the Charities Act are re-enactments of the Charities Act 1992, ss. 45–46, which came into force on 1 January 1993.
86 Pensions Act 1995, s. 29(5). This power is identical to that of the Charity Commissioners under the Charities Act 1993.
87 Charities Act 1993,, s. 4(1)(e). The Authority is also empowered to issue an order prohibiting a person from continuing as a trustee of a scheme in prescribed circumstances: Charities Act 1993, s. 3. Penalties for breach of either a prohibition or suspension order are set out in s. 6.
88 Police Act 1996, Schedule 2A.
89 Railways and Transport Safety Act 2003, s. 18 and Schedule 4.
90 See s. 91, Schedule 2, para. 3.
91 Criminal Justice and Police Act 2001, Schedule 3.
92 Police Reform Act 2002, s. 9 and Schedule 2.
93 This provision came into force on 1 October 1996. The Housing Corporation previously had power under the Housing Associations Act 1985 to remove a housing association committee member in certain circumstances (e.g. bankruptcy or mental disorder). The 1996 Act extends these powers to encompass persons disqualified under CDDA.
94 School Companies Regulations 2002.
95 School Companies (Private Finance Initiative Companies) Regulations 2002.
96 Education (Foundation Body) (England) Regulations 2000.
97 School Governance (Constitution) (England) Regulations 2002.
98 See School Standards and Framework Act 1998, s. 72 and New Schools (General) (England) Regulations 2003.
99 See e.g. SI 2002/2376; IS 2002/3038; SI 2002/3040; SI 2003/506; SI 2003/3059; SI 2003/3060; SI 2003/3190; SI 2003/2772; SI 2003/2773; SI 2003/3279.
100 See e.g. SI 2004/291.
101 Financial Services and Markets Act 2000, ss. 40–41 and Schedle 6, Part. I, para. 5. Equally, if a disqualified person applies for authorisation, it is open to the FSA to refuse the application if it does not consider the applicant to be fit and proper.
102 See CDDA, ss. 1, 1A and 17.
103 *Re Brian Sheridan Cars Limited* [1995] BCC 1035 at 1,046C; 1049B, H.
104 See CDDA, s. 17, but note that criminal courts often do not seem aware of this limit to their jurisdiction: see e.g. *R v. Creggy* [1998] 3 All ER 91.

105 *Re Amaron Ltd* [1998] BCC 264, at 277D.
106 *Re Amaron Ltd* [1998] BCC 264, at 277F–278E.
107 *Re TLL Realisations Limited* [2000] 2 BCLC 223, at 231a–c; *Re Barings plc (No 3)* [2000] 1 WLR 634, at 637F–G, 640H–641A, citing Arden J in *Re Tech Textiles Limited* [1998] 1 BCLC 259, at 267; *Re Westminster Property Management Limited (no 2), Official Receiver v. Stern (no 2)* [2001] BCC 305, at 258E–H.
108 E.g. *Re Westmid Packing Services Limited* [1998] 2 BCLC 646, at 652i–653b; 654i–655e.
109 Per Arden J in *Re Tech Textiles Ltd* [1998] 1 BCLC259, at 267e–f.
110 Per Ferris J in *Re TLL Realisations Limited (on appeal)* [2000] 2 BCLC 223, at 239e–g.
111 *Re Gibson Davies Limited* [1995] BCC 11 and the subsequent failure in that case: See Walters and Davis-White, *Directors Disqualification and Bankruptcy Restrictions*, paras 15-36–15-39.
112 See generally *Re Barings plc (No 3) Secretary of State for Trade and Industry v. Baker* [2000] 1 WLR 634; *Dawes & Henderson (Agencies) Limited (No 2), Secretary of State for Trade and Industry v. Shuttleworth* [1999] 2 BCLC 317; *Re Hennelly's Utilities, Hennelly v. Secretary of State for Trade and Industry* [2004] EWHC 34 (Ch); (2005) BCC 542. *Re Finelist Limited* [2005] EWCA 2479 (Ch).
113 See *Re Dawes and Henderson Limited* [1999] 2 BCLC 317; *Re TLL Realisations Limited* [2000] BCC 998.
114 See e.g. *Re Tech Textiles Limited* [1998] 1 BCLC 259.
115 *Re Westminster Property Management Limited (No 2), Official Receiver v. Stern (No 2)* [2001] BCC 305.
116 *Re TLL Realisations Limited* [2000] BCC 998.
117 *Secretary of State for Trade and Industry v. Renwick* (July 1997, unreported). *Re Amaron Limited* [1998] BCC 264; Re *TLL Realisations Limited* [2000] BCC 998.

20

Induction of directors and board evaluation

Introduction

20.1 This chapter examines the induction of directors and summarises the requirements for performance evaluation of the board and committees, and of directors.

Induction

20.2 The objective of induction is to 'inform the director such that he or she can become as effective as possible in their new role as soon as possible'. As Higgs noted in his original report: 'to be effective, newly appointed non-executive directors (NEDs) quickly need to build their knowledge of the organisation to the point where they can use the skills and experience they have gained elsewhere for the benefit of the company'.

20.3 It is with such thoughts of enabling a newly appointed director to 'hit the ground running' that the Combined Code raised the profile of induction. The Main Principle contained in section 1, paragraph A5 of the Combined Code simply states that 'all directors should receive induction on joining the Board'. However, the subsequent Revised Combined Code Provision elaborates on this to state that 'the Chairman should ensure that new directors receive a full, formal and tailored induction on joining the board. As part of this, the company should offer to major shareholders the opportunity to meet a new non-executive director'.

20.4 The need for effective induction has featured in a number of reports since the publication of Higgs' original Combined Code. In 'The Recruitment and Development of Non Executive Directors' (published in June 2003) Professor Laura Tyson echoed Higgs and observed: 'Companies should provide thorough induction programmes for all new NED appointees and should provide ongoing training opportunities for incumbent NEDs.'

20.5 Higgs had also commented that NEDs who were interviewed highlighted that visiting company locations and attending company events 'significantly developed their knowledge of the business and its people'.

20.6 In December 2004, the DTI-sponsored report 'Building Better Boards' suggested:

> 'Effective solutions (in this case for information flow – but the principle is the same) may lie in pairing or partnering NEDs with executive directors or senior managers in areas of mutual interest or expertise or building informal relationships between individual directors and middle managers, e.g. by arranging for directors to "adopt" a group company, plant or store.'

20.7 Higgs highlighted that a company should set aside adequate resources and ensure sufficient time is allowed for a thorough induction for directors. In practice, this means that a suitably comprehensive programme is compiled which is relevant to the company's business and combines presentations, meetings and the provision of information in an induction pack. The induction must also be specific to the director in question, taking into account whether the individual:

- is executive or non-executive;
- has prior experience or no experience as a director; and
- has prior experience within the industry sector of the company.

20.8 Any induction process should therefore incorporate:

- an understanding of the nature of the company, its business and the markets in which it operates;
- a link with the company's people; and
- an understanding of the company's main relationships.

20.9 In addition, an induction pack needs to provide a new director with certain basic information about the company. In this regard the ICSA produced a Guidance Note setting out comprehensive details of the materials that should be considered for inclusion. The ICSA devised a three-part approach, consisting of:

- the essential material that should be provided immediately;
- the material that should be provided over the first few weeks following the appointment; and
- items the company secretary might consider making the director aware of.

20.10 Irrespective of splitting the information in such a way, the director should be provided immediately with a comprehensive list (as set out below) of all the material which is to be made available to him.

Director's induction pack
20.11

Directors' duties

- Brief outline of the role of a director and a summary of his responsibilities and ongoing obligations under legislation, regulation and best practice.
- Copy of FSA's Model Code, and details of the company's procedure regarding directors' share dealings and the disclosure of inside information.
- The company's guidelines on:
  - matters reserved for the board;
  - delegated authorities;
  - the policy for obtaining independent professional advice for directors;
  - other standing orders, policies and procedures of which the director should be aware;
  - 'fire drill' procedures (i.e. the procedures in place to deal with situations such as hostile takeover bids).

The company's business

- Current strategic/business plan, market analysis and budgets for the year with revised forecast, and three-/five-year plan.
- Latest annual report and accounts, and interims as appropriate.
- Explanation of key performance indicators.
- List of major domestic and overseas subsidiaries, associated companies and joint ventures, including any parent company(ies).
- Summary details of major group insurance policies including D&O insurance.
- Details of any major litigation, either current or potential, being undertaken by or against the company.
- Treasury issues:
- Funding position and arrangements;
- Dividend policy.
- The corporate brochure, mission statement and any other reports issued by the company, such as an environmental report, with a summary of the main events (such as mergers, divestments, introductions of new products, diversification into new areas, restructuring, etc.) over the last three years.

Board issues

- Up-to-date copy of the company's memorandum and articles of association /constitution, with a summary of the most important provisions.

- Minutes of the last three to six board meetings.
- Schedule of dates of future board meetings and board subcommittees if appropriate.
- Description of board procedures covering details such as when papers are sent out, the normal location of meetings, how long they last and an indication of the routine business transacted.
- Brief biographical and contact details of all directors of the company, the company secretary and other key executives. This should include any executive responsibilities of directors, their dates of appointment and any board committees upon which individual directors sit.
- Details of board subcommittees, together with terms of reference and, where the director will be joining a committee, copies of the minutes of meetings of that committee during the previous twelve months.

Additional material to be provided during the first few months

20.12 The following information is crucial to assist the director to develop his knowledge of the company, its operations and staff, but is not necessary for him to commence his involvement. It is suggested, however, that a detailed schedule of the information available is provided, and the information is supplied either on request or within three months of appointment:

- copies of the company's main product/service brochures;
- copies of recent press cuttings, reports and articles concerning the company;
- details of the company's advisers (lawyers, bankers, auditors, registrars, etc.), both internal and external, with the name of the individual dealing with the company's affairs;
- the company's risk management procedures and relevant disaster recovery plans;
- an outline of the provisions of the Combined Code as appended to the UK Listing Rules, together with details of the company's corporate governance guidelines and any investor's corporate governance guidelines which the company seeks to follow;
- a brief history of the company, including when it was incorporated and any significant events during its history;
- notices of any general meetings held in the last three years, and accompanying circulars as appropriate;
- company organisation chart and management succession plans;
- a copy of all management accounts prepared since the company's last audited accounts;
- the company's investor relations policy and details of the major shareholders;
- details of the five largest customers with the level of business done over the last five years;

- details of the five largest suppliers to the company;
- policies as regards:
  - health and safety;
  - the environment;
  - ethics and whistleblowing;
  - charitable and political donations;
- internal company telephone directory, including any overseas contact numbers and names.

Induction briefings

20.13 Prior to the first board meeting, new directors should be briefed by the chairman, chief executive and senior independent director to discuss:

- overall group strategy and progress of strategy;
- current performance, and significant issues and challenges in relation to performance;
- role of the board and style of board meetings;
- role of board committees and current priorities;
- market perception of the company and significant influences on this.

The chairman should also outline the responsibilities and procedures of the nominations committee, and the company secretary should discuss with the new director matters relating to corporate governance and board procedures.

20.14 As soon as practicable after appointment directors should:

- attend briefing meetings with divisional chief executives to acquire a thorough overall knowledge of the group's businesses, their strategies and progress against strategy, their current performance and performance issues and challenges;
- attend briefing meetings with the chairman of the audit and remuneration committees to gain an understanding of the role of the committees, the responsibilities of committee members and current priorities;
- meet the finance director to supplement the briefing of the audit committee chairman and provide appropriate information on accounting policies, procedures and control issues;
- visit the corporate centre to gain an understanding of its role and organisation and to meet key heads of function;
- visit to major plant(s) in the UK/Europe/worldwide;
- attend an external course on the duties and responsibilities of a NED, if appropriate to his level of experience.

Appointment to committees

20.15 Prior to appointment as a member or chairman of the audit committee, directors should attend in-depth meetings with the finance director, head of corporate audit and other key in-house accounting staff and external auditors. He should also attend briefing meetings with the human resources director and external remuneration advisers to the committee if he is to be appointed to the remuneration committee. In each case arrangements should be made for him to attend external courses on audit and remuneration committee responsibilities and effectiveness if appropriate.

20.16 The responsibility for selecting whatever else might be appropriate falls in practice to the company secretary.

20.17 In terms of overall responsibility for compiling the induction programme, Higgs suggested that the chairman should take the lead in providing a properly constructed induction programme and this should be facilitated by the company secretary. This approach was subsequently reflected in the Combined Code.

Updating and refreshing skills and knowledge

20.18 When considering the training needs of NEDs, Higgs noted that there 'should be a step change in training and development provision so that it is suited to the needs of boards'. He emphasised that what he envisaged is continued professional development tailored to the individual.

20.19 Both the Tyson and the DTI reports subsequently addressed the need for evaluation and training; Tyson recommended companies need to invest more in NED evaluation and that NED training should be linked to the findings of such assessments. The Tyson Report reiterated Higgs: companies should undertake an evaluation of the performance of their boards on a regular basis. The report also observed that as NED responsibilities continue to expand, companies will need to provide more training for their board members.

20.20 So what are the training issues which the chairman and the company secretary need to consider? Higgs underlined the importance of the performance evaluation process to the formulation of a training schedule and also stated that NEDs themselves should regularly appraise their skills, knowledge and expertise to determine whether further professional development would 'help them develop their expertise and fulfil their obligations as members of the unitary board'. It is with this sentiment of self-responsibility that Higgs summed up his view that 'non-executive directors should be prepared to devote time to keeping their skills up-to-date'.

20.21 Examples of training for potential directors are understanding:

- the role of the board;
- the obligations and rights of directors of listed companies;
- the behaviours needed for effective board performance.

20.22 For existing directors these are:

- updating knowledge of strategy, management of human and financial resources and audit and remuneration;
- legal and regulatory updates;
- revisiting board behaviours.

Performance evaluation

20.23 The DTI report 'Building Better Boards' embraced the conclusions of the Higgs Report on performance evaluation and concluded: 'Regular evaluation of board performance represents a tool which, used positively, will not only produce a better board but improvements in company performance.'

20.24 Higgs provides for a 'formal and rigorous annual evaluation' of the board, the committees and the individual directors alike. The Supporting Principle in the Combined Code goes one step further and provides as follows:

> 'Individual evaluation should aim to show whether each director continues to contribute effectively and to demonstrate commitment to the role (including commitment of time for board and committee meetings and any other duties). The Chairman should act on the results of the performance evaluation by recognising the strengths and addressing the weaknesses of the board and, where appropriate, proposing new members be appointed to the board or seeking the resignation of directors.'

20.25 In recommending that resignations should be sought from under-performing directors, the principle was established that a performance- and results-led culture should prevail in the boardroom, as it has among the general workforce.

Board evaluation

20.26 In conducting a board evaluation, the following questions should help to form the basis of what issues to cover:

- Do the directors work as a team with all directors contributing?
- Is the chairman an effective leader?
- Do decisions take account of shareholders' views?
- Is the board capable of taking and sticking to difficult decisions?
- Do all members of the board have a clear understanding of their roles and responsibilities?
- How has the board performed against performance objectives?
- How has the board ensured robust and effective risk management?
- Is the composition of the board and its committees appropriate and effective?
- As a whole, is the board up to date with the latest relevant developments?

27.27 Whether the right processes and procedures are in place to produce high-performing boards, should also be assessed. For instance:

- Is the best use of time made at meetings?
- Are board procedures flexible enough to allow for unforeseen eventualities?
- Is the flow of information sufficient to consider issues, make decisions and have them implemented ?

Performance evaluation of the non-executive director

20.28 In evaluating individuals it is necessary to ask:

- How well prepared and informed are they for board meetings?
- Do they have a satisfactory record of attendance?
- Do they demonstrate a willingness to devote time and effort to understand the company and its business and a readiness to participate in events outside the boardroom?
- What has been the quality and value of their contributions at board meetings?
- How effectively have they probed to test information and assumptions?
- How resolute are they in maintaining their own views and resisting pressure from others?
- How effective are their relationships with fellow board members, the company secretary and senior management?

20.29 The role of the chairman is critical in any company and there are some specific issues relating to the chairman that should be included as part of an evaluation of the board's performance, for example:

- Is the chairman demonstrating effective leadership?
- Are relationships and communications with shareholders well managed?
- Are relationships and communications within the board constructive?
- Are the processes for setting the agenda working? Do they enable board members to raise issues and concerns?

- Are all directors allowed or encouraged to participate fully in board discussions?
- Is the company secretary used appropriately and to maximum value?
- Do they provide effective leadership, manage communications and relationships and encourage board members to participate fully in board discussions? (Further information on the role of the chairman, chief executive and senior independent director, see the ICSA Guidance at **Appendix 2**.)

20.30 While it is the chairman's responsibility to oversee the process of a board evaluation, in this, he (and the company secretary) should be supported by members of the company's nomination committee.

Evaluation of board committees

20.31 The Code also requires the chairman to undertake an evaluation of the board committees. It is not unusual for committee members to forget that they form a committee of the board – and are responsible to it; the following areas should be addressed as part of an evaluation process:

- Does each board committee have adequate and appropriate written terms of reference?
- Has the committee the correct composition of members?
- Is sufficient time allocated to committee meetings to allow it to handle the business delegated to it properly?
- Should other members of the executive team be invited to attend meetings?
- Does the committee achieve its remit?
- Is the reporting between committee and Board adequate for those who are not members of the committee to understand the work undertaken on their behalf?

20.32 The Combined Code lists a number of areas which fall under the remit of a nomination committee, including the general requirement to undertake evaluations which a properly conducted board, committee and individual assessment process would encompass. These include:

- evaluating the balance of skills on the board;
- performing an annual evaluation of time NEDs spend in their role;
- considering succession planning requirements;
- reviewing the structure, size and composition (including the skills, knowledge and experience) of the board.

20.33 Tyson further observed that the selection of NEDs should rest on the careful assessment of the needs and challenges of the company. Further, when identifying the criteria for any new NED, a nomination committee should instigate a broad, transparent and rigorous search that reflects their assessment. This in turn should foster greater diversity in the background, experience, age, gender, ethnicity and nationality of NEDs. In the words of the report: 'many UK companies would benefit from extending their searches for NEDs to new pools of talent.' The DTI's 'Building Better Boards' also expressed the opinion that a more diverse and effective board starts with identifying the skill sets and capabilities required for each new appointment.

20.34 The Combined Code is clear that it is also the responsibility of the nomination committee to make recommendations to the board concerning the re-election by shareholders of any director under the retirement-by-rotation provisions.

20.35 Principle A.7.2 of the Code is explicit:

> 'The chairman should confirm to shareholders when proposing re-election that, following formal performance evaluation, the individual's performance continues to be effective and to demonstrate commitment to the role.'

By extension, it appears logical that if a chairman is to give assurances to his shareholders, and he in turn is to receive recommendations from the nomination committee, that an individual director is suitable for re-election, the nomination committee should be in a position to support the recommendations by overseeing the evaluation procedures.

20.36 The ultimate motivation for a company to undergo an effective evaluation process should be the expectation of improved functionality. This could be improved performance of individual directors by identifying potential weaknesses which can be addressed through additional training or improvement in the way the board or a committee operates or by a change in administrative procedures.

20.37 The chairman is tasked by Higgs with selecting an appropriate and effective evaluation process and acting on its outcome. The Combined Code is clear on this: it is the chairman's overall responsibility to ensure that an evaluation of the board, its committees and individual directors is undertaken annually. In this, the chairman should be assisted by the nomination committee, supported by his board and company secretary, but in the final analysis it is the chairman who is responsible for identifying the skills base against which the board is to be judged and it is his responsibility to set the agenda to ensure that this objective is achieved.

20.38 Although not going as far as to suggest it should be compulsory, Higgs clearly indicated in the performance evaluation guidance to his Report that the 'use of an external third party to conduct the evaluation will bring objectivity to the process'.

20.39 Checklist – Leading the process

- Is the process being driven by the chairman? If the company secretary is simply 'spoon-feeding' a solution without proper buy-in from the chairman or the board, the exercise is unlikely to deliver optimal results.
- Is this to be an internal exercise – or can value be added by using external agencies?
- If the former, will the board be satisfied their responses will be treated confidentially?
- If the latter, what is their experience and are references available?

20.40 Evaluating individuals is likely to be a significantly more subjective exercise than discussing processes. Inevitably the questioning will touch on individual contribution and this can be an extremely sensitive issue, particularly when it is perceived that judgements are being made about personal 'performance'. It will require a very open approach from participants and a good degree of skill in conducting the assessment to gain any commitment to change.

20.41 As important as the qualities and contributions of individual directors, however, is the chairman's ability to achieve an effective balance of skills and experience on his board, which when brought together, contribute to the efficient and effective running of the company.

20.42 What the chairman should be seeking is a team that can operate within a culture of open exchange, constructive dialogue and an atmosphere of mutual trust and respect. The individual appraisal is likely to focus more on relationships, particularly among board members, but also between the board and senior management. It will tend to centre on skill sets – some of which may be generic (good communication skills) while others will be company-specific (understanding the business and its sector).

20.43 The individual evaluation will invariably need to address personal attributes in addition to assessing an individual's professional performance and contribution. Again, it will be the role of the chairman to explain that he is looking for a balanced board rather than one where every member excels at everything. It is also an opportunity to measure existing skill sets against the long-term objectives of the business to identify any gaps that could be addressed by the appointment of an additional board member.

Conclusion

20.44 Where appropriate, a company should ensure that a comprehensive induction programme is established and maintained for new directors so that they become effective in their new role as soon as possible.

20.45 Performance evaluation should be used to help establish the training needs of directors, to monitor the strengths and weaknesses of the board as a whole as well as of individual directors, and also to address any under-performance.

20.46 Continued professional development for a company's board should be tailored to specific needs and should cover both refreshment and extension of knowledge and skills.

20.47 Companies should aim to create a virtuous circle of continual enhancement of board and individual effectiveness based on regular objective evaluation of past performance and to relate this to the company's changing situation and requirements.

20.48 Professional development does not cease on appointment to a board. If anything, the need to continue to develop personal skills only increases. Ultimately, it is the responsibility of the individual director – and him alone – to ensure he remains proficient and competent in his role.

Appendix 1

The Combined Code on Corporate Governance (June 2008)

Preamble

1. Good corporate governance should contribute to better company performance by helping a board discharge its duties in the best interests of shareholders; if it is ignored, the consequence may well be vulnerability or poor performance. Good governance should facilitate efficient, effective and entrepreneurial management that can deliver shareholder value over the longer term. The Combined Code on Corporate Governance ('the Code') is published by the FRC to support these outcomes and promote confidence in corporate reporting and governance.
2. The Code is not a rigid set of rules. Rather, it is a guide to the components of good board practice distilled from consultation and widespread experience over many years. While it is expected that companies will comply wholly or substantially with its provisions, it is recognised that non compliance may be justified in particular circumstances if good governance can be achieved by other means. A condition of non compliance is that the reasons for it should be explained to shareholders, who may wish to discuss the position with the company and whose voting intentions may be influenced as a result. This 'comply or explain' approach has been in operation since the Code's beginnings in 1992 and the flexibility it offers is valued by company boards and by investors in pursuing better corporate governance.
3. The Listing Rules require UK companies listed on the Main Market of the London Stock Exchange to describe in the annual report and accounts their corporate governance from two points of view, the first dealing generally with their adherence to the Code's main principles, and the second dealing specifically with non-compliance with any of the Code's provisions. The descriptions together should give shareholders a clear and comprehensive picture of a company's governance arrangements in relation to the Code as a criterion of good practice.
4. In relation to the requirement to state how it has applied the Code's main principles, where a company has done so by complying with the associated provisions it should be sufficient simply to report that this is the case; copying out the principles in the annual report adds to its length without adding to its value. But where a company has taken additional actions to apply the principles or otherwise improve its governance, it would be helpful to shareholders to describe these in the annual report.
5. If a company chooses not to comply with one or more provisions of the Code, it must give shareholders a careful and clear explanation which shareholders should evaluate on its merits. In providing an explanation, the company should aim to illustrate how its actual practices are consistent with the principle to which the particular provision relates and contribute to good governance.

6. Smaller listed companies, in particular those new to listing, may judge that some of the provisions are disproportionate or less relevant in their case. Some of the provisions do not apply to companies below the FTSE 350. Such companies may nonetheless consider that it would be appropriate to adopt the approach in the Code and they are encouraged to do so. Externally managed investment companies typically have a different board structure, which may affect the relevance of particular provisions; the Association of Investment Companies' Corporate Governance Code and Guide can assist them in meeting their obligations under the Code.
7. In their turn, shareholders should pay due regard to companies' individual circumstances and bear in mind in particular the size and complexity of the company and the nature of the risks and challenges it faces. Whilst shareholders have every right to challenge companies' explanations if they are unconvincing, they should not be evaluated in a mechanistic way and departures from the Code should not be automatically treated as breaches. Institutional shareholders should be careful to respond to the statements from companies in a manner that supports the 'comply or explain' principle and bearing in mind the purpose of good corporate governance. They should put their views to the company and be prepared to enter a dialogue if they do not accept the company's position. Institutional shareholders should be prepared to put such views in writing where appropriate.
8. Companies and shareholders have a shared responsibility for ensuring that 'comply or explain' remains an effective alternative to a rules-based system. Satisfactory engagement between company boards and investors is therefore crucial to the health of the UK's corporate governance regime. Although engagement has been improving slowly but steadily for many years, practical obstacles necessitate a constant effort to keep the improvement going.
9. Companies can make a major contribution by spreading governance discussion with shareholders outside the two peak annual reporting periods around 31st December and 31st March and by raising further the general standard of their explanations justifying non-compliance. Shareholders for their part can still do more to satisfy companies that they devote adequate resources and scrutiny to engagement.
10. References to shareholders in this Preamble also apply to intermediaries and agents employed to assist shareholders in scrutinising governance arrangements.
11. This edition of the Code applies to accounting periods beginning on or after 29 June 2008, and takes effect at the same time as new FSA Corporate Governance Rules implementing European requirements relating to audit committees and corporate governance statements. The relevant sections of these Rules are summarised in Schedule C. There is some overlap between the content of the Code and the Rules, and the Rules state that in these areas compliance with the Code will be deemed sufficient also to comply with the Rules. However, where a company chooses to explain rather than comply with the Code it will need to demonstrate that it nonetheless meets the minimum requirements set out in the Rules.
12. The Code itself is subject to periodic reviews by the FRC, the latest of which was conducted in 2007 and was generally reassuring about the Code's content and impact. In the normal course of events the next review will take place in 2010.

Financial Reporting Council
June 2008

Code of Best Practice

Section 1 Companies

A. DIRECTORS

A.1 The Board

Main Principle

Every company should be headed by an effective board, which is collectively responsible for the success of the company.

Supporting Principles

The board's role is to provide entrepreneurial leadership of the company within a framework of prudent and effective controls which enables risk tobe assessed and managed. The board should set the company's strategic aims, ensure that the necessary financial and human resources are in place for the company to meet its objectives and review management performance. The board should set the company's values and standards and ensure that its obligations to its shareholders and others are understood and met.

All directors must take decisions objectively in the interests of the company.

As part of their role as members of a unitary board, non-executive directors should constructively challenge and help develop proposals on strategy. Non-executive directors should scrutinise the performance of management in meeting agreed goals and objectives and monitor the reporting of performance. They should satisfy themselves on the integrity of financial information and that financial controls and systems of risk management are robust and defensible. They are responsible for determining appropriate levels of remuneration of executive directors and have a prime role in appointing, and where necessary removing, executive directors, and in succession planning.

Code Provisions

A.1.1 The board should meet sufficiently regularly to discharge its duties effectively. There should be a formal schedule of matters specifically reserved for its decision. The annual report should include a statement of how the board operates, including a high level statement of which types of decisions are to be taken by the board and which are to be delegated to management.

A.1.2 The annual report should identify the chairman, the deputy chairman (where there is one), the chief executive, the senior independent director and the chairmen and members of the nomination, audit and remuneration committees. It should also set out the number of meetings of the board and those committees and individual attendance by directors[1].

A.1.3 The chairman should hold meetings with the non-executive directors without the executives present. Led by the senior independent director, the non-executive directors should meet without the chairman present at least annually to appraise the chairman's performance (as described in A.6.1) and on such other occasions as are deemed appropriate.

A.1.4 Where directors have concerns which cannot be resolved about the running of the company or a proposed action, they should ensure that their concerns are recorded in the board minutes. On resignation, a non-executive director should provide a written statement to the chairman, for circulation to the board, if they have any such concerns.

A.1.5 The company should arrange appropriate insurance cover in respect of legal action against its directors.

A.2 Chairman and chief executive

Main Principle

There should be a clear division of responsibilities at the head of the company between the running of the board and the executive responsibility for the running of the company's business. No one individual should have unfettered powers of decision.

Supporting Principle

The chairman is responsible for leadership of the board, ensuring its effectiveness on all aspects of its role and setting its agenda. The chairman is also responsible for ensuring that the directors receive accurate, timely and clear information. The chairman should ensure effective communication with shareholders. The chairman should also facilitate the effective contribution of non-executive directors in particular and ensure constructive relations between executive and non-executive directors.

Code Provisions

A.2.1 The roles of chairman and chief executive should not be exercised by the same individual. The division of responsibilities between the chairman and chief executive should be clearly established, set out in writing and agreed by the board.

A.2.2 The chairman should on appointment meet the independence criteria set out in A.3.1 below. A chief executive should not go on to be chairman of the same company. If exceptionally a board decides that a chief executive should become chairman, the board should consult major shareholders in advance and should set out its reasons to shareholders at the time of the appointment and in the next annual report[2].

A.3 Board balance and independence

Main Principle

The board should include a balance of executive and non-executive directors (and in particular independent non-executive directors) such that no individual or small group of individuals can dominate the board's decision taking.

Supporting Principles

The board should not be so large as to be unwieldy. The board should be of sufficient size that the balance of skills and experience is appropriate for the requirements of the business and that changes to the board's composition can be managed without undue disruption.

To ensure that power and information are not concentrated in one or two individuals, there should be a strong presence on the board of both executive and non-executive directors.

The value of ensuring that committee membership is refreshed and that undue reliance is not placed on particular individuals should be taken into account in deciding chairmanship and membership of committees.

No one other than the committee chairman and members is entitled to be present at a meeting of the nomination, audit or remuneration committee, but others may attend at the invitation of the committee.

Code provisions

A.3.1 The board should identify in the annual report each non-executive director it considers to be independent[3]. The board should determine whether the director is independent in character and judgement and whether there are relationships or circumstances which are likely to affect, or could appear to affect, the director's judgement. The board should state its reasons if it determines that a director is independent notwithstanding the existence of relationships or circumstances which may appear relevant to its determination, including if the director:

- has been an employee of the company or group within the last five years;
- has, or has had within the last three years, a material business relationship with the company either directly, or as a partner, shareholder, director or senior employee of a body that has such a relationship with the company;
- has received or receives additional remuneration from the company apart from a director's fee, participates in the company's share option or a performance-related pay scheme, or is a member of the company's pension scheme;
- has close family ties with any of the company's advisers, directors or senior employees;
- holds cross-directorships or has significant links with other directors through involvement in other companies or bodies;
- represents a significant shareholder; or
- has served on the board for more than nine years from the date of their first election.

A.3.2 Except for smaller companies[4], at least half the board, excluding the chairman, should comprise non-executive directors determined by the board to be independent. A smaller company should have at least two independent non-executive directors.

A.3.3 The board should appoint one of the independent non-executive directors to be the senior independent director. The senior independent director should be available to shareholders if they have concerns which contact through the normal channels of chairman, chief executive or finance director has failed to resolve or for which such contact is inappropriate.

A.4 Appointments to the Board

Main Principle

There should be a formal, rigorous and transparent procedure for the appointment of new directors to the board.

Supporting Principles

Appointments to the board should be made on merit and against objective criteria. Care should be taken to ensure that appointees have enough time available to devote to the job. This is particularly important in the case of chairmanships.

The board should satisfy itself that plans are in place for orderly succession for appointments to the board and to senior management, so as to maintain an appropriate balance of skills and experience within the company and on the board.

Code Provisions

A.4.1 There should be a nomination committee which should lead the process for board appointments and make recommendations to the board. A majority of members of the nomination committee should be independent non-executive directors. The chairman or an independent non-executive director should chair the committee, but the chairman should not chair the nomination committee when it is dealing with the appointment of a successor to the chairmanship. The nomination committee should make available[5] its terms of reference, explaining its role and the authority delegated to it by the board.

A.4.2 The nomination committee should evaluate the balance of skills, knowledge and experience on the board and, in the light of this evaluation, prepare a description of the role and capabilities required for a particular appointment.

A.4.3 For the appointment of a chairman, the nomination committee should prepare a job specification, including an assessment of the time commitment expected, recognising the need for availability in the event of crises. A chairman's other significant commitments should be disclosed to the board before appointment and included in the annual report. Changes to such commitments should be reported to the board as they arise, and their impact explained in the next annual report.

A.4.4 The terms and conditions of appointment of non-executive directors should be made available for inspection[6]. The letter of appointment should set out the expected time commitment. Non-executive directors should undertake that they will have sufficient time to meet what is expected of them. Their other significant commitments should be disclosed to the board before appointment, with a broad indication of the time involved and the board should be informed of subsequent changes.

A.4.5 The board should not agree to a full time executive director taking on more than one non-executive directorship in a FTSE 100 company nor the chairmanship of such a company.

A.4.6 A separate section of the annual report should describe the work of the nomination committee, including the process it has used in relation to board appointments[7]. An explanation should be given if neither an external search consultancy nor open advertising has been used in the appointment of a chairman or a non-executive director.

A.5 Information and professional development

Main Principle

The board should be supplied in a timely manner with information in a form and of a quality appropriate to enable it to discharge its duties. All directors should receive

induction on joining the board and should regularly update and refresh their skills and knowledge.

Supporting Principles

The chairman is responsible for ensuring that the directors receive accurate, timely and clear information. Management has an obligation to provide such information but directors should seek clarification or amplification where necessary.

The chairman should ensure that the directors continually update their skills and the knowledge and familiarity with the company required to fulfil their role both on the board and on board committees. The company should provide the necessary resources for developing and updating its directors' knowledge and capabilities.

Under the direction of the chairman, the company secretary's responsibilities include ensuring good information flows within the board and its committees and between senior management and non-executive directors, as well as facilitating induction and assisting with professional development as required.

The company secretary should be responsible for advising the board through the chairman on all governance matters.

Code Provisions

A.5.1 The chairman should ensure that new directors receive a full, formal and tailored induction on joining the board. As part of this, the company should offer to major shareholders the opportunity to meet a new non-executive director.

A.5.2 The board should ensure that directors, especially non-executive directors, have access to independent professional advice at the company's expense where they judge it necessary to discharge their responsibilities as directors. Committees should be provided with sufficient resources to undertake their duties.

A.5.3 All directors should have access to the advice and services of the company secretary, who is responsible to the board for ensuring that board procedures are complied with. Both the appointment and removal of the company secretary should be a matter for the board as a whole.

A.6 Performance evaluation

Main Principle

The board should undertake a formal and rigorous annual evaluation of its own performance and that of its committees and individual directors.

Supporting Principle

Individual evaluation should aim to show whether each director continues to contribute effectively and to demonstrate commitment to the role (including commitment of time for board and committee meetings and any other duties). The chairman should act on the results of the performance evaluation by recognising the strengths and addressing the weaknesses of the board and, where appropriate, proposing new members be appointed to the board or seeking the resignation of directors.

Code Provision

A.6.1 The board should state in the annual report how performance evaluation of the board, its committees and its individual directors has been conducted. The non-executive directors, led by the senior independent director, should be responsible for performance evaluation of the chairman, taking into account the views of executive directors.

A.7 Re-election

Main Principle

All directors should be submitted for re-election at regular intervals, subject to continued satisfactory performance. The board should ensure planned and progressive refreshing of the board.

Code Provisions

A.7.1 All directors should be subject to election by shareholders at the first annual general meeting after their appointment, and to re-election thereafter at intervals of no more than three years. The names of directors submitted for election or re-election should be accompanied by sufficient biographical details and any other relevant information to enable shareholders to take an informed decision on their election.

A.7.2 Non-executive directors should be appointed for specified terms subject to re-election and to Companies Acts provisions relating to the removal of a director. The board should set out to shareholders in the papers accompanying a resolution to elect a non-executive director why they believe an individual should be elected. The chairman should confirm to shareholders when proposing re-election that, following formal performance evaluation, the individual's performance continues to be effective and to demonstrate commitment to the role. Any term beyond six years (e.g. two three-year terms) for a non-executive director should be subject to particularly rigorous review, and should take into account the need for progressive refreshing of the board. Non-executive directors may serve longer than nine years (e.g. three three-year terms), subject to annual re-election. Serving more than nine years could be relevant to the determination of a non-executive director's independence (as set out in provision A.3.1).

B. REMUNERATION

B.1 The Level and Make-up of Remuneration

Main Principles

Levels of remuneration should be sufficient to attract, retain and motivate directors of the quality required to run the company successfully, but a company should avoid paying more than is necessary for this purpose. A significant proportion of executive directors' remuneration should be structured so as to link rewards to corporate and individual performance.

Supporting Principle

The remuneration committee should judge where to position their company relative to other companies. But they should use such comparisons with caution, in view of the risk of an upward ratchet of remuneration levels with no corresponding improvement in performance. They should also be sensitive to pay and employment conditions elsewhere in the group, especially when determining annual salary increases.

Code Provisions

Remuneration policy

B.1.1 The performance-related elements of remuneration should form a significant proportion of the total remuneration package of executive directors and should be designed to align their interests with those of shareholders and to give these directors keen incentives to perform at the highest levels. In designing schemes of performance-related remuneration, the remuneration committee should follow the provisions in Schedule A to this Code.

B.1.2 Executive share options should not be offered at a discount save as permitted by the relevant provisions of the Listing Rules.

B.1.3 Levels of remuneration for non-executive directors should reflect the time commitment and responsibilities of the role. Remuneration for non-executive directors should not include share options. If, exceptionally, options are granted, shareholder approval should be sought in advance and any shares acquired by exercise of the options should be held until at least one year after the non-executive director leaves the board. Holding of share options could be relevant to the determination of a non-executive director's independence (as set out in provision A.3.1).

B.1.4 Where a company releases an executive director to serve as a non-executive director elsewhere, the remuneration report[8] should include a statement as to whether or not the director will retain such earnings and, if so, what the remuneration is.

Service Contracts and Compensation

B.1.5 The remuneration committee should carefully consider what compensation commitments (including pension contributions and all other elements) their directors' terms of appointment would entail in the event of early termination. The aim should be to avoid rewarding poor performance. They should take a robust line on reducing compensation to reflect departing directors' obligations to mitigate loss.

B.1.6 Notice or contract periods should be set at one year or less. If it is necessary to offer longer notice or contract periods to new directors recruited from outside, such periods should reduce to one year or less after the initial period.

B.2 Procedure

Main Principle

There should be a formal and transparent procedure for developing policy on executive remuneration and for fixing the remuneration packages of individual directors. No director should be involved in deciding his or her own remuneration.

Supporting Principles

The remuneration committee should consult the chairman and/or chief executive about their proposals relating to the remuneration of other executive directors. The remuneration committee should also be responsible for appointing any consultants in respect of executive director remuneration. Where executive directors or senior management are involved in advising or supporting the remuneration committee, care should be taken to recognise and avoid conflicts of interest.

The chairman of the board should ensure that the company maintains contact as required with its principal shareholders about remuneration in the same way as for other matters.

Code Provisions

B.2.1 The board should establish a remuneration committee of at least three, or in the case of smaller companies[9] two, independent non-executive directors. In addition the company chairman may also be a member of, but not chair, the committee if he or she was considered independent on appointment as chairman. The remuneration committee should make available[10] its terms of reference, explaining its role and the authority delegated to it by the board. Where remuneration consultants are appointed, a statement should be made available[11] of whether they have any other connection with the company.

B.2.2 The remuneration committee should have delegated responsibility for setting remuneration for all executive directors and the chairman, including pension rights and any compensation payments. The committee should also recommend and monitor the level and structure of remuneration for senior management. The definition of 'senior management' for this purpose should be determined by the board but should normally include the first layer of management below board level.

B.2.3 The board itself or, where required by the Articles of Association, the shareholders should determine the remuneration of the non-executive directors within the limits set in the Articles of Association. Where permitted by the Articles, the board may however delegate this responsibility to a committee, which might include the chief executive.

B.2.4 Shareholders should be invited specifically to approve all new long-term incentive schemes (as defined in the Listing Rules) and significant changes to existing schemes, save in the circumstances permitted by the Listing Rules.

C. ACCOUNTABILITY AND AUDIT

C.1 Financial Reporting

Main Principle

The board should present a balanced and understandable assessment of the company's position and prospects.

Supporting Principle

The board's responsibility to present a balanced and understandable assessment extends to interim and other price-sensitive public reports and reports to regulators as well as to information required to be presented by statutory requirements.

Code Provisions

C.1.1 The directors should explain in the annual report their responsibility for preparing the accounts and there should be a statement by the auditors about their reporting responsibilities.

C.1.2 The directors should report that the business is a going concern, with supporting assumptions or qualifications as necessary.

C.2 Internal Control[12]

Main Principle

The board should maintain a sound system of internal control to safeguard shareholders' investment and the company's assets.

Code Provision

C.2.1 The board should, at least annually, conduct a review of the effectiveness of the group's system of internal controls and should report to shareholders that they have done so[13]. The review should cover all material controls, including financial, operational and compliance controls and risk management systems.

C.3 Audit Committee and Auditors[14]

Main Principle

The board should establish formal and transparent arrangements for considering how they should apply the financial reporting and internal control principles and for maintaining an appropriate relationship with the company's auditors.

Code provisions

C.3.1 The board should establish an audit committee of at least three, or in the case of smaller companies[15] two, independent non-executive directors. In smaller companies the company chairman may be a member of, but not chair, the committee in addition to the independent non-executive directors, provided he or she was considered independent on appointment as chairman. The board should satisfy itself that at least one member of the audit committee has recent and relevant financial experience[16].

C.3.2 The main role and responsibilities of the audit committee should be set out in written terms of reference and should include[17]:

- to monitor the integrity of the financial statements of the company, and any formal announcements relating to the company's financial performance, reviewing significant financial reporting judgements contained in them;

- to review the company's internal financial controls and, unless expressly addressed by a separate board risk committee composed of independent directors, or by the board itself, to review the company's internal control and risk management systems;
- to monitor and review the effectiveness of the company's internal audit function;
- to make recommendations to the board, for it to put to the shareholders for their approval in general meeting, in relation to the appointment, re-appointment and removal of the external auditor and to approve the remuneration and terms of engagement of the external auditor;
- to review and monitor the external auditor's independence and objectivity and the effectiveness of the audit process, taking into consideration relevant UK professional and regulatory requirements;
- to develop and implement policy on the engagement of the external auditor to supply non-audit services, taking into account relevant ethical guidance regarding the provision of non-audit services by the external audit firm; and to report to the board, identifying any matters in respect of which it considers that action or improvement is needed and making recommendations as to the steps to be taken.

C.3.3 The terms of reference of the audit committee, including its role and the authority delegated to it by the board, should be made available[18]. A separate section of the annual report should describe the work of the committee in discharging those responsibilities[19].

C.3.4 The audit committee should review arrangements by which staff of the company may, in confidence, raise concerns about possible improprieties in matters of financial reporting or other matters. The audit committee's objective should be to ensure that arrangements are in place for the proportionate and independent investigation of such matters and for appropriate follow-up action.

C.3.5 The audit committee should monitor and review the effectiveness of the internal audit activities. Where there is no internal audit function, the audit committee should consider annually whether there is a need for an internal audit function and make a recommendation to the board, and the reasons for the absence of such a function should be explained in the relevant section of the annual report.

C.3.6 The audit committee should have primary responsibility for making a recommendation on the appointment, reappointment and removal of the external auditors. If the board does not accept the audit committee's recommendation, it should include in the annual report, and in any papers recommending appointment or re-appointment, a statement from the audit committee explaining the recommendation and should set out reasons why the board has taken a different position.

C.3.7 The annual report should explain to shareholders how, if the auditor provides non-audit services, auditor objectivity and independence is safeguarded.

D. RELATIONS WITH SHAREHOLDERS

D.1 Dialogue with Institutional Shareholders

Main Principle

There should be a dialogue with shareholders based on the mutual understanding of objectives. The board as a whole has responsibility for ensuring that a satisfactory dialogue with shareholders takes place[20].

Supporting Principles

Whilst recognising that most shareholder contact is with the chief executive and finance director, the chairman (and the senior independent director and other directors as appropriate) should maintain sufficient contact with major shareholders to understand their issues and concerns.

The board should keep in touch with shareholder opinion in whatever ways are most practical and efficient.

Code Provisions

D.1.1 The chairman should ensure that the views of shareholders are communicated to the board as a whole. The chairman should discuss governance and strategy with major shareholders. Non-executive directors should be offered the opportunity to attend meetings with major shareholders and should expect to attend them if requested by major shareholders. The senior independent director should attend sufficient meetings with a range of major shareholders to listen to their views in order to help develop a balanced understanding of the issues and concerns of major shareholders.

D.1.2 The board should state in the annual report the steps they have taken to ensure that the members of the board, and in particular the non-executive directors, develop an understanding of the views of major shareholders about their company, for example through direct face-to-face contact, analysts' or brokers' briefings and surveys of shareholder opinion.

D.2 Constructive Use of the AGM

Main Principle

The board should use the AGM to communicate with investors and to encourage their participation.

Code Provisions

D.2.1 At any general meeting, the company should propose a separate resolution on each substantially separate issue, and should in particular propose a resolution at the AGM relating to the report and accounts. For each resolution, proxy appointment forms should provide shareholders with the option to direct their proxy to vote either for or against the resolution or to withhold their vote. The proxy form and any announcement of the results of a vote should make it clear that a 'vote withheld' is not a vote in law and will not be counted in the calculation of the proportion of the votes for and against the resolution.

D.2.2 The company should ensure that all valid proxy appointments received for general meetings are properly recorded and counted. For each resolution, after a vote has been taken, except where taken on a poll, the company should ensure that the following information is given at the meeting and made available as soon as reasonably practicable on a website which is maintained by or on behalf of the company:

- the number of shares in respect of which proxy appointments have been validly made;
- the number of votes for the resolution;
- the number of votes against the resolution; and
- the number of shares in respect of which the vote was directed to be withheld.

D.2.3 The chairman should arrange for the chairmen of the audit, remuneration and nomination committees to be available to answer questions at the AGM and for all directors to attend.

D.2.4 The company should arrange for the Notice of the AGM and related papers to be sent to shareholders at least 20 working days before the meeting.

Section 2 Institutional Shareholders

E. INSTITUTIONAL SHAREHOLDERS[21]

E.1 Dialogue with companies

Main Principle

Institutional shareholders should enter into a dialogue with companies based on the mutual understanding of objectives.

Supporting Principles

Institutional shareholders should apply the principles set out in the Institutional Shareholders' Committee's "The Responsibilities of Institutional Shareholders and Agents – Statement of Principles"[22], which should be reflected in fund manager contracts.

E.2 Evaluation of Governance Disclosures

Main Principle

When evaluating companies' governance arrangements, particularly those relating to board structure and composition, institutional shareholders should give due weight to all relevant factors drawn to their attention.

Supporting Principle

Institutional shareholders should consider carefully explanations given for departure from this Code and make reasoned judgements in each case. They should give an explanation to the company, in writing where appropriate, and be prepared to enter a dialogue if they do not accept the company's position. They should avoid a box-ticking approach to assessing a company's corporate governance. They should bear in mind in particular the size and complexity of the company and the nature of the risks and challenges it faces.

E.3 Shareholder Voting

Main Principle

Institutional shareholders have a responsibility to make considered use of their votes.

Supporting Principles

Institutional shareholders should take steps to ensure their voting intentions are being translated into practice.

Institutional shareholders should, on request, make available to their clients information on the proportion of resolutions on which votes were cast and non-discretionary proxies lodged.

Major shareholders should attend AGMs where appropriate and practicable. Companies and registrars should facilitate this.

Notes

1 Provisions A.1.1 and A.1.2 overlap with FSA Rule DTR 7.2.7 R; Provision A.1.2 also overlaps with DTR 7.1.5 R (see Schedule C).
2 Compliance or otherwise with this provision need only be reported for the year in which the appointment is made.
3 A.2.2 states that the chairman should, on appointment, meet the independence criteria set out in this provision, but thereafter the test of independence is not appropriate in relation to the chairman.
4 A smaller company is one that is below the FTSE 350 throughout the year immediately prior to the reporting year.
5 The requirement to make the information available would be met by including the information on a website that is maintained by or on behalf of the company.
6 The terms and conditions of appointment of non-executive directors should be made available for inspection by any person at the company's registered office during normal business hours and at the AGM (for 15 minutes prior to the meeting and during the meeting).
7 This provision overlaps with FSA Rule DTR 7.2.7 R (see Schedule C).
8 As required under the Directors' Remuneration Report Regulations 2002.
9 See footnote 4.
10 This provision overlaps with FSA Rule DTR 7.2.7 R (see Schedule C).
11 See footnote 5.
12 The Turnbull guidance suggests means of applying this part of the Code. Copies are available at www.frc.org.uk/corporate/internalcontrol.cfm
13 In addition FSA Rule DTR 7.2.5 R requires companies to describe the main features of the internal control and risk management systems in relation to the financial reporting process (see Schedule C).
14 The Smith guidance suggests means of applying this part of the Code. Copies are available at www.frc.org.uk/corporate/auditcommittees.cfm

15 See footnote 4.
16 This provision overlaps with FSA Rule DTR 7.1.1 R (see Schedule C).
17 This provision overlaps with FSA Rules DTR 7.1.3 R (see Schedule C).
18 See footnote 5.
19 This provision overlaps with FSA Rules DTR 7.1.5 R and 7.2.7 R (see Schedule C).
20 Nothing in these principles or provisions should be taken to override the general requirements of law to treat shareholders equally in access to information.
21 Agents such as investment managers, or voting services, are frequently appointed by institutional shareholders to act on their behalf and these principles should accordingly be read as applying where appropriate to the agents of institutional shareholders.
22 Available at www.institutionalshareholderscommittee.co.uk.

Schedule A: Provisions on the design of performance-related remuneration

1. The remuneration committee should consider whether the directors should be eligible for annual bonuses. If so, performance conditions should be relevant, stretching and designed to enhance shareholder value. Upper limits should be set and disclosed. There may be a case for part payment in shares to be held for a significant period.
2. The remuneration committee should consider whether the directors should be eligible for benefits under long-term incentive schemes. Traditional share option schemes should be weighed against other kinds of long-term incentive scheme. In normal circumstances, shares granted or other forms of deferred remuneration should not vest, and options should not be exercisable, in less than three years. Directors should be encouraged to hold their shares for a further period after vesting or exercise, subject to the need to finance any costs of acquisition and associated tax liabilities.
3. Any new long-term incentive schemes which are proposed should be approved by shareholders and should preferably replace any existing schemes or at least form part of a well considered overall plan, incorporating existing schemes. The total rewards potentially available should not be excessive.
4. Payouts or grants under all incentive schemes, including new grants under existing share option schemes, should be subject to challenging performance criteria reflecting the company's objectives. Consideration should be given to criteria which reflect the company's performance relative to a group of comparator companies in some key variables such as total shareholder return.
5. Grants under executive share option and other long-term incentive schemes should normally be phased rather than awarded in one large block.
6. In general, only basic salary should be pensionable.
7. The remuneration committee should consider the pension consequences and associated costs to the company of basic salary increases and any other changes in pensionable remuneration, especially for directors close to retirement.

Schedule B: Guidance on liability of non-executive directors: care, skill and diligence

1. Although non-executive directors and executive directors have as board members the same legal duties and objectives, the time devoted to the company's affairs is likely to be significantly less for a non-executive director than for an executive director and the

detailed knowledge and experience of a company's affairs that could reasonably be expected of a non-executive director will generally be less than for an executive director. These matters may be relevant in assessing the knowledge, skill and experience which may reasonably be expected of a non-executive director and therefore the care, skill and diligence that a non-executive director may be expected to exercise.

2. In this context, the following elements of the Code may also be particularly relevant.

(i) In order to enable directors to fulfil their duties, the Code states that:

(ii) Non-executive directors should themselves:

- Undertake appropriate induction and regularly update and refresh their skills, knowledge and familiarity with the company (Code principle A.5 and provision A.5.1)
- Seek appropriate clarification or amplification of information and, where necessary, take and follow appropriate professional advice. (Code principle A.5 and provision A.5.2)
- Where they have concerns about the running of the company or a proposed action, ensure that these are addressed by the board and, to the extent that they are not resolved, ensure that they are recorded in the board minutes (Code provision A.1.4).
- Give a statement to the board if they have such unresolved concerns on resignation (Code provision A.1.4)

3. It is up to each non-executive director to reach a view as to what is necessary in particular circumstances to comply with the duty of care, skill and diligence they owe as a director to the company. In considering whether or not a person is in breach of that duty, a court would take into account all relevant circumstances. These may include having regard to the above where relevant to the issue of liability of a non-executive director.

Schedule C: Disclosure of Corporate Governance Arrangements

Corporate governance disclosure requirements are set out in three places:

- FSA Listing Rule 9.8.6 (which includes the 'comply or explain' requirement);
- FSA Disclosure and Transparency Rules Sections 7.1 and 7.2 (which set out certain mandatory disclosures); and
- The Combined Code (in addition to providing an explanation where they choose not to comply with a provision, companies must disclose specified information in order to comply with certain provisions).

These requirements are summarised below. The full text of Listing Rule 9.8.6 and Disclosure and Transparency Rules 7.1 and 7.2 are contained in the Listing, Prospectus and Disclosure section of the FSA Handbook, which can be found at http://fsahandbook.info /FSA/html/handbook/.

There is some overlap between the mandatory disclosures required under the Disclosure and Transparency Rules and those expected under the Combined Code. Areas of overlap are summarised in the Appendix to this Schedule. In respect of disclosures relating to the audit committee and the composition and operation of the board and its committees, compliance with the relevant provisions of the Code will result in compliance with the relevant Rules.

Listing Rules

Paragraph 9.8.6 R of the Listing Rules states that in the case of a listed company incorporated in the United Kingdom, the following items must be included in its annual report and accounts:

- a statement of how the listed company has applied the Main Principles set out in Section 1 of the Combined Code, in a manner that would enable shareholders to evaluate how the principles have been applied;
- a statement as to whether the listed company has:
- complied throughout the accounting period with all relevant provisions set out in Section 1 of the Combined Code; or
- not complied throughout the accounting period with all relevant provisions set out in Section 1 of the Combined Code and if so, setting out:
  (i) those provisions, if any, it has not complied with;
  (ii) in the case of provisions whose requirements are of a continuing nature, the period within which, if any, it did not comply with some or all of those provisions; and
  (iii) the company's reasons for non-compliance.

Disclosure and Transparency Rules

Section 7.1 of the Disclosure and Transparency Rules concerns audit committees or bodies carrying out equivalent functions. DTR 7.1.1 R to 7.1.3 R sets out requirements relating to the composition and functions of the committee or equivalent body:

- DTR 7.1.1 R states than an issuer must have a body which is responsible for performing the functions set out in DTR 7.1.3 R, and that least one member of that body must be independent and at least one member must have competence in accounting and/or auditing.
- DTR 7.1.2 G states that the requirements for independence and competence in accounting and/or auditing may be satisfied by the same member or by different members of the relevant body.
- DTR 7.1.3 R states that an issuer must ensure that, as a minimum, the relevant body must:
  (1) monitor the financial reporting process;
  (2) monitor the effectiveness of the issuer's internal control, internal audit where applicable, and risk management systems;
  (3) monitor the statutory audit of the annual and consolidated accounts;
  (4) review and monitor the independence of the statutory auditor, and in particular the provision of additional services to the issuer.

DTR 7.1.5 R to 7.1.7 R explain what disclosure is required:

- DTR 7.1.5 R states that the issuer must make a statement available to the public disclosing which body carries out the functions required by DTR 7.1.3 R and how it is composed.
- DTR 7.1.6 G states that this can be included in the corporate governance statement required under DTR 7.2 (see below).
- DTR 7.1.7 R states that compliance with the relevant provisions of the Combined

Code (as set out in the Appendix to this Schedule) will result in compliance with DTR 7.1.1 R to 7.1.5 R.

Section 7.2 concerns corporate governance statements. Issuers are required to produce a corporate governance statement that must be either included in the directors' report (DTR 7.2.1 R); or in a separate report published together with the annual report; or on the issuer's website, in which case there must be a cross-reference in the directors' report (DTR 7.2.9 R).

DTR 7.2.2 R requires that the corporate governance statements must contain a reference to the corporate governance code to which the company is subject (for listed companies incorporated in the UK this is the Combined Code). DTR 7.2.3 R requires that, to the extent that it departs from that code, the company must explain which parts of the code it departs from and the reasons for doing so. DTR 7.2.4 G states that compliance with LR 9.8.6R (6) (the 'comply or explain' rule in relation to the Combined Code) will also satisfy these requirements.

DTR 7.2.5 R to 7.2.7 R and DTR 7.2.10 R set out certain information that must be disclosed in the corporate governance statement:

- DTR 7.2.5 R states that the corporate governance statement must contain a description of the main features of the company's internal control and risk management systems in relation to the financial reporting process. DTR 7.2.10 R states that an issuer which is required to prepare a group directors' report within the meaning of Section 415(2) of the Companies Act 2006 must include in that report a description of the main features of the group's internal control and risk management systems in relation to the process for preparing consolidated accounts.
- DTR 7.2.6 R states that the corporate governance statement must contain the information required by paragraph 13(2)(c), (d), (f), (h) and (i) of Schedule 7 to the Large and Medium-sized Companies and Groups (Accounts and Reports) Regulations 2008 (SI 2008/410) where the issuer is subject to the requirements of that paragraph.
- DTR 7.2.7 R states that the corporate governance statement must contain a description of the composition and operation of the issuer's administrative, management and supervisory bodies and their committees. DTR 7.2.8 G states that compliance with the relevant provisions of the Combined Code (as set out in the Appendix to this Schedule) will satisfy the requirements of DTR 7.2.7 R.

The Combined Code

In addition the Code includes specific requirements for disclosure which are set out below:
The annual report should record:

- a statement of how the board operates, including a high level statement of which types of decisions are to be taken by the board and which are to be delegated to management (A.1.1);
- the names of the chairman, the deputy chairman (where there is one), the chief executive, the senior independent director and the chairmen and members of the nomination, audit and remuneration committees (A.1.2);
- the number of meetings of the board and those committees and individual attendance by directors (A.1.2);
- the names of the non-executive directors whom the board determines to be independent, with reasons where necessary (A.3.1);

- the other significant commitments of the chairman and any changes to them during the year (A.4.3);
- how performance evaluation of the board, its committees and its directors has been conducted (A.6.1);
- the steps the board has taken to ensure that members of the board, and in particular the non-executive directors, develop an understanding of the views of major shareholders about their company (D.1.2).

The annual report should also include:

- a separate section describing the work of the nomination committee, including the process it has used in relation to board appointments and an explanation if neither external search consultancy nor open advertising has been used in the appointment of a chairman or a non-executive director (A.4.6);
- a description of the work of the remuneration committee as required under the Directors' Remuneration Report Regulations 2002, and including, where an executive director serves as a non-executive director elsewhere, whether or not the director will retain such earnings and, if so, what the remuneration is (B.1.4);
- an explanation from the directors of their responsibility for preparing the accounts and a statement by the auditors about their reporting responsibilities (C.1.1);
- a statement from the directors that the business is a going concern, with supporting assumptions or qualifications as necessary (C.1.2);
- a report that the board has conducted a review of the effectiveness of the group's system of internal controls (C.2.1);
- a separate section describing the work of the audit committee in discharging its responsibilities (C.3.3);
- where there is no internal audit function, the reasons for the absence of such a function (C.3.5);
- where the board does not accept the audit committee's recommendation on the appointment, reappointment or removal of an external auditor, a statement from the audit committee explaining the recommendation and the reasons why the board has taken a different position (C.3.6); and
- an explanation of how, if the auditor provides non-audit services, auditor objectivity and independence is safeguarded (C.3.7).

The following information should be made available (which may be met by placing the information on a website that is maintained by or on behalf of the company):

- the terms of reference of the nomination, remuneration and audit committees, explaining their role and the authority delegated to them by the board (A.4.1, B.2.1 and C.3.3);
- the terms and conditions of appointment of non-executive directors (A.4.4) (see footnote 8 on page 10); and
- where remuneration consultants are appointed, a statement of whether they have any other connection with the company (B.2.1).
- The board should set out to shareholders in the papers accompanying a resolution to elect or re-elect directors:
- sufficient biographical details to enable shareholders to take an informed decision on their election or re-election (A.7.1);
- why they believe an individual should be elected to a non-executive role (A.7.2); and

- on re-election of a non-executive director, confirmation from the chairman that, following formal performance evaluation, the individual's performance continues to be effective and to demonstrate commitment to the role, including commitment of time for board and committee meetings and any other duties (A.7.2).

The board should set out to shareholders in the papers recommending appointment or reappointment of an external auditor:

- if the board does not accept the audit committee's recommendation, a statement from the audit committee explaining the recommendation and from the board setting out reasons why they have taken a different position (C.3.6).

Additional guidance

The Turnbull Guidance and Smith Guidance contain further suggestions as to information that might usefully be disclosed in the internal control statement and the report of the audit committee respectively. Both sets of guidance are available on the FRC website at http://www.frc.org.uk/corporate/.

ANNEX

Overlap between the Disclosure and Transparency Rules and the Combined Code

DISCLOSURE AND TRANSPARENCY RULES

D.T.R 7.1.1 R
Sets out minimum requirements on composition of the audit committee or equivalent body.

D.T.R 7.1.3 R
Sets out minimum functions of the audit committee or equivalent body.

D.T.R 7.1.5 R
The composition and function of the audit committee or equivalent body must be disclosed in the annual report

DTR 7.1.7 R states that compliance with Code provisions A.1.2, C.3.1, C.3.2 and C.3.3 will result in compliance with DTR 7.1.1 R to DTR 7.1.5 R.

D.T.R 7.2.5 R
The corporate governance statement must include a description of the main features of the company's internal control and risk management systems in relation to the financial reporting process.
While this requirement differs from the requirement in the Combined Code, it is envisaged that both could be met by a single internal control statement.

DTR 7.2.7 R
The corporate governance statement must include a description of the composition and operation of the administrative, management and supervisory bodies and their committees.
DTR 7.2.8 R states that compliance with Code provisions A.1.1, A.1.2, A.4.6, B.2.1 and C.3.3 with result in compliance with DTR 7.2.7 R. This requirement overlaps with a number of different provisions of the Code:

COMBINED CODE

Provision C.3.1
Sets out recommended composition of the audit committee.

Provision C.3.2
Sets out the recommended minimum terms of reference for the committee.

Provision A.1.2:
The annual report should identify members of the board committees.

Provision C.3.3
The annual report should describe the work of the audit committee. Further recommendations on the content of the audit committee report are set out in the Smith Guidance

Provision C.2.1
The Board must report that a review of the effectiveness of the internal control system has been carried out.
Further recommendations on the content of the internal control statement are set out in the Turnbull Guidance.

A.1.1: the annual report should include a statement of how the board operates.
A.1.2: the annual report should identify members of the board and board committees.
A.4.6: the annual report should describe the work of the nomination committee.
B.2.1: a description of the work of the remuneration committee should be made available. [Note: in order to comply with DTR 7.2.7 R this information will need to be included in the corporate governance statement].
C.3.3: the annual report should describe the work of the audit committee.

Appendix 2

ICSA Guidance Note (September 2004)

The Roles of the Chairman, Chief Executive and Senior Independent Director under the Combined Code

Introduction

Corporate governance in the UK is regulated not by legislation but by the Combined Code, which is annexed to the UK Listing Rules and requires companies to either comply or explain why they are choosing a different course. This means that companies are entitled to have procedures that suit their business, rather than follow a prescribed legal structure, as long as they can give an adequate explanation in their annual report for not following the Code.

Some of the proposed changes to the Combined Code resulting from the Higgs review[1] which gave the most cause for debate related to what was seen as a weakening of the role of the Chairman. Many of these issues were resolved before the final version of the Code was produced in July 2003. This note looks to identify the respective roles of the Chairman, the Chief Executive and the Senior Independent (Non-Executive) Director.

The Chairman

The Higgs review sees the Chairman playing a pivotal role in the company, and creating the conditions for overall board and individual non-executive director effectiveness. The Combined Code clearly differentiates between the running of the company's business and the running of the board. The Code states that the chairman is responsible for:

- Leadership of the board, ensuring its effectiveness on all aspects of its role and
- setting its agenda;
- Ensuring that the directors receive accurate, timely and clear information;
- Ensuring effective communication with shareholders;
- Facilitating the effective contribution of non-executive directors and ensuring constructive relations between executive and non-executive directors, and
- Acting on the results of board performance evaluation by recognising the strengths and addressing the weaknesses of the board and, where appropriate, proposing new members be appointed to the board or seeking the resignation of directors.[2]
- To ensure that this happens the Combined Code now requires that the roles of the Chairman and Chief Executive be separated,[3] in addition the board needs to agree a high level statement of which decisions are to be taken by the board and those that are delegated to management.[4]

Appendix 1 to this guidance note details a suitable outline statement for the board to adopt.

The Combined Code now suggests that a Chief Executive should not go on to become Chairman of the same company.[5] This is because the detailed knowledge of the general running of the company will impede the handover of management responsibility to another individual. This may cause confusion among other executives and result in unwanted tensions between the Chairman and Chief Executive. It may also impact on the Chairman's ability to keep the non-executive directors informed, as they may take for granted that the nonexecutives have the same level of inside knowledge as they do. This does not mean that there may not be circumstances when, for a short period of time, the Chief Executive may be the best candidate to act as Chairman. For example this may be during a period of intense company reorganisation, where the board has promoted a new Chief Executive from within. The outgoing Chief Executive could provide valuable support to the new appointee, for a short period, before a new Chairman is found. This would be a clear example of the need to explain the company's non-compliance with the Code provision. In this case the Chairman could not be considered independent on appointment,[6] which would need to be disclosed in the annual report.

The Chairman, under the Code, is responsible for ensuring the efficient use of the board's time and that the agenda is forward looking, concentrating on strategy, rather than approving issues which should have been delegated to management. They must allow sufficient time to discuss complex or contentious issues and if necessary arrange for pre-board preparation. This should avoid non-executive directors being faced with unrealistic deadlines for decision-making.

The company secretary has a clear role to play in supporting the Chairman in the design of the agenda and ensuring that the non-executive directors are comfortable with the amount of information that they receive. The Combined Code states "The company secretary should be responsible for advising the board, through the Chairman, on all governance matters."[7]

The Chief Executive

The revised Combined Code does not specify a corporate governance role for the Chief Executive, but notes that the board should have a clear division of responsibilities and the posts of Chairman and Chief Executive should not be combined in one individual.

To facilitate the division of the responsibility of running the board and running the company the Combined Code recommends that a clear division of responsibilities is set out in writing and agreed by the board.[8] It is, however, recognised that there should be a strong executive representation on the board, so that power and information are not concentrated in one or two individuals.[9]

The Senior Independent Director (SID)

The Higgs review builds on the view expressed in Hampel[10] and codified in the Combined Code that a senior non-executive director should be identified in the annual report. The SID should be available to shareholders, if they have a concern that contact through the normal channels of Chairman, Chief Executive and finance director has failed to resolve or where such contact is inappropriate.[11] To be in a position to undertake this role, the SID should attend "sufficient meetings with a range of major shareholders to listen to their views in order to help develop a balanced understanding of their issues and concerns. The

Chairman should ensure that the views of shareholders are communicated to the board as a whole".[12] It must be emphasised that these are meetings that management would have as part of their normal Investor Relations programme, they are not special events or one to one meetings with the institution and SID, unless the shareholder has raised a concern with the SID that has not been dealt with in the normal manner.

Under the revised Code the SID should also lead a meeting of the non-executive directors at least once a year, without the Chairman present, to appraise the Chairman's performance and on such other occasions as are deemed appropriate.[13]

The purpose of this guidance note is not to be prescriptive but to provide a starting point to help ensure that all the issues are addressed. As with most aspects of corporate governance one size does not fit all and the detailed division of responsibilities will vary from one company to another according to each company's specific circumstances and the nature of the individuals involved. Examples of such differences may be the reporting lines of some individuals or whether charitable donations are considered separately or as part of the Corporate Social Responsibility policy.

APPENDIX 1

Role of Chairman

A. The Chairman is responsible for:

1. Meetings

- Chairing board and general meetings and those of the Nomination Committee.
- Running the board and ensuring its effectiveness in all aspects of its role, including regularity and frequency of meetings.
- Setting the board agenda, taking into account the issues and concerns of all board
- members. The agenda should be forward looking, concentrating on strategic matters.
- Ensuring that there is appropriate delegation of authority from the board to executive management.
- Ensuring that the directors receive accurate, timely and clear information, including that on the company's current performance, to enable the board to take sound decisions, monitor effectively and provide advice to promote the success of the company.
- Managing the board to allow enough time for discussion of complex or contentious issues. The Chairman should ensure that directors (particularly non-executive directors) have sufficient time to consider critical issues and obtain answers to any questions or concerns they may have and are not faced with unrealistic deadlines for decision making.

2. Directors

- Facilitating the effective contribution of non-executive directors and encouraging active engagement by all members of the board.
- Ensuring constructive relations between the executive and non-executive directors.
- Holding meetings with the non-executive directors without the executives resent.[14]

3. Induction, development and performance evaluation

- Ensuring that new directors participate in a full, formal and tailored induction programme, facilitated by the company secretary.

- Ensuring that the development needs of directors are identified and, with the company secretary having a key role, that these needs are met. The directors should be able to continually update their skills and the knowledge and familiarity with the company required to fulfil their role on the board and its committees.
- Identifying the development needs of the board as a whole to enhance its overall effectiveness as a team.
- Ensuring the performance of the board, its committees and individual directors is evaluated at least once a year and acting on the results of such evaluation by recognising the strengths and addressing the weaknesses of the board. Where appropriate, through the Nomination Committee, proposing that new members be appointed to the board or seeking the resignation of others.

4. Relations with shareholders

- Ensuring effective communication with shareholders.
- Maintaining sufficient contact with major shareholders to understand their issues and concerns, in particular discussing governance, strategy and remuneration with them.
- Ensuring that the views of shareholders are communicated to the board as a whole so that all directors develop an understanding of their views.

5. AGM

- Arranging for the Chairmen of board committees to be available to answer questions at the AGM and for all directors to attend.
- The Chairman's direct reports are the Chief Executive and the company secretary.

In addition, the Chairman should:

- Uphold the highest standards of integrity and probity.
- Set the agenda, style and tone of board discussions to promote effective decision making and constructive debate.
- Ensure that they are fully informed about all issues on which the board will have to make a decision, through briefings with the Chief Executive, the company secretary, and members of the executive management as appropriate.
- Ensure clear structure for, and the effective running of, board committees.
- Ensure effective implementation of board decisions.
- Promote effective relationships and open communication between executive and non-executive directors both inside and outside the boardroom, ensuring an appropriate balance of skills and personalities.
- Build an effective and complementary board, and with the Nomination Committee, initiate change and plan succession in board appointments (except that of a successor as Chairman) subject to board and shareholder approval.
- With the assistance of the company secretary, promote the highest standards of corporate governance, seeking compliance with the Combined Code. If full compliance is not possible, ensure that the reasons for non-compliance are fully understood, agreed by the board and explained to shareholders.
- Ensure an appropriate balance is maintained between the interests of shareholders and other stakeholders (employees, customers, suppliers and the community).
- Ensure the long-term sustainability of the business.
- Ensure the continual improvement in quality and calibre of the executives.

- Establish a close relationship of trust with the Chief Executive and Finance Director, providing support and advice while respecting executive responsibility
- Provide coherent leadership of the company, including, in conjunction with the Chief Executive, representing the company to customers, suppliers, governments, shareholders, financial institutions, the media, the community and the public.

APPENDIX 2

Role of Chief Executive

The Chief Executive is accountable and reports to the board and is responsible for running the group's business.

A. The Chief Executive is responsible for the following, within the authority limits delegated to them by the board:

1. Business Strategy and Management

- Developing group objectives and strategy having regard to the group's responsibilities to its shareholders, customers, employees and other stakeholders.
- The successful achievement of objectives and execution of strategy following presentation to, and approval by, the board.
- Recommending to the board an annual budget and [5 year] financial plan and ensuring their achievement following board approval.
- Optimising as far as is reasonably possible the use and adequacy of the group's resources.

2. Investment and Financing

- Examining all trade investments and major capital expenditure proposed by subsidiary companies and the recommendation to the group board of those which, in a group context, are material either by nature or cost.
- Identifying and executing acquisitions and disposals, approving major proposals or bids.
- Leading geographic diversification initiatives.
- Identifying and executing new business opportunities outside the current core activities.

3. Risk Management and Controls

- Managing the group's risk profile, including the health and safety performance of the business, in line with the extent and categories of risk identified as acceptable by the board.
- Ensuring appropriate internal controls are in place.

4. Board Committees

- Making recommendations on remuneration policy, executive remuneration and terms of employment of the senior executive team, including the company secretary to the Remuneration Committee.
- Making recommendations to the Nomination Committee on the role and capabilities required in respect of the appointment of executive directors.

5. Communication
- Providing a means for timely and accurate disclosure of information, including an escalation route for issues.
- Ensuring effective communication with shareholders.

6. Other
- Setting group HR policies, including management development and succession planning for the senior executive team and approving the appointment and termination of employment of members of that team.

B. The duties which derive from these responsibilities include:
- Leading the executive directors and the senior executive team in the day to day running of the group's business, including chairing the Executive Committee and communicating its decisions/recommendations to the board.
- Ensuring effective implementation of board decisions.
- Regularly reviewing the operational performance and strategic direction of the group's business.
- Regularly reviewing the group's organisational structure and recommending changes as appropriate.
- Formalising the roles and responsibilities of the senior executive team, including clear delegation of authorities.
- Supervising the activities of subsidiary companies' most senior executives.
- Developing senior teams within subsidiaries and ensuring succession planning.
- Developing the following policies for board approval and then implementing them.
- Codes of ethics and business practice.
- Share dealing code.
- Health and safety policy, risks and procedures (to be reviewed annually)
- Communications policy (including procedures for the release of price sensitive information).
- Investor relations policy.
- Corporate social responsibility policy (including environmental, employee communications and employee disability).
- Charitable donations policy.
- Ensuring that all group policies and procedures are followed and conform to the highest standards.
- Together with the Chairman, providing coherent leadership of the company, including, representing the Group to customers, suppliers, government, shareholders, financial institutions, employees, the media, the community and the public.
- Keeping the Chairman informed on all important matters.

APPENDIX 3

Role of the Chairman and Chief Executive – Alternative Approach

Statement of Division of Responsibilities between the Chairman and the Chief Executive

1. Reporting lines	
Chairman	Chief executive
Chairman Chief Executive 1.1 The Chairman reports to the board (the 'board').	1.1 The Chief Executive reports to the Chairman (acting on behalf of the board) and to the board directly.
1.2 The Chairman is not responsible for executive matters regarding the Group's business. Other than the Chief Executive and the company secretary, no executive reports to the Chairman, other than through the board.	1.2 The Chief Executive is responsible for all executive management matters affecting the Group. All members of executive management report, either directly or indirectly, to him/her.
2. Key responsibilities	
Chairman	Chief executive
Chairman Chief Executive 2.1 The Chairman's principal responsibility is the effective running of the board.	2.1 The Chief Executive's principal responsibility is running the Group's business.
2.2 The Chairman is responsible for ensuring that the board as a whole plays a full and constructive part in the development and determination of the Group's strategy and overall commercial objectives.	2.2 The Chief Executive is responsible for proposing and developing the Group's strategy and overall commercial objectives, which he does in close consultation with the Chairman and the board.
2.3 The Chairman is the guardian of the board's decision-making processes.	2.3 The Chief Executive is responsible, with the executive team, for implementing the decisions of the board and its Committees.
3. Other responsibilities	
Chairman	Chief executive
3.1 Running the board and setting its agenda.	3.1 Providing input to the board's agenda from himself and other members of the executive team.

3.2 Ensuring that board agendas take full account of the important issues facing the Group and the concerns of all board members. There should be an emphasis on strategic, rather than routine, issues.	3.2 Ensuring that he maintains a dialogue with the Chairman on the important and strategic issues facing the Group, and proposing board agendas to the Chairman which reflect
3.3 Ensuring that the board receives accurate, timely and clear information on: ■ the Group's performance ■ the issues, challenges and opportunities facing the Group and ■ matters reserved to it for decision.	3.3 Ensuring that the executive team gives appropriate priority to providing reports to the board which contain accurate, timely and clear information.
3.4 Ensuring, with the advice of the company secretary where appropriate, compliance with the board's approved procedures, including the schedule of Matters Reserved to the board for its decision and each Committee's Terms of Reference.	3.4 Ensuring, in consultation with the Chairman and the company secretary as appropriate, that he and the executive team comply with the board's approved procedures, including the schedule of Matters Reserved to the board for its decision and each Committee's terms of reference.
3.5 Arranging informal meetings of the directors, including meetings of the non-executive directors at which the executive directors are not present, as required to ensure that sufficient time and consideration is given to complex, contentious or sensitive issues.	3.5 Ensuring that the Chairman is alerted to forthcoming complex, contentious or sensitive issues affecting the Group of which he might not otherwise be aware.
3.6 Proposing to the board, in consultation with the Chief Executive, company secretary and Committee Chairmen as appropriate: ■ a schedule of Matters Reserved to the board for its decision ■ Terms of Reference for each board ■ Committee and ■ other board policies and procedures.	3.6 Providing input to the Chairman and company secretary on appropriate changes to the schedule of Matters Reserved to the board and Committee Terms of Reference.
3.7 Chairing the Nomination Committee, and, in that role, initiating change and succession planning in board appointments to retain and build an effective and complementary board, and to facilitate the appointment of effective and suitable members and Chairmen of board Committees.	3.7 Providing information and advice on succession planning, to the Chairman, the Nomination Committee, and other members of the board, particularly in respect of executive directors.

3.8 Proposing, in conjunction with the Nomination Committee, the membership of board Committees and their Chairmen.	3.8 If so appointed by the board, serving on the Nomination Committee.
3.9 Ensuring that there is effective communication by the Group with its shareholders, including by the Chief Executive, Finance Director and other executive management, and ensuring that members of the board develop an understanding of the views of the major investors in the Group.	3.9 Leading the communication programme with shareholders.
3.10 Taking the lead in providing a properly constructed induction programme for new directors, facilitated by the company secretary.	3.10 Commenting on induction programmes for new directors and ensuring that appropriate management time is made available for the process.
3.11 Taking the lead in identifying and seeking to meet the development needs both of individual directors and of the board as a whole, assisted by the company secretary.	3.11 Ensuring that the development needs of the executive directors and other senior management reporting to him are identified and met.
3.12 Ensuring that the performance of the board as a whole, its Committees, and individual directors is formally and rigorously evaluated at least once a year.	3.12 Ensuring that performance reviews are carried out at least once a year for each of the executive directors. Providing input to the wider board evaluation process.
3.13 Promoting the highest standards of integrity, probity and corporate governance throughout the Group and particularly at board level.	3.13 Promoting, and conducting the affairs of the Group with the highest standards of integrity, probity and corporate governance.
4 Status of this statement	
4.1 Any amendments to this statement are a Matter Reserved to the board. 4.2 This statement is to be annexed to the Chief Executive's Job Description. In the event of any conflict between this statement and the Chief Executive's Job Statement in so far as they may relate to his role as Group Chief Executive, this statement shall take precedence.	

APPENDIX 4

Draft Board Responsibilities Statement

To achieve the maximum effectiveness of the board, the board accepts that the roles of Chairman and Chief Executive need to be split and clearly defined. The policy statement adopted by the board on xx yyyy 2003 defines the role of the Chairman and Chief Executive.

The Chairman is responsible for leadership of the board and creating the conditions for overall board and individual director effectiveness, both inside and outside the boardroom. The Chief Executive is responsible for running the group's business.

It should be noted that this document does not supersede the authorities delegated in the matters reserved for the board document approved by the board on xx yyyy 2003.

APPENDIX 5

Role of the Senior Independent Director ("SID")

1. Shareholders

- The SID will be available to shareholders if they have concerns which contact through the normal channels of Chairman, Chief Executive or Finance Director has failed to resolve or for which such contact is inappropriate.
- They will attend sufficient meetings with major shareholders and financial analysts to obtain a balanced understanding of the issues and concerns of such shareholders.

2. Chairman

- The SID will chair the Nomination Committee when it is considering succession to the role of Chairman of the board.
- They will meet with the non-executive directors at least once a year to appraise the Chairman's performance and on such other occasions as are deemed appropriate.

Notes

1 The role and effectiveness of the non-executive director, by Derek Higgs published January 2003
2 Principles of Good Governance and code of Best Practice (The Combined Code as amended by the Higgs review), principles A.2 and A.6
3 Code provision A.2.1
4 Code provision A.1.1
5 Code provision A.2.2
6 Code provision A.2.2
7 Code principle A.5
8 Code provision A.2.1
9 Code principle A.3
10 Committee of Corporate Governance: Final Report (The Hampel Report) January 1998
11 Code provision A.3.3
12 Code provision D.1.1
13 Code provision A.1.3
14 This corresponds to provision A.1.3 of the Combined Code however experience suggests that the scope of such meetings may need to be carefully defined and controlled to ensure that executive directors are not made to feel that decisions are being made without their involvement.

Appendix 3

GC100: Companies Act 2006 – Directors' conflicts of interest (18 January 2008)

1. Introduction

1.1 From 1 October 2008 a director will have a statutory duty under section 175 of the Companies Act 2006 (the 2006 Act) to avoid a situation in which he has, or can have, a conflict of interest or a possible conflict of interest with the company's interests. There will be no breach of this duty if the relevant matter has been authorised by the directors. For a public company the directors can only authorise the matter if permitted to do so by the company's constitution.

1.2 There are a number of situations which put a director in a potential position of conflict with the company, for example, where he is a director of another company which becomes a competitor of, or a major supplier to, his company, where he represents a major shareholder or has a position with one of the company's advisers. A conflict must be authorised in advance to avoid a director being in breach of duty. Public companies will therefore want to have a power in their articles of association for the board to sanction conflicts.

1.3 As not all conflict situations can be anticipated and each situation will be different, the GC100 considers that most companies will want a general power to authorise conflicts. There are safeguards that will apply when a board decides whether to authorise a potential conflict in accordance with the articles of association. When a board is making this decision, each authorising director will need to have regard to his own duties including the duty to act in a way he considers, in good faith, will be most likely to promote the success of the company. Shareholders therefore have the assurance that the board will only use the power to sanction conflicts where it is in the interests of the company.

1.4 Currently when a material conflict of interest arises, the director concerned will take steps to mitigate the conflict by, for example, absenting himself from board discussions and, in extreme cases, standing down from the board. Under section 175 however, a director must not let the situation arise in the first place unless the board has given prior authorisation. This change in the law will require companies to operate more formal procedures regarding conflicts of interest but provided a potential conflict has been authorised, the change should not result in the relevant director behaving in a different way than he would at the moment when a real conflict arises.

1.5 The 2006 Act also preserves the effect of provisions in a company's articles dealing with conflicts. A director will not be in breach of section 175 (and the other general duties in Chapter 2 of Part 10) for anything done or omitted by the director in accordance with provisions in the articles dealing with conflicts. Where a company's articles include a power for the purposes of section 175 for a board to authorise conflicts, this will supplement any other general provisions in the articles dealing with conflicts.

1.6 As the statutory power for a board to authorise conflicts is a new one (previously the power lay with shareholders), the GC100 concluded that boards might find it helpful to have some guidance on the exercise of this power. This paper therefore sets out:

- a summary of the 2006 Act provisions on conflicts;
- an explanation of changes companies might make to their articles of association to reflect the 2006 Act provisions on conflicts and a paragraph to include in the AGM circular explaining those changes;
- guidance for directors on exercising the power to authorise conflicts including suggested procedures for authorising conflict situations and reviewing authorisations; and
- potential situations of conflict to provide boards and individual directors with a reference point.

1.7 It should be stressed that this note is intended as general guidance only and that each situation of conflict or potential conflict should be considered on its facts. Where there is any doubt, companies should consult their own legal advisers.

1.8 The ABI has reviewed this guidance paper and the suggested amendments to articles of association to reflect the conflict provisions in the 2006 Act. The GC100 expects that shareholders are unlikely to raise objections provided companies have an existing sound governance structure, have procedures in place as suggested in this paper for ensuring that a board's powers of authorisation of conflicts are operated effectively and commit to confirming compliance with the procedures.

2. The duty to avoid conflicts of interest

2.1 Section 175(1) of the 2006 Act states that a director of a company must avoid a situation in which he has, or can have, a direct or indirect interest that conflicts, or possibly may conflict, with the interests of the company.

2.2 Some points to note are:

a) there is no definition of "interest" or "conflict of interest", although a reference to a conflict of interest includes a conflict of interest and duty and a conflict of duties (section 175(7));

b) the conflicting interest can be direct or indirect – an example of an indirect interest would be where a director represents a major shareholder in the company whose interests conflict with those of the company;

c) the duty applies in particular to the exploitation of any property, information or opportunity, whether or not the company could itself take advantage of it (section 175(2));

d) the prohibition applies to the situation rather than the actual conflict. Section 175(1) refers to a situation in which the director has *or can have* an interest that conflicts *or possibly may conflict* with the interests of the company. However, the duty is not infringed *if the situation cannot reasonably be regarded as likely to give rise to a conflict of interest* (section 175(4)(a)); and

e) it appears that it is not necessary for a director to have any influence over a particular situation for a conflict to arise. For example, if a director of Company A is also a director of Company B, which is a competitor of Company A, it appears that the duty would be breached even if the director is not involved in any decision-making in the area in which the companies compete unless the boards of Company A and Company B have authorised the matter.

2.3 Arguably, any of the following situations could fall within section 175(1) (this list is not exhaustive):

a) if a director of Company A is a competitor in some respects of Company A;
b) if a director of Company A is a major shareholder in Company A;
c) if a director of Company A is a potential customer of, or supplier to, Company A;
d) if a director of Company A owns property adjacent to Company A's property, the value of which could be affected by the activities of Company A;
e) if a director of Company A has an advisory relationship (for example, financial or legal) with Company A or a competitor;
f) if a director of Company A is a director of Company A's pension trustee company;
g) if a director wants to take up an opportunity that had been offered to, but declined by, Company A;
h) if a director is in a situation where he can make a profit as a result of his directorship whether or not he discloses this to Company A; and
i) if in each of the above situations, the director is a director of another company and that other company has the relevant relationship with Company A or is in the situation described above.

2.4 The duty does not apply to a conflict of interest arising in relation to a transaction or arrangement with the company (section 175(3)). Conflicts arising in these circumstances are covered by two separate provisions of the 2006 Act that will replace section 317 of the Companies Act 1985:

a) under section 177, a director has a duty to declare an interest in a proposed transaction or arrangement with the company; and
b) under section 182, a director must declare an interest in an existing transaction or arrangement with the company – in this case, failure to comply is a criminal offence (section 182).

2.5 This paper does not consider sections 177 and 182 in any detail, except it should be noted that situations that initially appear to fall within section 175 could evolve to a situation falling within section 177, in which case section 175 may no longer apply. For example, if a director of Company A is also on Company A's list of preferred suppliers, the general relationship may fall within section 175, but the entering into of any supply contract between Company A and the director would fall within section 177.

2.6 The paper also does not consider section 176 (duty not to accept benefits from third parties). Boards will need to review their policies on, for example, corporate hospitality taken up by directors. Unlike section 175, there is no specific provision for boards to authorise the acceptance of benefits by directors. The duty not to accept benefits from third parties is not infringed if the acceptance of the benefit cannot reasonably be regarded as likely to give rise to a conflict of interest (section 176(4)).

2.7 There has been some debate as to whether the attempt to codify the law through section 175 has resulted in an over-simplification of the previous law. The Company Law Review pointed out that there appeared to be widespread misunderstanding of the previous law, and in particular the circumstances in which conflicts could be authorised. One part of the 2006 Act that is clearly an attempt to clarify the law is to give boards express powers to authorise conflicts, which is a welcome development.

2.8 Under section 175(4)(b) the duty to avoid conflicts of interest is not infringed if the matter has been authorised by the directors. In the case of a public company authorisation can only be given where:

a) its constitution includes provision enabling the directors to authorise the matter; and

b) the matter is proposed to and authorised by them in accordance with the constitution.

The authorisation is only effective if quorum requirements are met without the relevant director voting, or would have been met without his votes being counted. The transitional provisions for section 175 provide that for a private company incorporated on or after 1 October 2008, authorisation can be given by the board provided nothing in the company's constitution invalidates such authorisation (section 175(5)(a)). For a private company incorporated before 1 October 2008, authorisation can be given by the board provided shareholders have resolved that authorisation may be given in accordance with section 175(5)(a). The transitional provisions also deal with "situations" that arose before 1 October 2008. These are referred to in paragraph 4.8 below.

2.9 Provided a conflict situation has been authorised by the directors, it will not require approval by shareholders (section 180(1)). Where a transaction falls within Chapter 4 of Part 10 (transactions with directors requiring approval of members), it is not necessary for the director concerned also to comply with section 175 or section 176 (duty not to accept benefits from third parties). This is provided approval is given under Chapter 4 or the Chapter provides that approval is not required (section 180(2)). So compliance with the Chapter 4 procedures in this case effectively sanctions any conflict.

2.10 Some points to note on an authorisation under section 175(4)(b):

a) authorisation by the board cannot be retrospective; and

b) authorisation will apply to the conflict situation, but not other breaches of duty. For example, even if a director's conflict has been authorised, that will not absolve him from his duty to act in a way that he considers is most likely to promote the success of the company under section 172. There is however a safe harbour where a director acts in accordance with provisions in the articles dealing with conflicts (section 180(4)(b)).

2.11 The safe harbour in section 180(4)(b) provides that where a company's articles contain provisions for dealing with conflicts of interest, the general duties are not infringed by anything done (or omitted to be done) by the directors, or any of them, when following those provisions. Section 232(4) of the 2006 Act is also relevant in this context as it allows a company's articles to protect directors from liability by continuing to include provisions dealing with conflicts of interest where they were previously lawful. This means that companies can continue to rely on provisions in their articles dealing with conflicts (for example article 85 of Table A).

2.12 Where a company is amending its articles to reflect section 175(4) and incorporating the power for the board to authorise conflicts, it may want to consider how directors can take advantage of the section 180(4)(b) safe harbour in relation to conflict situations authorised by the board. A company may for example want to make it clear that a director will not be in breach of duty in respect of an authorised conflict situation:

a) if he receives confidential information as a result of the conflict situation from a third party and does not disclose this to the company or use it for the company's benefit; or
b) where he takes mitigating action when the actual conflict arises by, for example, not attending board meetings or reading board papers.

A company may want wider provisions in its articles, for example sanctioning conflicts that may arise as a result of directors' involvement with other companies in the group or joint venture companies.

3. Provisions for articles and paragraph of explanatory circular

3.1 The provision in the articles enabling the directors to authorise the matter giving rise to the actual or potential conflict must include the power for the board to authorise conflicts. In addition a company may want to set out in the articles:

a) how any matter is to be proposed to the board and how it is to be authorised by them (see section 175(5)(b));
b) the quorum requirements to approve any conflict (see section 175(6)); and
c) to take advantage of the section 180(4)(b) safe harbour both in relation to authorised conflicts and other non-material conflicts, deal with:
   - overriding the duty to disclose confidential information received in a capacity other than as a director or employee to the company, and the obligation to use such information for the company's benefit; and
   - the director's conduct in relation to an authorised conflict.

3.2 Companies may wish to note that there are differing views as to how to best take advantage of the safe harbour in section 180(4)(b). One view is that the articles themselves should specify that a director will not be in breach of duty by, for example, withholding confidential information from the company. The other view is that the articles should permit the board, when authorising a conflict, to provide that the director does not have to disclose confidential information received as a result of the conflict. In each case, the articles must contain the relevant provision. Companies will also need to consider appropriate changes to their articles to deal with sections 177 and 182 (duty to disclose interests in transactions or arrangements).

3.3 The following is a suggested paragraph for an explanatory circular to shareholders covering changes to the Articles to reflect the Companies Act 2006. This wording is based on the pro forma circular published in December 2007 developed by a number of law firms represented on the Company Law Sub-Committee of the City of London Law Society. The pro forma circular has been seen by the UKLA which has confirmed that the changes described can be regarded as not containing unusual features.

'The Companies Act 2006 sets out directors' general duties which largely codify the existing law but with some changes. Under the Companies Act, from 1 October 2008 a director must avoid a situation where he has, or can have, a direct or indirect interest that conflicts, or possibly may conflict, with the company's interests. The requirement is very broad and could apply, for example, if a director becomes a director of another company or a trustee of another organisation. The Companies Act 2006 allows directors of public companies to authorise conflicts and potential conflicts where appropriate, where the articles of association contain a provision to this effect. The Companies Act 2006 also allows the articles to contain other provisions for dealing with directors' conflicts of interest to avoid a breach of duty. The New Articles give the directors authority to approve such situations and to include other provisions to allow conflicts of interest to be dealt with in a similar way to the current position.

There are safeguards that will apply when directors decide whether to authorise a conflict or potential conflict. First, only directors who have no interest in the matter being considered will be able to take the relevant decision, and secondly, in taking the decision the directors must act in a way they consider, in good faith, will be most likely to promote the company's success. The directors will be able to impose limits or conditions when giving authorisation if they think this is appropriate.

[It is also proposed that the New Articles should contain provisions relating to confidential information, attendance at board meetings and availability of board papers to protect a director being in breach of duty if a conflict of interest or potential conflict of interest arises. These provisions will only apply where the position giving rise to the potential conflict has previously been authorised by the directors.]

It is the board's intention to report annually on the Company's procedures for ensuring that the board's powers of authorisation of conflicts are operated effectively and that the procedures have been followed.'

4. Guidance on exercising power to authorise conflicts

4.1 Before 1 October 2008 (and subject to what is said in paragraph 4.8 below) a board will want to consider the situation of each of the company's directors to determine if there are actual or potential conflicts of interest that need to be approved in accordance with section 175(4) to avoid that director being in breach of section 175. After that date, a director will be in breach of duty if he is in a situation that involves, or could involve, a conflict unless this has previously been authorised by the board, the situation cannot reasonably be regarded as likely to give rise to a conflict of interest or he acted in accordance with provisions in the articles dealing with conflicts. Potential situations of conflict are set out in Part 5 of this paper.

4.2 It should be stressed that each situation should be considered separately on its particular facts. It is not practicable to prescribe what conflicts should be authorised, or to what extent. This part of the note does, however, set out some suggested guidance that boards may find helpful.

4.3 It is suggested that the company secretary (or another appointed representative) writes to each director to explain the new duty in section 175 and that prior board authorisation will be needed for any conflict situation. Each director should be asked to prepare a list of other positions he holds (for example directorships) and also all other conflict situations that he thinks need authorising by reference to Part 5 of this note. He should also be asked to consider if any of his connected persons hold positions that could lead to the director being in breach of section 175. Companies might like to note however that Lord Goldsmith, the Government's spokesman on the legislation, regarded the situation of multiple directorships as capable of being authorised by the directors (see Hansard 6 February col. GC288).

4.4 Each director's situation needs to be considered by the board and the board must decide whether to approve any conflict situations taking account of their general duties set out in Chapter 2 of Part 10 of the 2006 Act. Where the board is asked to approve a potential conflicting position that brings clear benefits to the company, for example access to industry or sector expertise, it will usually not be an issue in deciding that they are acting in the interests of the company in approving the conflict. A board should be able to approve a matter if on balance the directors think it is in the interests of the company for the company to retain (or appoint) that director. A board should consider whether the matter they are approving would affect the relevant director's ability to act in accordance with his wider duties.

4.5 A board should consider how far the authorisation should go in relation to each matter it is asked to approve to avoid the director being in breach of section 175. Taking the example of a director seeking sanction for his role as a non-executive director of another company, the board may decide to approve his continuing in this role but may not want to sanction all consequences that flow from the role, for example if Company B decides to acquire the company or becomes a competitor. So in sanctioning any matter that gives rise to a conflict, a board needs to consider what consequences could flow from that matter and the stage at which the authorisation should no longer apply. Part 5 considers some of the consequences that could flow from various situations of conflict that a board may want to address when considering the extent of its authorisation of any particular matter.

4.6 A board also needs to consider what should happen if a real conflict arises post authorisation and the director has clearly conflicting interests. The options are:

a) exclude the director from the relevant information and debate;
b) exclude the director from the board (suspension); or
c) require the director to resign.

4.7 The board resolution approving a director's actual or possible conflict should:

a) set out the matter that has been authorised, for example the director's appointment as a non-executive director of Company B;
b) state the duration of the authority (it is suggested sufficient time, eg 15 months, for it to be reviewed annually) and that it can be revoked at any time;
c) set out any circumstances when the director must revert to the board (or any committee referred to in paragraph 4.10 below) for the authority to be reviewed;
d) include, where appropriate, provisions stating that the director may not receive information relating to the conflict or participate in board discussions where the conflict is relevant; and
e) include, where appropriate, provisions stating that where the director obtains information as a result of his position with Company B that is confidential to Company B he will not be obliged to disclose this information to the company, or to use the information in relation to the company's affairs, if this would breach that confidence. In certain situations a board may only want to give this effective release if Company B has also acknowledged that the director can keep the company's information confidential and not use it for Company B's affairs. The director is then able to "ring-fence" information received from each company.

4.8 Companies will need to consult their advisers on the timing of changes to their articles to reflect section 175 and, if deemed necessary, section 180(4)(b) and the timing of the board meeting to authorise conflicts. It is also worth noting that the transitional provisions relating to section 175 (paragraph 47 of schedule 4 to the Fifth Commencement Order) provide that the section applies where the situation arises on or after 1 October 2008. Therefore situations arising before 1 October 2008 are in theory outside section 175. However, it is not clear what the position is where a conflict arises after 1 October 2008 as a result of a situation that existed before that date, for example as a result of a cross directorship. Because of the uncertainty, it is likely that companies will take a cautious view and treat conflicts arising from 1 October 2008 as new situations requiring board approval. For this reason it is thought that most companies will want to use the new section 175 procedures for situations such as cross directorships that straddle the commencement date. Also this enables such situations to benefit from the new safe harbour provisions discussed in paragraph 2.12 above.

4.9 From 1 October 2008 the board's power to authorise conflicts will also be relevant when:

a) a new director is appointed to the board; and
b) an existing director proposes to take up an appointment that could lead to a conflict.

4.10 The board should consider appointing a committee, for example, the nominations committee, to be responsible for regularly reviewing conflict authorisations. Each director's section 175 authorisations should be reviewed annually (perhaps as part of the board performance review) to check it is appropriate for the relevant matter to remain authorised. Authorisation should, however, be formally considered by the board on the advice of the committee.

4.11 It is suggested that companies keep a list of authorisations granted to directors, setting out the date an authorisation was granted and the date it expires, its scope and any limitations or special circumstances.

4.12 Boards should also consider how they could give shareholders assurance that their powers of authorisation are being exercised properly and in accordance with the approved changes to the articles, for example, by providing an explanation in the company's Corporate Governance Report.

5. Potential conflict situations

5.1 **Where a director is on the board of, is a significant shareholder in, or is himself, a supplier to or customer of the company**. The board may decide to approve this relationship but will not want the director to be able to disclose "company" information to the supplier or customer or to use it for the supplier or customer's benefit. They also will not want him to be involved in board discussions concerning the relationship.

5.2 **Where a director is on the board of, is a significant shareholder in, or is himself, a major shareholder of the company**. This may be a situation the board is in favour of or it may be a hostile situation. Whichever it is, the board will want to ensure there are safeguards attached and that the director agrees not to disclose "company" information to the shareholder. If he is a director of the shareholder, the board will also want to be satisfied that the director's arrangements with the shareholder permit him to withhold confidential information from the shareholder. The board needs also to consider what should happen if the shareholder decides to increase its stake, to make an offer or to sell its stake to a potential bidder or if there is a difference of views between the board and the significant shareholder on policy matters or strategy.

5.3 **Where a director also has a role with one of the company's advisers**. The board needs to anticipate what to do when the director receives information as a result of his position with the adviser that his duties to the company would normally require him to disclose. In this situation, it would usually be appropriate for the director to be expressly authorised not to disclose the relevant information to the company having agreed not to disclose company information to the adviser.

5.4 **Where a director is also a director of the company's pension trustee company or a trustee of the pension fund**. Potentially there is a conflict whenever the board discusses a matter that could affect the ability of the company to fund the scheme, including paying a dividend or buying back shares. The board needs to consider what will happen when there are direct negotiations between it and the pension trustee on funding contributions and whether the director should be able to take one side. Note that the ICAEW has issued useful practical guidance on this situation – see Tech 06/07: Acting as a trustee for the pension fund of your employer, available from the ICAEW website.

5.5 **Where a potential bidder approaches a director and the director is offered a role with the potential bidding group**. It is unlikely that a board would be asked to sanction this sort of clear conflict until the situation arises.

GC100: background information

1. The GC100 was officially launched on 9 March 2005 and brings together the senior legal officers of more than 90 FTSE100 and former FTSE 100 companies. The formal name of the GC100 is now the "Association of General Counsel and Company Secretaries of the FTSE" as membership of the group was extended to company secretaries in the FTSE 100 in January 2007.
2. The main objectives of the GC100 are to:
   - Provide a forum for practical and business focused input on key areas of legislative and policy reform common to UK listed companies.
   - Enable members to share best practice in relation to law, risk management, compliance and other areas of common interest.
3. Officers to the GC100 for 2008 are:
   - Chair: Peter Maynard, Prudential
   - Vice-chairs: Grant Dawson, Centrica and Peter Kennerley, Scottish & Newcastle
   - Treasurer: Richard Bennett, HSBC
   - Secretary: Mary Mullally, PLC
4. Other members of the Executive Committee for 2008 are:
   - Rupert Bondy, GlaxoSmithKline
   - Alan Buchanan, British Airways
   - John Davidson, SAB Miller
   - Nick Folland, Kingfisher

- Andrea Harris, WPP
- Mark Harding, Barclays
- David Jackson, BP
- Tom Keevil, United Utilities
- Helen Mahy, National Grid

5. As a matter of formality please note that the views expressed in this paper do not necessarily reflect the views of all of the individual members or their employing companies.
6. The GC100 thanks the following for their assistance with this paper:
   - Lucinda Case, PLC Corporate;
   - Vanessa Knapp, Freshfields Bruckhaus Deringer, Nilufer von Bismarck, Slaughter and May and James Palmer, Herbert Smith; and
   - Michael McKersie and Marc Jobling, ABI for reviewing the paper and seeking feedback from their members.

For more information contact:
Nick Folland (Director of Governance and Corporate Services, Kingfisher plc) at nick.folland@kingfisher.com
Peter Kennerley (general counsel and company secretary, Scottish & Newcastle) at peter.kennerley@s-n.com
Lucinda Case (PLC Corporate) at lucinda.case@practicallaw.com
Mary Mullally (PLC) at mary.mullally@practicallaw.com

Appendix 4

GC100: Companies Act 2006 – Directors' duties (7 February 2007)

1. Background

1.1 The new Companies Act seeks to codify directors' duties for the first time, as well as introduce the concept of enlightened shareholder value. The GC100 has no issue with these proposals in principle. However, together with other bodies such as the CBI and City of London Law Society, we have expressed concerns that the Act (coupled with the new provisions making it easier for shareholders to bring derivative actions) could have the effect of increasing bureaucracy in companies, making the decision process more cumbersome and potentially increasing the liability of directors.

1.2 Whilst we made representations to the Government and to the DTI about our views during the legislative process, the Act was not amended and our concerns were met with a mixed response. This varied from 'this is no real change to what responsible companies are doing now anyway' to 'of course it's a change, and we want you to take this seriously – it's not just a box-ticking exercise.' We now wish to engage with interested parties to achieve clarity for UK plc.

1.3 As the Companies Bill passed through parliamentary debates, the Government tried to provide some comfort to directors on the intended impact of the provisions. For example, the Attorney General, Lord Goldsmith, said in the Lords:

> 'There is nothing in this Bill that says there is a need for a paper trail.... I do not agree that the effect of passing this Bill will be that directors will be subject to a breach if they cannot demonstrate that they have considered every element. It will be for the person who is asserting breach of duty to make that case good ... [Derivative claims] will be struck out if there is no decent basis for them.'

1.4 Against this background, we have decided that the GC100 should take a lead in identifying best practice guidelines for compliance with the new law.

1.5 This note is designed to set out that best practice. It considers the current law and practice and suggests how this may be adapted to the new law. Whilst it is not intended to be relied upon as legal advice, it represents the views of the GC100 as to how companies and their advisers can put the new law into practice.

2. The current law

The current law may be summarised as follows: directors must act in a way that they believe to be in the interests of the Company and its shareholders, both current and future, as a whole. This duty is owed to the Company itself, and not to individual shareholders. The current Companies Act states that directors are to have regard to the interests of the company's employees in general, as well as the interests of shareholders, but this duty is not owed directly to employees.

3. Current practice

1.1 Levels of decisions

The way that directors currently perform their functions varies widely, depending upon the nature of the issues in question and the company concerned.

(a) There are invariably some matters that are formally reserved for the board. This is a requirement of the Combined Code and, arguably, some provisions of the Companies Act. Examples include: approval of financial statements, recommending dividends, major transactions and board appointments.

(b) Companies often delegate authority for other issues to an executive committee, usually led by the Chief Executive. The terms of reference for such a committee will *authorise* the committee or individuals to take decisions which are not reserved for the board, but also *require* certain decisions to be submitted to the committee or individual for approval.

(c) Issues that do not require approval at board, executive committee or designated director level will usually be taken informally by directors or other managers within the authority delegated to them by virtue of their appointment. In practice, the vast majority of day-to-day business will be handled in this way.

(d) Companies also operate through subsidiaries, which may have their own governance structures, similar to those referred to above. The proposals put forward in this paper are designed to be adaptable, as companies see fit, through any part of a corporate structure and, if thought appropriate, cascaded down to subsidiaries.

3.2 Formalities

The formalities supporting and recording decisions taken by companies, again, vary depending upon the nature of issue, the level at which it is taken and the company concerned.

(a) Board or committee meetings.

In the case of a formal decision taken at a board or executive committee meeting, the process may typically involve:

(i) A briefing paper. This paper usually addresses all the issues which the directors are likely to take into account in making their decision, including for example the strategic rationale for the proposal, the financial effects, a summary of legal and regulatory issues, issues relating to employees and reputational issues. The precise form of paper varies from company to company and the detail depends on the type of proposal. The paper is circulated in advance of any meeting, unless the circumstances are exceptional, and is considered thoroughly by directors. Arguably it forms the most important documented support to the decision process.

(ii) A presentation. This may be used to supplement the briefing paper.

(iii) A discussion amongst board members leading to a decision.

(iv) A board minute. The minute may summarise the main points of any board or committee discussion, and will record any decision. Minutes may include wording to the effect that, taking all matters into account, the directors, consider that the proposal is in the interests of the Company as a whole.

However, this practice is really only followed in situations where formal board minutes have to be disclosed to external third parties, for example as a condition to drawdown under a banking facility, and is rarely thought necessary otherwise. As far as formal codification of factors that directors must consider stands today, whilst boards often discuss the effect of any proposal on employees, it is virtually unheard of for minutes expressly to refer to this. In fact, some companies, particularly those with exposure to US litigation, largely omit the details of discussion from any minute, and simply record the decision reached.

The process for full board meetings is likely to be more formal, the process for executive committee meetings much less so.

(b) Decisions taken by individual directors on matters specifically reserved for them.

Where decisions are taken by individual directors, the process may, legitimately, involve much less formality, although in order to show that internal processes have been followed, there may be some form of briefing paper and/or record of the decision concerned.

(c) Other decisions.

The way other decisions are supported or recorded varies as widely as the nature of the decisions concerned. In the vast majority of cases, it is simply not practicable for decisions to be supported by background papers or for the reasons, or in many cases even the decisions themselves, to be formally recorded. This has to continue to be the case if companies are to retain their operational flexibility and remain competitive.

4. The new legislation

Section 172 of the Companies Act will require a director to exercise his duties in a way that he considers, in good faith, would be most likely to promote the success of the company for the benefit of its members as a whole. So far, this is broadly in line with the current law. However, section 172(1) states that, in exercising those duties, directors must have regard to (amongst other matters) the following six factors:

(a) the likely consequences of the decision in the long term;
(b) the interests of the company's employees;
(c) the need to foster the company's business relationships with suppliers, customers and others;
(d) the impact of the company's operations on the community and the environment;
(e) the desirability of the company maintaining a reputation for high standards of business conduct; and
(f) the need to act fairly as between members of the company.

It is clear that these factors are subsidiary to the overall duty under section 172, and that the duty is owed only to the company, not to individual shareholders or to third parties. Whilst the wording of section 172(1) is mandatory (directors 'must act ... and in doing so have regard to'), it is also clear that the list of factors is not exhaustive. The GC100 is of the view that directors are not currently, and should not be, as a result of this legislative codification, forced to evidence their thought processes whether that is with regard to the stated factors or any other matter influencing their thinking. Apart from the unnecessary process and paperwork this would introduce into the boardroom, it would inevitably expose directors to a greater and unacceptable risk of litigation, especially in light of the new derivative action also being brought in by the Companies Act 2006.

5. Aim of guidelines

5.1 The GC100's aim is to develop best practice guidelines for boards of public companies to:

(a) assist them in complying with the new law relating to directors' duties;

(b) reduce their potential liability to the company, whether directly or by means of derivative action;

(c) minimise the administrative burden through aiming for a pragmatic approach;

(d) demonstrate to all stakeholders that public companies and their directors are taking their wider duties seriously.

5.2 Any guidelines should:

(a) recognise the diverse ways in which decisions are taken by directors;

(b) have broad support from all stakeholders, including companies and their legal advisers; and

(c) recognise that individual companies choose to have differing governance arrangements.

6. Outline guidelines

6.1 Generally

Given the wide range of circumstances in which directors exercise their duties, it will not be possible to recommend a particular process which will apply for all decisions. It would, for example, be completely unworkable to require all decisions, and the reasons for them, to be recorded in writing. The suggested approach is therefore that:

(i) companies should ensure that all directors are aware of their duties under the new Companies Act; and

(ii) where the nature of the decision being taken by directors is such that it is supported by a formal process, that process need only specifically record consideration of those duties where the particular circumstances make it particularly necessary or relevant. The default position should be not to include these references.

6.2 Ensuring directors are aware of their duties

Companies should ensure that all board members are aware of their duties under the new Act. This can be done in all or some of the following ways:

(i) As a transitional move, boards should be given a thorough briefing on the new duties introduced by the Companies Act.

(ii) On appointment, all new directors should be briefed upon their duties under the Companies Act.

(iii) The terms of appointment and description of the role of any director should specifically refer to their duties.

(iv) The terms of reference of any board or committee may also refer to those duties.

(v) Companies should review their existing policies in areas such as human resources, ethics, compliance and corporate responsibility against the background of the new duties.

(vi) Care will need to be taken to ensure the duties are not inadvertently extended to give new rights of action to third parties.

6.3 Board and committee decisions

(a) As noted above, board (and to a lesser extent, committee) decisions are likely to have the greatest degree of formal process.

(b) In general, if a proposal is to be put to a board for a decision, it is likely to be an important one for the company. It will nearly always be supported by a background paper which will have been thoroughly prepared by the management team; possibly with the help of advisers. In practice, therefore, a thorough analysis of all the issues reflecting on the decision will already have been made by management. It is the job of the directors, at that stage, to review the papers, and any recommendations made in them, both in the light of the information supplied to them and using their own business judgement and, following discussion, to reach a decision. Without detracting from the importance of thorough debate at the boardroom table and the need for the directors to apply their own business judgement, the background paper (and any management presentations made at the meeting) is a key way of assisting directors in properly taking into account all relevant factors relating to their decision.

(c) It should therefore be best practice for those members of the management team responsible for preparing the paper to ensure that each of the relevant factors, including those referred to in the Companies Act, are properly considered whilst the paper is being prepared. They can then, if necessary, be included in the paper or any presentation made. Responsibility for considering relevant factors can properly be delegated to the members of the management team preparing the paper in the usual way.

(d) In some cases, one or more particular factors may clearly be irrelevant. GC100 does not believe that best practice should be prescriptive by requiring a negative statement.

(e) Directors will, of course, continue to have to be satisfied that they delegate the task of compiling the briefing to the appropriate people. Moreover, whatever the contents of any briefing, the directors concerned would still have to use their business judgement in considering the proposal.

(f) Board minutes also form an important part of process, in particular to the extent that they reflect the actual debate at a meeting and the decision taken. However, minutes are, of necessity, simply a summary and can never, in practice, be prepared with the thoroughness of a board paper. In some cases, companies have very brief minutes, for example, where there is a specific need to avoid detailed references to legal advice to ensure privilege is not lost. It is therefore recommended that board minutes should not be used as the main medium for recording the extent to which each of the factors of the Companies Act were discussed. Board minutes do not, after all, do so today insofar as either the common law or statutory duties require directors to consider particular factors. The minimum requirement for minutes should only be that they clearly state the decision reached.

(g) Despite the importance of the briefing paper, its purpose should not be misunderstood; that is to assist directors in reaching a decision through exercising their own judgement – it should not be construed as the decision or a record of the directors' views.

(h) The advantages of this approach would be:

  (i) each of the factors relevant to a decision, whether those prescribed by the Companies Act or otherwise, will be properly considered by management before an issue is brought to the board;

(ii) the board will have a written report on each relevant issue – even if brief – and each director will have had the opportunity of considering it in advance and of raising any questions at or before the meeting;
(iii) it treats the factors as part of the overall commercial decision process;
(iv) there will be a clear written record of the issues addressed; and
(v) it will not be necessary to minute what was said on each factor, except to the extent appropriate to reflect points raised on them. This will avoid any substantial increase in the length of minutes.

6.4 Other decisions

When decisions are taken by directors in circumstances other than at a formal board meeting, it should be for the company concerned to decide, in its particular circumstances, the best approach to be adopted.

Where there is a clear scheme of delegation and a decision is to be taken by an individual director, it is unlikely to be appropriate for a paper to be prepared as described above. It has to be recognised that many decisions, even if taken in accordance with a formal scheme of delegation, have to be taken within a timeframe which does not allow for preparation of a formal paper; or for a formal minute of the decision. It is important that best practice recognises this – lack of formal process should not lead to any inference that factors have not been properly considered.

February 2007

Background information to the GC100

The GC100 was officially launched on the 9th March 2005 and brings together the senior legal officers of more than 70 FTSE100 companies (see below for a full list of member companies).

1 The main objectives of the GC100 are to:
- Provide a forum for practical and business focused input on key areas of legislative and policy reform common to UK listed companies.
- Enable members to share best practice in relation to law, risk management, compliance and other areas of common interest.

2 At the Group AGM on 16 January 2007 members voted in favour of extending membership to company secretaries in the FTSE 100. The formal name of the GC100 is now the 'Association of General Counsel and Company Secretaries of the FTSE 100' although it continues to be generally known as the GC100.

3 Officers to the GC100 for 2007 are:

Chair:	Helen Mahy, National Grid
Vice-chair:	Rosemary Martin, Reuters
Vice-chair:	Peter Maynard, Prudential
Treasurer:	Richard Bennett, HSBC
Secretary:	Mary Mullally, PLC

4 Other members of the Executive Committee for 2007 are:
Rupert Bondy, GlaxoSmithKline
Grant Dawson, Centrica
Nick Folland, Emap
Mark Harding, Barclays
Andrea Harris, WPP
Peter Kennerley, Scottish & Newcastle
Christopher Roberts, Reckitt Benckiser

5 As a matter of formality please note that the views expressed in this paper do not necessarily reflect the views of all of the individual members or their employing companies.

For more information contact:
Nick Folland (company secretary and group legal director, Emap) at
nick.folland@emap.com
Peter Kennerley (general counsel and company secretary, Scottish & Newcastle) at
peter.kennerley@s-n.com
Mary Mullally, secretary to the GC100, on 020 7202 1245 or at
mary.mullally@practicallaw.com

Glossary

The following explanations are not intended to be strict legal definitions.

Administrator A person appointed by the court to manage a company in financial difficulties in order to protect creditors and, if possible, avoid liquidation. The administrator has the power to remove and appoint directors.

Agent Someone who is authorised to carry out business transactions on behalf of another (the principal) who is thereby bound by such actions.

AIM Alternative Investment Market.

Annual general meeting (AGM) A general meeting of the company's members which must be held in each period of six months beginning with the day following its accounting reference date.

Articles Articles of association, a constitutional document setting out the internal regulations of the company. The articles cover matters such as directors' powers and responsibilities, decision-making by directors, their appointment and removal, decision-making by shareholders, the issue and transfer of shares, dividends and communications by the company. Unless modified or excluded, the specimen articles in Table A have effect. *See also* Table A.

Board (of directors) *See* Director.

Business Enterprise and Regulatory Reform The government department responsible for the administration of company law. The Companies Act confers certain powers on the Secretary of State for Business, Enterprise and Regulatory Reform (formerly the Secretary of State for Trade and Industry).

Case law The principles and rules of law established by judicial decisions. Under this system the decision reached in a particular case creates a precedent: that is, it is regarded as exemplifying rules of broader application which must be followed except by higher courts. *See also* Common law.

Class rights The rights attached to different classes of shares.

Combined Code The Code sets out good corporate governance recommendations and is issued by the Financial Reporting. Presently, two versions are in effect: the 2006 edition which applies to accounting periods beginning on or after 1 November 2006 and the 2008 edition which applies to accounting periods beginning on or after 29 June 2008. Listed companies are required to report how they have complied with the Code in their annual report and accounts.

Common law A body of law based on custom and usage and decisions reached in previous cases. The principles and rules of common law derive from judgments and judicial opinions delivered in response to specific circumstances, not from written legislation. *See also* Case law, Statute law.

Company secretary An officer of the company with a number of statutory duties, such as to sign the annual return and accompanying documents, and usually charged with a range of duties relating to the company's statutory books and records, filing requirements, etc. Until April 2008, every company was required to have a secretary who, in the case of a public company, must meet the qualification requirements laid down in the Companies Act.

Connected person Includes members of a director's family (including a spouse or civil partner; any other person with whom the director lives as partner in an enduring family relationship and that person's children or stepchildren under the age of 18 years; the director's own children and stepchildren; and the director's parents); a body corporate with which the director is connected (holds an interest in at least 20% of the share capital or may exercise or control the exercise more than 20% of voting power at any general meeting); a person acting as trustee of a trust of which the director is a beneficiary or may benefit; a partner of a director or person connected with the director; or any firm of which the director is a partner (CA 2006, ss. 252–256).

Director An officer of the company responsible for determining policy, supervising the management of the company's business and exercising the powers of the company. Directors must generally carry out these functions collectively as a board.

Dividends The distribution of a portion of the company's profits to members according to the class and amount of their shareholdings.

DTR Disclosure and Transparency Rules.

E-money issuer A person who has permission under the Financial Services and Markets Act 2000 to carry on the activity of issuing electronic money

General meeting A meeting of the company which all members (subject to restrictions in the Memorandum and Articles) are entitled to attend. *See also* Annual general meeting.

IFRS International Financial Reporting Standards.

Insider dealing Buying or selling shares on the basis of an unfair advantage derived from access to price-sensitive information not generally available.

Liquidation The process under which a company ceases to trade and realises its assets for distribution to creditors and then shareholders. The term 'winding up' is synonymous.

Listed company A company whose shares are dealt on the Official List of the London Stock Exchange.

Listing Rules Published by the Financial Services Authority, these detail the requirements that must be met by companies before their shares can be publicly traded on the Official List of the Stock Exchange. For the full requirements, readers should refer to and rely only on the latest edition, available from the FSA.

Memorandum Memorandum of Association, a constitutional document governing the company's relationship with the world at large, stating its name, domicile, objects, limitations of liability (if applicable) and authorised share capital. CA 1985 but under CA 2006 more limited purpose – *see* s. 8.

Misfeasance Improper performance of a lawful action.

MiFID investment firm A firm authorised under the Markets in Financial Instruments Directive.

Model Articles Draft articles published by the government in March 2008 and intended for use by private companies, public companies and companies limited by guarantee incorporated on or after 1 October 2009.

Non-cash asset Any property or interest in property other than cash and includes discharge of a person's liability and creation of an interest in property such as a lease (CA 1985, s. 739).

Officer Includes a director, manager or secretary of a company. An officer must have a level of supervisory control that reflects the general policy of the company, so not everyone with the title of manager is sufficiently senior to be regarded as an officer.

Ordinary resolution A resolution approved by a simple majority of votes cast in general meeting.

Ordinary shares The most common form of share in a company, giving holders the right to share in the company's profits in proportion to their holdings and the right to vote at general meetings (although non-voting ordinary shares are occasionally encountered).

Parent company A company that:

- holds a majority of the voting rights in another company; or
- is a member of it and can appoint or remove a majority of its directors; or
- has the right to exercise dominant influence over the other company (for example through provisions in the articles or a control contract); or
- is a member and has an agreement with other members that gives it alone the right to control a majority of the voting rights in the other company; or
- has the power to exercise or actually exercises dominant influence over the other company or is managed on a unified basis with it.

Preference shares Shares carrying the right to payment of a fixed dividend out of profits before the payment of an ordinary dividend or the preferential return of capital or both. The exact nature of preference shares are set out in a company's articles.

Private Company Articles The draft Model Articles published by the government in March 2008 and intended for use by private companies incorporated on or after 1 October 2009.

Prohibited name In relation to the appointment of a director, this means a name for a company which is the same as or similar to the name of a company that went into insolvent liquidation at any time within 12 months of the person being a director (refer to IA 1986, s. 216(1) and (2) for the full definition).

Prospectus Any prospectus, notice, circular, advertisement or other invitation to the public to subscribe for or purchase a company's shares or debentures. Essentially, a prospectus is a selling document.

Proxy A person authorised by a member to vote on his or her behalf at a general meeting.

Public Company Articles The draft Model Articles published by the government in March 2008 and intended for use by public companies incorporated on or after 1 October 2009.

Quasi-loan Where one party makes payment to another or incurs expenditure on their behalf without an agreement but on the understanding that the money will be repaid (*see* CA 2006, s. 199(1) for the full definition).

Quoted Company Defined in s. 361 of CA 2006 (by reference to s. 385(2) CA2006) as a company whose equity share capital is: (i) included on the Official List in accordance with Part 6 of the Financial Services and Markets Act 2000; (ii) officially listed in an EEA state; or (iii) is admitted to dealing on NYSE or NASDAQ.

Registered office The address at which legal documents may be served on the company and where the statutory books are normally kept. The registered office need not be the company's place of business and may be changed freely so long as it remains in the country of origin.

Registrar of companies The official responsible for maintaining the company records filed under the requirements of the Companies Act.

Regulated market Includes the main market of the LSE. AIM is not a regulated market. For a list of regulated markets, see the list of exchanges on the FSA register page at www.fsa.gov.uk.

Return date Either the anniversary of incorporation or the anniversary of the date shown on the previous year's annual return.

Secretary of State In this book, refers to the Secretary of State for Business, Enterprise and Regulatory Reform (formerly the Secretary of State for Trade and Industry).

Special resolution A resolution approved by 75% of votes cast.

Statute law The body of law represented by legislation, and thus occurring in authoritative written form. Statute law contrasts with common law, over which it takes precedence. *See also* Common law.

Statutory books The general term applied to the registers and minute books that the Companies Act requires a company to maintain.

Subscriber A person who subscribes to the memorandum and agrees to take up shares in the company on incorporation.

Table A The specimen articles of association for a company limited by shares set out in the Companies (Tables A to F) (Amendment) Regulations 2007. Unless specifically modified or excluded, the version of Table A in force at the time of a company's incorporation automatically applies to the company.

Turnbull Report The report 'Internal Control: Guidance for Directors on the Combined Code' issued in September 1999 by the Turnbull Working Party.

TVRs Total voting rights.

Tyson Report The Tyson Report on the Recruitment and Development of Non-Executive Directors (June 2003) commissioned by the DTI.

UCITS management company A company which manages undertakings for the collective investment of tradable securities

Written resolution Allows private companies to move almost any resolution without holding a general meeting (except, where the resolution concerns the removal of a director or auditor, for which a meeting is required). Only those members comprising the requisite majority for the resolution need to sign it to make it effective.

Index